The Philosopher's Stone

Peter Marshall is a former tutor in philosophy and has a doctorate in the History of Ideas. His many works include *William Godwin*; *Demanding the Impossible: A History of Anarchism*; *Natures's Web: Rethinking Our Place on Earth* and *Riding the Wind: A New Philosophy for a New Era*. His circumnavigation of Africa was made into a television series and a book, *Around Africa*. *Celtic Gold: A Voyage Around Ireland* was the subject of a BBC radio series. He has two children.

Peter Marshall

The Philosopher's Stone

A Quest for the Secrets of Alchemy

PAN BOOKS

For Elizabeth, fellow explorer

First published 2001 by Macmillan

This edition published 2002 by Pan Books
an imprint of Pan Macmillan Ltd
Pan Macmillan, 20 New Wharf Road, London N1 9RR
Basingstoke and Oxford
Associated companies throughout the world
www.macmillan.com

ISBN 0 330 48910 0

5 7 9 8 6 4

A CIP catalogue record for this book is available from
the British Library.

Typeset by SetSystems Ltd, Saffron Walden, Essex
Printed and bound in Great Britain by
Mackays of Chatham plc, Chatham, Kent

The Philosopher's Stone is called the most ancient, secret or unknown, natural, incomprehensible, heavenly, blessed, sacred Stone of the Sages. It is described as being true, more certain than certainty itself, the arcanum of all arcana – the Divine virtue and efficacy, which is hidden from the foolish, the aim and end of all things under heaven, the wonderful epilogue or conclusion of all the labours of the Sages – the perfect essence of all the elements, the indestructible body which no element can injure, the quintessence; the double and living mercury which has in itself the heavenly spirit – the cure of all unsound and imperfect metals – the everlasting light – the panacea for all diseases – the glorious Phoenix – the most precious of all treasures – the chief good of Nature.

Anon., *The Sophic Hydrolith* (1678)

Contents

List of Illustrations

1. Wei Boyang with his cauldron and dog. From: Richard Bertschinger (tr.), *The Secret of Everlasting Life* (Shaftesbury, Element, 1994).
2. Female Chinese alchemist making elixirs. From: Joseph Needham, *Science and Civilisation in China* (Cambridge University Press, 1954–), vol. 5, part 3, fig. 1350.
3. Jade girl carrying magic mushrooms. Fresco from the Taoist temple Yung-Lo Kung in southern Shansi, China. Needham, *Science and Civilisation in China*, vol. 5, part 2, fig. 1312.
4. Ko Hung. From J. Read, *Prelude to Chemistry* (G. Bell & Sons, 1936).
5. Rubbing from a stele in the White Cloud Temple, Beijing, China. *(Elizabeth Ashton Hill)*
6. Swami Yogi Prakash. *(Elizabeth Ashton Hill)*
7. Author and Dr Lobsang Tenzin next to his alchemical furnace. *(Elizabeth Ashton Hill)*
8. The Sphinx and the Great Pyramid, Giza, Egypt. *(Peter Marshall)*
9. Cleopatra's *Chrysopia* ('Gold Making'). From: MS 2325, Bibliothéque Nationale, Paris, reprinted from Marcelin Berthelot, *Collection des anciens alchimistes grecs* (Paris, Georges Steinheil, 1888).
10. The Stele of Metternich. From: E. A. Wallis Budge, *Egyptian Magic* (London, Kegan, Paul, Trench, Trubner & Co, 1901).
11. 'Maria the Jewess'. From: Michael Maier, *Symbola Aureae Mensae* (Frankfurt, Lucas Jennis, 1617), reprinted in Stanislas Klossowski de Rola, *The Golden Game: Alchemical Engravings of the Seventeenth Century* (London, Thames & Hudson, 1988).
12. Lady Tai with her attendants depicted on a silk banner from her coffin. Museum of Chinese History, Beijing. *(Elizabeth Ashton Hill)*
13. Taoist monk in the White Cloud Temple, Beijing. *(Peter Marshall)*
14. Thoth with pharaoh. Temple of Seti I, Abydos, Egypt. *(Elizabeth Ashton Hill)*
15. Anubis, guide to the Underworld. Tomb of Sennofer, Valley of the Nobles, West Bank, Luxor, Egypt. *(Peter Marshall)*
16. Golden mask of Tutankhamon. Egyptian Museum, Cairo. *(Elizabeth Ashton Hill)*
17. Kandariya Mahadev Temple, Khajuraho, India. *(Elizabeth Ashton Hill)*

Acknowledgements

I would like to thank first and foremost my family and friends for their support and encouragement during my long and fascinating quest: my children Dylan and Emily, my mother Vera, my brother Michael, my friends Colette Dubois, Richard Feesey, Jeremy Gane, Graham Hancock, Dei Hughes, David Lea, John Schlapobersky, Peter Tutt and Jenny Zobel. I am particularly grateful to Elizabeth Ashton Hill, who accompanied me on much of my journey, helped in the research and who took many of the photographs in the book.

I am grateful to Joy Brown, John. P. C. Moffett, Robert Temple, David and Brenda Thomas and John Anthony West for giving me some useful information and contacts. Robin Waterfield kindly read the entire text and made many helpful suggestions.

There are countless people who have assisted me in my quest; if they are not mentioned, it does not mean that I do not value their help. These include: in China, Professor Liu Dun, Professor Zhao Kuang-hua, Professor Zhou Jia-hua, Dr Hao Liu Xiang, Dr Yang Lifan, Ming Zhiting and Sun Tong Chang; in India, Tara Jauhar, Shivnath Mehrotra, Swami Yogi Prakash, Rati Shankar, Dr S. K. Saigel, Dr J. S. Shukla, Dr Losang Norbu Shastri, Dr Lobsang Tenzin, Professor Kamalesh Datta Tripathi; in Egypt, Sohiela Hasam, Dr Zahi Hawass and Ayman Whaby Taher; in Spain, Manuel Olmedo Checa and Mariluz Comendador; in Italy, Father Joseph Pittau and Dr Andrea Scotti; in the Czech Republic, Pavel Suchanek, Robert Vrum and Vladislav Zadrobílek; and in France, Jean and Josette Dubuis and Nadejda L. Loujine.

I am indebted to the staff at Macmillan for their help and advice: the editor in the early stages Rupert Heath, the desk editor Tess Tattersall, the publisher Jeremy Trevathan and his former assistant Stefanie Bierwerth. The associate publisher William Armstrong has been most insightful and encouraging. My literary agent Bill Hamilton has been supportive throughout.

In their different ways, all these people have helped me recover and reveal a magical tradition of great wisdom.

Peter Marshall
Bromebyd, Midsummer 2000

Part One

The Tiger and the
Dragon: China

1

A Strange and Ancient Mystery

A truly remarkable discovery was made in 1972 at Mawangui near Changsha in Hunan Province, China. Buried some 12 metres down in a large tomb, a coffin was excavated which contained three painted inner coffins. They were filled with a great variety of beautiful objects: figured textiles, painted silks, musical instruments, lacquer utensils, pottery, food, pouches of medicinal and aromatic plants, and a host of carved wooden statues of serving maids. The innermost coffin was draped with a beautiful T-shaped banner of painted silk depicting the dwelling place for immortal beings and a map of the heavens. In its centre writhed the god Fu Hsi with his serpent tail, surrounded by magical crane birds. When the archaeologists lifted the last coffin lid, they discovered a female body wrapped in more than twenty silk garments. The mouth was filled with a jade amulet.

The body has been identified as that of a Lady Tai (pronounced Di), the wife of the first Lord of Tai. When buried, she was aged about fifty years and had a broken rib. The burial took place around 186 BC. Although more than 2,000 years old, when first exhumed the body was found to be in a perfect state of preservation: its condition was that of a person who had died only a week before. Forensic scientists from London were astonished to find that when they pressed the skin it returned at once to normal when the pressure was released. The colour of the femoral artery was like that of a newly dead person. The fingers and toes were not shrivelled at all.

This perfect preservation was not achieved by embalming (using formalin, alcohol and other organic chemicals), by any kind of mummification (that is desiccation by natron as in Egypt), by tanning (as in Danish bog burials), nor by freezing (as with woolly mammoths). The only factual observations were that the innermost of the four coffins contained a certain amount of brownish aqueous solution which contained mercuric sulphide; the atmosphere was largely of methane under some pressure; all the coffins were remarkably airtight and watertight, sealed with layers of charcoal and a kind of sticky white clay; and the temperature had been a rather constant 13–14° centigrade. After lengthy and careful forensic tests, modern scientists and experts have been forced to conclude that they simply do not know how the perfect preservation of Lady Tai was achieved.[1]

What we do know is that the principal aim of the Chinese alchemists at the time was to discover a 'pill of immortality' – the Chinese equivalent to the Philosopher's Stone. It was thought that whoever took this supreme elixir would be able to leave his or her corpse as if emerging from a chrysalis and fly off to dwell among other immortals in the heavens. And a sign of success was to leave the body on earth preserved like a living person.

The preserved body of Lady Tai remains one of the greatest mysteries of world science and of ancient China. Could it be that she is an example of a successful alchemical experiment, illustrating the allegory depicted on the silk banner draped over her coffin? Who were the alchemists who attempted such feats and what did they know? Had they really discovered the Philosopher's Stone?

Inspired by the mystery of Lady Tai and the promise of lost ancient wisdom, I decided to set off on a worldwide quest to discover the essence of alchemy and to see whether it really does offer a key to everlasting life.

2

The Mirror of History

Whatever is contrary to the Tao will not last long.

Lao Tzu

I looked out of the window of my aeroplane and saw the snow-capped mountains of the Himalayas. To the north and east stretched the endless reddish-brown sands of the Gobi Desert. I then flew over the Great Wall of China which stretches for over 2,000 miles, the only man-made structure which can be seen from space. My destination was Beijing, capital of China.

China escapes the imagination. It not only has one of the oldest civilizations on earth, but with 1.2 billion people it contains a quarter of the world's population. Whereas Europeans think in terms of hundreds of years in their history, the Chinese think in terms of thousands.

To reach China in the old days on horseback and by camel, it would have taken months from Arabia along the Silk Road; now it was taking me ten hours in a great metal bird. The aeroplane was the ultimate development of the manned kites which the Chinese alchemists had perfected some 2,500 years ago.

I had come to China in search of the Philosopher's Stone and to discover the origins and nature of Chinese alchemy. Ironically, the day I flew to Beijing saw the crash of the Hong Kong Stock Market after the island's recent reunification with the mainland. It had a ripple effect on the financial markets throughout the world: the headlines of *The Times* of London declared 'Gold and Mine Stocks Battered' while an evening newspaper announced 'City Screens Drowned in Red'. It was yet another reminder of the fragility of the world's financial system and the near universal obsession with gold.

I flew to Beijing via Tashkent, capital of Uzbekistan in Central Asia, formerly a remote satellite of the Soviet Union. The Old Silk Route which ran through it had once linked China with the Middle East via India and Tibet, bringing alchemical ideas and substances with its precious and exotic goods. Under the Mongol conqueror Tamburlaine, its ancient cities had become great centres of Islamic learning and alchemy.

I stayed long enough in Uzbekistan to take the 'golden road' (grey with snow and pockmarked with police) to Samarkand in order to admire its splendid medieval turquoise mosques, university and mausoleum of Tamburlaine. I also visited the observatory of the early fifteenth-century astronomer and alchemist Ulugh Beg whose celestial observations had been published at the time in Oxford. Afterwards on the plane to China, a large Uzbeck woman with Mongoloid features gave me a great shock when she smiled: all her teeth were gold. I later learned that young Uzbecks had their good teeth pulled out and replaced with gold if they could afford it.

My initial impression of China was one of headlong development. The streams of black bicycles were there but they wove between slow-moving fast new cars. Modern palaces – luxury hotels and offices of transnational companies – were going up everywhere. The Communist Party was still in power, the State was as centralized and authoritarian as ever, but dreams of communism were fading like the Mao suits of the old men. Economic growth and wealth creation were the watchwords of the day.

I had arrived in Beijing with an introduction from the Needham Research Institute in Cambridge, England, to the Institute for the History of Natural Science which was part of the Chinese Academy of Sciences. Joseph Needham was the author of the monumental collection called *Science and Civilisation in China*, one of the greatest works of twentieth-century scholarship, a project which was still continuing after his death. His favourite subject had been alchemy.

I had great difficulty finding the institute in central Beijing. My taxi driver did not know it despite being given the address in Chinese characters. Eventually, I was deposited at the side of a busy and dusty road and pointed in the direction of a run-down neighbourhood of ramshackle houses and shacks. Asking directions from an old man who was cooking noodles outside his hut, he led me through the labyrinth of grey hovels until we at last came to a faded but imposing gateway.

The institute was housed in the dilapidated seventeenth-century palace of a minor prince and was known as the 'Ninth Lord's Mansion'. It was built in a similar style to that of the Forbidden City although on a much smaller scale. Its enamelled tiles were cracked and grass grew out of its gutters, but it had a tranquil inner courtyard and garden and many cloistered buildings. Its library stocked more than 120,000 volumes, including the famous *Taoist Patrology* (*Dao Zan*), a unique collection of alchemical writings. I liked the motto of the institute that 'history is a mirror'. By a strange coincidence, there was a visiting professor from Berlin University giving a series of lectures on Western alchemy.

As a scholar of ancient astronomy explained to me, the institute had only recently been reopened after the ravages of the Cultural Revolution. He himself had been forced to work as a peasant in a remote region for twenty years and then for five years in a factory. Although funds were scarce and water dripped into a bucket in his office from a beautifully painted ceiling, he was delighted to be able to undertake research once more.

I was recommended by the director of the institute to meet Professor Zhao Kuang-hua who was a retired professor at Beijing University and said to be the leading expert on alchemy in China. He agreed to meet me at his flat on the campus which was like a vast run-down suburban estate. His flat was situated on the second floor of a grey apartment block. He kept his precious books locked up in a glass cabinet. There was a statue of a flying horse on a table and a butterfly collection on the wall.

The professor was a gentle and mild-mannered man in his sixties, dressed casually in a woven jacket. I got straight to the point and asked him about the origins of Chinese alchemy. He replied through an interpreter from the institute:

'That's a very difficult question to answer. It was at least 200 years before Christ, but we do not know the place. It came from Taoism. Every alchemist is a Taoist but not every Taoist is an alchemist. Alchemy is one aspect of Taoism.'

My ears pricked up. Taoism is the oldest philosophy in China, first written down in the *Tao Te Ching* attributed to Lao Tzu in the fifth century BC. I knew it well. It contained some of the most profound and beautiful wisdom I had ever come across.

'Like the Taoists', the professor went on, 'the alchemists were searching for longevity and immortality. They had two approaches. One was to seek in nature minerals, stones and plants to prolong life and the other was to become a *hsien* – an immortal – in the Far Eastern Sea. When they had no success seeking it in nature, they tried to make themselves immortal.'

'Did they then look for the Philosopher's Stone?'

'Yes. We call it the "pill of immortality".'

'And did they try to make gold?'

'For alchemists, it is important to make gold, but the gold is not for the market but used as an elixir for immortality.'

I asked the professor about the special nature of Chinese alchemy.

'We distinguish between two aspects of alchemy in China, *wai tan*, the outer elixir, and *nei tan*, the inner elixir.'

He pronounced the former as 'way dan', and the latter as 'nay dan'.

'With the practice of *wai tan*, seeking outer elixirs in nature, the alchemists were already thinking of *nei tan*, developing an inner elixir. Before the practice of *wai tan*, there was a long tradition of qigong. Its medical and chemical results continue and the practice of qigong is still alive today.'

This was fascinating. Qigong is a form of gentle exercise which aims to regulate vital energy (chi) in order to cure illnesses and prolong life. Modern Chinese science makes extraordinary claims about the feats of the qigong masters; they are reputedly able to hold back four motorbikes, break walls with their heads and control their heart rate. I had myself been practising qigong exercises for some time and knew their beneficial effects.

Having read many Taoist texts on the intimate link between sex, health and long life, I asked him about the importance of the sexual techniques for the *nei tan* alchemists to nourish vital energy. While we were talking, I could hear children playing outside and recalled that the policy of the Chinese government was to limit one child per family.

'The history of sex practice in China is very ancient. The sexual techniques are just a branch of *nei tan* alchemy. They are still valuable today in sexual life. In Chinese medicine, sex is good for health. But overdo it!'

'Do you mean, *don't* over do it?'

'Yes. That's it! In moderation!'

I then asked the professor who were the best writers on alchemy in China. He immediately said Ko Hung who lived in the fourth century. He did not think so highly of his famous predecessor Wei Boyang since he did not practise much in his laboratory.

I also asked him whether I could see any existing alchemist laboratories.

'To my knowledge', he said, 'there is not one existing anywhere. Information about alchemy is to be found mostly in books, and that is very complicated and difficult!'

This news was not very encouraging. It would seem that the professor mainly had an academic interest in the *wai tan* tradition of the outer elixir, of the place of alchemy in the history of science. He did not seem to be working on an outer elixir in the laboratory of the university nor trying to develop the inner elixir in the reaction vessel of his own body. Alchemy was clearly not helping him or his family. His wife, he confessed, was very ill.

I asked him what he thought the main contribution of Chinese alchemy was to the history of science.

'Although alchemy in its search for the pill of immortality had no success, it had success in making drugs for human health. Most alchemists were doctors and they wrote up their results in medical books.'

I realized that I was not going to find the Philosopher's Stone in the flat of China's leading academic expert on alchemy at Beijing University. But before I got up to go he surprised me. Painfully aware that I had taken up most of his morning, I asked bluntly: 'Do you think humanity will ever discover the Philosopher's Stone?'

There was much laughter and merriment. After a pause, he replied: 'According to modern physics, it is possible in fact to make mercury into gold. As for the Philosopher's Stone for eternal life, I am not very optimistic. But according to today's knowledge, a person's life could be 200 years if we improve our environment and medicine!'

My last question was about the whereabouts of the 2,000-year-old body of Lady Tai. As far as he knew, the body had been destroyed. If this was the case, then the great mystery of its preservation, which Needham put down to the work of alchemists, would never be solved. All that remained was the testimony of the forensic experts and the film and photographs of the body. At least the mystery of her preservation had inspired my interest in Chinese alchemy and brought me to the country of her birth.

On my way back to my hotel, I suddenly realized that I had not asked the professor to clarify the process of transforming mercury into gold. This for thousands of years had been the goal of alchemy and he claimed that he knew the answer. In my attempt to record the interview faithfully I had not realized the full import of what had been said. Being off-guard for a moment, had I missed the great object of my quest? Had I stumbled on the truth only not to recognize it for what it was? I later wrote twice to the professor and the institute about the technique which could transform mercury into gold but got no reply.

*

Following the professor's advice, I visited the Museum of Chinese History in Tiananmen Square. The vast marble mausoleum recorded the many firsts in Chinese science and technology, especially in the discovery of the compass, gunpowder, paper-making and printing. I was excited to come across two artefacts closely associated with alchemy and the search for immortality.

The first was a beautiful jade suit, held together by gold thread, which had once enclosed the body of a prince. It was believed by alchemists and by the Chinese at large that jade preserves the body after death, thereby enabling the deceased to ride the wind and journey through heaven.

The second artefact was the T-shaped silk banner which had been found in the tomb of Lady Tai. It contained a map of celestial phenomena and depicted several ancient myths and legendary figures. Her body may have disappeared along with the evidence of its alchemical techniques, but at least the world view of ancient Chinese alchemy portrayed on her shroud was preserved for ever.

The banner is divided into three levels with the heaven of the immortals at the top, the earthly world in the middle and the Underworld at the bottom. The sun with its emblem of a crow is high up on the right, and on the left is the moon with its symbols of a toad and a rabbit. Sun and moon represent the cosmic forces of yin and yang, the female and male principles, which operate throughout the universe. Just below is a great dragon carrying Chang Ho with an elixir into the Palace of the Moon. In the centre is Fu Hsi, the organizer god with his serpent tail. At the gates of heaven sit two guardian immortals. Lower down, Lady Tai herself, leaning on a stick and attended by three maids, discourses with two immortal envoys. In the Underworld strange creatures, all forms of Thu Po, the Earth Lord, do battle with the forces of evil.

Lady Tai is clearly destined to become an immortal in the heavens, a destiny which all the Chinese alchemists hoped to achieve. Would I ever be able to acquire the knowledge and skills to follow her?

*

After visiting the museum, I sat on its steps overlooking Tiananmen Square in the weak autumnal sun. Were they the ghosts of dead students I saw amongst the businessmen with their phones, the girl army recruits with bright lipstick, and the dark-faced peasants from the provinces looking for work? Huge red flags still flew above a vast portrait of Chairman Mao on the imposing entrance to the Forbidden City. But his great experiment in social transformation had ground to a halt and his materialistic philosophy had failed to stamp out the ancient Chinese search for everlasting life.

I pondered over my recent findings. The practice of *wai tan*, the outer elixir, may have disappeared from sight, but I felt sure that at least the search for the inner elixir of *nei tan* alchemy was still pursued in contemporary China. Wherever I went in the palaces, especially the Forbidden City and the Summer Palace, there were gardens of longevity, stones of longevity and halls of longevity. It was a national passion. Everybody seemed to want to live long, and despite the official atheism of the State, to become immortal.

3

The Alchemical Way

As above, so below.

Emerald Tablet

After a favourable start in my quest for the Philosopher's Stone, it seemed that I was quickly grinding to a halt in China. But I was determined to continue. The stakes could not be higher. If the alchemists were right, the discovery of the Philosopher's Stone would bring untold material and spiritual riches.

I had been studying alchemy for years and the more I delved into it, the more intriguing I found it to be. It is one of those subjects which everyone has heard about and yet it remains one of the world's great mysteries. It has a strange fascination and spell, like the myth of a lost civilization or the possibility of making contact with other beings in the universe. It has a magical aura and an occult background and yet it promises profound philosophical and spiritual insights. Hermetically sealed for thousands of years, alchemy attracted me as something very ancient, very mysterious and very important.

In this age of uncertainty when people are looking for answers to the fundamental questions of life and death, it seemed to me that alchemy might have a crucial message for our time. What I had already read further suggested that it might offer profound insights into the character of the human psyche and the ultimate nature of the universe. I suspected that it might well be the remnants of something really important, of a highly advanced sacred science handed down from remote prehistory. It held the enticing prospect of discovering a body of ancient wisdom which could transform our lives and bring about a new dawn at the beginning of the third millennium.

But what exactly was the nature of the subject for which I was prepared to spend years of study and risk my life travelling to the four corners of the world? Alchemy is often defined as a form of early science and seen as a prelude to modern chemistry but it is much more and much deeper. First and foremost, alchemy is the art and science of transformation. It is an ancient body of beliefs and practices which seeks to transmute base metal into gold and produce an elixir to prolong life. But the final goal of all true alchemists is not to gain material wealth or power but to attain enlightenment and everlasting life. The agent to bring about this miraculous transformation is, as we have seen, called the pill of immortality in the East and the Philosopher's Stone in the West.

What is unique about alchemy, and what particularly appealed to me, is that it is a sacred science which combines philosophy and religion, psychology and art, theory and practice, vision and experiment. It is a very ancient science, yet highly relevant to our times. It addresses the heart as well as the head, reason and intuition, the imagination and the intellect. It is a holistic science which is concerned with the mind, body and spirit.

Alchemists refer to their work as the *Magnum Opus*, usually translated as 'The Great Work' or simply 'The Work'. It involves the 'outer work' of making experiments in their laboratories and the 'inner work' of perfecting themselves. No alchemical experiment in the laboratory is devoid of a moral or spiritual dimension. Alchemists agree with the ancient principles: 'As above, so below' and 'As within, so without'. The transmutation of external matter mirrors the inward transformation of the soul. Indeed, the discovery of the Philosopher's Stone is an outward sign of the alchemist's inner self-realization.

There are thus two traditions and two interpretations of alchemy, the 'exoteric' and the 'esoteric', which are interrelated like two faces of a coin. The exoteric deals with the practical science of preparing the substance – the Philosopher's Stone – which is endowed with the power of transmuting metal into gold and prolonging life. This aspect played a key role in the history and development of science. The esoteric tradition on the other hand sees the transmutation of gold as a symbolic activity, as an attempt to transform humans from base matter to refined spirit and to produce nothing less than the gold of spiritual illumination. From the earliest times, the esoteric tradition passed down truths about the structure of the world, the place of humanity within the universe and the nature of the mind and the purpose of life.

Despite its scientific and spiritual achievements, alchemy has not always had a good reputation. Its detractors maintain that it is just a wacky form of science and that its philosophical and spiritual claims are mere mumbo-jumbo. Many have dismissed its obscure writings as simply 'gibberish' – a word derived from the name of the great Arab alchemist Geber. Even worse, the orthodox and conventional fear alchemy as a dangerous heresy, a black cauldron of magic boiling behind the white altars of organized religion. It is common to dismiss it as part of the lunatic fringe of intellectual life.

It is true that not all those who call themselves alchemists can be relied on. Over the centuries, the prospect of prolonging life and obtaining untold riches has undoubtedly attracted a great number of quacks and puffers. On one level, alchemy would seem to offer an exemplary tale of the gullibility, folly and greed of humanity, a tragicomedy of their obsession with youth and riches.

The alchemists, too, have often been their own worst enemies. Many of the symbols of alchemy seem impenetrably obscure and deeply disturbing. What are we to make of dragons swallowing their tails, kings and queens copulating in water, naked bodies being dismembered, pelicans plucking their bleeding breasts, green lions swallowing the sun, crucified snakes, peacocks appearing in flasks, men giving birth, hermaphrodites with two heads?

But before dismissing the alchemists as deluded dreamers, devilish fanatics or scheming charlatans, it is worth recalling that they deliberately disguised their theories and findings in obscure language and bizarre symbols. This was partly to escape the persecution of those in Church and State who saw them as a threat to their rule and partly to guard the potentially explosive knowledge from getting into the wrong hands. The alchemists knew they were playing with fire, in more senses than one.

Even more to the point, if alchemy is nonsensical gibberish, why have so many great minds and powerful figures in history become engrossed in the subject? The Emperor Wen of China and the Holy Roman Emperor Rudolf II became so absorbed in the subject that they neglected their affairs of state. Among many others, the philosophers St Thomas Aquinas and Giordano Bruno, the artists Albrecht Dürer, Hieronymus Bosch, Botticelli and André Breton, the writers Johann

Wolfgang von Goethe, Victor Hugo and W. B. Yeats, and the psycho-analyst Carl Jung have all come under its spell.

Among the long roll-call of famous alchemists who have made a major contribution to science are Paracelsus, often called the father of modern pharmacy; Joan Baptista van Helmont, who proved the exist-ence of gas; and Johann Friedrich Böttger, the first in Europe to discover porcelain. Robert Boyle, who laid the foundations of modern chemistry in the seventeenth century, started out as an alchemist and continued to believe in many of its claims.

The most extraordinary case, however, is that of Isaac Newton, one of the most original minds of all time. It is not widely known that the main inspirer of the Scientific Revolution spent much of his life immersed in alchemical studies. The economist John Maynard Keynes, who acquired his private writings, perceptively observed that Newton was '*not* the first of the Age of Reason; he was the last of the magicians . . . the last great mind which looked out on the world with the same eyes as those who began to build our intellectual inheritance rather less than 10,000 years ago'.[1]

Ironically, it was the triumph of Newton's vision of the universe as a machine governed by fixed laws which forced alchemy underground at the end of the seventeenth century. But while the Scientific Revolu-tion and the 'Age of Reason' chased it into the shades, alchemy was kept alive by a few enthusiasts and semi-secret societies. In the twen-tieth century, however, it rose again like a phoenix out of the ashes of the reductionist and mechanical science which had threatened to replace it. Far from being confined to the museum of science, alchemy would seem to be at its frontiers, especially in its understanding of energy, matter and consciousness. And now at the dawn of the new millennium, alchemy speaks directly to the evolving awareness which challenges materialist and mechanical thinking and offers a holistic approach to nature.

The new physics of the twentieth century was the first to confirm ancient alchemical insights, depicting the universe as a field of force and a constant flow of transforming energy. Modern physicists agree with the ancient alchemists that we cannot speak about nature without speaking about ourselves. Ecology further presents nature as a complex web of relations, thereby confirming the old alchemical principle: 'All is One, and One is All.' To call the living organism of the earth Gaia is to stand in a very old alchemical tradition. Indeed, the concept of

the earth as an animated, self-sustaining and self-generating world is a
new version of the *anima mundi* (world soul) of ancient alchemy. It
recognizes the delicate network of hidden sympathies and correspondences in nature's bespangled web. The reverence felt by modern
ecologists and environmentalists for nature was always deep in the
heart of the alchemists.

This is not only true in the area of science. Alchemy has taken on
a new lease of life in the field of psychology. Alchemists were always
explorers of the darker and more remote realms of the mind but their
insights came as a revelation to the psychoanalyst Carl Jung when he
first began to read their texts. On discovering alchemy's deep mine of
symbolism, he was astonished to find images which matched the
archetypes in the dreams and fantasies of his patients, who knew
nothing of the subject. Indeed, alchemy gave him the key he had been
looking for to understand the unconscious region of the mind. Not
only is the Philosopher's Stone a perfect symbol of psychic wholeness,
but the alchemical process itself mirrors the stages of the integration
and realization of the self. Alchemy thus offers a rich seam of visionary
experience and opens the doors of perception to a new order of
consciousness.

Apart from contributing to modern science and psychology,
alchemy has become an essential part of holistic and alternative
medicine. It has always been associated with astrology in recognizing
the subtle correspondences between the microcosm and the macrocosm, the individual and the solar system, the person and the planet.
Homeopathy, too, has a common source in alchemy, recognizing the
importance of the subtle realm of consciousness in treating illness.
Many alternative therapists specifically talk in alchemical terms of
initiation, transformation and revelation, of creating a union between
male and female principles, of transmuting leaden feelings of
depression into the golden light of wholeness. Alchemy not only seeks
to heal the rift between the mind, body and spirit but proposes a
holistic view of human nature – sometimes known as the 'subtle body'
– which is neither physical nor mental but both.

Alchemy thus forms a central strand of the growing cultural movement which seeks to replace the crumbling mechanistic, rationalist and
materialistic world view with an organic, spiritual and holistic one. It is
a brightly coloured and volatile participant in the rebellion against the
arid intellect. Alchemy is now an essential ingredient of New Age

sensibility and an integral element of what has been called 'perennial philosophy', the wisdom of the ages. Its encoded message offers guidance on how to live long and well and combines deep thinking with high feeling. As we face the challenges of the twenty-first century, never before have its hidden truths been more relevant and urgent.

The deepening interest in the ancient wisdom of alchemy is a sign that a general reformation of the world is taking place as the third millennium dawns. It is a time of awakening and of exploration, of change and transformation. Although the insights of alchemy are potentially explosive, we are living in a time when the traditional cloak of secrecy is no longer necessary nor appropriate. Now is the time to open the key to its elaborate system of symbols, rituals and doctrines, and to reveal its hidden secrets to the world.

*

After spending years studying alchemy in books, I realized that its secrets lie scattered throughout the world, in distant libraries and neglected monuments, among small groups and with obscure individuals. I therefore decided to set off on a worldwide journey to the lands where alchemy had traditionally been practised in order to understand its origins, development and meaning. I hoped to find out whether it was still a living tradition and to track down adepts who guarded its secrets.

I knew my quest would inevitably involve historical investigation, literary archaeology and philosophical enquiry. It would be a marvellous and exciting adventure of ideas, symbols and images. I would have to explore dark chambers of hidden knowledge and enter rarely visited towers of history, philosophy and religion. It would take me through fascinating paths of the Occult, the Cabbala and the Hermetic tradition. I would have to decipher clues laid in my path, distinguish between false trails and real leads and overcome seemingly insurmountable obstacles.

My quest for the Philosopher's Stone would be a journey into the heart of a great and ancient mystery, a journey of body and soul, of intellect and imagination, of spirit and matter, of time and space. It would take me from the earliest times to the present, from the caves of the earth to the vaults of the heavens, from the darkest realms to the most resplendent. Like alchemy itself, it would no doubt be a process, an experiment, a transformation, involving despair and hope, disorder and harmony, darkness and light. I saw it as a physical journey with a metaphysical dimension, a personal vision quest, a 'wonder' voyage like those undertaken by ancient mariners who pulled themselves away from the comfort of hearth and home in search of enlightenment in the Isles of the Blessed across the wayward sea.

I wanted to investigate alchemy in all its aspects: the alchemy of matter, the alchemy of the psyche and the alchemy of the spirit. I planned to explore the practical and the spiritual, the exoteric and the esoteric traditions and engage in inner and outer work. I intended to consider the methods, processes and substances of alchemy as well as its metaphysical claims as an ancient sacred science. Above all, I hoped to evaluate the contribution which alchemy has made to science and philosophy as well as to our psychological understanding and spiritual awareness.

Wherever I went, I aimed to keep the central questions posed by alchemy at the forefront of my mind. Firstly, there is the mystery of its origins. Where does it come from? Why did it emerge independently in the Far East and the Middle East thousands of years ago? Why did it share such similar themes in such widely different cultures? Is there a common root from a lost civilization?

Secondly, there is the mystery of its fascination throughout the ages. Why has it seduced so many great minds? Why have so many powerful figures become obsessed with its study? Why has it been outlawed and defiled?

Thirdly, there is its promise as a repository of ancient wisdom. How far does it take the veil off nature? What light does it cast on the ultimate nature of the universe and our rightful place within it?

Fourthly, there are its psychological and spiritual claims. How far does it illuminate the mysteries of the soul? Does it offer a path of self-knowledge? Can it transform our lives? Does it really provide a key to everlasting life?

And finally there is the question of the relevance of alchemy to our own troubled times. Why are more and more people becoming interested in the subject? What has it got to offer us now? Will it be as significant for the future of consciousness as it has been for its past? Does it indeed contain a crucial message for our time?

With these thoughts and feelings in mind, I continued my journey in China with renewed vigour.

4

The Art of the Yellow and the White

> If one's life is prolonged, one will be able to meet the immortals.
>
> Li Shao-Chun, second century BC

So far I had found out that alchemy had played an important part in the history of Chinese science and medicine and that there was an important distinction to be made between the pursuit of the *wai tan* outer elixir and the *nei tan* inner elixir. My next task was to delve into the mysterious origins and development of alchemy in one of the world's oldest civilizations. It soon became clear that its principal aim of becoming immortal was of the greatest antiquity and that the roots of Chinese alchemy were to be found in the practices of the ancient shamans as well as in the philosophy of the Taoists. There may well have been another source from across the sea.

Chinese archaeology shows that in the earliest burials humans painted the remains of their ancestors with red, the colour of blood, as a form of sympathetic magic to ensure their immortality. Red ochre was used for colouring skulls and skeletons in Palaeolithic and Neolithic graves. Red cinnabar pigments have also been found on oracle bones. Tombs dating from the sixth century BC contained masses of cinnabar. All these discoveries show the early importance given to cinnabar as a symbol of immortality.[1] When heated, this bright red substance – mercuric sulphide – gives rise to the most volatile of metals, mercury. It is no coincidence that cinnabar was the most common ingredient in the elixir-making of Chinese alchemists.

There is a fascinating etymological clue to the origins of alchemy in the character for the Chinese word '*tan*'. From very ancient times it simply meant red, but it also means elixir or cinnabar. In alchemical texts and modern usage, it usually refers to a pill.

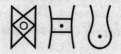

As shown in the above illustration, the Chinese character for *tan* could be a drawing of a globule of mercury in a crucible.[2] It demonstrates that the practice of alchemy was part of the language and culture of China from the earliest times. The general term for alchemy in Chinese is *lien tan*, meaning 'pill of transformation'.

In the remote prehistory of *Homo faber*, alchemy is undoubtedly rooted in the discovery of fire and the growing awareness of its transformational powers. It springs from the desire of early humans to transform nature rather than merely accept the given as inevitable. It was no doubt further stimulated by the establishment of settled agriculture which not only transformed nature on a large scale but also provided a surplus to support artisans and thinkers who pursued philosophical and scientific interests.

Alchemists undoubtedly shared a common ancestry with shamans, magicians, smiths and to a lesser extent miners, who were custodians of the magic arts of transformation and the secrets of the primordial forces of the earth. They all recognized that by interfering with nature they were playing with dangerous powers and their operations had to be carefully controlled through rituals and taboos. They also believed that as the source of life mother earth is sacred and that any violation of her must be appeased by sacrifices.[3] For this reason, the alchemists located their laboratories in safe places, such as retreats in sacred mountains, and purified themselves for the Great Work, undergoing fasting and ritual cleansing and making careful use of invocations and spells.

Chinese shamans and magicians, known as *wu* and *fang shih*, played an important part in Chinese life from the earliest times. They worked in many different fields as weather forecasters, star recorders, architects and smiths. In the old texts, they appear as experts in exorcism, magical healing, the interpretation of dreams, fortune-telling and prophecy. Their practices fused imperceptibly with other disciplines, especially astrology, geomancy and feng shui. In the cult of spirits, the Chinese shamans were considered intermediaries with other realms; indeed, they are sometimes defined as people who dance in order to bring down the spirits.[4] They not only made use of drugs which brought about trance-like states but also were specifically interested in finding a herb which banished death.

From the myths and rites of smiths and miners, the Chinese alchemists adopted ideas about the growth of ores, the natural transformation of metals into gold in the womb of the earth, and the mystical value of gold. And from their brotherhoods they acquired carefully guarded secrets only after long periods of preparation and initiation with a master.

These masters of fire did not set out to achieve 'mastery' over or the 'conquest' of nature as modern science attempts with its objective observation of neutral phenomena. Their aim was to collaborate with natural forces in order to improve and perfect nature. Above all, this involved the manipulation of time, by speeding up the formation of minerals and metals in their laboratories, and by slowing down the process of ageing of the human body.

*

But was there another source for alchemy in China apart from the local traditions of the shamans? It has long been thought in the Far East that there was a common cosmology throughout the world from an original civilization until a series of natural disasters 10,000 or 12,000 years ago broke it up. There is also an ancient Taoist tradition in China that around 10,000 BC there arrived a race of people from across the sea who were very tall and learned. Because of their unusual clothing which shone in the sun, they were called the 'Sons of Reflected Light' (*Fankuang Tzu*).[5] On their arrival, they collected together a group of skilled people and instructed them in arts and crafts which were technically far in advance of anything that previously existed. These included making glass and gunpowder, silk-weaving, pottery-making, the utilization of metals, medicine, and, yes, alchemy. This knowledge was reputedly passed down from generation to generation and dispersed by family groups throughout China until it was brought together again by the Taoists so that the advancement of knowledge was not hindered by local differences.

Lao Tzu may have been referring to these ancient masters in the *Tao Te Ching* which dates from the fifth century BC:

> The ancient masters were subtle, mysterious, profound and
>   responsive.
> The depths of their knowledge is unfathomable.
> Because it is unfathomable,
> All we can do is describe their appearance.[6]

He believed that the ancients understood the Tao – the Way of Nature
– better than his contemporaries and that true knowledge of it was
already being lost.

Where the 'Sons of Reflected Light' came from remains a deep
mystery. Could they have come from a lost civilization overtaken by a
sudden catastrophe, bringing with them the secrets of alchemy? Were
their fellow countrymen the Siddhas who allegedly landed in southern
India and the 'Companions of Horus' who came to Egypt at roughly
the same time? Although it cannot be proved, the idea cannot be
dismissed out of hand. China, India and Egypt all developed ancient
schools of alchemy without any known connections between the
countries at the time.

What did the 'Sons of Reflected Light' look like? Lao Tzu omits to
describe the 'ancient masters'. But there may be a recently discovered
clue. Were they like the figures found in two pits full of bronze,
gold and jade in Sanxingdui, Sichuan Province, dating from around
1200–1000 BC? Buried beneath a layer of ivory tusks and burned
animal bones, archaeologists were astonished to find a complete bronze
figure over 2 metres high on a tall square base, along with a large
number of heads, some covered in gold. They all shared similar features
– slanting eyes framed by bold outlines, strongly curled nostrils,
big ears and tight-lipped mouths.[7] The figures do not look at all like
the Chinese. They were clearly honoured ancestors. Were they the first
Chinese alchemists?

*

Whatever the exact origins of alchemy in China, whether from local or
foreign sources or from a mixture of both, the earliest written records
show that the belief in the possibility of physical immortality is clear
by the eighth century BC. By the fourth century BC it was widely held
that it could be attained by taking drugs as well as by performing
certain breathing, meditation, sexual and gymnastic techniques – methods developed by the shamans and the Taoists.[8] It was thought that a

person could nurture an imperishable body within the old one, rather like a butterfly in a cocoon. The actual preservation of the old body, as in the case of the Lady Tai, was therefore considered a real sign that immortality had been attained.

Chinese alchemy was crystallized in the school of scientists and philosophers known as the Naturalists during the fourth century BC. The pursuit of physical immortality was always far more important than transmuting gold. Indeed, there was no word for gold in China until about the fifth century BC. The Chinese were impressed by gold at the time not so much as a medium of wealth but for its psychological and spiritual aspects as a substance of brilliant radiance. It later became of interest as an ingredient to produce an elixir to prolong and to attain the 'pill of immortality'.

The first known practising alchemist was Tsou Yen, who lived approximately from 350 to 270 BC and wrote a short treatise known as *The Virtues by which the Five Emperors Ruled* (*Wu Ti Te*). An early biographer of Tsou Yen mentions the practice of becoming immortal by the use of magical techniques, so that 'their bodies would be etherealised and metamorphosed by some transmutation'. He drew on Taoism (the philosophy of yin and yang) and was in contact with shamans and magicians of the seaboard states of China to whom the earliest Chinese alchemists were greatly indebted:

> Tsou Yen was famous among the feudal lords [for his doctrine] that the Yin and Yang control the cyclical movements of destiny. The men who possessed magical techniques, and who lived along the sea-coast of Yen and Chhi, transmitted his arts, but without being able to understand them.[9]

During the third century BC, the appeal of attaining physical immortality was so strong that the Emperor Chin Shih Huang Ti sent several expeditions to search for the elixir in the legendary islands of the immortals – Pheng-Lai, Fang-Chang and Ying Chou – in the Eastern Sea:

> These three divine [island] mountains were reported to be in the Sea of Po, not so distant from human [habitations], but the difficulty was that when they were almost reached, boats were blown away from them by the wind. Perhaps some succeeded in reaching [these islands]. [At any rate, according to the report]

many immortals [*hsien*] live there, and the drug which will prevent
death is found there. Their living creatures, both birds and beasts,
are perfectly white, and their palaces and gate-towers are made of
gold and silver. Before you have reached them, from a distance
they look like clouds, but [it is said that] when you approach
them, these three divine mountain-islands sink below the water,
or else a wind suddenly drives the ship away from them. So no
one can reach them.[10]

The interest in alchemy grew to such an extent under the rule of
Emperor Wen that many charlatans became involved and 'deceptive
wonders, flatteries and illicit practices' abounded. The deception grew
to such a head that in 144 BC an imperial edict was issued which
prohibited alchemy and made the counterfeiting of gold an offence
punishable by public execution. Nevertheless, the Emperor Wu Ti,
who ruled from 140 to 86 BC, and his empress dowager took a great
interest in the teachings of the alchemists.

One Li Shao-Chun was granted an audience by the Emperor
because it was said that he possessed the art of making offerings to the
spirit of the furnace and knew how to live without cereals and without
growing old. Using apparently irrefutable logic, the alchemist declared
to the Emperor:

By making offerings to the Furnace [spirit] natural substances
can be changed. If one cause substances to change, cinnabar can
be transformed into gold. When gold has been produced it can be
made into vessels for eating and drinking, the use of which will
prolong one's life. If one's life is prolonged one will be able to
meet the immortals [of the isle] of Pheng-Lai in the midst of the
sea.[11]

The Emperor personally made offerings to the furnace spirit and
dispatched magicians and alchemists to search for the island of immortals. He was so convinced by Li Shao-Chun that when the adept fell ill
and died, the Emperor believed that he had not really died but had
merely undergone a transfiguration and disappeared.

The alchemical tradition was developed by masters passing down
the secrets orally and in coded writings to their most favoured pupils.
As a result the secrets of alchemy were guarded by a carefully chosen
group of adepts. They were part of the inner circle surrounding Liu
Nan, the Prince of Huai Nan (179–22 BC), a venerable forerunner

according to the great fourth-century alchemist Ko Hung. Ko also mentions an alchemist called Cheng Wei at the Han Imperial Court in the first century BC who had a great liking for 'the Art of the Yellow and the White'.

His wife came from a family of adepts skilled in the magical arts, and, it would seem, was more skilled than her husband. She had studied under one of Emperor Wu Ti's favourite concubines who was an expert in Taoist sexual techniques for prolonging life:

> Cheng Wei tried to make gold following the directions of the *Chen Chung Hung Pao* book, but without success. One day his wife went to see him just as he was fanning the charcoal to increase the heating in the reaction-vessel in which there was mercury. She said: 'Let me show you what I can do', and taking a small amount of some substance from her pouch she threw it into the vessel. After about the space of time in which a man could take a meal, she opened the vessel, and they saw that the contents had turned to silver.
>
> Cheng Wei was astounded and said: 'How is it possible that you could possess this Tao and never let me know about it?' She answered: 'It cannot be gained unless one has the right destiny.'[12]

The passage shows the prominence of women in alchemical circles from the beginning in China. It also describes the power of projection later attributed to the Philosopher's Stone in the West.

5

The Crucible

The Tao that can be told is not the eternal Tao.

Lao Tzu

China's leading expert on alchemy, Professor Zhao Kuang-hua, had told me that alchemy is one aspect of Taoism and that every Chinese alchemist is a Taoist. Even the first known practising alchemist, Tsou Yen, was famous for his doctrine that 'yin and yang', the two fundamental principles of Taoism, control the movements of destiny.

As I deepened my studies, it became clear to me that while shamanism provides the fire for Chinese alchemy (especially in its use of drugs, trances and magic), Taoism forms the philosophical crucible. It cannot be properly understood outside its context. I had long studied Taoism and found it to contain a repository of beautiful and profound wisdom which is highly relevant today.[1] Despite its great antiquity many of its insights have been recently confirmed by the findings of modern physics and ecology.

Taoism is the oldest philosophy in China. As their name implies, the Taoists are concerned with the Tao, often translated as the Way. The Tao is the order of nature. As a concept it cannot be clearly defined but rather sensed; indeed, as Lao Tzu says in the *Tao Te Ching*: 'The Tao that can be told is not the eternal Tao.' The universe is in a process of constant change, and we cannot stop it. We can attune to the Tao but we cannot grasp or alter it. Nevertheless the constant flux of nature forms a cosmic order in which All is One, and One is All. As Chuang Tzu, the other great philosopher of Taoism, asserted two centuries after Lao Tzu: 'He is a just man who regards all parts from the point of view of the Whole.'[2]

But it was not only the philosophy of Taoism but also the Taoists' approach to nature which encouraged the early development of alchemy and science in China.[3] The Taoists adopted a very receptive and open attitude to the world around them. They valued the qualities of yielding and tolerance. They did not try to impose their views on nature but rather contemplated it as they found it. By carefully observing its phenomena, they began to understand its ways.

They associated this receptive attitude with the 'feminine' approach to life. They called it the 'valley spirit'. Lao Tzu observed:

> The valley spirit never dies;
> It is the woman, primal mother.
> Her gateway is the root of heaven and earth.
> It is like a veil barely seen.
> Use it; it will never fail.[4]

In the original Chinese, 'woman' is literally called the 'Mysterious Feminine'. The feminine is not therefore a veil which hides nature but a thread which is woven throughout its fabric which if properly understood and tended can be used to accomplish great things. Indeed, the 'valley spirit' came to symbolize for alchemists the golden elixir itself.[5]

Chinese alchemy – and all Chinese science for that matter – is based on three basic ideas of the cosmos found in Taoism. The first is the notion of chi, the second is the concept of yin and yang, and the third is the theory of the five elements.

Chi is often translated as energy and is seen as circulating around the body as well as in the universe. It pervades all and is responsible for growth and regeneration rather like a life force. But it is not invisible. Material things are composed of chi which gives them their structure and qualities.

The second basic idea of Chinese alchemy is that the Tao divides into the two fundamental principles of yin and yang. They are two complementary forces operating in the universe which ebb and flow like a wave. In the *Tao Te Ching*, it is suggested that living creatures are surrounded by yin and envelop yang, and the harmony of their life depends on the harmony of the two principles. The Tao produces one energy from nothingness and then from that energy gives birth to yin and yang:

> The Tao begot one.
> One begot two.
> Two begot three.
> Three begot the ten thousand things.
>
> The ten thousand things carry yin and embrace yang.
> They achieve harmony by combining these forces.[6]

The process can be compared to the growth of plants and trees. First one sprout emerges from the earth and opens into two leaves. Then the stem grows between the two leaves, yin and yang combining to form three bodies. From these, all the other branches and countless leaves grow.

The Chinese written characters for them are connected with darkness and light. The ancient character for 'yin' (see below) involves pictographs for a hill and clouds; hence the association with the shady, dark and north side of a hill. In the character for 'yang', the upper part represents the sun and the lower part slanting sun rays or a flag fluttering in the sunshine; hence the association of the yang force with the sunny, bright and south side of a hill.[7]

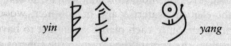

In the *Shih Ching*, a collection of ancient folk songs, yin evokes the idea of cold and cloud, of rain and dark, underground chambers and femaleness; while yang evokes the idea of sunshine and heat, of spring and summer, and maleness. In Chinese alchemical texts, yin is represented by the tiger, water and woman, and yang by the dragon, fire and man. The alchemist tries to reverse the original process of the division of the Tao into yin and yang and by bringing about their union in himself and the laboratory he can produce the golden elixir of immortality.

The third basic ingredient of Chinese alchemy, along with the notions of chi and yin and yang, is the theory that all the processes and substances in the universe are composed of five 'elements' (*wu hsing*). The five-element theory is of great antiquity. In the earliest Chinese record, the *Shu Ching* ('Historical Classic'), parts of which date from the tenth century BC, the theory is said to be one of the parts of the ninefold Great Plan which heaven withheld from Kun, father of Yu the Great. As for the five elements themselves, the first is called water, the second fire, the third wood, the fourth metal and the fifth earth. Water gives rise to saltiness, fire to bitterness, wood to sourness, metal to acridity and earth to sweetness. Each quality is associated with the five tastes.

To understand Chinese alchemy, it is essential to realize that the five 'elements' do not refer to five kinds of basic matter as in the Western notion of the four elements (fire, earth, air and water) but to five sorts of processes. Chinese thinking fundamentally works in terms of relation, not substance. The 'elements' are not passive but five powerful forces in ever-flowing cyclical motion. It was thought that when the five elements were aligned and associated in symbolic corre-lation, everything else in the universe would fall into a fivefold arrange-ment. The five intrinsic elements of a human being are essence, sense, vitality (*ching*), spirit (*shen*) and energy (chi). The first two give rise to consciousness while the other three came to be known as the three treasures.

A correspondence is established in Chinese alchemy between the five elements and the five planets (only five are visible to the naked eye) which are seen to be similar in spirit. The planet Mercury corresponds to the element water; Mars, fire; Jupiter, wood; Venus, metal; and Saturn, earth. Since each planet is thought to have its own pitch, circling together, they create the music of the spheres and show the inherent harmony of the universe.

There is also a correspondence between the five planets and the five main minerals used by the alchemists. While they do not exert a direct 'influence', the chi of a planet can stimulate a response in a metal or mineral on earth as if they are tuned to the same note in the universe. Magnetite is considered the essence of Mercury; cinnabar of Mars. Malachite is associated with Jupiter, arsenolite with Venus and realgar with Saturn. According to the author of the book *Huai Nan Tzu* (c.125 BC), a five-mineral elixir made from the 'essences of the five planets can give a man perpetual life, exempt from death for ever'.[8]

While chi, yin and yang and the five-element theory form the tripod of Chinese alchemy, the role of time is crucial in the experiments. It is seen in a cyclical rather than a linear way. Chinese natural philosophy emphasizes that everything in the universe is in a constant state of flux. The Tao is constantly changing and chi circulates throughout the universe. But all is not chaos; there is an underlying harmony and pattern. Momentary events are made sense of by fitting them into the cyclical rhythms of natural processes. The life cycle of the individual – birth, growth and death – thus mirrors the general cycles which go on regularly and eternally in the passage of the day, the seasons and the years.

In keeping with this approach, the alchemists believe that nature is a living organism and everything has a life cycle. Minerals and metals are believed to grow inside the earth, slowly developing towards perfection over an immense period of time. But unlike vegetable and animal growth cycles (whatever the efforts of farmers), the mineral cycle can be interrupted. The alchemist can manipulate time and speed up in his laboratory the growth of minerals and metals. And since the Way of Nature (Tao) is cyclical, correct timing is moreover the key in the alchemist's use of materials, apparatus and combustion. He must choose the right time, and proceed at the right pace.

The Great Work in the alchemist's laboratory thus mirrors the work in the womb of mother nature. While it may take 4,380 years (the number of double-hours in the 'round year' or cycle of 360 years) to form an elixir naturally, in the alchemist's reaction vessel it can be speeded up to one year. In addition, the elixir itself – the Philosopher's Stone – acts as a time-manipulating substance. It can speed up the growth of gold and slow down the process of ageing. At the same time, the attainment of immortality – the supreme goal of alchemy – will release the alchemist from the normal ravages of time.

At the root of Chinese alchemy is the belief in a complex and intricate web of correspondences between parts of the universe which make up the vast whole of the Tao. As we have seen, everything falls into the categories of yin and yang and the five elements in an ordered way. But it is not an order based on a static and mechanical model of the universe but on a kind of organic pattern.[9] Within the pattern, things move and react upon one another not so much by mechanical causation (like one billiard ball guided by a cue hitting another) or by chance collisions (like bumping into someone in the street) but by a kind of mysterious resonance. Things which belong to the same category give energy to each other. Events influence one another by association rather than by a chain of cause and effect. This may not be strictly logical or empirical, but it is a valid way of thinking; it works by intuition rather than by analytical reasoning.

The Chinese alchemists thus conceive of the universe as a vast organism in which the parts resonate with and energize each other. They all freely and spontaneously cooperate, the larger and smaller contributing according to their degree and no one more important than the other. No one has ever been seen to command the four seasons, yet they never swerve from their course. It is a great and glorious mystery:

> The Tao of Heaven operates mysteriously and secretly; it has no fixed shape; it follows no definite rules; it is so great that you can never come to the end of it; it is so deep that you can never fathom it.[10]

Joseph Needham beautifully likened the fluid, resonating and mysterious movement of the alchemists' universe to that of a dance:

> It was an ordered harmony of wills without an ordainer; it was like the spontaneous yet ordered, in the sense of patterned, movements of dancers in a country dance of figures, none of whom are bound by law to do what they do, nor yet pushed by others coming from behind, but cooperate in a voluntary harmony of wills.[11]

I found this one of the most exciting insights of Chinese alchemy, one which directly anticipates the modern notion of Gaia as a living organism.

The alchemists not only had the same world view as the Taoists but also shared their belief that it is possible to save the body from death. The idea centred on the search for material or physical immortality. The Taoists' goal is to become an *hsien*, a person who will never die and who will be able to fly to the heavens for ever. The *hsien* are often depicted as feathered men. There are countless stories of these immortals who can ride the wind, pass through star gates and tread the void.

The Taoists not only sought to prolong life but were fascinated by youth which symbolizes all that is supple and spontaneous. They believe there are techniques which can not only arrest the process of ageing but can also recover the physical condition of youth. In the *Tao Te Ching* of Lao Tzu, it is written: 'He who is filled with Virtue is like a new-born child.'[12]

What happens to the body after death? Chinese alchemists make no clear distinction between the body and soul; the difference is one of quality, rather than of kind. The 'soul' is simply a finer essence of the human organism which 'by nature' is immortal. Since the world consists of a continuum of energy from the grossest matter to the void, death is simply the separation of the finer essence from the coarser essence of the body. It was only one step further for the alchemists to argue that if the physical essence of the body could be refined it would become indistinguishable from the spiritual essence, and a person would then become an immortal being.

While the soul is not separate from the body, the soul itself does not form a unitary whole. From earliest times in China, it was thought to be made up of two parts, the *hun* which derives from the air and is associated with yang, and the *pho*, from the earth and associated with yin. These were later subdivided into three upper *hun* souls and seven lower *pho* souls. They are rather like chi, a rarefied and subtle form of energy.

Where did the immortals go after death? Early in the first millennium BC, the dwelling of the spirits was visualized as the Yellow Springs, somewhere underground. By the third century, they were thought to dwell in a heaven governed by a fully fledged celestial bureaucracy headed by a Jade Emperor, a state of affairs which clearly mirrored the hierarchical nature of the Chinese Empire. As we have seen from the silk banner found in her tomb, Lady Tai was clearly destined to travel to the land of the immortals.

What could she expect to encounter there? Lieh Tzu (c.370) describes it as the country into which pours the stream of the Milky Way. It is a region of great mountains and broad plains in which:

The towers and terraces upon them are all gold and jade, the beasts and birds are unsullied white; trees of pearl and garnet always grow densely, flowering and bearing fruit which is always luscious, and those who eat of it never grow old and die. The men who dwell there are all of the race of the immortal sages, who fly, too many to be counted, to and from one mountain to another in a day and a night.[13]

The alchemists not only conducted their experiments when the constellations were in a favourable position but they also claimed to be able to draw down power from the heavens. A sudden surge of supernatural energy was the reward of the adept who could dance 'the pace of Yu', sometimes called the 'shaman's step'. Great Yu's mother is said to have conceived him after seeing a shooting star in the constellation of Orion.

The nature of their star and planet worship is vividly illustrated in an invocation to the Year Star (Jupiter) from around 900. Choosing the correct cyclic day in the spring, the celebrant first 'rectifies his heart' in meditation and then fixes his gaze on the planet and declares:

> I desire that the luminous star in the eastern quarter support my cloud-soul, unite with my white-soul, and make my longevity like that of pines and cypresses – a life extended through a thousand autumns, a myriad of years.[14]

The alchemists also had immortals known as 'jade women' as protectors and guides. 'The Jade Women of the Luminous Star' await skilful adepts on Mount Hua, the sacred western prop of the sky, offering cups of the 'pale liquor' (the elixir of the alchemists) which gives everlasting life. They could also become directly involved with humans and live in mountain retreats and caves. After ritual banquets, they sometimes came with the secrets of immortality which existed in the arcana of 'Highest Clarity' beyond the sky. Some jade women were clearly librarians of alchemical texts: inside the 'Grand Supreme Sextuply Fitted Purple Chamber', they attended and protected the 'Cryptic Books of the Grand Cinnabar'.[15]

These fairy figures were said to be insubstantial as snowflakes, congealed out of cosmic breath, yet as clear and luminous as shining jade. But how could one be sure of their identity? Easy. They were distinguished from ghost messengers by a piece of yellow jade the size of a millet grain placed above their noses.

But how could I meet them? How could I be rejuvenated? Only through enlightenment. Only through the illumination of divine wisdom. In an alchemical poem, the Taoist poet Lu Yen describes the process:

Awake to clear apprehension of the scheme for extended life –
As lotuses in autumn open in place after place;
Golden lads will climb brocaded hangings;
Jade women will descend aromatic staircases.

The Tiger Whistle – and volatile souls of Heaven stand still;
The Dragon Chant – and residual souls of Earth will come.
Should a man become enlightened in this Way,
He will become once more an infant-babe![16]

Many of the alchemists allegedly flew beyond this world like the old shamans on their soul voyages, sometimes on the back of a dragon, sometimes on a star-raft, sometimes with their own burgeoning wings, sometimes with 'far-roving hats' and 'flying-cloud shoes', to pass through a star gate to the realm of the immortals. By marvellous feats of self-projection, they were capable of 'treading the array of stars to the limits of light'.[17]

The anonymous ode 'Yuan Yu', written around 110 BC, gives a wonderful description of the adventures of an alchemist who travels the world as an immortal. Before he sets off, his master gives him advice:

Keep your *hun* soul from confusion, and it will come of itself.
Unify the energy [chi] and control the spirit [*shen*],
Preserve them within you at the midnight hour . . .
This is the Door of Power.

Having heard this precious teaching, the alchemist departs on his journey towards immortality. The description is full of alchemical ideas and symbols. One wonders whether he had partaken of the famous magic mushrooms as an aid to his vision.

I met the Feathered Ones at Cinnabar Hill,
I tarried in the ancient Land of Deathlessness.
In the morning I washed my hair in the Hot Springs of Sunshine,
In the evening I dried myself where the ten suns perch.
I sipped the subtle potion of the Flying Springs,
And held in my bosom the radiant metallous jade.
My pallid countenance flushed with brilliant colour,
Purified, my *ching* of vitality began to grow stronger;
My corporeal parts dissolved to a soft suppleness,
And my spirit grew lissome and eager for movement.

During a grand tour of the universe, he visits the gods and the spirits of the stars, the earth and the ocean. But while he flies through the universe he is still within the world of nature, for there is nothing outside it. In the end, he attains the ultimate goal of all alchemists, enlightenment, immortality and union with the Whole:

> I attained the Clarity
> And entered the precincts of the Great Beginning.[18]

6

The Lover of Mystery

Being the source of yin and yang,
Its darkness cherishes a yellow shoot . . .
Thus the lead is black outside
Yet within it carries a golden flower,
Like a slab of jade being concealed
By someone coarse, dull and wild.

Wei Boyang

After exploring the origins and basic principles of Chinese alchemy to prolong life and attain immortality, I decided to take a closer look at the lives and works of the major alchemists to see if they could provide me with some further leads in my quest for everlasting life. I began with Wei Boyang who lived in the second century and has been called the 'father of alchemy'. In reality, he was one of its later sons, the beneficiary of an ancient tradition. He was summoned to the court but like a good Taoist refused to go. He had no taste for officialdom or imperial favours. His principal work was traditionally known as *Ts'an T'ung Ch'i* ('The Convergence of the Three'), and has recently been translated as *The Secret of Everlasting Life*. It was written in 141 and is the earliest known full alchemical text.

Wei Boyang was a son of the Kaomen clan, probably from an old family of shamans and magicians. He described himself and his work with endearing modesty:

In the State of Kuai, a common man,
Alone in a valley barely existing
Clasps to his bosom rough simplicity
And pleasures in neither circumstances nor honour . . .

> So there, dwelling in idleness and ease,
> Then I composed this work,
> To sing of the order of Great Change,
> The Three Sages' forgotten words . . .
> I looked at their one meaning,
> And saw one thread connecting the whole.[1]

The 'order of Great Change' is the Tao and the 'Three Sages' are the fathers of Taoism – Lao Tzu, Chuang Tzu and Lieh Tzu. By bringing their insights together, Wei Boyang found the alchemical way to immortality.

The 'Three' of his masterpiece refers to the alchemical operations, the Taoist theories which give them their meaning, and the system of changes which governs their dynamics.[2] The work is mainly devoted to the technical problem of timing the alchemical process in a sequence of phases derived from the sixty-four hexagrams of the *I Ching* ('Book of Changes'). At the same time, it offers a basic account of Chinese alchemical theory and practice. It stresses repeatedly the importance of the right theoretical framework and practical laboratory procedures in order to obtain the correct results. Like all Chinese works of alchemy, it is a philosophical study as well as an exploration of ancient mysteries.

Wei Boyang's greatest work resembles a piece of intricate Chinese embroidery, interweaving cryptic statements with stirring rhetoric and vivid imagery. He insists that it cannot be studied enough: a thousand readings will bring out some points, and 10,000 perusals will enable a person to see others. He uses the symbolism of alchemy to convey very ancient ideas about perfecting oneself in order to attain immortality, a process which requires combining both sides of oneself (yin and yang) in a series of transformations (symbolized by the *I Ching*) in order to become a complete being.

Much of the work describes the materials and procedures needed to produce the elixirs of long life and immortality. One of Wei Boyang's fundamental concepts is that of chemical affinity. He insists that the way to become an immortal through consuming elixirs lies in the use of substances of similar category. There can therefore be no success when substances of the wrong category or proportions are used:

> Even with the Yellow Emperor to build the furnace
> And Great Oneness himself to attend the firing,

> The Eight Lords to pound down the material
> And Huai Nan to stir them together;
> If you set up a High Altar
> Under cover, with white jade steps,
> And unicorn and phoenix meats offered up,
> With a lot of lengthy prostrations,
> Prayers to the earth-spirits,
> Wailing pleas to the ghosts and sprites,
> If you bathe, fast and abstain,
> Hoping for that so long hoped for;
> Even then, like mixing glue to repair a pot,
> Or sal ammoniac daubed on a sore,
> Adding ice to get rid of cold,
> Or using hot water to do away with heat,
> A flying tortoise or dancing snake
> Would be equally unreasonable![3]

The passage gives a vivid idea of some of the rituals and ceremonies that the alchemists practised in the second century in China. It also underlines the need for them to prepare themselves if the experiment is to succeed.

Wei Boyang is much given to sexual imagery to describe the alchemical process. He is the earliest advocate I came across of the 'chemical wedding'. To describe the combination of two chemicals in a reaction vessel, for instance, he calls it the union between the dragon and the tiger or the moon and the sun residing in the same palace. He makes a close parallel between chemicals combining in a reaction vessel and the act of love-making:

> Now see how this cock and hen
> Join in sexual union,
> Their firm and yielding flesh
> Bonds together and cannot be released.
> Just like matching sections of a tally
> No art or skill is involved in managing this.[4]

This is all very interesting, but what about the Philosopher's Stone? In one passage Wei Boyang seems about to reveal the ultimate mystery of alchemy and gives a recipe for the pill of immortality. The process is the classic alchemical one. First, the two main ingredients *chin* and *shui* are heated so that they dissolve and then coagulate, creating a substance called 'Yellow Carriage', which eventually is transformed into a powdery ash. After being carefully ground and mixed the ash is enclosed in a reaction vessel and then placed in a furnace. Entering through 'the red-coloured gate', it is heated with great care, night and day, first with a mild flame and then a fierce one. Finally, when the twelve divisions of the whole cycle are complete a change will be seen:

> Its breath is scattered, its life is cut short,
> The body dies and the soul departs –
> Then the colour turns to the deepest purple,
> Luminous and shining, a restored Elixir is made!
> Just the amount settling on a knife-point
> Will prove to be quite efficacious . . .[5]

Wei Boyang waxes lyrically about the wondrous effects of this supreme elixir:

> If even the herb *ch-sheng* can make one live longer
> Surely the elixir is worth taking into one's mouth
> Prepared as it is by cyclical transformations?
> Gold by its nature does not rot or decay
> Therefore it is of all things the most precious.
> If the alchemist includes it in his diet
> The duration of his life will become everlasting . . .
>
> Hairs that were white all turn to black.
> Teeth that had fallen grow in their former place.
> The old dotard is again a lusty youth,
> The decrepit crone is again a young girl.
> He whose form has changed escapes the perils of life
> And has for his title the name of the True Man.[6]

But there is a hitch. What are the original two ingredients? Their exact nature is not given. Their names of *chin* and *shui* can be interpreted in a variety of ways. Their most common meaning is 'gold' and 'water' but clearly in their normal state these substances cannot alone produce the reaction described. Some commentators have even interpreted them to be lead and cinnabar.

No other alchemical text has been so carefully studied by later alchemists as the many commentaries show. And it was still being studied in the twentieth century. The Taoist monk and alchemist Pien Tao-shi told John Blofeld during his travels in China in the 1930s that 'everything is there for the mixing of the elements that produce the gold and cinnabar pill'. An abbot also told him that it could be interpreted on three levels: 'first, the transmutation of cinnabar and lead into the miraculous elixir of immortality; second, the creation within the crucible of one's own body of a golden pill or foetus, as a means of cheating age and death; and third, a similar form of internal alchemy depending on an ingredient derived from sexual intercourse'.[7] The statement brings together perfectly the *wai tan* and *nei tan* aspects of Chinese alchemy, the production of the outer elixir in the laboratory and the inner elixir within the body.

Did Wei Boyang benefit from his elixir? Some say the master alchemist died at sixty, others at eighty. He may even have attained immortality. There is a lovely story about Wei Boyang and his dog. One day he

passed into the mountains to prepare numinous elixirs. With him went three disciples, two of whom were, he felt, lacking in faith and sincerity. When the elixir was achieved he decided to make a trial of them. 'The gold elixir is now made,' he said, 'but it ought first to be tested. Let us give it to this white dog; if the animal lives and can soar into the air then it will be safe for human beings, but if the dog should die then it is not to be taken.'

So Wei Po-Yang fed it to the dog, and the dog immediately fell down dead. Turning to the disciples he said: 'I fear the elixir was not perfected. As it has killed the dog it would seem that we have not grasped the full theory of spiritual power. If we take it now I am afraid that we shall go the same way as the animal. What do you think we should do?' The disciples, perplexed, replied by another question: 'Would you, sir, dare to take it yourself?' He answered: 'I abandoned worldly ways and forsook family and friends to enter into the mountains; I should be ashamed to return without having found the Tao of the Holy Immortals. To die of the elixir would be no worse than living without it. I must take it.' And he did, whereupon no sooner was it in his mouth than he fell dead . . .[8]

On seeing this, one of his disciples took the elixir and died. The other two decided to live for a few more decades in this world. So they went down the mountains to get coffins and other things for the burial of their teacher and friend. After they had gone, Wei Boyang revived and gave a drug to his disciple and the white dog and in a few moments they both regained consciousness. They all went further into the mountains to tread the path of the immortals.

7

The Day-dreamer

Cleanse the dark mirror of the mind.

Ko Hung

While appreciating the poetry of Wei Boyang and the manner of his passing I was none the wiser about the exact nature of the pill of immortality. I therefore turned with keen anticipation to Ko Hung who had been recommended by the professor from Beijing University as the greatest Chinese alchemist. I soon found out that Ko was not only the most famous but also the most colourful of the Chinese alchemists. Known as Pao Phu Tzu, the 'Simplicity-Embracing Master', he was a brilliant physician and natural philosopher working in the early fourth century. His principal alchemical work is called *Esoteric Chapters* (*N'ei P'ien*) which suggests the revelation of hidden truths. I was not to be disappointed.

Ko was born around 283. He came from an illustrious family. His first ancestor T'ien of Ko was an ancient king and his grandfather and father had both been governors. His father-in-law Pao Ching was a renowned scholar with alchemical interests while his uncle Ko Hsu was an alchemist who could allegedly appear in several places at the same time.

Being a third and late son, Ko says that he was spoiled early on by his parents, but at the age of thirteen his father died and he was obliged to fend for himself. He had to engage in farming for a while and educated himself by reading and copying anything that came his way – some 1,000 scrolls in all. Eventually, he became the pupil of the great alchemist Cheng Yin who allowed him to read the most esoteric texts in his possession and told him his secrets. Ko's own work was thus a product of the great oral and written alchemical tradition handed down from ancient China.

Living in violent times, Ko helped put down a rebellion in 303 and personally decapitated a minor leader and shot with bow and arrow two pursuing horsemen. He was made a marquis for his services. But to avoid the troubles in the north of China, he headed south to retire to the Lo-fou Shan mountains near Canton to 'nurture' his life and pursue his alchemical studies. He lived up to his Taoist ideal of the man who

> deploys his phoenix-dragon wings in the company of simple folk and nourishes his overwhelming vitality in a humble cottage. His garments may be patched and his belt a rope, but he would not exchange them for all the glory of the imperial robes ... He lets gems remain in Mount Sung's peak so that they will not be worked on the grindstone. He lets tortoise shells sink into the dark depths so that they will not suffer the drillings and scorchings of diviners. Whether active or resting, he knows when to stop; he is satisfied wherever he goes.[1]

Ko liked to depict himself as a dull and unsophisticated person – 'no better than a day-dreamer' – but in reality he was extremely learned and wrote a great deal. His work shows how closely alchemy, medicine, magic and astrology were interwoven at the time. His *Esoteric Chapters* form a wonderful tale of gods, immortals, elixirs, talismans and marvels. Like all Taoist alchemists, his aim was to live long and fully and to obtain enlightenment and everlasting life. He had no interest in gold as a medium of exchange but only as a means to endow himself with 'Fullness of Life' (*ch'ang sheng*), a form of immortality.

Ko underwent long training with his alchemical master Cheng Yin. In his view, selection of the right teacher is more important than hard study. The task is not to be taken lightly and failure in the Great Work is inevitable due to the lack of 'secret oral directions obtained from an enlightened teacher'.[2]

This was not the first time I had come across this caveat. Would I ever be able to find such a teacher? Alchemists in Ko's time believed that the ancients, especially the legendary Yellow Emperor, handed down their knowledge in deliberately obscure records so that they could only be understood by the initiated. Certainly in Ko's own case a direct affiliation can be traced from the alchemist Ho Shang Jen who lived in the second century BC to his master Cheng Yin in the fourth century.[3] Ko not only stands in a very ancient tradition of esoteric knowledge but his work contains the oldest and most comprehensive list of alchemical books.

Given the traditional commitment of Chinese alchemists to secrecy and deliberate obscurity, I wondered why Ko should express his alchemical ideas in such an accessible form for the general public. Then it became clear. It was because he feared that the tradition might be lost in his sceptical times:

> To ask the average man of the present to believe my teaching would avail be nothing. I have, therefore, with great diligence, entrusted my teachings to pen and ink with the fond hope that the scholars of a future age – such as love mystery and delight in truth – may examine my books, and earnestly deliberate upon the meaning of Tao.[4]

Much of his writing is therefore polemical and he tries to get his readers to consider the possibility of immortality with such enticing chapter headings as 'Resolving Hesitations', 'Clarifying the Basic', and 'Allay Your Doubts'.

Ko bases his case for alchemy on a close observation of nature. He was impressed by its evolutionary character and ecological diversity: 'In the myriad changes and transformations of creation, marvels may occur without limitation . . . We cannot treat all things the same way.'[5] Ko saw like Darwin the 'art of change' at work all around him. When material substances are broken down they are not destroyed but simply alter their form. Recalling the shape-changing abilities of the old shamans, Ko declares:

> Man is the noblest of all creatures, yet men or women may be transformed into cranes, stones, tigers, monkeys or turtles. Similarly, the transformation of high mountains into abysses, and the making of peaks out of deep valleys, are examples of change in huge things.

Since change is inherent in the nature of heaven and earth, Ko asks: 'Why then should we think that gold and silver cannot be made from other things?'[6] And if mercury can be transformed into gold, why can't humans become immortals?

It was a powerful argument and the best I had so far come across for alchemy, even though I found it difficult to believe that I could be turned into a crane or a turtle.

Despite his down-to-earth approach, Ko did not believe that observation and experience were the only sources of truth. To argue that something does not exist simply because we do not see it is absurd. Can a fly which only lives for a day judge the age of a tortoise? No wonder trying to persuade ignorant people to believe in the 'Fullness of Life' is 'like getting a gnat to carry a mountain or like describing the sea to a hoptoad in a well'.[7]

Ko felt that a knowledge of magic is essential for aspirants of immortality to protect themselves. The Great Work should be performed in secrecy in the dangerous wilderness of sacred mountains. Ko made full use of charms, talismans and rituals. His teacher Cheng Yin told him that after wearing 'Grand-Concealment' amulets for ten days, one may disappear by wheeling to the left, and reappear by wheeling to the right. By taking 'gold-merchant-Artemisia', it is possible to change shape: some adepts can turn into little boys, old men, birds, wild animals, grass, trees or domestic animals. Another sure way of protecting oneself on entering a mountain is to take a knife with your left hand, hold your breath, draw a square on the ground, and say a prayer. If you then lay the knife horizontal for ten days to the west, you will have nothing to fear.[8]

Ko delights in giving many stories of past alchemists who gained extraordinary powers or who achieved immortality. One Kan Shih put some elixir in the mouth of a fish and it could swim about in boiling oil; when he fed it to a silkworm it stopped developing even after the tenth month. When chickens and puppies ate it they grew no more, and when he gave it to a white dog it turned black. When another adept, Luan Ta, was presented to Emperor Wu, he made chessmen hit one another of their own accord. Even his teacher Cheng Yin in his late eighties had black hair and a full and cheerful face, could walk several hundred miles a day and drink two demijohns of wine without becoming drunk.[9]

Although Ko seems to share the ancient Chinese astrological belief that a person's fortune depends on whether one is conceived under a 'star of life' or a 'star of death', the whole direction of his alchemical work implies that each individual ultimately decides the length of his or her own life. He insists:

The span of life is up to me, not heaven.
The reverted cinnabar becomes gold, and millions of years are
    mine.[10]

I was intrigued to learn from Ko Hung that there are different orders
of immortals: some remain on earth and others mount to heaven. It
depends on the quantity and quality of the alchemically prepared
elixir. If one drinks only half a dose of 'reverted cinnabar' or 'potable
gold' one can remain in the world until one decides to take the rest.
It is quite possible to live to 800 years or more like the legendary
Old Pheng-Lai. Those who attain the highest form of immortality
sprout feathers and wings and can become 'coeval with the sky and
earth', travelling up and down in paradise, 'riding clouds or driving
dragons'.[11]

What is this paradise like, the paradise to which all the Chinese
alchemists sought the key? According to Ko, we could travel there in a
flying machine:

> We could mount into the air and tread upon the light, using clouds
> for our floor and the rainbow for the roof of our vehicle. We
> could taste dews fallen from the roseate clouds of morning and
> imbibe the pure essences of heaven and earth. Our drink would be
> jade juice and gold juice; our food, mushrooms of kingfisher blue
> and fruit of vermilion red; our dwellings, halls of beautiful stone
> and rooms of pink gems, our travels, fancy free in Paradise.[12]

Like all Chinese adepts, Ko insists on the need to prepare oneself for
the Great Work and to make sure the wider conditions are right
outside the laboratory. In order to become immortal, one must be calm
and impartial and free oneself from all covetousness and disturbing
thoughts and emotions. Adepts must 'clean the dark mirror of the
mind, maintain a feminine approach, and embrace Unity ... By
eschewing everything shallow, governing through joy and love, and
acting through perfect freedom they maintain the natural order
intact'.[13]

Ko explores many different methods of inner *nei tan* alchemy, such
as breathing exercises, gymnastics to circulate chi and blood, and
sexual techniques aimed at 'reverting the sperm to repair the brain'.
His dietary advice includes dispensing with starches made from the five
grains and eating certain roots, mushrooms and lichens. His recom-

mended herbal medicines range from 'tiger-gall' and 'heaven-male-crane-fat' pills to thistle abstract and absinthe. Echoing the ancient classics of Chinese alchemy, he says:

> Take the elixir and preserve Unity:
> With all heaven together end.
> Revert your sperm, breath like a foetus:
> Protect longevity peaklessly.[14]

At the same time, he insists that these methods cannot produce immortality by themselves. They are merely means of extending life by a couple of hundred years in order to have more time to perform the Great Work. Indeed there are three levels of attainment. Those who subsist on herbs and live for less than a thousand years are third class. Those enjoying 'Fullness of Life' through roots, mushrooms, callisthenics, and breathing disciplines are second class. Only those who make gold from cinnabar and attain immortality by taking it are first class.[15]

All three paths of the Chinese alchemical way seemed appealing but was there one sure way? I was startled to come across the statement:

> If you wish to seek divinity and immortality, you need only acquire
> the quintessence, which consists in treasuring your sperm, circulat-
> ing your breath, and taking one crucial medicine. That is all![16]

But what is this one crucial medicine? Among the thousands of recipes Ko examined, he concluded that the most important are 'reverted cinnabar' and 'potable gold' (*chin i*). Cinnabar produces mercury which after a number of successive transformations will revert back to cinnabar. Ko claims that if you take a spatula of 'reverted cinnabar' for one hundred days you will become an immortal. Like the Philosopher's Stone of Western alchemy, it can transform other substances by projection:

> If one spatula of it is mixed with one pound of mercury and fired,
> it will immediately turn into gold.[17]

Amongst his many recipes for elixirs culled from ancient texts and his teachers, Ko singles out nine main ones and gives careful instructions for their preparation. The most interesting recipe is for the 'elixir flower':

One should first prepare the 'mysterious yellow' [substance] [*hsuan huang*]. Add to it a solution of realgar [arsenic disulphide] and a solution of alum. Take several dozen pounds of rough Kansu salt, crude alkaline salt, alum, [powdered] oyster shells, red bole clay, [powdered] soapstone, and lead carbonate; and with it make the Six-One Lute [and seal the reaction-vessel with it]. After 36 days heating the elixir will be completed, and anyone who takes it continuously for seven days will become an immortal.

The method given of heating substances in a reaction vessel over a fire is the classic operation of alchemy East and West.

Did this elixir have the gold-making property of the Philosopher's Stone? I was not disappointed to read:

Now if this elixir is made into pills with 'mysterious fat' [*hsüan kao*] and placed upon a fierce fire, it will very quickly turn into gold. Gold can also be made by taking 240 *chu* [10 oz] of this elixir and adding it to it 100 catties [lbs] of mercury, then upon heating, it will all turn into gold. If this works we know that the elixir is right. If it does not, re-seal the constituents and heat for as long as before. This never fails.[18]

The problem of course is to discover the exact nature of the 'mysterious yellow' substance and the 'mysterious fat'. While the correct technique might be given, the crucial ingredients are omitted. Ko frequently mentions that such secrets are passed down only after a pupil has proved himself worthy and then only under an oath sealed with blood on the lips. The more I studied Chinese alchemical texts, the more frustrating I found this attitude to be. Did they really know the elixir of everlasting life or were they simply misleading their patrons and followers?

And what of Ko himself? Was he really a serious alchemist?

Unable to acquire real gold, Ko tried to prepare potable gold, using cinnabar and other reagents. He also produced mixtures and oxidations from the eight minerals: cinnabar, realgar, malachite, sulphur, mica, salt, saltpetre and orpiment. In one of the gold-making processes which he attributes to his venerable predecessors, he describes the earliest known preparation of stannic sulphide. Known as 'mosaic gold', it forms golden yellow glistening hexagonal scales or flakes which do not tarnish and are still used for gilding and bronzing. In this case Ko really succeeded in producing an artificial gold from substances manifesting none of the properties of the precious metal.[19]

And the 'Fullness of Life'? Did he discover the ultimate goal?

Ko was endearingly frank. He confessed that because of the difficulties in his life he was unable to be sufficiently single-minded and detached to attain his end. There were times when he obtained oral instructions for an important process or when he met an uncommon teacher, but then he found himself clinging to his old wife and children:

> Although knowing that Fullness of Life can be achieved, I was unable to undertake the work, for, even though I am concerned about the horrors of popular practices about me, I cannot quit them.[20]

As a result, the greatest of all Chinese alchemists is generally thought to have died at sixty in poverty. On the other hand, on the site of his laboratory in the Lo-fou Shan mountains there is near the 'Bridge of Immortals' the 'Tomb of the Empty Clothes and Cap'. Perhaps he did vanish into thin air after all and ride the wind with the immortals!

What is certain is that Ko Hung left a unique and rich list of alchemical recipes, a profound work of Taoist philosophy, and a marvellous collection of anecdotes and stories. He marked the zenith of the *wai tan* tradition of the outer elixir and explored the techniques of the *nei tan* alchemy of the inner elixir. He remained a profoundly spiritual man and shows how the scientific method need not banish the soul from the heart of nature. Magic can help in the search for truth, and meditation is essential. As his great teacher Cheng Yin taught him:

> If men Unity could know,
> Then they'd know all here below.[21]

My study of Ko Hung left me with more questions than answers. He pointed a way to the mountain top but I would still have to go through woods and over streams alone. Was I born under a star of death or a star of life? Was the span of my life really up to me? Would I ever be able to attain 'Fullness of Life'?

8

The Secret of the Golden Flower

Sit on the summit of a thousand mountains without leaving
the crossroads.

The Secret of the Golden Flower

After months of research, I eventually realized that the sun of Chinese
alchemy began to set after Ko Hung, although it still occasionally
continued to shoot off blazing rays. The golden age lasted roughly
from the end of the Sung (c.420) to the late Tang dynasty (c.800).
During this period, the prospect of discovering a pill of immortality
attracted and fascinated many a Chinese emperor. Tao Wu-ti of the
Northern Wei dynasty even established a professional chair in alchemy
and arranged for large-scale experiments at the beginning of the fifth
century. Yet little new emerged. One alchemist, however, stands out in
the early seventh century, the 'wonder worker' Sun Ssu-mo.

Many works were attributed to him, with such enticing titles as
*Records of the Pillow Book, Records of the Nourishing of Vitality for
the Attainment of Realization, Prescriptions Worth a Thousand*. The
best and most famous, however, is *Essentials of the Elixir Manuals for
Oral Transmission* which was written down about 640. As a practical
alchemist in the *wai tan* tradition, Sun describes his procedures and
laboratory equipment in simple language, avoiding the use of synonyms and obscure terms so beloved by his predecessors.

Sun Ssu-mo called himself a 'recluse scholar'. Born in Hua-yan in
581, he is reputed to have died a hundred and one years later. He
was something of a child prodigy: he had great powers of divination
and was by twenty able to discuss with insight the ideas of the great
Taoist philosophers. Refusing to accept offices from three emperors,
he withdrew to work in Mount T'ai-po.

For Sun, alchemy was mainly a branch of medicine. Like all Chinese alchemists of his day, he made ample use of magic, sympathetic procedures, invocations and taboos. He kept an open mind and was prepared to try all approaches to treating illness. Under a heading entitled 'Earwig', for instance, he describes how an insect urinated on a man's shadow and caused a sore to develop on the corresponding place on his body. To find a cure he drew a likeness of the earwig on the ground and with a knife cut out all the earth enclosed by its stomach. 'Then I spat into this earth, mixed it to the consistency of mud, and plastered it twice on [the afflicted spot], which healed forthwith.' And his conclusion? 'We must realize that everything in nature [interacts] by mutual resonance, although no one understands the causes [of particular instances].'[1]

Although a practical man, Sun does not question the possibility of immortality:

> I have read in succession the lore books of ancient times; they agree that, without exception, cases of men's bodies sprouting feathered wings and rising weightlessly in flight were due to the taking of elixirs. Never did I read or speak of these things without feeling an ardent longing in my heart. My sole regret was that the divine Way is so remote, the pathway through the clouds so inaccessible. I gazed in vain at azure heaven, not knowing how to ascend it.[2]

Sun began by using the traditional alchemical techniques of preparing elixirs by cyclical transformation and of fixing substances in the fire. He also tried the formulas for making liquid jade and potable gold. But he found the techniques abstruse and unpredictable and declared in exasperation: 'How can one without occult virtue comprehend them?' I knew exactly what he meant.

Many of the elixirs mentioned by Sun are clearly copies from older compendia of alchemical recipes. Of the thousand known names for Chinese elixirs of immortality, he lists only sixty-seven elixirs. As always they have wonderfully exotic names, such as 'Roseate Cloud Elixir of the Grand Immortal', the 'Grand Concord Dragon Elixir', and the 'Elixir of Ma the Immortal's Ascension to Heaven in Broad Daylight'. Sun decided to concentrate on the lesser elixirs. In all, his aim was never to chase 'mundane profit' but to 'save the sick, to aid the imperilled'.[3]

What are the elixirs like? The 'Formula for Making Scarlet Snow and Flowing Pearl Elixir' is made mainly from realgar, wine vinegar and salt and fired in a reaction vessel. In a rare burst of eloquence, Sun says that when the elixir is made, 'It will have a brilliant radiance. It will be of the shape of a pendant or string of pearls or of coloured silken threads. Again, its configuration will be that of stretched knotted netting. Its fresh brilliance dazzles the eyes. Those who see it will, unawares, feel a shock. But it is well to be calm.'

Sun recommends the elixir for those who have suddenly fainted, who are on the point of death, or have even expired, but he regrets that 'in these unsettled times there is no one who will understand its preparation and use'.[4]

To a modern chemist most of the elixirs appear extremely harmful as they invariably contain mercury or lead, and sometimes arsenic. On the face of it, they seem more likely to hasten than postpone death. Every ingredient, for instance, of his formula for 'Mixing Demon-Killing Pellets' is a poison. But then perhaps this is being too literal, and forgetting the power of the 'occult virtue' in them . . .

Sun's *Essentials of the Elixir Manuals* reads very much like a handbook for the laboratory bench. He describes the essential alchemical apparatus of the day, including the furnace and the two-part reaction vessel. He carefully explains the making of the sealing compound or lute which he calls a 'six-in-one paste'. The proper selection and preparation of raw materials are given. And although his main interest is in minor elixirs to heal illnesses and prolong life, he is not above giving recipes for augmenting brass and making artificial white jade, pearls and malachite.

China's *Old Standard History* (945) says that Sun died in 682 and was buried with a minimum of ceremony: 'After more than a month had passed there was no change in his appearance. The corpse, when placed in the coffin, was [light] as empty clothing. At the time this was much wondered at.'[5] A sure sign of apotheosis as an immortal! Did he go the same way as Lady Tai and Ko Hung?

*

My studies showed that from the eleventh century onwards in China, *wai tan* outer elixir alchemy went into decline, partly because of the difficulties of discovering the pill of immortality and partly because its elixirs, mainly based on mercury and lead, had poisoned many emperors, high officials and alchemists themselves. The *nei tan* alchemy of the inner elixir came to preponderate, with its stress on perfecting the self through meditation, regulated breathing and exercises. The human body became the true crucible, inner work on oneself taking precedence over outer work in the laboratory. The language and symbolism of practical alchemy were used to describe processes of inner transformation and self-realization. This at first sight seemed a more fruitful field for research.

The leading exponent of this new development was Chang Po-tuan, who founded the southern school of 'Complete Reality' Taoism (Quan Zhen) which contains elements from Cha'n Buddhism (known as Zen in Japan). The northern school was known as the 'Pure Serenity' sect because of its stress on quiet sitting and silent meditation. By contrast the southern school made more use of the 'water wheel' sexual techniques of *nei tan* alchemy to nourish the brain and prolong life.

Chang Po-tuan, also styled Tzu-yang, lived approximately 983–1082. Little is known about his life, except that he learned the esoteric lore of alchemy from his master Liu Ts'ao and produced the alchemical classic *Understanding Reality*.[6] Like the other great Chinese alchemists, Chang worked within the classic Taoist framework of the doctrine of yin and yang and the theory of the five elements. He recommended fostering yang while repelling yin. What on earth does this mean? I found out that it is a key operation in *nei tan* alchemy and is sometimes called 'yin convergence'. It means bringing about an inner state in which heavenly yang consciousness, what might be called the 'original mind', balances earthly yin consciousness which is the part of the human mind which is historically and culturally conditioned.

How could I do this? How could I escape my conditioned self and get back in touch with my 'original mind'? I learned that it can be achieved through a process of meditation which frees the mind from worldly entanglements. It is well described by Lao Tzu in the *Tao Te Ching*:

Empty yourself of everything.
Let the mind rest at peace.
The ten thousand things rise and fall while the Self watches their return.

> They grow old and flourish and then return to the source.
> Returning to the source is stillness, which is the way of nature.[7]

In this way worldly yin conditioning remains the 'guest' and not the 'host' in the mind and the individual retains his freedom and autonomy. Doing nothing, he leaves nothing undone. Stabilizing the wandering mind in this way will allow the seed of the 'golden flower' of the original mind to take root and put forth shoots.

The essence of *nei tan* inner alchemy is therefore to balance and reunite yin and yang and then escape from the ordinary world and live in the pure yang of heaven. As Chang describes it:

> Containing female substance within the male, bearing yin yet embracing yang, when the two are combined the medicine is then produced, changing the slightness in the yin spirit and the predominance in the yang spirit. Truly it is said of a grain of the gold elixir that a snake that swallows it is immediately transformed into a dragon and a chicken that eats it is then changed into a phoenix, flying into the pure realm of true yang.[8]

The text of *Understanding Reality* opens with sixteen verses, representing 'eight ounces' of yin and 'eight ounces' of yang, forming 'one pound of elixir'. The approach clearly echoes the principle of the *I Ching* that 'One yin and one yang is called the Tao'. Chang's work also contains sixty-four verses modelled on the number of hexagrams of the *I Ching*.

For those not familiar with the system, the symbols can at first appear confusing, but they form a beautiful and satisfying symmetry. The most common are the four called heaven and earth, water and fire. The trigrams for heaven (see below) and earth are the parent signs, representing pure yang and yin respectively. The fire sign refers to awareness, particularly the conscious knowledge of the human mind. By contrast, the sign for water is used to refer to the real knowledge of the 'original mind'. The yang component in the middle stands for the real heavenly knowledge that has been buried under worldly conditioning.

heaven   earth   fire   water   yang   yin

The basic operation of *nei tan* alchemy is to take the solid yang out of water and use it to replace the broken yin inside fire so as to produce the whole of heaven. In this way real knowledge is retracted from the overlay of artificial conditioning. Another way of expressing the operation is in terms of the 'inversion of fire and water' so that they interact: water 'cools' fire, in the same way that real knowledge stabilizes consciousness, while fire 'warms' water and brings real knowledge into action in everday life.

The equivalent of yang (fire) and yin (water) in Chinese alchemy is lead and mercury. Yang, sun, dragon, fire, lead, black, original mind and real knowledge go in one category; while yin, moon, tiger, water, mercury, white, conscious mind and conditioned knowledge go in the other. The aim is to bring the two categories together: the harmonization of the 'lead' of the real knowledge of the original mind and the 'mercury' of conscious knowledge of the human mind is needed to produce the golden elixir. 'True lead' depicts the 'mind of Tao' but, as the commentator Liu-I-ming observes, it has many synonyms:

> True lead is the primordial root of consciousness; it is also called the root of heaven, or the true unified vitality, or the true unified energy, or lead from the homeland of water, or metal within water, or black within white, or the yang soul within the yin soul, or the black tiger, or the metal man, or the method of immortality of that house.[9]

In order to practise this kind of inner alchemy, must I like Ko Hung and Sun Ssu-mo retreat to the mountains and lead an ascetic life? Chang insists that there is no need to withdraw into the wilderness or become a solitary; on the contrary, it can be undertaken in the 'furnace' of everyday life. At the same time, he warns against being too attached to family and possessions: '"That" and "this" both non-existent, myriad bubbles return to water.'[10]

His advice is simple and yet profound:

> Stay relaxed beside the alchemical furnace and watch the firing process; just settle your spirit and breath, and leave it up to nature. When all mundanity has been stripped away, the elixir is complete; leaping out of the cage of the ordinary, life is myriad years.[11]

As in Zen, sudden enlightenment is possible. For the right person the crystallization of the inner elixir of immortality can happen in a single moment.

But if you are going to practise this form of *nei tan* alchemy, Chang insists that only the 'gold elixir' of immortality is worthwhile. Everyone, he claims, originally has the 'herb of long life' within them; it's just that they don't understand it, and throw it away. There's therefore no need to take external elixirs or engage in complicated rituals:

> When the sweet dew descends, heaven and earth join; where the yellow sprouts, water and fire mix ... When the elixir is fully developed, naturally gold fills the room; what is the need to look for herbs and practise burning reeds?[12]

I warmed to Chang Po-tuan and his belief that the 'herb of long life' is within us all. We can develop it or let its yellow shoots wither, depending on how we lead our lives. If we allow our conditioning and the entanglements and worries of the everyday world to overwhelm us we are lost. But if we carefully combine yin and yang, mix and stabilize the 'mercury' of the conscious knowledge of our own mind with the 'true lead' of real knowledge of the original mind, gold will fill our dwelling place. Wandering freely, nothing can get us down. And we will then live for ever.

*

Reading Chang's *Understanding Reality* reminded me of another work I had come across before going to China – *The Secret of the Golden Flower*. Thanks to the interest of Carl Jung, it has become the most famous text of Chinese *nei tan* alchemy in the West. The reputed author Lu Yan is from the same Taoist school of 'Complete Reality' as Chang. He wrote down its esoteric teaching in 1668, claiming that it had been passed down orally as a 'special transmission outside of doctrine'.[13] It condensed thousands of years of Chinese *nei tan* alchemy. I turned to it again hoping to find more guidance on how to germinate the 'seed' of immortality within and nurture the 'golden flower'.

What is the golden flower? Gold represents light and the flower stands for the opening up of the light of the mind. It refers to the awakening of the hidden potential of the real self independent of its worldly conditioning.

The light is a very special kind of light, 'the absolutely unified real energy of celestial immortals'. The whole work is devoted to a particular form of meditation known as 'turning the light around'. It recalls the *nei tan* technique of making the semen (*ching*) return to nourish the brain and the practice of circulating energy (chi) throughout the body. Yet it also refers to the Buddhist exercise of mentally looking inward towards the source of consciousness – the 'original mind' which is beyond the passing thoughts and emotions of the 'conscious mind' and its psychological, cultural, historical and environmental influences.

The process of 'turning the light around' is a method of reversal, switching from the limited realm of the 'conscious mind' to dwelling in the 'original mind'. It means turning the primary attention from involvement in mental objects to focus on the source or ground of the mind. It means forsaking all discriminating thoughts and feelings. It means polishing the mirror of the mind until there is nothing there. Then the light begins to shine from within.

This form of meditation in *The Secret of the Golden Flower* is expressed in specifically alchemical terms:

> The highest secrets of alchemy are the water of vitality, the fire of spirit, and the earth of attention. The water of vitality is the energy of the primal real unity. The fire of spirit is illumination. The earth of attention is the chamber of the centre, the celestial mind.[14]

The alchemical way of *The Secret of the Golden Flower* is to sublimate the pure, 'original mind' out of the conditioned 'conscious mind'. Making the traditional Chinese distinction between the upper *hun* soul with its three aspects and lower *pho* soul with its seven forms, the text recommends 'turning the light around' as a means of dissolving darkness and refining the higher soul and controlling the lower soul. Again, the imagery of alchemy is used to describe the method of meditation: 'the water of vitality will be full, the fire of spirit will ignite, the earth of attention will stabilize, and thus the embryo of sagehood can be solidified'. The higher soul is defined as yang, male energy that is light and clear; the lower soul is yin, female energy that is dense and opaque. The adept therefore attempts to transform yin into yang: 'If learners refine the dark lower soul completely, then it will be pure light.'[15]

'Turning of the light' in meditation is thus the alchemical 'firing process' which produces the inner elixir. It is done not by the eyes or hands in the laboratory but in the mind of the adept.

The process requires regulating the breathing. By resting the mind on the breath, one can get rid of the potential pitfalls of oblivion (such as dulling the mind or falling into drowsiness) and distraction (where thoughts run off). When the mind is calm, so is the breath and vice versa. The advice is to sit, lower your eyelids and then establish a point of reference. Then let go of entanglements and objects of desire so that nothing disturbs your mind.

How can I be sure that I have successfully turned the light around? When there is uninterrupted quiet, your spirit becomes joyful and happy, as if you were intoxicated or in a bath. This is called positive harmony pervading the body. Once 'myriad pipes are all silent', and 'the bright moon is in mid sky', you feel the whole earth as a realm of light.[16]

This is called the 'great stabilization' of the golden flower. The mind is alert but detached, the light of the eyes blazes up, the physical body becomes like silk or jade. If you find the 'unified energy' in yourself, the 'elixir immediately crystallizes'. This is the 'secret of freedom'. Indeed, it is claimed that the whole practice described in *The Secret of the Golden Flower* does not go beyond the words 'emptiness of mind'. This single statement can save 'decades of seeking'.[17]

How can I know that I have successfully 'turned the light' and germinated the golden flower within? When the original mind first stirs in the midst of darkness, it is called 'living midnight', a state of deep mental stillness which is pregnant with energy and promise. As you progress in the meditation of turning the light around, spontaneous observation occurs: gazing inward, suddenly you forget the gazing. At that moment body and mind are in a state of great freedom, and all objects of desire disappear: 'Then you don't know where the furnace and cauldron in your spiritual room are.' One then attains a sense of calm abiding and clear seeing.

How long will it take to reach this level? It is possible, the text claims, to set up the foundation of this kind of meditation in a hundred days. The vital energy will be sufficient for 'true yang' to rise spontaneously, so that there is 'true fire naturally existing in water. If you carry on the practice this way, you will naturally achieve intercourse and formation of the embryo. You are then in the heaven of unknowing, and the child thus develops.'[18]

It is not necessarily a static form of meditation. The method of 'turning the light around' can be carried on whether you are walking, standing, sitting or reclining. You can work on this alchemical way whatever you are doing. There is nothing to stop you; you can even 'sit on the summit of a thousand mountains without leaving the crossroads'. And there is no need to retreat to a remote mountain or wood for you can practise it wherever you happen to be.

Because of the warmth of his 'cinnabar heart' to liberate the world, the author of *The Secret of the Golden Flower* offers at the end a 'Song to Inspire the World'. It is a poetic summary of his argument:

> The pervasive principle of the centre
> Bears universal change;
> The very being of true poise
> Is the mysterious pass.
> Midnight, noon, and in between,
> If you can stabilize breathing,
> The light returns to the primal opening,
> So all psychic functions are calm.
> There emerges the unified energy
> Of the river source that produces the medicine.[19]

But does the meditation work? Does it really germinate the 'golden flower'? The success of the method of 'turning the light around' can be measured by its effects. My own experience has taught me that it can clarify and awaken the mind in the midst of everyday life. Everyone can practise it; everyone can become an alchemist in the inner chamber of their mind and manufacture their own elixir, thereby prolonging life and improving its quality. While Jung warned readers away from the practice of *The Secret of the Golden Flower*, I would warmly recommend the form of meditation. And remember: 'if you do practise for a single breath, then you are a realized immortal for a single breath'.[20]

Is the 'golden flower' another name for the Philosopher's Stone? It is written: 'The golden flower is the same thing as the gold pill. The transmutation of spiritual illumination is guided by the mind.'[21] It enables you to enter eternity in the midst of time, to experience immortality here and now. It is not a pill of immortality to be fashioned in a crucible in a laboratory; it is a seed which can be grown in the inner chamber of the mind. By turning the light around, light shines from within to illuminate the world.

9

The Arts of the Inner Elixir

Know the strength of man,
But keep a woman's care!
Be the stream of the universe!
Ever true and unswerving,
Become as a little child once more.

Lao Tzu

During my stay in China, every morning at dawn crowds of people would gather in the groves and by the lake of the Purple Bamboo Park near my hotel in Beijing. The same was happening all over China. Dressed against the autumn frost, they came to practise qigong exercises and tai chi. Some practised alone, but most joined small groups who copied the movements of an expert who wore white gloves. Like supple dancers they turned in slow motion, very relaxed, but following a carefully rehearsed and precisely ordered organic pattern. They extended and contracted their bodies in a mild and gentle way: it was like a moving meditation. They were in fact practising *nei tan* alchemy of the inner elixir, continuing a tradition which is at least 3,000 years old.

The Chinese alchemists long practised this mild form of gymnastics (qigong) and self-massage (*tao yin*) to unblock the flow of energy, to nourish the life force and to circulate the chi. The exercises were probably derived from the dances of the shamans but they were well developed by the second century BC. The tomb of the son of Lady Tai at Mawangui contained at least forty coloured drawings on silk of the exercises, including those mentioned by the sage Chuang Tzu, such as the 'bear rambling' and the 'bird stretching'.[1]

The famous third-century physician Hua Tho taught that the body should be exercised in every part but this should not be overdone in any way. 'Exercise', he said,

> brings about good digestion and a free flowing of the blood. It is like a door-pivot never rotting. Therefore the ancient sages engaged in *tao yin* exercises, [for example] by moving the head in the manner of a bear, and looking back without turning the neck. By stretching at the waist and moving the different joints to the left and right one can make it difficult for people [to grow] old. I have a method known as the 'play of the five', the tiger, the deer, the bear, the ape and the bird.[2]

The mild exercises of qigong and tai chi almost 2,000 years later are very similar and have the same beneficial effects.

They are only part of a whole variety of techniques used by Chinese alchemists in order to prolong life. These include meditation, regulated breathing, special diets and certain sexual techniques. The practices are all directed to nourish and preserve the three primary 'vitalities' known as the three treasures: *shen* (spirit or mental activity), chi (energy or the breath of life) and *ching* (semen or seminal essence). In terms of modern Western physiology, *shen* may be compared to the components of the brain; chi, to the nervous impulses and dissolved gases in body fluids; and *ching*, to the fluids themselves. The Chinese alchemists believed that their all-round development would result in a healthy and harmonious person who would live long. How the techniques actually work remains mysterious but their extraordinary effects can be measured and tested. They lower blood pressure and keep the body supple and lithe and the mind clear and alert. I have practised them myself and can vouch for their effectiveness, although at first they are not easy to perform and require long and regular practice.

The most important element of all is to cultivate a state of serene calmness. This can be done by letting go troubling thoughts and feelings and by becoming centred and focused in all that one does. Developing this inner repose is a very ancient art. In the oldest Chinese medical classic, the *Yellow Emperor's Manual of Internal Medicine*, collated over 2,000 years ago, the imperial physician-alchemist Qi Bo declares:

> If you can be quiet and remain indifferent to things, and be completely humble and empty – then the true breath will follow.

> When the mental powers are guarded within, how can disease
> arrive? Breathing the essence of life, one stands alone, guarding
> the spirit, flesh and sinews as one.[3]

Meditation is the key to this inner calm. The alchemists developed
techniques of meditation which were partly inherited from the states
of trance and ecstasy of the early shamans. The main form of meditation involves 'visualizing the Unity', that is the Unity of the Tao. This
enables the meditator, as in *The Secret of the Golden Flower*, to open
the 'mysterious pass', which lies midway between the eyes, in order
to reconnect with the 'original mind' beyond the conditioned mind of
everyday consciousness. This is the lair of spirit (*shen*) and energy
(chi). This form of meditation is similar to the process of 'seeing
essence' in Zen. It is a kind of sitting forgetfulness in which, lost to the
external world, one can visualize the wholeness of things. The alchemists believed that a settled mind in a quiet body was the best way to
cultivate the golden elixir of everlasting life.

An important part of meditation is breathing, or 'harmonizing the
chi'. Chinese alchemists believed that you are given all the breath
or chi you need at birth. You can waste it or conserve it. When it runs
out you die. The breathing techniques are of great antiquity and go
back well before the sixth century BC. They are still widely practised:
Taoist monks and nuns in Beijing, Hong Kong and Taiwan and in
obscure temples in remote mountain retreats can hold their breath for
three minutes and reduce the heartbeat to 20 times a minute.

The aim of the breathing exercises is to become like an embryo in
the womb, that is, to breathe quietly and hold the breath closed for as
long as possible, so quietly that the air passing through the nostrils
will not disturb a soft feather. Some of the more advanced techniques
are highly elaborate and involve breathing in various rhythmic ways
and chasing inner chi around the body.

The alchemist Ko Hung claimed that regulated breathing worked
wonders. He gave his own advice:

> By practising the circulation of the chi, one can cure the hundred
> diseases, one can walk through the midst of plagues and epidemics,
> one can ward off snakes and tigers, stop bleeding from wounds,
> stay under water or walk across it, free oneself from hunger and
> thirst, and protract one's years. The most important thing is simply
> to [know how to] breathe like an embryo. He who can breathe

like a foetus will respire as if still in the womb, without using nose or mouth; thus the Tao will be achieved ... After continual practice one may very gradually increase the number of heartbeats [during which the breath is held] to as much as 1,000, and when this proficiency is reached, an old man will be able to grow younger daily, returning to youth by one day every day.[4]

Apart from meditation and regulated breathing, the Chinese alchemists went in for sun and moon bathing. Moon bathing tended to be for women and sun bathing for men. Both sexes also walked the symbolic constellations, such as the Great Bear, to draw the chi from the planets and the stars. One such walk is known as the 'dance of Yü'. Absorbing the chi from the planets and stars as well as from the centre and the four directions of space helps strengthen the corresponding organs in the body.

The alchemists also experimented with diet to prolong life and restore vitality. They recommended, in particular, the consumption of plants such as peach gum, pine needles and ginseng, minerals such as mica powder, and animal products such as crane, bird blood, chicken, tortoise and rhino horn in order to prolong life. Abstention from foods for a period, notably cereals and plants of the *Allium* genus, was widely practised. The macrobiotic variation of the intake of foods, especially of rice, according to a monthly cycle was adopted. Many alchemists were also vegetarians, believing that the chi of blood and meat is bad for the souls inhabiting the body and thus encourages the process of ageing.[5]

An integral part of diet is the consumption of elixirs, which, as we have seen, is the main concern of *wai tan* alchemy. Ko Hung tried to convince his sceptical contemporaries of their efficacy:

If flesh and blood could mount up into the heavens after swallowing the chi and taking [medicinal substances] for a single day, or if feathers and wings were to sprout after a mere month's practice of the gymnastic exercises, there is no one in the world who would fail to believe in the adepts of the Tao ... Yet not knowing that the fault lies in themselves, men turn against the Taoist processes, declaring that they are profitless; and soon they abandon the pile of pills and powders, and stop practising the respiratory techniques.[6]

Ancient and medieval Chinese alchemists made great use of elixirs. Many were thought to have aphrodisiac properties as well as being capable of averting hunger, lightening the body and prolonging life. Sulphur, for instance, was considered to increase virility for it 'stiffens and edifies the male essence, dissolving the yin and modifying the influence of the *pho* soul'. Mercury was used for male exhaustion, while blue vitriol was considered beneficial for fertility by 'warming the uterus'.[7] From the sixth to the twelfth centuries, people consumed a great deal of alchemical elixirs, generally made from a mercury or arsenic base. Although small doses were always recommended, there were many cases of poisoning.

It seems certain that alchemists made use of hallucinogenic drugs. While Chinese alchemy from the beginning mainly focused on metals, it included the art of growing marvellous plants (*ling chih*), including hemp, which were believed to prolong life and even bring about immortality. The most famous was the 'magic mushroom', which was pictured in the hands of alchemists, both female and male, in many popular portraits. The fact that mushrooms were so prominent in alchemist lore suggests that there was a ritual use of hallucinogenic substances; indeed, as many alchemical poems show, visions and ecstatic trances of riding the wind with the immortals were common in ancient China. Ko Hung made no bones about it: 'All the numinous fungi can bring men to longevity and material immortality – and this belongs to the same category as the making of gold.'[8] In many ways, the Chinese alchemists were forerunners of the turned-on hippies of the second half of the twentieth century who used drugs to open the doors of perception and to explore different realms of consciousness.

Although I had long known about the physical exercises and techniques of meditation and breathing used by Chinese alchemists, the importance they gave to sex as a means to health and long life came as a surprise and revelation to me. Could it be that the Philosopher's Stone is to be found in sex? Sex is one of the most important aspects of *nei tan* alchemy of the inner elixir. It goes to the heart of the most intimate structure of the universe. It is a sacred act in which the union of man and woman mirrors the union between yin and yang in the cosmos.

The Chinese alchemists recognized that the cooperation of the sexes is necessary for health and longevity and that sex benefits both. The female element is considered as important as the male for they are complementary and interdependent. As we have seen, the alchemists celebrated the 'Mysterious Feminine' and the 'Valley Spirit' as part of a much wider philosophy which sees yin and yang as equal and complementary forces in the universe.

Since to prolong life is to follow nature, then it is logical for alchemists to see sexual intercourse as a means of increasing the vitality of both partners through the mutual nourishment of yin and yang. And as everything in nature has male and female properties, continence is regarded as contrary to the great rhythm of the Tao. To have sex is thus going with the flow of our true nature.

The sexual techniques of the Chinese alchemists were highly systematized from very early on. They are called 'the method of nourishing the life by means of the yin and the yang'.[9] Their basic aim is to conserve as much as possible the seminal essence (*ching*) and stimulate the spirit (*shen*), especially by 'causing the *ching* to return' and nourish the brain. *Ching* in men is regarded as semen and in women as menstrual blood, following the ancient saying that 'the male sows the white, the female the red'. The notion of vital energy suffusing the mind-body is central to alchemist physiology.

In alchemical symbolism, the act of making love between a man and a woman is often depicted as a dance between a dragon (yang) and a tiger (yin); it was called coiling the dragon and playing the tiger. Recognizing that all men have yin and women yang within them at a deeper level, in several illustrations a girl is shown riding the dragon (the yin within the yang) while the young man rides a tiger (the yang within the yin) on either side of a reaction vessel in which an elixir is being prepared.[10]

I found this equality between male and female at the heart of Chinese alchemy to be one of its most attractive aspects. I also found a study of the ancient sex manuals, sometimes known as 'pillow books', to be highly relevant to anyone wishing to lead a healthy and long life. And who knows, if the Chinese alchemists are right, the arts of the bedchamber may help you attain immortality.

In a work entitled *The Yellow Emperor's Canon of the Nine-Vessel Spiritual Elixir*, probably dating from the second century, it is written:

> If he [the alchemist] only takes the Medicine, and does not obtain
> the essentials of the Art of the Bedchamber, then it will be
> impossible for him to live for ever . . . [if they] give free rein to

their emotions and desires, without knowing that they can equita-
bly regulate the dispersion [of their chi], they are hacking at the
trunk of their lives.[11]

The sexual techniques developed by Chinese alchemists were practised
from ancient times, long before they were written down around
300 BC. A few of the oldest texts, including *Su Nü' Ching'* ('The
Immaculate Girl') and *Hsu'an Nü'* ('The Mysterious Girl'), are associated with the legendary Old Man Pheng Tzu who was said to owe his
longevity to his mastery of sexual techniques. One text attributed to
him declares:

> Many are the things which harm men – vaulting ambition, mourn-
> ing and melancholy, joy and jubilation, anger and frustration,
> inordinate desire, apprehensive anxiety, unseasonable heat and
> cold, abstention from sexual life – many indeed are these things,
> and what happens in the bedchamber is mainly responsible [for
> their effects]. How people are deluded by this! Man and woman
> naturally complete each other, just as heaven and earth mutually
> generate each other, and so the Tao nourishes the *shen*, the chi,
> preventing human beings from losing their harmony. Heaven and
> earth have always had the [true] Way of union, therefore they are
> everlasting, but men and women have lost this Way, therefore
> their time has been broken and injured by mortality. Thus to
> obtain the Art of the Yin and the Yang is to avert all the harmful
> dangers and to tread the path of life eternal.[12]

There are repeated warnings in the pillow books about the need to
practise the techniques with skill and care. The joys of sex should be
moderate and well-ordered. In a work called *Ten Questions*, the
following advice is given on how to master energy through sexual
intercourse:

> By care, education, consideration, nutrition, making the erection
> strong yet going about the act in a slow and relaxed manner, not
> being premature when full of desire, not ejaculating at the peak of
> pleasure. Vitality will build up, energy will be stored up, and even
> though one lives to be a hundred one will be healthier than ever.[13]

In general, preparations take on a ritualized form. Some times and
places, such as after midnight in a chamber of relaxed calm, are better
than others. Sex should not be accompanied with an excess of wine or

food. Meditation is recommended to put away all worldly thought and feeling. Incense is burned, music on the lute is played and prayers are offered up for harmonious success.

By preparing in this way, both partners can benefit from the union, circulating and harmonizing the *ching* and chi in each other. At the same time, spontaneity, naturalness and freedom are central parts of the practice.

In the work entitled *Important Matters of the Jade Chamber* (the jade chamber is a metaphor for the vagina), Liu Ching advises men on the proper way of uniting with a woman:

> It [is] essential first to embrace in mutual play, unhurried, gentle, and relaxed, so as to bring the spirits [*shen*] into accord, and let the minds resonate together perfectly, and only when this has been achieved for a long time should intromission take place. Entrance should be made when the Stalk of Jade is still only partially erected, rapid withdrawal when it is fully so. In between, the movements should be restrained and slow, and spaced at suitable intervals. A man should not throw himself violently about, for that turns the five viscera upside down, does permanent injury to the tracts and vessels, and brings on the hundred diseases. But intromission should not be accompanied by emission.[14]

Advice is not only given from a man's point of view. Legend has it that 'in the beginning' the techniques were taught to men by five goddesses or wise women. In the ancient text attributed to one of them called 'The Immaculate Girl', it is written:

> Debility in men can always be attributed to a faulty exercise of the sexual act. Now woman is superior to man in the same way that water is superior to fire. And those who are expert in the arts of sex are like good cooks who know how to blend the five tastes into delicious dishes. Those who know the Tao of Yin and Yang can fully achieve the five pleasures. Those who do not know it die untimely, without ever having experienced sexual joy. Is this not something that should be guarded against?[15]

The woman's benefit from sexual union is as important as the man's. The 'flowery contest' of female and male, yin and yang, fire and water, should lead to equal mutual nourishment. It is often implied that both women and men can 'feed on' their copulations with different partners.

The legendary Hsi Wang Mu (Mother Queen or Goddess of the West) was a woman who allegedly obtained immortality by making love with hundreds of young men and boys. Equally, the immortality of the Yellow Emperor was said to have been achieved by absorbing the vital fluid of no less than 1,200 women. Whatever the truth of these legendary lovers, the importance of sex to increase their vitality, health and longevity is clear.

The status of orgasm for women is not entirely clear. A few pillow books advocate multiple orgasm, but the majority recommend avoiding orgasm for both sexes since a leakage of seminal essence or *ching* leads to a loss of vitality. *Ching* is considered the most precious thing in the world and should not be emitted, except of course to procreate.

This is particularly stressed in the case of men. The adepts developed a special technique known as the 'waterwheel' exercise which was a 'way of making the *ching* return to nourish the brain'. It involves suppressing ejaculation, either by internal muscular contraction or external pressure, to create an extremely intense and prolonged orgasm, the heat of which is then conducted by concentration up the spine into the brain, where the experience of bliss burns away mundane thoughts and feelings. The technique involves applying pressure with the two middle fingers of the left hand at the moment of ejaculation to the urethra between the scrotum and anus. At the same time the breath should be fully expelled through the mouth and the teeth gnashed several dozen times. Some adepts could perform the act with their heel rather than their hand.

Although physically the semen is diverted into the bladder and eventually lost with the urine, the alchemists thought that the seminal essence (*ching*) travelled through the 'cinnabar fields' – the abdomen, thorax and head – via the spinal column to nourish and rejuvenate the brain. It was kept as a great secret only for the advanced adepts. 'This procedure', claims *Important Matters of the Jade Chamber*, 'has always been transmitted by the immortals to one another, but they who receive it swear a solemn oath sealed in blood not to hand on the method lightly, under the pain of suffering calamity themselves.'[16]

The pillow books give detailed instructions for the preparation and union in love making. One called *Joining Yin and Yang* recommends ten manners of penetration, eight movements, ten styles, and ten signs of consummation. They are all developed to a refined art. The different styles of love making, for instance, are known as the tiger roaring, the cicada clinging, the inchworm, the deer nudging with his antlers, the phoenix stretching, the monkey climbing, the toad, the rabbit running and the fish feeding.[17] The alchemists clearly used their close observations of nature to full effect.

The sexual techniques used by the alchemists are all part of their overall search for perfection and everlasting life. Sex is never an end in itself but always a means to an end. Quoting the *Manual of Immortals*, Ko Hung makes clear that sex – 'making the sperm return' – is one of the key methods of prolonging life along with elixir taking, meditation and regulated breathing:

> Those who take chymic elixirs
> And guard the primal unity
> Will come to a stop from living
> No sooner than Heaven itself;
> Making the sperm return,
> Breathing like babe in womb,
> They will lengthen their days in peace
> And blessing, world without end.[18]

I found many aspects of the approach to sex of the Chinese alchemists very attractive. It stresses the equality of men and women and their mutual pleasure and nourishment. It is free from asceticism and guilt: sex is seen as a sacred and beautiful thing. It is not considered merely as a means of procreation but as an exciting and imaginative venture of man and woman to create 'the holy embryo of eternal life' within themselves. Making no distinction between the body and soul, it involves the whole personality. While requiring certain skills and following certain rituals, there is room for spontaneity and naturalness.

From my own experience, I am certain that many of the methods of Chinese *nei tan* alchemy, especially tai chi exercises, breathing and the 'golden flower' meditation of 'turning the light around' are highly beneficial. The sexual techniques, too, seem sensible, although I must confess that I have not yet mastered the method of making the *ching* return in the recommended way. Modern sexual therapy confirms the ancient alchemical wisdom that sex is natural and to be enjoyed. Just as its absence can make us wither, so its presence can make us blossom.

There can be no doubt the techniques of *nei tan* alchemy can prolong life, but whether they lead to immortality I have yet to find out . . .

10

White Clouds

The span of life is up to me, not heaven.

Ko Hung

Before I left China, I wanted to see whether alchemy was still a living tradition. Matteo Ricci, leader of the Jesuit mission to China in the late sixteenth century, observed in a passage on superstitions and bad customs:

> We may conclude all these distressful things by speaking of two rather fantastic obsessions common in all the fifteen provinces of China, where there are many who give themselves over to them. One is the claim that from mercury and other substances it is possible to make true silver. The other is the belief that by means of various medicines and exercises it is possible to attain perpetual life without ever dying. Ancient tradition holds that the two systems have been handed down by those who have been considered saints, men who having, they say, accomplished many good works, flew up body and soul together at last into the heavens. At the present time the books on these two sciences circulate in ever-increasing and enormous numbers, some printed, and others, more greatly prized, in manuscript form.[1]

Had these alchemical interests survived the coming of Western chemistry in the nineteenth century and the rigours of Marxist indoctrination in the twentieth century? I thought the best place to find out was at the Taoist Association of China in the White Cloud Temple in Beijing. This headquarters of Taoism had been turned into an army barracks during the Cultural Revolution but had now been allowed to return to its former state. I remembered that the professor at Beijing University had said that every alchemist is a Taoist in China.

My taxi driver suddenly swerved into a side road, narrowly missing a stream of cyclists in the bustling Beijing streets. We came to a halt outside the magnificent, many-coloured gateway to the White Cloud Temple – Bai Yun Guan – with its two fabulous lions standing guard.

The White Cloud Temple had long sheltered many adepts amongst its monks. The American E. V. Cowdry, later professor of anatomy in Peking Union Medical College, reported around 1917:

> The priests sometimes attempt to distil mercury. When the distillation has been successfully repeated nine times, the resulting substance will be the "elixir of life". One of the priests of the White Cloud Temple is said to have been killed by an explosion during the sixth distillation.[2]

When the scholar Joseph Needham visited the White Cloud Temple in 1964, he did not see an alchemical laboratory but confirmed that there was a rich collection of Taoist alchemical books in the library, including the classic collection *Dao Zan*, which includes texts more than 2,000 years old.[3] Needham also recorded reading reports of government agencies of the communist regime condemning obscure Taoist sects for practising alchemy.

The temple consisted of a large rectangular compound with a series of pavilions dedicated to different Taoist patriarchs and divine immortals. Along the sides were cloisters where the monks lived and at the far end there was a tranquil 'Cloud-Gathering Garden'. Monks quietly did their rounds, dressed in white gaiters, dark grey trousers and jackets, with wooden needles through their top knots. Some raised fine dust with their long brooms as they brushed the immaculate courtyards while others tended the large bronze incense burners. Colourful flags with their famous Taoist 'yin-yang sign' (see below) fluttered in the cool breeze which blew in from the Gobi Desert covering the whole of Beijing with a fine yellow dust.

People came to the White Cloud Monastery to ask for protection and favours from the brightly coloured statues of divine immortals and patriarchs in the pavilions rather like Catholics pray to particular saints. In front of all the pavilions there were beautiful bronze incense burners where the devout burned several bundles of joss sticks at a time. The smoke billowed out across the temple grounds, filling the air with its sweet fragrance. An ancient hymn to incense, considered the most important rite in the Taoist liturgy, was still being chanted:

> Official Envoys of the incense, Lords of the Dragon and Tiger to the left and right, Golden Girls and Boys attending upon the fragrance, and all Divine Beings, cause that at this place where I have today conducted an audience, the divine mushroom of immortality, cinnabar and jade green, may spontaneously grow from out of the golden liquor, and that the host of Perfected Immortals may meet in unity at this ardent incense burner. May the Immortal Youths and Jade Girls of the Ten Directions attend upon and protect this incense, and transfer swiftly all that I have said before the heavenly throne of the Supremely Honoured . . . Jade Emperor.[4]

Exploring the temple complex, I discovered that the main pavilion was devoted to the Jade Emperor, the supreme deity in heaven, the counterpart of the emperor on earth. Behind it was a large pavilion housing lacquer carvings made in the Ming dynasty (1368–1644) of the Three Purities who presided over the three phases of the Creation, known as the Celestial Worthy of Original Beginning, the Celestial Worthy of Numinous Treasure, and the Celestial Worthy of the Tao and its Virtues (none other than Lao Tzu). These three make up the supreme trinity of Taoism as an organized religion. They also represent the three powers (heaven, earth and humanity), the three virtues (compassion, frugality and humility) and the three treasures *ching*, *shen* and chi (vitality, spirit and energy).

I chatted to one of the monks who was sweeping a courtyard under a pine tree and wanted to practise his English. I could hear the haunting sound of a flute being played from one of the cloisters.

What did the monks do? I wondered. They listened to the visitors' troubles and tried to exorcize their ghosts. They meditated, studied the scriptures, played music, painted, tended the gardens, practised qigong exercises and tai chi. Above all, they were like their ancient ancestors seeking to prolong their lives and attain immortality.

*

In a small, dark, simply furnished room in the heart of the temple, I was first introduced to Sun Tong Chang, the director of the Liaison Department of the Chinese Taoist association. He was dressed in a dark lounge suit and sported a brightly coloured silk tie decorated with yin and yang symbols. We were then joined by Ming Zhiting, the abbot of the White Cloud Temple and the vice-president of the Taoist Association of China. Despite his slight stature, his calm presence filled the room.

Dressed in black flowing jacket and trousers, Ming Zhiting had a matching hat with a small jade tablet on its front – a symbol of immortality. He looked to be in his sixties and had a sparse goatee beard. His features were fine, with high cheekbones. His hands were thin and delicate; on the third tapering finger of his left hand, he wore a ring. He looked at me steadily with dark grey eyes which shone with an inner light.

We sat next to each other. Quiet and mild-mannered, he answered in a clear and precise way my questions through our interpreter, Yang Lifan from the Institute for the History of Natural Science. The abott refused firmly to have our conversation recorded and would not allow any photographs to be taken. Here was a 'simplicity-embracing' master if there ever was one. I felt he had achieved a profound degree of serenity after many years of study and meditation.

I told him that I had come to China to see if alchemy was still a living tradition.

'You have come to the right place! The main idea of Taoism is immortality,' he replied unhurriedly, pausing to let himself be translated. 'In China, Taoism is different from other religions because it seeks immortality. You can prolong life and become immortal!'

Looking at me steadily, he added firmly after a long pause: 'My life is grasped in my hand, not by heaven.'

I knew that I had heard something like that before; yes, it was the famous saying of the fourth-century alchemist Ko Hung.

This was really exciting. I was clearly in contact with someone who took the alchemist pursuit of immortality seriously, so seriously that he was prepared to devote his whole life to it and to suffer from the authorities for his beliefs if need be.

'What do I have to do to live for ever?' I asked.

'There are three ways to live for ever. The first is to activate the body. Our body is made up of three factors, *ching*, chi and *shen*. The first, *ching*, is the good things in the body.'

My translator explained that *ching* not only includes semen but also bodily fluids such as blood and saliva.

'You know if you are hurt,' she added, 'it is good to wake up in the morning and to lick your wound before you wash your teeth. We Chinese do not like to give blood since we think that it weakens us.'

The abbot Ming Zhiting, one of the most respected authorities on Taoism in China, continued: 'The second factor is chi. You can regulate chi in aspiration and respiration.'

'The third factor is *shen*,' continued the abbot. '*Shen* is usually translated as spirit or soul, but it is different from the Western concept. It is not separate from the body for the body itself is a form of gross *shen*. We have *shen* rather like a cat has nine lives; they are not separate from its being, but an aspect of it.'

'How can I use them to live for ever then?'

'By integrating these three factors, *ching*, chi and *shen*, into one being we can prolong life. In the body is yin and yang. Through exercises and other ways, we can turn yin into yang. We can make it very pure by transforming yin into pure yang. We can then move freely around the universe. This is the first way to live for ever.'

Again, I was hearing echoes of Chang Po-tuan and of *The Secret of the Golden Flower*. Yang Lifan added afterwards: 'All common bodies, including you and me, have a lot of yin. By making it into yang, we make ourselves pure.' I also remembered that in Chinese alchemical literature yin is represented by mercury, yang by gold. Transforming yin into yang mirrored the alchemists' dream of transmuting mercury into gold!

The abbot continued with his simple and straightforward exposition of his beliefs. If it lacked detail, it was admirably clear: 'The second way to live for ever is through our works. We should be kind; do very great kind things. When you die the things you did live on for ever.'

This clearly echoed the Buddhist doctrine of karma: the cosmic law of cause and effect which states that we reap what we sow.

'The third way to attain immortality is through *nei tan* alchemy.'

He mentioned Needham as a reliable guide. I assumed he was referring to meditation, regulated breathing, diet, sexual techniques and the other methods I had already explored.

The Taoist sage paused; I expected more; but then he smiled and said emphatically: 'That's all!'

It was as simple as that. The final word had been said on the subject. He had given me an admirable summary of the work I had been doing on the alchemical way in China.

I liked the way the vice-president of the Taoist Association of China declared: 'That's all!' as if his exposition was self-evident and irrefutable. At least he knew his own mind. He had the certainty of one who stood in an ancient tradition and had come to some clear conclusions which he believed were universally valid, for him and all humanity.

He made as if to go, but I rather impertinently posed another question. I had not come all the way to China, flown across the Himalayas and the Gobi Desert, to leave it at that. I hoped he might clarify some of my own difficulties with the notion of immortality. I also wanted to find out more about the link between Chinese alchemy and Taoism. I therefore asked the venerable abbot whether there were any practising alchemists in China.

'At present the main alchemist people are Taoists. I practise *nei tan* [the inner elixir]. Outside this place there are some who do research on *wai tan* [the outer elixir]. Taoists are devoted to *nei tan*.'

'How long can you prolong your life with *nei tan* alchemy?'

'I'm not sure. I'm seventy-four. I think I'm very young. There are many people here over one hundred years old.'

'Does the spirit, *shen*, leave the body when you become immortal?'

'In Chinese philosophy, the body and spirit are one. When you become immortal, there is still some body. It is not the common body, but a special one. We call it chi. You can make the body take shape or disappear very freely. You can become invisible.'

'Is it up to me whether I become immortal or not?'

'To become immortal, this depends on you. Some conditions are given to you when you are born, but it depends on you.'

'At what age does your body become immortal?'

'When you're mature. At only fifteen you can get out of your common body. It depends on you. Someone at one hundred still cannot get out of the body. You have to wait until the body becomes mature.'

Ming Zhiting got up, bowed slightly, and disappeared. He did not leave his clothes behind him.

*

I stayed on at the White Cloud Temple and talked to Sun Tong Chang, director of the Liaison Department of the Taoist association. He explained that an immortal keeps his or her appearance at the moment of becoming immortal, whether the person is seventeen, thirty or ninety years old.

I asked him what the Tao is. He replied: 'I have no understanding of the Tao.' Quite rightly so, for as the classic masters of Taoism point out the Tao is beyond words and concepts; it cannot be described but only sensed. As Lao Tzu says in the *Tao Te Ching*: 'The Tao that can be told is not the eternal Tao.'[5]

I asked what was so special about Taoism as a religion.

'Taoism is a unique religion which originated in China. There are not so many Taoists today, but you cannot separate Taoism and Buddhism now. Some people go to Buddhist temples with Taoist beliefs.'

'What is the difference between Taoism and Confucianism?'

'Both originated at the same time. The main difference is that Confucians like to make rules for society, while the Taoists want to make themselves immortal, to live for ever. The Taoists want to do good things. They always want to separate themselves from society. They live a very free, very clear life.'

'And the immortals? What are they like?'

'If they are thirsty, they drink the juice of flowers; if they are hungry, they eat the flowers. They always sit on a donkey and go riding around the world!'

And that was that.

*

The place I most enjoyed in the White Cloud Temple was the Cloud-Gathering Garden in its innermost courtyard. Carefully placed trees offered shade and contrasted with the rectangular layout and the irregular stone of a large rock garden which looked like a miniature version of the rugged mountains from southern China immortalized in so many Chinese paintings. On its summit was perched a small 'Pavilion of Friendly Cranes': traditionally cranes are creatures of wisdom and long life.

In the centre of the garden, I sat meditating by a pond. A few white clouds in the blue sky were mirrored in its clear water. Small goldfish floated motionless amongst its lilies. A gentle breeze rippled its surface.

From a tree above, yellow fan-shaped leaves fell on my head and into the water. I was reminded of the lines of Lao Tzu, the first philosopher of Chinese alchemy:

> The highest good is like water.
> Water gives life to the ten thousand things and does not strive.
> It flows in places which men reject and so is like the Tao.[6]

Water assumes the shape of any vessel and finds its way around any obstacle. Its still surface mirrors the face of nature. It is yielding and yet overcomes the hardest rock. The watercourse way is the way of Taoism and the way of alchemy.

On the walls of the cloisters surrounding the Cloud-Gathering Garden, I discovered a beautiful 'Diagram of the Internal Texture of Man' (*Nei Ching Thu*) engraved on a stone tablet. It had been made in 1886 from an ancient silk scroll found in a temple in Kao-sung Shan.[7]

The diagram is a graphic illustration of the *nei tan* Chinese alchemy which had developed over thousands of years. The body is pictured as a mountain with crags projecting from the spinal column and the skull. It depicts the circulation of chi through the three main energy centres in the abdomen, thorax and head – the so-called 'cinnabar fields' in Chinese alchemy. The heart is represented as a ring of seething blood with a calm centre. The kidneys are symbolized by a weaving girl at her wheel which sends up the chi to the throat (a seven-storeyed tower) and the head (a mountain summit). In the central pivot of the body in the abdomen, known as the Dantian point, there is an ox and plough with four turning yin-yang symbols. At the bottom is a waterwheel, sending up seminal fluids from the genitals to nourish the brain and prolong life. And as there should be, a sage calmly meditates in the head.

Could it be that this stele in the Cloud-Gathering Garden in the White Cloud Temple contained the secrets of everlasting life?

My visit to the White Cloud Temple was the high point of my journey to China. Abbot Ming Zhiting seemed to embody the wisdom of at least 3,000 years of Chinese alchemy. I had at last met a practising alchemist who was clearly well advanced on the way to immortality. His words may have been enigmatic and his answers short, but they hinted at profound mysteries and truths. As I walked out of the temple gateway into the bustle and noise of Beijing, I felt a lightness of being and sense of calm which stayed with me for a long time afterwards.

*

My journey to China had already taken me far in my quest. I had discovered that alchemy was a very ancient tradition and may have been brought to China from a lost civilization across the sea by the Sons of Reflected Light. It also had deep roots in the practices of the ancient shamans and in the philosophy of Taoism.

I had learned that the Chinese alchemists working in their laboratories believed in the intimate correspondences between earth and the heavens, in the growth of minerals within the earth, and the possibility of manipulating time. They were aware that they were imitating the natural process of nature itself. By bringing yin and yang together, they hoped to recover the original unity of the Tao and produce the golden elixir, the pill of immortality. They also believed that what goes on in the reaction vessel represents the processes of the cosmos itself; if it does not, the elixir will fail. At all times, an inextricable link was recognized between the personal growth of the alchemist and the development of his experiment. Ultimately, the alchemist is the subject and object of his own experiment.

I was struck by how close the world view of the Chinese alchemists was to that of modern physicists and ecologists. The notion of the Tao is like the idea in quantum physics that all things orientate themselves according to a 'cosmic field of force'.[8] The yin and yang principles anticipate the positive and negative electricity at the very foundations of the natural world, the subatomic elementary charged particles, the protons and electrons. The Taoist philosophy at the heart of Chinese alchemy also echoes the many mysteries of growth and regeneration of modern ecology, particularly the subtle network of relationships between things and beings in nature's intricate web.

In its search for the pill of immortality and other lesser elixirs to prolong life, Chinese alchemy had undoubtedly made some major contributions to chemistry, biology and medicine. Alchemists had produced some real results in endocrinology, especially in the preparation of steroid sex-hormones, and increased an understanding of the biochemistry of ageing.[9] Above all, in the pursuit of the inner elixir, they developed some remarkable techniques, especially in the area of meditation, breathing exercises and sex in order to tune the body and focus the mind.

Although the abbot of the White Cloud Temple had assured me that some *wai tan* 'outer elixir' alchemy was being undertaken by his fellow monks elsewhere, I was unable to trace it. At the same time, it was clear that despite decades of materialist indoctrination by the Communist Party and the ravages of the Cultural Revolution, the tradition of *nei tan* 'inner elixir' alchemy was still alive and well in China. Not only are all alchemists Taoists, but all serious Taoists today are practising alchemists. They take the Great Work seriously, the work of refining and perfecting themselves in order to become immortal. They make their own inner elixir through good works, meditation and other exercises.

I left China more convinced than ever that whatever is contrary to the Tao will not last long. If one finds one's centre, if one is in harmony with the great rhythms of nature, free from anxiety and obsession, indifferent to so-called success or failure, one is more likely to live long. And if one can nourish the three treasures of vitality, spirit and energy, one will live well.

I may not have found the pill of immortality – the Chinese Philosopher's Stone – but I felt sure that a seed had taken root deep in my being. I continued to practise qigong exercises and tai chi. I meditated by 'turning the light around'. Perhaps these ancient methods of the Chinese alchemical way would encourage the seed to put forth one day some golden shoots.

What I had found in China made me even more eager to visit its great and equally ancient and mysterious neighbour: India.

Part Two

Ganga: India

11

Older than History

> Benares is older than history, older than tradition, older than
> legend and looks twice as old as all of them put together.
>
> Mark Twain

India is so vast and old that it escapes the imagination. It is more like
a continent than a country. It embraces the greatest religions and
cultures of the world: Hinduism, Buddhism, Jainism, Islam and to a
lesser extent Christianity. Even Taoism has made its presence felt.
Alchemy, I soon learned from Prafulla Chandra Ray's classic *History
of Hindu Chemistry* (1902), evolved chiefly in India as 'a handmaid of
medicine'. Above all, it is central to the yoga of transformation which
is at the heart of Indian religion and philosophy.

I had a difficult time travelling to India. Having flown comfortably
to China on Uzbekistan Airlines via Samarkand, I decided this time to
try the national carrier of Kyrgystan, another fledgling state in Central
Asia created after the break-up of the Soviet Union. After nearly 24
hours' delay at Birmingham Airport, I eventually boarded an ancient
Russian aircraft which seemed to be falling to bits. It was so small that
we had to stop to refuel in Kishinev in Moldova near the Black Sea.
Unable to land at Bishtek because of dense fog over the snow-bound
capital of Kyrgystan, we were redirected to Osh, a remote military
base near the Chinese border. Here we were kept on board the freezing
aircraft overnight by an armed guard, without blankets, food, drink or
information. Outside it was −20°. I asked the Russian air hostess
when we might leave and she giggled hysterically: 'One hour, one day,
two days, maybe three!'

The next morning we took off and flew over a spur of the

Himalayas only to turn back to Osh again because of fog. Eventually, in the afternoon, we managed to land in Bishtek to take another plane to India. It had taken two and a half days to complete the usual eight-hour flight.

'Excuse the inconvenience,' the hostess said with a false smile, trying to disguise her dejection.

I arrived with bronchitis in New Delhi, the capital of India, to confront the most polluted city in the world. Just walking down the streets, where so many people live, is equivalent to smoking forty cigarettes a day. Half the population is suffering from heart problems, a third from respiratory diseases. The doctor of the ancient system of Ayurvedic medicine with whom I stayed was in despair: he could no longer rely on the quality of the medicines he used and was unable to struggle against the rapidly deteriorating environment. His preoccupation was no longer with prolonging life but with trying to help children reach maturity.

Having failed to track down an alchemist guru whose name had been given to me by a Sri Lankan in London, I decided to travel on to Benares (now officially Varanasi). Bordering the River Ganges (known as Ganga), it is the holiest and oldest city in India. As a place of pilgrimage, it is to Hindus what Mecca is to Muslims and Jerusalem is to Christians.

One foggy morning before dawn, I joined the devout down at the river. I shivered in the cold damp in my small boat as grey mist swirled across the flowing green waters. My boatman rhythmically pulled against the current; with a dull thud the pink carcass of a bloated cow bumped into us, turned over and disappeared. A dead dog floated by. 'Killed by the cold,' was the boatman's comment, resting his arms on the oars. As we drifted awhile, turning hither and thither, I launched a little candle on a bed of marigolds in a round paper boat and watched it float in the dawn light downstream towards the Indian Ocean.

Then the miracle happened. The red orb of the sun suddenly appeared, perfectly round in the morning mist. Swallows skimmed across a line of gilded water. I turned towards the west bank. The sun's rays lit up a line of towering buildings at the top of terraces of steps which ran down to the water's edge. These were the famous 'ghats' – ghats for bathing, for washing clothes, and for cremation. It is the ideal of every Hindu to be burned on a wooden pyre on the river bank at Benares and to have his or her ashes scattered in the holy waters of Ganga. The maharajas had built the great palaces, with their elegant domes and ornate balconies, to witness the burning of their relatives, but now they are dilapidated and falling down, mainly the haunts of rats, pigeons, dogs, monkeys and lepers. Holy cows and goats wander at will along the terraces.

On the steps of the ghats at the water's edge swarms of people of all ages were taking their early morning dip. Just downstream of a sewer, I could see a group of men in loincloths immersing themselves and rubbing their teeth with their forefingers. Children played and splashed. An old woman in a sari turned in the water with her hands clasped together, chanting mantras. A lone young white woman washed her blonde hair amongst the scum and filth and lotus petals. Dhobi wallahs hit grey clothes on stones in a futile attempt to clean them. Sadhus, holy men who had abandoned all material attachments, sat meditating, their serene faces turned towards the rising sun. Their hair was matted, their dark naked bodies were impervious to the cold.

The devout of Benares were taking the holy waters of Ganga which would purify and preserve them for ever. They were practising spiritual alchemy. Along the bank of the river and in the adjoining maze of alleys holy men, priests, monks, gurus, magicians, herbalists, astrologers, alchemists and con men abounded. What crazy wisdom, what magical cures, what extraordinary beliefs could be found there! I decided to see if any of them could enlighten me about Indian alchemy and the Philosopher's Stone.

In one tiny room in Annie Besant Road, opposite the entrance to the headquarters of the Theosophical Society, I came across a thin and ancient astrologer and phrenologist surrounded by yellowing books in Sanskrit, Hindi and English. He said he could read my past and future by the contours of my head and the lines on my palms. His name was Shivnath Mehrotra and he placed in my hands a pamphlet entitled 'Rays of Astrology' in which he claimed that Varanasi is 'the seat of the Metaphysical Sciences'. He was a former astrologer for the *National Herald*. He lamented that none of his children was interested and he could not find a decent apprentice to whom he could pass on his special knowledge and skills.

'I learned all over India with the best gurus. Everything will be lost,' he said with a deep sigh. 'There will be no more true astrology in India.'

Shivnath Mehrotra offered me 'a perfect guidance, step by step' to my problems. 'You may obtain the desired happiness and success by applying meditational and occult measures as guided by ancient scriptures of sages.' He also offered talismans, prepared according to Indian *sastras* (holy scriptures), which removed the bad effects of the planets.

'Do you know anything about alchemy?' I asked him.

'I don't practise it but a friend of mine did. He died five years ago. He spent most of his life trying to get gold from copper. He also prepared something with the help of mercury. It was the aim of his whole life but he never found it.'

'Do you know any recipes?'

'He had them. But they are never the complete story. There's still some secrets not said; there's always something missing. He had no one to carry it on.'

My ears pricked up. I was already on the trail in my quest. At least it would seem that alchemy in Benares was still a living tradition.

'About ten or fifteen years ago there was a series of articles on alchemy called *Vanu Dharmayug* in *The Times of India*, but it was written in Hindi and you'll need a translator to understand. They were about people who had made real gold with a strange formula.'

'One last question. Have you heard of the Philosopher's Stone?'

'Yes. There's a stone called the *Sphadick* Stone. It's the stone of Sarasvati, the goddess of learning. The Stone helps you to become conscious. It's real gold . . .'

'Where can I find it?' I asked, carefully hiding my excitement.

The old astrologer spoke in Hindi to my driver. We left his tiny, dark, book-lined room with its wooden bed and braved the seething humanity, wildly dashing rickshaws, sauntering holy cows and belching cars of the sun-drenched streets. We eventually pulled up outside a jeweller's shop in a back alley.

'Philosopher's Stone here,' said my beaming driver, nodding his head from side to side. We went inside. The Sphadick Stone turned out to be a garland of glass-like beads which the devout pass through their fingers like a rosary whilst reciting mantras. It was not exactly what I had in mind.

*

Within a few days of arriving in Benares, I had not only seen holy men purifying themselves in the Ganges and meditating in the rising sun, but had established that alchemy was still a living tradition in India. It was also an important part of the tantric tradition.

I clearly needed to consult a guru to enlighten me further about these matters. A guru is not only a teacher; he is meant to be heavy with wisdom and a dispeller of darkness. I did not look one up in the telephone directory. There is an Indian proverb that when the pupil is ready the guru will appear. He did. A local actor friend of a French choreographer whom I had met in Delhi introduced me to Swami Yogi Prakash.

The yogi lived in two simple rooms on the third floor of a half-built apartment block. A young boy opened the door and asked me to take off my shoes. His master was a medium-sized, middle-aged, slightly plump man with a long black beard and flowing black hair beginning to recede at the temples. The flat was simply furnished, with a bed and low table. The only luxury was a large black television in a recess. Behind a curtain was a small meditation room with an ornate shrine to Shiva, the third god of the Hindu Trinity, the Destroyer, who carried a trident to chase away evil spirits.

Swami Yogi Prakash described himself on his card as a 'Yoga expert, Tantrist, and Astrologer'. He had recently returned from a tour of Canada. After obtaining a PhD in philosophy, he had abandoned the academic life for the spiritual path. His own guru lived in the Himalayas.

The yogi sat cross-legged behind a low table which had a small portrait of Lord Rama, mandalas and yantras, symbols used for meditation. Where he was propped up by soft cushions, I had to sit in the lotus position on a hard wooden board in front of him. 'You should not sit on the ground,' he observed. 'You should not earth your *prana* – energy – too much, but keep it within. If you direct your *prana* inward, you enter the kingdom of God which is within you!'

I told him that I had been on a dawn boat ride on the Ganges and had seen the devout taking a dip. 'It's not just a question of taking a dip,' he insisted. 'The bath is psychic. The water of Ganga is not common water. It purifies. In five minutes the bacteria have gone from it. In *puja* [rituals] the devout use water as a way of worshipping the Lord. We call it nectar.'

Was the water of 'Ganga' the equivalent of the elixir of the alchemists?

*

Swami Yogi Prakash called himself a Tantrist. On his white and yellow
card was a figure of a yogi meditating cross-legged on a lotus flower
with a serpent of energy unfurling from his genitals to his head, with
symbols of the planets and metals cascading down his arms. I asked
him to explain the meaning of the tantra, especially as I had read in
Ray's *History of Hindu Chemistry* that alchemy was an 'adjunct of the
Tantric cult'. I knew that tantra was a school in Hinduism which
emphasizes the female aspect of nature and makes great use of sexual
symbolism.

'There are two ways towards enlightenment and salvation. One is
to negate, negate, negate. The other is to accept, accept, accept. The
Vedic tradition negates, the Tantric accepts. It accepts immanent
phenomena and what you are as a form of the divine. Wine, for
instance, is not normally good for consciousness or the liver, but the
Tantrist will take some wine but first offer it to the deity. Tantra
embraces the whole world.'

'And sex?' I asked, thinking of the Chinese alchemists and their
method of nourishing the brain.

'The Tantrist does not reject passion, but only satisfies his appetites
in a disciplined way. The passionate person loses his consciousness and
stillness. The Tantrist may worship the vagina and breasts but he does
not use a woman. He relates certain mantras. During intercourse,
he does not forget his consciousness or lose his identity. In this way, he
can purify his body and mind. If you lose consciousness by becoming
passionate or angry, you separate yourself from divinity.'

'And the body? Is that considered evil?'

'The body is not an end but a means. Why did God give you a
body? The body is only a staircase to uplift you to consciousness.'

'So the Tantrist practises a kind of spiritual alchemy in which he
purifies and transforms himself?'

'Yes. Tantra believes in a supreme cosmic energy hidden in man in
a certain form known as Kundalini. It is represented as a female
serpent with its mouth pointing downwards to the junction of the
spinal chord. Through certain disciplines, by the grace of a guru or a
deity, the cosmic energy can be awakened and pass up the spinal chord
through the seven chakras to the crown of the head. As it passes, it
purifies. It enables you to cross the border of nature, to free yourself
from the empirical world, to reach the kingdom of heaven.'

'Are you transformed in the process?'

'Of course. When you go into the Ultimate, your inner being is transformed. Your spiritual, astral body is purified. You leave your physical, causal body. When your destiny is wiped out, you have *samadhi*, enlightenment.'

'How can I achieve this?'

'There are many ways in tantric yoga. It's not child's play. Everyone needs a yogi; you can't do it yourself. You need a guru to explain to you how to awaken cosmic energy. When you cross over, you get bliss, bliss irrespective of the passions, senses, intellect and mind!'

'Can it take a long time? Is there a quick way?' I was thinking of the sudden enlightenment of *satori* in Zen or the dry path in Western alchemy.

'Where there's a will, there's a way. If you're truly interested, you will be realized sooner or later. There's a story of Saint Ramana Maharshi. He met a boy who was a spiritual bomb. The boy was immediately realized. One of his old disciples asked why it was taking him so long to reach enlightenment. "I was not knowing", replied Ramana Maharshi, "that you were thirsty for the divine!"'

Wanting to find out more about how to awaken Kundalini energy and how it might fit in with alchemy, I said: 'I have read that in Indian alchemy mercury is considered to be "the seed of Shiva" and that when he joins with his consort Shakti they produce gold.'

'Shiva and Shakti are within you, male and female principles. They are equal in both sexes. If you use a woman, she becomes negative energy and eats you. Your energy will be neutralized in the same way that if you overeat you have to use up energy to digest the food. You should not eat a woman but give pleasure to her, just as she should not eat you. You can give each other energy; it can be very fruitful. But as the German philosopher Kant said, you should see people as ends in themselves, not use them as means.'

'So sexual energy can be important in the spiritual path of alchemy?'

'Yes. You can use energy in sex and transform it and purify it in the chakras. But the real Tantrists keep the seed within them. Eventually, they leave behind sex like a ladder as they develop pure energy and cosmic consciousness . . .'

Again, I was hearing strong echoes of Chinese *nei tan* alchemy, especially in their arts of the bedchamber and waterwheel sexual techniques.

'What do you understand by the Philosopher's Stone?'

'It's a symbol of pure consciousness, of the journey of your mind to enlightenment. I pour my whole energy into realizing myself. Yoga is a very practical path. The chakras can always be purified. Although I have a home life and have consciousness of the world I am not attached to them. If you surrender your life to the divine, you will never live in vain. You will have all the features of a realized *gita*.'

'Will you be able to prolong your life in this way?'

'At birth your span of life is given you, but you can decide how to use it. If you use your breath in the proper way you can prolong your life and decide when to die. It's like a game of football. The goal is a hollow space like your breath. You can decide when to kick your body into the goal and expire.'

Again, I was hearing the same argument of Ko Hung and the abbot of the White Cloud Temple. But I still found it difficult to square the idea of being born with a predetermined number of breaths in your life and free will.

'It's something like TV,' said Swami Yogi Prakash, smiling warmly at my difficulty and pointing to the inert black box in the recess above his head. 'When we come into the world of phenomena, it's just like a script of someone's life which has been written and filmed. But you can jump out of the script. You can escape this circle of dependence, you can be free of *sansara*, the bondage of rebirth, by purifying your energy and reaching cosmic consciousness.'

'Do you know anyone who has managed to prolong his life?' I asked.

'Many people,' he said without hesitation. 'Tailang Swami lived to 300 years in Benares. There's a yogi who is 800 years old in the Himalayas. I've met one who is over 200 years old; he doesn't see anyone, he's drunk in himself.'

I found his turn of phrase revealing. One description of *samadhi* or realization is self-intoxication.

'You can even invert the rhythm of your body and cross death,' Swami Yogi Prakash continued. 'In *samadhi*, the body is stopped but does not decay. Not all can do it. As it says in the Bible, many are called, few are chosen . . .'

There were clear echoes here of Lady Tai's perfectly preserved body.

'How can you do this?' I asked eagerly.

'There are three ways to attain *samadhi* and have a glimpse of the Lord: through mantras, meditation and medicine. By repeating mantras, you pray without ceasing so as not to forget the Lord. In meditation, you direct the flow of energy within you. In karma yoga, your consciousness is at one with the Lord. You can then have deep sleep, which is so difficult in your civilization. You also act well. As Socrates said, knowledge is virtue.'

'And medicine? How does that help?'

'The Gutika Siddhas know how to prepare something which they keep in the mouth and which gives them the power to fly in the air like aeroplanes . . .'

A Gutika Siddha, I later found out, is a Realized One (Siddha) who uses pills of mercury (*gutikas*). Again, I was reminded of the Chinese alchemists who were able to ride the wind after taking the pill of immortality. Clearly there was an important overlap here in Indian and Chinese alchemy.

*

I spent two days with Swami Yogi Prakash discussing tantric yoga and alchemy. At our last meeting, he said the key to his philosophy was love.

'Love is pure and unconditional. If you love, whatever you do, even intercourse, it's not bad. If love is there, nothing's bad. Love purifies you. If I love you, I cannot cheat you!'

I asked him whether he believed that the Philosopher's Stone exists.

'Of course, of course!' he said enthusiastically. 'It's the jewel of the sages which you can get! It's a practical process, involving the alchemy of the body. But its aim is to transcend this world and to achieve balance and harmony.'

Thinking of all the beggars, lepers, deformed and homeless people I had seen on the ghats by the Ganges, I asked: 'With all its imperfections and afflictions, is it possible to be happy in this world?'

'It's a hundred per cent possible to be happy, but only through detachment. I see the world as a mirror. Nothing affects me, neither sorrow nor pleasure. I might have a pain in my arm, but I am not the pain. There are many problems in the world but they do not affect me.'

Again, thinking of the entrenched caste system, the abject squalor and growing pollution I had encountered everywhere in India, I asked whether things would ever get better.

'A very harmful time is coming for mankind,' Swami Yogi Prakash prophesied. 'It's coming soon, in ten or fifteen years. We are out of balance; women are being used and men are treated like things. There's a growing lust for money and lust for sex.'

'Will it mean the end of the world?'

'The world is not going to end but about two-thirds of it will go. Then there will be a new beginning. Have faith. As Leigh Hunt said: "All is well and wisely put"!'

12

Rasayana

The *chugchi* [yogis] who live for 150 or 200 years ... These people make use of a very strange beverage, for they make a potion of sulphur and quicksilver mixed together and this they drink twice every month. They say this gives them long life, and it is a potion they are used to take from their early childhood.

Marco Polo

Yogi Prakash's comment about Indian alchemists taking pills of mercury and living to 200 years reminded me of this remarkable passage in the travels of Marco Polo which had been written towards the end of the thirteenth century. He was not the only traveller to remark on the use of mercury as a poison, a restorative and a tonic. At the close of the seventeenth century, François Bernier wrote disapprovingly of 'strange fellows, almost constantly travelling hither and thither; these people scoff at everything, and whom nothing troubles. They are people with secrets, who, it is said, know how to make gold and to prepare mercury so admirably that one or two grains taken every morning restore the body to perfect health . . .'[1]

These strange fellows were part of a very ancient tradition which goes back to the earliest known civilization in India which was already advanced by 2500 BC. Excavations at Mohenjo-Daro in the Indus Valley have unearthed many figurines which suggest that its inhabitants worshipped a mother goddess. It was probably from this *devi* that the figure of spiritual power known as Shakti evolved.[2] Figurines of a male god in the position of a meditating yogi have also been found. He was often surrounded by animals and may well be the original form of the god Shiva.

Shiva and Shakti came to represent consciousness and energy and the alchemists sought to combine these forces to recover the original wholeness of the universe and live for ever. The *Kulacudamani Nigama* says: 'By the union of Shiva and Shakti, Creation comes . . . All this universe is of Shiva and Shakti.'

At its most fundamental level, Hinduism believes that the entire universe is in a constant process of creation, preservation and transformation, processes which are identified with the gods Brahman, Vishnu and Shiva respectively. By trying to transmute matter, Indian alchemists, like their Chinese counterparts, are therefore merely mirroring the universal transformation of energy which is taking place and trying to bring together the male and female principles of Shiva and Shakti.

The Indus Valley civilization declined in the middle of the second millennium BC, probably due to the invasion of a people known as the Aryans who spoke a language from which Sanskrit is derived. Their religion, as presented in the *Vedas*, was polytheistic like that of the Celts. They worshipped in the open air and performed their rites around water. Their main gods represent the elements and forces of nature: sun, moon, wind, rain, fire and water. Two of their most popular are Indra, god of rain and thunder, and Agni, god of fire.

The *Vedas*, written sometime between 1500 and 800 BC, form the bedrock of Hinduism and Hindu civilization.[3] They are collections of prayers and hymns meant for incantation. They already show that at least 3,000 years ago Indians were interested in producing an elixir of immortality. In the oldest Vedic period the hymns of the *Rig Veda* celebrate the *Soma Rasa*, the juice of the soma plant, which was also known as *amrita* or nectar. Probably extracted from the climbing plant *Asclepias acida* or *Ephedra*, when mixed with milk, butter or honey it was thought to give inexhaustible strength and vitality. The hymn exclaims: 'We have drunk *Soma*; we have become immortal; we have gone to the light; we found the gods . . .' Another hymn in the *Rig Veda*, addressed to divine physicians called Asvins, says: 'O King Varuna! A hundred and thousand medicinal drugs are thine.'[4]

Indian alchemy crystallized the ancient Vedic longing for immortality. It first evolved mainly as a handmaiden to Ayurveda, the 'science of longevity', one of the oldest systems of medicine in the world which is still widely practised.[5]

The fourth Veda, the *Atharva Veda*, is the earliest literary record of Indian medicine. It combines a heady brew of magic, astrology and alchemy and the therapeutic value of gold is already recognized: 'The gold, [endowed by] the sun with beautiful colour, which the men of yore, rich in descendants, did desire, may it gleaming envelop thee in lustre! Long-lived becomes he who wears it!' Gold was a symbol of purity and imperishability. A Vedic ritual of restoring the exhausted body of the creator god Prajapati involved placing a golden image of a man behind the altar with the priest intoning: 'He is Prajapati, he is Agni, he is made of gold, for gold is light and fire is light; gold is immortality and fire is immortality.'[6]

The theory of compounds in Indian alchemy is based on the doctrine elaborated by Ayurvedic medicine, particularly in the *Charaka* (80–180). It maintains that all substances have a combination of five original subtle elements: earth, water, fire, air and ether (space). In ascending order, these were depicted as a square, circle, triangle, crescent moon and sun.

The early alchemical experiments were mainly aimed at reducing substances to their primary form which was thought to be the original stuff of the universe. This was done by either burning solids to ash or boiling liquids to obtain their sediments. After this process of purification, the 'ash' was then dissolved in *rasa* or mercury. Of all the substances, *rasa* was considered to be the quintessential. Indeed, Indian alchemy is known as *rasayana*, 'the way of mercury'. From the earliest days in the Ayurvedic tradition, the term *rasa* or *rasayana* was the watchword of a 'mercurial elixir cum philosopher's stone'.[7]

In order to make elixirs, specially prepared *rasa* was mixed early on with herbs, blood and semen, with the minerals sulphur, mica, orpiment, pyrites and cinnabar, and with the metals gold, silver, zinc, copper and arsenic. It was also combined with acids. As in China, the alchemists, however, always combined drinking their elixirs with exercises, breath control and meditation in order to prolong their lives, to transform themselves, and to attain self-realization.

India's early fascination with alchemy may well have been given a boost by contacts with China during the period when India was exporting Buddhism to China. The contacts were through the two Indian spurs of the Silk Road and the seaports along the coasts of Tamil Nadu and Gujarat. In 520, the King of Udyana in the Swat region (now Pakistan) interrogated two visiting Chinese Buddhists about the 'Taoist matter' of medicine and science and about the silver and golden palaces of the immortals. Around 646 the Chinese offered the King of Assam a Sanskrit translation of the *Tao Te Ching*, the greatest text of Taoist philosophy and spiritual alchemy.[8]

The father of Indian alchemy is widely held to be the great Buddhist philosopher Nagarjuna. He is said to have undergone twelve years of asceticism to know the hidden secret of longevity and to have sailed to the intermediate continent on a fig-leaf boat to recover a 'gold-making elixir'.[9] He certainly seems to have lived a long time for works ascribed to him date from the second to the ninth centuries. Tibetan historians allow that a single figure named Nagarjuna prolonged his life by alchemical means from 529 to 1,000 years.

The most famous work attributed to Nagarjuna is called the *Mahaprajnaparamitashastra*. When translated into Chinese by Kumarajiva, it introduced the Madhyamika (Middle Path) school of the Mayahana (Great Vehicle) Buddhism into China in the fourth century. The works insist that the *dharmas* (elements of existence) are unreal; the only reality is Emptiness itself, the Ultimate Void. The work mentions among the miraculous powers (*siddhis*) of the Buddhist adepts the transmutation of 'stone into gold and gold into stone'. This can be achieved by the use of herbs and by the power of yoga practice.[10]

India's first alchemical classic, the *Rasaratnakara*, was also attributed to Nagarjuna. It is usually dated to around 800 but it might go back to as early as the second century. While it has been called India's first alchemical classic, it is probably a conflation of three different texts.[11] It describes the ideal adept as 'intelligent, devoted to his work, without sin and master of his passions'. Such a person can prolong his life and provide remedies against 'wrinkles and white hair and other signs of old age'.[12] Information is given about different preparations of mercury, including red crystalline sulphide of mercury, and ways of extracting mercury and zinc from zinc ore. More than two dozen pieces of apparatus are described. The descriptions are often quite specific, as the following passage on fixing or 'killing' mercury vividly shows:

When the mercury assumes colours after having given up its fluidity, it is known as 'swooned'. Killed mercury is that which does not show signs of fluidity, mobility or lustre. When the quicksilver, which has acquired the colour and lustre of the rising sun, stands the test of fire, then it is to be regarded as fixed.[13]

Practical alchemy reached its zenith in India from about 700 to 1300 after which adepts of tantra come to the fore with their highly specialized techniques of yoga and meditation to produce the inner elixir. The *Rasarnavakalpa* or *Manifold Powers of the Ocean of Mercury* probably dates from the eleventh century.[14] Borrowing a number of verses from Nagarjuna's *Rasaratnakara*, it offers a rich compilation of alchemical practices. It not only describes the powers of different substances to transmute base metals like lead and copper into silver and gold but also provides recipes for elixirs which are said to give extraordinary psychic powers to human beings. These include curing diseases, preventing decay, rejuvenation, perennial youth and beauty, immense strength, sexual power, grace, supernatural vision, invisibility, material immortality, levitation, and the ability to fly in the air and to observe at will the 'three worlds'. About one elixir it is written: 'He who uses it becomes free from wrinkles and grey hair, and is cured of all diseases. He is endowed with strength like that of a young elephant, becomes omniscient and victorious.'[15] If only it could be found!

The text is mainly concerned with the methodical treatment of mercury (*rasa*) and its powers. It shows how mercury can be abstracted from cinnabar, how the juice of different plants 'kills' mercury and increases it powers. It makes a distinction between *rasayana* (the way of mercury) and *rasavidya* (the science of mercury) but both are concerned with the perfection of metal and the perfection of man. Of the twenty-nine substances described in the text, twenty-one are from plants, six refer to certain types of soil and water, and only two deal with sulphur and arsenic sulphide. Water collected on a full moon day or from certain mountains is said to confer eternal youth and immortality.

The text opens with the claim that mercury is endowed with the properties of all metals. Of all known substances, it alone has the capability of making silver, gold and gems and preparing the drug of immortality. Although it is recognized that it can act like a poison, if certain procedures are followed it may be turned into a 'nectar'.

Mercury is so powerful that transmutation can be achieved by the vapour, the touch or the sight of it. Indeed, a man who takes processed mercury internally can transmute metals by his mere touch. The text speaks of mercury as having the power of transmuting 10 million times its weight of base metal into gold and silver.

The context for the operations is important if success is to be achieved. The preparations are considered best when performed in 'a well-situated place having a beautiful environment on an auspicious and excellent day'.[16] The adept should revere Shiva, the father of *rasayana*, whose seed is considered to be mercury, and his consort Pavarti (a manifestation of Shakti). The same paradox appears which runs through nearly all texts on alchemy: the author gives disguised recipes for the preparation of mercury elixirs but warns against divulging the secret: 'O great Goddess [Parvati]! I have indicated the path to *moksa* [deliverance] in order to please you. This *rasayana* is worthy of being kept secret and should be done so with special effort.'[17]

Another key Indian alchemical work from the eleventh century is known as the *Rasanarva* ('The Flood of Mercury') (c.1200). While it shows how alchemy was becoming a direct precursor of medical chemistry, it has been described as the 'greatest work of tantric alchemy'.[18] 'Mercury and breath [control]', it declares, 'are known as the Work in two parts.' Both aspects are repeatedly interwoven, as in the passage:

> Liberation [arises] from gnosis [*jnana*], gnosis [arises] from the maintenance of the vital breaths. Therefore, where there is stability, mercury is empowered and the body is stabilized. Through the use of mercury one rapidly obtains a body that is unageing and immortal, and concentration of the mind. He who eats calcinated mercury truly obtains both transcendent and mundane knowledge, and his mantras are effective.[19]

A thirteenth-century treatise known as the *Rasaratna-samuccaya* also offers detailed descriptions of the location, construction and equipment of chemical laboratories. These later works show that the Indian alchemists use the processes of calcination, distillation, sublimation, steaming and fixation for chemical composition and decomposition. They are also familiar with the metallurgical operations of extraction, purification, incineration, powdering, solution, precipitation, rinsing, drying, melting, casting and filling. Yet within these procedures there always runs the thread of spiritual alchemy, and the ultimate goal of self-realization is never forgotten.

Whilst studying the history and texts of Indian alchemy, it quickly became clear to me that the elixirs made principally from mercury are only one part of a whole raft of techniques and practices to prolong life and to attain immortality as in Chinese alchemy. The most important are *asanas* (postures), *pranayama* (controlled breathing), mantras (repeated chanting of sacred sounds) and mandalas (symbolical diagrams) used by tantric adepts and hatha yogis to transmute their bodies into incorruptible ones. Tantra, yoga and alchemy all see the transformation of the everyday body as a process of death and resurrection in which the 'divine body' is eventually delivered from the laws of nature and time.

The most famous tantric Siddhas or Realized Ones, notably Capari, Kamari and Vyali, were all alchemists. Madhava moreover looked on *rasayana* not simply as a eulogy of metal, but as 'an immediate means – by preserving the body – of attaining the supreme goal, which is deliverance'.[20] The parallel between yoga and the preparation of mercury is obvious. The attempt to 'fix' or 'kill' the fluidity of mercury is similar to the yogi's attempt to still his desires and reach a steady state of heightened consciousness. Again, as the extraordinary claims made for the mercurial preparations in *Rasarnavakalpa* show, the language of alchemy is used to describe the miraculous powers of hatha yoga, tantra and spiritual therapy. As the oriental scholar Mircea Eliade pointed out, Indian alchemy is not so much an early science but 'a technique of the same order as the other methods of "subtle physiology" elaborated by Hatha-yoga and tantrism and pursuing a similar goal – the transmutation of the body and the conquest of liberty'.[21]

There can be no doubt that Indians were great scientists and capable of observing nature in an objective way. Ayurvedic medicine was using metals and minerals as drugs from ancient times. As early as the twelfth century, Indians recognized the importance of the colour of flame in the analysis of metals. They were the first to invent steel and were describing accurately metallurgical processes long before the West.[22] Nevertheless, I quickly realized that it is misleading to see Indian alchemy as proto-chemistry in the Western sense.

Indian alchemists developed their scientific knowledge not only by careful observation of natural phenomena but also by intuitive insight and yogic visions.[23] Substances are never considered inert, as particles of dead matter, but as different stages of the manifestations of Prakriti, the primordial form of the goddess Shakti, symbol of creative energy. Plants, stones and metals are believed to be related and living; they are, as Eliade put it, 'different moments of a same cosmic process'.[24]

As such, the alchemist-yogi saw it as his task to help them to pass from one stage to another, to be transmuted from one form into another. To work on substances was not just a physical operation of manipulating nature but a psychic act with spiritual consequences. The alchemists knew this when they contemplated the naked body of a woman as much as when they observed the movement of mercury in a flask.

13

Ayurveda and Siddha

Many young men have sex many times at night and thus waste this essence of life recklessly. With small production and heavy drainage, supply will exhaust soon and critical consequences will have to be faced.

Gupta rog clinic, late twentieth century

Throughout India in the last few decades clinics have mushroomed offering a cure for *gupta rog*, the 'secret' or 'hidden affliction'. These clinics specialize in 'sexual disorders' and use traditional techniques of Ayurvedic medicine to restore vitality and virility. Ayurveda is, as we have seen, the 'science of longevity' and Indian alchemy mainly developed as its handmaiden.

Whilst staying in Benares, I visited the Ayurvedic hospital and college at the Samparnanand Sanskrit University to find out more about this ancient system which is attracting growing attention in the West. I was welcomed by a group of doctors having tea and cake in a room which had faded paintings of alchemical apparatus used for distillation and sublimation on the walls. When I mentioned my interest in alchemy, a middle-aged doctor in a double-breasted suit and thick-rimmed glasses laughed loudly and slapped his leg:

'You have come to the right place. You are in the Department of the Mercurials!'

He was called Vaidya (Dr) J. S. Shukla and he was a lecturer in surgery. I returned to see him the next day. As we sat on a terrace in the cool shade of some great mango trees, he spent a long time explaining to me the fundamental principles of Ayurvedic medicine. Like alchemy, it is based on the Samkhya school of philosophy founded by Kapila, who probably lived in the seventh century BC. It comes through in the Upanishads which were written down a century later. At first it appears complicated but soon you realize there is an elegant symmetry amongst its subtle web of relationships.

According to this system, the universe evolved from a single point and grows in stages layer after layer. The first stage is a vibratory element called *akasa*, which gives rise to heat. Heat turns into a gaseous substance and liquefies, and finally the gas is turned into solid matter. When the cycle is complete it reverses itself and the universe devolves to a point again. The whole process then repeats itself, endlessly, in eternal recurrence. This scheme mirrors the modern principles of physics known as the conservation, transformation and dissipation of energy. Because of this endless process of change in the world alchemy is possible.

The Absolute is called *Brahman*. The cosmos itself results from the union of *Purusha* and *Prakriti*, loosely speaking, consciousness and nature or spirit and matter. *Purusha* is endowed with all aspects of life and responsible for the recurring cycles of the universe. The Katha Upanishad says:

> Beyond the senses is the mind, and beyond mind is reason, its essence. Beyond reason is the Spirit in man, and beyond this is the Spirit of the Universe, the evolves of rall. And beyond is *Purusha*, all-pervading, beyond definition. When a mortal knows him, liberation is attained . . .[1]

While *Purusha* is unknowable, *Prakriti* as nature consists of five elements: space or ether, air, fire, water and earth. The Upanishads say: 'All beings arise from space and into space they return.' As for the other four elements which form the basis of Western alchemy: 'from space came air. From air, fire. From fire, water. From water came solid earth. From earth came living plants. From plants, food and seed, and from food and seed came a living Being, man'.[2]

But how do the elements come about? *Prakriti* contains three principles known as *gunas*: *sattva* (essence of intelligence), *rajas* (essence of energy) and *tamas* (essence of matter). At the beginning of the cosmic cycle, they are in perfect equilibrium until disturbed and impregnated by *Purusha*. The *gunas* then combine in different forms and produce the diversity of the world.[3]

Dr Shukla told me that Ayurveda recognizes that the individual is made up of the three *gunas*, defining *sattva* as goodwill and ideas, *rajas* as dynamic vitality and *tamas* as stagnation. 'All aspects are omnipresent,' he declared. 'The combination of *sattva* and *rajas* gives rise to the five sensory organs, while the combination of *rajas* and *tamas* results in the five functional organs.' These in turn link up to produce the mind, which he insisted is the finest organ in humans:

> The mind relies on our functional and sensory organs, but it is very fast. You are sitting here in India. Without seeing your house in Great Britain, you can move to your house in your mind and think it's very lovely. Although the mind appears as one, there are actually three in the body. There is one situated in the brain, one in the heart, and one in the sole of the foot. The mind is very fine and moves very fast. If it doesn't send an order through your body, you won't be able to move your finger!

Ayurveda clearly does not share the mechanical view of the body of Western medicine but takes a holistic view of mind, body and spirit.[4] Dr Shukla maintained that Ayurvedic doctors accept the traditional Hindu view that the self (*atman*) consists of a mind as well as a body which cannot be separated. The psychological aspects are as important as the physical in both disease and health. As I read in an Ayurvedic work on *kayachikitsa* (internal medicine), 'spiritual therapy' must be used along with surgery and drugs. This involves incantations (mantras), sacred herbs, precious gems, propitiatory rites, offerings, sacrifices, vows, ceremonial penitence, fasts, prostration and pilgrimages.[5]

The five elements which make up matter in Indian alchemy and science are classified in the human body in three main groupings or vapours known as *tridoshas*: *vata* (combining space and air) gives rise to movement and enthusiasm; *pitta* (air and fire) provides heat, radiance, vision and cheerfulness; and *kapha* (earth and water) offers support, sustenance and strength. When they are in balance a person is healthy but their derangement produces diseases. Too much *vata*, for instance, leads to strokes; *pitta* to fevers; *kapha* to coughs. All the functions of the body, the states of health and disease and the remedies for them are described in terms of the *tridoshas*.[6]

Diseases in the Ayurvedic system, Dr Shukla explained, are classified in seven categories which consist of different combinations of the *tridoshas*. There are also accidental diseases influenced by external causes, such as a blow to the head. Mental disorders occur when there is an imbalance between *rajas* (dynamic activity) and *tamas* (stagnation) in the will.

'How does karma fit into this?' I asked, remembering the central place of reincarnation in the Hindu scheme of things.

'The effect of karma of your past lives is important. If you have inherited some wrong things from a previous life, this can affect your health.'

Treatment in Ayurvedic medicine seeks to redress the balance between the *tridoshas*, by either reducing or increasing one of them. But the first task, the surgeon told me, is to clean the channels of the body and clear out the toxins. This is sometimes seen as purifying the body from its gross to its subtle level. The drugs used in Ayurvedic medicine are made from oils, herbs, minerals and metals. But in keeping with its holistic approach the curative treatment invariably calls for changes in diet and lifestyle.

I asked the surgeon for a typical example of Ayurvedic drugs. He mentioned the use of aconite to treat cirrhosis of the liver, paralytic intestines and gastric ulcers. It was also a traditional alchemical elixir for long life.

'It has a very Indian preparation,' he had said with a smile. 'You soak the aconite seeds in cow's urine for seven days. The cow who carried Lord Shiva, as you know, is very sacred in India. You then remove the husks from the seeds, grind them and fry them in pure ghee – the fat left after boiling butter. Next you boil it in cow's milk and dry it into a powder. If you take 125 milligrams of it a day, you'll feel much fitter and stronger!'

Alchemy assists Ayurvedic medicine in the use of metals in the preparation of drugs. Mercury is still considered the king of the therapeutically usable metals.[7] Indeed, the modern discipline of geriatrics, one of the eight major clinical specialities practised in Ayurveda, is called *rasayana*, the 'way of mercury', the traditional Indian name for alchemy. Its therapy is used to promote strength and vitality and to prolong life and bring about rejuvenation.[8] The branch of Ayurveda dealing with the processing and therapeutic use of metals and minerals is also called *Rasa Sastra* and includes the use of mercury, mica, sulphur, stibnite and arsenic, as well as the seven metals and a variety of gems.

'We use mercury for many preparations and medicines,' Dr Shukla explained proudly. 'It's our main ingredient.'

'How do you prepare it?' I asked eagerly, feeling that I was entering the inner sanctum of Indian alchemy.

'You take some mercury – *rasa* or *parada* – and put it into a stone pot and add some calcium hydroxide and pound them together. You filter it and obtain mercury without impurities. You then mix it and rub it with garlic which further detoxifies it. You repeat the process eighteen times and finally distil it. It's now ready to make the medicine. You add sulphur to the purified mercury – sulphur has a great affinity with mercury and gold.'

As the surgeon spoke in the shade of a mango tree, I could hear direct echoes of medieval European alchemists.

'You then burn the sulphur and mercury and get *kajjali*, that is black mercury or mercury sulphide. It's now non-toxic and if you add it to other medicines it makes them very powerful!'

'Is this the Philosopher's Stone then?' I asked, wondering whether he knew the term.

'Yes, it's the jewel of the wise. It prolongs life!'

*

As my researches deepened, it became clear to me that apart from Ayurveda there was another ancient tradition of medicine and alchemy known as Siddha which had developed in southern India. Whereas the original texts of Ayurveda were written in Sanskrit, the Siddha system of medicine and alchemy was written in Tamil. Both shared a belief in the continuum between the macrocosm and the microcosm, the five elements, and the theory of the *tridoshas*.

But there are differences. Ancient Ayurvedic medicine mainly used herbs, plant products and organic treatments and *Rasa Sastra* was a late development, whereas from the beginning Siddha placed a great stress on the use of salts, metals and minerals.[9] They not only aimed at the prevention and cure of disease, but also tried to conquer death and render the body perfect and immortal by becoming a *jivanmukti*, a liberated person.

How could this be done? The 'perfect body' could be made by using medicines called *kalpas*. In order to prevent the body from perishing, to arrest decay and to prolong life, they made use of minerals and metals which are imperishable themselves. As in Chinese alchemy, their key materials are mercury and to a lesser extent sulphur; sulphur is often used to control the fluidity of mercury and to form a sulphide.

The Siddha system classifies drugs as *satru* (enemy) and *mitra* (friend), not unlike the modern notion of compatible and incompatible drugs. In their diagnosis, they examine the eight entities, namely pulse, eye, voice, touch, colour, tongue, faeces and urine. The examination of urine is especially important; it is tested by the behaviour of an oil drop on the surface tension of samples collected over a period of 24 hours.[10]

But where did this medicine and alchemy come from? The Tamil alchemists trace their knowledge back to a civilization which was destroyed by a great flood some 10,000 years ago. This lost continent allegedly stretched from Madagascar to Australia; Sri Lanka is its central surviving land mass. The legend not only recalls the lost civilization of Atlantis, first mentioned by Plato, but has extraordinary parallels with the Chinese alchemists who claimed that their knowledge was brought by the 'Sons of Reflected Light' from across the seas.

Legend has it that Shiva taught Siddha medicine to his consort Parvati who then passed it on to Nandi Deva. His disciple Agastya is claimed to have presided over two academies on the lost continent. He is not only seen as the father of arts and sciences but as the founder of the Tamil language and grammar which appeared fully fledged as one of the most sophisticated literary systems on earth. At least twenty-six classic authors wrote under Agastya's name. It is still believed that he frequents the Pothigai Hills and occasionally makes himself visible to true yogis.[11]

The teaching of Agastya was allegedly transmitted to eighteen saints. Writing in an obscure and allegorical style, they mocked the caste system, temple rule and ritual worship of the Brahmins. Not surprisingly, they earned a reputation for being dangerous radicals amongst the Hindu orthodox. Believing that the ability to prolong life is a sign of self-realization, they became masters of yoga, medicine and alchemy. They presented their beliefs and practices in poetic works which are full of tantric imagery and references to Kundalini yoga.

One of the most fascinating saints was the legendary third-century sage Bogar, to whom are attributed 7,000 verses on alchemy, medicine and Kundalini yoga. Born into a family of goldsmiths, he was initiated by the Natha yogi Kalangi. Bogar is said to have taught the guru Babaji at Katiragama in Sri Lanka. He greatly contributed to Siddha medicine, especially in the use of poisonous herbs and minerals. Murals at the hill-top shrine at Palani record his marvellous feats which allegedly include inventing an aircraft and a steam engine for a boat.

Legend further has it that Bogar was a master of astral projection and soul transmigration. Local residents at Palani even claim that he was incarnated as the great Taoist philosopher Lao Tzu. On the other hand, the scholar Joseph Needham considered Bogar to be a Chinese sage who came to the region to study Siddha medicine and alchemy.[12] The story certainly confirms the view that Chinese alchemy may have come to southern India along the maritime trade routes.

Bogar taught that in the climax of the 'gold-coloured alchemy' of Kundalini yoga the male and female principles of Shakti and Shiva are united in ecstasy:

> You can go anywhere,
> wandering freely
> throughout the three worlds.
>
> The dull-hued body
> will mellow
> and shine.
> All impurities
> will be removed
> and the six chakras
> will become visible
> to the eye.
>
> The gold-coloured alchemy
> will heed your every word.
> In the Sleepless Sleep
> all subtlety
> can be perceived.
>
> Look and See.[13]

14

Tantra

> The tantra ... is from its very nature an encyclopaedic science. It is practical, and has no concern with wordy warfare. It lights the torch and shows the way, step by step, until the sojourner comes to the end of his journey.
>
> Arthur Avalon (Sir John Woodroffe)

What is the 'gold-coloured alchemy' which Bogar talks about? After my conversations with Swami Yogi Prakash and Dr Shukla, I decided to visit the Benares Hindu University (BHU) to find out more about the link between tantra and Indian alchemy. Where Ayurveda and Siddha draw on the practical side of Indian alchemy with its mercury-based drugs, tantra is mainly concerned with spiritual alchemy and with developing the inner elixir. The body itself is taken as the reaction vessel as in *nei tan* Chinese alchemy.

BHU is the largest university in Asia and is scattered over a sprawling campus full of fields and trees. Parakeets screech in the bright green foliage bordering the dusty tracks. My first port of call was the huge grey Viswanath Temple which was built in 1964. Bus loads of devotees were coming from all over India to pay homage to Shiva and Parvati (Shakti) in the small central shrine. Holy water from the Ganges dripped there from a pot on to a huge sculpture of Shiva's *linga* (penis) which stands on a pedestal in the shape of Parvati's *yoni* (vulva). A priest sprinkled water on the foreheads of the bowed pilgrims who made offerings of flowers to the idols.

These symbolic sexual organs represent the union of the male and female principles in the universe, the Hindu equivalent of yang and yin in Chinese alchemy. Another shrine in the temple contained the hermaphrodite figure of Ardahanarisvara which symbolized the union of Shiva and Parvati, mirroring the original unity of the cosmos.

This was a fascinating example of India's spiritual alchemy but the most extraordinary thing for me about the Viswanath Temple was a small marble plaque on one of its walls. It stated that one Krishna Pal Shastri, an associate of the industrialist Birla who paid for the building of the temple, had manufactured by alchemical means gold worth more than 70,000 rupees. It seems that BHU had long been a place of practical alchemy and *rasayana*.

With great excitement, I discovered that there was a well-documented case of transmutation carried out in 1940 by Krishna Pal Shastri, a doctor from Jamnagar in Gujarat. The experiment was performed in the laboratory of the chemistry professor Phaldevasahaya Varma at BHU. It took place in the presence of nine or ten Ayurvedic scholars and practitioners and, yes, the great industrial Birla himself who paid for the Viswanath Temple. One of the scholars present, Yadunandan Upadhyaya, reported to the American scholar David Gordon White:

> Shastri hollowed out a soap nut, which he filled with mercury, two or three grams of borax, and a grain of secret powder. He sealed the nut with a paste of lime and molasses and put it inside a crucible, which he placed on a charcoal fire. He fanned the fire until the nut inside the crucible began to burn. When the smoke cleared, he split the nut open with an iron wedge. Inside was a metal that looked like silver. Half of this metal was taken by Professor Varma and the other half by Mr Birla. Varma tested it at BHU and Birla at one of his firm's laboratories in Calcutta. In both cases, the metal tested out as pure silver, with only the spectroscopy showing a slight variation from that of natural silver. Shastri had informed those who were present that he could also produce gold by the same procedure, by merely substituting ammonium chloride for borax. Later on, at Birla's instigation, he produced the gold in this way. He continued to make gold in this way; at the rate of three grams per week, to cover his laboratory and personal expenses.[1]

What is one to make of this? The description of the experiment resembles several I was later to find in the accounts of European alchemists. The fact that so many scientists and scholars were present gives credence to the claim. Was Shastri simply a brilliant hoaxer or a genuine alchemist? I found it highly significant that Shastri should have come from Jamnagar in Gujarat. A report in the 8 June 1968 issue of the *Navabharat Times* of Ahmedabad gave a story of an Ayurvedic pharmacist called A. C. Acharya who had produced in a few days pure gold from mercury at Jamnagar. The story was corroborated by an Ayurvedic scholar at BHU called Siddhinandad Misra who claimed that it was carried out under the eyes of ten goldsmiths, ten chemists and six government ministers. The secret ingredient was said to be 'perfected mercury'.[2]

BHU had clearly been a hotbed of alchemy. I wanted to find out more. The best person to talk to, I was told, was Professor Kamalesh Datta Tripathi. I managed to track him down with the help of an ancient postman on a rickety bicycle. He lived in a modest villa down a dusty lane shaded by trees on the campus. He was the head of the department of Dhamaga (Religious and Agamic Studies) in the Faculty of Sanskrit Learning and Theology. *Agama*, I learned, means 'revelation' and refers to the tantric texts which usually take the form of Shiva addressing Parvati.

Professor Tripathi was a tall, slender, middle-aged man who sat quietly and composed with a white scarf around his head. He practised the Hindu and Buddhist principle of right speech, carefully choosing his words and expressing himself slowly and clearly. He described himself with a self-deprecating smile as a jack of all trades and a master of one or two.

The professor came from a family which had been physicians for at least twenty-five generations. His brother was an Ayurvedic doctor and still prepared medicines in his own pharmacy.

'I have seen very desirable results with medicines prepared from mercury, iron and copper,' he said. 'Alchemy is very much a living tradition here. It is also very ancient. In the eighth, ninth and tenth centuries, there was an important philosophical school of *rasayana* or alchemy, and several texts were produced by certain branches of Siddhas and Nathas. Nagarjuna, the celebrated Buddhist philosopher and logician, is well known for his work on alchemy.'

I asked him about the connection between alchemy and tantra.

'In India, the tantric terminology is highly symbolic. The metallurgical and the mystical points of view are interrelated.'

'It's the same in China and the West,' I said. 'For his experiments to succeed, an alchemist must be morally worthy.'

'In India the person working with metals has to be pure. Contemplation and meditation are required in all areas of knowledge, especially in those disciplines which deal with the deeper spiritual attainment. Where in Greek philosophy and Western science the prime preoccupation has been with the discovery of the secrets of nature, in the Indian tradition it has been with the deeper secrets of the self. It is rather more metaphysical than physical. In the West, there is a very narrow concept of "I", confining it to the physical ego, which is the source of all human suffering. The Hindu notion of the self – *atman* – needs to be rediscovered; we need to go deeper into the nature of the self. This can be achieved by purity in our speech, our mental behaviour and our bodies through grammar, yoga and Ayurveda.'

'Certainly,' I agreed, having written two books called *Nature's Web* and *Riding the Wind* on the same theme. 'We have a very fragmented view of the self in the West and an exploitative attitude to nature which is seen as separate.'

'In Western philosophy after Descartes there was a dichotomy between the ego and phenomena, "I" and "that", the self and the entire universe. This bifurcation at the cosmic level influenced Western science in the nineteenth and twentieth centuries. We in India are working for the removal of this dichotomy. Nature is not separate from man. That is the way of the original philosophy. You need meditation to reach a more central level of the "I". This science of meditation is at the basis of Indian alchemy.'

'Is the science of alchemy very old in India?'

'India is credited with the making of the first high-quality steel in the fifth century BC. The secret of steel was known to the Indian metaphysicians of alchemy. It was a precious gift we gave to the Persian emperors. On the medicinal side, the use of metals has long been established. Even in folklore and ordinary life, there's a living tradition of alchemy. It's fantastic!'

I asked him again about tantric yoga and its connection to alchemy. The learned and meditative professor held his slender fingers together and paused before answering with careful deliberation:

'Tantra is a philosophy out and out. There are two streams of Indian philosophy. Vedanta which says away with the world, and

Agamatantra which explains this world. The former says the world is an illusion, the latter says it is real. A charge against Indian philosophy is that it is too idealistic, but tantra says that the self and the universe are real. There are some magical aspects in tantra, but they are insignificant. Tantra is an integral system of philosophy.'

'I believe there is a left-handed path and a right-handed path.'

'Yes. The right hand is moral and recognizes certain inhibitions, while the left hand has no problem about what one should do or not do. It teaches to forget about inhibitions in life, including the enjoyment of sex, wine and meat. But they are only experienced to be transcended.'

Our meeting ended there as we were both late for other appointments. It had touched on some central themes of my quest and had emphasized once again the close connection between practical Indian alchemy and Ayurveda and between spiritual alchemy and tantra. Yet despite my conversations with Swami Yogi Prakash and Professor Tripathi, the spiritual and scholarly custodians of the tradition, I still did not have a clear understanding of tantra. It was as if they were so steeped in tantra, like fish in water, they could not jump out of the pond to define it. I returned to my books for further enlightenment. The great Tibetan Buddhist teacher Gampopa claimed:

> The Tantras represent a philosophy comprehensive enough to embrace the whole of knowledge, a system of meditation which will produce the power of concentrating the mind upon anything whatsoever, and an art of living which will enable one to utilize each activity of Body, Speech and Mind, as an aid to the path of Liberation.[3]

The art of living would seem to be crucial. Tantra does not advocate renunciation, detachment and asceticism; its aim is not a withdrawal from life, but an acceptance of life in this world as part of the ultimate goal of transcending it.

Tantra is a Sanskrit word derived from the root '*tan*' meaning 'to stretch' as one would a thread on a loom. It implies a process of 'weaving' or 'expansion'. Tantra thus came to mean 'the warp (of reality)'.[4] Whereas 'yoga' means union – the union between the inner and the outer, the microcosm and the macrocosm – tantra is the practice of weaving such a union, of expanding the self to embrace the Universal Self. Not surprisingly, in its earliest form its rituals were shamanistic and magical, and some of these elements remain.

The tantrikas follow the cult of Shiva and Shakti, who represent consciousness and energy, and the male and female principles in the universe. Through the ritual of love-making, they hope to overcome the duality of themselves and the world and recover the original wholeness. The most advanced are known as Siddhas (Realized Ones), many of whom develop occult and magical powers known as *siddhis* (realizations). These are said to include communicating with animals, controlling hunger and thirst, reading other people's minds, thought transference, having knowledge of past lives and distant universes, levitation and flying in the air.

The alchemists of medieval India (known as Rasa Siddhas and in the north as Nath Siddhas) developed practices involving sexual fluids, often in an attempt to become a 'second' Shiva, that is an immortal super being. It was thought that in the bliss of sexual orgasm the 'gross body' could be transformed into the 'subtle body'. The doctrine of the Rasa Siddhas was summed up in the phrase: *'yatha lohe tatha dehe'* ['as in metal, so in the body'].[5] They practised hatha yoga, the ancient Indian system of exercises, to raise energy from the genital region through the seven chakras – energy centres known as 'wheels of transformation' – to the head.

These wizards of alchemy used the language of the transmutation of base metals into gold to describe the transformation of mortal man into a perfected being. The twelfth-century guru Gorakhnath Bani compared his subtle body to the goldsmith's workshop:

I take the gold [the void] in the gold smithy [the cranial vault] – I am a goldsmith by trade. Pumping the bellows [of my breaths], and stabilizing my mercury, I have fixed it and then mixed it together with mica.

I the goldsmith am in my gold. The root chakra is my fire pot. I forge it on the anvil of vibration, using my drop hammer to press out the gold.

In an ever-verdant forest my poisoned charcoal [burns, with its fire] blowing upwards naturally, through the bellows' twin jet.

Harmonizing [the jets of] sun and moon [up breath and down breath], I stop the breath, and breath is merged into breath . . .

Gold above, gold beneath, gold in the midst of gold. He who

makes the triadic void his dwelling-place has a body that is neither pure nor impure.[6]

As with the Chinese alchemists, the tantric teachings and yogic instructions for the inner purification and transformation of the body were carefully guarded and passed down orally from teacher to disciple after a long period of initiation. Most of the written tantras are disguised in a language using symbols, allegories and metaphors known as *sandhyabasa*, or the 'twilight language'. Some metaphors are impossible for the uninitiated to understand: 'placing his foot on the guru's head', or 'pressing his sister's breasts', for instance, refer to the brain chakra and the heart chakra respectively.

Tantra uses techniques of hatha yoga as a means of attaining inner unfoldment and self-realization. The word '*hatha*' is a compound of the syllable '*Ha*', which stands for sun, and '*Tha*' for moon.[7] It brings the male and female principles in the universe into a harmonious whole, especially through the practice of postures (*asanas*) and breath control (*pranayama*). Tantra also involves the use of sounds (mantra), diagrams (yantra), magic circles (mandala), and gestures (*mudras*). In this spiritual alchemy, the body is seen as a 'laboratory' for worship (*sadhana*). In meditation, it is also common to visualize and concentrate on an assisting deity within. All these techniques can help remove the obscuring factors of ignorance which encourage people to take *maya*, the conditioned world of external phenomena, to be real. The ultimate goal is *samadhi*, enlightenment and absolute realization, in which the individual self (*atman*) merges with the Universal Self (*Brahman*).

The tantric use of mantras is very specific. Mantras are formulae of sound, stringing together vibrations using the fifty words of the Sanskrit alphabet. The mantra, usually given by a guru, can be audible or inaudible, and repeated in *sadhana*. *Om* is perhaps the most famous, the primal sound and the basis of all evolution. In Benares, I was given the mantra '*Om Namah Shiway*' to say with a *mala*, a kind of rosary made from 103 Rudraksa seeds collected in the Himalayas. It is used for *jupa*, the repetition of mantras. Tantrikas believe that sound can be 'struck' or 'unstuck', that is to say, with or without vibrations. The former gives pleasure while the latter leads to liberation.

A yantra is the physical form of a mantra, used as another tool to help meditation or to depict a deity. They are usually composed of geometrical shapes, such as the square, triangle and circles, often in labyrinthine patterns. The circle is a symbol of wholeness.

A central ritual performed in tantric worship of Indian alchemists is *bhuta-suddhi* which purifies the elements. By reciting the appropriate mantras for earth, water, fire, air and ether, the elements of the material body are dissolved and purified step by step. Each element is dissolved by the one which follows in ascending order. Ether is finally absorbed into the subtle body until the ultimate source of all – the Absolute or *Brahman* – is reached.

Apart from seven main chakras or energy centres of the subtle body, Indian alchemists recognize five main primary channels of energies called *pranas*. They are sometimes called branches of the Nadi (vitality) tree. When blocked they lead to mental and physical sickness. They are associated with colours, planets and elements, and are therefore central in the alchemy of well-being. Prana, 'The Holder of Life', is concentrated in the heart region: its colour is emerald-blue, its planet Mercury, its element earth. Udana, 'The Upwards Moving', is centred in the throat region: reddish violet, it is associated with Saturn and air. Apana, 'The Downwards Moving', concentrates around the genital region: orange red, it is identified with Venus and the moon, and water. Samana, 'The One Like Fire', concentrates around the navel: its colour is red, its planets Mars and the sun, its element fire. And finally, Vyana, 'The Encompasser', which flows around the body, mainly the head: it is blue-white and has Jupiter for its planet and ether for its element. A tantrika-alchemist will activate and visualize these channels and chakras of the subtle body according to the tradition of his or her guru. As the *Prasna Upanishad* declares:

> One who knows the Prana . . . from where it comes, how it enters
> the body, how it lives after dividing fivefold, and what are its
> inner workings . . . such a one attains immortality.[8]

The way of tantra used by Indian alchemists is thus a strict form of self-discipline to obtain enlightenment and immortality and as such is a form of spiritual inner alchemy. It proceeds first by purification, transforming the gross body into the subtle body; by sanctification, developing the divine spark within; by equilibrium, seeking harmony between the male (Shiva) and female (Shakti) principles; and finally by unity, attaining oneness with the cosmos. Its ultimate aim is to transform physical energy into spiritual energy.

This was all very exciting. Before practising Chinese tai chi and qigong exercises, I had for years been doing hatha yoga, but mainly as a way of keeping supple and centring myself. I had not realized before coming to India its full potential for personal transformation. Nor had I known about tantra as a form of spiritual alchemy and its central relevance in my quest for eternal life and the Philosopher's Stone. In particular, I wanted to find out more about the 'left-handed' path of tantra which involves Kundalini yoga and seeks the symbolic union of Shiva and Shakti through sex.

15

Shiva and Shakti

This gem of the *sansara*, possessed of the properties of the
five desires, becomes like poison in its unpurified state, but
when purified, it becomes ambrosia.

Hevajra Tantra

In my conversations with Swami Yogi Prakash and Professor Tripathi,
they had both distinguished between a left-handed path (*vama*) and a
right-handed path (*dakshina*) in tantra. The right-handed approach is
the mainstream and is concerned with detachment and renunciation;
in the alchemy of spiritual transformation, it seeks to purify the
elements of the self. The left-handed practice, however, embraces all
aspects of the world, including sex which is often held to be a snare. It
has clear echoes of the sexual techniques of the Chinese alchemists
who bring together the female and male principles of the universe (yin
and yang) in order to prolong life and transform the self.

The first thing I realized was that the god Shiva and the goddess
Shakti are central figures in the practice. Shiva is an expression of
Purusha and represents male energy while Shakti is a manifestation
of *Prakriti* and symbolizes female energy. Only on the relative plane in
this conditioned world are Shiva and Shakti separate. Together they
form a seamless and indivisible whole.[1]

The male practitioners of tantra call themselves Shivas and worship
the god Shiva while the female adepts call themselves Shaktis and
worship the goddess Shakti. The serpent fire energy of Kundalini Shakti
lies coiled in the lower centres of humans. When activated, its energy
surges and spirals through the subtle body and its chakras. It rises
from the *Muladhara* (between the anus and the genitals), through the
centres situated at the navel, heart, throat and between the eyebrows.

Finally, it reaches the *Sahasrara* on the crown of the head, the white lotus of a thousand petals where Shiva resides as cosmic consciousness.

The union of Shakti and Shiva here releases *amrita*, nectar of the purest gold, as radiant as the sun. It is the drink of the gods, the 'elixir of immortality'.[2] It opens the gate of the heavens. And it is accompanied by a sense of utmost bliss. As the *Hevajra Tantra* says: 'There are Moon and Sun, and between them the Seed. This last is that Being, whose nature is Joy Supreme.'[3]

Pattinattar, the Tamil Siddha poet, describes beautifully the experience:

> the eight-fold Yoga
> the six regions of the body
> the five states
> they all have left and gone
> totally erased.
> And in the open
> Void
> I am left
> amazed.
> There is but a red rounded Moon
> A fountain of white milk
> for delight
> The unobtainable Bliss
> has engulfed me:
> A precipice
> Of light.[4]

I was told by the tantrist Swami Yogi Prakash that awakening the sleeping power of Kundalini is not to be taken lightly. It requires careful initiation and long practice. To raise its energy is literally playing with the fire of the cosmos. It is often forgotten by Western seekers that Shiva is the Lord of Destruction. As another Indian guru warned:

> When Kundalini awakes, a man becomes a Yogi. To awaken it a man has to proceed very carefully along the path of Yoga observing many restrictions. If it is awakened and its mouth is not turned upwards, a man will not live. Hence the person who awakens it must have great power.[5]

Kundalini yoga can be practised alone, in which case the visualization of the union of Shakti and Shiva plays an important part. The fourteenth-century female Siddha mendicant Avaiyar in her work *Vibayag Agaval* evokes Ganesh, the elephant-headed god of wisdom and son of Shiva and Shakti. As the gatekeeper to the inner world, he became the patron saint of Kundalini yoga in southern India:

> He had concentrated my mind,
> clarified my intellect,
> and said,
> 'Lightness & Darkness
> share a common place.'
> He presses me down
> into the grace of ecstasy . . .
> He has revealed the Shiva Linga
> within the mind.
> And he has revealed that . . .
> The smaller than the smallest,
> The larger than the largest,
> stands within . . .
> like ripe sugar cane.[6]

Most tantrikas on the left-handed path perform the worship (*sadhana*) as a couple, although it can take place in groups. The female partner is usually called Bhagya-Shakti, meaning 'to be enjoyed', or Pujya-Shakti, 'to be worshipped'. The best Shakti for a yogi is considered to be his wife.

Kundalini energy can be raised by the yogic methods of *pranayama* (breath control) and mantras as well as by the use of *rasas* (alchemical elixirs). But the most common and central way is to use sexual *asanas* (postures) as a means of transcending the human condition. Although imagination and empathy play their part, the attitude to sex is generally free from sentimental impulses or moral inhibitions. The body is used as an instrument, a yantra, in order to develop higher consciousness. The end of sexual union is not sensual pleasure but to blend the polarities of the conditioned world and to reach a transcendental union which brings pure joy.

The cosmic purpose of the *sadhana* practice should always be uppermost in the minds of the participants. During the ritual, the adepts control their minds, their breathing and their sexual desires. As

with the Chinese alchemists, special techniques are used to retain
sexual energy in both partners. Referring to the volatile substances of
mercury and semen in tantric alchemy, the guru Gorakhnath observed:
'Penis in the vulva's mouth, mercury in the mouth of fire, he who can
retain these, him I call my guru.'[7]

After ritual bathing and gentle massage with perfumed oils, the
ritual begins with the practice of mantras, *pranayama* and *mudras*
(gestures) to purify the elements of the body. Yantras are drawn.
Small offerings of meat, fish, parched cereal and wine are placed in
ritual bowls to invoke the Kundalini energy and then taken, either
in small amounts or by simply touching them. Usually considered
impure, they are used to symbolize an acceptance of the world. Ganja
is sometimes smoked, and bhang, a tea made from hemp, is often
drunk.

I found all this fascinating. I had long come to see the sexual act as
a spiritual ritual uniting the male and female principles of the cosmos.
Nevertheless, as a vegetarian I could not see why meat, fish, parched
cereals and wine (known with intercourse as the five 'M's' after the
first letter of their Sanskrit names) should be offered, even symbolically, before embarking on the ecstatic voyage of love. In the Hindu
and Buddhist tradition, they are usually seen as barriers. Right-handed
tantrikas will only visualize them symbolically or use material substi-
tutes; the act of intercourse (*maithuna*), for example, can be symbolized by two flowers representing the *yoni* and *linga* side by side. The
left-handed adepts, however, employ small quantities of the actual
substances. They believe their use is necessary to cut the knots of
shame and fear.

Perhaps this aspect of the ritual is the Hindu equivalent of what
Jung called confronting the 'shadow' or dark side of the personality –
a necessary stage in the development of a fully integrated self. It is no
doubt for this reason that some tantrikas will sit meditating on
decaying corpses at midnight in cremation grounds or in the lotus
position on human skulls. By confronting death and darkness, they are
able to purge fear and terror from their minds. It is part of the goal of
going beyond feelings of attraction and repulsion, of accepting this
world in its beautiful and repulsive aspects, in order to reach a
profound sense of detachment. I had to do the same confronting the
rotting bodies, both human and animal, by the ghats on the banks of
the Ganges. No doubt the young white woman I had seen washing her

hair downstream of an open sewer and cremation ghat was doing the same.

After meditating long about this aspect of the Shakti–Shiva ritual, I concluded that the very aspects of human nature which bind us to our lower state in this world can be stepping stones to liberation. To explore the senses rather than to shun them can further one's alchemical journey of spiritual transformation. Sexual impulses, carefully directed, can provide a pathway towards cosmic consciousness and oneness with the universe.

Back to the *sadhana*, the alchemy of love. After ritually taking the 'forbidden' substances, the male partner worships his partner's *yoni*, while she worships his *linga* with mantras and offerings. She then places her hands over his head and recites three times:

> Get up. Wake up. Be strong. Realization of the everlasting and original self. Now I am giving you the command to immerse yourself within me. I am your guru, and enjoy yourself now with the full bliss within me. I am your Shakti and you are mine . . . Think that at this moment you are not my husband; you are Shiva . . . May my divine self bless you and lead you to the eternal joy of bliss.[8]

He then places his 'jewel' in her 'lotus' and sexual union finally takes place. The male tantrika works through rather than against the energy of the female and vice versa. During the act, he might sometimes recite:

> Om, thou the Goddess, resplendent by the oblation of *dharma* and non-*dharma*, into the fire of the self, using the mind as sacrificial ladle, along the path of *susumna* [the central subtle nerve], I who am engaging in harnessing the sense organs, constantly offer this oblation.[9]

Complex and exact postures are described in tantra for the ecstatic love-making in which a balanced flow of energy passes between two embracing bodies.

Female orgasm is sometimes considered positive as it circulates energy. Male tantrikas on the other hand try to retain the semen so as to prolong the act of union and to avoid loss of energy. Special techniques of balancing breath, thought and sexual energy are employed. Like the Chinese alchemists, the Tibetan Buddhists in

particular seek to have an internal orgasm by pressing a point between
the anus and the scrotum so that the semen may pass up the spinal
column to nourish the brain. The Hindu tantrikas do not place so
much stress on retention. If ejaculation takes place, it is considered to
be a final sacrifice to the goddess, an ultimate blissful blending of the
cosmic elements. As the *Kulacudamani Tantra* says: 'From the union
of Shiva and Shakti unfolds the world.'[10]

*

Tantric alchemy has inspired some of the greatest temple sculptures in
India from at least the second century BC. Indian sutras have long
declared that carvings of couples making love are propitious symbols
which render the temples indestructible. Erotic scenes of love are found
in shrines all over India, especially in Gujarat, Rajasthan and Orissa,
all centres of tantric alchemy. When Europeans first discovered them
they were greatly misunderstood.

In 1838 a British engineer called T. S. Burt stumbled across some
abandoned temples hidden under the dense canopy of the jungle near
Khajuraho on the central plains of India. They were the haunt of
peacocks who fanned their wings on their spires and tigers who silently
padded through their cool and dim interiors. Naked figures embraced
in ecstasy on the honey-coloured walls of the temples. Far from being
awe-inspired by their sensuous beauty, the engineer was horrified by
their explicitness: 'Some of the sculptures here', he wrote, 'are
extremely indecent and offensive, which I was at first much surprised
to find in temples.'[11]

The temples of Khajuraho are supreme artistic expressions of the
tantric alchemy of love. Their origins are still shrouded in mystery.
One legend proclaims that a beautiful young woman called Hemvati,
the daughter of the royal priest of Kashi (Benares), was bathing in the
waters of a lotus pond at night when the moon god fell in love with
her. He came down to earth in human form and ravished her.
Consumed with guilt, he promised that she would have a son – the
first of the Chandela kings – who would rule over Khajuraho and
build magnificent temples. The moon god added that he would perform
a ritual sacrifice which would include the depiction of loving figures.
In this way, he would free Hemvati from the stains of guilt. Their son
grew up handsome and strong. By the time he was sixteen he could
kill lions with his bare hands. Delighted with the young man, the

moon god presented him with an alchemical touchstone which could turn iron into gold.[12]

The Chandela kings, who claimed descent from the moon god, started to build the temples from the ninth century. In the twelfth century, they suddenly abandoned the site. At one time, there were eighty-five temples in the vicinity, but when I visited them only twenty remained. Standing on terraces, made from granite and sandstone, they loom above the trees. They have successive waves of towers, some of which are pyramid-shaped. All culminate in a soaring spire. They are intended to link earth with heaven and to remind the worshipper that there is a continuum between the world of humans and that of the gods.

Each temple may be compared to the human body. The inner shrine with its deity is the equivalent of the soul, the base represents the legs, the mid portion the waist, and the spire the head. On its crown is an *amalak*, a jar which contains nectar (*amrita*), the elixir which the devotee seeks to bring about the final release from this world of death and decay.[13] The alchemy of spiritual transformation is thus crystallized in the stone of the temples.

I walked many times around the temples of Khajuraho with my right shoulder towards the walls – recommended by the temple guardians as the right side of a man is considered to be his purest. I soon realized that the sculptures on the walls reflect an ascent from the everyday world at its base to the sublimity of the divine at its summit. The temples also vividly represent the transformation of the gross sex of the physical body to the creative energy of the subtle body which is at the heart of tantra, Kundalini yoga and Indian alchemy. While the temples undoubtedly celebrate the arts of love, the joy of sex and the fecundity of life, ultimately sexuality is presented as a means of deliverance from mortal coils.

The lowest sections on the outside walls, running in horizontal bands around the base, show scenes of everyday life and war. Graphic acts of lust are depicted: on a frieze in the Lakshman Temple, for instance, a man copulates with a horse while another man masturbates nearby. Women couple with animals, including the tiger and the wild boar. Some women perform fellatio, while other couples engage in the intricacies of soixante-neuf. A woman hides her sex from an excited monkey: she has 'no glad mouth', the temple guardian observed. The carving is often crude like the scenes themselves and the pained faces of the participants suggest the path of unadulterated lust leads to despair.

The higher the temple ascends, the more beautiful and graceful are the figures and the more accomplished and exquisite the carving. The middle sections are most clearly tantric in inspiration and demonstrate how sex can be transformed into a spiritual exercise. The figures are highly stylized. The men are young, graceful, tall and virile. The women have curvaceous hips, narrow waists and full, round breasts. Some have scorpions on their thighs as symbols of passion. Many are familiar figures in the Hindu mythology: *apsaras* (celestial dancers) *surasundaris* (heavenly attendants) and *nayikas* (human beauties) as well as fabled beasts like the dancing *shardul*, half horse and half lion. Some of the women are engaged in mundane activities, like washing their hair, applying make-up, taking a thorn out of a foot, writing a letter or even fondling themselves. The equal weight given to women and men suggests that there was a relative equality between the sexes at the time.

The many amorous scenes involving couples and groups illustrate highly skilled examples of tantric *asanas*. In the Vishvanath Temple, for example, a woman standing on her head makes love to a man who faces the other way above her; she fondles in turn the genitalia of one of the two women who are supporting them. In the Kandariya Mahadev Temple, the order is reversed, with the man fondling both attendants. Women on top, women underneath, men in front, men from behind, the whole spectrum of creative and imaginative love-making is portrayed with uninhibited abandon. It is the very exaltation of the life force itself. The expressions on the faces of the graceful lovers are almost trance-like, exuding mutual tenderness and an inner stillness.

Finally, towards the summit, the closest to the heavens, come images of deities. As the temples soar from the dark inner chamber of their lower regions to the resplendent, sunlit peaks, their shape and ornamentation represent the ecstatic ascent of Kundalini energy from the genitals to the thousand-petalled chakra on the crown of the head. The sculptors and architects of Khajuraho managed to find a perfect balance between the spiritual and the physical and express the final union of higher consciousness and creative energy, of Shiva and Shakti. Their exquisite tantric temples celebrate human beings as made in the image of the divine, and honour the human body as the dwelling of god.

16

Under the Bodhi Tree

And how would he illuminate it? So as not to reveal. Therefore it is said, 'he would illuminate'.

Diamond Sutra

One afternoon I meditated under a Bodhi tree in Sarnath, about 10 kilometres north-east of Benares. It was grown from a cutting of the very tree under which Buddha attained enlightenment some 2,500 years ago. It was at Sarnath that Buddha preached his first sermon known as 'Turning the Wheel' on the 'Middle Path'. The place has been a centre for Buddhist pilgrims ever since.

There is a huge bell-shaped stupa decorated with floral and geometrical patterns standing at Sarnath, its underlying brickwork dating from around 200 BC. The first great Indian Buddhist emperor Ashoka (272–32 BC) is said to have meditated in the shrine built where Buddha first meditated. I, too, sat quietly amongst the old stones which had been daubed with gold as a sign of purity and enlightenment and watched children and birds play amongst the ruins of the ancient monastery.

I recalled the event in Buddha's life which had led him to the theme of his famous sermon which established him as one of the world's greatest spiritual teachers and earned him the honour of being the first of a long line of Buddhist alchemists. Having encountered for the first time the suffering of the world outside the walls of his palace in the form of an old man, a sick man and a dead man, he left his young wife and child and became an ascetic living in the forest . One day he heard a young woman tuning her stringed instrument. He noticed that if the strings were too taut, they would break; if they were not tight enough, they would not produce music. From this observation, Buddha realized the importance of the 'Middle Way' and gave up fasting unto death.

I also visited the Buddhist temple at Sarnath. A tall, thin old man with a long white beard came over to me. It was midwinter and cold and he wore a heavy overcoat. 'Buddhism was born here,' he said. 'Buddha gave his first sermon to his five disciples on the four noble truths: that life is full of suffering, that the cause of suffering is wrongly directed desire, that suffering can be cured, and that can be achieved by the removal of the cause of suffering through the eightfold path.'

'And what's that?'

'Right views, right intention, right speech, right action, right livelihood, right effort, right mindfulness and right concentration.' The old man looked at me through his thick glasses and nodded slowly.

'Is its way still relevant today?' I asked.

'More than ever,' came his firm reply. 'We live in an age of atomic war, pollution and hunger. Many are dying because of lack of medicines. Buddhism can offer a lasting remedy and peace. We should do no fighting and no injury. If we use our resources for necessities and not luxuries, by sacrificing some of our possessions, there will be enough for all!'

*

There is not only a Buddhist temple and stupa at Sarnath but also the Central Institute of Higher Tibetan Studies, a university and cultural centre. People from all over the world come to study there. It is set in beautiful grounds, with well-kept lawns, mature shady trees and flower borders full of chrysanthemums, marigolds and gladioli. Its buildings are boldly painted in blue, yellow and red. It has an excellent computerized library, with many books on alchemy. After the dirt, pollution and bustle of the streets of Benares, it was a real oasis of green and quiet. The Dalai Lama stays there regularly and I just missed him by a couple of days.

Wanting to discuss Tibetan alchemy, medicine and philosophy, I was introduced to a monk called Losang Norbu Shastri. He was a stocky middle-aged man with a shaved head and saffron robes. I quickly became aware in our conversations that he was not only a great scholar but a deeply spiritual man.

Although he had all the appearance of being strong and robust, he admitted that he suffered from asthma: 'We are mountain men and love the cold. It is difficult for us to breathe down here on the plains, especially in the summer when the temperature reaches the forties!'

Losang Norbu Shastri had clearly suffered much in his life and continued to suffer. Forced into exile after the Chinese occupation of Tibet, he had to look on and see its ancient Buddhist culture deliberately undermined. There seemed no short-term likelihood of returning. Yet he was gentle, mindful and full of fun. His lined face was forever breaking out into a boyish grin.

I asked him about Tibetan alchemy and medicine.

'In Tibetan medicine, alchemy is used to make elixirs. It is called *rasayana*. We believe the life within you is propelled by your past actions. But you can avoid untimely death through meditation and by holding your breath and breathing from the whole. Buddha showed the way of transforming our negatives into positives and the flowering of goodness.'

'Can you prolong your life to, say, 200 years?'

'I think so.'

'Do you use elixirs?'

'Only if we are ill and if we wish to restore vitality. If the elements in us are out of balance, we use herbs and metals such as mercury and gold to restore the deficiencies.'

'Are there any side effects?'

'No. The physician will treat the patient holistically. He is also very specific; every person is different. There is the gross body of flesh, blood and marrow and the subtle body with nerves and channels for energies which we cannot see. The mind is central. If the mind is in the right way, the five winds in the body flow in the right direction.'

'How can you get the mind right?'

'Stability of mind is enhanced by inner meditation and steadfast sharpness of thinking. Morality, concentration and wisdom can eliminate negativity and bring about enlightenment. If the intention is not good, it will not happen.'

'What do you understand by morality?'

'Transforming the mind into love and great compassion for all things.'

'What is concentration?'

'Fixing the mind on one point,' the scholar-monk said without hesitation.

'And wisdom?'

'Wisdom is understanding phenomena as they are.'

'And how are they?'

'All phenomena are in interdependent relationships. Nothing is solitary. We call it "dependent origination". It's the same with people. Everyone's equal and interdependent. We all share and want peace and happiness. We're all parts and parcels, causes and factors. All people sustain me; there are even animal helpers like cats and dogs.'

'How should we act towards others then?'

'Since I'm indirectly connected, I am responsible for others, I feel compassion for them, I have a duty to serve them. The bottom line is if we cannot help someone, at least we don't harm them.'

I was amazed to hear this; it was the same point I had made in my last book *Riding the Wind*. I continued the interrogation, eager to learn more.

'Is this possible for all people?'

'Yes. The rich often suffer more than others. Those who sleep on the railway station probably have a more sound sleep. Their suffering leaves them with more stamina to help others.'

'Is there a limit to our compassion?'

'We have a universal responsibility. If we can't act globally we can act locally. The problems of the world are made by humans. We are the most dangerous animals. The choice is ours. We can choose violence or non-violence, to survive or to be destroyed. But I have hope. We will survive. There are growing signs of international cooperation.'

Before I left, I brought the conversation back to our discussion of medicine and alchemy. I asked the monk what caused disease.

'If I'm diseased,' he said, smiling broadly, 'I am not at ease; my ease is disrupted. The mind becomes diseased if we think badly. If you kill, steal, lie, and indulge in too much sex; if you have divisive talk and harsh words, then the meaning of life is lost. Grasping is no good. Motivation is very important. I am at ease when my mind, speech and body are in the right direction. Mind is the forerunner!'

I had heard the same sentiment from Swami Yogi Prakash and Professor Tripathi. The value placed on the mind was clearly at the centre of Indian and Tibetan culture.

'And what about spiritual alchemy – is there a quick path to enlightenment?'

'You can obtain Buddhahood in a very short period. After being initiated, you must practise the sutras within your life by meditating and right living. You must raise the energy inside you, transforming the negativities into positives. Like that you can become a hot furnace!'

'Do you need a guru?'

'A guru can put you on the right path. He can tell you important details and techniques. But Buddha taught what he saw: potentiality, compassion and wisdom. You need to make them real. Concentration, meditation, manifest morality and wisdom are all intertwined.'

As I made to go, he said with a broad grin: 'Buddha is in all things!'

*

We arranged to meet again in his home, this time to discuss Tibetan alchemy and medicine with a doctor from the institute. I found my way to his first-floor flat in a low apartment block overlooking a garden. We sat at a table on the balcony in the warm morning sun. Birds chirped in the trees. A smiling young Tibetan woman served us small earthenware cups of traditional Tibetan tea made with butter.

I was shocked to see his face. Losang Norbu Shastri explained that he had had a 'little accident' the day before. A hit-and-run driver had knocked him off his scooter.

'If I hadn't been wearing a helmet, I probably would have been killed,' he said.

There was a large suppurating wound on his cheek and when he smiled, I could see that he had broken a front tooth. He had been badly bruised and cut and could move only with difficulty. And yet despite his pain, the Sanskrit scholar and monk was as calm, clear and cheerful as ever.

He introduced me to Dr Lobsang Tenzin, one of two *lhajes* looking after the 400 people who lived on the campus of the Central Institute of Higher Tibetan Studies. He wore a shirt and tie and a green and purple jacket. He had a smiling face with perfect white teeth. His hands were delicate with long fingers.

I asked him to explain the fundamentals of Tibetan medicine.

'Everything is made from the five elements: space, fire, earth, water and air. In the body, when there is a deficiency of one element, the body is out of balance and not at ease.' I recalled that 'ease' in Sanskrit

is *sukha*, which means not so much happiness as absence of suffering
and annoyance. As he spoke, I also thought how close Tibetan
medicine was to Indian Ayurvedic medicine.

'The treatment is to restore the balance. If there's too much of one
element, we subtract; if too little, we add. We do this through diet and
medicine, with fruits, plants, herbs, stones and earth.'

Referring to Losang Norbu Shastri, who sat painfully with us on
the balcony, I said:

'Our friend has recently had an accident. How should he be
treated?'

'After an accident, there's a disturbance of bone and blood. The
blood pressure and temperature are high. I will clean the blood
with flowers, herbs, fruit, minerals and salt.'

'How does alchemy fit in?'

'*Rasayana* – the use of mercury – is a perfect way of enhancing
other medicines. Mercury is a poison in its natural state, but as in
homeopathy a poison can be used to cure. There are many processes
to make the supreme nectar.'

'Has it been used long in Tibet?'

'Buddha talked of *rasayana* in the wisdom chapter of the *Kala
Chakra Tantra*, known as the "Wheel of Time".'

In the work, Buddha had indeed declared that man's own body is
the true cosmos. It is also a temple and a laboratory for the inner work
of self-perfection so that it can be transmuted into an 'incorruptible
diamond body'.

'And as a medicine?' I asked, not wanting to lose my theme.

'Mainly from the twelfth century. A Tibetan scholar and sage
called Ugyempa learned about it then in Udiyana in the Swatvali valley
in Afghanistan which was a centre of great learning. It was said that
knowledge of how to prepare *rasayana* was received there from female
deities. It can lessen diseases and prolong life. It is said that Nagarjuna
prolonged his life for 600 years.'

'Why should someone wish to live so long?'

'To have time to find life meaningful. The nectar produced by
rasayana can do many things, like transforming metals into gold. It
enables the life of the person who discovers it to escape the chain of
cause and effect and to become totally free. One who is free, is free
from fear, free from afflictions. He can fly. It's easy!'

Again, I heard echoes of the Chinese Taoists who believed that if

1. Wei Boyang, second-century Chinese alchemist, with his cauldron and dog.

2. Female alchemist outside her laboratory making elixirs. Women played an important part in Chinese alchemy.

3. Jade girl carrying a magic mushroom amongst a group of immortals.

4. Ko Hung (c.283–343), the greatest of all Chinese alchemists.

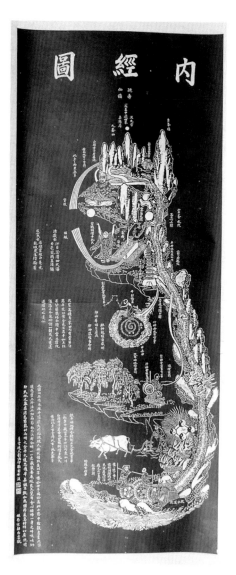

6. Swami Yogi Prakash, adept of the tantric tradition of spiritual alchemy, who lives in Varanasi (Benares), India.

5. Rubbing from a stele in the White Cloud Temple, Beijing, China, depicting a 'Diagram of the Internal Texture of Man' taken from an ancient silk scroll. It shows the principal energy centres of *nei tan* Chinese alchemy of the inner elixir.

7. Author with Dr Lobsang Tenzin next to his alchemical furnace in the grounds of the Central Institute of Higher Tibetan Studies, Sarnath, India.

8. The Sphinx and the Great Pyramid, Giza, Egypt. Not only is the Great Pyramid a laboratory for transforming the soul, but a chamber under the Sphinx may well contain the secrets of Egyptian alchemy.

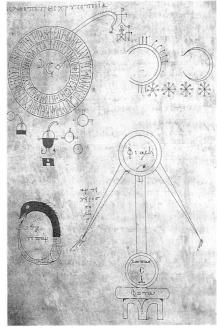

9. Cleopatra's *Chrysopia* ('Gold Making'), depicting the classic symbols and apparatus of Egyptian alchemy. The Ouroboros serpent encircles the phrase in Greek: 'One the All'. The alembic with two beaks over a furnace stresses the importance of work in the laboratory.

10. The fourth-century BC Stele of Metternich which depicts the magical healing of the infant Horus. It is a gigantic talisman, containing the most important gods of Egyptian mythology.

11. 'Maria the Jewess', the great second-century Alexandrian alchemist and inventor of the *bain-marie*. The fumes rising and falling between the vessels represent the circular process of 'dissolution' and 'fixation' which precedes the growth of the Philosopher's Stone.

sufficiently developed one could ride the wind with ease. I asked him how the 'nectar' was prepared in order to have such marvellous effects.

'To make nectars you need a lot of items. It takes a long time, at least two months day and night. There's also special timing; in Tibet, we prepare it in a place where you cannot see the sky.'

'What metals do you use?'

'Eight different kinds of metals, especially mercury, lead, silver and gold. *Rasayana* is the most important part of Tibetan medicine. To get rid of the poison, you need to clean mercury with six or seven herbs by cooking it and making it into ash. Next you add saltpetre – what you make matches and gunpowder from – and mix it until it becomes black. Then you grind it for five to seven days, adding water. You grind it so fine that in the end it won't mix with water. Then it becomes nectar. You can add it to any kind of medicine and it will increase the potency. If you have all the ingredients the process takes two months.'

'Is the process in Tibet different from the one in India?'

'In India, *rasayana* is not so elaborate. The process is shorter. The same substances are used, but not so many items. The result is in Indian medicine the poison is still there; it's not a good one. The supreme way is the long way; that is the way to prolong your life.'

Before I left the institute, the doctor showed me his pharmacy. He prepared all his medicines with plants, minerals and metals brought down from the Himalayas.

'Tibetan medicine makes precious pills for different ailments,' he said, showing me the brown pea-sized pills neatly stacked in large steel containers in a dark room. Outside in a courtyard, two men were grinding some special bark in large bowls.

I asked him about transforming ordinary metal into gold.

'People talk about it a lot in Tibet. I've seen some of the special gold.'

Rather shyly, the doctor then showed me a large furnace made from bricks in the corner of the courtyard where he had for the last two years been trying to transmute mercury into gold. He had refined and distilled it many times.

'How far have you got?' I asked him.

'I have a long way to go, but I believe it's possible!'

'Is there another way to prolong life other than taking the nectar?' I asked.

'If you're not pure, if you don't have the power within, if you don't develop your self, you have to rely on outside nectars. But the person who meditates, purifies his negativities, who cleans his subtle channels, he does not need them. He practises *rasayana* of the spirit. He is his own nectar!'

It had been an amazing experience. I had come to the main centre of Tibetan scholarship outside Tibet. I had not only been able to discuss Buddhist philosophy and medicine with a learned monk and doctor, but had come across a practising Tibetan alchemist. And he was not a crank, but steeped in Tibetan science, medicine and pharmacy.

*

The idea of a supreme elixir or 'nectar' – the equivalent of the Chinese pill of immortality and the Western Philosopher's Stone – had long been part of Tibetan culture. The earliest reference to it I had come across was in a memorial by the Chinese Buddhist Ho-Shan addressed to a Tibetan king in 792. Defending the Zen notion of sudden enlightenment, Ho-Shan declared: 'The *Nirvana Sutra* speaks of a medicine called Agada, a panacea which heals sicknesses whatever they may be. Likewise with non-thought and non-reflection . . . all we have to do is to abandon all discursive thinking and discrimination, and that thereby we are automatically endowed with all the spiritual practices.'[1]

An elixir of life, so sought after by the alchemists, is also mentioned in *The Tibetan Book of the Dead*. If during your voyage, during the intermediate state after death and before liberation or rebirth, you have a suicidal impulse, the anti-death potion of *amrita* ensures that you stay alive and on your path.[2] The guardian of the gate to the north is called Amritakundali, 'The Coil of Nectar'.

The Tibetan scholar and monk Losang Norbu Shastri had recommended as essential reading *The Tibetan Book of the Dead* and the *Diamond Sutra* for an understanding of Tibetan Buddhist alchemy. From my earlier studies, I knew that Tibetan Buddhists believe that life does not finish with the death of the body. Indeed, we are condemned to *sansara*, turning the wheel of life and rebirth, until we can escape from it by becoming enlightened and realizing that the self and the world do not strictly speaking exist. The goal is not to prolong life – that is automatic as long as we continue to be reborn – but to escape from a life of suffering and to reach the state of nirvana, the radiant luminosity of emptiness which is without centre or circumference.

Known in Tibetan as the *Bardo Thötröl* ('Book of Space'), *The Tibetan Book of the Dead* describes the 'bardos' or intermediate states that a person can expect to experience after the death of his or her body. Its subtitle is 'The Great Liberation through Hearing in the Bardo'. It claims that consciousness can take up to four days to leave the physical body and may travel for forty-nine days and nights. During this time one is a 'mental body of unconscious tendencies', nine times more perceptive than in the physical world. One can expect to encounter great and terrifying beings from the six different realms, including peaceful gods, jealous gods, animals, hungry ghosts, and hell beings. They represent different psychological states as well as the possible realms of existence in *sansara*.

The death experience itself is described in terms of the elements of the body reverting back to space from which they originally came. The dead person travels deeper and deeper into the intermediate state as earth dissolves into water, water into fire, fire into air. When air dissolves into space you lose contact with the physical world; when that goes, there is a final inner luminosity. Tibetans also believe that when the corpse of an enlightened person is burned, shining round stones, white or greenish in colour, are left. They are often kept as relics and sometimes eaten before death.[3]

Not everyone has to pass through the realms of being and the cycle of rebirth. When breathing is just about to stop, the advanced tantric yogi can perform the 'Transference of Consciousness', which will enable him to depart immediately by the 'Great Straight-Upward Path'.[4] It involves the realization of the Great Symbol, a mandala which unites the male and female aspects of the universe within the practice of meditation. It is the best kept secret of all the orders of yogis, the most difficult to achieve, for it enables one to attain nirvana instantaneously.

If this is not possible, liberation can still be achieved at any stage after death as one travels through the intermediate states. The key is to keep calm and steady and to avoid yearning for this life and to reject attachment to possessions: 'The true, profound, essential secret is to enter into the supreme state of equilibrium in which there is no good or bad, acceptance or rejection, passion or aggression.'[5] Above all, it involves realizing that the beings of the different realms are all merely 'projections' of one's own mind induced by karma from previous lives and from unconscious tendencies. All the wrathful or peaceful gods, the hungry ghosts or hell beings, are illusory. They are no more real than a stuffed lion, an echo, or the reflection of the moon on water:

> All phenomena appear as lights and images; by recognising all these appearances as the natural radiance of your mind, your own radiance will merge inseparably with the lights and images, and you will become a Buddha. O son, whatever you see, however terrifying it is, recognise it as your own projection; recognise it as the luminosity, the natural radiance of your own mind. If you recognise in this way, you will become a Buddha at that very moment, there is no doubt. What is called perfect instantaneous enlightenment will arise on the spot. Remember![6]

In this spiritual alchemy, there is ultimately no self as a centre of existence. If one can realize this, one can achieve immediate liberation from the cycle of rebirth.

The other key text recommended to me by Shastri was the *Diamond Sutra*, the first book to be printed in 868. While *The Tibetan Book of the Dead* gives advice on how to cope after death and attain liberation, the *Diamond Sutra* illuminates the essence of reality. The original title of the *Diamond Sutra* is *Vajracchedika Prajnaparamita*, which literally means 'The perfect wisdom which cuts like a thunderbolt'. It probably dates from the fourth century. It is attributed to the Buddhist philosopher Nagarjuna, the father of Indian and Tibetan alchemy.

The *Diamond Sutra* is an extraordinary work, short, disjointed and cryptic, which aims at nothing less than the complete annihilation of the self. Like so many alchemical texts, it talks in riddles. Referring to the '*dharma*' of ultimate reality, the sutra states: 'This dharma which the Tathagata [Buddha] has fully known or demonstrated – it cannot be grasped, it cannot be talked about, it is neither a dharma nor a non-dharma'.[7] By even talking about it, I am attempting the impossible. As with the Tao or *Purusha*, it is trying to think the unthinkable.

The work is concerned with the unconditioned Absolute, Emptiness or the ultimate Void of nirvana. It cannot be revealed but only illuminated. How can this be done? By showing forth the wise attitude to adopt towards the conditioned things in this world. When a complete understanding of them is attained, their impurities will no longer have any affect and nirvana is achieved.

The sutra takes the form of a dialogue in front of an assembly of monks between Subhuti and Buddha, who is called Tathagata, the 'Fully Enlightened One' or the 'Well-Gone'. Its teaching is intended for the Bodhisattvas – the 'awakened beings' – destined to become like Buddha. They leave greed, hate and delusion behind them and seek to purify themselves and all sentient beings everywhere.

The paradoxical message of the *Diamond Sutra* is that a truly enlightened person will realize that he or she has no self (as an ego), no being (as a continuous separate individual), no living soul (as a vivifying force within an individual), no person (as a permanent entity who migrates from rebirth to rebirth). The 'signs' of experience do not correspond to realities; the 'marks' of merit are not marks. They are just verbal conventions which do not refer to anything real. All conditioned things are illusory; only the Absolute is; only nirvana is free from deception. The All is Emptiness. If a person realizes this he or she attains the spiritual goal and reaches the realm of nirvana which leaves nothing behind.

It is written in the *Diamond Sutra*: 'Subhuti the Bodhisattva, the great being, should produce an unsupported thought, i.e. a thought which is nowhere supported, a thought unsupported by sights, sounds, smells, tastes, touchables or mind-objects.'[8] It was meditating on this passage that Hui-Neng, the sixth patriarch of the Southern Ch'an (Zen) sect in China, attained enlightenment.

The *Diamond Sutra* makes clear that the merit derived from teaching perfect wisdom to others is immeasurably greater than making a gift of all the seven precious things of the world sought by many alchemists: gold, silver, lapis lazuli, coral, gems, diamonds and pearls. But again just as perception is no perception and the self is no self, ultimately merit is no merit. Buddhas, the Enlightened Ones, leave all such notions behind, along with karma and the conditioned world. Dwelling in peace, they do not dwell anywhere. They do not come from anywhere nor go anywhere. They are and they are not in the transparent luminosity of the Void.

The most profound stanza in the *Diamond Sutra* is the last:

> As stars, a fault of vision, as a lamp,
> A mock show, dew drops, or a bubble,
> A dream, a lightning flash, or cloud,
> So one should view what is conditioned.[9]

When a wise person awakens to reality, he realizes in the moment of enlightenment that his normal experience of things was as unreal as in a dream. As Nagarjuna, the great alchemist and Buddhist philosopher, observed: 'There is no reality in a dream, and yet, while one dreams, one believes in the reality of the things one sees in the dream. After one has woken up one recognizes the falseness of the dream and laughs at oneself.'[10]

Meditating on the meaning of the *Diamond Sutra* the question slowly formed in my mind: 'Is the Philosopher's Stone a symbol of perfect wisdom?'

The alchemists who were seeking to transform base metal into gold were interested in refining and purifying nature. Those who were seeking to prolong life and to attain immortality were trying to transform their base nature into a more spiritual form, their gross body into a subtle body. Their quest – and mine – started with a search for untold riches and eternal life. But my recent conversations with Indian Hindus and Tibetan Buddhists, my moments of meditation on the banks of the Ganges and under the Bodhi tree, made me realize that untold riches – the seven precious things – are nothing compared to the wealth of perfect wisdom.

Perhaps the search itself for eternal life is illusory. Perhaps the Philosopher's Stone like all concepts and things is as unreachable as the stars, unreal as a dream, and as changing as the clouds. Perhaps. But I was not yet convinced and decided to continue on my quest. This time it was to a country closer to home and the source of all Middle Eastern and European alchemy: Egypt.

Part Three

Secrets of the Sands:
Egypt

17

So Many Marvels

Concerning Egypt I will now speak at length, because
nowhere are there so many marvellous things, nor in the
whole world besides are there to be seen so many things of
unspeakable greatness.

Herodotus, *Histories*, fifth century BC

I set off to Egypt with great excitement and anticipation. My journeys
to China and India had shown me the great antiquity of alchemy and
that while it may have had a common source in a lost civilization the
two countries had developed their own distinct traditions. I wanted to
find out how Egypt fitted into the emerging pattern of a worldwide
alchemical way and what light it might throw on my quest for the
Philosopher's Stone and everlasting life.

Egypt was not only the fountainhead of Middle Eastern and
Western alchemy but its ancient Arabic title *Al-Kemia*, meaning 'The
Black Land', gave the whole subject its name. Alchemy is, literally, the
science of Egypt. Moreover, the Egyptian wisdom god Thoth, known
as Hermes to the Greeks, was considered by later alchemists to be the
father of alchemy. He gave his name to and inspired the whole
Hermetic tradition of esoteric knowledge.

During my flight to Egypt, I quickly realized I was surrounded by
ancient alchemical symbols. The emblem of *Egypt Air* was the falcon-
headed god Horus, son of Osiris and Isis, the legendary founder of
Egyptian civilization who embodied the aim of all Hermetic teaching:
the return to the divine source. His Egyptian name Heru means 'He
who is Above'. The cabin of the aircraft was also decorated with the
emblem of an ankh below a winged scarab beetle, representing life and
rebirth respectively. I was therefore protected by ancient alchemical

talismans as we flew 10,000 metres high over the Mediterranean towards the cradle of Western alchemy in Africa.

War was threatening yet again in the Middle East between Iraq and the Western powers. The British Foreign Office had also warned visitors to Egypt to be extremely vigilant after the recent massacre of tourists by Muslim fundamentalists. On my arrival in Cairo, all was calm, although there was a heavy presence of armed men at the airport. As we sped in the early hours through Africa's largest city, we passed through a panorama of Egyptian history. The wealthy suburbs of Heliopolis were built on the ruins of the ancient City of the Sun. After passing by the mausoleums of the City of the Dead, where the living homeless sleep at night, the twelfth-century battlements of the citadel of Saladin (the scourge of the Crusaders) rose upon a hill. It was dominated by the nineteenth-century mosque of the Turkish ruler Mohamed Ali.

The mud-brick houses and narrow alleys of Old Cairo gave way to the new city skyscrapers. Under the new moon, their dark silhouettes were reflected in the swirling, eerie waters of the Nile which flowed down from the Ethiopian highlands to the wide delta and the Mediterranean Sea. And then 8 kilometres west of the Nile, beyond the suburbs and on the edge of the desert, rose the unmistakable forms of the Pyramids of Giza under the star-studded sky. It was not the first time I had seen them but the thrill and awe they evoked were as intense as ever.

In my earlier studies of Egyptian mysteries, it had become clear to me that Egypt, and not Greece, was the crucible of Western civilization and alchemy. The Greeks, who conquered Egypt in 332 BC under the leadership of Alexander the Great, considered the Egyptians to be the healthiest and most religious people in the world. Although Egyptian civilization after some 4,000 years was already in serious decline, the Greeks were the first to acknowledge their debt. Plato in his work on metaphysics *Timaeus*, written around 448 BC, makes an old Egyptian priest tell Solon, the founder of the laws of Athens, during his travels in Egypt that his fellow Greeks are all children: 'You are all young in mind . . . you have no belief rooted in old tradition and no knowledge hoary with age.'[1]

The Egyptian priest went on to say that the age of their institutions was given in their sacred records as 8,000 years.

But where did Egyptian civilization itself come from? The eminent

Egyptologist E. A. Wallis Budge, formerly Keeper of the Egyptian and Assyrian Antiquities in the British Museum, was puzzled why such a civilization with a complex religion, writing, monumental architecture and science should have taken off so quickly in a relatively simple society.[2] Could it be that Egypt was the inheritor of the sacred science of a lost civilization? Certainly Egyptian myth mentions exceptional individuals known as the 'Companions of Horus' bringing their knowledge across the sea and founding the civilization. And as we have seen, both the ancient Chinese and Indian alchemists believed that their knowledge came from a lost civilization which was overwhelmed by some catastrophe.

Plato called the civilization Atlantis which, following 'earthquakes and floods of extraordinary violence', was 'swallowed up by the sea and vanished'.[3]

*

I pondered on these matters as I began to climb the Great Pyramid at Giza one afternoon late in February. The stones were hot and the sun burned on my back. I started from the south-west corner, hauling myself from one waist-high block to another.

It is now strictly forbidden to climb the Pyramids. I was fortunate enough to have obtained written permission from Dr Zahi Hawass, Director-General of Antiquities at Giza, whom I had interviewed for a TV series during my earlier circumnavigation of Africa. Before my solo ascent, an inspector of the Pyramids had advised me: 'When you climb, don't look behind you and if you hear anyone shouting at you, ignore it. OK, go now!'

About a quarter of the way up my ascent, I was spotted and all hell was let loose. The police below started shouting and blowing their whistles and every car in the vicinity started to sound their horns. Remembering the inspector's advice, I just slowly continued to climb without looking back, concentrating on the next stone block and carefully pulling myself up. I was soon sweating profusely. At any minute, I expected a bullet to ricochet on a stone near me. By the time I had reached halfway, the din below subsided. The police had given up; I assumed they would arrest me on my return.

It took me about twenty-five minutes to reach the summit of the Great Pyramid at Giza which is now about 138 metres high. When I looked down, I almost fell over. What had been great blocks of stone now appeared as a sheer cliff face. The top part of the pyramid had long disappeared and there was a platform about 6 metres square. In the middle was a large mysterious stone coloured blue.

I sat down and contemplated the view. To the south-west were the other two great pyramids of Giza: the Pyramid of Chephren (Khafre), with some of its limestone casing forming an apex which sparkled in the sun, and beyond the smaller Pyramid of Mycerinus. I recalled the hypothesis of Robert Bauval, whom I had met earlier, that the alignment of the three pyramids corresponded to the pattern of the three stars of Orion's belt, the cosmic man forever striding across the heavens. If this were the case they illustrate the ancient alchemical principle of 'As above, so below.'[4]

To the north was the sprawling city of Cairo, with its 6 million inhabitants, built on the ruins of Heliopolis, the City of the Sun. To the west, beyond burial grounds, stretched the light brown sands of the Libyan Desert – lone, lifeless and without end. To the east, beyond the green ribbon of the Nile, rolled the Sinai Desert. To the south-east the body of the Sphinx stretched out, eternally facing the direction of the rising sun. I could clearly make out in the distance the Pyramids of Saqqara which predate the Pyramids of Giza. I was literally at the apex of one of the greatest civilizations the earth had ever seen or would probably ever see again.

As I sat meditating facing the setting sun, it gradually dawned on me that the pyramid was a living organic being below me, scarred superficially perhaps, but still vital and powerful. Over thousands of years, its strength was undiminished, its light undimmed. It seemed to me that it was not, as most archaeologists maintained, a burial chamber for the pharoah but a wondrous instrument of initiation and transformation, a crucible of spiritual alchemy.

When I faced the seemingly sheer face of the descent, this time I was without fear. Looking outwards, I jumped down from one ledge to another. Armed guards were waiting for me at the base, as I expected, but they did not arrest me. The stamped piece of paper from the director had performed its magical work.

*

The Great Pyramid clearly shows great minds at work, minds who had an advanced and profound knowledge of astronomy, mathematics and architecture. Even the idea of choosing a pyramid was an unparalleled advance. It has been variously described as an astronomical observatory (to track the stars before it was completed), an almanac (an enormous sundial to mark solstices and equinoxes), a gigantic chronometer (recording the precession of the equinoxes), a geographic marker and geodesic repository (as a scale model of the northern hemisphere, with its apex representing the north pole and its perimeter the equator).[5] With its perfect proportion, the pyramid embodies in a supreme way the principle of cosmic order, represented by the Egyptian goddess Ma-at, often depicted as a woman with outstretched wings. It is an emblem of the harmony which all alchemists seek.

Inside the Great Pyramid, there are three main chambers, the so-called subterranean chamber, the Queen's Chamber and the King's Chamber. From the entrance to the Queen's Chamber, there is a Grand Gallery which leads to the King's Chamber. I was again given special permission by Dr Zahi Hawass to visit the subterranean chamber, access to which is strictly forbidden.

I was accompanied by the Inspector of Antiquities, Ayman Whaby Taher. We entered the Great Pyramid by way of the rough passage forced by Khalif Al-Mamoun in the ninth century. After the inspector had opened a barred grill, we descended a passage which connected to a smooth ramp which dropped from the entrance 105 metres to the subterranean chamber some 183 metres below the summit.

It consists of a rectangular chamber with a circular pit on the eastern side and some rough-hewn blocks. In the south-east corner there is a short square passageway which runs about 10 metres to a dead end and can only be entered on hands and knees. It was very hot and illuminated by one light. Nowhere had I come across such complete stillness. I sat down on a ledge of rock overlooking the well.

Meditating, I just barely breathed the sacred Sanskrit mantra 'Om' when to my astonishment it boomed and reverberated for a few seconds in the subterranean chamber! The acoustics were perfect. It was like being inside a vast amplifier. I imagined the sound vibrating throughout the massed stone of the pyramid, eventually passing through the blue stone at its apex and continuing in ever-widening waves to the cosmos. Perhaps the whole pyramid was tuned like a great musical instrument, the timbre of which had been impaired by the damage done to the external casing stones.

Although their building still remains a profound mystery, the Pyramids and other great monuments of ancient Egypt are a sublime expression of their sacred science which did not departmentalize architecture, religion, philosophy and science but saw them all as integral parts of divine knowledge of cosmic harmony. The ancient Egyptians undoubtedly possessed an ancient wisdom which we have largely lost but which alchemy and the Hermetic tradition carry on in a fragmented and disguised form.

*

After leaving the subterranean chamber of the Great Pyramid, we climbed up the smooth incline set at a perfect angle which joins the forced passage which leads to the so-called Queen's Chamber at the base of the Great Gallery. Although closed to the public, Inspector Ayman opened the Queen's Chamber for me. About halfway along on the right-hand side, he knocked on some stones: they had a distinct hollow sound. In 1980 a French team inserted a fibre-optic camera through the masonry and indeed found a chamber. It was half full of sand, without treasure, but most mysterious of all, the sand was radioactive! No one has yet worked out why this should be the case. Could alchemy have anything to do with it?

The Queen's Chamber itself is a large vaulted rectangular shape exactly at the centre of the pyramid. There is an alcove in the eastern side orientated towards the rising sun. I asked Ayman why it was called the Queen's Chamber.

'That's the name given to it by earlier Egyptologists, but it was probably never intended for Cheops' queen.'

'What was it for then?'

'Cheops changed his theory and developed his plan as he went on,' Ayman said, as if there was no challenging this received truth. 'He started off with the subterranean chamber, built the Queen's Chamber, and then wanted to be closer to Re the sun god and built the King's Chamber above. He considered himself to be Re and called himself the horizon Aten, that is, the disc of the sun.'

This is the conventional wisdom. But it seems inconceivable to me that the builders who usually worked everything out to a master plan in the Pyramids with such accuracy and foresight should change their minds twice. Unlike contemporary builders in Egypt, the ancients had every detail pre-planned and never made a mistake. The care in the execution is as great as in the conception. The subterranean chamber, the Queen's Chamber and the King's Chamber as well as the Great Gallery clearly had a function within the pyramid.

In the Queen's Chamber, I noticed on the north and south sides a shaft at chest level which was 15 centimetres square. The sides of the shafts, which go through vast slabs of carefully laid stone, are perfectly finished. I knew they were the subject of much controversy and asked Ayman for his view which must represent, partially at least, the agreed view of Egyptian Egyptologists.

'The shaft on the south side leads to the star Sirius. For the dead pharaoh, his *ba* soul at night goes to Sirius to visit his grandfather souls and takes power, energy and support from them to be king in the afterlife. His *ka* soul goes to the Underworld where he travels with Re. In the morning his *ba* spirit comes down from the sky and returns through the shaft on the south side to join up with his *ka* soul in the tomb.'

With his talk of *ba* and *ka* souls, sometimes translated as the 'double' and 'heart-soul' respectively, Ayman was touching on very deep and complex matters. The ancient Egyptians distinguished between nine different aspects of the self. They believed that while the body of a person remained after death on earth, his or her immaterial part would go to heaven. They mummified the body because they thought that it could germinate within it a spiritual body (*sahu*) rather like an embryo in a womb or a butterfly in a chrysalis.[6] The Chinese alchemists shared the same view.

The *ab* or 'heart' was considered the centre of the spiritual, thinking and moral life of the individual and played a role similar to our conscience. It was carefully preserved after death and examined at the final judgement. It is notable that like the ancient Chinese, the Egyptians saw the heart as the organ of speech as well as thought and recognized the intelligence of the heart.

The complexity of the ancient Egyptian notion of the self reflects the subtlety and depth of their sacred science which is at the foundation of alchemy.

The northern shaft of the Queen's Chamber was orientated around 2500 BC towards the Star Beta Ursa Minor which was associated with the immortality of the soul. The southern shaft was in line with the Dog Star, Sirius, associated with Isis, Osiris' consort. The dead pharaoh was thus identified with Osiris and by pointing to

Sirius the pharaoh in the Great Pyramid would be able to re-enact symbolically the union between Isis and Osiris in a cosmic orgasm. If this is the case, it would seem that the Great Pyramid is a gigantic reaction vessel of cosmic alchemy, joining together the male and female principles in the universe.

*

I directed my torch up the southern shaft in the Queen's Chamber but its dim light was soon lost in total blackness. A German team led by Rudolf Gantenrink had recently placed a tiny robot on wheels, named after the ancient god Upuat ('Opener of the Ways'), to explore the southern shaft. About three-quarters of the way to the exterior, some 65 metres in, the shaft was blocked. It had all the appearance of a door. What is behind the threshold? Could it throw light on the origins of Egyptian sacred science and alchemy? The door seems to have corroded copper handles and there is a small aperture at one side through which a fibre-optic camera might be inserted.

I later asked Dr Hawass about the project and he said that they would go ahead with it if possible: 'If there's anything there,' he added, 'we'll see it!'

We left the Queen's Chamber and climbed up the steep incline of the Great Gallery towards the King's Chamber. The gallery is huge and looks like the vault of a very narrow cathedral. It may well have served as an observatory before the pyramid was covered over; the fourth-century Neoplatonist philosopher Proclus from Alexandria certainly thought so. It reminded me of the semi-circular pit of the observatory of the fifteenth-century Islamic astronomer and alchemist Ulugh Beg which I had seen in Samarkand on my way to China.

It was the second time in my life that I had entered the King's Chamber. I was no less impressed by its size. It measured 10.49 by 5.24 metres and 5.84 metres in height. Its walls and floors are covered with huge polished granite blocks and the ceiling consists of nine vast granite monoliths. I was able to be alone and something of its ancient symmetry (expressing the geometrical formula phi) touched me to the core. The lightness of being which I had experienced in the subterranean chamber had not left me. I felt centred, complete and harmonious. Were invisible and subtle forces at work in this reaction vessel? It certainly exerts a deep influence on those who enter. After spending a night within it, Napoleon emerged white and shaken and refused to talk about his experience. Perhaps it has a way of revealing the state of one's inner being.

As in the Queen's Chamber, there are shafts in the King's Chamber. Around 2500 BC the southern shaft was aimed at the brightest star of Orion's belt (Zeta Orionis), associated with Osiris, while the northern shaft pointed to the ancient Pole star (Alpha Draconis). Ayman thought they were for the souls of the deceased pharaoh to come and go freely to the Underworld:

'The ancients thought that the world was flat and that during the night the sun travelled under it from west to east. They imagined another world under ours, like this one with rivers, plants and trees, but better. Osiris, the father of Horus, is the king of the Underworld. But it is a difficult journey to get to paradise . . .'

One intriguing idea is that the passages and chambers of the Great Pyramid make up a chart of the Underworld through which the deceased must pass in order to reach paradise.[7] I felt sure that the journey through the Underworld mirrored the different stages of the alchemical process, passing from death to rebirth, darkness to light.

In building the Great Pyramid the Egyptians may well have created a finely honed instrument of spiritual engineering to perform the most important of all experiments, the transformation of matter into spirit. If this is the case, the Great Pyramid is nothing less than a laboratory of the soul, aimed at attaining the supreme goal of alchemy – immortality. Just as the builders of the pyramid transformed rough stone into a work of perfect symmetry, so the Egyptian priests used it to transform the bodies of the deceased into immortal souls. The Great Pyramid thus stands as a great monument to both the alchemy of matter and the alchemy of spirit. Indeed, on a massive scale, it might well be a symbol of the Philosopher's Stone itself. Millions of people have entered the Great Pyramid and have been deeply moved by the experience, but how many have recognized it for what it really is – the ultimate alchemical laboratory?

*

How does the Great Sphinx fit in with this scenario? I visited the Sphinx next to the Pyramids on the Giza plateau many times during my stay in Egypt. On my last day the *Egyptian Gazette* celebrated the completion of its restoration which had taken nine years and been supervised by Dr Hawass. Archaeologists, it claimed, could now 'heave a deep sigh of relief for seeing this part of Egyptian history retrieve its bloom of youth'.[8]

Inspector Ayman told me that the Sphinx was erected as a symbol of power to protect the funerary temple of Cheops by his son Chephren. Just sitting in the presence of the Sphinx and contemplating its face and body for several hours I found it impossible to believe that it stood for imperial might. Its far-seeing eyes, looking eternally east to the rising sun, hint at prophecy and illumination, not strength and force.

How old is the Sphinx and the knowledge it might contain? It is a great riddle which perhaps contains the key to the genesis of Egyptian civilization and alchemy. It has recently been suggested, on the evidence of water erosion at its base and of its orientation, that it could have been built as early as 10000 BC.[9] It may well be that the civilizers who came across the sea – the 'Companions of Horus' – built the Sphinx, the mortuary temple and laid out the ground plan of the Pyramids of Giza before the rains fell at the end of the Ice Age and called off play. Work was only started again by later generations around 3500 BC when it is generally thought that the Pyramids of Giza were built. The evidence is far from conclusive, but it is a fascinating hypothesis, and points once again to the great antiquity of Egyptian civilization and the alchemical tradition which it contained.

While examining the body of the Sphinx closely, I noticed a small square passage in the bedrock at its rear. It has long been known that the Sphinx contains inner chambers. More recently, a seismographic survey revealed a rectangular chamber, measuring 12 by 15 metres, between the paws of the Sphinx. Could it contain the records of Horus, the wisdom of Thoth and the secrets of alchemy? A team of archaeologists from Florida University were given permission to investigate but when I asked Dr Hawass about the opening of the chamber, he replied curtly: 'The project has been cancelled. It's too dangerous to disturb the stone. The team was only interested in making a movie, not in science.'

I asked his colleague Ayman whether any documents had been found.

'That's what everybody is looking for! The secret of the sands! Hawass did some excavations ten years ago and discovered four crypts but there was nothing inside except an old shoe. No box containing an ancient atlas has yet been discovered!'

Not yet. Not all the known chambers under the Sphinx have been explored. Could the Sphinx contain the secrets of alchemy and a crucial message for our time from an even older civilization than Egypt itself? For millennia, we have been cut off from our roots in Egypt, by the difficulty of understanding the hieroglyphs, by the loss of ancient papyri, by the destruction of its tombs and temples. We have only fragments of alchemical texts to sift through. As Dr Hawass told me, we may know only a third of all the secrets and monuments which still lie buried under the sand.

During the late afternoon of my last day at Giza, I went for a ride on a fiery Arab stallion in the desert by the Pyramids and the Sphinx. Usually only an inch of rain falls over Giza, but dark nimbus clouds began to gather, riding low in the sky. The sun was blacked out. There was a sudden flash of lightning behind the Great Pyramid and a loud clap of thunder reverberated across the lonely sands. The heavens opened and thick drops of rain fell, drenching the dust. My horse reared up, snorted wildly and galloped across the desert towards the south where the Nile rises in the highlands of Ethiopia.

Did it augur the end of our own fragile civilization? Will the earth once again be engulfed by fire and water? Will we have to start again in our search for eternal life? Before this happens, I wanted to find out what more light ancient Egypt could throw on the Philosopher's Stone and the alchemical way . . .

18

Journey to the Underworld

I stand before the masters who witnessed the transformation
of the body of a man into the body in spirit, who were
witnesses to resurrection when the corpse of Osiris entered
the mountain and the soul of Osiris walked out shining . . .
when he came forth from death, a shining thing, his face
white with heat . . . And when the story is written and the
end is good and the soul of a man is perfected, with a shout
they lift him into heaven . . .

The Egyptian Book of the Dead

After my exploration of the Pyramids and the Sphinx at Giza, I
travelled south to visit the sacred enclosure of King Zoser at Saqqara,
three hours away by horse from Cairo. Built over 5,500 years ago,
Saqqara is justly famous for its Step Pyramid, the first large-scale
pyramid in Egypt, still standing over 60 metres high. It is believed to
be the work of the legendary Imhotep, architect, high priest, doctor,
sage and alchemist. The ancient Greeks called him Asclepius and
celebrated him as the father of medicine.

I was chiefly interested, however, in the nearby Pyramid of the
pharaoh Unas. It is now a pile of rubble, but the walls of its subterranean chambers are covered with chaste and delicate hieroglyphs.
They are known as the *Pyramid Texts* which, along with the later
Coffin Texts, form the basis of *The Egyptian Book of the Dead*.
Literally translated as 'Chapters on the Coming Forth by Day', its
subject matter – the transformation of the body into spirit and the
quest for eternal life – is the fundamental aim of all spiritual alchemy.
The theme of the Egyptian funerary texts further mirrored my own
quest for the Philosopher's Stone. It would seem that they are the
original source of all quest literature.

The work is inspired by the cosmology of the ancient Egyptians which is expressed principally in myth and symbol and forms the background to the world view of alchemy. It was elaborated by the priests of Heliopolis after the unification of Upper and Lower Egypt around 3000 BC. According to the great creation myth of ancient Egypt, in the beginning was the Primeval Waters, known as Nun, the father of the gods and the basic matter of the universe. Out of the Primeval Waters rose the Primeval Mound, the 'First Place' of the 'First Time'. The High God Atum 'was at first alone, very weary and inert' but, desiring a companion, 'that great He/She' created the first creatures, Shu (space) and Tefnut (moisture), male and female.

There are two versions of how this first creation took place: one is that Atum masturbated; the other is that he spat them out of his mouth.[1] Shu and Tefnut then produced the next pair of elements, Geb (earth) and Nut (sky). The sky Nut is female and the earth Geb is male. Nut gives birth to the stars and lets them sail across her belly. This story of creation clearly shows the origins of the elements of space, water, earth and air.

The Book of the Dead is a guide for the journey beyond the grave which passes through various stages in the Underworld to the realm of new life. The chapters are principally intended to help the deceased to overcome his foes in the Underworld, to draw on the help of friendly beings, and eventually, when regenerated and made immortal, to roam at will with the gods throughout the universe.

This, however, could only be possible if his mummified body remained undisturbed in its tomb. The preservation of the physical body, as in China, was considered essential to any continued existence in the afterlife. The physical body can germinate the immortal spiritual body (*sahu*) only if the physical body does not decay. For this reason, mummification was developed into a high art and science which in turn greatly contributed to the development of practical alchemy.

The process followed certain clearly demarked stages. First the brain was removed through the nostrils. Next the viscera – liver, lungs, stomach and intestines – were extracted, cleaned, dried and coated with molten resin before being placed in jars, usually made from alabaster, to be buried with the body. In the meantime, the body was packed for at least forty days with natron, a naturally occurring mixture of carbonate, bicarbonate, chloride and sulphate of sodium with strong drying and preserving properties.

This alone shows the advanced chemical knowledge of the ancient Egyptians. The body was anointed with unguents before being wrapped in fine linen gauze and adorned with amulets, magical symbols and jewellery, especially made from gold. The body was then placed in at least one coffin in a stone sarcophagus. This in turn could be placed in a series of nested shrines covered with gold leaf, as in the case of Tutankhamon.

The process of transformation, rebirth and immortality at the heart of spiritual alchemy is illustrated by the central Egyptian myth of Osiris. Born of the earth and the sky (Geb and Nut), Osiris was, according to the Greek historian Plutarch, the King of Egypt and the instrument of its civilization: 'He weaned the inhabitants from their barbarous ways, taught agriculture, formulated the laws and taught the worship of the gods. Having accomplished this, he set off to impart his knowledge to the rest of the world.'[2]

The Osiris myth is the founding myth of Egyptian civilization. After killing him, his brother Set cut up his body and scattered the pieces. His wife Isis, however, gathered them together and reunited his body while their son Horus enacted his revenge. Osiris is the very emblem of resurrection, symbol of the cosmic cycles of death and rebirth. He declared:

> I am the Great One, the son of the Great One; [I am] Fire, the son of Fire, to whom was given his head after it had been cut off . . . I have knit myself together; I have made myself whole and complete; I have renewed my youth. I am Osiris, the lord of eternity.[3]

The pharaoh in death is associated with the fallen Osiris, who in the texts and illustrations of *The Book of the Dead* is shown face down on the ground. He is exhorted to 'Cast the sand from thy face!' By turning towards the heavens, he will eventually be transformed and resurrected as his son Horus in his guise as a hawk of gold.

The myth of Osiris is reflected in the alchemical process itself. After the dismemberment of substances, they are brought together with the use of fire in a refined and immortal form. It marks the passage from chaos to order, dissolution to coagulation, darkness to light, death to everlasting life. The wisdom god Thoth, the father of alchemy, also plays a key role in 'establishing Osiris' in his spiritual transformation and purification in the Underworld. He acts like the Philosopher's Stone in an alchemical experiment: 'I am Thoth,' he announces, 'the guide of heaven, and earth, and the Underworld, and the creator of life of [all] nations and peoples. I gave air unto him that was in the hidden places by means of the might of the magical words of my utterance, and Osiris triumphed over his enemies.'⁴

*

Given the Egyptian belief in the afterlife, what might the deceased expect to face in the Underworld? To find out more, I left Saqqara and travelled up the Nile to Luxor, site of the ancient city of Thebes. In three parched valleys on the West Bank lay the elaborate burial places of the ancient kings, queens and nobles of Egypt cut deep into a barren escarpment of the desert. I managed again to obtain special permission from the Director of Antiquities at Luxor to visit the closed tombs of Tuthmosis III (1479–25 BC) which contained the complete version of the Egyptian funerary text known as *The Book of What is in the Duat*. The *Duat* is the Egyptian name for the Underworld.

Crossing over the Nile and travelling through the alluvial plain of the West Bank, I was struck by the ancient rhythm of the life of the farmers. It had not changed greatly since biblical times: donkeys, camels and oxen munched harvested clover and grass in the courtyards in front of the mud-brick houses at the side of the road. I passed by the Ramesseum, where lay the fallen colossal statue of Ramesses II which had inspired Shelley's great poem 'Ozymandias' on the folly of power. It was on the edge of the alluvial plain of the Nile: the dark green swathes of sugar cane suddenly gave way to the light yellow sand and stone of the desert.

CLOSED FOR RESTORATION said an old sign at an angle. I was at the entrance of the tomb of Tuthmosis III, so small that it could easily be missed. It was hidden in a steep defile at the head of the Valley of the Kings and could only be reached by a long ladder. Although only late February it was already very hot in the valley and hotter still as we descended into the tomb. The local inspector of antiquities unlocked a great padlock and after much struggling forced open an iron grill. Small stones rattled into the dark interior. An ancient generator was started up and some dim lights flickered on. We descended a long sloping corridor, with a ceiling depicting the starry night, and crossed a deep pit into a central chamber with its roof supported by two pillars. I was astounded by what I saw as my torch swung around the chamber. The walls were covered with hundreds of stick-like figures of some 740 different *neteru*, gods and goddesses of ancient Egypt. In the middle of the chamber was the large empty sarcophagus of the pharaoh.

Then there was a sudden smell of burning fuses and the lights went out. We were plunged into complete darkness, the darkness of the tomb. The nervous laughter of my guide echoed through the empty passages and chambers. I was deep in the tomb, unsure of the way out. I recalled tales of the Pharaoh's curse on those who violated his tomb but for some reason I did not feel frightened. I waited in the bowels of the Egyptian desert to see what would happen. Eventually, the lights flickered back on, casting shadows across the painted hieroglyphs and figures of gods still in a state of perfect preservation. The pitch-black darkness and bone-dry warmth of 3,500 years had not affected them.

The interior burial chamber with its empty sarcophagus was in the oval shape known as a 'cartouche', the hieroglyphical sign for a pharaoh and for eternity. Unfurled in a clockwise direction around the walls was the complete text of *The Book of What is in the Duat*. It was written 3,500 years ago, inspired by the early pyramid texts drawn up nearly 1,000 years earlier. Like *The Book of the Dead*, the work is a guide to the Underworld as well as a work of spiritual alchemy, showing the various steps and transformations that the soul of the deceased must undertake in order to attain immortality. He is at first associated with the dead Osiris but if he overcomes all the challenges and obstacles, he will come to life again and be identified with Re, the cosmic principle of all energy.

The journey takes the form of the twelve hours of the night. It was thought that the deceased descended like Re to the western horizon. His passage into the realms of the night in the Underworld is depicted as a journey of the soul on a solar boat through the body of Nut, the sky goddess, who gives birth to the deceased in the morning as she does the sun god Re. Figures of different gods, all manifestations of the supreme god Re, illustrate the hieroglyphs of the text rather like a stained-glass window in a medieval cathedral illuminates the Gospel.

In the middle of the northern wall of the burial chamber, the most striking figure was a large Ouroboros serpent, the oldest known representation of a key alchemical symbol. In this case, the serpent forming the circle with its tail in its mouth has three other heads. It also encircles a giant scarab which pulls along with its pincers the head of a man whose body is as big as the insect itself. Known as Khepri, the scarab is a manifestation of Re. As a flying creature emerging from a ball of dung, it is a symbol of the resurrection of the soul from the dead body. The encircling snake, like the shape of the tomb, is a symbol of eternity. Taken together, there could not be a more apt symbol for attaining immortality, the central theme of alchemy.

An introductory text called 'The Writings of the Hidden Chamber' on the walls of the tomb shows the contents of this ancient guide to spiritual alchemy and how it can be used:

> The places where the souls, the gods, the shadows and the spirits stand. What they do. The beginning of the Horn of the West, the Gate of the Western Horizon, the end of utter darkness. The Gate of the Western Horizon.
>
> [This is] the knowledge of the power of those in the Netherworld.
>
> [This is] the knowledge of what they do; knowledge of their sacred rituals to Re; knowledge of the mysterious powers; knowledge of what is in the hours as well as their gods; knowledge of what he says to them; knowledge of the gates and ways on which the GREAT GOD passes; knowledge of the movement of the hours and their gods; knowledge of the powerful ones and the annihilated.[5]

The journey takes the deceased through a series of trials and obstacles before he can attain immortality. Sitting in the penumbra of the tomb surrounded by sacred texts and visionary illustrations, I realized that it was a journey into the innermost recesses – the caves and pits, the heights and the depths – of the mind itself. It is also a philosophical journey, a bold attempt to penetrate and understand the reality underlying all phenomena. The journey into the Underworld is nothing less than a voyage into the heart of Being.

The deceased must encounter great challenges and terrifying characters; in the third hour, for instance, he must face 'She Who Cuts Up the Souls' and pass through the 'Place of Destruction'. This clearly mirrors the early stage in the alchemical process of dissolution. The appearance of Khepri, the scarab beetle, anticipates the rebirth in the fourth hour. After passing by the Abyss, in the seventh hour the Great God tells Osiris: 'Thou art a soul, thy soul is made spirit on earth.'[6]

In the twelfth hour, in the middle register a huge snake ridden by twelve gods pulls the solar barque. Its name is the Great Ka, Life of the Gods. The Great God travels inside the spinal column of the serpent, recalling the Kundalini yoga of the Indian alchemists in which energy works its way up through the chakras to the head and the practice of the Chinese alchemists of redirecting sexual energy through the 'cinnabar fields' to nourish the brain. The journey now reaches its climax: Khepri is born, pushing the disc of the sun through the sands of the eastern desert. Osiris is risen in the form of his son and heir Horus, the principle of light. The experiment of the twelve hours is complete.

As I sat in the gloom of the burial chamber next to the rifled sarcophagus of Pharaoh Tuthmosis III, the dim, flickering light sending long shadows across the funerary text, I realized that Egyptian civilization was not about darkness and despair but light and hope. The ancient Egyptian could expect to join his ancestors in the afterlife and live carefree in an eternal realm modelled on earth, or his soul could soar up to join the stars in their endless circuit of the heavens. It was no coincidence that Re was the supreme source of light in our galaxy: the sun. The apparent preoccupation of alchemy and of Egyptian civilization with death was really a preparation for an eternity of light.

Looking at the graceful, dignified figures of the gods and the elegant beauty of the hieroglyphs, it suddenly occurred to me that the Underworld – the *Duat* – is not some unknown world after death but this world, the world we live in, here and now. We must all like Osiris undertake a perilous voyage, passing through various gates, facing enemies on the way, encountering tests and challenges. We can all too easily fall into the Abyss, pass through the Place of Destruction, and swim across the Flood of Despair. The worst of all is to become a lost one, turned upside down and annihilated for a second and last time. It therefore makes sense to be a well-equipped soul before embarking on the final voyage, and to have a heart which is light with good deeds before standing before the gods in the final judgement. But there is no need to be dejected. Through the correct use of the sacred science of alchemy we, too, can undergo a spiritual transformation and resurrection like Osiris himself.

*

Before leaving Luxor, I was determined to visit the temple dedicated to Osiris at Abydos built by Seti I (1301–1290 BC), 145 kilometres to the north. It was situated at the heart of the present troubles, a stronghold of the Muslim brotherhood who were opposing the government. I was fortunate enough to form part of the first armed convoy which the government allowed to travel after the massacre months earlier at Queen Hatshepsut's Temple. I took my regular driver Ahmed in his old taxi and met the armed guards in the centre of town at eight o'clock on a beautifully warm and sunny morning. The only other vehicle in the convoy was a minibus with four German archaeologists.

We set off at high speed, a pick-up of heavily armed plain-clothed guards clearing our path and another protecting our rear. As we weaved around swaying donkeys and camels, lorries, carts, horns blaring at every opportunity, I noticed that our driver was having trouble changing gear. After about an hour, we were forced to stop at a police checkpoint outside a village by a bridge on the Nile to await a change of guard. As we coasted to a halt, the gearstick flopped off in Ahmed's hand. He leapt out and pushed the car off the road. I recalled the British Foreign Office advice: 'local driving conditions and poor vehicle maintenance make road travel outside the main cities hazardous . . . In the event of an accident emergency medical facilities are limited'. Osiris may have met many obstacles in his journey in the Underworld, but I was encountering similar ones in my quest for the Philosopher's Stone.

During our enforced wait, I began chatting to one of the German archaeologists. I asked her about the difficulties of interpreting the meaning of the hieroglyphs in the tombs and temples.

'There's no need to interpret texts,' was her reply. 'We must simply record what is left.'

'But how can you understand the nature of Egyptian civilization if you don't ask why the temples were built and for what purpose?'

'It's impossible to do that. Religious texts are very mystical. To try and understand them is a waste of time! Egyptology is a science. You have to be scientific!'

If that was science, it was certainly a dismal science. I recalled the words of the Egyptologist and alchemist R. A. Schwaller de Lubicz: 'Egyptology can be a profession for grave diggers and tomb vandals, or else the most marvellous source of knowledge for the world to come.'

While I was mulling over all this, Ahmed suddenly appeared. He was dusty and greasy but had a wide smile across his sweating face: '*Imshallah!* No problem! Car good! We go!'

At that very moment, the new armed guard turned up for the

convoy. We sped off to Abydos, the pick-up trucks again full of police with automatic weapons.

The temple with its huge columns is set in the desert below a rugged escarpment. Traditionally, Egyptian temples were closed to the public but the major ceremonies of the year took place in their courtyard. As I entered the vestibule, birds were twittering and flying amongst the forest of huge columns. A few shafts of light shone through small squares in the high, flat stone roof, creating a remarkable chiaroscuro effect. After the heat, dust and argument of the road, it was delightfully cool and calm.

Abydos was the main place of worship of Osiris, Lord of the Underworld, and it became the centre of his cult. The theme of the temple is the reincarnation of Osiris. An annual festival, which lasted eight days, took place during the last month of the flood when the waters of the Nile were beginning to recede. It began with the ritual of the 'Opening of the Ways', followed by three days and nights of lamentation – the period of passion when Osiris lay inert. After the symbolic trial of Set before the tribunal of the gods, Osiris was returned to the temple. The final and most symbolic act was the raising of the Djed column, supposed to represent the back of the god, a sign that Osiris was risen.

To join the company of Osiris, to 'become' an Osiris, required a righteous life and the correct funerary rites and mummification. But there was also a way for the initiated through acquiring alchemical knowledge, especially in the form of magic. In the early *Coffin Texts*, there is a 'Spell for becoming the first to enter and the last to leave among the banqueters at the feasts of Osiris'. A scribe of the twelfth dynasty added the rubric: 'If anyone learns this spell he will complete one hundred and ten years of life, of which the last ten years will be without weakness and impurity, without transgression or lies, and he will continually consume meals beside the helpful god, every day.'[7]

The Osiris Chapel deep within the temple at Abydos depicts the many forms and aspects of the god. It also has a fine relief of the Benu bird, the Egyptian phoenix, symbol of another resurrection. The Egyptians believed that the soul assumed the form of a bird in order to fly from the darkness of the tomb to the light of the heavens. In the Sokar sanctuary there are explicit portrayals of the posthumous impregnation of Isis with the seed of Osiris. In one tableau, Isis holds the head of Osiris while he masturbates to stimulate orgasm.

To the north of the main temple stands the so-called Oseirion, the alleged tomb of the head of Osiris. It is a deeply mysterious place. It only came to light at the beginning of the twentieth century from the drifting sands of the desert but it may well have been made much earlier than the temple. Built on an artificial mound, it would seem to express the creation myth of the Primeval Mound emerging from the Primeval Waters. Its massive structure consists of huge rectangular pillars which support massive architraves; some are 3 metres by 3 metres by 6 metres and weigh as much as 100 tons. Made from red granite they were brought down by ship from Aswan and carried across the alluvial plain of the Nile.[8]

How old is it? No one knows for sure. The crumbling rock around the great stone blocks are not bedrock but silt from ancient floods. The last great floods in Egypt occurred at the end of the last Ice Age, around 10000 BC. Does this mean that it was built at the time of the Sphinx, 6,000 years before the orthodox chronology for ancient Egypt? Does the passion of Osiris, and the roots of alchemy it contains, go that far back? The Oseirion will no doubt stand for thousands more years but the deep mystery remains.

19

Stars and Books

Egypt has recorded and kept eternally the wisdom of the old times. The walls of its temples are covered with inscriptions and the priests have always under their own eyes that divine heritage . . . from time immemorial when gods governed the earth in the dawn of civilization.

Plato

The next step in my quest was to see two extraordinary temples along the Nile which were built in Ptolemaic times after the conquest of Egypt by Alexander the Great in 332 BC. Their very existence demonstrates that the sacred science of the temple priests was still being kept alive at a time when the first alchemical texts were being written down in Greek.

The first was at Dendera, only about 50 kilometres and an hour north of Luxor. Because of the recent attacks on foreigners by the Muslim fanatics, I still had to leave in an armed convoy. After the dusty town of Qena, we crossed the Nile to Dendera. The approach to the temple was stunning. Almost intact, it stands at the edge of the desert. Its harmonious proportions rose out of the yellow sand and stood out against the dark blue sky. Four identical rows of huge columns, each topped with the head of the goddess Hathor, dwarfed the onlooker.

The temple is dedicated to Hathor, daughter of Re, the goddess of love and fertility, who was later identified with the Greek Aphrodite. She is often depicted with a sun between horns on top of her head, with cow ears or even in the form of a cow. While she can have a destructive role, like the Hindu goddess Kali, Hathor is usually considered a patroness of healing. Dendera was once a place of pilgrimage where all kinds of alchemical elixirs were made and magical therapies performed.

Dendera was a late temple, begun in the first century BC, and completed under the Roman Emperor Augustus around the time of the birth of Christ. Like most late temples it was erected on an earlier site and artefacts from the Old Kingdom have been found. An inscription in one of the subterranean crypts further states that it was built 'according to a plan written in ancient writing upon a goat skin scroll from the time of the Companions of Horus'.[1] This refers to those exceptional beings who allegedly ruled Egypt in the 'First Time' and who may have come across the sea with the knowledge of alchemy from a lost civilization.

The crypts of the temple have ceremonial and religious meaning: the statue of the *ba* soul of Hathor was kept there until her birthday on the new year when the golden goddess emerged from the cramped primeval darkness. She was carried at dawn up the spiral staircases, into the wide open space of the temple roof top so that, as one text puts it, 'the goddess Hathor might be united with the beams of her father, Re'. The new year celebrations would then begin: 'The sky rejoices, the earth dances, the sacred musicians shout in praise.'[2] The movement from darkness to light and her transformation were clearly alchemical in character.

Dendera is a golden temple. As the daughter of the sun god Re, she was known as 'The Gold' or 'The Golden One'. Mirrors were made of gold and decorated with an image or symbol of Hathor, thereby representing the sun and the goddess by virtue of their substance and form.[3]

In the second room on the left of the Hypostyle Hall, there are hieroglyphs describing the preparation of copper, electrum and gold. The priests must have used this room as an alchemists' laboratory. In the chambers surrounding the inner sanctuary there was also a perfume laboratory which manufactured the unguents and incense essential for the ceremonies. In the treasury opposite reliefs depict pieces of jewellery as well as unworked stones such as feldspar, granite and other minerals not yet identified.

The whole Temple of Hathor is focused towards the inner sanctuary, the Holy of Holies. The ceiling lowers and the floor rises as you travel deeper towards it. The hieroglyphs refer to this part as 'the hidden, secret chambers', surrounded by the 'Mysterious Corridor'.

The sanctuary forms a separate temple within the temple. It was called the 'Great Seat'. Here rested the golden image of Hathor and the sacred solar barque on which she was carried.

Apart from being dedicated to the golden goddess Hathor, the temple at Dendera is of great alchemical interest because of its astrological elements. The timing of an experiment in accordance to the right position of the stars was always an essential part of the success. The most interesting feature is in a small chapel in the north-eastern corner of the flat roof, dedicated to the 'Resurrection of Osiris'. There on the low ceiling I could just make out the famous Dendera zodiac, the only circular zodiac discovered in Egypt. Blackened by soot, the original is now in the Louvre. The zodiac is similar to the one developed by the Chaldeans, except the symbols are Egyptian. In the centre are personifications of the circumpolar stars: Draco is depicted as a hippo, the haunch of an ox is the Great Bear and Anubis is the Little Bear. Cancer the Crab is just off centre with Leo placed behind it and followed by the other signs of the zodiac in a counter-clockwise direction.

The Dendera zodiac has complex origins. As a map of the night sky, it reflects the fundamental belief of alchemy and astrology that there is a correspondence between the heavens and the earth: 'As above, so below.'[4] This close relationship between heaven and earth is expressed in the mythology of ancient Egypt and in the many illustrations of Nut, the goddess of the sky, stretching over the recumbent body of Geb, the earth, who often has an erection. Her arms and legs form the four pillars of the sky while her body is spangled with the stars and constellations of the firmament. Across it travels the sun god Re in his boat from sunrise to sunset.

The division of the zodiac into twelve 30° angles emerged amongst the Chaldeans in southern Babylonia, Mesopotamia around the fifth century BC. After the conquests of Mesopotamia and Egypt by Alexander the Great in the fourth century BC, Babylonian beliefs and Greek ideas were adopted by Egyptian astrologers and astronomers and passed down to the Greeks and Romans in Ptolemaic times. The Egyptian astrology of the third century BC thus developed the planetary sequence known as the 'Chaldean order', the model of the universe adopted by alchemists down to the time of Copernicus and the Scientific Revolution in the seventeenth century. It places the visible planets according to their apparent motion and supposed distance from the earth in the following order: moon, Mercury, Venus, sun, Mars, Jupiter and Saturn.

The most fundamental idea of Egyptian astrology, one which is at the heart of alchemy, is the profound correspondence between the macrocosm of the great world above and the microcosm of the little world below. As in China and India, a comprehensive system of correspondences was discovered between the planets and signs of the zodiac and different objects on earth, such as metals, animals, herbs and colours. A human being is the microcosm par excellence. There are stars in our bodies as well as in the heavens.

Astrology thus became the art of interpreting the influences of the macrocosm on the microcosm, exploring the cosmic correspondences and sympathies. As such, astrology was a handmaiden of alchemy. Medicine further linked the signs of the zodiac with different parts of the body. Character traits were associated with the planets, as the terms saturnine, mercurial, Martian and venereal indicate. The alchemists not only associated the seven metals with the seven planets but used the astrology so beautifully expressed at Dendera to determine the best times for conducting their different experiments.

*

After Dendera, I travelled to Edfu, the most intact temple in Egypt from Ptolemaic times which is about 95 kilometres south of Luxor. While built on earlier temples – some portions of the western enclosure wall date from the Old Kingdom – work on the existing building was begun in 237 BC and finished in 57 BC. Most temples are orientated east–west, but Edfu is unusual in that it faces south. This was probably to link it with Dendera which faces north: they look at each other and although some 145 kilometres separates them, they seem to have shared certain myths, rituals and ceremonies as well as common beliefs.

Surrounded by the brightly coloured mud-brick houses of a new village, its splendour and power are still undimmed. The temple shows that at the end of at least 4,000 years of building unparalleled monuments, the Egyptian priests, architects and craftsmen had not lost their skills. Indeed, the temple at Edfu is the best preserved temple of the ancient world so far discovered.

The temple is dedicated to Horus, represented by a falcon. Like his father Osiris, he symbolizes the different stages of rebirth. In the great founding myth of Egyptian civilization, he avenges the dismemberment of his father Osiris by his uncle Set. Just as Set is associated with the cycles of time and the embodiment of spirit in matter, Horus represents the triumph of spirit over matter and time.

Many temples in ancient Egypt had a 'House of Life' inside or close to the sacred enclosure. It acted as a school and university and the subjects studied included medicine, astronomy, astrology, magic and alchemy. Some Houses of Life were particularly famous for their libraries. There is one such library in Edfu, known as the 'Chamber of Writings'. It is the size of a small chapel, hardly 2 metres square, attached to the eastern inner wall of the vestibule. As I bent my head to enter the small stone chamber, I felt my heart beating. Could it be that papyri were once kept here, handed down from one generation of priests to the next, which contained the key to the Philosopher's Stone? Would I ever come closer to it in my quest?

We know that the chamber in Edfu was a library because it has a card catalogue inscribed upon the wall which refers to 'numerous chests containing books with large rolls of parchment'. The catalogue mentions twenty-two works. Most are 'magical' in that their titles indicate some form of protection or are concerned with divination. Some are distinctly astronomical and astrological, such as the '[Book] of knowing the return to their stations of the Sun and the Moon', 'Book which regulates the return of the stars', 'Detailed account of all places and knowledge of what is in them', 'All the reckonings of the rising of His Majesty Horus in the retinue of thy house in thy festivals'.[5]

Apart from the astrological works, the most interesting book in the library at Edfu has the enticing title 'Book of All the Mysteries of the Laboratory'. Did this book contain the secrets of alchemy? I could find no trace of it in all the known literature of Egypt. I had come to the right place in my quest but I had come 2,000 years too late.

There are also some intriguing texts on the walls of Edfu Temple, known as the *Building Texts*, which suggests that the origins of alchemy may well be in a lost civilization which sent envoys to Egypt. Inscribed around 200 BC, they mention repeatedly the remote golden age known as the 'First Time' and imply that the historical temple was a continuation of 'a mythical temple that came into existence at the beginning of the world'.[6] The introduction reveals the tradition that the contents of the records were a 'Copy of the writings which Thoth made according to the words of the Sages', who were seven in number.

The *Building Texts* also refer to the 'Great Primeval Mound' of the central Egyptian creation myth, the place where time began, which emerged out of the 'Primeval Waters'. It is made clear that this 'Homeland of the Primeval Ones' was an island which was later destroyed in a flood and only a few escaped to Egypt to become 'lords of light . . . who raised the seed for gods and men . . . the Senior Ones who came into being at the beginning, who illumined this land when they came forth unitedly'.[7]

Are the Edfu texts referring here to civilizers who came across the sea to Egypt and who were known as the 'Companions of Horus'? Could they be compatriots of the 'Sons of Reflected Light' who landed in China and the Siddhas who settled in southern India after their civilization had been destroyed by a flood? Is the 'Homeland of the Primeval Ones' and the ultimate source of alchemy to be found somewhere under the waves of the Indian Ocean?

Just as the Egyptian priests in their temples were heirs of the wisdom of the 'Companions of Horus', so the later Middle Eastern and European alchemists inherited the teaching of the Egyptian temple priests. They may therefore form part of an unbroken tradition which goes back to the 'First Time' before the flood. As members of an initiated group, they ensured that the sacred knowledge from a lost civilization in the earliest times was passed down through the ages. If this is true, it means that the esoteric teaching of the Hermetic tradition and alchemy comes from the very dawn of civilization on earth.

20

Mother of Magicians

Egypt was the mother of magicians.

Clement of Alexandria

As I travelled through Egypt and deepened my studies, I increasingly became aware of how central magic was to Egyptian alchemy. Every Egyptian alchemist was a magician; indeed, he was an alchemist-magician. Magic was closely entwined with religion, philosophy and myth. It permeated every aspect of Egyptian life and can be found in temples, alchemical and medical texts, spells, folk tales, funerary artefacts and jewellery. The Egyptian priests were renowned throughout the classical world for their magical powers.[1]

Magic is the art of invoking spiritual powers or harnessing occult forces. It assumes that there is an essential energy circulating around the universe which with skill can be manipulated to a particular end. According to the Instruction for Merikara, which may have been written as early as 2000 BC, 'the Creator gave magic to repel the thunderbolt of what is to come'.[2] Through the use of magic, humans need not therefore be victims of destiny or playthings of chance but can shape their future to a degree.

The Egyptian word '*heka*' is usually translated as 'magic'. It is one of the forces used by the High God (Atum) to create order out of the primeval chaos. Every act of magic continues this creative process.[3] All the gods had their own *heka*, considered as much part of them as their bodies or names.

In ancient Egypt, sympathetic magic made use of 'words of power'. It was believed that the uttering of the name of a being or object could bring it into existence. From the earliest times, the repetition of magical formulae, usually the names of gods and supernatural beings, was considered an essential part of the ritual in preserving the dead and ensuring their immortality. The power of the word derived from the activity of the High God in the 'First Time' when he gave Thoth the words to bring the world and all its creatures into existence. The *Coffin Texts*, which date from the third millennium BC, present the magician as 'one who controls the Word'.[4] Although the magician might use different amulets, it is the word which gives them their power.

Every Egyptian died with the conviction that he or she would be given *heka* or 'words of power' which would enable them to travel unhindered in the journey through the Underworld. I came across a remarkable incantation which suggests that the ancient Egyptians knew that light took time to travel: 'Behold, I gather together the word of power from wherever it is, and from any person with whom it is, swifter than greyhounds and quicker than light.'[5] The magical power of literature was thus known to the Egyptians from the earliest times.

Amulets were widely used by the Egyptian alchemists and priests for protection and strength. Among the most powerful were the ankh, utchat eye, and the scarab. The ankh is an emblem of life and with its oval shape over a 'T' probably represents the union of male and female organs. The utchat eye, looking from another world, is a symbol of creativity and insight: the hieroglyph for 'to create' is written with an eye. The scarab, symbolizing rebirth, is the most alchemical of all. The Egyptian name for a scarab is *kheper*, a word which also means 'to grow, to become, to change oneself'. Its symbolic name derives from its habit of laying eggs in a small ball of dung which it then pushes along with its hind legs. From the dung emerges new life, just as lead is transmuted into gold, and the dead body is transformed into spirit.

After the ritual of mummification, *The Book of the Dead* recommended placing a scarab of green stone, washed with gold, in the heart of the deceased man, reciting over it the words: 'My heart, my mother; my heart, my mother!'[6] It will perform for him 'the opening of the mouth', the most important part of the ritual in which the priest touched the mouth, feet and hands of the deceased in order to animate the spiritual body in the afterlife.

Amongst the ingredients of his art, the priest-magician-alchemist in ancient Egypt would make use of the magical power of metals and stones. Amongst the metals, gold was given pride of place and associated with the sun god Re. It was placed on the flesh of the deceased to preserve the body and to enable his spirit to attain everlasting life. After the process of mummification, the final act was the gilding of the nails of the fingers and the toes. The following address was then made to confirm the alchemical transformation of the body into spirit:

> O, Osiris, thou receivest thy nails of gold, thy fingers of gold, and thy thumb of *smu* metal; the liquid of Ra entereth into thee as well as into the divine members of Osiris, and thou journeyest on thy legs to the immortal abode. Thou hast carried thy hands to the house of eternity, thou art made perfect in gold ... O Osiris, the gold of the mountains cometh to thee; it is a holy talisman of the gods in their abodes, and it lighteneth thy face in the lower heaven ... those who are in the funeral chest rejoice because thou hast transformed thyself into a hawk of gold [Horus] by means of thy amulets of the City of Gold.[7]

This papyrus, now held in the Louvre, probably dates from a late period of Egyptian history but it draws on a more elaborate work dating from the period when the Great Pyramid was built some 5,000 years ago. It is the earliest recorded statement that I could find of the direct link in the Middle Eastern alchemical tradition between gold and immortality.

Other substances were used by the magician-alchemists. In the tomb of the High Priest Petosiris at Hermopolis, the centre of the cult of the great father of alchemy Thoth, there is a resurrection scene in which Osiris, Lord of the Underworld, becomes transformed into the sun god Re. Radiating gold, he illuminates the world. I was astonished to discover that the initiates of the mysteries of Thoth reveal that Re gave birth to a 'stone of light' and a gum intended to make the mummy of the deceased imperishable and incorruptible. This 'stone of light' may well be the first recorded reference to the Philosopher's Stone.[8]

The 'gum' may also be the 'black powder' referred to in other texts which has the power of transmuting base metal into gold and ensuring immortal life. According to the Greek writers, the ancient Egyptians used mercury to separate gold and silver from their ores. 'From these processes,' wrote Professor Wallis Budge, there resulted a black powder which was supposed to possess the most marvellous powers, and to contain in it the individualities of the metals; and in it their actual substances were incorporated. In a mystical manner this "black" powder was identified with the body which the god Osiris was known to possess in the Underworld, and to both were attributed magical qualities, and both were thought to be sources of life and power.[9]

There were many legendary magicians amongst the gods and priests of Egypt. The supreme magician was Isis, wife of Osiris, who restored his severed limbs and was impregnated posthumously by him through her arts. Isis went to Thoth when she was in trouble. Among his many powers, Thoth was known as the Master of Magic and other magicians owed the revelation of their knowledge to him. In his cult centre at Hermopolis, a great temple was built which housed magical papyri allegedly written by him in its secret crypts.[10]

The first renowned human magician from the third millennium BC was Imhotep, a high priest who served King Zoser and oversaw the building of the famous Step Pyramid at Saqqara. He was also considered to be the author of works on medicine and the Greeks identified him with their god of medicine Asclepius. In a story of the second century BC, Imhotep becomes a priest-magician who had the skill to read the ancient records in the library in the Temple of Thoth at Hermopolis. Later alchemists honoured him as one of their great ancestors and a key Hermetic text appeared in Alexandria under his name.

The continuity of the magical tradition in Egypt is confirmed by the reputation of the last Egyptian-born pharaoh, Nectanebo II (360–43 BC), as a great magician and sage. Nectanebo was deeply learned in all the wisdom of the temple priests and skilled in working magic of every kind. To combat his enemies he made wax figures of their ships and his own, put them in a bowl of water and then worked his magic. When one day he saw the gods of Egypt steering the ships of the enemy he knew that the end was nigh.[11]

From the fourth century BC, the Stele of Metternich, the most famous of magical stelae, tells of the magical healing of the infant Horus, stung by a scorpion in the marshes of the Delta. Isis threatens Atum the Creator that if her son is not healed, light will no longer shine. The god says, 'Awake Horus,' and the poison loses its power. Order is restored. The stele itself is a gigantic talisman, containing all the most important gods and most hostile beings of Egyptian mythology.[12]

*

It came as no surprise to find that magic and medicine in ancient Egypt were as inextricably entwined as they are in later alchemy. Magic makes medicine preventative. Since illnesses are caused by male and female enemies, the doctor must fight against them like a warrior, like Horus fighting Set. Magic spells were regarded as a key part of his armoury. Thoth, the master of words, was again the principal mentor of doctors as he was of magicians and alchemists. But the knowledge was carefully guarded and hidden beneath secret signs which only initiates could understand. A long period of training was required. Nevertheless, aspects of the mysteries were written down in disguised form and emerged in the work of later alchemists.

Egyptian medical practitioners took a holistic approach to health and were profoundly aware of the subtle links between the mind, body and soul. The heart is not only considered to be the organ of thought but its movement is 'the beginning of the secret of the doctor'.[13] The powers of the ancient Egyptian doctors are impressive, even in the light of modern knowledge. They often used to fight like with like, as in homeopathy. Their use of excrement against putrefaction was once derided but it is now recognized that it contains antibiotics. They had a profound knowledge of plants and were expert in ointments and perfumes. As I had seen at Edfu, Egyptian temples contained universities, libraries, laboratories and perfumeries in which they practised their alchemy and made their medicines. One elixir, known as 'the great secret ointment of the House of Life', served to protect the buildings as well as maintaining the harmony of the human body.[14]

These doctor-magician-alchemists claimed not only to prolong life but also to rejuvenate their patients. A spell from the sixteenth century BC proposes 'to transform an old man into a young man twenty years old'.[15] There is also a long recipe in the 'Beginning of the Book of Transforming an Old Man into a Youth', concerning the use of fenugreek fruit as a cream to eradicate wrinkles. It ends: 'Found effective myriads of times.'[16] Again, after careful funeral rites, the deceased would be told: 'You are going to begin to walk again, as a little child, because of what has been done for your *ka* [soul] according to the decree of the Sovereign of the four pillars of the sky.'[17]

As with the ancient Chinese and Indian alchemists, the Egyptian adepts could do extraordinary things. The *Coffin Texts* say how by knowing the name of the god who is responsible for the ladder of the sky it is possible to reach paradise and attain immortality. If the adept can achieve mastery over the four winds he will have the power to explore the entire universe. His clothing becomes the life-giving breath and the measure of his stride is the breadth of the sky. Not only can he manifest himself in the storm clouds but he can also transform the darkness into luminous sky.[18]

A key passage in *The Book of the Dead* directly echoes the Chinese alchemists who wished to join the immortals and ride the wind:

> Let me journey on in peace; let me pass over the sky; let me adore the radiance of the splendour [which is in] my sight; let me soar like a bird to see the companies [?] of the Spirits in the radiance of Re day by day, who vivifieth every human being that walketh upon the regions which are upon the earth.[19]

The literature of ancient Egypt repeatedly says that worthy humans in the future life will be able to assume the form of any god, animal, bird, plant or living thing at will. Indeed, this power was one of the greatest delights they could look forward to. I for one would love to perch as a bird on Re's solar 'boat of a million years' . . .

*

The magical power of words and objects was a key part of the practice of later alchemists. But according to the Greeks, the excessive use of magic was one of the principal causes of the collapse of Egyptian civilization. As I wandered amongst its ruins, 2,000 years later, I was keen to find out whether magic was still closely linked to alchemy.

John Anthony West, the author of the best guide to the sacred places of ancient Egypt, had told me: 'Magic is very much part of everyday life in Egypt. Everybody consults magicians – diplomats, politicians, army officers – before they make a move!'

He put me in touch with a friend, an intelligent woman who regularly visited magicians. I met her in a modern hotel built above the ruins of Heliopolis in Cairo. When I mentioned that I had come to Egypt in search of the Philosopher's Stone, she lowered her voice and said she might be able to get me a special substance known as Red Mercury . . .

'Many people know about it but it's a secret! You have to be very discreet. There's a shadow about it. With a fraction of a gram you can become very rich.'

'Who told you about it?'

'A magician who became a friend. All the big shots in Egypt have some of it. If you have it, you'll have a storeroom of treasures at your disposal. I've dreamt about having a touch of it myself. Another guy told me that high officials have it. He gave me their names. The very rich can get it and become even richer!'

'How much does Red Mercury cost?'

'A million dollars . . .'

'Where can you get it from?'

'A friend of mine who's a magician in Komombo, north of Aswan. He's really powerful. The Aswan people are gifted for magic.'

'Can I contact him?'

'No. It's secret. The ones who prepare the metaphysical force are called kings. You can't do it without Nigerians.'

'How does it work?'

'You take a bit of it on the tip of a knife and prepare it for food for a genie. The Nigerians know how to call a genie for it. The genie licks some of it and then you can ask him anything, anything, all the money you need . . . anything!'

It sounded too good to be true. But I didn't have a million dollars, and I didn't know any Nigerian magicians. The story at least showed that belief in the Philosopher's Stone was widespread in contemporary Egypt.

Whilst I was in Luxor, I mentioned Red Mercury to a dentist from South Africa who was on holiday with his family in the same hotel. One evening, he rushed up to me in the lobby of our hotel and said excitedly: 'You must meet our guide. When we were visiting the tombs in the Valley of the Kings, he said that they used Red Mercury in the mummification process. The tomb robbers would take it and grind it down and use it for healing purposes!'

That evening the dentist introduced me to the guide, a well-educated man in his thirties who had once shown a Russian prime minister around the tombs and temples of the West Bank. He was a member of the local church of Plymouth Brethren. I asked him about Red Mercury.

'Red Mercury was used in mummification. It's as expensive as gold, maybe more expensive. They say it changes clay into gold. People on the West Bank get it from the cloth of mummies. Forty years ago it used to be smuggled out of Egypt. It's very dangerous to trade it. I've heard about it many times. A lot of people believe in it. It has something to do with magic, with bad spirits . . .'

This was fascinating. Did the ancient Egyptians use a 'gum' in the process of mummification in the same way that the Chinese Taoists used some undiscovered substance in preserving the body of Lady Tai? Was this Red Mercury the modern equivalent of the 'black powder' which the ancient Egyptian alchemists made? During my stay in Luxor, I asked the guide repeatedly to find out more about Red Mercury and to see if I could obtain some. But he said his contacts were away. When I left, he said: 'If I find it, I'll let you know.' I have not yet heard from him and I suspect that I never will.

Does Red Mercury hold the key? Is the secret of the Philosopher's Stone still hidden in an unknown tomb in the desert of the West Bank of the Nile or in the bandages of a mummy in a museum somewhere in the world? It sounds highly fanciful, but many people still clearly believe in its magical effects.

While I was in Luxor, I tried to have a meeting with the Coptic bishop whom I had been told was a practising alchemist. When I went to his church, I was told by a Coptic priest who acted as his secretary that he would not see me to discuss the subject. Whether or not he was an alchemist I was unable to find out. I decided to head north to Alexandria, the capital of ancient alchemy.

21

Lady of the Dew

> We must prepare the matter with the aid of minerals alone,
> without using other substances. Just as I have told you,
> wheat engenders wheat, man engenders man, and similarly
> gold engenders gold. See there is the whole mystery.
>
> *Isis the Prophetess to Her Son Horus*

I left the tombs and temples near Luxor, passed by the Pyramids at
Giza and sped in a taxi down through the desert to Alexandria,
situated on the shores of the Mediterranean. On the outskirts of Cairo
the yellow sands and stones of the desert stretched out towards Libya,
shimmering under the baking sun. I could easily see why the Egyptians,
who loved the green waters of the Nile, considered the desert a place
of chaos and sinister spirits. After a couple of hours, palm trees in the
distance showed that we were approaching the Nile delta. And then
over the brow of a hill and beyond the great lake the city of Alexandria
rose along a thin strip of land like a mirage, its white skyscrapers
trembling in the heat against a dark blue sky.

I had come to the capital of unburied memories. I had been there
before and was delighted to be back. It had been founded by Alexander
the Great who had conquered Egypt in 332 BC, bringing about its
demise as an independent nation until the middle of the twentieth
century. After his death a general called Ptolemy seized control and
established a dynasty which was to last for almost 300 years. Ptolemy I
issued gold coins which depicted Alexander with the horns of Ammon
on one side, and Zeus holding an eagle on the other, neatly combining
Egyptian and Greek gods and confirming the power of the new rulers.

Although Greek-speaking, the Ptolemies soon adopted much of
the religion and way of life of the Egyptians. The local culture was

maintained by the hereditary priesthood of the temples. They elaborated the hieroglyphic script, collected myths, and wrote down temple rituals. Literature flourished. Some Greek scholars became interested in Egyptian religion, magic, astrology and alchemy, while some Egyptian priests learned to speak and write Greek. Magnificent temples to the Egyptian gods were built during the rule of the Ptolemies as I had seen at Edfu and Dendera. Indeed, on the rear facade of the main temple of Dendera was added a portrait of Cleopatra VII, the last of the Ptolemaic pharaohs.

Under the Ptolemies Alexandria became one of the greatest cities of the ancient world, comparable only to Athens and Rome. Scholars from all over the Greek world were attracted to the new capital and its growing library. During the first three centuries, an extraordinary range of religious and philosophical movements flourished in the multicultural society. Although different communities lived in separate districts, they overlapped socially and culturally. The city managed for a while to reconcile the irreconcilable. The key philosophical question for all its thinking inhabitants – whether Egyptian, Jew, Greek, Roman or Christian – was the nature of the relationship between humanity and God. Out of this intellectual and cultural hotbed emerged the first written texts on alchemy. They were saturated with an extraordinary mix of Greek philosophy engrafted on to Egyptian sacred science.

The library in Alexandria, which had been maintained by Cleopatra but burned in 391 by the Christians who had seized the city state, was the greatest library of the ancient world, a unique treasure chest of wisdom passed down from great antiquity. It would have undoubtedly contained works of sacred science and alchemy. Its destruction was one of the greatest losses to humanity; it has cut us off in the West from our intellectual roots in ancient Egypt. It also meant that only a few papyri and fragments of alchemical texts have survived from this formative period.

The library was a stimulus to a remarkable circle of thinkers and artists who were interested in mathematics, astronomy, geography, religion and alchemy; indeed, they did not distinguish between the different branches of knowledge. They were all philosophers in the original Greek sense: lovers of wisdom. The roll-call of famous thinkers is staggering: the Jewish philosopher Philo; the poet Theocritus; the mathematician Euclid; Eratosthenes who correctly measured the circumference of the earth; Aristarchus of Samos who first proposed the theory that the earth revolves around the sun; Claudius Ptolemy, who developed the opposite theory and who drew up the first world map on a grid which included China.

Ancient Egyptian beliefs were slow to die and many were incorporated in the new Hellenic philosophy. Although disapproved of by the Coptic Church, embalming continued well into the Christian era. In the Graeco-Roman museum in Alexandria I came across a fine collection of gold leaves from a mummy discovered in the catacombs of Kom el-Chugafa. They were used to cover different parts of the body (the eyes, lips, tongue, breast, navel and fingertips) to ensure its re-animation in the afterlife.

The catacombs of Kom el-Chugafa had been discovered when a horse and cart fell down a covered well at the beginning of the twentieth century. I descended 99 steps which spiralled around a central well to find a number of corridors and chambers in two storeys running in different directions 20 metres below the surface of the earth. It was the vault of a rich Roman family in the second century which had once housed 300 skeletons. The most interesting feature of the catacombs was the peculiar mixture of Egyptian and Graeco-Roman elements, which reflect the hybrid nature of Alexandrian culture at the time. It is the last known building works to express the ancient Egyptian religion.

In the central chamber there was a tomb surrounded by statues of gods. The entrance was flanked by two guards with the bodies of Roman soldiers but with the head of a jackal (Anubis) and one of a crocodile (Sobeck). The familiar figures of Horus, Anubis, Thoth and a priest in a panther skin were there overlooking the sarcophagus which had once contained a mummy. The Ptolemaic god Serapis (a combination of the Greek Apis bull and Osiris) was flanked by Hathor and Osiris himself. To the traditional Egyptian scene were added Medusa heads, bunches of grapes and other baroque Roman elements.

The workmanship in rough limestone was crude and lifeless. Standing in the gloom, my feet damp, breathing the fetid air, I thought of the wonderful images I had seen of the Egyptian gods in the temples along the Nile. After 4,000 years of unparalleled splendour, Egyptian civilization had finally come to this crepuscular world of decrepitude. But the legacy was not lost and the ideas and beliefs which inspired it lived on in the writings and practices of the alchemists.

*

After much research, it became clear to me that in Alexandria during the Graeco-Roman times, two principal elements came together to form the peculiar compound of alchemy: Greek philosophy and Egyptian sacred science. While alchemy ultimately finds its origins in ancient Egypt, it took on board many ideas from the new Greek philosophy, especially in its views of matter and the four elements. Ironically, it was a philosophy which was greatly indebted to Egypt in the first place, as the outstanding Greek philosophers Plato and Pythagoras were the first to acknowledge.

At the beginning of Greek philosophy, thinkers struggled with the idea of there being one underlying aspect of the universe. Empedocles argued, however, that all natural objects are made up of the four 'elements': earth, fire, air and water. Unlike the Chinese and Indian alchemists who worked with five elements, Middle Eastern and European alchemists all accepted Empedocles' view that the universe is composed of four elements. Aristotle added ether as a fifth element.

But what did the Greeks think of the nature of matter? The two principal thinkers who most influenced the alchemists were Plato and Aristotle. In the *Timaeus*, Plato used the term 'ideas' or 'forms' to describe the objects of true knowledge which are beyond sensory experience and which can be comprehended only by the mind. Material objects in nature are imperfect copies of these ideas: my horse in the field is a shadowy copy of the 'idea' of horsiness. Only the knowledge of these ideas in the world of thought, beyond the world of sensation, is real, eternal and divine. For the Egyptian alchemists, steeped in sacred science, it was obvious.

Plato also asserted that the four elements of Empedocles could not be considered distinct and complete in themselves as they easily passed from one into another: 'Let us begin with what we now call water. We see it, or we suppose, solidifying into stones and earth, and again dissolving and evaporating into wind and air.'[1] The statement contains the central alchemical belief of the transformation of the elements. It is therefore better to talk of these elements as qualities, that is to say, the flames of burning wood are not fire, but have a nature such as fire. The same is true with the other elements. Qualities are like colours which consist of 'a kind of flame that streams off bodies of various kinds'.[2] This view was adopted by all subsequent alchemists. Metals do not owe their particular properties to a material cause (a permanent substance) but to different qualities.

Aristotle accepted a modified version of Plato's theory of forms but as a biologist he was interested in change and evolution. In Aristotle's classification of the world, the individual being or thing, as the first subdivision of the species, has definite 'qualities'. When matter has been 'informed by the ideas', the resulting natural objects are real: 'As forms are to matter, so also is Soul to Body.'[3] In the case of humans, the soul can bring the potential body to active realization of the happy life.

Whereas Plato thought that all things partake of the universal essence which is good ('Nothing exists which is not good'), Aristotle with his evolutionary approach argued that qualities are forever becoming more perfect: 'Nature and God are working towards an end, striving for what is perfect.'[4] Nature therefore does nothing in vain but aims at perfection which is its final cause: 'Everything is striving to gain perfection – that ultimate union of the All in the One.'

All nature is living for Aristotle and constantly changing. He distinguished in the process of growth four essentials: a material, an individualizing tendency, a formula, and an end of the process. In the cycle of an oak, for instance, from acorn to a mature tree to acorn, the most important essentials are the tendency and the final product, with its power of reproduction.[5] The alchemists similarly believed that since all nature is alive, metals are as living as trees. They are striving to complete their cycle as they gradually move towards the perfection of gold.

Aristotle claimed that while there are different objects in the world they are all made of the same primary matter. Everything came out of it and everything could go back into it. This means that everything can be transformed into everything else – the fundamental belief of all alchemists and the basis of their confidence in the possibility of transmuting base metal into gold.

Aristotle argued like Plato that the four elements of Empedocles are not distinct but can be transformed into each other; indeed, there is a qualitative change of matter in the process. He explained this by the claim that they have common properties: fire is hot and dry, air is hot and moist, water is moist and cold, and earth is cold and dry. At a deeper level, the properties hot, cold, wet and dry are really only two, hot and moist (and their opposites). Heat is due to fire and moisture to water; fire and water are therefore the most important elements, ones which oppose each other. In alchemy, the two opposed elements fire and water correspond to sulphur and mercury, the one combustible and the other liquid. They also represent the male and female principles in the universe which can come together in a chemical wedding.

The alchemists thus followed Aristotle in thinking that humanity and nature have a *telos*, or purpose. Just as humans strive to become fully conscious and rational (the end of man) so all metals 'strive' to realize their potential and reach their purest state which is gold (the end of metal). The alchemists saw it as their task to assist nature with their art to bring it to perfection. They did not see this as improving on nature, but simply as speeding up natural processes.

While accepting Plato's view that the four elements appear as qualities and can be transformed from one into the other and Aristotle's notion that all substances strive for perfection, the Alexandrian alchemists were also exposed to other exotic beliefs. In the philosophical hothouse of their cosmopolitan city, the followers of Aristotle vied with the Neoplatonists (Plotinus and Porphyry), who argued that we should realize our divine potential and become godlike, and the Gnostics (Cerinthus, Basilides and Valentine), who thought that the world was a mistake and that we should transcend the body in order to become spirit. They debated with Egyptian priests, Jewish philosophers and the new Christian thinkers. They were exposed to Pythagoreanism and the Greek Mysteries. They were offered a vision of the One, the experience of mystical ecstasy, and the possibility of spiritual transformation through gnosis, the illumination of knowledge.

*

These philosophical and religious influences undoubtedly helped the alchemists to clarify their view of nature and confirmed the spiritual goal of their work. But they always acknowledged their debt to the mysteries of the temple. In a remarkable allegory I came across called *Isis the Prophetess to Her Son Horus* (written down at the end of the first century in Alexandria), it is said that the secrets of alchemy came from an 'angel of the first firmament' called Amnael. When Horus decided to go and fight with Set to avenge the killing of his father Osiris, Isis says that she went off to Hormanouthi (the City of Hermes) 'where the Sacred Art of Egypt is practised in secret'. On the way she met an angel who tried to ravish her: 'He came near, preparing to accomplish his purpose but I did not yield to him, wishing to learn from him the preparation of gold and silver. I asked the latter of him, he told me he was not allowed to explain this on account of the great importance of these mysteries but that the next day there would come a greater angel, the angel Amnael, and he would be able to give me the answer to the question.'[6]

When Amnael came, he had a strange sign on his head and a vase that had been coated with pitch and filled with water which he held between his hands. Before revealing the mysteries, Amnael made Isis swear that she would never communicate the revelation except to her son Horus 'so that he might be you, and you, he'. The angel then declared: 'I adjure you by heaven and earth, light and darkness. I adjure you by fire, water, air and earth. I adjure by the height of the heaven and by the depth of the Tartaros. I adjure you by Hermes and Anubis, and by the roaring serpent Ouroboros and the Three-headed dog, Kerberos, guardian of Hades. I adjure you by the Ferry and by the Boatman who crosses Acheron. I adjure by the Three Goddesses of Fate, by their Whips and their Sword.'

We can see here the beliefs of ancient Egypt translated into Greek names and symbols. The oath is the kind likely to have been used in secret alchemical circles at the time, especially during the persecution by the Roman authorities.

Isis then tells Horus in typically cryptic language: 'So go then, my child, to a certain labourer [Achaab] and ask him what he has sown and what he has harvested, and you will learn from him that the man who sows wheat also harvests wheat, and the man who sows barley harvests barley.' This apparent truism expresses the profound truth of the doctrine of karma: a person reaps what he sows.

Isis continues: 'For Nature rejoices in Nature, Nature contains Nature.' She then infers: 'We must prepare the matter with the aid of minerals alone, without using other substances. Just as I have told you, wheat engenders wheat, man engenders man, and similarly gold engenders gold. See there is the whole mystery.'[7]

Isis finally gives various recipes, beginning with mercury.

The Hermetic overtones of the story are strong. There is a tradition, mentioned by Plutarch, that Isis was the daughter of Thoth–Hermes. As for Amnael, he may well be the same legendary father of alchemy. Finally, the main argument of Isis that like begets like ('gold engenders gold') became a favourite axiom amongst Arab and European alchemists. It was clearly time for me to get to grips with the legacy of Hermes and to find out his precise role in alchemy.

22

The Way of Hermes

It is impossible, in whatever matter you may wish, to find
such a wise man as the Egyptian; and so of all philosophers
and men versed in the wisdom of letters, the best have been
those who have always dwelt in that country.

Iamblichus, *Expositio Totius Mundi*

The alchemical way is the way of Hermes. Down the ages, he has not
only been hailed as the father of alchemy but gave his name to the
esoteric wisdom of the great Hermetic tradition. More than any other
figure, Hermes inspired me and countless other generations as they
embarked on their alchemical journeys. Indeed, alchemy is often just
called the 'Hermetic Art'.

Who was Hermes? As we have seen, Hermes was the Greek name
for the Egyptian god Thoth. He was usually depicted by the Greeks
with winged sandals and a caduceus – a magic staff with intertwined
serpents – and he was considered the messenger of the gods and the
protector of travellers. As an alchemist and sage, he was called Hermes
Trismegistus. The epithet 'Trismegistus' – 'the thrice great' – was the
title given to Thoth as early as the second century BC.[1] The Hermetic
tradition, which draws inspiration from the writings and teachings of
Hermes, has always been esoteric in the Greek sense of *esoterikos*
meaning 'inner'. It is intended for an enlightened and initiated few;
hence its apparently abstruse and obscure nature to those standing
outside the tradition.

Thoth, of course, was the wisdom god of ancient Egypt. His name
was a Greek rendering of the Egyptian Djehuti. He uttered the words
commanded by Re to create the world and gave the names for
everything within it. He invented writing, arithmetic, music, sculpture,

astronomy and alchemy. As the 'heart of Re', he was Re's source of wisdom. An ancient passage ascribes his birth to the sun god: 'I am Thoth, the eldest son of Re, whom Atum has fashioned, created from Khepri . . . I descend to the earth with the secrets of "what belongs to the horizon".'[2] Thoth was indeed the bearer of powerful secrets.

Re appointed him his deputy and gave him the moon to balance his own sun. As a moon god, he was the creator and regulator of the laws of cosmic harmony and delineated the seasons and regulated time.

Thoth played a key role in the Underworld as well as on earth and in the heavens. The oldest surviving reference to him is found in the *Pyramid Texts* which describe him as ferrying the deceased across the 'winding waterway' to the Underworld where he protects the dead pharaoh. He plays a part in the process of posthumous justice, standing beside the scales in the ceremony of the weighing of the heart and recording the judgements of the gods with quill and papyrus. In the *Coffin Texts*, he is called the 'Bull of Justice'. He was chiefly known as a peacemaker, especially for ending the conflict between the arch rivals Horus and Set. He takes on two physical forms, as a baboon and more often as an ibis, the common white bird with a long curved beak still seen in the fields along the Nile. His chief place of worship was called Hermopolis by the Greeks. His fame was so wide and his origins so well known that he was often simply called 'The Egyptian'.[3]

His most important work, The Book of Thoth, allegedly contains the secrets of alchemy. Unfortunately, it is lost. Its length has been the subject of much controversy. Some sources claim there are only two pages to the book – one concerned with magic to influence nature, and the other giving magic to control the world of the dead. These, of course, are the two powers attributed to the Philosopher's Stone in its ability to transform base metal into gold and to confer immortality. Other sources claim that there were forty-two books which covered the whole gamut of the sacred science of ancient Egypt.[4]

Hermes Trismegistus is credited with the authorship of the famous Hermetic writings known as the *Hermetica*, which includes the Greek *Corpus Hermeticum* and the Latin *Asclepius*. It is a profound collection of mystical and philosophical writings which had a great influence on Middle Eastern and Western alchemists. They were composed in Egypt and written in Greek from around the first to the fourth century. Most of the doctrines of the *Hermetica* clearly come from Egyptian sacred science, but they are blended with elements from Neoplatonism, Zoroastrianism, Gnosticism and Judaism. While the outward dress may be imported, the body of ideas is fundamentally Egyptian in origin.[5]

To make sense of the *Hermetica* is no easy task. It took me months to grasp the meaning but it was well worth the effort. The more I studied the Hermetic texts, the more profound and enlightened I found them to be. They not only contain great wisdom, the culmination of at least four millennia of Egyptian civilization, but offer a crucial message for our time. Above all, they provide a key to the understanding of the world view and fundamental principles of all subsequent alchemy.

The *Hermetica* is intended to teach the 'way of Hermes', that is the successive steps on the path to enlightenment. It is aimed at those spiritual seekers who yearn for union with God and who wish to attain immortality. In the process, it explores the nature of humanity, of the world and of God.

It makes clear that the path to enlightenment can only be completed under the guidance of a master. The teaching is usually presented in the form of a dialogue between master and pupil, or parent and child. Hermes, for instance, instructs his son Tat (another form of Thoth) and his pupil Asclepius (Imhotep). In another dialogue, Isis teaches her son Horus. Knowledge from ancient times was passed down in this way, but where there was a danger of the succession being broken, then it had to be written down. Hermes bids his pupil Tat write the whole dialogue down 'for the temple of Diospolis in hieroglyphic characters . . . on steles of turquoise'.[6]

The Egyptian temple priests and alchemists both stressed the need for secrecy and initiation. The doctrine, Hermes insists, 'cannot be taught; it is a secret kept in silence'.[7] This no doubt increased the reputation of masters, but it was also motivated by a genuine fear that the knowledge might get into the wrong hands. The ideal was therefore a small group of initiates inspired and guided by an exceptional teacher. Such an affinity group was less prone to prosecution by the State, however subversive the doctrines might be.

The key question of the *Hermetica* is 'How can I know God?' Reason alone is not enough. It is made clear that the Logos guides the intellect only to a certain point; the intellect must then embrace intuition if it is to attain faith: 'To understand is to believe, and not to believe is not to understand.'[8] The *Hermetica* further makes a key distinction between two types of knowledge, episteme (science) and gnosis (illumination), the results respectively of reason and understanding. One leads to the other. But full understanding is only possible with the mind and the heart. To have a vision of God you must understand 'with the eyes of your heart'.[9] The ancient Egyptians not only saw the heart as the seat of thinking, but celebrated the intelligence of the heart as a reliable guide in the search for truth.

In order to know God, I must know myself and understand the world in which I live. Knowledge of God's Creation is an essential preliminary to knowledge of God. Science, philosophy and religion – which are uniquely combined in alchemy – are therefore mutually supportive in the path towards enlightenment.

Although the *Hermetica* accepts, like the ancient Egyptians, Greeks and Romans, that there is a hierarchy of daemons (semi-gods) and gods, it is stressed over and over again that the supreme God is the 'one and only'.[10] He is the source of light, mind, life and the good which are all interconnected. He is immanent, permanently pervading the universe. He is not only full of the fertility of both sexes but 'ever pregnant' with his own will which is all goodness.

God creates the world through an offspring, a demiurge who, combining both male and female principles, is androgyne: 'The mind who is god, being androgyne and existing as life and light, by speaking gave birth to a second mind, a craftsman, who, as god of fire and spirit, crafted seven governors [planets]; they encompass the sensible world in circles, and their government is called fate.'[11]

While the ancient Egyptians represented the earth as male (Geb) and the sky as female (Nut), the influence of Greek thought in the *Hermetica* reversed the order. In the process of the creation of the seven planets and the sensible world: '[Earth] was female. Water did the fertilizing. Fire was the maturing force. Nature took spirit from the ether and brought forth bodies in the shape of man. From life and light the man became soul and mind; from life came soul, from light came mind, and all things in the cosmos of the senses remained thus until a cycle ended [and] all kinds of things began to be.'[12]

Like the Middle Eastern and Western alchemists, the *Hermetica* follows the Greek philosophers in asserting that the whole of matter has been formed by the four elements: fire, water, earth and air. They all come from one root which is God. The earth is the storehouse of all matter while the sun, the centre of the cosmos, sends 'essence' below and raises matter above, thereby binding above and below.

Just as the sun god Re was the supreme god in the Egyptian pantheon, so the sun is given a central role in the *Hermetica*. The sun not only makes immortal beings eternal but enlivens and wakens all things to becoming and change: 'It brings transmutation and transformation among them, as in a spiral, when changes turn one thing to another, from kind to kind, from form to form, crafting them just as it does the great bodies.'[13]

This belief is at the heart of the alchemist's hope of transforming base metal into gold. The fire of his furnace transforms things from kind to kind and from form to form. And by trying to perfect metals he is only following the whole trend of nature which strives for perfection: God prepared matter as 'a receptacle for omniform forms, but nature, imagining matter with forms by means of the four elements, causes all things to reach as far as heaven so that they will be pleasing in the sight of God'.[14]

In the endless process of transformation throughout the universe, nothing is destroyed. Death is not the destruction of things that have been combined but merely 'the dissolution of their union'. Expressing a view shared by every alchemist, the *Hermetica* asserts the dissolution of composite bodies is simply the 'dissolution of an alloy'.[15] In dissolving all things, the cosmos renews them. Indeed, in the entire cosmos there is a fullness of life, and throughout the whole 'recurrence of eternity' there is nothing that does not live, neither in the whole of it nor in its parts: 'For there never was any dead thing in the cosmos, nor is there, nor will there be.'[16]

The *Hermetica* assumes like all alchemy that all phenomena in the celestial and the terrestrial realms are linked together by sympathetic 'powers' or 'energies'. The idea reflects the ancient Egyptian notion of *heka* as a magical power that pervades the universe and is similar to the Greek Stoic doctrine of universal sympathy. This cosmic sympathy comes from God, who is the creator and sustainer of all things. The 'energies' linking heaven and earth are like 'rays from god'.[17] Energy is the essence of the daemons, those demigods who dwell in the stars and revolve the eight spheres of the fixed stars, the seven planets and the earth.

In the cosmos, there is a plenitude of beings and everything is thus interconnected, from stones, plants, animals, humans, daemons, to gods. Sympathetic energies, affinities and correspondences connect the most disparate aspects of nature. The human soul, for example, corresponds with a planet and a metal, the sun and gold. The alchemist seeks to understand these correspondences and to influence the energies. Through his knowledge of the workings of nature and by magical words of power, he can manipulate them to transform base metal into gold. By true understanding, by seeing with the eyes of his heart and the mind, he can obtain a vision of God and achieve immortality.

Given this Hermetic view of God and the world, what is the nature of humanity? The central Hermetic doctrine, one shared by all alchemists, is that a human being is animated by a divine spark and is therefore a 'godlike living being'.[18] Indeed, 'a human being is a great wonder, a living thing to be worshipped and honoured: for he changes his nature into a god's as if he were a god . . .'[19]

Human beings are made in the image of God: 'Mind, the father of all, who is life and light, gave birth to a man like himself whom he loved as his own child.'[20] While he shares a soul with other living beings on earth, the nature of a human being is uniquely twofold: his body is mortal but his essential self is immortal. The body is therefore the principal obstacle to immortality. Because of our bodies we are slaves within the world and subject to fate (that is, the rule of the daemons via the stars). We have knowledge before we are born, but we forget when the body drags the soul down to its grossness. Hermes therefore declares: 'Leave the senses of the body idle, and the birth of divinity will begin. Cleanse yourself of the irrational torments of matter.'[21]

A human being is made up of a mind, a soul and a body. Mind is the highest for 'when mind has entered a reverent soul, it leads it to the light of knowledge'.[22] God is in mind, mind is in soul, and soul is in matter. The body is matter, the soul is the individual self, while the mind partakes of God. But what is spirit? It is the source of all life. The 'spirit mixes with everything and enlivens everything'.[23]

To complicate matters further, the *Hermetica* makes a distinction between understanding, which we share with other sentient animals, and consciousness, which is unique to humans and raises us up to the divine. If we see with our understanding, we see heaven as if through a mist, but with our consciousness we can see the light. Indeed, the human mind shines with the 'light of consciousness'.[24] Hermes at the end of the *Asclepius* discourse gives thanks to God for the gift of consciousness, reasoning and understanding: 'consciousness, by which we may know you; reason, by which we may seek you in our dim suppositions; knowledge, by which we may rejoice in knowing you'.[25]

Humans have extraordinary abilities and powers if they so wish to develop them. Echoing the claims of the Chinese and Indian alchemists, 'Mind' tells Hermes:

> Command your soul to travel to India, and it will be there faster than your command . . . Command it even to fly up to heavens, and it will not lack wings. Nothing will hinder it, not the fire of the sun, nor the aether, nor the swirl nor the bodies of the other stars. Cutting through them all it will fly to the utmost body . . .[26]

The *Hermetica* accepts the ancient Egyptian view that after death, when the soul withdraws from the body, a person will be judged for his deeds on earth. The 'chief daemon' weighs and judges the merit of his or her soul. If sullied with vice, it will be sent tumbling down to the depths below and consigned to 'the storms and whirlpools of air, fire and water in their ceaseless clashing', to be swept back and forth between heaven and earth in 'the streams of matter'.[27] As with the Indian notion of karma, one will pay the penalty precisely in proportion to one's wrongdoing. On the other hand, the person who has lived well without harming others and has developed his mind and revered God will be blessed with the divine light.

How can we realize our potential divinity? In a unique passage, the *Asclepius* suggests like the Taoist and tantric alchemists that sex can be a sacred act which raises the mind to heaven. God, it claims, devised and granted to all things 'this mystery of procreation unto eternity, in which arose the greatest affection, pleasure, gaiety, desire and love divine'. Indeed, Hermes describes orgasm as an exchange of male and female energy, as the moment when 'females gain the potency of males and males are exhausted with the lethargy of females'. In the act of this mystery, 'so sweet and vital', arises divinity in both natures.[28]

But this is said only in passing. The principal way to enlightenment – the way of Hermes – is through the illumination of true knowledge. Since the human mind partakes of God's mind, the more we develop our mind, the more divine we become. We can all understand our true nature and realize ourselves. Through self-knowledge, we can attain knowledge of the mind of God.

The ultimate goal is thus to apprehend God which is a return to the divine source. The *Hermetica* sees this in terms of a spiritual 'rebirth'. It is not a repetition of our physical birth but a sudden rising to a new level of being and consciousness. The process recreates the essential person, the divine self within. This rebirth liberates the soul from the body so that it can transcend the realm of fate in order 'to be made god'.[29] The alchemical way of Hermes is thus to attain immortality as the purified soul is absorbed into the one and only God.

Closing the radiant pages of the *Hermetica*, I recalled the advice 'Mind' gives Hermes about divine knowledge:

> To be ignorant of the divine is the ultimate vice, but to be able to know, to will and to hope is the [straight and] easy way leading to the good. As you journey, the good will meet you everywhere and will be seen everywhere, where and when you least expect it, as you lie awake, as you fall asleep, sailing or walking, by night and by day, as you speak or keep silent, for there is nothing that it is not.[30]

It had been a long and arduous process of understanding, but I hoped my immersion in the sacred knowledge of the *Hermetica* would stand me in good stead as I continued my journey in pursuit of the Philosopher's Stone amongst the Egyptian alchemists.

23

Nature Contains Nature

Nature rejoices in Nature, Nature contains Nature, and
Nature overcomes Nature.

Ostanes

Having examined in the crucible of alchemy the elements of Egyptian
sacred science and Greek philosophy and the Hermetic writings which
emerged from them, I turned my attention to a third crucial ingredient
– the techniques and skills of the Egyptian artisans. Early in the
twentieth century, the American Professor A. J. Hopkins declared that
alchemy was 'a form of philosophy applied to a technique' which
developed in Alexandria some time after the beginning of the Christian
era.[1] Although the roots of alchemy were much deeper and more
complex, he was pointing to an essential aspect of practical alchemy.

There can be no doubt that the Egyptian artisans and artists were
extremely accomplished. A multitude must have been engaged in
building, furnishing and decorating the great monuments. The recent
findings in the tomb of Tutankhamon show the superb level of
craftsmanship, especially the draperies dyed with 'royal purple' and
interwoven with silver and gold threads or studded with gold buttons
or jewels. Craftsmen also worked exquisitely in bronze and wood. As
the exquisite murals I had seen in the tombs and temples vividly
demonstrated, they knew how to mix wonderful colours and cut stone
reliefs which have not faded for at least 5,000 years. In this respect,
Egypt undoubtedly excelled in arts as well as science.

Not all Egyptians, of course, could enjoy the quality of the articles
found in the tombs of the pharaohs. In Graeco-Roman Egypt, where
alchemy first came to light, the artisans were involved in imitating expensive dyes and falsifying silver and gold. They did not see

themselves as counterfeiters but as legitimately satisfying the desire of
a people hungry for colour and decoration in their lives.

Ironically, the earliest known text referring to the practical techniques of alchemy unashamedly offers recipes for imitation purple dye
and for making false gold and silver. Known as the Leiden papyrus
after the town where it is now kept, it was written in Greek and
discovered in the tomb of a magician in Thebes. It probably dates from
around 300.[2] It essentially consists of a collection of notes for the
laboratory bench which an alchemist probably compiled from much
earlier works which are now lost. It offers 101 recipes, followed by ten
paragraphs from Dioscorides, the celebrated physician who studied in
Alexandria in the first century and who wrote the sober *De Materia
Medica*. Ninety of the recipes deal with the preparation of alloys
coloured silver or gold, the bronzing of metal, and so on. The
remaining eleven at the end show how to prepare a false 'royal purple'
dye.

The work takes a two-pronged approach to producing metals
which are coloured like gold or silver. The first is to increase the body
of the precious metals without changing their appearance or colour,
that is the 'increase of gold'. The second is to change the colour of
cheaper metals or alloys so that they look like silver or gold. One
recipe describing the preparation of calcium sulphide was particularly
favoured by later alchemists:

> Discovery of Water of Sulphur. Having mixed a handful of lime
> and as much sulphur, in fine powder, place them in a vase
> containing strong vinegar or the urine of a young child. Heat from
> below until the supernatant liquid appears like blood; decant this
> carefully to separate it from the dregs and use.[3]

The Leiden papyrus recommends preserving the shine of false metals
by applying a thin layer of wax or varnish. The papyrus also shows
that the alchemists used mordants, usually salt solutions, to vary and
fix the colour of dyes. The technical terms of the dyer were carried
over to the work on metals. By similar methods, the alchemists were
able to imitate silver and gold, understanding the use of a small
quantity of gold as a ferment by adding it to a large quantity of fused
base metal. When cooled, it was then made into the required shape.
The surface of a ring made in this way, for instance, could be dissolved

by a mordant salt, leaving granules of gold in relief to make it look like pure gold.

In the Leiden papyrus, there is no pretence of philosophy and no apology for trying to imitate gold or silver. Indeed, referring to an alloy made from tin, copper, gold and silver, the author proudly declares that it will be like *asem* (electrum, a mixture of gold and silver) and will 'deceive even artisans'. The recipes were clearly the work of counterfeiters who wanted to make money for themselves and provide cheap jewellery and dyes. They are very different from those of the true alchemists in Alexandria who were never interested in financial gain and who saw the methods of the practical technicians only as a way of imitating and illustrating the cosmic process.[4]

The first known direct discussion of alchemical ideas and practices comes in a Greek treatise called *Physika kai Mystika*. It exists only in fragmentary form in a papyrus manuscript which probably dates from around the time of Christ. The work is attributed to Democritus, the early Greek philosopher of atomic theory, but it now seems likely that many of the works attributed to him were probably those of Bolos of Mendes who lived around 320–250 BC in Egypt.[5] Little is known of his life, although the later Alexandrian alchemists all knew of his work.

In his passionate quest for knowledge Democritus explored the hidden secrets of Egypt's sacred science. According to the third-century Alexandrian alchemist Synesius, he was initiated into 'the mysteries of the great Ostanes in the temple of Memphis – by him and his disciples, priests of Egypt. Learning his principles from him, Democritus composed four books – on Bronzing, on Gold and Silver, on Stones and on Purple [dye]'.[6] Memphis at the time was the principal place of worship of the creator god Ptah.

It is not clear who the legendary alchemist Ostanes was. He is sometimes called the Mede, that is a member of the people who established an empire in south-west Asia in the seventh century BC. He lived in Memphis where Democritus met him and his deepest secret is said to have been left in the inner sanctuary of the temple there. He was well known for his secrecy and the Roman historian Pliny criticized him for creating a mania for magic amongst the Greeks.[7] Synesius claimed that Ostanes' pupil Democritus called the Philosopher's Stone 'the many named and nameless' thereby launching a paradoxical definition taken up by countless later alchemists.[8] It was the first direct reference to the Stone that I had so far come across.

In speaking of the 'great Ostanes', Synesius claims that Democritus 'testifies that this man did not use the projection or heatings of the Egyptians but that he operates on substances by surfacing from without; and with heat, effects his preparation . . .' This implies that the ancient Egyptians had their own techniques to transform other substances from within, a power usually attributed to the Philosopher's Stone.

The 'Egyptian method' probably worked by projection (with powder) or sublimation (conversion to vapour by heat and back again). In the first case, chemicals were projected into the body to be changed after being prepared by roasting. In Democritus' method the bodies are changed by embedding them in chemicals which penetrate them in a prolonged heating of the mass. In the second case of sublimation, Synesius emphasizes the importance of transforming metals through dissolving and removing the 'liquidity' of bodies: 'Take the water which escapes from the end of the eduction tube and keep it for decomposition. It is what is called Sulphur Water [or Holy Water].' This operation brings out the hidden nature of substances and is called 'the solution of metals'.[9]

Democritus revealed that in a dream he conjured up his master from the Underworld. When he asked Ostanes how to 'combine natures', he told Democritus that 'it was difficult for him to speak; the daemon wouldn't allow it. He said only, "The books are in the temple."' Democritus and his fellow adepts searched the temple without success, and gave themselves a great deal of trouble trying to learn 'how substances and natures were united and combined in a single substance'. Nevertheless, during a banquet in the temple

all of a sudden a column of its own accord opened up in the middle. But at first glance there seemed nothing inside. However, [the son of] Ostanes told us that it was in this column his father's books had been placed. And, taking charge of the situation, he brought the thing out into the open. But when we bent to look, we saw in surprise that nothing had escaped us except this wholly valuable formula which we found there. 'Nature rejoices in Nature, Nature contains Nature, Nature overcomes Nature.' Great was our admiration for the way he had concentrated in a few words all the Scripture.[10]

This temple myth clearly demonstrates the deep roots of alchemy in ancient Egypt and implies that the temple not only contains the wisdom of alchemy but that it is, in a profound sense, an alchemical text in stone. At the end of *Physika kai Mystika* the ancient Egyptian credentials of alchemy are reaffirmed: 'This method of gold-making, accomplished by natural means, is that of Pammenes who taught it to the Egyptian priests.'[11] I was unable to find out who Pammenes was.

It is misleading to translate the title of Democritus' work as simply 'Physics and Mysticism'. It offers that peculiar blend of science and religion, physics and metaphysics, philosophy and theology, which is immediately recognizable in the literature of later alchemists. It is a work of initiation which explores the hidden forces in nature, especially their dynamic sympathies and antipathies. On the strength of his surviving writings, Democritus was clearly a philosopher as well as an experimenter. He warns that there is no quick path to enlightenment and criticizes 'those who, on an unconsidered and irrational impulse, want to prepare a remedy for the soul and a release from suffering, and do not think of the harm they will come to'.[12]

Yet despite the air of mystery, initiation and revelation of *Physika kai Mystika*, it opens rather flatly with recipes for making the false purple dye which is mentioned in the Leiden papyrus. It then falls into two parts: 'Chrysopy', or gold-making, and 'Argyropy', or silver-making. These were often known as the 'Yellowing' and 'Whitening' of metals.

An early recipe in the section on gold-making declares:

> Copper is made clear and brilliant, free from tarnish and of silvery sheen, by use of arsenic, antimony or mercury . . . But by adding electrum [gold-silver alloy] there is produced a gold colour; by adding gold, 'Gold coral' is the result.

Such chemicals were to become favourites of later alchemists. The notion of transmuting one metal from another is also clear: in the section on silver-making, it is asserted:

> Taking the vapour [mercury or arsenic] previously described, rub it with alum and misy [a kind of mushroom] and having sprinkled the metal with vinegar, cast on it also white cadmia [calamine] or magnesia or chalk *in order that one metal may be made from another*.[13]

Democritus calls the primary matter used in the alchemical process 'our lead'. It was probably antimony, the lead which is richest in water and therefore most fusible. The later Alexandrian alchemist Zosimus stressed the importance of the substance and the value given to it by the Egyptian priests from whom Democritus learned his knowledge:

> Demokritos has named as substances the four metallic bodies, that is, copper, iron, tin, lead . . . All these substances are employed in the two tinctures (of gold and silver) . . . All the substances have been recognized by the Egyptians as produced by lead alone. For it's from lead that the other three bodies come.[14]

The classic stages in the alchemical process established by the Alexandrian alchemists usually begin with taking some solid, alloy or base metal like lead, the *tetrasomia* (lead, tin, copper, iron) or 'metal of magnesia'. The alchemist then tries to infuse in these bodies the qualities of liquidity (water), fusibility (air) or brilliancy (fire).

The challenge for Democritus and the other Alexandrian alchemists was to change the colour of the base material in order to make it look like silver or gold. Colour was one of the simplest ways of identifying ores; it also had a powerful magical resonance. Colour was considered the determining characteristic of a superior metal. It was said to reflect the degree of excellence: yellow is superior to white which in turn is superior to black. The alchemical process acts as a ferment to improve the natural colour of metals as they struggle towards the perfect colour of the highest metal gold – the colour which corresponds to fire, the highest of the four elements.

Colour was considered a form of activity, a 'spirit' (*pneuma*) which could be taken from one substance and infused into another. Mercury, for instance, was considered a 'spirit'; it is 'accidental' in that it does not show its properties until associated with metals. Mercury, Synesius wrote, 'robs all metals of their appearances. Just as wax takes the colour which it has received, so mercury whitens all metals and attracts their souls. It refines them and is diffused.'[15]

The first stage of the alchemical process is called blackening (*melanosis* in Greek), when the metal or material is broken down into a 'body', a degeneration which might be achieved by fusing it with sulphur. Fire is used to break it up, liquefy it, change its colour and drive it up the scale of nature towards silver or gold. This primary level is a condition of chaos, similar to the state of the cosmos at the beginning of Creation.

The second stage is called whitening (*leukosis*), which is often achieved by a fusion with the 'ferment' or 'seed of silver', using ingredients like arsenic or mercury. It involves the union of sympathetic metals, a chemical wedding of male and female substances with a magical affinity. In the famous triadic formula of Ostanes discovered by Democritus in the pillar of the temple: 'Nature rejoices in Nature.' But in order for this stage to be transcended and the colour transformed 'Nature contains Nature'.

The last stage is the production of a purple or violet colour (*iosis*). This ferment is thought to change the gold into an *iosis* of gold, a permanent tincture which if cast on common gold would create more. Hence the third part of Ostanes' formula 'Nature overcomes Nature'.

The alchemical operation is therefore fundamentally a dialectical process in three stages: on the original level, there is a mixture, to which is introduced a dynamic factor, which in turn changes the original relations and advances the mixture to a new and quantitatively different level.

Some alchemists saw the process as involving a third stage of yellowing (*xanthosis*) between the white and the violet. The colour sequence of transforming base metal to gold would then be black, white, yellow and finally violet.

The Egyptian alchemist identified with his experiment, concentrating his whole being – mind, body and spirit – in the work. No dispassionate observer, he experienced the transformation of the materials in himself, so much so that he often felt himself being torn apart (dissolution) and then put together (coagulation) before being finally reborn in a new form. This undoubtedly explains the significance of a dream reported by Democritus in which he is dismembered. It is a dimension which is entirely lost to many modern scientists who hide behind a cloak of impassive objectivity.

In his commentary on the *Physika kai Mystika* of Democritus, Synesius acknowledged him to be the great authority on the Hermetic art of alchemy. Synesius himself studied science and philosophy in the 390s under the philosopher Hypatia, the daughter of the celebrated Neoplatonist Theon, who was killed by a Christian mob in the streets of Alexandria. He was also in contact with the temple tradition of ancient Egypt, as the opening of one surviving letter shows: 'Synesius the philosopher to Dioscorus, priest of Great Serapis in Alexandria, greetings . . .'[16]

Synesius attributes to Democritus the saying that with alchemy 'you will conquer poverty, that incurable malady'.[17] It probably comes from earlier sources, but it does not mean that alchemy will produce personal wealth; true alchemists are never interested in that. It implies that alchemy will enable the adept to deliver himself from the snares of this world and prepare his soul for the next. But it also had wider social implications, reflecting a revolt against the prevailing social system in Egypt under the Romans which was expressed in apocalyptic prophecies. The sacred science of alchemy would, if properly developed, enable a new golden age to be realized.

24

Women of Fire

See, you wise men, and understand. See the fulfilment of the
art in the joining-together of the bride and bridegroom and
in their becoming one.

Cleopatra

I was pleased to find out that alchemy in Egypt was not a men-only
affair. As in China, women played an important role, not only as
assistants but in their own right. Indeed, the invention of some of the
main alchemical apparatus was attributed to two women in Egypt.
One was Cleopatra, not the lover of Pompey and Mark Anthony
whose nose changed the course of history, but a profound philosopher
and experimenter. The other was Maria, sometimes known as 'Maria
the Jewess' or 'Maria Prophetissa'. The two women were probably
associated with the same school of alchemy in Alexandria in the
second century.

The alchemist Cleopatra was called 'Queen Cleopatra' by the
Arabs and was credited with books on poisons and cosmetics as well
as on weights and measures. Without doubt, she was an experienced
alchemist standing in the ancient Hermetic tradition of Egypt. She
describes her teacher Komarios as a high priest of the Egyptian temple
and her own teaching takes the form of a revelation. Her principal
text, known as the *Dialogue*, is addressed to a circle of philosophers.
Egyptian in all essentials, it not only recalls the Creation myth of the
Primeval Waters, but evokes the darkness of the mummified dead in
their tombs and of the souls in the Underworld awaiting the divine
light of life and resurrection.

Her audience of philosophers includes the legendary magus Ostanes. He says to her at the beginning of the *Dialogue*:

In you is hidden a strange and terrible mystery. Enlighten us, throwing your light on the elements. Tell us how the highest descends to the lowest, and how the lowest rises to the highest, and is united with it, and what is the element that accomplishes these things. And tell us how the blessed waters visit the corpses lying in Hades fettered and afflicted in darkness, and how the Medicine of Life reaches them and rouses them as if woken by their possessors from sleep; and how the new waters, both brought forth on the bier and coming after the light penetrates them at the beginning of their prostration and how the cloud supporting the waters rises from the sea.

The alchemical processes in the flask clearly mirror the resurrection of the deceased in the Underworld. Cleopatra says to the philosophers listening to her every word:

The waters, when they come, awake the bodies and the spirits that are imprisoned and weak. For they again undergo oppression and are enclosed in Hades, and yet in a little while they grow and rise up and put on various glorious colours like the flowers in spring and the spring itself rejoices and is glad at the beauty they wear.

For I tell this to you who are wise. When you take plants, elements, and stones from their places, they appear to you to be mature. But they are not mature till the fire has tested them. When they are clad in the glory from the fire and the shining colour of it, then rather will appear their hidden glory, their sought-for beauty, being transformed to the divine state of fusion. For they are nourished in the fire and the embryo grows little by little nourished in its mother's womb; and when the appointed month comes near is not held back from coming out. Such is the procedure of this worthy art. The waves and surges one after another in Hades wound [awake?] them in the tomb where they lie. When the tomb is opened, they come out from Hades as the babe from the womb.[1]

Conveying her meaning through an elaborate allegory, Cleopatra then urges her philosophers to go up to a rock among the trees on the rugged mountain and to take arsenic for the 'divine process' of 'whitening'. She also makes a veiled reference to the famous axiom of the legendary Ostanes:

And look, in the middle of the mountain, below the male there lies the mate with whom he is united and in whom he delights; for nature rejoices in nature, and without her there is no union.

Then they should go down to the Egyptian sea (the Red Sea) and find natron (used in mummification) in the sand to unite with other things:

See how nature corresponds with nature, and when you gather together all things in equal measure, then natures conquer natures and delight in one another. See, you wise men, and understand. See the fulfilment of the art in the joining-together of the bride and bridegroom and in their becoming one.

The sexual imagery not only anticipates the chemical weddings illustrated in so many medieval European manuscripts but recalls the pillow books of the Chinese alchemists.

Cleopatra describes the lower part of the alchemical flask as the Underworld of the dead and sees it as a womb in which the process of transformation takes place. As divine spirit (*pneuma*) enters the deceased body so the blackness of base matter is whitened. The soul of the alchemist passes from darkness to light:

And the soul, calling to the body now full of light, cries out, 'Awaken from Hades! Rise up from the tomb and rouse yourself from darkness! For you have clothed yourself with spirituality and divinity, since the voice of resurrection has sounded and the pharmakon [medicine] of life has entered into you!'[2]

The mystery of rebirth is accomplished as the body, the soul and the spirit are all united in love and become one. Divine light is now its home.

I was greatly impressed by Cleopatra and delighted to come across a remarkable single-page document called Cleopatra's *Chrysopia* ('Gold-making') which is now kept in the Bibliothèque Nationale in Paris.[3] It depicts the classic symbols of the apparatus and doctrines of alchemy. At the top of the page three concentric circles enclose Hermetic axioms. The first states in Greek: 'One is the All and by it the All and in it the All and if it does not contain the All it is nothing.' In the inner ring, it says: 'The Serpent is One, he who has the Venom with two Compositions.' In the centre are the signs for mercury, silver and gold. Below on the right is an alembic with two beaks, stressing the importance of the work in the laboratory.

On the left at the bottom of the manuscript is the famed serpent Ouroboros, whom I had seen in the tombs of the West Bank, making a circle with his tail in his mouth and enclosing the principle: 'One the All'. I was unable to decode the mystical signs on the top right of this unique document. More than any other symbol, the Ouroboros, of course, symbolizes the Philosopher's Stone. As the fifth-century Alexandrian Olympiodorus observed: 'the Egyptian hieroglyphs, wanting to denote the world on obelisks in sacred characters, depict there the serpent Ouroboros'.[4]

Cleopatra wrote in a poetic and exuberant way which is rare amongst the early alchemists. She revealed a deep intuition of the dynamic unity of natural processes and their transformation. Later alchemists appreciated and developed the intimate link she made between the transformation of metals and the resurrection of the soul, her description of the alchemical process in terms of the sexual imagery of conception and childbirth, and her belief that fire brings to 'maturity' the vegetables and minerals, plants and stones found in nature. She not only had a real sense of the beauty of the cosmos but a passionate belief in the possibility of attaining harmony with nature through the alchemist's sacred art.

*

Drawing on the Hermetic philosophy and alchemical practices of the Egyptian temple priests, 'Maria the Jewess' or 'Maria the Prophetess' was also steeped in the Jewish tradition of alchemy. It gave the 'royal art' a semi-divine origin and saw it as a product of that superior race of humans mentioned in the Book of Genesis 6.4: 'There were giants in the earth in those days; and also after that, when the sons of God came in unto the daughters of men, and they bare *children* unto them, the same *became* mighty men which *were* of old, men of renown.'

According to the Book of Enoch it was Ayayel, one of the rebellious and lustful angels, who taught men the arts of metallurgy and dyeing. He showed them how 'to make swords and knives and shields and breastplates and made known to them the metals in the earth and the art of working them; and bracelets and armaments and the use of antimony and the beautifying of the eyelids; and all kinds of costly stones and all colouring tinctures'.

The violation of mother earth, the transformation of natural substances, and the beautifying of the body through artifice all clearly marked the downfall of 'cosmic man' and the degradation of humanity. It was not only accompanied by the arts of war but led to sin: 'And there arose much godlessness.'[5] For this reason, it was necessary to purify oneself before attempting to transform nature or else disaster would follow – a view still held by blacksmiths in parts of Africa.

The Old Testament also contains many references to the work of the smelters and smiths who used the 'refiner's fire' and the technique of cupellation. Some references are very ancient, such as the 'dross of silver' in Ezekiel 22.18 (c.720 BC). The most famous passage is in Malachi 3.2:

> But who may abide the day of his coming? and who shall stand when he appeareth? for he is like a refiner's fire and like fuller's soap: and he shall sit as a refiner and purifier of silver: and he shall purify the sons of Levi, and purge them as gold and silver . . .

Maria made great use of the refiner's fire. As a thoughtful innovator, she perfected the distillation of liquids and was profoundly interested in the instruments used in alchemical experiments. She is credited with inventing the *bain-marie* (*Baleneum Mariae*) or water-bath for gentle and steaming heating which is still widely used in kitchens and laboratories throughout the world. Maria described its construction in considerable detail, even down to explaining how to make the necessary copper tubes from sheet metal.

The bath is clearly a symbol of purification and baptism and many medieval illustrations depict Sol and Luna as king and queen sitting naked together in a bath.

Maria was celebrated for inventing the *tribikos*, a still with three funnels and receivers in which the distilled vapours are condensed. The *kerotakis* is also attributed to her, a reflux apparatus for treating metals with vapours, probably in order to colour them.[6] Zosimus describes the use of Maria's *kerotakis* in an alchemical experiment:

> Taking some arsenic [i.e., the sulphide], whiten it in the following manner. Make a soft clay disc of the thickness of a little mirror and pierce it with little holes, like a sieve. Place above, adjusting it, a recipient into which put one part sulphur; and into the sieve as much of the arsenic as you wish; and having covered with

another recipient and luted the joints, after two days and nights
you will find white lead [white arsenic]. Cast on a quarter mina
[pound] of this and heat a whole day, adding a little bitumen and
you will have [the result]; and such is the construction of the
apparatus.[7]

With Maria's instruments all the processes of the alchemists could be
carried out. They underwent little change down the ages. The classic
alchemical still consists of the 'cucurbit', the lower flask or 'gourd'
which contains the substances to be distilled; and the 'alembic', the
upper part of the still, whose beaker or spout conveys the vapours to a
receiver known as an 'aludel'. The word 'alembic' was often used to
describe the whole still. Maria's development of this apparatus was
undoubtedly a major contribution to the history of alchemy and
chemistry.

The word '*kerotakis*' used by Maria to describe her apparatus was
derived from the Greek word for wax. It was also associated with the
artist's palate. In ancient Egypt and Greece, colours were mixed in
wax and softened by gentle heating. The ancient artist like the alchemist had four colours at his command: black, white, yellow and red.
When the addition of mercury over a fire made metals into a soft alloy
or amalgam, it was called 'softening of the metals' and at the moment
of softening they assumed a new colour as on the artist's palette. The
four original colours indicated the different stages of the alchemical
process. The alchemist in his laboratory was thus mirroring the artist
in his studio and both were following the Creator in his Creation.

As an alchemical authority, Maria was credited with the saying:
'Unless you strip bodies of the corporeal state, you will not advance.'
That is to say, you will make no progress unless you take the metallic
state from metals. She also spoke of 'Our Lead' as distinct from
common lead, probably referring to antimony or some metallic sulphide. It became normal for subsequent alchemists to talk of 'our
water', 'our lead', 'our mercury', 'our sulphur' and even 'our gold' to
distinguish their materials from substances found in nature.

True to the tradition of her native land, Maria taught that the
Great Work of alchemy could only be performed in the Egyptian
month of *Pharmuthi*, which corresponds to March–April. The
materials had to be wrapped in linen and cooked in the 'water of
Pontus'. According to Olympiodorus, she called the *tetrasomia*

(copper, iron, lead and zinc) the 'four in one', the same name given to the 'egg of the philosophers' since the egg is one thing which comprises four parts: the shell, the skin, the egg white and the yolk.[8]

Maria was not only a brilliant experimenter and inventor; like Cleopatra she was a philosopher in her own right. She developed the Hermetic doctrine of the relationship between the microcosm and the macrocosm by giving it a dynamic illustration in the process of distillation in her *bain-marie*. She was also renowned for her mystical exultation and credited by later alchemists with the famous axiom: 'One becomes two, two becomes three, and out of the third comes the one as the fourth.' It describes the dialectical movement of thesis, antithesis, and synthesis in which the final synthesis becomes the thesis for a new threefold development. It also reflects the alchemical notion of the union of male and female principles which at first produces the partial unity of a hermaphrodite which in turn creates the real unity of the Philosopher's Stone.

As a thoughtful and imaginative woman, it is not surprising that Maria should have conceived of the combination of substances in sexual terms. An anonymous early seventh-century alchemist usually referred to as Christianos mentioned her method: 'Combine together, says Maria, the male and female and you will find that which you seek.'[9] The Arabs developed her analogy between the alchemical process and conception and birth. The womb was associated with the alchemical vessel and the union of substances as a chemical wedding. Even her still had sexual symbolism, with the spout as a penis entering the narrow opening of the receiver vessel as a vagina.

With Cleopatra and Maria Egyptian alchemy reached its maturity and their work shows that they combined philosophical and spiritual concerns with great practical skill. But it was with Zosimus that it reached its zenith. He admired Maria's work and used her instruments but he took alchemy to a new level of understanding. As a result his name has become synonymous with the very word alchemist.

25

The Crown of Philosophers

[God] will take his stand against the vices and perversions in
everything, righting wrongs, washing away malice in a flood
or consuming it in fire or ending it by spreading pestilential
disease everywhere. Then he will restore the world to its
beauty of old so that the world itself will again seem deserv-
ing of worship and wonder . . .

Asclepius

I found Zosimus the most inspiring and profound of all the Egyptian
alchemists. Olympiodorus called him accurately the 'Crown of Philosophers' and his language the 'Depth of the Abyss'.[1] By combining the
practice of the Egyptian craftsmen, the sacred science of the temple
priests, Greek philosophy and Hermetic ideas, he laid the foundations
for all later alchemy. Although only fragments of his works survive in
Greek and Syriac, his treatment of the subject is fascinating, both in its
practical and spiritual aspects.

Little is known of his life. He was probably born at the end of the
third century in Panopolis (Akhmim) in Upper Egypt and later lived in
Alexandria. He saw himself standing in an ancient Egyptian tradition,
referring to the 'fathers' of his sacred science as sages of long ago. He
acknowledged Democritus as a teacher and mentions Ostanes as a
forerunner of alchemy. But instead of using sulphur like Democritus,
he claims to have accomplished the whitening of copper by the use of
arsenic or mercury. Among his many alchemical successes, he dissolved
a solvent of metal in sulphuric acid, described accurately the nature
of mercury ('holy water'), and produced oxygen gas from red oxide of
mercury.

In his main treatise *On Apparatus and Furnaces: Authentic Com-*

mentaries on the Letter Omega, Zosimus illustrates the *tribikos,* the three-pointed alembic, with the Hermetic axiom: 'Above, the heavenly, below the earthly.' He adds like Maria: 'By the male and the female, the work is accomplished.'[2] Referring to the Jews, he says: 'the First Man, who is Thouth among us, these peoples have named Adam, with a name borrowed from the tongue of angels'.[3] Only the Jews, such as Maria, were able 'secretly, to operate, write and publish things' about alchemy while the Egyptian alchemists were prophets who were obliged to keep silent as 'friends of the Kings of Egypt'.[4]

Zosimus was very much in contact with the alchemical tradition of the Egyptian temples. He not only saw a priest in a vision but visited a temple in Memphis, a well-known centre of alchemy and magic, in order to see a special furnace. His fellow alchemist Theosebia, who attracted a secret circle of initiates, was a priestess. He regrets that the ancient Egyptians did not publish their knowledge about the 'timely tinctures', those alchemical operations carried out at the astrologically right time and place: 'they engraved them on their stelae in the darkness and depths of the temples in symbolic characters – both the tinctures and the chorography of Egypt – so that, even though one carried boldness to the point of penetrating into those dark depths, if one had neglected to learn the key, one could not decipher the characters for all one's boldness and trouble'.[5]

Zosimus refers several times to the role of priests as guardians of alchemical learning. Although many later alchemists tried to attach their own names to alchemical formulae, everyone knew, he insists, that they were really written by Hermes and the Egyptian writers.

Zosimus had strong spiritual yearnings and his greatest concern was to attain the divine vision. He also had powerful and vivid dreams. He left a description of one which greatly fascinated Jung. Falling asleep during the day, Zosimus saw fifteen steps heading up to a bowl-shaped altar attended by an Egyptian priest. The priest said to him:

> I have completed the descent of the fifteen steps of darkness and the ascent of the steps of light, and it is he that sacrifices who renews me casting away the coarseness of the body, and, being consecrated priest by necessity, I became a spirit . . . I am Ion, the sanctuary's priest, and I have survived intolerable violence. For in the morning one came headlong, dismembered me with a sword, and tore me apart according to the rigours of harmony. And

flaying my head with the sword held fast in his grip, he mingled my bones with my flesh, and burned them in the fire of the treatment – till I learned by the transformation of the body to become a spirit.

While he spoke these words, 'his eyes became like blood and he vomited up all his flesh. And I saw him as a mutilated little image of a man, tearing himself with his own teeth and falling away'.[6]

With its overtones of masochism, this passage no doubt refers to the initial stage of decomposition of base matter and its final restoration as the spirit leaves the body. The bowl-shaped altar is the alembic-womb of transformation and recalls the 'mixing bowl' discourse of the *Hermetica*.[7] It enacts the universal human drama of suffering and renewal and shows how the alchemist identified with his experiment. Made from semen and metals, the homuncular 'little image of a man' stands as a symbol of transformation from the non-living to the living. The theme of dismemberment and the creation of a homunculus became common in Western medieval alchemy.

Zosimus meets the same priest later on in the guise of a 'man of copper'. He presides over an altar bowl filled with boiling water in which many people are being burned. A witness explains to him that it is the place of 'preserving', that is, embalming. 'For those men who wish to obtain spiritual perfection come hither and become spirits, fleeing from the body.'

The priest tells Zosimus to build a 'Temple Made from One Stone' with neither beginning nor end in its construction, and with a spring of pure water glittering in the sun. At the entrance, he will find a serpent which he must sacrifice, dismember and then reunite its parts to make of them a stepping stone. He will then find in the temple what he seeks: 'you will not find him as a man of copper; for he has changed the colour of his nature and become a man of silver. If you wish, after a little time you will have him as a man of gold.'

Zosimus tries several times to ascend seven steps to the 'place of punishments' but keeps losing his way in despair – no doubt symbolizing his own failed experiments. He comes across a whitened old man who is sacrificed and dismembered. The vision ends with a voice telling Zosimus that 'once lead is projected amongst all the liquids the work is completed'.[8]

The vision not only graphically expresses the Hermetic doctrine of the soul's purification and ascent to God but also illustrates Zosimus' belief that a correct alchemical understanding of the properties of matter is essential if the soul is to be liberated from the coils of the body. The individual incidents and characters of his terrifying dream symbolize the different stages of the alchemical process. The man of metal recalls the living statues of the pharaohs with their *ba* souls while his experience mirrors the trials and suffering they must undergo in their journey through the Underworld. And the 'Temple Made from One Stone'? Could it be the Philosopher's Stone, symbol of the universe as a field of living forces?

Zosimus had clearly immersed himself in the *Hermetica*. He criticizes those mindless individuals who know nothing of the incorporeal and are 'only marchers swept along in the procession of fate'.[9] Philosophers like Hermes, on the other hand, are superior to fate because they are never affected by grief or by joy. Fate only controls the body, not the divine part in humanity. By releasing himself from the passions, by imitating God, the sage is no longer prey to fate. 'See him becoming all – god, angel, vulnerable man. For, since he can do all, he becomes all he wishes. Penetrating the body, illuminating the intellect of each man, he gives him the impulse to climb towards the happy region where this intellect is found before becoming corporeal, it makes him follow in its track, puts him in a state of desire, and serves him as guide up to that supernatural light . . .'[10]

Zosimus' work *On Apparatus and Furnaces* forms part of a treatise in twenty-eight books dedicated to Theosebia called *Alchemical Matters*. He also addressed to her his autobiographical memoir known as the *Final Quittance*. This priestess of the temple clearly played a major role in his life: he treated her as an equal and regarded her as a 'sister'.[11]

Both alchemists firmly believed that the true end of alchemy is not the manufacture of gold but the purification of the soul and the contemplation of God. He urged her not to follow Aristotle and restrict herself to the visible and mortal sphere, but to help 'the souls you will save and direct towards the incorporeal and incorruptible nature'.[12] He also warns her against the wiles of those daemons hostile to human happiness who 'hunger after your soul' and urges her to take control of herself, to calm her passions and to offer sacrifices to the good daemons which repel them. 'So doing', he continues, 'you will attain the true and natural [tinctures] that are appropriate at certain times. Perform these things until your soul is perfected. When you realize that you have been perfected, and have found the natural [tinctures – those operations carried out in the same way as nature], spit on matter and, hastening towards Poimenandres [sic] and receiving baptism in the mixing-bowl, hasten up towards your own race [of perfected souls].'[13]

Like most alchemists, Theosebia chose to work with a small circle of initiates who were bound by oath to secrecy. Zosimus (as I do) took the opposite line. He inveighed against the jealous, vain and mean-spirited character of those who concealed their wisdom for only a few. 'If the mysteries are necessary,' he argued, 'it is all the more important that everybody should possess a book of chemistry, which should not be hidden away.'[14] Nevertheless, Zosimus was not above using allusive language himself at times and, as we have seen, he often expressed himself in allegory and through dreams.

But what does Zosimus have to say about the Philosopher's Stone which was first mentioned 500 years earlier by Democritus? Zosimus' paradoxical definition was to reverberate down the centuries: 'This stone which isn't a stone, this precious thing which has no value, this polymorphous thing which has no form, this unknown thing which is known to all' (*'lithon ton ou lithon, ton agnoston kai pasi gnoston'*).[15]

Zosimus believed that the quality of gold is a 'spirit' independent of the metallic substance just as a dye is separate from cloth. It is the discovery of the material in which this spirit resides – the Philosopher's Stone – which can enable one to transmute base metal into gold.

In another passage, Zosimus describes the action of the Philosopher's Stone and by doing so establishes the fundamental principle of Western alchemy: 'All sublimed vapour is a spirit and such are the *tinctorial* qualities . . . The vapour is a Spirit – the spirit which penetrates into the Bodies.' He then adds the Hermetic axiom: 'Above, the things celestial and below the things terrestrial.' When the adept has completed his work, the spirit has not been destroyed but has 'penetrated into the depths of the metal'. In the same way, when the preparation is coloured, it colours other metals in turn. Zosimus specifically calls the transformation in terms of 'spiritual substances' taking on a 'bodily [metallic] form' as transmutation and traces the process back to the old Egyptian authors.[16]

Zosimus also developed the notion of a 'ferment'. In order to transmute metal into gold, one should add a little portion of gold.

Since every metal is 'striving' to reach the perfection of gold, by adding it as a catalyst the alchemist speeds up the natural process: 'just as yeast, although in small quantity, raises a great quantity of dough, so also a little quantity of gold or silver acts by aid of this reagent'.[17] The resulting 'true' gold is superior to the gold found in the earth: 'our gold which possesses the desired quality can make gold and tint [transmute] into gold. Here is the great mystery – that the quality becomes gold and then it makes gold.'[18] Whereas normal gold has 'only sufficient yellowness for itself', alchemical gold can impart yellow to other metals. Zosimus called this 'spirit of metallicity' *ios* or 'coral of gold'. It not only has a colour purer than the yellow of gold but its power as a kind of super ferment to transmute base metal into gold is precisely that of the Philosopher's Stone.

Despite Zosimus' declaration of openness and his description of the Philosopher's Stone, I was disappointed to find that the surviving fragments of his work do not show clearly how it can be made or discovered. Perhaps the answer still lies in papyri hidden in the sands of Egypt or in the secret chambers of its pyramids, temples and Sphinx.

*

During the lifetime of Zosimus alchemy became so widely practised that it was seen as a threat to the existing order. The Roman Emperor Diocletian issued a decree in 292 expelling the practitioners of alchemy from Egypt and ordered their books to be burned. According to John of Antioch:

> Because of the revolutions, Diocletian treated the Egyptians harshly and cruelly and having sought out the books written by their forefathers on the chemistry of gold and silver, burned them lest wealth should accrue to the Egyptians through this art and lest they emboldened by riches should in the future revolt against the Romans.[19]

The Roman persecution of the Egyptian alchemists seems to have forced them underground for a while. In a letter probably addressed to Emperor Justinian, Olympiodorus gave many disconnected citations from practitioners of the 'ancient art' but claimed that he was living in a time too far removed from real alchemy to be able to give practical details of transmutation.[20] This may have been his way of not revealing the truths of the sacred science to an unworthy person, but it also attests to the fact that in Egypt already by the fifth or sixth century alchemy was widely considered to be of great antiquity.

*

Stephanus of Alexandria, in the seventh century, was the last major writer who was directly exposed to the Egyptian alchemical legacy. A Neoplatonist deeply influenced by Plato's *Timaeus*, he shared the view of his mentor that 'the elements are transmuted because the qualities are opposed, not the substances'. A Christian mystic in the Hermetic tradition, he also lectured on Plato and Aristotle, geometry, astronomy and music.

After leaving Alexandria he taught philosophy and alchemy in Constantinople. His first lecture on alchemy has a typically rhetorical flourish: 'Stephanus of Alexandria the Universal Philosopher and Teacher of the Great and Sacred Art of Gold making. Lecture I, with God's help.' He begins by praising God as the cause of all good things and 'earnestly' beseeches his Son, 'resplendent before the ages with Holy *Pneuma*', for the illumination of his knowledge. He then launches into an inflated rendering of the formula of the old pagan Ostanes: 'O nature superior to nature conquering the natures. O nature becomes superior to itself, well-regulated, transcending and surpassing all natures. O nature one and the same yielding and fulfilling the All.'[21] And so on.

Stephanus expresses the by now traditional alchemical view that chemical reagents destroy the body (metal) and release the soul, but the dead metal (some compound) could be revived with a new soul and be transformed into another metal. He also holds firm to the ancient doctrine expounded by Zosimus that 'Mercury takes all forms, as wax attracts every colour. So mercury whitens all, attracts the soul of everything . . . It remains, while they do not; even if it does not appear to remain, it persists, held in the metal.'[22]

Although he adds little new to Zosimus, Stephanus transmitted Egyptian alchemy to Byzantium and the wider world and showed later alchemists how they could draw on the ancient wisdom of pagan Egypt and express it in Christian terms without attracting prosecution. He also encouraged their unfortunate tendency for rhetoric and obfuscation.

*

Ironically, alchemy first came to light in Alexandria at the very time that the ancient Egyptian civilization which had given birth and cradled it was coming to an end. The conquest of the Greeks and then the Romans had undermined it and then Christianity dealt it its final blow. The great Hermetic treatise *Asclepius* ends with dire prophecies. Hermes forewarns: 'Speaking as a prophet, I will tell you that after us will remain none of that simple regard for philosophy found only in continuing reflection and holy reverence by which one must recognize divinity.' He then goes on to lament the passing of Egyptian civilization of which the *Hermetica* was the last great flower:

> A land once holy, most loving of divinity, by reason for her reverence the only land on earth where the gods settled, she who taught holiness and fidelity will be an example of utter [un]belief ... They will prefer shadows to light, and they will find death more expedient than life. No one will look up to heaven. The reverent will be thought mad, the irreverent wise; the lunatic will be thought brave, and the scoundrel taken for a decent person. Soul and all teachings about soul ... will be considered not simply laughable but even illusory ... Such will be the old age of the world: irreverence, disorder, disregard for everything good ... The gods who rule the earth will [withdraw], and they will be stationed in a city founded at Egypt's farthest border toward the setting sun, where the whole race of mortals will hasten by land and sea.[23]

What Hermes did not foresee was that the new torchbearers of sacred science were to be the Arabs who carried alchemy and the Hermetic tradition to the West.

*

After my study of the roots and development of alchemy in Egypt I was still left with the question of whether alchemy originated in the East or the West. The first texts on alchemy in China and Egypt both came to light in the second century. They not only acknowledged a very ancient tradition but were clearly recording knowledge which had been passed down orally for generations. Neither texts referred to any influence from the other. This is not surprising since the first known direct contact made by the Arabs with China was when Arab sailors reached Canton in 714.

It is clear from my own work that alchemy developed in China and Egypt independently before the fifth century BC.[24] India, too, as we have seen, had its own alchemical tradition from very ancient times. Certainly after the arrival of the Arabs in China, Islamic and then Western alchemy was influenced by Chinese ideas and methods in the Middle Ages. There was a further stimulus in the sixteenth century when many Chinese philosophical texts, including the *I Ching*, were translated by the Jesuits and distributed in Europe.

But if there is no evidence of early cross-fertilization why did China, India and Egypt develop schools of alchemy roughly at the same time? Why did they explore such similar themes and experiments? We are back to the old dilemma. Can this be explained by our common human condition: born to die in a world of scarcity, is it not inevitable that we should dream of abundance and of living for ever? Or are the symbols of alchemy universal archetypes welling up from our collective unconscious? Or does alchemy find a common root in survivors from a lost civilization overtaken by some catastrophe? My travels and researches in Egypt, India and China, with their legends of sages coming with the knowledge from across the sea, tell me that the last explanation is the most likely.

Whilst travelling in these countries, I had come into contact with some very profound wisdom which was beginning to change my life, but I often felt that the essence of alchemy continued to elude me. In moments of self-doubt it seemed like I was only touching the surface of ancient mysteries. I could have remained in Egypt for the rest of my life but I was determined to continue in my quest. My next task was to see how the Islamic world took up and developed the Hermetic tradition and to see what they had to say about the Philosopher's Stone.

Part Four

The Sister of Prophecy:
Islam

26

The Summary of Perfection

Alchemy is the sister of prophecy.

Imam 'Ali ibn Abi-Talib

Ever since the Crusades, Islam has been seen as a threat to the Christian West, but I was fascinated to find out that the Muslims were the great heirs of Egyptian alchemy and the principal channel for its knowledge to Europe. When Muslims conquered Egypt in the seventh century, they still found in Alexandria a lingering tradition of learning and discovered many works of the dispersed remnants of the city's libraries. Muslim alchemists recognized ancient Egypt as the crucible of their art.

When the tenth-century Arab scholar An-Nadim drew up a cata-
logue of works of the 'Alchemists and Seekers of the Philosopher's Stone', he called Hermes the inventor of alchemy and said that his tomb was in the Great Pyramid. He further claimed:

> in Egypt there are buildings called *Barabi* [Temples], built of huge stones, that surpass all measures. Such a temple consists of apart-
> ments of various shape in which there are places for grinding, pulverizing, dissolving, coagulating and distilling, which shows that the temple was erected for [carrying out] the Alchemical Art ... There were also found subterranean treasure-houses, wherein these sciences were written on parchment treated with lime, on [papyrus made of] bast from the white poplar such as are used in bowmakers, on plates of gold and copper, and on stone.[1]

The Muslims also knew and venerated the Alexandrian alchemists Democritus, Cleopatra, Maria, Zosimus and Stephanus. To these were added the legendary 'alchemists' such as Moses of the Jews, Zoroaster and Ostanes of the Persians, and Pythagoras, Plato and Aristotle of the Greeks.[2]

While alchemy in Egypt was in decline, new centres of learning in the Near and Middle East were developing. The pagan Sabeans of Harran, renowned stargazers, played an important role in carrying the esoteric doctrines of the Hermetic tradition into the Islamic world. The persecuted Christian Nestorians also played a special part in keeping Egyptian and Greek learning alive. After settling in Edessa in the north of Syria, they were expelled in 489 and moved on to Nisibis in Mesopotamia and finally settled in Judi-Shapur in Persia. They translated works written in Greek, including those on alchemy, into Syriac, a language long spoken in Egypt.

After the Islamic conquest of Asia Minor, North Africa and Southern Europe, Greek works of philosophy, mathematics, science and alchemy were translated into Arabic. The translators could hardly satisfy the growing thirst for learning. It was not long before Islam was producing its own scholars, philosophers and scientists.

Syria was the most dynamic of the new Islamic States, a meeting ground of different cultures and tongues, but it was Baghdad in Iraq under the Abbasid caliphs from 750 which became the greatest centre of learning in the Muslim world.

The town was planned as a perfect circle: the caliph's palace and the main mosque surrounded by gardens were placed in the centre with residential quarters at the circumference. Greek, Christian and Muslim thought flourished in the academy known as the House of Wisdom. A separate school of translators included Sabeans from Harran and was supervised by a Christian Nestorian. Indians and Chinese who had travelled along the Silk Road, displaced Syriacs from Antioch, Jews from Byzantium and Nestorians from Edessa all flocked to the city to seek shelter and enlightenment. The postmaster general of Baghdad, Ibn Khurdadbih, described these unprecedented comings and goings of scholars between Babylonia, Syria, Egypt and Spain in *The Book of the Ways* (847).[3]

Islam was very accommodating to alchemy and the new philosophy. It saw no conflict between religion or science, revelation or reason; indeed Muslims believed that reason would lead to *tawhid* ('unity') – Unity of Being – rather than a denial of the divine. The ultimate aim of all science and philosophy for Muslims was to free the mind from dependence on physical appearances and to prepare it for its voyage to the intelligible realm and for a vision and experience of Unity.[4] Alchemy was therefore considered a 'sacred' science in that it revealed the Oneness of the universe.

Philosophy for the Muslims was associated with the name of Hermes, who was known as the prophet Idris. Hermetic philosophy was early accepted by the Shiahs, who opposed the rationalist aspects of Aristotle's philosophy, and to a lesser extent by the Sunnis. The Sufis, especially the great mystic Ibn 'Arabi, also adopted many Hermetic doctrines and symbols. Said of Toledo (d.1069) wrote:

> Sages affirm that all antediluvian sciences originate with the first Hermes, who lived in Sa'id, in Upper Egypt. The Jews call him Enoch and Muslims Idris. He was the first who spoke of the material of the superior world and of planetary movements. He built temples to worship God ... After the Flood the sciences, including alchemy and magic, were carried out at Memphis, under the more renowned Hermes the Second.[5]

The most influential group of Muslims who were steeped in Hermeticism were known as the Ikhwan al-Sufa – the Brethren of Purity. They were a Shiah group with Sufi tendencies and produced a widely influential encyclopaedia of philosophy and science called the *Rasai'l* ('Epistles') in 909–65. Like the authors of the Hermetic writings and latter medieval Muslim and Christian alchemists, the brethren believed the 'Universal Soul is the spirit of the world. The four elements are the matter which serve as its support. The spheres and the stars are like its organs and the minerals, plants and animals are objects which make it move.'[6] The aim of alchemy (as well as of philosophy and science) for the brethren was to awaken the initiate from the 'dream of negligence' and to help him pass through the hierarchy of sin in order to be transformed into an angel and finally to experience the light of God.

Islamic alchemy is full of colourful stories of genuine seekers and legendary adepts. The earliest known Muslim alchemist emerged in Damascus in Syria. His name was Khalid ibn Yazid, an Ummayyad prince who lived from 660 to 704. He was in line to be made caliph but after his mother killed a rival relative, he was so upset by this intrigue that he abandoned the court and spent the rest of his life in alchemical study and research. He summoned scholars from Egypt and asked them to translate books on alchemy and science from Greek and Coptic – the first translations of alchemical, astronomical and medical writings in Arabic.[7] On his orders, court records were kept in Arabic rather than in Persian.

Khalid is reported to have studied alchemy under Morienus, a Christian hermit living in the mountains near Jerusalem. Morienus had studied in turn with the Alexandrian alchemist Stephanus, thereby ensuring that the wisdom of the ancient Egyptians was transmitted directly to the Arab scientists as part of a living tradition.[8] Khalid's relationship with Morienus was complex and not without difficulty. When the hermit was summoned, he agreed to come, hoping to convert the young prince to Christianity. He was received warmly and proceeded to perform an alchemical experiment of transformation. When Khalid saw the brilliance of the alchemical gold produced, he ordered all the fraudulent alchemists who had surrounded him to be executed. In the ensuing confusion, Morienus disappeared. He was eventually brought back to the court and was persuaded, still in the hope of converting Khalid, to reveal the insights of alchemy. But again Morienus vanished soon afterwards, taking the secret of the Philosopher's Stone with him.

According to An-Nadim, the prince went on to write many alchemical works in verse, including The Book of the Testament to his Son on the Art and The Great and the Small Books of the Scroll.[9] His most famous work was The Paradise of Wisdom, said by a seventeenth-century Muslim biographer to run to 2,315 verses. He is also considered to be the author of The Book of the Secret of Alchemy. Khalid was undoubtedly a real historical figure but like so many earlier alchemists, he became a legend and many later alchemical texts were attributed to him.

*

If Khalid was the first major Muslim alchemist, Jabir ibn Hayyan – later known to the West as Geber – was undoubtedly the greatest. The details of his life and work are not always certain and many of the works attributed to him were probably written by other hands. Nevertheless, he stands forth as a major figure in the history of alchemy.[10]

Jabir ibn Hayyan means 'Jabir the son of Hayyan'. A druggist who was involved in overthrowing the Omayyad dynasty, his father settled in Tus in Khurasan where his son Jabir was born in 721 or 722. The young Jabir was sent to Arabia where he studied the Qur'an and mathematics. Despite his scientific and rationalist training, Jabir shares the ancient Chinese and Egyptian view that 'The intelligence has its seat in the heart, because that is what precedes all other organs.'[11] Without the heart, the brain simply cannot be awakened to a vision of the Unity of Being.

Jabir became an alchemist in the court of Harun al-Rashid and was the personal friend and disciple of the sixth imam, Ja'far al-Sadiq (700–65), a man of great learning, a Sufi and one of the chief authorities on all esoteric knowledge.[12] There was a long connection between alchemy and Shiah mysticism. The first imam, Ali ibn Abi-Talib, said that alchemy is 'the sister of prophecy; for there is an immunity which keeps prophecy from being desecrated, which is that ordinary people do no more than discuss its literal outer meaning'.[13]

Jabir was also called Al-Sufi, referring to his adherence to Sufism, the ascetic form of mysticism within Islam. Sufism takes its name from the Arabic *suf*, for wool, because its early followers, rebelling against the luxury and licentiousness of the court, wore coarse woollen garments. Influenced by Neoplatonism and the Hermetic philosophy, the Sufis sought ecstatic union with God which they achieved through meditation, prayer, exercises and dance. Humankind, they believed, is infinitely perfectible. It was the thirteenth-century Sufi mystic and poet Rumi who later founded the order of Mevlevi, the so-called whirling dervishes. By using the body as an axis, they sought to transform through dance and music their own chemistry. The dance itself represents the harmonious turning of the cosmos in which the dancer finds stillness at the heart of movement.

Jabir was friendly with the viziers of the caliph Harun al-Rashid, known as the Barmecides, who were descended from the priests of the Afghan Buddhist shrines, some of whom appeared in the *Thousand and One Nights*. He met the caliph himself for whom he wrote a book on 'the noble art of alchemy' called *The Book of Venus* (*Kitab al-Zuhra*) which described 'wonderful experiments of a very elegant technique'. Jabir offered his esoteric knowledge to the Barmecides. When one of the favourite concubines of the minister Yahya, a woman 'unequalled' in beauty, intelligence and accomplishments, fell ill, Jabir was called in. He recalled:

> I had a certain elixir with me, so I gave her a draught of two grains of it in three ounces of vinegar and honey, and in less than half an hour she was as well as ever. And Yahya fell at my feet

and kissed them, but I said, 'Do not so, O my brother.' And he asked about the uses of the elixir, and I gave him the remainder of it and explained how it was employed, whereupon he applied himself to the study of science and persevered until he knew many things; but he was not so clever as his son Ja'far.[14]

This was only a minor elixir, not the grand elixir of the Philosopher's Stone, but it certainly got the minister out of his boudoir and into his laboratory.

When the Barmecides fell out of favour at the court, Jabir moved to Kufa were he set up his laboratory. When it was rediscovered two and a half centuries after his death a golden mortar weighing two and a half pounds was found. Whether it was made from natural or alchemical gold is not known. Jabir died in Tus in 815, with The Book of Misericordia (*Kitab al-rahma*) under his pillow. He wrote his own epitaph:

> My wealth let sons and brethren part,
> Some things they cannot share –
> My work well done, my noble heart,
> These are mine own to wear.

The works that go under Jabir's name fall roughly into four groups. The first is The 112 Books which are dedicated to the Barmecides and include the famous *Emerald Tablet*. The second are The 70 Books, most of which were translated into Latin in the Middle Ages. The third group, known as The Ten Books of Rectification, claims to describe the work of 'alchemists' such as Pythagoras, Socrates, Plato and Aristotle. The fourth group which contains *The Books of Balance* elaborates Jabir's famous theory of equilibrium in nature. It is difficult to determine for certain what were his authentic works and what were those of his disciples, but as a whole they definitely form a Jabirian school of alchemy.[15]

As his principal sources and authorities in alchemy, Jabir mentions the Egyptian and Greek gods and the philosophers Hermes, Agatho-daimon, Pythagoras and Socrates. He stresses the long history and development of alchemy. He traces it back to Arius, not the Greek Christian philosopher but an alleged precursor of Hermes: 'Arius was the first who spoke in an allegorical language about this art; it was he who applied to the Stone the first treatment . . . [He] appeared and declared that man possesses the ability to imitate the action of Nature.

He gave an example of this by reducing things to their primitive nature: he melted metals, and submitted them to perpetual coction, analogous to the perpetual and unchanging coction that Nature uses.'[16]

Like the Alexandrian alchemists, Jabir divided the substances he knew into three groups: spirits (volatile bodies like mercury, sulphur, arsenic and sal ammoniac), metallic bodies (metals), and bodies (non-volatile solids). He regarded metals as a combination of body and spirit.

Of the metals, Jabir recognized seven: gold, silver, lead, tin, copper, iron and *khar sini*. The last means 'Chinese iron'. The actual substance was probably white copper known to the Chinese as *pai-t'ung*.[17] It would seem that it was included in the list of metals to make them up to the magical number seven to match the seven planets, since mercury was classified by Muslim alchemists as a spirit and not a body. Its important place amongst the metals shows that there was not only considerable trade of the substance from the eighth century along the Silk Route between the Islamic world and China but that the alchemists in the Middle and the Far East must have known of each other's work at this time.

Jabir developed his theory of the formation of metals from Aristotle. All minerals contain two 'exhalations' – 'moist' and 'dry' vapours – in the form of mercury and sulphur. They combine in rocks to form metals. This idea of vapours remained a central part of alchemy and chemistry until as late as the eighteenth century. Jabir maintained that metals are all composed of mercury and coagulated with sulphur:

> They differ from one another only because of the difference of their accidental qualities, and this difference is due to the difference of their varieties of sulphur, which in turn is caused by variations in the earth, and in their expositions with respect to the heat of the sun in its circular motion.[18]

Again, like Aristotle, Jabir supposed that metals are ultimately composed of the four elements – earth, fire, air and water – and have the qualities of these elements – dryness, heat, moisture and cold – in different proportions. The union of two of these qualities gives:

warm + dry + substance	>	fire
warm + moist + substance	>	air
cold + moist + substance	>	water
cold + dry + substance	>	earth

Jabir made a distinction between the internal and external composition of a metal. Gold, for example, is 'hot-moist' on the outside and 'cold-dry' within. Silver is the other way round. In order to transmute silver into gold, one must therefore reverse the relationship, a process which involves turning nature 'inside out'. This can only be achieved with an *al-iksir* (elixir), the Arabic word for essence. Where the Alexandrian alchemists had sought the *pharmakon* (medicine) to bring about a transmutation, Jabir looked for the 'grand elixir' – the Philosopher's Stone – to achieve it.

The cosmology of Jabirian science is based on his famous method of balance as well as the four elements. It has two aspects. On the one hand, it is an attempt to establish a qualitative base to the sciences of nature; on the other, it attempts to explain movement and change in the universe. There are 'balances' for minerals, vegetables, animals and stars, as well as between the nature, the form and the soul of the world and the celestial mind. The balance seeks to discover the equilibrium between the external appearances (the exotic) and the hidden reality (the esoteric).[19]

The alchemist's initial task is to find out the exact proportions of earth, water, fire and air in any given body. He can then alter the proportions to convert the body into another body. This can be done by adding an elixir made from the pure elements combined in the right proportion which will correct and supplement any excesses or deficiencies. In theory, the process seems startlingly simple, but in practice it is extremely difficult to measure the supposed elements in the bodies. This could be done in the case of organic bodies, such as animal and vegetable products, through distillation, but not with minerals or metals.

Although the elements supposedly have two qualities, Jabir's aim was to make 'pure elements' with only one quality which he could then add to a metal; coldness, for instance, without adding moisture. To obtain this from common water, which is cold and moist, he redistilled repeatedly, adding very 'dry' substances to absorb the moisture. In the end, he claimed that he produced the 'pure' element of water which he described as white, brilliant and solidified like salt.

While Jabir sought a balance of water and fire, he suggested that there is a 'dry path' which can lead directly to the final red stage in the alchemical process. This 'balance of Fire' is 'a royal operation, prompt and quick' but it is also 'extraordinarily difficult and perilous'. It should therefore be reserved for 'princes' amongst adepts.[20] I found this intriguing and it reminded me of the sudden path to enlightenment in Zen. I was unable, however, to find out more about this alchemical way at this stage.

Jabir was not only interested in balances in nature, but also in numbers; indeed, he shared with the Brethren of Purity a love of esoteric numerology, adopting a theory first elaborated by the Egyptian temple priests and developed by the followers of Pythagoras. They saw numbers as aspects of the Unity of Being, with their relationships reflecting the harmony of the various tendencies of the World Soul.[21] The Universe begins with One which multiplies into the many while remaining one. The theory of numbers is therefore a form of divine wisdom.

Jabir used numbers exclusively as the basis of his method of balance. He introduced a number system to Aristotle's notion of the degrees of hotness, coldness, dryness and moisture of bodies. He also assigned a 'value' to each substance: if gold is worth one, then the elixir is worth 5. He denoted the power of each treatment by a particular fraction. A fusion is worth 1/200, for instance, whereas a sublimation is only worth 1/50. According to his calculation: Gold (1) X Fusion (1/200) X 1,000 = the Elixir (5). A thousand fusions therefore would be needed to convert gold into the elixir.

Jabir was also interested in sacred geometry. Geometry not only reveals the character of numbers but is a means of knowing the universe.[22] The final aim of geometry is to allow the faculties of the soul to reflect and meditate so that it can separate itself from the external world and join the spiritual world of eternity. Geometrical shapes are different images of the One: a triangle is a symbol of harmony; the square, of stability; the circle, of everlasting life. The alchemical image of squaring the circle is the symbol of a circle inside a triangle inside a square. The circle can be squared and lead can be transmuted into gold because they are different images of the same Unity.

Jabir was fascinated by the magic square and wrote a treatise about it. It has the special property of combining number and shape. Throughout his work, he gave great importance to a series of numbers, namely 1, 3, 5, 8 (totalling 17), and 28. Everything in the world, he believed, is governed by the number 17. It provides the key to understanding all nature. The series of numbers adding up to 17 forms a key part of the magic square which contains the first nine digits:

4	9	2
3	5	7
8	1	6

Every line in whatever direction adds up to 15, including the diagonals. The total is 45. If we analyse the square gnomically, we find that the parallelogram consisting of the numbers 1, 3, 5, 8 adds up to 17. The geometric figure of the remaining upturned 'L' on the right of the parallelogram – the gnomon – is 28.

As I sat working this out in my study in North Wales, I was astounded to find that my own house, designed by the Cambridge architect Keith Garbett, was based on the magic square, with nine squares within one square.

Jabir's alchemical theory is great fun but it is obscure and complex. I could understand why later philosophers should associate the word 'gibberish' with his writings. But the word also probably derives from the Arabic word 'gharbala', meaning 'to sift the fine from the coarse'. Jabir undoubtedly made a major contribution to alchemical theory and practice. His method of balance involved the careful weighing and measuring of quantities. He reinvented aqua fortis and discovered sal ammoniac from distilling the dried dung of animals. Above all, his works not only ensured the transmission of alchemical knowledge from ancient Egypt to the Arabic world but formed the basis of European alchemy.

But while Jabir emphasizes the importance of experiment, it is difficult to know how to repeat his experiments under controlled conditions. What are those very 'dry' substances he used to draw out the 'moisture' from water? In some experiments, hundreds of distillations are required. The question arises of whether his experiments were ever meant to be performed. While studying his writings, I often had the feeling that the attempt of a Jabirian alchemist to liberate nature was really undertaken in order to liberate his soul.

*

Jabir was known to the West as Geber. He became a cultural hero and many alchemists no doubt used his name as a pseudonym. No Arabic original of his famous *Summa Perfectionis Magisterii* ('Summary of the Perfection of the Mastery') attributed to him has been found and it may well have been written by a Christian scholar in Moorish Spain who had access to his works. It was the most important alchemical text in Christendom in the Middle Ages and was among the first alchemical treatises to be printed in 1485.[23]

In the British Library in London, I came across an intriguing book called *The Works of Geber, the Most Famous Arabian Prince and Philosopher, of the Investigation and Perfection of the Philosopher's Stone* (1686), translated from Latin by Richard Russell. Apart from 'The Summ of Perfection, or the way to make the perfect magistery of the Art', it contained many intriguing titles: 'The Investigation of secret things corrupting and perfecting Metallick Bodies, for the Stone of the Philosophers', as well as 'A Confutation of the Reasons of those Men which deny this Art, imitating Nature'.

Geber insists that the alchemist must know 'natural principles' as a root for his intentions: '*Art* cannot imitate *Nature* in all *Works*, but imitates her as exactly as it can.'[24] He fully appreciated the value of careful experimentation and observation in the laboratory. He defines alchemy as a science which teaches how to perfect the '*imperfect Bodies of Minerals*', adding, like the ancient Chinese and Egyptian alchemists, that the perfection of metals is a natural process which takes place in the earth but can be speeded up by the art of alchemy.[25]

But what is it that can execute the transformation of metals in so short a time? The Philosopher's Stone of course. My lagging attention in the warm bowels of the British Library immediately picked up on reading this. Geber insists that there is only one Stone which brings to perfection the 'mercury' and 'sulphur' which are in all bodies. Of the two substances, I learned, mercury is superior: the more mercury present, the nobler the metal. The Stone projected on to a base metal perfects this inherent mercury. But how can the Stone be produced?

It is, Geber says, extracted from many different bodies and is prepared according to the different substances used: 'For experience hath taught us diverse ways of acting, *viz. Calcination, Sublimation, Descension, Solution, Distillation, Coagulation, Fixation* and *Inceration*: All of which we sufficiently declare in the *Sum of the Perfection* of the *Magistery*.'[26] But while he lists the common techniques of the alchemists, he does not say what substances are to be used in the preparation of the Stone.

He is more forthcoming on the properties that it must have. They are seven in number: oleaginy (oiliness), tenuity of matter, affinity, 'radical humidity', 'clearness of purity', a 'fixing earth', and tincture. After the projection of the Stone, its first function is sudden and easy fusion due to its oleaginy. Then the tenuity of the Stone – the fact that it is a very thin liquid when fused – enables it to penetrate throughout the material which is being transmuted. Next, affinity is essential between the Stone and the material, otherwise they would not adhere, and 'radical humidity' permanently congeals the similar parts of the material together. The 'clearness of purity' gives splendour. At this stage in the process, the dross can be purified by fire. Two properties remain, a 'fixing earth' and tincture. The former makes a permanent fixation in the solution of the body. The latter 'giving a splendid and perfect *Colour*, or intensely *Citrine*, and *Lunification*, or *Solification* of *Bodies* to be transmuted; because after *Fixation*, a splendid *Tincture*, and *Colour* tinging another *Body*, or a *Tincture* colouring the *Matter* convertible into true *Silver*, or *Gold* (with all its certain and known differences) is absolutely necessary'.[27]

But although the Latin Geber undoubtedly worked according to a definite plan, I looked in vain amongst his recipes for a clear way of making the Stone. Perhaps the true formula still lies in one of the countless works in Arabic and Latin under his name mouldering away in the archives of Europe or in the libraries of the Middle East. Or perhaps the Stone is really formed in the mind, when its different elements (salt, mercury and sulphur) have been combined and transformed, thereby bestowing power to live for ever and to see the light of God.

27

The Secret of Secrets

The astrology of the lower world.

Rhazes on alchemy

Despite the originality of Jabir and his school, I was still far from discovering the Philosopher's Stone. I next delved into the work of other Islamic alchemists, of whom there were many. I found the most outstanding to be Abu Bakr Muhammad ibn Zakariya, or simply Al-Razi – the 'man from Ray' named after Ray near Teheran in Persia where he was born in 866. He went on to study at Baghdad in Iraq. He was known to later European alchemists as Rhazes. He was not only a scientific genius but the first of the great encyclopedists of Islam. What did he get up to?

According to An-Nadim, Rhazes asserted that 'no one can succeed in the science of Philosophy, nor can a scholar be called a philosopher, unless he [first] succeeds in the science of the Alchemical Art, so that he becomes by this independent of everybody, whilst everybody else stands in need of him by reason of his knowledge and resources'.[1] The passage is fascinating because it shows how philosophy, science and art were not clearly separated at the time. Rhazes excelled not only in alchemy but also in medicine and his books became classics throughout the Islamic world.

The work of Rhazes best known in the Christian world was his treatise on measles and smallpox; he was the first to identify the latter and to treat it successfully. He isolated and used alcohol as an antiseptic. He was also the first to use mercury as a purgative, known in the Middle Ages as '*Album Rhasis*'. As his work *The Spiritual Physick* shows, he was a master of psychosomatic medicine and psychology.[2]

A fine story illustrates his method of treatment. On one occasion he was summoned to the Amir Mansur in Bukhara who was suffering from a mysterious ailment. Rhazes treated him with a form of psychological shock. On arriving at the River Oxus which was in flood, Rhazes refused to cross, not wanting to risk his life. The Amir had him bound and forcibly placed in a boat and brought to Bukhara. After his diagnosis – 'an extreme failure in the natural caloric' – Rhazes asked him to be ready to sacrifice two of his swiftest horses and mules. He took the Amir into a hot bath, gave him a draught, and then reviled and threatened him with a knife. The furious Amir rose from his bath – and found himself cured. Rhazes then leapt on the horse and rode off with his servant on the mule. The treatment was such a success that the Amir sent Rhazes a fully caparisoned horse, a cloak, a turban, arms, a slave boy and a handmaiden. He further commanded that he should be given in Ray a yearly allowance of 2,000 dinars in gold and 200 ass-loads of corn.[3]

There is a lovely description of Rhazes in old age seated in the courtyard of his hospital surrounded by students in rings, with the older students passing on his words of wisdom – and no doubt their misinterpretation of them – to the younger ones on the outside. Rhazes eventually became blind, some said because of his excessive love of beans. He died in 925. His pupils edited his unfinished *Al-Hawr*, an encyclopaedia of practical wisdom, later translated into Latin as the *Liber Continens*.

A score of books on alchemy are attributed to Rhazes but only a few have survived. His most important, *The Book of the Secret of Secrets* (*Kitab Sirr al Asrar*), was translated into Latin as *Secretum Secretorum*. Although the terms used are often obscure, he describes clearly practical operations, apparatus and substances. Indeed, Rhazes places greater emphasis on the work in the laboratory than in the mind, and was more interested in developing the outer elixir than the inner elixir.

Despite its tantalizing title, *The Secret of Secrets* mainly offers practical recipes. Describing sublimation, for instance, he wrote:

There are two methods of subliming Mercury, one for the 'Red' and one for the 'White'. In subliming it there are two secrets, one the removal of the moistness, and the other to make it dry, so that it may be absorbent. The removal of its moistness is by either of two processes. After triturating it with what you wish to sublime it, you heat it over a gentle fire in a phial luted with clay, and then triturate and [again] heat it, doing this seven times till it completely dries. Then sublime it with whatever you wish to sublime it with, and heat it gently and place it in the aludel. Over the aludel there should be an alembic of green pottery, or glass, with a short wide spout, for the purpose of distilling all the moisture out of the mercury. Under [the spout] is placed a dish.[4]

As the passage implies, Rhazes had a very well-equipped laboratory, including athanors, aludels, alembics and cucurbits. He further describes many other alchemical instruments, such as beakers, flasks, phials, casseroles, naptha lamps, shears, tongues, pestles and mortars. As a result, his alchemical works may be considered the first treatises on chemistry.

Rhazes had access to all known metals. He divided minerals into 'spirits' and 'bodies' and then gave the first systematic classification of substances into animal, vegetable and mineral – the triad so beloved of later quizmasters. He drew up another list of 'derivatives', such as cinnabar and litharge.[5] He is credited with reinventing sulphuric acid and aqua vitae. He also experimented with animal preparations and extracted sal ammoniac from hair. Here is his recipe for those who would like to cut their tresses:

Take washed black Hair, and put it in an iron pan with a cover, and close the joint, and cover the pan with small pieces of charcoal, ignite them, and let them burn until they are extinguished. Then pour upon it [i.e. the calcined residue of hair], after placing it in an iron [pot], 20 times [its weight] of distilled water of Hair – and it is Spirit – and let it [the mixture] undergo coction for one hour. Then filter it, and coagulate with it the Spirits which whiten by means of coction, if you so desire. But if you need Sal-ammoniac, coagulate the solution, and it will turn into solid Sal-ammoniac.[6]

Rhazes called the science of alchemy 'the astrology of the lower world'.[7] In his cosmology, he was a rationalist and an atomist. He believed that there are five eternal principles: the Creator, Soul, Matter, Time and Space. He rejected Aristotle's notion of space, asserting that there were absolute space and matter before the Creation. Like Jabir,

he believed that all substances are composed of four elements and
therefore capable of transformation but he rejected Jabir's complicated
theory of balance. An atomist like the Greek philosopher Democritus,
he thought that substances have different degrees of density due to the
empty space between the indivisible atoms which make up the elements. This determines their movement: the amount of space between
the atoms causes air and fire to rise and water and earth to fall.

In his alchemy, Rhazes believed like Jabir that all metals contain
mercury and sulphur to differing degrees, though he added a third
'salty' substance. This novel idea was taken up by Paracelsus and later
European alchemists. His work on salts and alums *De Salibus et Alubis*
was renowned in the Middle Ages throughout Europe.[8]

Rhazes did not doubt the possibility of transmuting metals. Since
all metals are composed of four elements, they can be transmuted from
one to another by the use of elixirs which change the degree of sulphur,
mercury, and 'salt' within them. In the same way, he believed that
common minerals like quartz and even glass could be converted into
emeralds, rubies, sapphires and other precious stones.

For the process of transmutation, Rhazes gives the following
procedure. The substances should first be purified by distillation,
calcination and amalgamation. Next they should be reduced to a
fusible condition by ceration (softening) so that they can be easily
melted. The result is further reduced by solution, that is dissolved by
'sharp waters' (usually alkaline and ammoniacal solutions rather than
acids). Depending on the proportions of the 'bodies' and 'spirits' in
the solutions, they are then brought together in the final process of
coagulation or solidification.

If the experiment is a success, hey presto, you end up with an elixir
which should be able to transform a small amount of gold into a
considerable amount – depending on its strength – from 100 to 20,000
times its weight . If the operation is not successful, then it is because the
right quantities of substances or the timing of the experiment are wrong.
Although Rhazes offers the classic account of the different stages of the
alchemical process that was first recorded by the Alexandrian alchemists, I looked in vain for a clear and exact description of his elixirs.

Rhazes died when he was about sixty. Despite his thirst for
knowledge, it seems that he was unable to find an elixir to prolong his
own life. Nor was he certain that he would achieve the ultimate
transformation in the afterlife. Just before he died, he wrote:

> This feeble form decaying day by day
> Warns me that I must shortly pass away.
> Alas! I know not wither wends the soul
> When it deserts this worn and waste clay.[9]

Jabir thought that there was a grand elixir, but either failed to find it or declined to tell his readers about it. The more practical Rhazes only believed in elixirs to transmute base metal into gold. Even more sceptical was the eleventh-century Islamic scientist, the Persian Abu Ali al-Husain ibn Sina, known to Europeans as Avicenna. The million-word *Canon of Medicine* of this 'Aristotle of the Arabs' became the bible of medical students during the Middle Ages and the Renaissance and is still taught in the Middle East. He accepted that all metals contain mercury and sulphur and their different proportions give them their specific character. Yet he was guarded about the claim of the alchemists to make artificial gold. They might be able to make very good imitations but could not perform a real change in metals:

> I do not deny that such a degree of accuracy in imitation may be reached to deceive even the shrewdest, but the possibility of transmutation has never been clear to me. Indeed, I regard it as impossible, since there is no way of splitting up one metallic combination into another. Those properties that are perceived by the senses are probably not the differences which distinguish one metallic species from another, but rather accidents or consequences, the essential specific differences being unknown. And if a thing is unknown, how is it possible for any one to endeavour to produce it or to destroy it?[10]

Avicenna's objections to alchemy excited a heated controversy but they did not prevent Islamic alchemists from following their vocation. They were also overlooked by later European alchemists who celebrated him along with Jabir and Rhazes as a revered forerunner of the Hermetic art. In a work by Daniel Stolcius published in Frankfurt in 1624, Avicenna appears with a large book under his arm pointing to an emblem illustrating the saying: 'Join together an earthly toad and a flying eagle; you see the magisterium in our art.'[11]

*

Avicenna based his objection to the transmutation of metals on sound reasoning. It cannot be denied that the behaviour of some would-be alchemists gave ample grounds for scepticism. There were plenty of charlatans and puffers travelling through the Islamic world claiming to have discovered the grand elixir of the Philosopher's Stone. A typical character turned up in Damascus dressed as a Sufi dervish. He first made some pellets from a paste of gold filings, charcoal, various drugs, flour and fish glue and sold them to a druggist under the name of 'tabarmaq of Khorassan'. After engaging a servant, the stranger then put on a rich cloak and went to the mosque where he declared that he was an alchemist who could make unimaginable riches between the rising and the setting of the sun. On hearing of his boasts, the sultan summoned him to court and insisted on a demonstration of his alleged skills. Not surprisingly, an essential ingredient of his recipe for the transmutation of metals was a certain substance known as 'tabarmaq of Khorassan'. It was only after a long search of the druggists in town that it was discovered.[12]

The stranger then set about his experiment, placing the pellets and other drugs in a crucible which he ordered to be heated fiercely. When the time was right, he had the crucible taken off the fire, cooled and then turned upside down. Out fell a fine nugget of gold. The sultan was charmed and ordered a further supply of the precious *tabarmaq*. When none could be obtained in Damascus, the stranger said that a large quantity could be found in a certain cave in Khorassan. Fearful that others might find out the secret source, the sultan ordered the man to travel alone to obtain some more. He equipped him handsomely for the journey, with a tent, carpets, silks, a travelling kitchen, sugar, and a large sum of money. The alchemist, who had arrived in Damascus as an impoverished ascetic, set off in grand style – and was never heard of again.

Were there any other Islamic alchemists who got close to the Philosopher's Stone? Dubais ibn Malik seems to have come across it by chance – or was it by Allah's design? The alchemist relates:

> I was living in Antioch, where I had settled, and there I had a friend who was a jeweller by profession, to whose shop I often resorted. Now, as we were talking together one day, a man came in, and, having saluted, took his seat. After a while he removed from his arm an armlet which he handed to my friend. It was set with four jewels, and an amulet of red gold fitted into it. On the amulet was inlaid a clear inscription in green emerald, which read

as follows: Al-Hakim bi-amrillah puts his trust in God [Al-Hakim was the King of Egypt from 996 to 1020]. I was astounded at the fineness of the jewels, the like of which I had never before seen, nor had I ever thought to see the like in the world, and it occurred to me that this amulet must have been stolen from the treasury of Al-Hakim, or it might have fallen from his arm, and this man had picked it up, since such jewels are to be found only in the treasuries of kings, or among their heirlooms.[13]

Ibn Malik bought the amulet and inside found a manuscript on which he recognized the shaky handwriting of the King of Egypt. It contained an account of two ways of making the Red Elixir, according to the method of Moses and the rest of the Prophets as handed down by imam Ja'far al-Sadiq – Jabir's friend and patron. Ibn Malik claimed that he was successful in carrying out the two ways. In the Lesser Way, the elixir converted 500 times it own weight of base metal into gold, while in the Greater Way, it was only necessary to use one dirham of the elixir to convert 3,000 dirhams of base metal. Unfortunately, Ibn Malik kept both ways to himself.

I was astounded on reading this tale. Was the Red Elixir the father of the Red Mercury that I had been offered in Luxor and Cairo which allegedly turned sand into gold and brought you all you wished? Even if it were not, it shows the vitality and continuity of the tradition. The fact that the grand elixir was attributed to Moses rather than Hermes reflects the strength of the Islamic tradition in which Dubais ibn Malik stood. The fact that it was from an amulet of the King of Egypt also confirms the importance of the country as the birthplace of alchemy.

Clearly alchemy was widely practised throughout the Islamic world from the eighth century, especially in Persia, Syria and Iraq. But it was not until the Muslims conquered Spain in the same century that it found its way into Europe. To find out more about the transition, I decided next to travel to southern Spain which was occupied by the Moors until the late fifteenth century. During this period, there was a continual exchange between Muslim, Jewish and Christian scholars who were interested in alchemy and steeped in the Hermetic tradition.

28

The Earthly Paradise

You who live in Al-Andalus, with its waters, its shade, its rivers, its trees – how blessed are you!

The Garden of Bliss is nowhere else than in your country, and if it was possible for me to choose between them it would be your country I would choose.

Ibn Khafaja (d.1139), *Diwan*

Sitting in the ornamental gardens of the Moorish palace of the Alhambra, it was difficult not to believe that I was in the earthly paradise described in the Qur'an. I had come to the Alhambra in Granada in southern Spain because the Moors, during their occupation of southern Europe, were the main conveyors of alchemy to the West. Thanks to the Islamic philosophers and scientists, the torch of knowledge which had gone out in Athens, Rome and Alexandria was rekindled. It illuminated the Dark Ages in Europe at a time when the intellect had taken refuge in a few scattered monasteries. The wisdom of the ancient world brought and developed by the Muslims helped trigger in Europe a revolution in learning with alchemy at its centre.

The Alhambra stands on a hill which dominates the city of Granada. Its surviving Alcazaba or citadel, built in the eleventh century, shows how life in Andalusia in Moorish Spain, however pleasant, was always under threat from the Christian north. By the thirteenth century, Granada was the capital, with a population of 200,000, four times that of London. The palace, built in the following century, was a masterpiece of delicate and sensitive architecture.

I entered it early one morning in spring, when the sun lit the long rectangular pond in the first courtyard. The fountain in the centre of the inner courtyard was held up by nine small lion statues and sparkled in the sun. Swallows swirled around the cloisters. The play of light also brought out the wonderful filigree effect of the intricately carved woodwork windows in the cool Salon of the Ambassadors.

The terraced gardens with their ponds continued the sense of harmony and ease which must have marked the everyday life of the Moors. The trembling water which flashed in the sun was brought by viaducts from the snow-capped Sierra Nevada some 30 kilometres away. I particularly liked the contrast between the formal gardens with their geometric shapes made by bright green myrtle hedges and the rough red-brown terrain of the hillside beyond the palace walls. Even the pathways were made from small black and white pebbles placed to make herringbone and swirling patterns. I could see why the Muslim alchemists were drawn to the sacred numerology and geometry.

Much of the interlaced ornamentation on the walls had the inscription: *Wala ghaliba ill Allah* ('Allah alone is Conqueror'). After six centuries of struggle, the Catholic kings eventually captured the magnificent palace in 1492. Carlos V observed judiciously: 'ill-fated was the man who lost all this'. He then proceeded to destroy the delicate grace and symmetry of the Moorish palace by building a brutish square block right in its centre. As for the Moors, banished from their Andalusian paradise, they retreated to the inhospitality, struggle and sand of the Moroccan desert.

I lingered on a balcony off some small rooms overlooking a small inner courtyard full of flowering shrubs. When the triumphant Catholic monarchs Isabella and Ferdinand entered the Alhambra in 1492 they wore Muslim dress and stayed in the rooms. Stories of its former Moorish inhabitants lived on. The American writer Washington Irving occupied the same quarters in the early nineteenth century when the Alhambra had been abandoned and Granada had shrunk to a population of 40,000. A local man called Mateo Jimenez told Irving about the 'Legend of the Arabian Astrologer' which reflects the continuity of the alchemical tradition from ancient Egypt, and its vigour during the Islamic period in Spain.

It tells the story of King Aben Habuz, who ruled over Granada but was in a constant state of vigilance and alarm, not knowing from what direction his Christian enemies might appear. One day an ancient Arabian physician arrived at his court, who had travelled from Egypt mostly on foot. His name was Ibrahim Ebn Abu Ajub. He was said to have lived ever since the days of Muhammad and to be the son of Abu

Ajub, the last of the companions of the Prophet. As a child he followed
the conquering army of Amur into Egypt, where he had remained
many years studying 'the dark sciences and particularly magic among
the Egyptian priests'.[1]

More than two centuries old, the astrologer seems also to have
been an alchemist for he had discovered the secret of prolonging life.
Although offered an apartment in the king's palace in the Alhambra,
he preferred to live in a cave with a circular hole in the roof where he
could see the heavens and even the stars at midday. The walls of his
cave were covered with Egyptian hieroglyphs, Cabalistic symbols and
the signs of the zodiac.

Ibrahim relates how he discovered the ancient wisdom of Egypt:

> After the victorious Amur (may he rest in peace!) had finished his
> conquest of Egypt, I remained among the ancient priests of the
> land, studying the rites and ceremonies of their idolatrous faith,
> and seeking to make myself master of the hidden knowledge for
> which they are renowned. I was one day seated on the banks of
> the Nile, conversing with an ancient priest, when he pointed to
> the mighty pyramids which rose like mountains out of the neigh-
> bouring desert. 'All that we can teach thee', said he, 'is nothing to
> the knowledge locked up in those mighty piles. In the centre of the
> central pyramid is a sepulchral chamber, in which is enclosed the
> mummy of the high priest who aided in rearing that stupendous
> pile, and with him is buried a wondrous book of knowledge
> containing all the secrets of magic and art. This book was given
> to Adam after his fall and was handed down from generation to
> generation to King Solomon the Wise, and by its aid he built the
> Temple of Jerusalem. How it came into the possession of the
> builder of the pyramids is known to Him alone who knows all
> things.'[2]

With the help of Arab soldiers and local Egyptians, Ibrahim broke
through the solid mass of the pyramid, penetrated its 'fearful labyrinth'
and reached the sepulchral chamber of the high priest. Unravelling the
bandages of the mummy, he eventually found the book of wisdom on
its bosom. It was clearly the legendary Book of Thoth, although Islamic
tradition attributes it to Adam and Solomon.

Whilst in Egypt Ibrahim also saw a great marvel devised by the
priests above the city of Borsa on the Nile. The figure of a ram was

placed above the figure of a cock, both made of molten brass, which turned on a pivot. Whenever the country was threatened with invasion, it turned to the direction of the danger and the cock would crow. The astrologer-alchemist devised a similar talisman for the King of Granada on a specially built tower on the hill of Albaicín opposite the Alhambra. In this case, it consisted of a bronze figure of a Moorish horseman with an elevated lance which turned towards the Christian invaders. At each window of the tower, facing every point of the compass, a magic board was placed on a table with a mimic army. The King, on seeing the point of danger, could move the figures on the board and defeat his enemies.

The talisman worked well until the caliph and Ibrahim fell out with each other. They were both undone by the wiles of a Visigoth sorceress who appeared in the guise of a beautiful princess. The Visigoths had ruled Spain before the arrival of the Moors. It was a lovely story. I had come across a similar tale about Nectanebo II, the last Egyptian-born pharaoh, who could defeat his naval enemies by moving wax models of boats in a bowl of water. Clearly, the wisdom of the Philosopher's Stone escaped them.

*

After visiting the Alhambra and Granada, I moved on to Córdoba. It had been an emirate from 756, then a caliphate from 929, and finally the capital of the independent Omayyad dynasty until 1031. At the time it was rivalled in prosperity and splendour only by Baghdad and Constantinople. At its height, Córdoba boasted magnificent palaces, gardens and fountains, 50,000 mansions of the aristocracy and rulers, 900 public baths and 700 mosques. Among its architectural jewels was the third largest mosque in the Islamic world. When his fellow Christians imposed a cathedral on its delicate symmetry even King Carlos V said to them: 'You have built here what you or anyone might have built anywhere else, but you have destroyed what was unique in the world.'[3]

I could see why. The Mesquita, as it is known, has a wide walled courtyard full of fountains, orange trees and doves. Coming from the bright noonday light, at first all is lost in the penumbra of the mosque, but then gradually shafts of suffused rosy light reveal row upon row of delicate arches, not more than 30 metres apart, above a forest of stone columns. A honeycombed central vault has beautiful blue tiles decorated with stars. The *mihrab*, pointing towards Mecca, is a masterpiece of carving, decorated with geometrical and flowing vegetable patterns.

I sat for a long time on the cool marble floor, my back against a pillar. Was the Mesquita, like the Great Pyramid itself, a laboratory of the spirit, a sacred place for the transformation of the soul? It felt like it. I recalled the distinction made by the Chinese alchemists between the inner and outer elixir and thought that perhaps the Philosopher's Stone is to be found more within the self than in the external world. The intuition remained with me long after I left the liquid coolness of the mosque and went out into the harsh glare of the midday sun.

*

The Mesquita is not the only great remnant of Moorish civilization in Spain and of the alchemy which nurtured it. About 8 kilometres west of Córdoba I visited the ruins of Medina Azahara on an escarpment overlooking a fertile valley. It had been the fortified palace of Abd al-Rahman III (912–61), the first independent caliph of Andalusia, who named it after his favourite wife, Zahra. It is said that it took 10,000 masons and labourers, 2,600 mules and 400 camels to build it over twenty-five years. I wandered down its three descending terraces and amongst its beautifully laid out gardens, full of bougainvillea, jasmine, hibiscus, oleander, cedars and myrtle hedges. I again marvelled at the size and splendour of the palace, with its marble and jasper facades and its black and rose marble arches.

Of particular alchemical interest was a mercury fountain which had once stood in the centre of the hall. When the sun rays penetrated the room and shone on to the mercury, the brightness blinded anyone present. The story goes that whenever the caliph wanted to frighten one of his subjects, he would get his slaves to move the mercury fountain around the room: it then seemed to be full of lightning and the building seemed to go round and round in circles.[4]

Al-Hakam II, who ruled from 961 to 976, was a philosopher, poet and great lover of learning. Paper was introduced by the Moors in Europe and his library was stocked with 600,000 volumes, making Córdoba the book centre of the world. It was the greatest library since the library of Alexandria, and contained all the known wisdom which had survived from ancient Greece and Egypt. Al-Hakam summoned scholars from all over the Middle East to teach in Córdoba, especially those who could translate from Greek into Arabic.[5] The Talmudic school in the city was among the foremost centres of Hebrew scholarship. The Christian *mozarabes* – 'almost Arabs' – were soon outnumbered by the *muladies* or converts. The Catholic Bishop Alvaro of Córdoba lamented: 'Alas, all the Christian youths who become famous for their talent know only the language and the literature of the Arabs; they read and study zealously Arabic books, of which by dint of great expenditure they form extensive libraries, and proclaim aloud on all sides that this literature is worthy of admiration.'[6]

Despite the wavering battle front with the Catholic kings, during the second half of the tenth century in Andalusia, a brilliant group of Islamic and Jewish alchemists flourished. Glass had been discovered in Córdoba in the previous century and the city had many alchemical laboratories. The writer Ibn Suhayd (d.1035) has left a vivid description of one of his friends, Abu Abd Allah al-Faradi: 'a blackened room, full of vapours . . . in which collected the stinking smell of arsenic, sulphur, cinnabar and sarcocolla [gum]'.[7] I tried to find existing remnants of the laboratories or signs of alchemists in the old Jewish quarter around the Mesquita but without success.

The most brilliant alchemist to be born in Córdoba was Abu'l Qasim Maslamah ibn Ahmad (d.1009). He was also known as Al-Majriti, 'The One from Madrid', because he later lived there. He was typical of the cosmopolitan nature of the scholars in Spain at the time. It seems that he was partly educated in the eastern Islamic Empire, where he came into contact with the Shiah cult known as the Brethren of Purity with whom Khalid and Jabir had been associated. He brought back to Spain a version of their remarkable tenth-century encyclopaedia *Rasai'l*. He also adapted the Persian astronomical tables into an Arabic chronology which started with the birth of Muhammad. But Al-Majriti's most important works were on alchemy and magic which were closely intertwined at the time.

The work called *The Final Aim of the Wise* (*Gayat al-hakim*) was attributed to him. It was translated into Castilian in 1256 by order of Alfonso X, the King of Castile and Leon, and later rendered into Latin under the name of *Picatrix*. As a manual of astral magic for seances, it became hugely popular in magical circles during the Renaissance.[8]

In the history of alchemy Al-Majriti is best known for *The Sage's Step*. Despite its intriguing title, it is primarily a work of practical alchemy, a manual for the laboratory. There is a description, for

instance, of the careful preparation of mercuric oxide using a quanti-
tative method – an approach which became the hallmark of modern
chemistry. There are also clear recipes for purifying gold and silver by
cupellation and other means.

Above all, the work outlines the proper training for an alchemist.
He should first study the mathematics of the Alexandrians Euclid and
Ptolemy and the natural sciences of Aristotle and Apollonius of Tyana.
He should then practise in the laboratory, observing and reflecting on
substances and reactions. In this he can follow nature and rely on her
operations, for he can be confident she never deviates.

*

I found a contemporary of Al-Majriti in Spain, Muhammad Ibn Umail
(or Ibn Amyal), to be a much more promising alchemist. He knew the
work of the Alexandrian alchemists and had interpreted Maria's
description of distillation in terms of a mystical wedding involving the
coitus of the soul and the spirit. Little is known about him except that
he produced *The Book of Silvery Water and Starry Earth* (*Kitab al-
ma' al-waraqi wa al-ard al-najmiyya*). It is a beautifully-titled commentary on his ode called 'Epistle of the Sun to the Crescent Moon'.

The commentary is particularly interesting for the quotations given
from earlier alchemical authors. Some of the 'Sayings of Hermes' are
from Greek originals and show that the Islamic alchemists were clearly
aware of and developing the Hermetic tradition. *Silvery Water and
Starry Earth* was still considered influential enough to warrant a long
commentary by the fourteenth-century alchemist Aidamur Al-Jildaki
who lived some time in Cairo and travelled throughout the Middle
East collecting alchemical texts. It was translated into Latin as the
Tabula Chemica and attributed to Senior Zadith. It later excited the
interest of the psychoanalyst Carl Jung.[9]

Ibn Umail in his introduction to the *Silvery Water and Starry Earth*
gives a remarkable allegorical description of the processes which lead
to the creation of the Philosopher's Stone. He recounts how on two
occasions he went to Busir al-Sidr in Egypt and from there walked to
an ancient temple. After the guardians had opened the door for him,
he saw nine eagles on the ceiling of a long chamber. Their wings were
outstretched and in their long claws they held bows and arrows. On
the left and the right of the chamber stood handsome men, richly
dressed in different coloured robes, who pointed towards an old man

seated on a throne. I took him to be none other than Hermes Trismegistus.

On his knees was a stone tablet which looked like an open book. It was divided into two parts: on the bottom right, there was the image of two birds with touching chests; the one underneath had its wings cut, the other outstretched. Each held the tail feathers of the other. They formed a circle. Above the flying bird was a circle, and above the two birds, at the top of the tablet, was the image of a crescent moon. At the side of this is another circle. The whole contained five symbols: three below (two birds and a circle) and two above (the crescent and the other circle).

On the right of the stone tablet was the image of the sun with two rays; next to it, there was another sun, with a descending ray. These sun rays surrounded a black circle, of which a third was separated. One of the thirds within the circle had the form of a white crescent. There were also two suns at the top. In this way, there are five elements on either side of the tablet, which make ten and correspond to the number of the eagles and the black earth.

The complex allegory symbolizes the different stages of the alchemical processes and the substances involved in making the Philosopher's Stone, especially the union of sun and moon, Sol and Luna. The two birds forming a circle and the two rays of the sun symbolize the principle of 'Two in One'. A poem follows this description, called the 'Letter of the Sun to the Moon', as well as a prose commentary which attempts to elucidate its meaning. The works of 'Senior' certainly impressed the medieval European alchemists but they did not take me a great deal further in my quest for the Philosopher's Stone.

*

Whilst researching the Muslim alchemists in Moorish Spain, I discovered that there were many Jewish philosophers and scientists involved in alchemy. The Visigothic monarchy had persecuted the Jews but the Muslim Umayyads who replaced them took them under their protection. Many Jews prospered, learned Arabic and assimilated Arabic culture. The result was a renaissance in Jewish philosophy, science and poetry which had no parallel elsewhere.

The most famous Jewish philosopher interested in alchemy was Rabbi Moses ben Maimon (1135–1204), known as Maimonides. Like Avicenna, he became one of the great intellectual figures of the Middle

Ages and codified Jewish law in the Mishnah Torah. He was born in Córdoba and educated under an Arab master. He eventually ended up as a philosopher and physician in Cairo. In his *Guide for the Perplexed* written in Arabic, he argued that there is no conflict between the revealed truths of religion and the *natija* or conclusions of reason. The techniques of the alchemists and physicians to prolong life are not an infringement of divine authority because God, being omniscient, would already have foreseen the intention and the action.

Very different in outlook was Moses of León (c.1250–1305), a Cabalist scholar who is now thought to be the author or the compiler of the *Zohar*. Purporting to be an ancient manuscript handed down from a second-century sage, it is a vast rambling mystical discourse on the Torah.[10] Moses ben Shem Tov, to give him his full name, settled in Guadalajara around 1275 where he wrote *midrash* (commentaries) on the Torah, a *Book of Lamentations* and the main bulk of the *Zohar* in Aramaic. The word 'Zohar' means 'splendour' or 'enlightenment'.

The Cabala became a powerful factor in Jewish religious life and an integral part of medieval alchemy. The Cabala is the occult teaching of the Jewish 'Secret Tradition'. Some say it was handed down from Moses or Abraham, others that it finds its source in the Egyptian temples. The Hebrew word '*qabalah*' is usually translated as 'tradition'. The root of the word 'cabala' means 'accept' which may also refer to the need for the initiate to trust his master. It probably finds its source in the Talmud as developed by the Geonim (elders) of the two great Jewish academies which flourished in Babylonia from the sixth to the tenth centuries.

From this milieu emerged the key Cabalist text known as the *Sefer Yetzirah* ('Book of Creation'). By the tenth century it was sufficiently well known to provoke an Arabic commentary. It describes God as entrusting the task of the Creation to ten emanations, the male and female *Sephiroth*. Between God's Light (*Pleroma*) and our world there are four levels which divide into ten spheres. The cosmic tree, with its roots in God and whose top reaches our world, interconnects them all.

Like the *Hermetica*, the Cabala concerns itself with the fundamental questions of God, the universe and the place of humans within it. God is called *Ejn-sof, baruch hu* ('The infinite one, the blessed'). God cannot be fully comprehended but we can understand the lower stages of his Creation through meditation, contemplation and ecstatic experience.

The Cabalists shared a similar world view with the alchemists, believing in the Hermetic doctrine of 'As above, so below.' Sharing the Arabic classification of animal, vegetable and mineral, they believed in the transmigration of souls up and down the Great Chain of Being. They were therefore theoretically predisposed to take up alchemy. The *Zohar* directly echoes the alchemical classic known as the *Emerald Tablet*:

> Every thing which is on the earth is also up above. In this world, there does not exist anything, even the smallest thing, which does not depend on another thing up there, which is superior to it. Therefore if the thing down here starts to move, the thing standing up there also starts to move – because everything is connected and united together.[11]

The Cabala holds that we are not just passive mirrors of the higher worlds but can directly affect them. If we are good, the flow of love increases; if we are evil, the severity of judgement grows. We can activate love in the universe by loving God and others. We are born with a lower biological soul (*nefesh*) but it is up to us to invite the ethical soul (*neshama*) down from the higher worlds. We must therefore work for our immortality in the laboratory of our selves. The Cabala implies that the genesis of the world was some kind of catastrophe, and that it is for humans to work with God as partners to restore the original universal harmony. In this way, the world will go back to God whence it came.

The most famous doctrine of the Cabala is the symbol of the Tree of Life with its different centres of energy which recall the Hindu notion of chakras. Since each person is a microcosm of the macrocosm, the Tree of Life represents one's inner spiritual world as well as the universe. Whereas the Tree of Knowledge in the Old Testament brings about the downfall of humanity, the Tree of Life in the Cabala enables us to re-ascend to our divine origins.

29

Bezels of Wisdom

A world dwells in the heart of a millet seed.
In the wing of a knat is the ocean of life,
In the pupil of an eye a heaven.

Mahmud Shabistari, *The Mystic Rose Garden*

On my return to Wales I was surprised to find out that my neighbour was a great admirer of Ibn 'Arabi, a Sufi poet and thinker who was born in Murcia in south-east Spain in 1165. Islamic spiritual alchemy reached its supreme expression in his works, but she warned me that he was not easy to understand. He would often quote the prophet Muhammad: 'The first gift God gave me was reading between the lines!' In his own writings, as in other alchemical works, it is necessary 'to read between the lines' since there are many levels and hidden meanings. They are all journeys of the soul towards God.

His full name was Abu Bakr Muhammad ibn 'Ali Muhyi al-Din al-Hatimi al-Andalus. In his youth, Ibn 'Arabi was exposed to the gnostic and mystical tradition of the Sufis in Andalusia. He had a thorough grounding in the Qur'an but was not deeply impressed by philosophers, preferring the works of 'sages' (*hakim*). His one exception was the 'divine Plato'. He felt theology and philosophy were not entirely in vain, but those who relied on their intellect could only grasp a tiny part of the truth. In Ibn 'Arabi's view 'there is not one single thing that cannot be known through revelation [*kashf*] or spiritual experience [*wujad*]'.[1] Only the man of faith would be able to reach the seventh heaven and experience the full light of God.

Ibn 'Arabi remained for thirty years in Seville, the capital of the empire of the Almohades dynasty. He travelled widely throughout the Islamic world, from Spain to Morocco, Egypt, Saudi Arabia,

Iraq, the Holy Land and Asia Minor. He eventually ended up in
Damascus in Syria where he died in 1240. His travels led him to
believe that God reveals himself in this world whatever one's religion:

> My heart is capable of every form:
> A cloister for the monk, a fane for idols,
> A pasture for gazelles, the votary's Ka'ba [temple],
> The tables of the Torah, the Qur'an.
> Love is the creed I hold: wherever turn
> His camels, Love is still my creed and faith.[2]

As a devout if unorthodox Muslim, he made the great pilgrimage to
Mecca. But his real travelling was within. From an early age, he
experienced visions of divine light. Indeed, his works – which run to
more than 400 – are records of his spiritual development and inner
transformation.

Ibn 'Arabi wrote no direct works on practical alchemy, but the
spirit of spiritual alchemy pervades his writings. In his *Bezels of
Wisdom* (*Fusus al-hikam*) and the *Meccan Revelations* (*al-Futahat al
Makkiya*), he expressed his belief in the Oneness of Being: the One in
the Many and the Many in the One. He gave the most important
exposition of this central Sufi conception of nature in terms drawn
from the Qur'an and from the Hermetic sources. There is no separation
of God from the Creation; he *is* the Creation. All things and beings are
his emanations. Whereas the Qur'an says: 'there is but one God', Ibn
'Arabi asserts: 'there is nothing but God'.[3] He rejects the notion of
there being any intermediaries such as a First Cause or Demiurge; there
is but the 'One and Only'.

God is Light and the objects in the world – animals, trees, microbes
– are all manifestations of His Light. In the *Meccan Revelations*, Ibn
'Arabi describes the resplendent vision which the blessed can hope to
experience as they gather on a snow-white hill in the presence of God:
'The Divine light pervades the beings of the elect and radiates from
them, reflected as if by mirrors, on everything around them. The
spiritual enjoyment produced by the contemplation of this reflection is
even greater than that of the Vision itself.'[4]

At the same time, the notion of the Logos or the Word plays an
important part in Ibn 'Arabi's thought. The archetypes of all things
are aspects of God's Names and Qualities which exist in a latent state
in the Divine Intellect. God gives them being so that they become

manifested, yet what is seen in the sensible world is only the shadow of the archetypes. The Qur'an says that the Absolute reveals itself in ninety-nine Divine Names but Ibn 'Arabi suggests that they are numberless. The Logos, however, consists of the twenty-two Divine Names which take the form of different energies and are manifestations of the divine essence. The 'Great Waves', he says, are called gold and silver.

They are all expressed in the spirit of Muhammad who is the supreme model of the Perfect Man (al-Insan al-kamil).[5] He is an ideal which ordinary humans can emulate in the processing of realizing their divine nature. By reaching the centre of himself, the seeker has knowledge of God and of all things. In the Qur'an, it is written: 'He who knows himself knows his Lord.' The more one approaches one's inner reality, the more one is in tune with the cosmos. As humans we descend from the Absolute – a devolution – but we can also ascend to the Absolute – an evolution – with the Perfect Man as our ideal.

This involves the Sufi goal of 'passing away' (al-fana) which is not so much an annihilation of the self but the passing away of ignorance and a growing awareness of the oneness of all things. Ibn 'Arabi says that you must 'die before you die', that is, pass away from the illusion of separateness. He uses the metaphor of a mirror to illustrate this point. When a person of ordinary intellect looks at a mirror he sees a reflected image of himself but not the mirror. The mirror is veiled from him. But at a higher lever of understanding, the mirror is not a veil for in it he sees not only himself but the Form of the Absolute assuming his own form. Indeed, God is never to be seen in immaterial form. 'The sight of God in woman,' Ibn 'Arabi says, 'is the most perfect of all.'[6]

In the Qur'an it is written: 'All men are asleep; only when they die do they wake up.' Ibn 'Arabi went further and said: 'The whole of life is a dream within a dream.' He also calls this world the 'shadow' of God: the archetypes are dark because they are distant from the light of Being just as a faraway mountain appears black. But even when we wake up and mystically experience the Absolute in 'unveiling' (kashf) and 'immediate tasting' (dhaq), the Absolute is unknowable in itself, and remains the mystery of mysteries.[7]

It was the aim of Ibn 'Arabi's life, as it was with all the Sufis, to stand in the light of God. Dreams and visions played a particularly important role for him: they are the 'inward eye' of the heart through which one can see everyday experiences as reflections of the archetypal ideas of the Absolute. He relates one such vision in the *Journey through the Night* (*Kitab al-isra*) which describes the ascent of the body to the Throne of Light through the seven heavens where he meets different prophets (including Idris–Hermes). On the journey, he is asked:

> Tell me, friend, which place you want me to take you to . . .
> —I want to go to the city of the Messenger, in search
> Of the Station of Radiance and the Red Sulphur.

Red Sulphur is clearly a synonym for the Philosopher's Stone.

I found the work to be a wonderful example of spiritual alchemy. The journey not only has the goal of finding the Red Sulphur but clearly reflects the different stages of the alchemical process in spiritual terms. It begins with the dissolution of the seeker's corporeal nature and the release of his spirit, which is then followed by a period of punishment by fire. He continues the ascent through the heavens until eventually he becomes 'nothing but light' in the seventh heaven. He then obtains the meaning of all the Divine Names and sees that they all 'referred to one and the same Object Named and to a single Essence: this Named was the object of my contemplation, and this Essence was my very own being'.

Ibn 'Arabi realizes that the whole journey is within, a process of realizing his true self: 'The journey I had made was only inside myself, and it was towards myself that I had been guided: from this I knew that I was a servant in a state of purity, without the slightest trace of sovereignty.'[8] He discovers the Red Sulphur and is totally transformed by the experience. It is a moment of absolute knowledge of the self and of the universe: 'For when you know yourself, your "I-ness" vanishes and you know that you and God are one and the same.'[9] The quest for the Red Sulphur is not so much the attainment of a goal, but simply the realization of who and where you are, of rediscovering your essential nature as part of the Oneness of Being.

On reading the work, I felt that Ibn 'Arabi had truly attained the goal of spiritual alchemy, union with the divine ground of our being and a vision of eternity. The supreme experience still eluded me but at least I had a stronger sense of the goal and of what I might expect.

Despite their different historical and cultural backgrounds, I was struck by the similarities between Sufi and Taoist spiritual alchemy and between their greatest exponents Ibn 'Arabi and Lao Tzu. While the former was prolific and the latter wrote nothing they seem to have come to the same conclusions about the inner transformation of the sage or Perfect Man. Although they believed that the Absolute or the Tao existed, the ultimate ground of existence remained the mystery of mysteries for both of them.[10] I felt they had both touched on fundamental truths about the universe and our place within it which are valid for all cultures and times.

*

Despite the struggle between the Christian kings and the Muslim caliphs in Spain, there were periods of peace when there was considerable coming and going of Christian scholars to the Islamic centres of learning across the wavering frontiers. They were not only eager to obtain Arabic translations of Greek works of philosophy, but keen to acquaint themselves with the Muslim contribution to science in general and to alchemy in particular which was an entirely new subject for them. The first Arabic work on alchemy to appear in Latin manuscripts in Europe in the thirteenth century was the anonymous *Turba Philosophorum*, or *The Assembly of the Sages*, a remarkable work of great philosophical interest and literary merit. It may well have been written around 900 by Uthman ibn Suwaid, of Akhmin in Egypt. The author quotes from the Alexandrian alchemists so he must have been in touch with the fountainhead of the Hermetic tradition in Egypt. Hermes and Zosimus are mentioned and Panoflus cites the famous triadic formula attributed to Ostanes and first mentioned by the Alexandrian alchemist Democritus: 'Nature rejoices in Nature, Nature contains Nature, and Nature overcomes Nature.'[11]

The *Turba* takes the form of a dialogue between twelve philosophers who meet to discuss the nature of alchemy. The speeches are full of rhetorical flourishes and are often addressed to 'O, all ye Seekers after this Art'. The sages have Greek names and some refer to real historical characters, such as Pythagoras, Socrates, Aristotle and Democritus. The author clearly knew his early Greek philosophy for they express theories which they were reported to have espoused. Pythagoras, for example, discusses the relations between numbers and the 'alchemical symbol of Man'. In fact, the *Turba* is the earliest evidence of Greek philosophy in Arabic literature.[12] But while the Hermetic cosmology is given as a context for alchemy, the author makes his Islamic faith clear. He asserts that nature is uniform, that all creatures of the upper and lower world are composed of four elements, but also that the creator of the world was Allah.

The work contained the first full discussion of the Philosopher's Stone that I had come across since Zosimus. The philosopher Belus declares:

> A report has gone abroad that the Hidden Glory of the Philosopher is a stone and not a stone, and that it is called by many names, lest the foolish should recognise it. Certain wise men have designated it after one fashion, namely, according to the place where it is generated; others have adapted another, founded upon its colour, some of whom have termed it the Green Stone; by some other it is called the Stone of the most intense Spirit of Brass, not to be mixed with bodies . . . some have distinguished it astronomically or arithmetically; it has already received a thousand titles, of which the best is: – 'That which is produced out of metals'. So also others have called it the Heart of the Sun, and yet others have declared it to be that which is brought out of quicksilver with the milk of volatile things.[13]

At first sight all this is very bewildering, but the names are not mutually exclusive; indeed, they describe different aspects and properties of the Philosopher's Stone. This is made clear at the end of the work by Agmon, who suggests that the names are multiplied so that the 'vulgar' might be deceived. Rest assured, he tells us, that 'the Stone is one thing'. But how can we recognize it? By its properties, of course, which are indeed impressive:

> The strength thereof, shall never be corrupted, but the same, when it is placed in the fire, shall be increased. If you seek to dissolve it, it shall be dissolved; but if you would coagulate it, it shall be coagulated. Behold, no one is without it, and yet all do need it! There are many names given to it, and yet it is called by one only, while, if need be, it is concealed. It is also a stone and not a stone, spirit, soul and body; it is white, volatile, concave, hairless, cold, and yet no one can apply the tongue with impunity to its surface. If you wish that it should fly, it flies; if you say that it is not water, you speak falsely.[14]

It is clear here that the Islamic alchemists saw their art as a form of spiritual transformation in the same way as the ancient Egyptians.

What applies to metals also applies to humans. The 'Philosopher' mentioned in the following passage would seem to be our old friend Zosimus:

> the definition of the Art is the liquefaction of the body and the separation of the soul from the body, seeing copper, like man, has a soul and a body. Therefore, it behoves you, O all ye seekers of the Doctrine, to destroy the body and extract the soul therefrom! Wherefore the Philosopher said that the body does not penetrate the body, but that there is a subtle nature, which is the soul, and it is that which tinges and penetrates the body. In nature, therefore, there is a body and a soul.[15]

The *Turba Philosophorum* played a pivotal role in the transition of Egyptian alchemy via the Muslims to Europe. It also ensured the continuity of the Hermetic tradition. Its special combination of philosophy, religion and science became typical of medieval European alchemy.

*

The other famous text bequeathed by the Islamic alchemists to the West is the *Tabula Smaragdina*, better known as the *Emerald Tablet*. In my opinion, it is the most profound single work of spiritual alchemy to emerge from the whole Hermetic tradition. An Arabic version exists in the works of Jabir which dates it to at least the eighth century. Translated from Arabic into Latin, it was reprinted countless times in the Middle Ages in Europe. It is one of the most influential documents to emerge from the Hermetic tradition and a key text in the understanding of all subsequent alchemy. Nothing stands so powerfully as the words themselves:

The Words of the Secret Things of Hermes Trismegistus

1. True it is, without falsehood, certain and most true. That which is above is like to that which is below, and that which is below is like to that which is above, to accomplish the miracles of the one thing.
2. And as all things were by the contemplation of the one, so all things arose from this one thing by a single act of adaptation.
3. The father thereof is the Sun, the mother the Moon.
4. The Wind carried it in its womb, the Earth is the nurse thereof.

5. It is the father of all the works of wonder throughout the whole world.
6. The power thereof is perfect.
7. If it be cast on to the Earth, it will separate the element of the Earth from that of Fire, the subtle from the gross.
8. With great sagacity it doth ascend gently from Earth to Heaven.
9. Again it doth descend to the Earth, and uniteth in itself the force from things superior and things inferior.
10. Thus thou wilt possess the glory of the brightness of the whole world, and all obscurity will fly from thee.
11. This thing is the strong fortitude of all strength, for it overcometh every subtle thing and doth penetrate every solid substance.
12. Thus was the world created.
13. Hence there will be marvellous adaptations achieved, of which the manner is this.
14. For this reason I am called Hermes Trismegistus, because I hold three parts of the wisdom of the whole world.
15. That which I had to say about the operation of the Sol is completed.[16]

The work is attributed to our old friend Hermes Trismegistus the 'Thrice-blessed' who has 'three parts of the wisdom of the whole world' and access to the three realms of being: the earth, the Underworld and the heavens.

There have been countless interpretations of the *Emerald Tablet* and I thought long and hard about the elusive meaning of this mystical text. First, I found a familiar idea from ancient Egypt: 'that which is above is like to that which is below' or, to put it more succinctly: 'As above, so below.' The same forces work through the earth as they do throughout heaven, in the microcosm of humanity and in the macrocosm of the universe. There is a correspondence and a sympathy between the two which only have the appearance of separation: 'that which is below is like to that which is above'.

What are 'the miracles of the one thing'? They are the miracles of the universe as a whole, of its unity in diversity, of the fact that All is One, and One is All, 'as all things were by the contemplation of the one'. A single consciousness permeates all beings and things, known as God, *anima mundi*, Universal Mind, Great Spirit, world soul. In the Hermetic tradition the universe is often represented by the circle, the symbol of eternity and of gold.

What follows next in the *Emerald Tablet* would seem to be a version of the creation myth of ancient Egypt. Re, symbolized by the sun, told the names of the creation to Thoth, symbolized by the moon, who by uttering them brought them into existence – the 'single act of adaptation'. The Wind is the goddess Nut, and the nurse is Earth, the god Geb, reversing as the ancient Egyptians did the familiar notion of mother earth and father sky.

At the same time, this would seem to be an alchemical allegory of the chemical wedding of the sun and the moon, Sol and Luna, who represent the universal male and female principles as well as gold and silver, sulphur and mercury. They produce the 'one thing', the power of which is perfect – the Philosopher's Stone . If cast on earth (*prima materia*) it dissolves it, separating the 'element of the Earth from that of Fire, the subtle from the gross'. In the process of distillation, it ascends to heaven (as vapour) and descends to earth (as sublimate). In addition, it unites through coagulation 'the force from things superior and things inferior', the great and the small.

Of course, the whole alchemical process of the transformation of the elements is a spiritual allegory, describing the separation of the soul from the body ('the subtle from the gross') and its transformation into a purer form. If the work is successful, you become enlightened: 'all obscurity will fly far from thee'.

What does the *Emerald Tablet* tell us about the nature of the Philosopher's Stone? It focuses the power of the universal mind, it is 'the strong fortitude of all strength, for it overcometh every subtle thing and doth penetrate every solid substance'. The alchemist thus mirrors the work of the Creator in the Creation; 'thus was the world created'. And if the alchemist can discover the Philosopher's Stone he or she will be able to achieve 'marvellous adaptations', not only with matter, but also with spirit, not only in the laboratory but in him or herself and in the world at large.

In a sense, the writing of the *Emerald Tablet* is an alchemical experiment itself. At the end, the Great Work is done. Thus Hermes finishes by saying: 'That which I had to say about the operation of the Sol is completed.'

Throughout the *Emerald Tablet* there is a deep awareness of the beauty and magnificence of the Creation. It celebrates 'all the works of wonder throughout the whole world' and 'the glory and the brightness of the whole world' which the enlightened and transformed person, awakened from the dark slumber of ignorance, freed from the dross of material things, will be able to contemplate. It charts the voyage of the soul as it returns to its divine ground across the sea of materiality.

The exact origins of the *Emerald Tablet* are not clear. One probably Jewish legend claims that it was discovered by Sara, the wife of Abraham, who entered a cave near Hebron after the Flood and found it engraved in Phoenician characters on an emerald plate held in the hands of the corpse of Hermes Trismegistus. Other European commentators in the Middle Ages ascribed it to Alexander the Great or to the Pythagorean sage Apollonius of Tyana, giving it a Greek rather than a Middle Eastern origin.[17] An Arabic writer, on the other hand, claims that there were three philosophers called Hermes, one who built the pyramids in Egypt (Thoth?), one who came from Babylon and who taught Pythagoras, and a third who lived in Egypt and wrote on alchemy. In fact, the 'three' Hermes would seem to describe the ancient origins, diffusion and continuity of the Hermetic tradition.

The exact date and authorship of the *Emerald Tablet* are also unknown. Apart from the abridged Arabic text of it discovered in the works ascribed to Jabir, a version came to light in *The Secret of Creation*, wrongly attributed to Apollonius of Tyana, which was written in the ninth century.[18] It was probably translated from Syriac but may have been based on a much earlier Greek original. Whatever the exact origins of the text, when it was translated into Latin by Hugh of Santillana in the twelfth century, it became the bible of the medieval alchemists in Europe. It remains the greatest document of the Hermetic tradition.

But where did all this leave me in my search for the Philosopher's Stone? I had heard again the elusive voice of Zosimus in the *Turba* that it 'is a stone and not a stone'. I had been told by the *Emerald Tablet* that 'it overcometh every subtle thing'. But would obscurity ever fly from me? Would I really be able to witness those 'marvellous adaptations' held tantalizingly before my vision? Would I ever on my journey find the Red Sulphur of Ibn 'Arabi and the divine light deep within myself? I decided to continue my quest amongst the extraordinary characters and arcane texts which brought alchemy from the Middle East to Europe in the twelfth century.

Part Five

The Green Lion:
Europe

30

The Wisest Philosophers in the World

I learned from my Arabian masters under the leading
of reason; you, however, captivated by the appearance of
authority, follow your halter. Since what else should authority be called than a halter?

Adelard of Bath

Alchemy clearly had a wide currency throughout the Islamic world.
Taken up from Egypt, developed in Iraq, Persia and Syria, it came to
fruition in Spain. For the Muslim natural philosophers, alchemy was
the key science since it was thought to open up all the mysteries of
Creation and to be the foundation of medicine.

The common language of Arabic meant that writers from different
nations could contribute to its development. Their innovations were
reflected in the technical terms the Muslims bestowed on alchemy.
Amongst substances, they gave words for alcohol (*al-kohl*, the powder
of antimony used to darken eyelids from Egyptian times), alkali (*al-
qali*, for plant ashes), usifur (*zanjifar*, for cinnabar), lacquer (*lac*, for
resin), elixir (*al-iksir*, in turn from the Greek *xerion* for medicine). For
alchemical apparatus, they bequeathed the words for athanor (*al-
tannur*, a furnace), aludel (*al-uthal*, a pear-shaped vessel) and alembic
(*al-anbiq*, the head of a still which in turn comes from *ambix*, Greek
for cup). Above all, the very word 'alchemy' came from the Arabic *al-
kemia*, the name for Egypt, the Black Land.

As alchemists, the Muslims were great optimists: if their experiments failed, it was not because of any inadequacy of their theory but
because not all of the conditions for their experiments were right.
These included the quality of the substances used, the favourable time,
the correct position of the stars and their worthiness as experimenters.

258 *The Green Lion*

At the same time, their observations on the progress of science offered solid grounds for their hopes. If grains of opaque sand could be transformed into clear glass, as the alchemists in Córdoba had shown, then it seemed reasonable to expect mercury could be transformed into silver or gold which appeared outwardly much more similar. Again, if human skill could produce iron and steel to different degrees of quality and purity why should it not be able to make gold which develops naturally in the earth?

The alchemists in the Islamic Empire had practised alchemy for 500 years before the Europeans. They not only translated the Greek texts from Alexandria and transmitted them to Europe, but made their own original and substantial contribution. European alchemy in the Middle Ages was thus entirely founded on the Islamic legacy which in turn was mainly based on ancient Egyptian sacred science. Although the early Islamic contacts with China had brought to light a great civilization and an awareness of another alchemical tradition, the Chinese had a minimal effect on the development of alchemy in Europe.

The eruption of Islamic alchemy in Europe was a complete novelty, a novelty which appeared to be full of promise as well as full of difficulty. Its practices offered new information about scientific instruments and its theory made available fresh knowledge about metals and minerals but its coded language undoubtedly acted as a barrier to the integration of learning.

The first mention of alchemy in the West is often taken to be in a passage from the chronicle *Adame de Brême*, reporting a fraudulent transmutation of gold to the Bishop of Hamburg around 1050 by a Byzantine Jew called Paul. But the first certain reference is to be found in a famous passage about Spanish gold in the *Diversarum Artium Schedula* ('Brief Description of Diverse Arts') written around 1225 in Saxony by the monk Theophile, the pseudonym of the Benedictine Roger de Helmarshausen. In the passage, he writes: 'There is also a gold called Spanish which is composed of red copper, basilic powder, human blood and vinegar.'[1] It is almost certainly a coded recipe. Human blood was probably liquid mercury taken from red cinnabar. To obtain basilic powder would have been more difficult: the basilisk was a fabulous reptile alleged to be hatched by a serpent from a cock's egg; its breath and even its look were considered fatal!

The first known Latin translation of an alchemical text also came from Spain. It was made by Robert of Chester who became Archdea-con of Pamplona. In 1141 he was asked by Peter the Venerable, the Abbot of Cluny, to translate the Qur'an into Latin which he did in two years with his friend Hermann of Carinthia. He went on to introduce a new branch of mathematics by translating the ninth-century Al-Khwarizmi's *Algebra* (from whose Arabic name comes the word 'algorithm'). He completed the translation of *The Book of the Composition of Alchemy* from Arabic into Latin on 11 February 1144 and called it the *Liber de Compositione Alchemiae de Morienus*. It could not have been a better choice to maintain the continuity of the Hermetic tradition from ancient Egypt for it contains the story of the first major Islamic alchemist Khalid ibn Yazid being taught by the Christian adept Morienus who had in turn been a pupil of Stephanus of Alexandria.

Recognizing that the Latin world knew nothing about alchemy, Robert of Chester explained:

> I have given this word [alchemy], although unknown and surpris-ing, so that it can be clarified by a definition. The philosopher Hermes and his successors define the word in the following manner, for example in the book of the transmutation of sub-stances: alchemy is a corporal substance taken from one and composed of one, joining between them substances most precious by affinity and effect, and by the same natural mixture, transform-ing them naturally into better substances. In the following, what we have said will be explained, and we will treat in detail its composition.[2]

Robert of Chester also notes that the word 'alchemy' was often called 'the Stone', but defines it as transmuted silver.

The work was sufficiently intriguing to excite a demand for any-thing on alchemy which the scholars who knew Arabic could translate. The trickle soon became a stream and then a flood. The fountainhead was at Toledo in central Spain. Under the Moors, it had been an important centre of learning. After Alfonso VI had captured the city in 1085, it became the capital of Castile but the population still contained many Muslims and Jews and the main language continued to be Arabic. Archbishop Raimundo set up the School of Translators in Toledo to transmit Arabic learning to the West. The Arabic-speaking Christians known as *mozarabes* – almost Arabs – joined their ranks.

Even more important were the Jewish translators who knew Arabic and Latin as well as Hebrew.[3] Daniel of Morley in Norfolk claimed that after finding the professors in Paris childish, in Toledo he came across 'the wisest philosophers in the world'. He returned to England with the abundant supply of precious texts which formed the basis of his own philosophy.

Wanting to find out more about this magical city, I travelled north from Andalusia to Toledo. In the late afternoon I entered the walled city on the hill by the *Puerta del Sol* (the Gateway of the Sun). It was a twelfth-century Moorish (*Mudejar*) gatehouse rebuilt in the fourteenth century by the Knights Hospitallers. The bright rays of the setting sun lit up the extraordinary symbols above the portico: a group of figures was carved within the unmistakable alchemical symbol of a triangle within a circle. Within the circle on the left-hand side was an image of the full sun and on the right an image of the crescent moon – Sol and Luna. As I entered I was acutely aware that many alchemical manuscripts had passed through the gate to transform the intellectual world of medieval Europe.

The Knights Hospitallers had renamed the nearby Bab al-Mardun mosque Cristo de la Luz church when the city fell to the Christians. Built in 1000, its graceful square building with nine doors reflected the chaste elegance of the Moorish way of life at the time.

I wondered where the famous 'Cave of Hercules' might be, which was said to contain fabulous treasures as well as the *Table of King Solomon* and the *Emerald Tablet*. I looked in vain for the underground laboratories of the alchemists, both Moorish and Jewish, which flourished in the twelfth and thirteenth centuries in the walled city. I did find, however, the daughter of the School of Translators in a palace in the labyrinth of cobbled streets of the old city.[4] When I asked the chief librarian Mariluz Comendador about the Arabic manuscripts, she said that most had been lost: 'After the conquest of Granada, the victors burned nearly all the manuscripts in public bonfires. From time to time a few Arabic or Hebrew texts hidden in walls and floors come to light. But most Arabic texts from this period can be found in Morroco, in Fez or Marrakesh.'

As I was about to leave, she said: 'Let me know if you find the *Piedra Filósofal*, the Philosopher's Stone. Everyone's looking for it!'

The greatest of the translators – certainly the most prolific – was Gerard of Cremona from Lombardy. He is said to have translated seventy-six books whilst residing in Toledo, including at least three books on alchemy: Jabir's *Book of Seventy*; *De Alumibus et Salibus*, a work on sulphates and salts re-edited in Spain in the spirit of Rhazes; and the *Liber Luminus Luminum*, an obscure work of occult theory. The Jewish scholar Avendauth of Toledo also translated *Kimya al-sa'ada* ('Alchemy of Happiness') by the Persian Sufi Muhammad Al-Ghazali (the Spinner). It was a great work of spiritual alchemy which became very popular in the Middle Ages. I took his point: 'Alchemical gold is better than gold, but real alchemists are rare, and so are true Sufis.' I also took heart from his observation: 'A man, then, who has a capacity for acceptance of a perfection of Being will prefer the contemplation of this. Even in the present life the happiness of the right-seekers is incomparably greater than can be imagined.'[5]

The fine tradition of learning continued in Toledo in the next century under Alfonso X, King of Castile and Leon. He was known as *el Sabio* ('the Wise') for his love of knowledge. He employed Jewish scholars to translate Arabic alchemical, astronomical and scientific texts into Castilian.[6] He was also responsible for the drawing up of lists of planetary movements by the two Jewish scholars Isaac Ibn Sid and Jehuda ben Moses Cohen, which came to be known as the *Alfonsine Tables*. They were not only consulted in alchemical and astrological work but also formed the foundation of modern scientific astronomy.

The freedom of enquiry, the mixing of Muslim, Jewish and Christian traditions, and the work in the 'occult arts' of alchemy and astrology earned Toledo a dubious reputation amongst Christian fanatics who began to seek out any signs of heresy. The Cistercian monk Helinando de Froidmont (d.c.1229) wrote: 'The clergy find in Paris liberal arts, in Orleans authors, in Bologna laws, in Salerno doctors of medicine, in Toledo demons and good customs nowhere.'[7]

*

The most influential work to emerge from Toledo was the *Picatrix, Libro de la Magia de los Signos*. It was a translation of the Arabic work called *Gayat al-hakim* ('The Final Aim of the Wise') attributed to the tenth-century alchemist Al-Majriti. Translated into Castilian in 1256 by order of Alfonso X, its Latin title *Picatrix* was probably a corruption of Hippocrates via the Arabic name Buqratis.[8] The work contains an exotic mix of incantations from many different sources, including Egyptian, Hebrew, Greek and Chaldean. It draws heavily on the astrology of the Sabeans of Harran and the philosophy of Hermes. Its author claims it is a compilation of 224 books of philosophy and magic which required seven years of study and meditation to assimilate. The work had a very wide readership throughout Europe and was hugely popular in magical circles during the Renaissance.[9] It was so well known that the French writer Rabelais in the sixteenth century jokingly wrote in his burlesque novel *Pantraguel*, 'the reverend father of the Devil Picatris, rector of the diabolical faculty of Toledo'.

The *Picatrix* is fundamentally a work of talismanic magic. Whereas in ordinary magic the magician has no need to call on any external aid, the magician using talismans seeks help from the spirits of the planets, the secrets of numbers, and the positions of the celestial spheres. Since rays from celestial bodies transmit power to objects, it was believed that careful rituals were necessary to ensure the transmission of their power into the talismans.

The adept in the *Picatrix* appears as a philosopher and a Perfect Man who combines a favourable birth, a competent education and ascetic training. His magic is the activation of the One and, by definition, is good. In this respect, it has nothing to do with devilish arts but seeks to co-ordinate actions within the general laws of nature. The skill of the magician is to discover the hidden secrets of nature and to direct them to beneficial ends. To the medieval mind the science of magic lay very close to the magic of science.[10] Indeed, medieval science was usually called 'natural magic' or 'natural philosophy'.

The *Picatrix* opens with the familiar Hermetic doctrines: there is One Truth and One Unity. Lower things are raised to higher things and higher things descend to lower things. Man is a little world mirroring the great world of the cosmos but through his intellect can raise himself above the seven heavens to reach God. The 'virtues' of the superior bodies (*spiritus*) are the form and power of the inferior bodies (*materia*).The art of magic is to channel the *spiritus* into the *materia*.

From an alchemical point of view, I found the most fascinating passage of the *Picatrix* in the fourth book. It relates to Hermes Trismegistus who is described as the first magician and the founder of a magical city in Egypt. Trismegistus appears in his triple role of Egyptian priest, philosopher and king and declares:

Hermes was the first who constructed images by means of which he knew how to regulate the Nile against the motion of the moon. This man also built a temple to the Sun, and he knew how to hide himself from all so that no one could see him, although he was within it. It was he, too, who in the east of Egypt constructed a City twelve miles long within which he constructed a castle which had four gates in each of its four parts. On the eastern gate he placed the form of an Eagle; on the western gate, the form of a Bull; on the southern gate, the form of a Lion; and on the northern gate he constructed the form of a god. Into these images he introduced spirits which spoke with voices, nor could anyone enter the gates of the City except by their permission. There he planted . . . a great tree which bore the fruit of all generations. On the summit of the castle he caused to be raised a tower thirty cubits high on the top of which he ordered to be placed a light-house [*rotunda*] the colour of which changed every day until the seventh day after which it returned to the first colour, and so the City was illuminated with these colours . . . The name of the city was Adocentyn.[11]

Did the statues above the four gates of the four directions represent the Egyptian gods Horus, Apis, Sekhmet, and Anubis respectively? Did the lighthouse, perhaps inspired by the ancient pharos of Alexandria, offer a permanent weekly light show of the stages of alchemy? Is the great tree the Tree of Life of the Cabala? Is the city a planned image of the world in which Hermes Trismegistus arranges the images from the lighthouse to channel the influences of the heavens so that the inhabitants live a healthy and virtuous life? The Hermetic Utopia harks back to memories of Heliopolis with its animal-shaped gods, living statues, and wonder-working priests.

*

Whilst researching the origins of the *Picatrix* in the New School of Translators in Toledo, the librarian placed in my hands an intriguing article about necromancy in the city.[12] It contained a reference to Wolfram von Eschenbach, the author of *Parzival*, the account of the Holy Grail which appeared from around 1200 to 1210. Wolfram claims that Chrétien de Troyes' version of the Grail story – *Le Roman de Perceval ou le conte du Graal* – was inaccurate and that he obtained the true story from one Kyot of Provence, who in turn received it from an adept called Flegetanis, a converted Jewish astrologer who lived in Toledo. Following up the lead, I read in Wolfram's *Parzival*:

> Flegetanis saw with his own eyes in the constellations things he was shy to talk about, hidden mysteries. He said that there was a thing called the Grail, whose name he had read clearly in the constellations. A host of angels left it on earth.
>
> Since then baptised men have had the task of guarding it, and with such chaste discipline that those who are called to the service of the Grail are always noble men. Thus wrote Flegetanis of these things.

Expressing the prevailing view of the Church in its struggle against Islam and Judaism, Wolfram writes that only by the sacramental force of baptism is it possible to decipher and correctly understand the secret of the Grail:

> Kyot, the well-known master, found in Toledo, discarded, set down in heathen writing [i.e. Arabic] the first source of this adventure. He first had to learn the abc's, but without the art of black magic . . .[13]

The fact that the story of the Grail was found in Toledo, the point of contact between the East and the West, Islam, Judaism and Christianity, suggests a Middle Eastern origin of the Grail legend. As an alchemical ritual connected with the cycle of the seasons, death and rebirth, and renewal of the year, the story has a direct echo of the drama of Osiris in the Underworld.

The connection between the Grail and alchemy became even more intriguing when I discovered that Wolfram describes the Grail directly in terms of the Philosopher's Stone. When it first appears during Parzival's stay in the Fisher King's Castle, it is vaguely called 'a thing called the Grail, which surpasses all earthly perfection'. It brings healing and food to those who touch it and can be found only by the absolutely pure. When I came to the description given by Parzival's uncle, a hermit, I was astonished to read:

> Well I know that many brave knights dwell with the Grail at Munsalvaesche. Always when they ride out, as they often do, it is to seek adventure. They do so for their sins, these templars, whether their reward be defeat or victory. A valiant host lives

there, and I will tell you how they are sustained. They live from a stone of the purest kind. If you do not know it, it shall here be named to you. It is called *lapsit exillis*. By the power of that stone the phoenix burns to ashes, but the ashes give him life again. Thus does the phoenix molt and change its plumage, which afterwards is bright and shining and as lovely as before. There never was a human so ill but that, if he one day sees that stone, he cannot die within the week that follows. And in looks he will not fade. His appearance will stay the same, be it maid or man, as on the day he saw the stone, the same as when the best years of his life began, and though he should see the stone for two hundred years, it will never change, save that his hair might perhaps turn grey. Such power does the stone give a man that flesh and bones are at once made young again. The stone is also called the Grail.[14]

The phrase *lapsit exillis* could be a corruption of *lapis ex caelis*, meaning 'a stone from the heavens', but the whole passage, with the symbol of the phoenix for rebirth and the Grail's ability to prolong life, point clearly to the *lapis elixir*, the Philosopher's Stone.[15]

The Explosion in the Cathedral

The infinite ocean of eternal light and luminous eternity.

Bernard, Abbot of Clairvaux

In my research into the possible Arabic source of the Grail legend and its link with the Philosopher's Stone, I was intrigued to find out that the Grail was protected by the Templars in the Wolfram von Eschenbach version. Another anonymous Grail romance known as *Perlesvaus*, written between 1190 and 1212, has much more direct alchemical symbolism. During his travels, Percival is received in a mysterious castle by two 'masters' who clap their hands to call thirty-three other 'initiates' who are of the same age and are clad in white garments with a red cross on their breasts. They recall the Order of the Knights Templar; indeed the tale may well have been written by a Knight Templar.[1]

The Templars have long been a mysterious and shadowy presence in the Hermetic tradition. It would seem that with the Moors they played an important role in transmitting ancient alchemical knowledge from the Middle East to Europe during the early twelfth century. And they may well have made a crucial contribution to the sudden and explosive development of the Gothic cathedral. After Spain, I travelled to France to find out more.

The Gothic appeared in France after the First Crusade; more specifically, after the return in 1128 of six or more of the original nine Knights Templar from Jerusalem. Abbot Suger of St Denis built the first Gothic vault on the Romanesque foundations of his abbey. The cathedrals of Notre Dame in Chartres and Paris followed soon after. This implies that there was a Gothic 'school' of building which spread

12. Lady Tai with her attendants receiving immortal envoys. Detail from the painted silk banner buried in her coffin around 186 BC.

13. Taoist monk tends an incense burner outside a pavilion in the White Cloud Temple, Beijing. Many of the monks are practising alchemists.

14. Pharaoh with Thoth, the ibis-headed god of wisdom and the legendary father of alchemy, known to the Greeks as Hermes. Temple of Seti I, Abydos, Egypt. Nineteenth dynasty (1306–1290 BC).

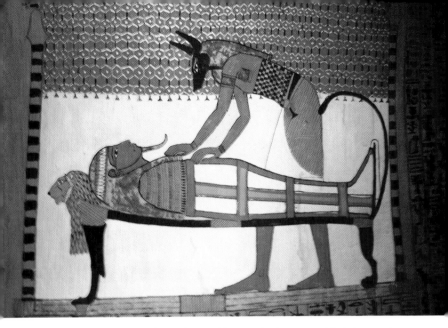

15. Anubis, guide to the Underworld, attends the mummified deceased. Tomb of Sennofer, Valley of the Nobles, West Bank, Luxor. Eighteenth dynasty (1427–01 BC).

16. The solid gold funerary mask of Tutankhamon, inlaid with semi-precious stones and coloured glass. A spell from *The Egyptian Book of the Dead* is engraved on the back of the shoulders to ensure immortality. Eighteenth dynasty (1333–23 BC).

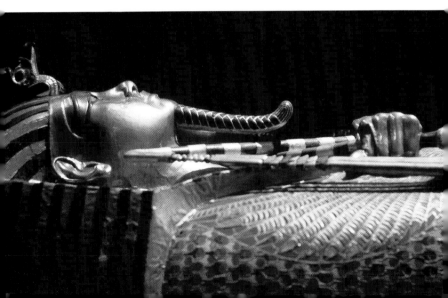

17. Tantric practitioners raising kundalini energy depicted on the outside wall of the eleventh-century Kandariya Mahadev Temple in Khajuraho, India.

18. Modern shrine of Shiva, god of destruction and key figure with his consort Shakti in the Hindu tradition of spiritual alchemy.

19. Marble floor panel of 'Hermes, Mercurius Trimegistus, Contemporaneus Moysi' laid by Giovanni de Stefano in 1488 on the threshold of Siena Cathedral. Hermes Trismegistus, dressed as an Oriental sage, offers an open book to two philosophers. He rests his hand upon a tablet supported by two winged sphinxes which declares that the wisdom of Egypt has a divine origin.

20. *The Alchymist in Search of the Philosopher's Stone* (1771 & 1795)
by Joseph Wright. The German alchemist Hennig Brandt discovered
phosphorus in 1669 whilst mixing gold with an extract of urine.

throughout Europe from its centre at St Denis after the return of the Knights Templar.[2]

The nine original Knights Templar ostensibly travelled in 1118 to the Holy Land to offer their services to King Baldwin II of Jerusalem to secure the safety of the routes for the pilgrims. But why should they want to do this since the task was already being performed by the Order of Hospitallers of Saint John of Jerusalem?

Baldwin lodged them in the mosque called Masjid-el-Aksa built in the wing of his palace on the original site of the Temple of Solomon. It was for this reason that they were called Knights of the Temple or Templars. After pondering on these curious facts for some time, I felt sure that the protection of the highways was a smokescreen, and that the real mission of the Templars was to search for the wisdom of Solomon in the tables of the law which had once been housed in his temple in Jerusalem.

*

It is written in Exodus 31.18 that God gave the tables of the law to Moses on Mount Sinai – 'two tables of testimony, tables of stone, written with the finger of God'. But when Moses came down from the mountain, he found the people making sacrifices to the Golden Calf. Furious, he smashed the tables, reduced the calf to powder, spread the powder on water and made the people drink it. He performed in fact what alchemists, East and West, have done in their attempt to find an elixir in potable gold. But the result did not prolong life but created a thirst for gold.

This was not the end of it. When the anger of Moses and God subsided, fresh tables were 'written on both their sides' and hidden in the Ark of the Covenant. Could it be that these tables of the divine law contained the laws of measure, relationship and number mentioned in Genesis? To know the tables would thus be to know the divine law of unity and its system of proportions which holds the cosmos together.

The statement that the 'laws' were written 'on both their sides' of the stone suggests that they had an exoteric and esoteric meaning to them. Even more interesting is the fact that medieval alchemists held Moses as well as Hermes to be one of their fathers. Moses himself came from Egypt, leading the Israelites out of captivity to the Promised Land. He was 'learned in all the wisdom of the Egyptians' (Acts 7.22).

He would therefore have inherited the Hermetic sacred science from the priests of the Egyptian temples.

King David, of course, later ordered Solomon to build the Temple to house the Ark of the Covenant and the secret knowledge it contained. Solomon, also acknowledged with Moses as a father of alchemy in the Middle Ages, was a 'strong man'. As it is written in I Kings 4.29–31:

> And God gave Solomon wisdom and understanding exceeding much, and largeness of heart, even as the sand that is on the sea shore. And Solomon's wisdom excelled the wisdom of all the children of the east country, and all the wisdom of Egypt. For he was wiser than all men . . .

Solomon possessed the Tables and Aaron's rod, and as a sage and initiate versed in the wisdom of the Egyptians, he could decipher the divine law of perfect proportion. His building of the Temple to house the Ark of the Covenant assumed knowledge of cosmic standards of measurement. And to complete the building he addressed himself to Hiram, King of Tyre, for Phoenician builders who probably drew their knowledge from the Egyptian temples.

The last reference to the Ark after it was placed in the 'most Holy place' is in I Kings 8.12–13:

> Then spake Solomon, the Lord said that he would dwell in the thick darkness. I have surely built thee an house to dwell in, a settled place for thee to abide in for ever.

It was widely assumed that when Nebuchadnezzar took Jerusalem in 587 BC he burned down the Temple and the Ark with it. But could the Ark of the Covenant have been buried during the siege before the final onslaught?

If so, the journey of the Knights Templar to Jerusalem and their billeting in the mosque on the site of Solomon's Temple raise many intriguing questions. Did they find the tables placed in the Ark of the Covenant on the site of the Temple of Solomon and return with the sacred knowledge of number and measure and weight to France? Was it this knowledge which enabled the Gothic cathedral to take off so quickly and so superbly? We shall never know for certain, but the connections and repercussions are endlessly fascinating.[3]

Abbot Suger, who built the first Gothic building at St Denis, admitted that apart from the Hagia Sophia in Constantinople his source of inspiration was the Temple of Solomon.[4] Moreover, Adelard of Bath, who was linked with the School of Chartres, called Solomon's Temple God's 'regal palace' and as such, the image of the heavenly Jerusalem.[5] He argued that its dimensions, given in I Kings 6, were as much pervaded by divine harmony as the celestial spheres. He further suggested that the proportions were those of the musical consonances and it was this 'symphonic perfection' that made it an image of heaven.

Solomon left a commentary in ciphers on the divine laws in the form of 'The Song of the Songs'. Is it a coincidence that the work inspired 120 of the sermons of Bernard of Clairvaux? It was Bernard who established the Order of the Knights Templar, whose first name was *Templum Salomonis*, or Solomon's Temple. He also founded the Order of the Temple of Solomon, which included monks, soldiers and craftsmen, and his Cistercians instructed the building fraternity called the 'Children of Solomon'. These were the first guilds of masons which later developed into the Freemasons.

*

As I deepened my research into the origins of the Gothic, I came across another deep enigma. How did a small town like Chartres, with only 20,000 inhabitants, manage to raise enough money to pay for the building of the cathedral? Were the Knights Templar behind it? And did alchemy contribute to their enormous wealth in any way?

Although the Templars vowed not to own property (*sine proprio*), this did not mean that they were poor. Far from it. Indeed, the order amassed vast riches – so much so that they were seen as a threat to the French monarchy and were suppressed by King Philippe IV in 1307. The order received wealth but never gave, 'not a section of wall nor an inch of ground'. They protected the routes in France, set up tolls, and farmed great tracts of land. Moreover, they were not liable to taxes or tithes. They also acted as bankers and treasurers. But was this their sole source of wealth? The knowledge they acquired during their stay in Jerusalem may well have included the secrets of making alchemical gold.

There can be no doubt that many Templars studied the secrets of the Great Work. They were also exposed to the Hermetic tradition through their contact with dissident Muslim sects during their stay in Jerusalem. It would seem that they knew the Order of Assassins, so nicknamed by the Crusaders because of their fearlessness, partly inspired no doubt by their practice of smoking hashish before going into battle. The Muslim orthodox waged war on them for their mystical pantheism. The Assassins may well have been the source of some of the heretical beliefs of the Templars.[6]

Among the many accusations levelled against them was the denial of Christ and defiling the Cross, adoring an idol called Baphomet, immorality and ritual kissing, and perverting the sacrament. 'They have a chamber, or cave', it was reported, 'excavated in the ground, very dark, where they have an image in the form of a man, over which is a human skin, and shining carbuncles for its eyes.'[7]

Baphomet has often been identified as Muhammad but it is more likely that he stood for 'the God within' in keeping with the Hermetic doctrine of the microcosm mirroring the macrocosm. The word 'Baphomet' may be traced to two Greek words meaning Baptism of Wisdom.[8] It would seem that, in common with Hermetic texts and alchemy, they believed in the possibility of becoming godlike. Indeed, they may well have discovered the Gnostic Dead Sea Scrolls and the Hermetic Nag Hammadi texts which supported the view that Christ was not the 'crucified one'.

The Knights Templar were not the only ones interested in the new alchemical knowledge held by the Muslims. The Cluniac Order, founded in Burgundy in 810 by twelve Benedictine monks, also made its own contacts. Following the launch of the First Crusade in 1095, and during the building of the Gothic cathedrals, Peter the Venerable dreamt of uniting the religions of the Christians, Muslims and Jews into a Hermetic philosophy. He not only got Robert of Chester to translate the Qur'an but also consulted converted Jewish scholars about the Talmud.

Although Bernard of Clairvaux opposed him, Peter had the backing of Abbot Suger. They were deeply interested in news of the Hermetic tradition which was emerging from their contacts with the Muslim world in the Holy Land, Sicily and Spain. Peter built up a vast collection of manuscripts in Greek, Latin, Hebrew and Arabic known as the *Cluniac Corpus*. The Cluniac Order spread rapidly from Spain to Poland, disseminating much of this esoteric and alchemical knowledge through its string of monasteries.

*

These connections fired my imagination, and I was determined to find out more about the link between alchemy, the Philosopher's Stone and the Gothic. Unfortunately the great Gothic cathedral at Cluny was destroyed during the French Revolution. I therefore decided to go to Chartres. I had a hunch that the message of alchemy was written in stone in the Gothic cathedrals, an ideal medium for the vast majority of people who could not read at the time.

As I travelled across the flat and featureless plains of Champagne, two sharp arrows suddenly appeared on the grey horizon, shooting up into the dark and menacing sky. Then it came into view, the Cathedral of Chartres, with its turquoise roof and two great western towers. Only when we were nearly upon it did it become clear that the Cathedral of Chartres was built on a small hill surrounded by a town.

It was late October and cold rains swept in from the north. In the deserted square, I walked slowly in an anticlockwise direction around the great cathedral, with its delicate flying buttresses, great rose windows and lancets, and enigmatic figures carved on its portals. I noted that the roses mirrored the three main stages of alchemy and reflected the nature of the alchemical process itself. The roses unfold in a circular progression from the northern shadows which represent the initial black stage, to the southern light which symbolizes the middle white stage, to the final red of the western sunset.

I entered the cathedral from the western 'Royal Portal' – the most beautiful of all medieval facades. In the silent gloom of the vast building, I was overwhelmed by the coloured light which swirled around the higher parts of the vault in a dance of light and space. The walls of the cathedral seemed translucent, the roof floating, as if held up by air rather than stone. The stained-glass windows, with their famous reds and blues, seemed to glow with their own inner luminosity.

Was Chartres an alchemical experiment in stone? As a means of transforming the human soul, did it work in the same way as the Philosopher's Stone?

There are many enigmas in Chartres: the black Madonna in the crypt which local chronicles say was an ancient statuette of Isis sculpted before Christ and may represent the *prima materia* of the Great Work; the nail in a flagstone in the southern transept which is lit up by a shaft of light through a small hole in a stained-glass window on the summer solstice; the 2,000-year-old veil in the treasury, said to have been worn by Mary when giving birth. It was sent from Constantinople as a gift to Charlemagne and given by his grandson Charles the Bald in 876 to the original church at Chartres.[9]

Then there is the labyrinth, the largest and best preserved in medieval France. It would seem the master builder used the labyrinth as a mathematical key to decide the plan, measurements and proportions of the whole cathedral. The diameter of the labyrinth, for instance, is equal to a tenth of the interior length of the whole building. The distance is the same from the centre of the labyrinth to the centre of the transept and from there to the end of the four columns of the choir.[10]

A copper plaque in the centre of the labyrinth used to say that it represented the labyrinth of Theseus and the Minotaur. But the labyrinth is clearly symbolic of the pilgrim travelling in this world towards the celestial Jerusalem. Where the pagan labyrinth represented the deceased in the Underworld seeking paradise, for Christians it came to mean the world through which they wander in order to reach heaven. Early pilgrims walked around the labyrinth on their knees. For this reason, the Renaissance Hermetic philosopher Comenius entitled his work *The Labyrinth of this World and the Paradise of the Heart.*

The symbolism of the labyrinth is undoubtedly alchemical. The path is complicated and requires perseverance. It is best taken in rhythm for it forms a dance pattern inscribed on the ground. The person who reaches the centre of the labyrinth is transformed by the process. At the same time, there is a direct path to and from the centre of the labyrinth, just as there is a wet and dry path in alchemy and a gradual and sudden path to enlightenment in Zen.

The labyrinth is thus symbolic of the whole labour of the Work, with its main obstacles to overcome, especially the fight with the fabulous beast, all of which cannot be achieved without Ariadne's thread of special wisdom.

*

For all these enigmas, the greatest mystery at Chartres still remains the origins of the cathedral itself. It was built out of the ashes of the old Romanesque cathedral after the fire of 1194 and completed in less than thirty years. Within a year, the ground plan, the material, the labour force and the finance were in place. Funds poured in. In a great surge of energy, thousands of labourers, chanting and praying, dragged carts carrying stones from limestone quarries 5 miles away. Aristocrats, wealthy citizens, and merchant confraternities sponsored windows. And there in the background was the support of the Knights Templar.

Although many aspects associated with the Gothic were already developed – the pointed arch, the great height, the cross-ribbed vault, flying buttresses, the wide window, the tall clerestory and the tracery – they came together in Chartres in a unique way. It was one of those rare moments in history when the technical engineering, the architectural vision, the spiritual life and the energy of thousands all fused in a coherent whole. It is for the balance of its parts and its supreme simplicity that Chartres is the most perfect cathedral ever created.

One aspect was entirely new: the use of light. It was not merely for ornament since beauty was perceived by contemporary scholars as the *splendor veritatis*, the radiance of truth. Chartres in fact was a place of great learning, especially since Bishop Fulbert had founded the Chartres Cathedral School in 990. It seems unlikely that Gothic art would have come into existence without the Hermetic cosmology cultivated at Chartres. The masters of Chartres discovered in the Arabic literature of Spain and the Maghreb many aspects of ancient thinking and science which were hitherto unknown in Europe.[11] The brilliant scholar Bernard of Chartres acknowledged that his contemporaries were 'dwarfs sitting on the shoulders of giants, the ancients'. Although we might be able to see further, without the philosophers of antiquity, we would be nothing.

Bernard's younger brother, Thierry of Chartres, compiled an encyclopaedia of the Seven Liberal Arts, four of which were concerned with matter and three with spirit. On the right bay of the Royal Portal of the cathedral, surrounding the black Madonna, I saw carvings of these seven arts and the authors who best represent them from the classical world: Geometry and Euclid, Rhetoric and Cicero, Dialectic and Aristotle, Arithmetic and Boethius, Astronomy and Ptolemy, Grammar and Donatus, and Music and Pythagoras. On the left bay, the signs of the zodiac surround a carving of Christ ascending. Classical learning is recognized and incorporated at the entrance and in the heart of the great Gothic cathedral at the centre of Europe.

To the philosophers of Chartres, God appeared as the great architect who created the cosmos out of the prime chaos of matter according to 'measure, number and weight' in perfect proportions. The world was thus a work of architecture. God had provided its sacred proportions to Noah for his Ark, to Moses for the Tabernacle, to Solomon for the Temple. The human architect could therefore discover and emulate them, and thereby create a building in the image of heaven. The builders of Chartres Cathedral thus attempted to imitate the Temple of Solomon in its perfect proportions. In doing so, they believed they were giving a model of the inner nature of reality itself. They exemplified the 'measure, number and weight' which Thierry of Chartres saw in the primordial principle of Creation.

The proportions throughout the cathedral are extraordinary and they all interrelate as one harmonious whole. This is because the overall design was determined from the first parts laid out. The width of the window openings, for instance, was made the same as the thickness of the piers, thereby creating a kind of a contrapuntal harmony down the nave. Another example is the spaces in the aisle. The voids of the aisle, measured between the piers on one side and between pier and wall shafts on the other, relate in the proportion of the Golden Mean – the ratio said to underlie the proportions of most growing things.[12]

I suspected that the harmonious proportions reflected a continuous tradition – the Hermetic tradition – of sacred science inherited by Europe from Egypt via the Middle East at the time of the building of the Gothic cathedrals. It is a tradition which Solomon took from the Egyptian priests and which the Knights Templar may well have uncovered during their sojourn in Jerusalem.

Just like the Great Pyramid, Chartres Cathedral appeared to me to be a finely tuned musical instrument with many resonances. Goethe once called architecture 'frozen music'; in the case of Chartres, it is a living symphony of light and music and stone. It is indeed the very image of heaven.

*

For me the defining characteristic and the glory of Chartres was the light. The thirteenth-century alchemist Robert Grosseteste maintained that the beauty of light is due to its simplicity and, like unison in music, is 'most harmoniously related to itself by ratio of equality'. St Bernard, too, described the mystical union with God as the 'immersion in the infinite ocean of eternal light and luminous eternity'.[13]

The stained-glass windows of Chartres turn the cathedral into a living jewel. Light does not so much pass through them but rather radiates from within. The windows show a double transmutation: of matter by the fire of the furnace in their manufacture and, once in place, the transmutation of the cathedral by the fire of the sun. The same *spiritus mundi* which the alchemists saw as 'staining' their substances with different colours seems to be present in the stained glass of the windows of Chartres.

True stained glass first emerged in Persia towards the eleventh century and came from the laboratories of the Muslim alchemists. In Europe, it appeared suddenly in the first quarter of the twelfth century. It was first used in the Abbey St Denis, the birthplace of the Gothic, after repairs were made to the basilica. For a while all windows of this quality were gifts from Abbot Suger. But it was not long before the centre of stained-glass-making shifted from St Denis to Chartres which in turn produced them for the cathedrals at Sens, Paris, Rouen and Bourges. Towards 1140 the source of the stained glass at Chartres mysteriously began to dry up. Was this due to the disappearance of the master glazier-alchemist who felt he had completed his Work?

According to a twelfth-century German monk called Theophilus (lover of God), the glass was made from one part river sand to two parts pot-ash of dried beechwood.[14] The rich iridescent colours were created by adding metal oxides. Purple was obtained from manganese oxide, yellow from soot or sulphur, green from iron oxide, and the ruby red from copper oxide. All these would not have been found without the activities of the alchemists. The famous blues of Chartres were produced partly from cobalt oxide but no one has been able to reproduce the peculiarly luminous quality which makes the glass glow from within.

What was the source of the secret recipe used by Abbot Suger's master glazier? It may well have been the same source as the knowledge of Gothic building itself – documents taken from Jerusalem by the Knights Templar who had been in clandestine contact with adepts in the Middle East.

*

There were other enigmas at Chartres which enthralled me. Could it be that the return of the Templar Hugues de Payns and at least six of his fellow knights escorting a very precious object from Jerusalem in 1128 is portrayed on the north porch of Chartres known as the 'Door of the Initiates'? One small column carved in relief would seem to show the transport of the Ark in a cart drawn by a couple of oxen. It has the description *Archa cederis* – 'You are to work through the Ark.' Another portrays a man covering the Ark with a veil, near a heap of corpses amongst whom is a knight in a coat of mail. It has the inscription *Hic amititur Archa cederis* which means: 'Here things take their course; you are to work through the Ark.'[15]

On the same 'Door of the Initiates', St Anne, who has a black face and carries a fleur-de-lys, is surrounded by renowned adepts of the Old Testament. These include Melchizedek, the Chaldean magus who passed to Abraham the Grail chalice; Aaron, the Egyptian magus, 'brother' of Moses, who erected the Golden Calf in the desert; and David, the musician-king who was inspired by the Ark which contained the tables of divine law. And there again is Solomon, the builder of the Temple of Jerusalem, wiser than Moses and full of all the wisdom of Egypt.

The carving of St John the Baptist carrying a lamb on the same door has been called 'perhaps the most moving image of this saint in Christian art'.[16] But why does the figure crush a dragon with his bare feet? It would seem to be an alchemical allegory showing how the energy of prime matter, represented by the dragon, can be transformed into spirit, symbolized by the saint.

*

As the dark winter evening drew in, I pondered on these matters in front of the west rose window which appeared like a great coloured mandala. Its subject is the Last Judgement. Christ is at the centre surrounded by the first series of petals, containing eight angels. They are placed in pairs between four apocalyptic animals who represent the four evangelists at the cardinal points. Quietly focusing my gaze on the whole rose, a sense of calm and peace descended on me. The darkening gloom of the church was suffused by a deep blue from on high. I was within the womb of a mysterious and beautiful creature, gently breathing, emanating a diaphanous light. The interior was as dark as moonlight. I realized that in the pillars, arches and buttresses of the cathedral energy was not only descending but also rising as the breath within me. It circulated around the building and through my being.

Then quite unannounced, the rose was transformed. Its luminous blues suddenly broke into a rainbow of colour created by the bright rays emanating from the setting sun behind the dark winter clouds. The cathedral, and I within it, were transfigured. The finely tuned building, a symphony of stone, light and sound, came together in that sudden and unexpected epiphany. The masons and glaziers had attained the end of their Great Work with the divine help of the source of all energy and life: the sun.

In that moment it became clear that the cathedral was the symbol of heaven on earth: As above, so below. The spiritual end of alchemy and of the Gothic cathedral are the same: to enable the seeker to leave the labyrinth of this world and to pass through the celestial gates into the light of heaven.

32

The Mirror of Nature

Then bring the elements into balance and you will have it.

Roger Bacon

Having studied the transmission of alchemy to Europe and the link with the Gothic cathedrals and Templars, I began next in my quest for the Philosopher's Stone to pore over the histories and texts of early Western alchemy. As I had found out in Spain, alchemy had not existed in Europe outside Islamic Spain and Sicily before the first translations from Arabic into Latin in the twelfth century.

At first compilers were largely content to classify and edit the new material from Islam. The scholar Vincent de Beauvais (c.1190–1264), a Dominican who was librarian and chaplain to Louis IX and tutor to his two sons, was much admired by later alchemists. His major work *Speculum Maius* ('The Greater Mirror') was intended to summarize existing knowledge. For his account of alchemy, he mainly drew on Rhazes and accepted the Muslim sulphur-mercury theory of metals. Bartholomew the English (Bartholomaeus Anglicus), a Franciscan who studied at Oxford in the first half of the thirteenth century, mentions alchemy in his widely circulated encyclopaedia *De Proprietatibus Rerum* ('On the Properties of Things'). It declares that mercury is the element common to all metals and is made from heating 'minium' which is cinnabar.

While Bartholomew and de Beauvais were compilers and introduced alchemy to a Christian audience, they added little new. But it was not long before European philosophers began to make their own discoveries and adapt alchemy to Christian theology. Roger Bacon (c.1220–92) dominated the intellectual landscape of the thirteenth century in Europe. His reputation as a magician earned him the title Dr Mirabilis.

Born in Somerset, Bacon went to Oxford to study Greek. There he came under the influence of the alchemist Robert Grosseteste, Chancellor of Oxford and Bishop of Lincoln, who had probably studied with Bartholomew and was reported to have a talking bronze head. His laboratory tower in Oxford stood, not inappropriately, on Folly Bridge, combining the elements of earth, water, fire and air. Around 1257, he joined the Franciscan Order. He lectured at the University of Paris and went to Spain, where he read the works of Jabir and met Sufi masters. He later returned to Oxford where he fell out with the authorities for his independent thinking. After spending more than £2,000 on *libros secretos* (occult books) and instruments, he had to abandon his researches because of his lack of funds. But he still felt it was worthwhile.

In his *Opus Maius* (1268, 'The Greater Work'), Bacon attempted a new classification of science and a new method based on 'experience' rather than 'argument': 'There are two modes of knowledge, through argument and experience. Argument brings conclusions and compels us to concede them, but it does not cause certainty nor remove doubts in order that the mind may rest in truth, unless this is provided by experience.'[1] Although Bacon's experimental approach is usually seen as a precursor of the modern scientific method, his much-vaunted 'experience' is more akin to Sufi gnosis, involving divine inspiration and spiritual intuition. The experimenter is never outside the experiment. He considered this kind of mystical experience to be 'much better' than the experience of philosophy or science.

Bacon believed that the ancients had made great achievements in technology and saw no reason why the moderns should not emulate if not surpass them. In his *De Mirabili Potestate Artis et Naturae* ('On the Wonderful Power of Art and Nature'), published in 1542, Bacon defines alchemy as the 'Science of a certain Medicine or Elixir'. Adopting the mystifying style of the Islamic masters whom he read in the original Arabic, he gives an alchemical recipe in the form of a conundrum:

Take salt and rub it diligently with water, and purify it in other waters. Afterwards by diverse contritions, rub it with salts and burn it with sundry assation, that it may be made a pure earth,

separate from other elements. Understand me, if thou art able, for
it shall be composed undoubtedly of the elements, and therefore it
shall be a part of the Stone which is no Stone and is in every man;
which thou shalt find at all times of the year in its own place.[2]

In his *Opus Tertium* ('The Third Work'), he defines alchemy as part of
'experimental science' and distinguishes between 'speculative' and
'practical' alchemy. The former 'treats of the generation of things from
the elements and of all inanimate things and of simple and composite
humours, of common stones, gems, marbles, of gold and other metals,
of sulphurs and salts and pigments, of lapis lazuli and minium and
other colours, of oils and burning bitumens and other things without
limit, concerning which we have nothing in the books of Aristotle'.

Practical alchemy is more important than all the other sciences
because it brings greater material benefits, especially in medicine. It
teaches how 'to make the noble metals, and colours, and many other
things better or more abundantly by art than they are made in nature'
as well as 'how to discover such things as are capable of prolonging
human life for much longer periods than can be accomplished by
nature'.[3] It therefore confirms theoretical alchemy through its works
and supports natural philosophy and medicine as can be seen in the
books of physicians. Bacon's interest in prolonging life – what he
called 'The glory of going on and still to be' – was a new development
in European alchemy and only later became a major concern.

Before abandoning my studies of Bacon, I came across a fascinating
reference to alchemy in Rhazes' *Secretum Secretorum* which Bacon
lovingly edited. In a long note to the manuscript, he observes: 'All
writers, because of the greatness of the secrets, conceal the science of
alchemy in words and metaphors and figurative work, and God
inspires them to this so that only the most wise and good men perceive
it achieving the good of the republic. So the *Lapis* is to be taken first
of all metaphorice, for that upon which the *operacio alchimica* works.'

He then goes on to say that the alchemical process can operate on

mineral things, like sulphur and arsenic, but better is the vegetable
realm, like fruits and parts of trees and herbs, and especially the
parts of man, amongst these blood, in which four humours are
distinguished to the eye: flegm, cholera, blood and melancholia.
The alchemist, then, seeks to separate these humours in turn and
to purge one from the other. And when through difficult works

they are reduced to their pure simplicity, then they are mixed in a secret proportion and most certain; to which is added quicksilver after it is mortified and sublimated several times . . . And then it is projected onto the baser metals liquefied and becomes nobler. But in all this are most difficult works only the wisest and happiest can attain.[4]

Even if I did accept his view that the parts of man were the best ingredients to work on, the problem remained with that 'secret proportion and most certain'. Moreover, I did not think I was yet capable of joining the ranks of the 'wisest and happiest'. My researches had so far directed me in favour of mineral substances as the most likely source of the Philosopher's Stone, but the conviction of such a great natural philosopher as Bacon was both revealing and inspiring.

The Renaissance alchemists greatly honoured Bacon as a precursor. Some thirty alchemical works are attributed to him, including one called the *Speculum Alchimiae* which was translated into English by Ralph Rabbards in 1597 as *The Mirror of Alchimy*. In his *Symbola Aureae Mensae* ('Symbols of Gold'), published in Frankfurt in 1617, Michael Maier depicted Roger Bacon as a hooded friar holding a large pair of scales, with water on one side and fire on the other. The caption reads: 'Bring the elements into balance and you will have it [the Philosopher's Stone].' If only it were so easy.

*

Impressed by Bacon, I turned with great eagerness to Albertus Magnus, the other outstanding mind of the thirteenth century, who earned such a reputation for knowledge that he was called Dr Universalis. Born in Lauingen in Swabia probably in 1193, the young Count of Bollstädt became a member of the Dominican Order at Padua. He went on to become Bishop of Ratisbon in 1262 only to retire soon after to a cloister in Cologne where he remained until his death in 1280. Practising voluntary poverty, he often walked barefoot during his official journeys.

Although a great admirer of Aristotle, Albertus recognized that knowledge advanced. He took a great interest in natural science, adopting a strongly empirical approach. He claims to have witnessed the following experiment:

An emerald was recently seen among us, small in size but marvellous in beauty. When its virtue was to be tested, someone stepped forth and said that, if a circle was made about a toad with the emerald and then the stone was set before the toad's eyes, one of two things would happen. Either the stone, if of weak virtue, would be broken by the gaze of the toad; or the toad would burst, if the stone was possessed of full natural vigour. Without delay things were arranged as he bade; and after a short lapse of time, during which the toad kept its eye unswervingly upon the gem, the latter began to crack like a nut and a portion of it flew from the ring. Then the toad, which had stood immovable hitherto, withdrew as if it had been freed from the influence of the gem.[5]

In his *Book on Minerals*, Albertus Magnus mentions visiting alchemical laboratories. In his view, alchemy cannot change species but only imitates them. He personally tested alchemical gold and found that after six or seven ignitions it was converted into powder.[6] While apparently accepting the possibility of transmutation, he admitted that he never saw it successfully performed himself.

Many alchemical manuscripts were attributed to Albertus, including *Libellus de Alchimia* ('The Little Book of Alchemy'), also know as the *Semita Recta* ('The Straight Path'). Although I could not find the quote in my Bible the preface allegedly cites Ecclesiastes: 'All wisdom is from the Lord God, and hath been always with Him, and is before all time.'[7] The author supports his divine inspiration by travelling throughout Christendom and the Middle East, consulting Arabs and Jews alike. He also claims to have witnessed many alchemical experiments – 'decoctions, sublimations, solutions, and distillations'. The standard Islamic theory of the generation of metals is given. Gold results from the combination of red sulphur and mercury, while silver can be made with white sulphur and mercury. The resulting alchemical metals are 'the equal of natural metals in almost all their qualities and effects'.[8]

Like Bacon, Albertus was celebrated as a great forbear by Renaissance alchemists. In his *Symbola Aureae Mensae* (1619), Michael Maier depicts him with his bishop's staff and hat pointing to a naked hermaphrodite with two heads, explicitly showing both sexual organs, with the motto: 'All are united in one, which is divided into two parts.'

*

I was intrigued to learn that the most famous pupil of Albertus Magnus was St Thomas Aquinas (1225–74), the Dominican friar and philosopher, who believed in the possibility of the transmutation of metals 'by true alchemical art'. According to tradition, Albertus owned a talking head of brass, recalling the Egyptian belief in living statues, but Aquinas smashed it because it disturbed his studies. Sir Thomas Browne in his *Religio Medici* ('A Doctor's Religion'), written around 1635, suggested that the bust was the bubbling head of an alchemical still.

Michael Maier has Aquinas pointing with approval to an illustration of the sulphur-mercury theory, in which natural vapours are depicted rising under the earth's crust inside a mountain, with an alchemist imitating the process in his furnace at its summit. The caption reads: 'As nature produces metals from sulphur and mercury, so does art.'

Aquinas recognized that the task of the alchemist to imitate this process in his alembic is a difficult one for the generation of metals involves the occult operations of celestial virtue which are not easily manipulated. He must therefore create the most propitious conditions for this virtue to operate. In his *Summa Theologiae* (1267–73), the first attempt at a comprehensive system of theology, Aquinas expressed his firm belief that alchemists can produce gold although alchemical gold is not usually the same as real gold.

As with Albertus, several alchemical works were ascribed to Aquinas after his death. One fourteenth-century manuscript known as *Aurora Consurgens* attracted the attention of psychoanalyst Carl Jung and his followers.[9] Magnificently illustrated, it offers a medley of quotations from the Bible as well as Senior (Ibn Umail), Morienus and the *Turba Philosophorum*. The text, however, is something of a puzzle. While attributed to Aquinas, it reads as if it were written by someone undergoing a profound visionary experience alternating between heaven and hell. It has a strange, haunting and mythical quality.

The Jungian Marie-Louise von Franz pointed out that a few weeks before the death of St Aquinas, he suffered a strange alteration of personality with long periods of absent-mindedness. She concluded that the work might well have originated in the notes of his last seminar.[10] It is an extraordinary suggestion and worth pursuing.

The title of *Aurora Consurgens* means 'rising dawn'. The text interprets its meaning in different ways. Firstly, 'the dawn is between day and night and has two colours, namely yellow and red, and thus our science, or alchemy, produces the yellow and the red colours, which are between black and white'.[11] The allusion here is to the classic stages of the alchemical process demarcated by changes in colour: *nigredo–albedo–citrinas–rubedo*. Secondly, there is the dawn after the long night sea journey of the soul.

The first five chapters are all concerned with the female apparition of the Wisdom of God who evokes the Gnostic figure of Sophia, the Goddess of Wisdom. She represents the 'eternal ideas in God's mind' when he created the world. As such, 'Long life and health are in her right hand and glory and immense riches in her left . . . She is the tree of life for everybody who understands her and light which is never extinguished . . .'

Throughout the work the Wisdom of God is identified with the Philosopher's Stone. The celebrated alchemists are quoted:

> Hermes and the other philosophers say that if a man had this knowledge for a thousand years and had to nourish seven thousand people daily, he would still have enough, and Senior [Ibn Umail] says that such a man is as rich as the man who possesses the philosopher's stone from which you can get, and so give, fire to whomever you wish.[12]

Unfortunately this science of God and secret of the philosophers is despised by fools who do not know what it is and for that reason there will always be poverty and unhappiness in the world.

In a chapter called 'Exciting the Ignorant to Search for Wisdom', the text describes the Wisdom of God as the Queen of Sheba. The author then experiences depression, despair and confusion, the dark cloud of unconsciousness which corresponds to the initial *nigredo* stage in alchemy. He cries likes Osiris: 'Who can save my soul from the Underworld?' The section ends on a positive note in which the tormented soul anticipates being unearthed, resurrected and whitened. The allusion to the union of Sol and Luna and the *albedo* state of alchemy is underlined by the quote from Senior: 'After you have distributed those seven [metals] through the seven stars, and attributed them to the seven stars, and cleansed them nine times till they look like pearls, that is the state of whiteness.' The text goes on to say that the spirit softens and liquefies the hardness of the earth, as 'the woman dissolves the man, and the man congeals the woman'.[13]

The different stages of alchemy thus mirror the long process of inner development of the tormented and fragmented self towards integration and wholeness. Out of the dark prison of depression (*nigredo*), one emerges cleansed and whitened (*albedo*). After combining the male and female principles within (Sol and Luna), the final red stage (*rubedo*) sees the formation of a firm nucleus within, the Philosopher's Stone of the self, which comes with a new awareness and a sense of freedom. The Stone stands for the centred wholeness of the personality, no longer swept away by emotion or overwhelmed by the unconscious. Alluding to Proverbs 9.1–5, the fifth parable in *Aurora Consurgens* describes 'The Treasure House which Wisdom Builds on the Rock'.

The fully integrated self combines like the Philosopher's Stone the elements of earth, water, air and fire:

> water conserves the embryo during three months within in the womb, air nourishes and sustains it for three months, and during the last three months fire preserves it. And the child shall not come to light before all these months are fulfilled, but then it shall be born and receive life from the sun who is the resuscitator of all dead things.[14]

The new self is full of creative energy like fire, firm and solid like earth, and yet flowing and flexible like water. Above all, it has a certain lightness of being like air, an alert constancy and playful spontaneity.

In the sixth and last parable of *Aurora Consurgens* the deceased calls from his tomb:

> I will arise and go into the town and will seek in the alleys and streets if I may find a chaste virgin, beautiful in face and body and more beautifully clothed, who shall roll away the stone from my tomb and give me feathers like the dove, and with her I will fly up to Heaven. And I will say to her that now I live in eternity and will rest in her, for she will stand at my right dressed in a golden garment.[15]

The author finally visualizes the Goddess of Wisdom entering his body through his ear – a reference to a quaint medieval theory about the conception of Christ in the Virgin Mary. She clothes his black body with a purple robe. With Sol and Luna united within, he has reached the final red stage of *rubedo*. She tells her 'red bridegroom':

> I am the cleverest among the virgins who come forth like the aurora, the morning dawn, chosen like the sun and beautiful as

the moon without mention of what is within . . . I am the land of
promise in which the philosophers have sown their gold and silver
. . . I am the whole work and the whole science is hidden in me.[16]

In this hallucinatory parable of St Aquinas as he faced death, every
alchemist would see reflected – as I did – the struggle to attract the
Goddess of Wisdom and the quest to bring forth the Philosopher's
Stone and attain immortality.

33

The Rosary of Philosophers

I would transmute the sea, if it were mercury.

Arnald of Villanova

Dr Mirabilis and Dr Universalis had held up a mirror of nature for me and a Catholic saint had revealed the dark night of the soul before being transformed, but were there any other medieval alchemists to enlighten me? A name I kept coming across was the thirteenth-century Catalan Arnald of Villanova.

According to a letter he wrote to Pope Boniface VIII, Arnold came from an obscure background.[1] Born in Valencia around 1240, he was educated at a Dominican convent. He taught theology in Montpellier for a while and then travelled to study medicine in Salerno medical school, the first to be established in Europe. His reputation as a physician grew rapidly, and he attended kings (Peter III and James II of Aragon and Frederick III of Sicily) as well as popes (Boniface VIII, Boniface IX, and Clement V). Although he fell foul of the Inquisition for his view of the imminent arrival of the Antichrist and was imprisoned for a couple of years, he continued to travel throughout southern Europe. He died at sea in 1316 on a return journey from Naples to Genoa.

Able to read Arabic, Hebrew and probably Greek, Arnald could read all the available alchemical texts in the original. Many alchemical legends circulated about him. These included the story that he made bars of gold in the court of Boniface VIII and that Ramon Lull received under secret seal from King 'Roberto of England' (Robert Bruce of Scotland?) an account of his alchemical experiments.[2] As with the Muslim alchemists, it is extremely difficult to determine what works attributed to Arnald were written by his own hand. He reportedly burned many of his alchemical writings later in life.

Works attributed to Arnald include the *Perfectum Magisterium* ('The Perfect Mastery') addressed to the King of Aragon which contains chapters later rearranged under the title *Semita Semitae* ('The Path of the Path'). His *Flores Regis* ('The Flowers of the King') was dedicated to the King of Naples. The *Novum Lumen* ('The New Light') is thought to be his quotes from the Latin translation of the famous Arabic text of *Turba Philosophorum*. But much of the alchemical literature attributed to Arnald would seem to belong to the fourteenth, fifteenth and sixteenth centuries.[3]

Like Jabir and Rhazes, Arnald did not treat alchemy and medicine as separate disciplines and explored the possibility of chemical and metallic remedies for illnesses, especially antimony in the form of stibnite.[4] He accepted Galen's notion that the healthy body is made up of a proper balance of the four humours (sanguine, choleric, melancholic and phlegmatic) which corresponds to the Aristotelian theory of the four elements constituting matter. But like Jabir he extended the notion of balance to metals. Just as ill health is caused by the upset balance of humours, so imperfect metals can be helped to attain their ideal internal balance through the use of elixirs. In this way, both alchemy and medicine can be employed to improve health and prolong life.

While Arnald stressed the importance of experiment and the study of the natural sciences, the influence of the Egyptian and Muslim alchemists comes through in his use of magic and astrology in the treatment of illnesses. He not only used a seal in the form of a lion for curing Boniface XIII of his gallstone (the Pope was not above making use of pagan magic) but wrote a treatise on seals and amulets. If a seal does not work in the case of mania, then Arnald proposes the more nuts-and-bolts method of trepanning: drilling a small hole in the skull to permit the escape of noxious vapours affecting the brain.

Arnald's longest and most famous alchemical work was the *Rosarius Philosophorum* ('The Rosary of the Philosophers'). It deals with the theory and practice of alchemy in two parts. Like Jabir, he presents the sulphur-mercury theory of the constitution of metals, but argues that ordinary sulphur is harmful to metals and that 'philosophical' sulphur is hidden in the mercury. Mercury is the 'medicine' of metals.

The best mercury is 'mercurial liquid', Arnald maintains, which comes from Spain in sealed containers. It can be used for transmuting base metals as well as preparing elixirs. In the former case, you should use four parts of liquid to one of metal. In the latter case, the preparation should be a ratio of 12:1 of gold or silver. Such elixirs can transmute one thousand times their own weight of base metals into precious ones, so well that they will be able to pass a complete assay. The crucial ingredient of course is the Spanish 'mercurial liquid' and the crucial question is where can it be obtained and of what does it consist? I for one was unable to find it in Spain.

Another method given is the separation of the mercury into the four elements by using a ferment and then the recombination of them in the form of gold. As with Jabir, the elements must be recombined in specific proportions by weight. Gold needs the ratio of 1:1; water and air, 2:1; water and fire, 3:1; and water and earth, 3:2. In addition, their relative heat, cold, dryness and moistness must be known. The stages to pass through are solution, purification, reduction and fixation. And as with the Alexandrian alchemists, the changes in colour are signs of a correct transmutation: the creation of a red powder is the sign of success in the preparation of the great elixir.

Arnald's elixir became renowned as a panacea for maladies and for rejuvenation. Just as the Philosopher's Stone was considered a 'medicine of metals', healing their defects and raising them to the perfection of gold, so it was thought that the elixir as a healing medicine could not only prolong life but reverse the process of ageing. If only it could be found.

I was struck by a new emphasis in Arnald's alchemy: its Christian framework and symbolism. He compares the different stages of the alchemical work with the conception, birth, crucifixion and resurrection of Christ. The easy transition to Christian symbolism, however, shows that a specific religion is not important for a belief in alchemy, even in its spiritual dimension. My quest so far had vividly shown that spiritual alchemy can be expressed in pagan, Taoist, Hindu, Egyptian, Muslim, Sufi or Christian terms. The symbolic language might be different but its fundamental beliefs in the living soul and in the possibility of self-transformation remain the same. Alchemy translates from religion to religion as it does from language to language, containing its core message in many different forms and guises. It confirmed my view that at the most fundamental level all religions are one.

Arnald was not just a theoretician but performed himself some of the chemical operations he described. He is credited with being the first to distil alcohol (*aqua ardens*) from wine by distilling it several times through copper-sided tubes, and of extracting the 'quintessence' of plants and herbs by dissolving them in alcohol. Working in a smoky laboratory, he was probably the first to observe the harmful effects of carbon monoxide. His account of the distillation of human blood from an alembic is recognizable, although as a good alchemist he associated the changing colours with the elements: the initial liquid with water, the second yellow distillate with air, and third red distillate with fire. He also claimed that the 'fire' obtained from the blood has special virtues: he managed to revive a count on his deathbed with it so that he could make a confession before expiring once and for all.

Although it comes from the ancient alchemist Ostanes, the alchemical saying 'Nature overcomes Nature' was often attributed to Arnald. His works had a new wave of popularity in the sixteenth century and were reprinted in Leiden in 1520 and 1532. In the seventeenth century, he appears along with Hermes, Rhazes and Geber as the main alchemical authorities in an engraving in Elias Ashmole's *Theatrum Chemicum Britannicum* (1652). In Michael Maier's *Symbola Aureae Mensae*, he points to the alchemical marriage of the philosopher Chabritius and Beia, representing the male and female principles, from which the Stone is born.[5]

*

Whilst searching for Arnald's remedies for a long life, I unearthed in the British Library a 'new boke' translated by Jonas Drummond, but with no date, called 'the degence of age and recovery of youth translated out of the famous Clarke and ryght experte medycyne Arnold de Nova Villa very profytable for all men to knowe'. I was disappointed to find that it was a mainly medical tract on the importance of choosing good meat and wine in order to live well.

A much more fascinating book was entitled *LONG LIVERS: A CURIOUS HISTORY OF Such Persons of both Sexes who have liv'd several AGES and grown Young again: with the rare SECRET of REJUVENESENCY of Arnoldus de Villa Nova, And a great many approv'd and invaluable RULES to prolong LIFE: AS ALSO, How to prepare the UNIVERSAL MEDICINE.* It was dedicated to 'the Grand Masters, Masters, Wardens and Brethren of the most Antient and Most Honourable Fraternity of the Free-Masons of Great Britain and Ireland'. It was a dark leather-bound book, well printed, with stained dark pages. On the title page the author is given as Eugenius Philalethes, FRS, author of the *Treatise of the Plague*. The British Library gives the author as one Robert Samber but it could also have been the alchemist and priest Thomas Vaughan, twin brother of the metaphysical poet Henry Vaughan, who used the same pseudonym.

What are the recommendations for a long life? In the first place, peaceful repose and moderation. But what of the 'Secret of Rejuvenesency' of Arnoldus de Villa Nova? It is a grand operation which should appeal to all alchemists, homeopaths and herbalists. It is to be 'renewed' every seven years. It is worth quoting the method in full:

> Immediately when you begin the Operation lay upon your Heart going to Rest, a Plaister made with an Ounce of the best oriental Saffron, half an ounce of Red Roses, two drams of Red Sanders, one Dram of *Lignum Aloes*, and as much of good Amber; these being all reduced to fine powder incorporated with the best Virgin Wax.
>
> The grand operation consists chiefly of two procedures. The first is to feed on pullets fed on best wheat and cooked in viper broth and herbs. The second is to bath three times a week, especially in April and May since it is the season of the renewal of nature. The water should be clear and warm and mixed well with a Decoction of Rosemary, and Elder Flowers, two Sthecas, Camemol, Melilot, Red Roses, and Nenuphur, or Water-lilly, of each one Pound; add to these the Roots of Bistorte or Snake-weed, Burdony, Elicampe, Patience and Iris, of each a handful well picked and bruised, put all of these into a linen Bag to boyl in one or two Waters in a great Kettle of River Water.

And to complete the operation use for twelve days in succession the following concoction:

> Take four Ounces of Calx Auri dissolved philosophically, Lignum Aloes, and of three Sanders, Seed Pearl, Saphires, Hyacinth, Emeralds, Topazes, red and white Coral, the finest Ivory Raspins, of the Bones of a Stag's Heart, of each half a Dram; of the best Musk and Amber of each six Grains.[6]

Clearly the method of Arnoldus de Villa Nova was not for the poor or faint-hearted. The 'Calx Auri' – Gold Powder – would be difficult to find and I had no idea what it was to dissolve it 'philosophically'.

Unable to obtain all the necessary ingredients, I was unable to see whether it rejuvenated me. As a vegetarian, I was not given to eating the pullets and would prefer to eat the best wheat direct. I give the recipe for others to try and may they give thanks to Arnald if it works!

*

What happened to Arnald's legacy in the thirteenth century? According to one treatise Ramon Lull met Arnald in Naples just before he died on his return sea journey to Genoa, and his arguments and experiments convinced Lull of the power of alchemy. Another claims that he was a student of Arnald.[7] Whatever the truth of these claims, Lull was certainly well placed to learn alchemy from the Muslims in Spain. Born in Majorca of Catalan parents around 1232, he largely educated himself. As a young man, he became a troubadour and writer of romances – a manual of chivalry under his name was translated into English by Caxton around 1484.

The most crucial event in his life occurred in 1272 when he underwent a visionary experience on Mount Randa in Majorca. Dr Illuminatus, as he came to be known, served as tutor to the sons of James I of Aragon, *el Conquistador*, but his vision was so powerful and his Christian conviction so strong that he decided to become a missionary amongst the Muslims. He spent nine years in Majorca learning Arabic from a slave allegedly to refute the Muslim philosophers; in reality he learned a great deal from them. He is said to have been stoned to death by the Saracens in North Africa.

Lull developed a kind of rationalistic mysticism in which he tried to defend the profoundest revelations of Christianity by reason. In his principal work *Ars Magna* ('The Great Art), written in 1305–8 when in his seventies, Lull depicted the causes of phenomena in the Creation as the *Dignitates Dei* – Divine Names or attributes (such as wisdom, will, virtue, glory and justice). The historian Frances Yates has suggested that this derives mainly from the Cabala and the work of the scholastic philosopher John Scotus Erigena.[8] Yet for me – and I realized later for Idries Shah – his philosophy bears an uncanny resemblance to the Islamic tradition which was still so alive in Spain, especially in the teachings of the Sufis. In his *Blanquerna*, Lull confessed that he adopted his devotional methodology from the Sufis, whom he called religious even among the Saracens.[9]

The famous 'Lullian Art' is a universal method, based on geometrical figures and letter-notations, which allegedly reflects the structure of the universe.[10] He designated the 'Divine Dignities' by letters of the Latin alphabet and placed them on a series of revolving concentric discs. Any combination of letters could thus represent a possible form in the universe. These relationships and categories could be extended by analogy to other fields, such as principles, virtues, mental faculties and even medical ideas.[11]

Alchemists made great use of Lull's method, especially his symbolic names, numbers, diagrams and alphabets. Many alchemical works appeared under his name. Thomas Le Myésier in France produced an exquisite edition of his works called *Electorium*, a part of which reached the Italian Hermetic philosopher Pico della Mirandola. A vast corpus of 143 alchemical works are attributed to Lull, yet it is by no means certain that he wrote any of them.[12] It would seem that his name, like that of Hermes and Geber, was used to give authority to the writings of later anonymous alchemists who shared common beliefs. In the seventeenth century, he was honoured by Michael Maier as one of his dozen alchemical heroes. He depicted him as gesturing towards a man and a woman holding a naked child between them, with the caption: 'The child's body [the Philosopher's Stone] comes into motion from the masculine and feminine.'[13]

I came across a magnificent fifteenth-century manuscript entitled *Opera Chimica* attributed to Raimondo Lullo in the National Library of Italy in Florence. It is a beautifully scripted Latin work on vellum and illustrated by Girolamo de Cremona, one of the greatest illustrators of the day. The details are so precise and carefully wrought that they need a magnifying glass to appreciate them fully. The work also has erudite marginal notes in Latin in another hand.[14]

The work opens with the words '*Deus qui gloriosus et omnipotens existis*' ('God, you who exist glorious and omnipotent'). In the accompanying illustration, Lull is shown as an elderly sage with a long beard standing before the archangel Raphael who leads by the hand a woman who doubtlessly represents nature. The first letter of the text has an angel carrying a sphere, a symbol of the Philosopher's Stone. It shows that it is no mere collection of alchemical recipes but rather a work of divine origin offering a method capable of revealing the profoundest secrets of the Philosopher's Stone. The Christian tone changes in the following illustration where Lull is depicted with Hermes ploughing a field behind oxen, practising celestial agriculture in an earthly paradise. The 'field' as earth stands for the conditions and possibilities contained within matter. The seed is the base metal of the ordinary personality which when placed in the earth dissolves and is reborn as the alchemical gold of the transformed self.

Other illustrations show the alchemist observing male twins boiling in a fiery pot, holding a scarf between his hands which contains a naked praying homunculus, giving a solution in a vase to a cardinal and working with alchemical apparatus. A tree with a king demonstrates the different stages of the process itself. Mercury, always quick and volatile, makes an appearance playing a flute.

The *Opera Chimica* was the most beautiful text ascribed to Lull that I unearthed during my research. The most fascinating appeared under the title of *Testament*.[15] Its form became a model for many subsequent alchemical works. Divided into three parts, the Theoretical, the Practical and the Codicil, it offers a systematic account of alchemy. Although it makes use of Lull's 'Art' with a table in which principles, materials and operations are represented by the alphabet, the work has little which is deliberately allegorical or arcane.

The author of the *Testament* claims that God used the original matter of *argentum vivum* (mercury) to create all things. The finest part formed the bodies of angels, the coarser part the heavenly spheres, planets and stars, and the coarsest the terrestrial bodies. Part of the mercury became the four elements of fire, air, earth and water. But there is a fifth element, the *quintessence*, found in its purer state in heavenly spheres. It is also to be found in all bodies on earth and is responsible for their generation, movement and corruption. One of the aims of the Lullian adepts was to manipulate this 'fifth element' and to increase its activity in this world. This seemed to me a genuine new development in alchemy.

Aqua ardens or alcohol was considered to be an impure form of the 'active' fifth element. They believed that its isolation and manipulation could increase the beneficial influence of the planets and stars on the sublunary scene. To purify the *aqua ardens* and obtain the quintessence of the fifth element, it was recommended to pour the alcohol (probably about 90–95 per cent proof) in a 'pelican' – a kind of reflux condenser – and place it on a large bed of fermenting matter, such as horse's dung. The warmth volatilized the alcohol which then 'circulated' in the pelican. It was claimed that *aqua ardens* separated into two layers, a lower dull, turbid mass, and an upper one which was clear and blue as the sky – the quintessence. Although modern science has been unable to repeat this experiment, it clearly represented the release of the purified 'spirit' from gross matter and had great symbolic importance for the alchemist. Sipping his 'brandy of the angels', he may well have had wondrous visions of the Whole.

The author of the *Testament* further claims that he obtained the congelation of common mercury by means of its 'menstrual' – a universal solvent thought to work like the menses in the ovum. The successful experiment was allegedly performed near Naples 'in the presence of a natural philosopher and faithful associates'. Unfortunately, I was not present and was none the wiser.

However, my attention lit up when I discovered that the Ashmolean collection in the Bodleian Library in Oxford held a manuscript known as *The Experiments of Raymond Lully of Majorca the most learned philosopher, wherein the operations of the true Chymicall Philosophy are plainly delivered.*[16] I was even more excited to discover that it contained several recipes for the Philosopher's Stone. One begins with gold (Sol), silver (Luna) and that most crucial and elusive of ingredients – 'philosopher's mercury'. The thirty-third alchemical experiment of Sol caught my eye. It reads as follows:

Take *aqua fortis* [nitric acid] with his form, as I have taught you before, and in it dissolve 3 ounces of Lune [silver]; then purify it 20 days, then take 3 oz. of ☉ [gold] and dissolve it in 18 oz. of the same *aqua fortis* with his form in which yet 4 oz. of the fixed salt of Urine [mainly common salt] ought to be first dissolved, as you have it in his Experiment. Then putrefy these 2 bodies by themselves severally for 20 natural days. Then exanimate [remove the spirit of] them both severally by themselves, as well Lune [silver] as ☉, even to the rule delivered you before. Now when every one shall be exanimate by themselves and their quickened waters shall be severally kept by themselves and also the earth [dry salts] shall yield no more smoke, then shall there be a sign that the ☉ and ☽ [silver] do suffer eclipse [distilled to dryness]. Beate then the earth of either of them, and likewise mingle them then in a little glass ball strongly luted. Put him to a fire of reverberation 24 hours.

Then take it out and give it first the water of [nitric acid] quickened and rectified first 7 times by ashes. And when it shall drunke up all his Water little and little, in the same order as you

had it before in the other experiments, then give it the Water of
☉, without any rectification, by little and little after the order
which you kept in imbibing that earth with water of. Then you
shall ferment it in this manner. Take one part of ☉ and 3 parts
of ☿ [mercury] and one part of the medicine, that is to say as
much as there was gold. Put it all together in a glass vessel upon
warm ashes, and in a short time it shall be turned into powder
[gold amalga with admixture of gold and silver salts]. Then shall
you incere it with the 3rd oil of ☉ [the solution of gold chloride
in hydrochloric and nitric acids]. Now when it is all very well
cerated and brought into the forme of oyle [a paste of mercury,
gold and silver salts], project one part thereof upon 100 of
mercury: and it shall be all turned into medicine. Of which take
againe one part and project upon 500 parts. It shall turn the
mercury into ☉ better and purer than mineral gold.[17]

The operation is quite understandable in terms of modern chemistry as
indicated in the brackets. Professor Sherwood Taylor, former director
of the Science Museum in London, has suggested that the powder
obtained would be gold amalgam with an admixture of gold and silver
salts. When mixed with 'oil of gold' (usually a solution of gold chloride
in hydrochloric and nitric acids) much of the metal will dissolve and
form a thick oily solution or paste of mercury, gold and silver salts.
This is the 'medicine' as described and understood by modern chemistry. He concludes: 'By throwing one part on 100 parts of mercury a
very weak gold amalgam would result, which when added to 500 parts
of mercury would have no effect whatever.'[18]

No doubt. But the mercury – *argentum vivum* – used by the
alchemists is, as I had long realized, no ordinary mercury. It is
'philosophic mercury' which has very different properties.

I could easily see why the special properties of mercury should
endear it to the alchemists. Firstly, it can easily be released from its
solid red sulphide ore known as 'cinnabar' and with the application of
gentle heat can readily be vaporized. Its vapour was called the 'spirit
mercury' and understandably inspired speculation about the release of
the spirit from the body. Secondly, since it was known that other
metals liquefy under heat, it was reasonable to infer that they are all
essentially mercury. Thirdly, the fact that mercury is the only metal
which is liquid at room temperature and that it is both fixed and
volatile suggested that it was a 'divine principle' in the world, a

hermaphrodite substance uniting both male and female principles. Since mercury is the source of the Philosopher's Stone, it has been called the '*alpha* and *omega*', the beginning and the end. But what about that 'philosophical mercury'? For all my researches, it remained the central mystery of the Great Work and the most difficult substance to find – a fugitive stag indeed.

*

The reputation of Dr Illuminatus and the vogue for the 'Lullian Art' during the Renaissance inspired many alchemical stories. In his own remarkable *Testament*, John Cremer claims that after wasting thirty years perusing the unintelligible writings of alchemists he met Lull ('Master Raymond') in Italy and persuaded him to return to England and live with him for two years. During this time, he revealed 'the whole secret of the work'. He further claims that Lull was able to transform himself into a red cock at will.

Cremer describes himself as a Brother of the Benedictine Order and Abbot of Westminster. He says he introduced Lull to King Edward III and the alchemist managed to transmute 22 tons of base metal into gold in the Tower of London on the condition that it was only used to finance a crusade against the Turks. After the experiment Edward broke his promise, made war on France and clapped Lull in the Tower. He managed to escape to France by making himself 'a leaper' – which may mean that he obtained a pole vault or that he disguised himself as a leper.

Another story, 'affirmed by an unwritten verity' according to Elias Ashmole, has it that Edward III had rose nobles struck from the alchemical gold made by Lull, although they were not minted before 1465.[19] The reverse of the coins were inscribed with *Iesus autum transiens per medium eorum ibat* ('But Jesus passing through the midst of them went this way'), Luke 4.30. I have looked for the nobles, but to no avail. Again Ashmole asserts that Cremer had an alchemical device painted on a wall of Westminster Abbey, depicting in graphic form 'the Grand *Misteries* of the *Philosopher's Stone*'. It is nowhere to be found, long washed over with plaster, but perhaps one day a workman will reveal it to the world.

34

Poets of Gold

The philosophres sworn everychoon
That they sholden discovere it unto noon . . .

Geoffrey Chaucer, 'The Canon's Yeoman's Tale'

The discovery of Elias Ashmole's marvellous *Theatrum Chemicum Britannicum* (1652) in the British Library was one of my greatest finds during my quest. Subtitled 'Severall Poeticall Pieces of our Famous English Philosophers, who have written the Hermetique Mysteries in their owne Ancient Language', it is a treasure trove of arcane knowledge. What I found most remarkable about the developing alchemical tradition after Roger Bacon in Britain was that it was expressed in verse. Ashmole's work not only evokes the lively world of the alchemists in the Middle Ages but also gives new life to many of the traditional alchemical emblems such as the black toad, the peacock's tail, the green lion, the fountain and the union of Sol and Luna.

The first and most hilarious account of alchemy comes in Geoffrey Chaucer's 'The Canon's Yeoman's Tale' in *The Canterbury Tales* (c.1387–1400). It anticipates the satire of Ben Jonson's play *The Alchemist* (1610). Chaucer's knowledge of alchemy is profound. He not only mentions Hermes, Senior Zadith (Ibn Umail) and Arnald of Villanova but gives a detailed description of the alchemical process itself. He clearly felt the lure of the Philosopher's Stone. A manuscript attributed to him describes in Middle English several alchemical experiments in allegorical terms.[1] It has even been suggested that Chaucer might have been an alchemist himself; certainly he knew how in 'Our elvysshe craft, we semen wonde wise' and could use their terms 'so clergial and so queynte' with ease. Ashmole for one thought Chaucer to be a master of the Art.[2]

It seems unlikely that he would dismiss alchemy, the principal medieval science, as an imposture simply because of some unscrupulous practitioners any more than he would reject Christianity because of some corrupt priests and sellers of indulgences. His acerbic comments suggest that he may well have been taken in by a puffer and lost some money in the process; some point a finger at William Shuchirch, the Canon of the Royal Chapel at Windsor who was an alchemist.[3]

'The Canon's Yeoman's Tale' is told by the laboratory assistant of the alchemist canon who joins at a mad gallop the pilgrims on their way to Canterbury. In the prologue, he tells his fellow travellers that his master is a man of 'high discreioun' who 'can switch subitilee'. He had such mastery of the Art that he could turn 'upside down' all the ground they rode along to Canterbury and pave it with silver and gold. Not surprisingly, they are immediately intrigued and demand to know more. The yeoman, one of Chaucer's most vivid characters, then relates how he set out to learn the art of 'multiplying'. After seven years of incessant labour and trials at 'that slidynge science' he has ended up threadbare, stinking and ill. His colour had once been 'both fressh and reed'; now he is 'wan and of a leden hewe'.

Although the tale is intended to be a cautionary one, it is clear that Chaucer knew all about the alchemical apparatus, such as 'sublymatories, cucurbites and alembikes', as well as the procedures, such as 'calicinacioun and of watres albificacioun'. The yeoman further reveals to his spellbound fellow pilgrims some of the substances used by medieval alchemists:

> The firste spirit quyksilver called is,
> The seconde orpyment, the thridde, ywis,
> Sal armonyak, and the ferthe brymstoon.
> The bodyes sevene eek, lo! hem heere anoon:
> Sol gold is, and Luna silver we thrape,
> Mars iren, Mercurie quyksilver we clepe,
> Saturnus leed, and Juppiter is tin,
> And Venus coper, by my fader kyn!

Orpiment is arsenic sulphide, used as yellow dye, while brimstone is sulphur. Although the canon 'can don craftily' his experiments invariably go wrong. On one occasion when his pot broke, fellow alchemists offered their advice: one said that it was on the fire too long; a second that the bellows had not been properly operated (the yeoman's task); a third that the mixture was not prepared properly; a fourth that the fire was not made of beech-charcoal. In the yeoman's own view, being the closest to the matter, the pot was cracked.

When they get together to discuss their subject, the alchemists think they are as wise as Solomon. The yeoman suggests that his master is not ignorant or fraudulent but too learned in that he misuses his learning. He then tells his fellow pilgrims of the antics of another canon he worked for who deliberately tricked a gullible priest by slipping silver or gold filings into some mercury in his crucible at a crucial moment in the preparation. He would also hide a silver ingot up his sleeve which he would produce at the end of the experiment.

After seven years of failing to reach a conclusion, the yeoman ended up like all other alchemists 'stynken as a goot'. He has seen all the tricks of the trade of puffers. He declares that the quest for the 'philosophres stoon, Elixer clept' is hopeless. His advice is to give it up:

> Thanne conclude I thus, sith that God of hevene
> Ne wil nat that the philosophres nevene
> How that man shal come unto this stoon,
> I rede, as for the beste, lete it goon.[4]

I could understand his position. But I had no intention of giving up my enthralling quest. There before me were some wonderful alchemical poets to explore, full of vivid imagery and mystical visions. And, who knows, maybe they could provide me with some further clues which would lead to the Philosopher's Stone.

*

Like Chaucer, Sir George Ripley knew of the continental alchemists but where the author of *The Canterbury Tales* joked about practical alchemy, Ripley took its spiritual dimension very seriously. Ashmole rightly called his most famous treatise *Compound of Alchymy* 'a most, excellent, learned and worthy worke'.

Born in the village of Ripley near Harrogate in Yorkshire in the early fifteenth century, Ripley studied theology in Louvain and Rome before becoming a canon at Bridlington in Yorkshire. But he continued to travel. He stayed with the Knights of St John, also known as Knights Hospitallers, on the island of Rhodes. They had an extensive alchemical library and active laboratory, no doubt drawing on the knowledge they acquired in Jerusalem, where they protected the pilgrim routes during the Crusades. Ripley is reputed to have contributed a great deal of money each year to support them. It is said that he was one of the last to leave when the island fell to the Turks. He sought patronage from the powerful in Church and State, dedicating his *Medulla Alchemiae* (1476, 'The Marrow of Alchemy') to George Nevill, the Archbishop of York, and his *Compound of Alchymy* to King Edward IV.

The original version of Ripley's principal work was written in 1471 and published in English thirty years later. It is divided into 'twelve gates' which recall the gates in *The Egyptian Book of the Dead* which the soul in the Underworld must pass through in order to reach paradise. Ripley describes them as the twelve stages of the Great Work: calcination, dissolution, separation, conjunction, putrefaction, congelation, cibation, sublimation, fermentation, exaltation, multiplication, projection. Congelation is crystallization; cibation is 'feeding the matter'; exaltation is the elevation of a substance to a higher virtue; and multiplication is the increase in the amount or power of the Stone. They are all clearly physical operations which mirror spiritual development, stages on the path of the soul towards enlightenment. Ripley further likens the trinity of the Godhead – the Father, Son and Holy Ghost – to the three aspects – magnesia, sulphur and mercury – which make up the one substance of the microcosm of man.

The *Compound of Alchymy* contains a famous mandala diagram known as 'Ripley's Wheele' which claims to contain 'all secrets of the Treatise both great & small'. It also includes Ripley's famous poem about his vision of an alchemical toad:

> When busie at my booke I was upon a certeine night,
> This Vision here exprest appear'd unto my dimmed sight;
> A *Toad* full rudde I saw, did drinke the juice of grapes so fast,
> Till overcharged with the broth, his bowells all to brast;
> And after that from poysoned bulke he cast his venome fell,
> For greif and paine whereof his Members all began to swell,
> With drops of poysoned sweate approaching thus his secret Den,
> His cave with blasts of fumous ayre he all be-whyted then;

And from the which in space a golden humour did ensue,
Whose falling drops from high did staine the soile with ruddy
   hew:
And when this Corps the force of vitall breath began to lacke,
This dying *Toade* became forthwith like Coale for colour
   blacke . . .

He placed the carcass on a gentle fire which was pierced with rare colours until it became white and finally red. He then made a medicine from its venom which 'kills and saveth such as venome chance to take'.[5]

The toad imbibing its own venom is clearly a poetic conceit for the alchemical process itself. Ripley was following directly in the steps of the Alexandrian alchemists when he described the succession of colours which mark the different stages in the alchemical process. The dying toad becomes black, the preliminary *nigredo* stage of putrefaction, mirroring the conversion of a substance into an apparently inert mass. When Ripley in the poem heats the putrefying carcass, he sees the colours of the *cauda pavonis*, the peacock's tail, the multi-coloured stage. The substance then passes through the white (*albedo*) and red (*rubedo*) stages which produce the white and red elixirs and silver and gold respectively. From the poison (no doubt symbolizing mercury), he makes an elixir which can heal the body and purify metals.

Another visionary and surreal work of Ripley's was *Cantilena*, written in imitation of Ramon Lull, with the subtitle *De Lapide Philosophorum, seu de Phenice* ('On the Philosopher's Stone, or On the Phoenix'). Ripley offers the alchemical allegory of a king who seeks a son – *the filius philosophorum*, the Son of the Philosophers. By dissolving himself in the *materia prima*, he returns to the primal womb. His mother becomes pregnant and

> Meanwhile she of the Peacock's Flesh did Eate
> And Dranke the Greene-Lyons Blood with that fine Meate,
> Which Mercurie, bearing the Dart of Passion,
> Brought in a Golden Cupp of Babilon.[6]

As a result, she gives birth to the Son of the Philosophers who combines the female and male principles of Luna and Sol and changes from lunar radiance to the splendour of the sun. As the personification of the Philosopher's Stone, he becomes a reformer of sins and a great healer.

Eirenaeus Philateles, probably a pseudonym for George Starkey, revived Ripley's work in the second half of the seventeenth century after the publication of Ashmole's alchemical compilation *Theatrum Chemicum Britannicum*. He summarized Ripley's Hermetic philosophy for his contemporaries in five conclusions:

Conclusion 1: That as all things are multiplied in their kind, so may be metals which have a capacity of transmutation from imperfect to perfect state.

Conclusion 2: The possibility of transmutation is because metals can be reduced to their first mercurial matter.

Conclusion 3: That two Sulphurs only are related to the work, and that their mercuries are united to them essentially.

Conclusion 4: Whoever understands the two Sulphurs and Mercuries shall find that the one is most pure Red Sulphur of Gold – which is Sulphur *in manifesto* and Mercurio *in oculto*, – while the other is most pure white Mercury – which is true Quicksilver *in manifesto* and Sulphure *in oculto* – these being our two Principles.

Conclusion 5: That if a man's principles be true and his operations regular, his Event will be certain, which Event is not other than the True Mystery.[7]

Dating from the same period is the famous *Ripley Scrowle*. The only surviving copies I could trace are in the British Library and in the Fitzwilliam Museum, Cambridge. The work contains two marvellous and often reproduced emblems. The first shows an old adept with a phial in his hand from which arises vapours represented by feathers. Beneath is a wheel representing the stages of the Work. A ribbon flowing from the vessel declares the 'Fountain of the Philosophers' from which comes the philosophical mercury which produces the Stone.

The second emblem has a castle with seven towers (the seven metals) with the king (Sol) and queen (Luna) climbing out of the waters up a philosophical tree (symbol of their union). On the wall of the castle are a toad and a dragon, representing the first stage of the Work and the transformations brought about by fire. Seven processes are illustrated by a monk at his furnace in circles, all connected to the red essence of the Stone in the middle.[8]

*

The English alchemists like their continental counterparts passed on their knowledge from generation to generation through pupils. Ripley instructed Thomas Norton of Bristol (c.1433–1513). A fifteenth-century manuscript of Norton's principal work *Ordinal of Alchemy* shows a disciple, possibly Norton himself, swearing to 'serve the holy secrets of alchemy'.[9]

Norton came from a renowned Bristol family; his great-grandson Samuel says that his illustrious forbear was a member of the Privy Council of Edward IV. He once accused the Mayor of Bristol of high treason (his own grandfather had been an earlier mayor and MP), and challenged him to a duel in the council chamber. In the ensuing dispute he was in turn accused of haunting taverns, neglecting divine service and, sin of sins, playing tennis on Sunday afternoon. He lost the case.

Interested in alchemy from an early age, Norton corresponded with George Ripley. The older alchemist agreed to make him 'heire unto this Arte' but insisted that they met face to face. Norton travelled a hundred miles to Bridlington and after forty days he allegedly learned all the secrets of alchemy. He was twenty-eight at the time. On his return to Bristol, he put his knowledge to the test and managed to prepare the Great Red Elixir but he says a servant stole it from him. With a heavy heart, he bid adieu to alchemy. But his despair passed off and he started work again and attempted to make the Elixir of Life. Again he was successful, but again it was stolen, this time by a woman. It is said that she was the wife of William Canynges, a master mason who rebuilt the Church of St Mary Redcliffe in Bristol with money made from the elixir.

Norton's *Ordinal of Alchemy* was begun in 1477. He intended it to be 'Of Alkimy the Ordinal, the *Crede Mihi*, the Standard Perpetuall'. He professes to speak more plainly than his predecessors, among whom he mentions Hermes, Khalid, Rhazes, Geber, Democritus, Morienus, Bacon and Arnald. But while he says much about furnaces and other alchemists, he is vague about the exact procedure to transmute metals. Believing that the secret philosophy can only be truly communicated by a personal teacher, he declares that he will express himself in a way that the initiated will understand while the layman will be led astray. He insists that the 'sibtile science of holy Alchymye' if properly understood improves the morals:

> It voydeth vaine Glory, Hope, and also dreade:
> It voydeth Ambitiousnesse, Extorcion, and Excess:

> It fenceth Adversity that shee doe not oppresse.
> He that thereof hath his full intent,
> Forsaken Extremities, with Measure is content.

Unfortunately many in Church and State undertake the study of alchemy out of an appetite for riches, such

> As Popes with Cardinalls of Dignity,
> Archbyshopes with Byshopes of high degree,
> With Abbots and Priors of Religion,
> With Friars, Heremetes, and Preests manie one,
> And Kings with Princes and Lords great of blood . . .[10]

Warning against charlatans and puffers, Norton insists that most books of recipes for making the elixir are better called 'deceipts'. A true alchemist must understand the how and why of alchemical operations: 'Nothing is wrought but by proper Cause.' In his view, the 'multipliers' are wrong who argue that it is possible to make metals grow and increase. Only in nature can the influence of the sun's rays slowly convert the subterranean 'vertue Minerall' into metals and only in 'certain places of eligible ground'. The goal of alchemy must therefore be to transmute already existing metals which is possible because of their 'propinquity of matter'.

All this is well and good but what of the Philosopher's Stone? Was I to discover anything in Norton to help me in my quest? He raises the subject in the form of replies to an unsuccessful alchemist, a 'labourer in the fire' who for sixty years has tried herbs, gums, roots, grass, antimony, arsenic, honey, wax, wine, quicklime, vitriol and other ingredients but all to no avail. Norton reluctantly reveals that for the White work or the preparation of silver, two substances are necessary. The first is a mineral which cannot be bought (there's the rub!) and which must be prepared by the alchemist himself. It is a 'subtle earth', at first dull and reddish brown, known as litharge; when suitably treated, it becomes white and is known as marcasite. Litharge is another name for lead monoxide, but I suspect Norton was thinking of its Greek origin: *lithos* for stone and *arguros* for silver.

The second substance is a stone described as 'gloriouse faier and bright . . . glittering with perspecutie, being wonderfull Diaphanitie'. It can be bought and is known as 'magnetia' (magnesia). It was a vague term for several mineral substances, including manganese dioxide and magnesite. It was sometimes used as a synonym for the Stone itself. Be that as it may, Norton says that when magnesia and marcasite are mixed with sal ammoniac (ammonium chloride) and sulphur and heated, they will produce the White Elixir.

But it was not a simple process which I could do on my own. The work of transmutation of a reasonable quantity, Norton tells us, requires eight servants who must be sober, diligent, attentive, obedient and clean. As the operations take place for 24 hours a day, they must work in shifts, with four on duty while the others sleep or go to church. I would have to purchase many different vessels made of clay, stone, glass and lead. Then there is a special furnace for every part of the process. Norton himself seems to have invented a multiple furnace with 'stopples' (dampers) which enable the operator to regulate the heat. So much for the materials, labour force and equipment.

That is not all. The conditions must be right on earth and in heaven. An appropriate place must be found for the experiment. The environment should be dry for some operations, moist and cold for others, while wind is always bad. At one stage a dim light is necessary; at another as much light as possible is best. And since the sublunary scene is affected by the heavens, the astrological relationships must be propitious. With all these variables, it is easy to see that it would be very difficult to get them all right, let alone repeat them.

Despite his warning against puffers, Norton could not prevent himself from telling the cautionary tale of Thomas Daulton. He led a peaceful life in Gloucester Abbey but had in his possession the Red Medicine – 'neer English man had more'. The word spread and he was summoned by the courtier Thomas Herbert to go before King Edward IV. Daulton confessed that he had the elixir which would have been enough to equip and maintain 20,000 Crusaders in the Holy Land but since it had caused him much worry he had thrown it into a muddy lake near the River Severn. The King asked him to make some more, but Daulton insisted that he had been given it by a canon of Lichfield. Although he was freed by the King, Thomas Herbert had him seized in the streets of London and carried off to Gloucester Castle. Herbert put him in jail in order to make him reveal his secrets. After four years, he even threatened him with the scaffold. When Daulton finally accepted his end cheerfully, his jailer repented and set him free, deeply impressed by his refusal to divulge the Hermetic mystery.

*

One of the most curious and likable English poets of the Art was the Elizabethan Thomas Charnock. Born in Faversham in Kent in 1526, the self-styled 'unlettered Scholler' travelled throughout England looking for the secrets of the Philosopher's Stone. It seems that he became like Chaucer's canon's yeoman a laboratory assistant to one 'James S., a spiritual man', possibly James Sauler from Salisbury.[11] His master initiated him into the operations of the Work and allegedly handed on the secret of the Philosopher's Stone on his death in 1554. Unfortunately, on New Year's Day in the following year, a fire broke out in Charnock's laboratory when the wooden casing of a vessel caught alight. The resulting fire destroyed his laboratory together with the secret.

The would-be alchemist was not deterred. He tracked down the blind William Holway (also known as Gibbs), the former prior of Bath Abbey, who had been initiated into the secrets of the Art by George Ripley. Holway had spent a great deal to rebuild the Abbey which was destroyed in 1090 and perhaps was drawn to alchemy to raise more funds. Ashmole later reported that when some stonework was pulled down in the abbey the workmen discovered a lost elixir: 'a Glasse found in a Wall full of Red Tincture, which being flung away to a dunghill, forthwith coloured it, exceedingly red'. When the manure was carted away and spread on a field, 'for a long tyme after, the Corne grew wonderfully ranke, thick and high: insomuch as it was there look'd upon as a wonder'.[12]

Charnock began his *Breviary of Naturall Philosophy* on 1 January 1557, two years after the great fire. He completed it on 20 July 1557, and dedicated it to Elizabeth I and delivered a copy to her chief secretary, William Cecil, first Baron Burghley.[13] It was not completed without interruption: a man who bore him great malice had him press-ganged into Mary Queen of Scots' army in Calais to defend it against the Duke of Guise. Charnock was so incensed that he destroyed his whole laboratory, not this time with fire but with a hatchet. He cannot have been well-off for he was unable to buy himself out of military service.

On his return he settled in Stockland, Bristol and married Agnes Norton in 1662, who bore him a daughter, Bridget. After 1565 they moved to Combwich near Bridgewater in Somerset. His new laboratory there upset his neighbours, who looked on him as no better than a conjuror. Hoping to purify his *materia prima*, he noted that he once repeated an alchemical operation 476 times, believing that it would be

transformed by the time he reached 500. He claimed that the long
years of study and laboratory work were eventually crowned by
success in the Great Work in 1574. In a fragment in his own hand
found amongst his papers, he wrote:

> Looke you conceive my words a right
> And marke well this which I have sede;
> For Black is Ferment unto the Whyte,
> And Whyte shal be Ferment unto the Rede:
> Which I never saw till I had whyte heres upon my head.
>
> T.C., 1574, The 50 yeare of my age.[14]

Charnock died seven years later. A neighbour recalled that his daughter
Bridget once let his fire go out during his temporary absence and all
his work was lost.

About a hundred years after Charnock's death a roll of parchment
about 2 metres long and 23 centimetres wide was discovered in the
wall of a room in his house at Combwich, which still stands. A
clergyman called Andrew Pascal, an antiquary and friend of Ashmole,
enquired about the discovery and after a visit to the house wrote to
John Aubrey, FRS:

> I saw on the dore of his little Athanor-room (if I may so call it)
> drawne by his owne hand, with course colours and worke, but
> ingeniously, an Embleme of his Worke, at which I gave some
> guesses, and soe about the walls in his Chamber, I think there was
> in all 5 panes of his worke, all somewhat differing from each
> other, some very obscure and almost worne out. They told me
> that people had been unwilling to dwell in that house, because
> reputed troublesome, I presume from some traditionall stories of
> this person, who was looked on by his Neighbours as no better
> than a Conjuror.[15]

The parchment roll in English and Latin (which is now in the British
Library) has the almost illegible note at its foot:

> Thomas Charnock of Stokeland, Bristow, who travelled all the
> realm of England over for to obtain unto the secrets of this science,
> which, as God would, he did attain unto, anno Domini 1555; as
> it appeareth more plainly in the Book [named the Breviary of
> Philosophie] which I dedicated unto Queen Elizabeth of England.
> Born at Feversham in Kent, 1526.[16]

35

Hieroglyphic Adventure

Our Work is the conversion and change of one being into
another being, as from one thing into another thing, from
debility to strength . . . from corporeality to spirituality.

Nicolas Flamel[1]

After investigating the works of the English alchemists, I crossed the
Channel to see what enlightenment I could gain from their French
counterparts. I had already visited Chartres Cathedral. In Paris I was
intrigued to come across the priest Claude Frollo in Victor Hugo's
great novel *Nôtre Dame de Paris*, who sat 'in the cavern at this
mysterious table of alchemists, astrologers, Hermeticists, of whom
Averröes, Guillaume de Paris, and Nicolas Flamel come at the end in
the Middle Ages'.

Frollo was taken by a singular passion for the symbolic portal of
Nôtre Dame, '*cette page de grimoire*' written in stone by Bishop
Guillaume de Paris, the man responsible for raising the great Gothic
cathedral. The priest would spend hours, seated on the parvis, contemplating the sculptures of the main portal, examining the virgins with
their lamps, and at other times, calculating the angle of the glance of
the crow on the left side which looks into the church at 'a mysterious
point where certainly is hid the Philosopher's Stone'.[1] It was precisely
these aspects of the cathedral that the mysterious alchemist Fulcanelli
tried to decipher in *Le Mystère des cathédrales* (1926). After my visit
to Chartres I had also reached the conclusion that the great Gothic
cathedrals of France were built in order to ensure the transmission of
alchemical symbols and doctrines down the ages.

Nôtre Dame de Paris is a 'Philosopher's Church'.[2] Like Hugo's
priest Frollo, I spent a long time exploring the statues on the main

portal, known as the 'Porch of Judgement'. On the pier, there is an intriguing carving representing the medieval sciences. In pride of place is Alchemy herself. Sitting on a throne, she is holding between her knees a nine-runged ladder, the *scala philosophorum*, symbolizing the different stages of ascent to the illumination of the Philosopher's Stone. In her right hand, she has an open and a closed book, representing the exoteric and esoteric paths, and in her left a sceptre, symbolizing her magical power. On her right side is a woman holding up a phial and on her left a woman holding a square within a square representing the unity of the four elements. Other figures on the central porch have hidden alchemical themes. A fountain at the foot of the old oak represents the fountain of mercury which contains the seed of gold. Women hold discs with different alchemical symbols: a serpent around a caduceus (philosophic mercury), a salamander (calcination), and the Stone itself. On the threshold of one of the world's greatest monuments thus stands the symbol of the Great Work of alchemy.

In the north portal, known as the 'Portal of the Virgin', I noticed in the centre of the tympanum on the middle cornice a sarcophagus which depicts an episode in the life of Christ. On the sarcophagus where the dead Christ is lain there are seven circles depicting the seven planetary metals: sun (gold), Mercury (quicksilver), Saturn (lead), Venus (copper), moon (silver), Jupiter (tin), Mars (iron).

According to the alchemist Fulcanelli, the south portal known as the 'Porch of St Anne' describes the shortest practice of alchemy – the 'dry' as opposed to the 'moist' way.[3] On the thin jamb known as the St Marcellus Pillar, a bishop would seem to perch over a furnace in which 'philosophical mercury' is being sublimated. His stick holds down a dragon which from an esoteric point of view depicts the destruction of prime matter and its transformation into pure energy.

Before leaving the Cathedral of Nôtre Dame de Paris, I climbed at dusk up a small spiralling staircase to its towers – itself an emblem of the spiritual path. I emerged on the second gallery to find myself on a narrow parapet surrounded with tall statues of monstrous creatures from a nightmare: devils, griffins, golems and even a character which looks remarkably like an alien. They seemed to have escaped from the devil's workshop, or more likely from the shadows of the masons' unconscious – a counterpart to the divine light of the stained-glass windows.

Next to the north tower, leaning out from the parapet looking over the vast panorama of Paris below, was the alchemist, stroking with one hand his flowing beard. He wore a Phrygian cap, made famous by the extreme *sans culottes* during the French Revolution, but which was used much earlier by adepts as a sign of initiation. Known as '*la chimère*', the figure is not in the meditative pose of a monk, but has the earnest, searching gaze of the alchemist at his athanor.

I suspected that he might be looking down to the old house of Nicolas Flamel in Rue Montmorency or perhaps at 51 Rue Nicolas Flamel or Rue Pernelle named after his wife. Their house I found out dates from 1407. It has Hermetic symbols on its facade and you can even enjoy the alchemy of food in the Restaurant Nicolas Flamel within.

Not far from Nôtre Dame is the tower of the Church of St Jacques-la-Boucherie with its gargoyles and angels. When Victor Hugo described Nôtre Dame Cathedral as 'the most satisfying summary of Hermetic science', he added, 'of which the Church of Saint-Jacques-la-Boucherie was such a complete hieroglyph'.[4] A plaque records that since the tenth century millions of pilgrims of all nationalities started here on their way to the tomb of St Jacques (St James) in Compostella in northern Spain.

Flamel was one of them. According to Abbé Villian: 'On the west post of the portal a little sculptured angel is seen, holding a circle of stone in her hands; Flamel had a circular piece of black marble incorporated in it, with a thread of fine gold in the form of a cross . . .'[5] This would seem to represent the four elements, a motif found in the central porch of Nôtre Dame. Flamel recorded that he had himself and his wife Perennelle painted on the door of the chapel, giving thanks at the feet of St Jacques of Compostella and at those of Saint John to commemorate his safe return from his pilgrimage.[6]

In his will, Flamel left funds to found fourteen hospitals, to build three chapels and to endow seven churches. Some forty deeds still survive concerning these gifts and donations. Where did this immense wealth come from? From alchemical gold, it was widely rumoured. Flamel's marble tombstone, which at one time was used as a chopping block for herbs, reflects his alchemical interests. It has carvings of St Peter and St Paul on either side of a figure of Christ with symbols of Sol and Luna. In the Cimetière des Innocents in Paris, there are bas-reliefs ordered by Flamel which depict the different operations of the Great Work in esoteric images.[7]

Born in Pontoise in 1330, Flamel started life as a public scribe and notary, at first near the Charnier des Innocents, and then, when the guild of scribes moved as a whole, to a road opposite the Church of St Jacques-la-Boucherie, which became known as the Rue des Ecrivains. He opened a shop in a nearby house called A la Signe de la Fleur de Lys for copying manuscripts and books.

It was while quietly earning a living this way that one night in a dream an angel came to him and showed him a book with strange hieroglyphs on every seventh page. 'Flamel,' said the angel, 'look carefully at this book; you'll understand nothing in it, nothing, neither you nor many others, but one day you will see there what no one else would be able to see.' As he stretched out to seize the book, the angel disappeared into a golden cloud.

Many years later a very large gilded book came into his hands with curious symbols engraved on leaves of thin bark. The cover was of finely-worked copper, with curious letters and figures. Flamel recognized it as the book which had appeared in his dream. It declared on the first pages in golden letters that it was written by 'Abraham the Jew, Priest, Levite, Astrologer and Philosopher, to the Nation of the Jews, by the Wrath of God dispersed among the Gauls, Salutations'.[8]

Flamel bought the curious work on the spot for two florins. It consists of twenty-one pages. Every seventh leaf has only images. On the first is a rod with two serpents swallowing one another; on the second, a cross on which a serpent is crucified; and on the last, a beautiful fountain from which issue many serpents in a desert.

The book contained other images. On the fourth leaf appears an image of Mercury with an ancient figure of winged Saturn with hourglass and scythe sweeping down on him. A second image on the same leaf depicts a mountain at the top of which is a flower bush, with a blue stalk, white and red flowers and golden leaves. Dragons and griffins make their abodes on the mountainsides. On the fifth leaf a flowering rose tree climbs around a hollow oak tree in the midst of a beautiful garden. Water gushes out of its foot only to disappear into the earth; blind people dig in search of it. On the other side of this leaf soldiers on the orders of a king are killing little children and gathering their blood in a great vessel in which Sun and Moon come to bathe themselves.

Flamel could make neither head nor tail of the images. The letters of the text did not help, for they were not in Latin. It would not have been too difficult to understand the images if he had met a knowledge-able alchemist. The old man with the scythe is Saturn or lead trying to cut the feet of Mercury – that is trying to 'fix' philosophical mercury. The fountain usually represents a vessel in which mercury is trans-formed and the spring at the foot of the rose bush gushes forth the life-giving *fons mercurialis* itself. Snakes are the classic symbol of mercury, the source of the Philosopher's Stone. The white and red flowers stand for the White and Red Elixirs. The blood of the innocents symbolizes the spirit of metals.

Flamel believed the author was revealing to the Jews the art of transmuting metals so that they might help pay taxes to the Roman Emperor. He also suspected that the book gave the recipe of the Great Work but it did not explain the *materia prima* to use. After twenty-one years of fruitless experiment, he suddenly realized that since the book was written by Jews for Jews the best person to interpret would be a Jew steeped in the Cabala. Where better to find one than by joining the pilgrims who left every year from the Church of St Jacques-la-Boucherie to travel to Compostella in Spain, the land of ancient Hebrew and Arab wisdom?

He set off in 1378. After paying homage to St Jacques at his shrine in Compostella, he visited many synagogues in Spain with his cherished book but to no avail. His luck – or destiny – changed on his return journey. He met in León a merchant from Bologne who directed him to a friend called Maître Canches, a converted Jew steeped in the Cabala. He recognized the work as the long-lost *Aesh Mezareph* by Rabbi Abraham, a text which the Cabalists believed had been lost for ever. The new friends, discoursing in Latin, decided to travel to Paris to decipher the original document. After being seasick during the journey, the master died but not before initiating Flamel into the secrets of the Great Work.

It still took Flamel another three years to bring his experiments to success. When it came to the penultimate stage with the substance in a 'philosophical egg' (glass flask) in his athanor (furnace), he watched the changing colours with a beating heart and bated breath. They came in the correct order: from grey to black (the 'crow's head'), from black to white. The white appeared like a halo round the edge of the black while white filaments shot towards the centre until the whole was a perfect white. He had reached the stage of the White Elixir.

With the help of his wife Perennelle, he recorded that around midday on Monday, 17 January 1382, they managed to achieve transmutation by projecting the white substance on to half a pound of melted lead in a crucible. The result was 'pure silver', purer than the natural silver of mines.

Having attained the magistery of the art, Flamel put the rest of the White Elixir back in a flask and continued heating. One after the other, the rest of the correct colours emerged, this time the white changing into the iridescence of the peacock's tail, and then to yellow, orange, purple and finally to the red of the Great Elixir.

Then again alone with his wife in their house, around five o'clock in the evening on 25 April in the same year, he performed the Great Work. Following word for word the instruction in his book, he transformed with the 'Red Stone' a similar quantity of mercury into virtually as much pure gold. It was, he recorded, 'certainly much better than common gold, softer and more pliable'.

Flamel and his wife are a model of the close collaboration between male and female alchemists, mirrored in the work of the Alexandrian alchemists 1,500 years earlier and with the Curies nearly five centuries later. In his account, he insists: 'Perennelle understood it as well as I, because she helped me in my operations, and without doubt if she had undertaken to do it herself she would have attained to the end and perfection thereof.'[9]

With the gold obtained from three more transmutations, Flamel allegedly became one of the richest men of Paris. His reputation reached Charles VI, King of France, who sent the Chief Tax Inspector to investigate his circumstances. He was reported to be living with his modest wife out of the barest earthenware crockery. His fortune remained a great mystery.

It is said that Perennelle died in 1397 or 1404 and was buried in the Cimetière des Innocents. Flamel himself lived on to eighty in his house in Rue Montmorency. Another version claims, however, that troubled by the interest of the powerful, envious and curious, he dissimulated her death, escaped for Switzerland and then travelled to India.[10] Paul Lucas in his *Voyage au Levant* met an Uzbeck dervish who claimed to have seen the Flamels alive and well in 1705. In 1761 they were reported to be at the opera in Paris. Having discovered the Philosopher's Stone are the couple still travelling the world? Comte St Germain in the eighteenth century and Fulcanelli in the twentieth century were reputed to have similar ability to transcend time and place.

Certainly myth and history combine in the story of the Flamels. There may well be hidden symbols in their own lives and names. Was the work of Flamel one of fiction or fact or a mixture of both? The description of his wife Perennelle is very much like alchemical mercury, passive but indispensable, while Flamel appears to be like active and creative sulphur. The Jewish teacher who dies would seem to represent the *prima materia* which must be destroyed before Mercury and Sulphur can have their chemical wedding.

Even their names might hide Cabalistic meanings. 'Flamel' invokes 'flame' while 'Perennelle Flamel' suggests *'flame pérennielle'* (perpetual flame) or even *'pierre'* for the Stone. Her maiden name is Perrier which also suggests *pierre*. Taken together, Flamel and Perennelle would seem to evoke *'flame'* and *'pierre'*, fire and stone, the means and goal of alchemy.

In a collection called *The Hermetic Museum*, first translated into English in 1678, I came across a work attributed to Flamel called 'Short Tract or Philosophical Summary'. The author asserts like most medieval alchemists that all metals have been formed out of sulphur and mercury, which are the seeds of all metals. One represents the male and the other the female principle, which are also in fire and air, and earth and water. If the two seeds are united by 'triumphant Nature' the result is mercury, the 'Mother of Metals'. The first coagulation of mercury is lead which according to Flamel is most suitable for fixing it and bringing it to perfection:

> For lead is never without some fixed grain of gold and silver, which are imparted to it by Nature for the purpose of multiplication and development.

Flamel is convinced like his forbears – whom he calls 'the Sages' – that 'if gold and silver be joined through their proper mercury, they have power to render all other (imperfect) metals perfect'. The alchemist cannot therefore create matter, but only perfect what is already created. Flamel insists:

> I will not say that man by his art can make natural things; but I do say that human art can impart greater perfection to that which Nature makes.

But where are we to obtain the 'mercury of the Sages', the first substance in the production of the Stone? This is the greatest difficulty. 'If they would obtain it', Flamel declares,

> they must go to the seventh mountain, where there is no plain, and from its height they must look down upon the sixth, which they will behold at a great distance. On the summit of that mountain they will find the glorious Regal Herb, which some Sages call a mineral, some a vegetable. The bones they must leave, and only extract its pure juice, which will enable them to do the better part of the work. This is the true and subtle mercury of the philosophers which you must take. Now, first it prepares the white tincture, and then the red. For the *Sun* and the *Moon* are prepared by the same method, and yield the red and white tincture respectively . . .[11]

Once you have obtained the mercury of the Philosophers, the rest is easy. The alchemist must simply follow the example of a hen on her eggs and warm the mercury with a gentle heat. The problem remains that the seventh mountain is as difficult to find and scale as the seventh heaven. But Flamel, according to his own account, attained it.

Part Six

The Hermetic Enlightenment

Bulls and Alembics

Poor themselves, the alchemists promise riches which are not
forthcoming; wise also in their own conceit, they fall into the
ditch which they themselves have dug . . .

Spondent Pariter (1317), bull issued by Pope John XXII

Climbing the steps to the piazza designed by Michelangelo in the
Capitol on one of the seven hills of Rome, I was struck by the presence
of two lions in black granite taken from a Temple of Isis in Ptolemaic
Egypt. They reminded me how the ancient Romans appreciated the
civilization of Egypt, especially when it became part of the Roman
Empire after the defeat of Cleopatra. During their occupation of the
Middle East and North Africa, the Romans not only imposed their
administration but absorbed many of the beliefs of the conquered.
There was a considerable vogue for Egyptian styles and gods, evidence
of which I had seen in the ruins of Pompeii near Naples. And when
the Muslims occupied Sicily from the early ninth century, they brought
with them their philosophy and science, including alchemy.

Despite the overthrow of the Muslim rulers of Sicily, Frederick II
(1194–1250) continued to be very hospitable to Islamic learning – so
much so that when he crowned himself King of Jerusalem the Pope
excommunicated him for being so sympathetic to the Muslims. He
declared himself Emperor of the Romans, of Germany and Sicily.
He founded the University of Naples and supported the medical school
of Salerno. He surrounded himself with Muslim, Jewish and Christian
scholars and alchemists. Not a man to rest in theory, the half-
Hofenstaufen and half-Sicilian emperor conducted his own bizarre
experiments, on one occasion locking a man in a box to die in order
to see if his soul would emerge through a hole in the lid.

Attracted to such intellectual ferment, many scholars from the north descended to his court. Michael Scotus (the Scot) was amongst them. He so impressed Frederick that he was made one of his astrologers. Whilst residing at the court, he also wrote two works on alchemy: *The Magistery of the Art of Alchemy* and *The Lesser Magistery*. They give detailed descriptions of alums, salt, vitriols, and spirits as well as many recipes for transmutation. One such involves five toads which are 'shut up in a vessel and made to drink the juices of various herbs with vinegar as the first step in the preparation of a marvellous powder for the purposes of transmutation'.[1] He clearly practised his own experiments and seems to have collaborated with Jewish and Muslim adepts. The broad range of substances which he used included herbs and minerals from Calabria, India and Alexandria as well as the dust of moles and the blood of an owl. Opium figured prominently which may also have inspired some of his wilder recipes.

Michael Scotus earned a serious reputation as a magus. He is mentioned by Dante as a practitioner of 'magical deceits' and by Boccaccio as a 'master of black magic'. The learned Pope Gerbert described him as

> A wizard, of such dreaded fame,
> That when, in Salamanca's cave,
> Him listed his magic wand to wave,
> The bells would ring in Notre Dame![2]

He was reported to have ridden through the air on a demon horse and sailed in a demon ship. It seems that he was a dab hand at foretelling deaths. He predicted that Frederick would meet his death in Florence; the Emperor refused to enter the city, but finally died in Fiorentino or 'Little Florence'. He foresaw that he would himself be killed by a small stone falling on his head. As a precaution, he henceforth wore a cerebrerium or steel helmet, but one day when he took it off in church to receive the host, a two-ounce stone fell from the roof and finished him off. His astrology was clearly more powerful than his alchemy: he could predict events but not prolong his life.

*

Despite the Muslim transition of alchemy to Europe and the association of some of its practitioners with the devil, popes and cardinals became directly involved in the subject. Pope Clement IV requested to see Roger Bacon's *Opus Maius* and was sent three of his works. Arnald of Villanova dedicated an *Epistola* to Pope Boniface VIII, to whom he was a physician for a year, and the *Semita Semitae* to Pope Benedict XI. The Avignon Pope John XXII was rumoured to have amassed a fortune through alchemy, yet in 1317 he issued the bull *Spondent Pariter* forbidding alchemy as a science and imposing heavy fines on counterfeiters. It declared with a rhetorical flourish:

> They dissimulate their failure so that finally, though there is no
> such thing in nature, they pretend to make genuine gold and silver
> by a sophistic transmutation; to such an extent does their damned
> and damnable temerity go that they stamp upon the base metal
> the characters of public money for believing eyes, and it is only in
> this way that they deceive the ignorant populace as to the alchemic
> fire of the furnace.[3]

The bull announced that anyone making counterfeit gold or silver, or helping to make it, would have to pay the same amount in real gold or silver or face imprisonment and be 'branded with the mark of infamy'. As for clerics found to be engaged in alchemy, they were to be deprived of any benefices.

John Dastin, an obscure monk and adept, was incensed. He wrote to John XXII explaining the real nature of 'the most noble matter, which according to tradition of all philosophers, transforms any metallic body into very pure gold and silver' and which 'makes an old man young and drives out all sickness of the body'. Adopting the Muslim theory of the generation of metals from sulphur and mercury, he claimed that purified gold could be used as a ferment in order to transmute 'fixed' mercury into gold by combining it with 'very pure sulphur'. Using homely metaphors he declared:

> Gold is more valuable than all other metals, because it contains in
> itself the essence of any metal. It tinges them and vivifies them,
> because it is the ferment of the elixir, without which the philoso-
> phers' medicine can by no means be perfected, like dough cannot
> be fermented without a ferment. It is indeed as leaven to dough,
> as curd to milk for cheese, and as the musk in good perfumes . . .[4]

Dastin went on to expound his theory in letters to Cardinal Orsini, insisting that the 'red sulphur' to be found in gold is sufficient to convert suitably prepared mercury into the 'Red Elixir'. In another work ascribed to him, he describes the mercury as the sperm and material of metals and of the Philosopher's Stone. At the same time, he insisted that the elixir has a spiritual nature for it occupies no space and yet can be manipulated. It follows that 'This magistery is for kings and the great of this world, because he who possesses it has a never-failing treasure.'[5] Dastin was reported to have lived in extreme frugality. If he discovered the Philosopher's Stone in his lifetime, it was not to amass riches.

*

Despite the papal bull forbidding alchemy in 1317, Petrus Bonus composed around 1330 the *Pretiosa Margarita Novella* ('The New Pearl of Great Price'), one of the greatest works of alchemy to come out of Italy in the fourteenth century. He was a member of the Avogadrus family of Ferrara, a town north of Bologna, although the book itself was composed in Pola, a city of the Italian province of Istria (known as Pulji in the former Yugoslavia). Petrus only mentions classical and Muslim authorities for his work. But he also claims that many ancient poems and myths have hidden alchemical themes, singling out Ovid's *Metamorphoses* as an esoteric treatment of the Philosopher's Stone.

Petrus is a believer, but he is not a naive believer. While the essential knowledge can be acquired in a very brief time, he stresses that the quest for it can be very difficult – something which I had found out the hard way. He observes that adepts use words in enigmatic and even ironical ways, especially figures of '*aequivocationis, allegoriae et metaphorae*'.[6] Alchemical writers further contradict each other and use different methods in the laboratory. Yet if you strip away the figures of speech, Petrus claims the message could be written down in some eight or twelve lines. If only it were true!

As a good medieval schoolman, Petrus states and answers many of the principal arguments against alchemy. To the objection that the alchemists do not know the exact composition of metals and cannot therefore reproduce the experiments, he replies that the constituents of all metals are known, namely sulphur and mercury. The alchemists can cure impure metals by releasing their superfluous sulphur to obtain silver or gold. Above all, transmutation brought about by the Stone is the work of nature assisted by Art and directed by the Divine Will. Faith is essential; without it any experiment is doomed to failure.

The principles of alchemy, Petrus recognizes, are both natural and artificial. The former are the causes of the four elements and of the metals. The latter are the processes used in the laboratory as well as the tests, signs and colours employed to ensure that the operations are successful.

In the composition of metals, the supreme ingredient is mercury which contains an 'intrinsic' non-combustible sulphur within it. Apart from gold, all metals have 'extrinsic' burning sulphur which is the reason for their imperfection. Mercury can thus be purified in the furnace by the removal of the outward sulphur, restored to its original condition and transmuted into gold. 'We may justly conclude from these considerations', Petrus declares,

> that when the Philosopher's Stone is projected upon iron or copper in a liquefied state, it mingles in a moment of time with all the particles of quicksilver existing in them, and with these only, and perfects them into the purest gold, while all the particles of external sulphur are purged off, because they are not of a nature homogeneous with that of the Stone . . . So we see that, in the case of milk, the coagulant clots only those parts of the milk that are of a nature homogeneous with its own.[7]

In order to clarify the nature of the Philosopher's Stone, Petrus used the analogy of smoke, something perpetually swirling in the alchemist's laboratory, which could become fixed or condensed as soot.

Although I looked in vain in *The New Pearl of Great Price* for the exact method of preparing the Stone, Petrus does at least explore the meaning of the 'ferment' which is used in projection. The alchemists, he observes, use it in two senses, to refer to the Stone itself or to that which perfects the Stone. Using another homely analogy, he writes that in the first sense the Stone is 'the leaven of all other metals' which changes them into its own nature just like a small piece of yeast transforms a lump of dough. In the second sense, the ferment may be invisible to the eye but it can be seen by the mind. Petrus continues the long Hermetic tradition of spiritual alchemy when he explores the subtle relationship between the body, soul and spirit:

> It is the body which retains the soul, and the soul can shew its power only when it is united to the body. Therefore when the artist sees the white soul rise, he should join it to its body in the same instant, for no soul can be retained without its body.

> This union takes place through the mediation of the spirit, which
> gives permanence to their union, and this conjunction is the end
> of the work ... The body is the form, and the ferment, and the
> Tincture of which the sages are in search.[8]

The passage makes clear that the Stone is an unstable substance and
that a critical operation must be performed at a precise moment just
before the completion of its preparation. The entire substance – the
soul united to the body by the spirit – is of the pure nature of gold.

The ability of gold to reproduce itself after being dissolved and
coagulated is illustrated in *The New Pearl of Great Price* in a series of
disturbing engravings. An old king is first depicted enthroned and
honoured by his six kneeling sons. One of them then murders him
with a sword and collects his blood. He is buried but the king rises
likes Osiris from his tomb, sits on his throne and shows his power by
giving golden crowns to his sons and making them kings in their own
right. Parricide, or the 'killing' of Mercury, thus leads to rebirth and
multiplication.

*

Although Petrus was convinced that the whole secret of transmutation
could be learned in a single hour and expressed in a few lines, he is
rare amongst alchemists in admitting that he was never successful in
the art. By keeping a low profile, Petrus managed to escape the fate of
his fellow Italian alchemist Cecco d'Ascoli, author of *L'Acerbe*, who
was burned at the stake by the Inquisition in Florence in 1327, three
years before the composition of *The New Pearl of Great Price* and ten
years after the declaration of Pope John XXII's bull against alchemy.

The bull gave rise to a whole series of ecclesiastical works against
alchemy. In his *Epistola Contra Alchimistas*, Eymerich the Inquisitor
of Aragon declared that alchemy was a heresy, since it was based on
an implicit pact with the devil. Yet throughout the fifteenth and
sixteenth centuries, Rome was a hotbed of alchemy and the occult.
Popes kept private astrologers and diviners, and red-capped cardinals
and black-frocked monsignori haunted the laboratories of the alchemists in the back streets around the Vatican.

I came across one whilst in Rome in the Hospitale di Santo Spirito,
the oldest hospital in the city, founded in the thirteenth century in a
time of plague, only a stone's throw from St Peter's Square. It is now

part of the Museo Storico dell'Arte Sanitaria, a small museum dedicated to the history of alchemy and medicine. The alchemist's laboratory is in a small and dark room, lit only by a high latticed window and by the fire in the furnace. There is a clay lute as round and white as an egg. A lioness stalks across the ornate fireplace. Mortars and pestles and coloured glass bottles line the shelves. Scattered on the workbenches are pewter pots, bulbous glass jars, alembics and pelicans with their graceful protruding spouts. Among the more bizarre exhibits is a spherical 'Bezoar' in an ornate case, the gallstone of a virgin camel valued as a remedy against all poisons, and an embossed leather case containing the alleged horn of a unicorn from France.

37

Mysteries of Divinity

Whatever is small, trivial or mean serves to complete the
splendour of the whole.

Giordano Bruno, *De l'Infinito, Universo e Mondi* (1584)

The contradictory attitude of the Vatican to alchemy and the Hermetic
tradition became even more apparent during the Renaissance. I had a
strong reminder of this early one morning in Rome in late July. The
sun was only beginning to warm the pavements of the city as I passed
through the semicircle of cool colonnades into the great circular
courtyard in front of St Peter's where hundreds of thousands of
Christians would gather to listen to the Pope. There, right in the
middle of the vast courtyard in front of the world's largest church, was
a colossal Egyptian obelisk, its tapering point glinting in the rays of
the early morning sun.

It was one of forty-eight obelisks which had been taken from Egypt
to Rome after the defeat of Cleopatra. Standing 25 metres high and
weighing 26 tons, it was first erected by Augustus in the Julian Forum
in Alexandria. It was then brought across the sea by Caligula and
placed on the site of the Roman Circus where it witnessed the
martyrdom of St Peter around 65. Aware of its symbolic value, Pope
Sixtus V had the obelisk moved to the great piazza in front of the
Basilica of St Peter in 1586.[1] The Pope placed his personal emblem of
the holy star and a cross on the orb at its top to symbolize the triumph
of the new religion over the old.

But was it really triumphant? The more I studied the Hermetic
tradition during the Renaissance, the more it seemed to me that the
obelisk in front of St Peter's was a symbol of the ancient wisdom of

Egypt thriving at the heart of Christendom. There was undoubtedly a concerted effort amongst the Renaissance thinkers both within and outside the Church to restore the Egyptian religion and the sacred science which fired it.

Giordano Bruno, the most original Italian philosopher of the period, was at the forefront of the underground movement. Bruno was born at Nola, near Naples in 1548, and later talked of the 'Nolan' as a prophet who would change the world. As a young man, he became a Dominican friar but after being accused of heresy he abandoned his habit. He began the life of the travelling scholar, lecturing at Toulouse, Paris (where he caught the attention of Henri III), Oxford (where he lectured to the dons), and then Prague (to see Emperor Rudolf II). Although he was not a practising alchemist in the laboratory, he was a great exponent of the alchemy of the spirit.

Bruno believed the Hermetic philosophy to be the true religion, with its worship of 'God in things', its 'profound magic', and its view, expressed in *Asclepius*, that '*magnum miraculum homo est*'. He worshipped the Egyptians for worshipping the One in All: 'You see, then, how one simple divinity which is in all things, one fecund nature, mother and preserver of the universe, shines forth in diverse subjects, and takes diverse names, according as it communicates itself diversely.'[2]

In *De l'Infinito, Universo e Mondi* (1584), Bruno presents the living earth revolving around the divine sun with other innumerable worlds in an infinite universe moving by a kind of magical animism. Nothing in the living world is immobile; everything moves in an inherent circular motion. There is no death in nature, only change.

Bruno made it his life's task to propagate the old religion in the hope of bringing about a cosmological and moral revolution throughout Europe which would bring to an end its wars and persecutions. In his dedication to the doctors of the University of Oxford, he boldly described himself as 'the waker of sleeping souls, tamer of presumptuous and recalcitrant ignorance, proclaimer of a general philanthropy'.[3]

Bruno was greatly influenced by the *Hermetica*, the Cabala and the art of Lull (which he felt he understood better than Lull himself). In a work called *Articuli Adversus Mathematicos* (1588, 'Articles against Mathematics') full of geometrical shapes and diagrams, Bruno developed his own idiosyncratic version of magical numerology which he called 'mathesis'. It has dotted across its pages the alchemical gold sun sign for *mentus*, the silver moon sign for *intellectus*, and the five-pointed star for *amoris*.

In Bruno's view the 'Temple of Wisdom' was built first among the Egyptians, and the wisdom of the Cabala of the Jews came from the Egyptians. He not only implied that the Egyptian religion was the true religion, superior to Christianity, but argued that the Cross was a symbol – presumably the ankh – taken from the Egyptians. He accepted the heliocentric view of Copernicus 'that the earth did go round' and urged the worship of the sun in a splendid passage:

> Some men, resembling the dim-eyed mole, who the moment he feels upon him the open air of heaven, rushes to dig himself back again into the ground, desire to remain in their native darkness ... But those who were born to see the sun, being full of thanksgiving when they come to the end of the loathsome night, dispose themselves to receive in the very centre of their eyes' crystal globe the long-expected rays of the glorious sun, and, with unaccustomed gladness in their hearts, they lift up hands and voices to adore the east.[4]

Bruno praised the 'sacred letters' of the hieroglyphs which were images taken directly from 'things of nature'. By using such writings and voices the ancient Egyptians were able to capture with marvellous skill 'the language of the gods'. But when the modern alphabet was invented it brought about a rift both in memory and in the divine and magical sciences. In order to overcome this, he developed an original method for training the memory based on the imagination. Since the mind of God is present in the mind of humans, the magus can discover the secrets of the universe within his own memory.[5] By engraving on the memory celestial images which are 'shadows' close to the 'ideas' of the divine mind, one can become godlike and gain divine powers. Bruno considered this way of thinking to be a genuine 'Egyptian' experience and I could see his point.

With his celebration of the sacred science and religion of the ancient Egyptians, it is easy to see why Bruno was persecuted by the Catholic Church. Yet he returned to Italy in 1591 in goodwill, with a manuscript on the seven liberal arts to be dedicated to Pope Clement VIII. He was arrested in Venice by the Inquisition. Although he recanted his heresies at a trial, he was sent for a retrial in Rome. This time he refused to recant, and after eight years in prison he was burned at the stake in 1600. It was probably as a Hermetic magus and as an 'Egyptian' that Bruno was condemned to death.[6]

*

Bruno was not the only Hermetic philosopher to be persecuted. The Inquisition tortured and imprisoned for more than twenty-seven years the Dominican priest Tommaso Campanella (1568–1639) for trying to bring about a general revolution based on Hermetic principles of his *La Città del Sole* (1602, 'City of the Sun'). The work written in prison has clear echoes of the ideal city of Adocentyn in the Arabic *Picatrix*. A Hermetic believer in the World Soul and in the intimate correspondence between heaven and earth, Campanella saw the 'descent of the sun' closer to the earth in his own day as a celestial portent of a new age.

The design of his City of the Sun is circular, recalling the Egyptian City of the Sun (Heliopolis) and the original plan of Baghdad. Like a Celtic cross, it has four roads going towards the four directions of the compass. At its centre is a round Sun Temple on a hill. The greatest stars of the heavens, with their names and their powers over earthly objects, are painted on the ceiling of its great dome. Its seven concentric walls, known as *giri*, represent the seven planets and depict aspects of the natural and the celestial worlds.[7]

How is the City of the Sun organized within this sacred architecture? It is run by adepts called Solarians who in the name of Hermes Trismegistus practise benevolent magic and ensure that the city is in harmony with the celestial influences so that its inhabitants enjoy health, happiness and virtue. The name of the high priest of the Solarians – in the manuscript written whilst Campanella was in prison – is represented by a circle with a dot in the centre, the alchemical symbol for gold. He is assisted by three priests representing Power, Wisdom and Love. The people in the city are well educated and virtuous, living in communal love and sharing all their possessions.

*

The Vatican had good reason to be fearful of Bruno and Campanella in their desire to bring about a religious, moral and social revolution based on the Hermetic philosophy. Thomas Aquinas had defended magic and alchemy and many priests, especially in Dominican circles, were being won over to the new vision. Even popes were not immune.

The Hermetic philosophy was a great attraction and a huge threat. It placed the sun and not the earth at the centre of the universe. It awakened fears of a revival of the old religion of sun worship. It seemed as if the ancient pagan religion of Egypt, which the early popes had done so much to suppress, was about to burst like a tree through the marble pavements of the Renaissance and scatter the fragile edifice of their hard-earned power to the four winds.

With this growing interest in the ancient Egyptian religion and philosophy, Pope Innocent X called upon the Hermeticist Athanasius Kircher (1602–80) to decode the hieroglyphs on his obelisk. Kircher was a Jesuit father and a professor of mathematics at the College of Rome and was therefore considered reliable. But was he? He not only recorded having undertaken trance journeys through the spheres of the planets but celebrated at every opportunity ancient Egyptian wisdom.

Kircher published the first Coptic grammar and saw in the Egyptian hieroglyphs 'the highest mysteries of Divinity'.[8] He also believed that within Egyptian symbols and myths lay hidden universal and sacred truths. Indeed, he was convinced that Egypt was the post-diluvian cradle of all arts, sciences and wisdom. In his 'Sphere of Love', a diagram of a circle enclosing dark and light pyramids, Kircher presented the 'Egyptian' philosophy in which the World Soul infuses the whole cosmos with a ray of Love, causing it to live and move around its axis. Towards the end of his *Oedipus Aegyptiacus*, Kircher asserts in an outburst of Hermetic faith:

> Hermes Trismegistus, the Egyptian, who first instituted the hiero-glyphs, thus becoming the prince and parent of all Egyptian theology and philosophy, was the first and most ancient among the Egyptians and first rightly thought of divine things; and engraved his opinions for all eternity on lasting stones and huge rocks . . . And this Trismegistus was the first who in his Pimander and Asclepius asserted that God is One and Good, who the rest of the philosophers followed.[9]

Kircher's position on alchemy was more circumspect. Although he claimed to have performed palingenesis – the resurrection of plants from their ashes – he raised doubts about the possibility of transmuting metals into gold in his *Mundus Subterraneus* (1665, 1678). But was this his true position? While outwardly rejecting magic, in *Oedipus Aegyptiacus* he offered a veritable textbook of planetary magic. Drawn to the heliocentric view of the universe, he adopted Tycho Brahe's position that the stars and planets circle the sun which, with the moon, revolves around the earth.

These caveats may well have been because he did not want to appear too unorthodox in Jesuitical circles and at the Vatican. He was, after all, a member of the religious order in Rome which burned Giordano Bruno, tortured and imprisoned Campanella, and condemned Galileo. His protestations against some of the conclusions of magic and alchemy appear as a smokescreen, allowing him to expound heretical doctrines without being hauled before the Inquisition. He undoubtedly knew and believed more than he was prepared to reveal. The colophon at the end of *Oedipus Aegyptiacus* represents Harpocrates, the son of Isis and Horus, holding his finger to his lips, as if to whisper to the reader: 'If you understand, keep your peace!'

*

Pope Innocent X called on Kircher to decode his obelisk, but what he did not realize is that the Holy Catholic Church was built on Egyptian remains. St Peter's is a fascinating example of the layers of architecture reflecting layers of thought and belief over time. In 1950 Pope Pius XII announced on a radio broadcast after eleven years of secret excavations that they had discovered the tomb of St Peter.[10] It was situated directly under Bernini's ornate canopy and the great dome of Michelangelo which dominates the Roman skyline. But the excavations had also revealed a much older and greater continuity of tradition, a tradition which I suspect the present Vatican would rather forget.

After much ado, I managed to get special permission to visit the necropolis below the marbled floors of the grottoes of St Peter's where past popes had been buried. The necropolis had been first discovered in 1939 when an attempt was made to find room for the tomb of another pope. The workmen revealed a marble monument below the floor of the church built in 326 on Vatican hill by the first Christian Roman emperor, Constantine. Ironically, it was after founding the Church of St Peter's that Constantine moved the centre of the empire to Constantinople, bringing to an end a thousand years of Roman pre-eminence.

My official guide to this Underworld was called Magdalene, a woman with a German accent and well-rehearsed arguments. No photographs were allowed. We passed through a small side door off the marbled corridors and entered a cool, damp, dark labyrinth of corridors made of red brick and earth which had openings into small mausoleums. The necropolis survived because it had been covered with rubble and earth when part of Vatican hill was flattened by Constantine in order to build the first basilica on the site.

The chamber I was most interested in along the narrow lanes was the so-called 'Egyptian Tomb'. Although faded and crude, I could make out the unmistakable shape of Horus with his staff in the centre of the north wall of the tomb. The figures of Osiris and Isis which had formed part of the fresco had disappeared since the discovery of the tomb.[11] Horus would follow them soon. As Magdalene observed dryly: 'Unfortunately, excavation means destroying. The frescoes were perfect when first exposed fifty years ago.' She implied that it would be no great loss. But for me they were a wonderful illustration of the fact that the might of Rome and Christendom had Egyptian foundations, archaeologically, historically and culturally.

As we continued down the narrow, dark corridors of the necropolis, I saw an intriguing artefact in the middle of the Tomb of Aebutius. It was a square plinth topped by a decorated stone casket or cinerary urn. On one side, it had a carving of a 'cup' and a lighted lamp in the shape of a swan. Magdalene remarked jokingly:

'It looks like an incense burner or a chalice. I've heard some people say it's the Holy Grail but that's very controversial! I don't believe in that sort of thing. It's all very Indiana Jones. People like that find what they want to find . . .'

Her easy dismissal was highly suggestive. When I asked her again about it at the end of our visit, she said that the object was nothing more than a cup. It was probably not a chalice because early Christians did not use them. But what was it used for? Could it have anything to do with the chalice of the Holy Grail? Could it even have been an image of the Philosopher's Stone itself? I recalled that in the Parzival story of Wolfram von Eschenbach, the Grail is described as a stone, the *lapsit exillis* of the alchemists.

*

The presence of Hermes and his tradition was to be found not only hidden in the necropolis below St Peter's but openly for all to see in Vatican City. Climbing the stairs of the Vatican Palace, I was confronted on the first floor with two colossal statues of Egyptians, guarding an inner room containing a sculpture of Jason with the Golden Fleece. The Egyptian Museum nearby contained a mummy with a gold-winged scarab Khepri on its chest, a colossal bust of Isis, a seated black granite statue of the Sekhmet from the temple at Karnak, and a statue of Serapis and Bes, popular gods of Ptolemaic times in Alexandria.

Perhaps the most extraordinary example of 'Egyptianism' in the Vatican and the subterranean influence of the Hermetic tradition are the frescoes painted by Pinturicchio for Pope Alexander VI in the Appartamento Borgia. In the Room of the Saints, a series of frescoes begins with the Egyptian worship of the Apis bull who personifies the power of Ptah, the Cosmic Architect. Since the family emblem of the Borgia was the bull, it indirectly associates Ptah with the Borgia Pope Alexander VI. The frescoes then depict Mercury (identified by Cicero as Hermes Trismegistus) killing Argus who was set to guard Io by Juno who had turned her into a cow. After being rescued, Io escapes into Egypt where she becomes the goddess Isis. She is depicted in the frescoes on a throne with Moses on her left and Hermes on her right, who were considered to be contemporaries.

Why should the Borgia Pope Alexander VI find this acceptable in his loggia? It would appear that he believed that the Egyptian *Hermetica* and the Jewish Cabala, Hermes as well as Moses, supported the Christian religion.[12] The Apis bull in stucco relief is shown worshipping the Cross, implying that Christianity is the heir to Egyptian religion.

*

Given this contradictory attitude of the Vatican to alchemy and the Hermetic tradition, I was determined to find out its official position and to discuss its involvement in the Great Work. It was not easy. Before my visit to Rome I telephoned the Vatican from Wales eight times before I managed to speak to someone who could help me. At first, I was passed on to the 'Social Communications Office'. On one occasion, I ended up in an echo chamber. On another I was serenaded by liturgical music. On another, I was suspended in limbo. When I did get through to someone and mentioned the word 'alchemy', I was asked 'Do you want authorization?' The Holy See Press Office seemed more forthcoming but after several more telephone calls I was told that the only expert on alchemy in the Vatican was a Jesuit priest who had died the previous year.

I decided that the only way to get into the Vatican would be a frontal attack in person during my stay in Rome. I therefore marched up to the brightly coloured Swiss mercenaries who were holding back the masses with their swords and halberds and said firmly that I had come to visit the Pontifical Academy of Sciences. To my surprise, I was let in and obtained a pass with ease and was then directed to the other side of Vatican City behind St Peter's. In contrast to the noise and rush and hot stone of Rome, this was a green oasis of beauty and peace. Fountains sung in grottoes, birds flitted in the trees, and swathes of immaculate, well-watered lawns stretched up the hill scattered with ancient statuary. I was stopped twice by security guards but eventually found my way to the sixteenth-century palace known as the Casino di Pio IV which housed the Pontificia Academia Scientum.

Here I met a short, middle-aged Jesuit priest called Joseph Pittau who introduced himself as the Chancellor of the Academy of Sciences. His office was richly decorated with brightly coloured frescoes and exuberant stucco figures. On the walls were panels representing scenes from the Life of Moses. At the centre of the vaulted ceiling was an Angel coming down to make the Annunciation to the Virgin. What a laboratory of the imagination!

Father Pittau was extremely polite and spoke excellent English. He had spent twenty-nine years at Sophia University in Tokyo.

After I explained my interest, the chancellor admitted that in the Middle Ages popes and cardinals had been involved in alchemy. He also accepted that the Inquisition had persecuted and burned alchemists and Hermetic philosophers like Giordano Bruno.

'Certainly it was one of the main issues, alchemy, even with the Galileo case. They were afraid of this kind of thing and so they wanted to be very sure that it was scientific.'

'Is there an official view of the Church on alchemy as there is on Darwinism, for instance?'

'No, just that if it's not science, we don't recognize it.'

'You wouldn't recognize alchemy as a science?'

'No. Today that would be out of place.'

'So it's just seen as part of the history of science . . .'

'Yes, as with magic and other things. In this sense, the Church today accepts science if it is proved through experiments. It's not that we don't recognize spiritual events, but what you might call superstition, we don't.'

'So you want to keep science and religion quite separate?'

'Yes. Just let the scientists and theologians take up their own fields. They can collaborate, but certainly you cannot prove religious things through experimental science.'

This seemed to be the crux of the matter. The chancellor was calling for science and religion to be kept as quite separate disciplines. This had not been the case during the Middle Ages and the Renaissance. The Church, and its arm of the Inquisition, had rejected the findings of science and persecuted their practitioners if they conflicted with the official dogma. The controversy over the Copernican theory that the planets revolve around the sun and not the earth, which led to the persecution of Galileo and the execution of Bruno, resulted from the Church insisting on the biblical interpretation which states that the earth is at the centre of the universe. The new science of the Renaissance with its heliocentric theories not only threatened traditional Catholic dogma but raised old fears of the ancient Egyptian cult of the sun god.

The chancellor went on: 'The dogmas of religion cannot be imposed – which is a new thing. Sometimes, before, we didn't take the advice of St Thomas Aquinas who said if a thing is proved scientifically we cannot with theological or philosophical reasons say that it is not true. If necessary, we should change our interpretation of the Bible because two proofs cannot contradict themselves. We cannot use, let's say, theology to define a scientific thing. But also we cannot use science to define some mysteries of theology. They can complement each other, they can help each other . . .'

The Chancellor of the Academy of Science paused and then turned to a subject which was clearly close to his heart and worrying him: 'Certainly Giordano Bruno was not condemned because of science. Mostly it was because of superstition. The fear of alchemy and all those things might have led some people to condemn Bruno.'

'But what about the Church's interest in the Hermetic philosophy? Why is there an Egyptian obelisk in front of St Peter's?'

'You might say the same thing about these walls here, these frescoes. It's always a combination of Christian and sacred with pagan and profane things. That was the experience of the Renaissance and of

Humanism. Pius the IV thought that everything beautiful, everything good, everything truthful should be put together in Christianity so that it could reach you. So that's how different times bring together different conclusions!'

It was now time for Father Pittau to leave. Our conversation had been very revealing. Clearly the Vatican was eager to explain away the past errors of the Inquisition in condemning Hermetic philosophers and alchemists and was now keen to keep science and religion quite separate and distinct. But as far as the Chancellor of the Academy of Sciences was concerned, alchemy was another form of superstition like magic or astrology; it had nothing to contribute to either theology or science.

As I left the Pontifical Academy of Sciences, I looked at the facade of the loggia of the Casino di Pio IV for the last time and was struck by the pagan nature of the papal palace. At the top of the centre was Aurora with the four horses of the sun: Pyrois, Eous, Aeon and Phlegon. Around them were the signs of the zodiac and beyond two female figures, one holding flowers and the other fruit. At the top was an ancient statue of Salus dressed as a female figure, with a serpent winding around one hand and drinking from a cup. She was an old Roman goddess, associated with the Greek Hygieia, the attendant of the Egyptian magus Asclepius. So sun worship was pagan and alchemy a superstition?

38

Magnum Miraculum

> Man is an intermediary between creatures, the intimate of
> higher beings and the king of the lower beings, the interpreter
> of nature by the sharpness of his senses, by the questing
> curiosity of his reason, by the light of his intelligence, the
> interval between enduring eternity and the flow of time.
>
> Pico della Mirandola, 'Oration on the Dignity of Man' (1486)

After visiting Rome, I decided to continue my search in Florence. I was
stunned by the skyline of the city from the roof garden of my hotel
next to the Palazzo Pitti south of the River Arno. To the north
Brunelleschi's immense dome of the cathedral soared above the terracotta roofs of the city, while to the west the dark bell tower and dome
of the Church of Santo Spirito stood out against waves of bright
orange light. The gardens and scattered villas stretched up the hills,
with cypresses and pines silhouetted on the fading skyline in the golden
glow of the last rays of the sun. It was still very hot: the dry sirocco
wind was blowing in from North Africa. Swallows dived and swirled
across the rooftops; cicadas set up their steady calls in the darkening
gardens; and a cat slinked across a deserted courtyard. The landscape
blended with the city, combining harmoniously eight centuries of the
works of man with those of nature. By comparison with Luxor,
Alexandria and Rome, Florence was a young city, but it had given
birth to some of the greatest art and architecture of the Renaissance. It
had not only been the cradle of Humanism but had helped to develop
the Hermetic tradition and alchemy.

I saw evidence of this in the Palazzo Vecchio. The Studiolo of
Francesco I, now known as the 'Salon of Elements', has murals created by Vasari and his Mannerist school on each of the four walls

representing one of the four elements. They are decorated with paintings which celebrate Francesco's interest in alchemy and the natural sciences. On the right wall, dedicated to Fire, there are paintings of a glass-blowing factory, a goldsmith's workshop and, most interesting of all, an alchemist's laboratory by Giovanni Stradano (also known as Jan van der Straet).

I found an intriguing collection of alchemical and astrological drawings in the Biblioteca Laurenziana in the Church of San Lorenzo, the site of the oldest church in the city and the final resting ground of the principal members of the Medici family. The vestibule to the peaceful library has a free-standing staircase designed by Michelangelo and executed by Vasari. The inlaid desks in the reading room are also by Michelangelo. I came across a drawing of Hermes as an Oriental sage and an alchemical furnace designed like a castle, with alembics, tongues and bellows. The most extraordinary was a fourteenth-century painting of a dead naked man, struck by an arrow in his chest, with a huge erect penis in the form of a tree bearing fruit. It depicts the fallen Adam as *prima materia*, from which emerges new life. The drawing shows the first and last stages of the alchemical process.[1]

I also saw many rare and beautiful alchemical works in the Biblioteca Nazionale Centrale in Florence. It was a delight to turn the pages of Ramon Lull's *Opera Chimica*, beautifully illustrated by Girolamo de Cremona.[2] Another fascinating work was the *Elixir Vitae* by Donato D'Eremita, dedicated on 7 October 1624 to Fernando II de' Medici, the Grand Duke of Tuscany and brother of Cardinal Leopoldo. Unlike most books on alchemy at the time, it was written in Italian rather than Latin and while its illustrations are painted by hand in watercolours, it is printed rather than in manuscript form. The author mentions the alchemist heroes Stephanus, Dioscorides, Aristotle and Galen amongst the Greeks, Rhazes and Geber amongst the Muslims, and Vincent de Beauvais, Arnald of Villanova and Albertus Magnus amongst the moderns. The author also recognizes the different meanings and names given to the 'Noblissimo Antidado del Elyxir Vitae' and lists among its numerous synonyms: 'Acqua celeste; ciclo noftro; Stella Diana; Quinta essenza; Prolungatione dell vita; Viva forza, e potenza celeste; Spirito, ed anima; Aether; and Mercurio vegetabile'.[3]

*

Cosimo de' Medici (1389–1464) founded the first modern library in Europe. During his ascendancy, Florence reached its zenith as the intellectual and artistic centre. Scholars dedicated themselves to the study of the Classics as artists delved into the pagan sculpture of Greece and Rome. And it was not long before their attention turned to ancient Egypt. Cosimo's mantle was passed on to his grandson Lorenzo. First and last a financier, he was also known as *il Magnifico* for his patronage of learning and the arts. His son Giovanni was ordained a cardinal at the age of thirteen and became Pope Leo X in 1513.

Cosimo surrounded himself with men of letters, poets and philosophers. In his Careggi villa outside Florence, he established with the Neoplatonist Marsilio Ficino in 1462 an academy or 'round table' of philosophers, which came to be known as the 'Platonic Academy'. Wanting Florence to become a 'New Athens', Cosimo tried to recreate the kind of debate and enquiry which had flourished in Spain under Islamic rule five centuries earlier and which was symbolized by Raphael's magnificent painting *The School of Athens* which I had seen in the Vatican. Ficino had inscribed around the walls of the villa at Careggi a maxim which had echoes of Lao Tzu: 'All things are directed from goodness to goodness. Rejoice in the present; set no value on property; seek no honours. Avoid excess; avoid activity. Rejoice in the present.'

In the gardens Ficino and his fellow philosophers Pico della Mirandola, Poggio Bracciolini and Angelo Poliziano were joined by scholars and philosophers who had come from Constantinople with rare manuscripts after its fall to the Turks in 1453. Together they drew on Hermetic and Greek philosophy to inspire the Humanist movement of the High Renaissance.

The Renaissance philosophers were deeply interested in the Hermetic tradition which they knew went back to Egypt. Indeed, it was Cosimo who ordered Ficino in 1462 to abandon his translations of Plato into Latin and turn to the fourteenth-century manuscript in Greek he had obtained of the first fourteen treatises of the *Corpus Hermeticum*. Originating in Alexandria, the texts had been brought to Florence from Byzantium. They are now in the Biblioteca Laurenziana.

Ficino finished his translation in 1463 and it was published in 1471 under the name of *Pimander*, two years after the first edition of the Hermetic text *Asclepius* in Latin appeared. Ficino's translation of the Hermetic writings had an immediate impact. By the mid-sixteenth century Ficino's *Pimander* had seen two dozen editions and had been translated into French, Dutch, Spanish and Italian. It remained the most influential presentation of the *Corpus Hermeticum* until the nineteenth century. Hermes became fashionable throughout Europe, an integral part of what Agostino Steuco called the 'perennial philosophy'.[4] Despite Isaac Casaubon's philological attempt in 1614 to deny the Egyptian origins of the *Hermetica*, Hermolatry reached its apogee in the productions of the alchemists Robert Fludd and Michael Maier in the early seventeenth century.

Ficino makes it clear in his preface to his translation, entitled *Book on the Power and Wisdom of God, Whose Title is Pimander*, why he and his patron Cosimo turned from Plato to Hermes: 'They called him Trismegistus or thrice-greatest because he was the greatest philosopher and the greatest priest and the greatest king . . . Just as he outdid all philosophers in learning and keenness of mind, so also he surpassed every priest . . . in sanctity of life and reverence for the divine . . .' Like the alchemists with their love of philosophical ancestors, Ficino placed Hermes as the first of a succession of ancient sages which ended with the 'divine Plato'.[5]

Ficino was a physician as well as a philosopher. I particularly liked his *Libri de Vita* (1489) intended primarily for those scholars whose excessive study made them susceptible to illness and melancholy. Since contemplation and abstract thought belong to Saturn, he advised them to surround themselves with plants, herbs, stones, animals and people belonging to the cheerful, vital, and fortunate planets, especially the 'three Graces' Sol, Jupiter and Venus.

Ficino believed in natural magic and the use of talismans which marry higher virtues to lower things. Between the soul of the world and its body there is a *spiritus mundi* through which the influences of the stars come down to earth. Through the *spiritus*, which is a kind of fine air and fine heat, the magus can draw down the life of heaven like the ancient Egyptian priests.

This can be achieved not only through talismans but also through visualization. To prolong life, for instance, you should make an image of Saturn on a sapphire: 'An old man sitting on a high throne or on a dragon, with a hood of dark linen on his head, raising his hand above his head, holding a sickle or a fish, clothed in a dark robe.' For happiness and physical strength, Ficino recommends an image of a young Venus, holding apples and flowers, dressed in white and yellow. As for Mercury, he imagines 'a helmeted man sitting on a throne, with eagle's feet, holding a cock or fire in his left hand'.[6] They not only evoke the allegorical paintings of the Renaissance but the images illustrating the alchemical texts which burst into print in the sixteenth and seventeenth centuries.

In his famous opening to his 'Oration on the Dignity of Man', Ficino's friend Pico della Mirandola declared that '*magnum miraculum homo est*'. Pico presented man not as the fallen seed of Adam but as the bearer of the divine spark. Man is a great miracle because of his position in the cosmos, allied by his nature to the 'race of daemons' and therefore able to draw down their cosmic powers. Pico glorifies man as the Magus, who can operate the forces and affinities which hold together the different parts of the universe. In a passage echoing the visions which illuminated the dingy laboratories of the alchemists, he declared that man is endowed with seeds of all kinds of life. If they are rational, 'he will become like a heavenly creature; if intellectual, he will be an angel and son of God. And if, content with the lot of no created being, he withdraws into the centre of his oneness, his spirit, made one with God in the solitary darkness of his spirit, which is above all things, will surpass all things'.[7]

Pico was a younger contemporary of Ficino who shared his interest in Hermetic philosophy, and his belief in *magia naturalis* (natural magic). By the age of twenty-four, he had already attempted to draw up a synthesis of all knowledge. His 'Oration on the Dignity of Man' was intended to open the debate on his twenty-six *Conclusiones Magicae* and 900 theses which he took to Rome. It was an attempt to create a new *gnosis*, a path to spiritual enlightenment through knowledge. It was Pico more than anyone else who persuaded Pope Alexander VI to allow Hermes Trismegistus into the Catholic Church and encouraged the Renaissance marriage between magic and religion.[8]

To Ficino's Hermetic *magia naturalis*, he added an interest in Cabalist magic which offered ways of tapping spiritual powers beyond the natural powers of the cosmos. These involved drawing down the powers of the planets, by invoking angels, archangels, the ten *Sephiroth* (names or powers of God) and God himself through the power of the sacred Hebrew language.[9] The *Sephiroth* are connected with the ten spheres of the cosmos (the seven planets, the spheres of fixed stars, and the higher spheres beyond). It was thought that this secret doctrine had been handed down from Moses to a few initiates.

The Cabala, Hermeticism and alchemy all shared the view of the Creation by the Logos, the Word. In the beginning was the Word: God 'spoke' to form the created world. Indeed, a whole branch of Cabalist magic known as the *gematria* was based on the numerical values assigned to the twenty-two letters of the Hebrew alphabet which through complicated calculations could depict in number the organization of the world.

Pico not only took a great interest in Cabalistic magic, but was quite open about his reverence for Hermes. In his 'Oration on the Dignity of Man', he openly declared: 'It is the magic of the *Asclepius* that I am really talking about, and I glory in Man the Magus as described by Hermes Trismegistus.'[10]

*

During the Renaissance, Hermes appeared in many guises. In Botticelli's *Primavera* (1482), held in the Palazzo Uffizi in Florence, he appears with the three Graces (Sol, Jupiter and Venus) in a complex allegory. With his winged sandals, he raises his finger and points through clouds to the divine origin of the light of knowledge.

In Siena Cathedral, his appearance is even more striking. As you enter the great metal doors of the cathedral, you must walk over a huge marble floor carving of Hermes Trismegistus dressed as an Oriental sage in flowing robes and turban. He offers a book to two other philosophers who accept it respectfully. The pages of the open book declare: '*Suscipite o licteras et leges Egiptii*', a form of medieval Latin which appears to mean 'Take up the letters and laws of Egypt'. Hermes rests his hand upon a tablet supported by two winged sphinxes. Inscribed on it is a sentence ascribed to the Hermetic work *Poimandres* which says that the wisdom of Egypt has divine origin (*Sanctum Verbum*) and that the first object of the human search for knowledge is the divine Creation. Beneath the figure a scroll announces, '*Hermes, Mercurius Trimegistus, Contemporaneus Moysi*' (Moses). It is thought that Giovanni di Stefano laid the panel in 1488.[11]

*

Before I left Italy, I still had one more place to visit in Florence. It was the Museum of the History of Science in the Palazzo Castellani. Based on a collection of the Medici family, it had some fascinating artefacts, including Arab astrolabes and early mathematical instruments. I managed to look through the same cracked lens through which Galileo first saw the four satellites of Jupiter, the roughness of the moon's surface, and the phases of Venus. These and other celestial phenomena confirmed the theory of Copernicus that the planets rotate around the sun and not the earth. In his study of sunspots observed by others, Galileo had further concluded that the sun was not as perfect as medieval philosophers had maintained. His discoveries did not prove the Copernican theory to be true, but they provided strong arguments against the traditional theories. Since it challenged the received Catholic doctrine that the earth is at the centre of a perfect universe, the Inquisition was not amused. Galileo spent the last part of life under virtual house arrest, although at least he escaped the fate of the Hermetic philosopher Giordano Bruno who shared his heliocentric views.

In the adjoining National Institute of Science, I met Dr Andrea Scotti, who was just completing the first bibliography of scientific manuscripts for the National Library of Italy. He wore shorts and sandals and had long hair. He spoke perfect English. His mother was Irish and he had grown up in New York before the family moved to Italy. By an extraordinary coincidence (or was it our destiny to meet?), his chief interest was alchemy. In a room at the top of the Renaissance palace, he showed me how, with the latest computer technology, he was putting the finishing touches to his analytical bibliography. When the institute closed, we adjourned to a cafe on the banks of the River Arno.

I asked him how he first got interested in alchemy.

'When I was sixteen or seventeen, I came across it in a work by Walter Benjamin on Baroque drama. Later at university, I did a doctorate on truth and representation in the works of Jacob Boehme, John Dee and Johann Valentin Andreae. The field was so great that it proved impossible to deal with all the documentation and to reach a conclusion. I said as much in my thesis. My examiner Umberto Eco said: "Why don't you go for it! Why don't you go and draw up the lists!" By the way, Eco himself is a great collector of alchemical texts . . .'

Taking the advice of the author of *The Name of the Rose*, he had been travelling ever since making bibliographies of alchemical and other scientific works. He had visited Israel and Egypt and drawn up bibliographies in Hungary and Czechoslovakia before the lifting of the Iron Curtain.

'In Prague, it was a nightmare. At night, when the lights went out, it was just like Kafka's castle. I was arrested eight times and put into jail. They accused me of smuggling manuscripts out of the country!'

I told him of my difficulties in getting into the Vatican. 'If they can block you, they will.' He smiled knowingly. 'The officials are all trained Jesuits. They have 1,600 manuscripts, but they have only catalogued 300 of them.'

Scotti had also gone to France to work with Professor Robert Halleux, scholarly editor of alchemical texts, who dismissed the subject as 'the history of an error'.

'The first question Halleux asked me was "Are you a believer?"'

'Are you?' I asked, seizing the moment.

After a long pause, he said: 'Alchemy is a bomb which can explode. The meanings shift and constantly multiply. There's no consistency. Sometimes, if you read a text in a straight line, it means nothing, but if you read it backwards, it makes sense. Alchemy is a bomb which can explode!'

'How do you approach the subject then?'

'I think it's important to take a historical line. As you know, as well as practical alchemy, there is philosophical and mystical alchemy. To understand it you have to understand the intellectual world of the Middle Ages.'

Before we parted, I said to Scotti: 'Do you know of any practising alchemists or laboratories in Italy?'

'No!' was his firm reply.

Scotti knew what he was talking about. But I had the impression of someone overwhelmed by the vast array of alchemical documents and the enormity of the task of making any sense of them. He had nearly drowned in his researches. He was now doing the only thing he knew in order to bring the documents under control: to list, catalogue and classify them. He would leave it to others who were either daring or foolhardy enough like myself to attempt to interpret them.

*

Sitting in the café by the River Arno after Scotti had left me I, too, felt overwhelmed by the amount of work to be done. As Scotti's bibliographies had demonstrated, there was a vast number of texts which I had not yet seen. Would I ever be able to bring together my researches and come to a conclusion?

I justified my work in thinking that there were two ways of approaching the sea of alchemy. One was to try to take the water out bucket by bucket and examine the contents. To do so, as Scotti had realized, would take several lifetimes. The other way was to become a deep-sea diver and search for specific treasures. I had a rough map to direct me which other historians, scholars and alchemists had drawn up. To search and explore was undoubtedly better than to sift. Only with this approach could I avoid drowning in the sea of alchemical documents, texts, illustrations and commentaries. As I proceeded, I had to rely on my judgement, my intuition, my good fortune, and a little help from my library mermaids. They seemed to be helping me along and I felt I was beginning to see the pearls amongst the seaweed.

But was I any nearer to discovering the Philosopher's Stone? I had now travelled to China, to India, to Egypt, to Spain and to Italy. I still intended to go to the Czech Republic and France. But was all this a diversion? Was I looking in the right places? Was I talking to the right people?

These questions came tumbling out as I strolled along the banks of the Arno. When I sat at last in the roof garden of my hotel, watching the last golden rays of the sun light up the domes and towers of Florence, I felt that deep within me, after several years of travelling, researching, reading and meditating, a transformation was slowly beginning to take place. My inner landscape was beginning to change, the darkness and confusion I had felt at the beginning of my quest was gradually giving way to light. A new dawn of understanding was beginning to break. Or so I sensed and hoped.

Faith, that was an important point. My conversation with Scotti had raised the key question: was I a believer?

Yes, in the sense that I believed in the possibility of spiritual transformation, of changing the dross of our lives into something more perfect and enduring. I also believed like the alchemists that change takes place and wholeness can be achieved through the reconciliation of opposites, through the mysterious and ecstatic union of mercury and sulphur, of Sol and Luna.

And the Philosopher's Stone? Yes, that too exists, though perhaps not as a pebble on the beach. The contradictory epithets – that it is a stone and not a stone, that it is priceless and worthless – all pointed to something intangible. As a concept, as a symbol of transformation, it exists. I still had to find out more and had a long way to go.

39

The Monarch of Arcana

I am different: let this not upset you.

Paracelsus

As my studies into alchemy during the Renaissance deepened, I kept coming across the name Paracelsus. Who was this revolutionary intellectual who changed the history of medicine and spawned a cultural and social movement? Where did he come from? Was he really the 'greatest alchemist of all times'?[1]

He adopted the name Paracelsus to show the world that he was greater than – 'beyond' – Celsus, the renowned first-century Roman writer on medicine. His real name was Philippus Aureolus Theophrastus Bombastus von Hohenheim and he was born in Einsiedeln near Zurich around 1493. He certainly lived up to his name. He went beyond Celsus and was undeniably 'bombastic' – the word originates from his vitriolic attacks on his contemporaries. But he paid dearly for his rebellion, dying prematurely in poverty in 1541. If some pronounced him mad, he was a brilliant madman, shining like phosphorous in the stagnant water of his times.

Paracelsus went out of his way to overthrow the old order in science and society. He was imprisoned in Salzburg in 1526 for his open support of the peasants' revolt. In order to pull down the Bastille of cultural privilege, he provocatively chose to lecture in his German-Swiss dialect rather than in Latin. He invented new words of his own which caught on. He took the Arabic word 'alcohol' for the spirit of wine and he created the word 'zinc' from *zinne* (tin) and *kupfer* (copper) because it seemed to share the properties of both. He called his own brand of alchemy 'spagyric' and his followers went on to call themselves 'spagyrists'. It comes from *spao* (to divide) and *ageiro* (to bind), illustrating the old alchemical motto 'dissolve and coagulate'. He searched for the universal solvent and named it the 'alkahest' from the German *'allgeist'* (all spirit). For his favourite painkiller, he invented the word 'laudanum' (opium). He also used the word 'azoth', the arcane name for 'philosophical mercury', the beginning and end of alchemy. It is a Cabalistic acronym of the first and last letters of the Greek, Roman, Arabic and Hebrew alphabets:

AZѠTT

Paracelsus says that his father, a physician, first taught him alchemy and medicine. His motto was: 'Learn and learn, and ask and ask, and be not ashamed.' The young Paracelsus had direct experience of metallurgy in the mines and workshops of the alchemist Sigismund Fugger in the Tyrol. He also knew the works of Georgius Agricola from Glachau in Saxony, the so-called father of metallurgy.[2] Agricola's most intriguing work, *De Animantibus Subterraneis* (1549, 'On Subterranean Living Things'), reflects the alchemists' belief in 'living' matter and in the 'spirits' of mineral substances.

Paracelsus claimed that he had 'great experience for a long time with many alchemists who have investigated these arts'. It seems that he came under the influence of Abbot Trithemius (Hans von Trittenheim) who lectured at the University of Basle. The Benedictine monk was steeped in alchemy, natural magic, Neoplatonism, Gnosticism and the Cabala. His most famous work *Steganographia* (1606) was on angel magic and ciphers. He wanted to use his angelic network rather like the modern Internet for transmitting messages and gathering knowledge 'of everything that is happening in the world'.[3] He was much given to secrecy and wrote an entire history of magic in pentacles.

Amongst Trithemius' other students was the great Renaissance magus Henry Cornelius Agrippa from Cologne. Trithemius proofread his *De Occulta Philosophia* (1533), a survey of Renaissance magic in its natural, celestial and ceremonial forms. As a good Hermetic philosopher, he worshipped the One beyond the many forms taken by the gods and angels. In Agrippa's view, the hidden virtues in things are infused 'by the Ideas through the World Soul and the rays of the stars'.[4] As for alchemy, he declared that the blessed subject of the Philosopher's Stone was not to be spoken of without perjury. He condemned all alchemists who did not practise the spiritual Art.

Paracelsus shared with Trithemius and Agrippa the Hermetic belief that magic could manipulate the hidden forces in the universe. As a young man, he travelled throughout Europe, studying in Vienna and Ferrara where he received his doctorate in 1515. If his own account is to be believed, he spent seven years travelling, visiting Russia, the Balkans, Rhodes, Constantinople and Alexandria in search of Hermetic wisdom. Wanting like his father to heal as well as to learn, he served for a while as a military surgeon in Scandinavia and to the Venetians. He returned to stay in Salzburg and Strasbourg. He had great success in curing patients, including Johannes Frobenius, the publisher and friend of Erasmus. His growing reputation led to him being appointed City Physician and Professor of Medicine in Basle.

He soon upset the university authorities by lecturing in German instead of Latin. He celebrated his appointment as City Physician by publicly burning the works of Avicenna and Galen in a brass pan with sulphur and nitre to show that he was his own man. He insisted that his students throw away their old books and study the 'Book of Nature'. In a characteristic speech, he exclaimed:

> O you hypocrites, who despise the truths taught you by a great physician, who is himself instructed by Nature, and is a son of God himself! Come then, and listen, impostors who prevail only by the authority of your high positions!

His praise of himself was matched by his contempt for his adversaries. He wrote to one critic:

> So then, you wormy and lousy Sophist, since you deem the Monarch of Arcana a mere ignorant, fatuous, and prodigal quack, now, in this mid age, I determine in my present treatise to disclose this honourable course of procedure in these matters . . .[5]

Not surprisingly, his bombastic vituperation rebounded on him. After a dispute over a fee, he was dismissed in 1528 and was reduced to wandering in rags through Switzerland, Germany and Austria. He died worn out in 1541 at the age of forty-eight. In the *Credo* of his vast

Astronomia Magna (1537–9) he declared: 'I am different: let this not upset you.'

*

Standing firmly within the Hermetic tradition, Paracelsus raised the edifice of his revolutionary thought on the twin pillars of alchemy and astrology. In his *Astronomia Magna*, he saw the whole universe as a kind of vast crucible in which the original Creation had been the Great Work of God.[6]

As the supreme alchemist and 'the true physician and the true medicine', God had created all things in a raw condition expecting humanity to continue his work and to perfect them. He

> created the ore but did not carry it to its perfect state; He has charged the miners with the task of refining it. In the same way, He enjoined the physician to purify man's body, from which purification man emerges as indestructible as gold. This is an action which, like that performed by fire on gold, frees man from the impurities that he himself does not know. And it is like such fire that medicine should act.[7]

Nature for Paracelsus is a living, flowing, dynamic whole. The source of everything is the *Mysterium Magnum* ('Great Mystery'). It reminded me of the Chinese concept of Tao. He believed in an *anima mundi* or world soul: the universe and all the beings and things within it are imbued with life. In the intermediate world between the immaterial and the material are beings with bodies and spirits but no souls: the nymphs of the water, the salamanders of the fire, and the sylphs of the air. Although he accepted that material substances are ultimately composed of the four elements, he rejected the idea that diseases result from an accidental imbalance of the four 'humours'. Moreover, he added a third ingredient to the sulphur-mercury theory of matter – salt.

The idea was not new amongst alchemists, but Paracelsus makes it central to his scheme. The trio of salt, sulphur and mercury is to be found in all substances whether animal, vegetable or mineral. They correspond respectively to body, soul and spirit: mercury is the spirit; sulphur, the soul; and salt, the body. Salt is the principle of incombustibility and non-volatility; sulphur is the principle of combustibility; while mercury is the principle of fusibility and volatility. It becomes more complicated when Paracelsus claims that sulphur and salt are the parents of mercury, the child of sun and moon. At the same time, sulphur is found 'in the depths of the nature of Mercurius' and they are brother and sister. Both have the power to bring metals to life and to heal.

The *tria prima*, the fundamental trinity underlying all phenomena, are not like elements in the modern sense but rather like active principles of creation. Indeed, these 'hypostatical principles', as Paracelsus calls them, vary in different substances: 'As there are many kinds of fruit, so there are many kinds of sulphur, salt and mercury.' The sulphur in wood, for example, is different from the sulphur in copper:

> You should know that all seven metals originate from three materials, namely from mercury, sulphur and salt, though with different colours. Therefore Hermes has said not incorrectly that all seven metals are born and composed of three substances, similarly also the tinctures and the Philosopher's Stone. He calls these three substances, spirit, soul, and body. But he has not indicated how this is to be understood nor what he means by it ... you should know that they mean not other than the three *principia*, that is mercury, sulphur, and salt, out of which all seven metals originate.[8]

If the three are not properly balanced in the body, illness results. Too much sulphur, for instance, causes fever and plague, and not enough leads to gout. Too much mercury causes paralysis and depression; too much salt gives rise to diarrhoea and dropsy. The physician as an alchemist of the body therefore should try to re-establish the natural harmony of health by encouraging the right proportions of salt, mercury and sulphur.

It is, however, a delicate task. Adopting the Hermetic principle of 'As above, so below', Paracelsus insists that sickness as well as health are influenced by the heavens. Given the correspondence between the macrocosm and the microcosm, there are planets, constellations and stars – *astra* – within humans as there are in the heavens. The role of the physician-alchemist is to restore the natural harmony between the heavenly *astra* and the *astra* within the patient. According to Paracelsus, the sun rules the heart; the moon, the brain; Venus, the veins; Saturn, the spleen; Mercury, the liver; Jupiter, the lungs; and Mars rules the gall.

Physicians must therefore know about astrology in order to understand the causes of illness, and about alchemy in order to prepare secret remedies or *arcana*. A medicine might be material, but the *arcanum* within it is spiritual. Paracelsus writes:

> For what is more noble in a doctor than a knowledge of the concordance of both *astra*? – for there lies the basis of all diseases. Now alchemy is the outer stomach which prepares for the stars its own. The purpose of alchemy is not, as it is said, to make gold and silver, but in this instance to make *arcana* and direct them against diseases; as this is the outcome, so is also the basis. For all these things conform to the instruction and test of nature. Hence nature and man, in health and sickness, need to be joined together, and to be brought into mutual agreement. This is the way to heal and restore to health. All this shall be achieved by alchemy, without which these things cannot be done.[9]

Paracelsus was not a man to rest in theory alone. 'What light do you shed, you doctors of Montpellier, Vienna, and Leipzig?' he asked rhetorically. 'About as much light as a Spanish fly in a dysentery stool!' He praised on the other hand the 'artists' who tend their work at the fire patiently day and night, who are 'sooty and dirty like the smiths and charcoal-burners', and who learn the various operations of alchemy: 'distillation, solution, putrefaction, extraction, calcination, reverberation, sublimation, fixation, separation, reduction, coagulation, tinction, and the like'.[10]

As a result of such sentiments, Paracelsus gave a new direction to medieval alchemy and revolutionized traditional medicine. By seeking mineral rather than herbal remedies, he ensured that chemistry became an essential part of medical training. He established the science of medical chemistry known as iatro-chemistry and was a forerunner of antisepsis, microchemistry and chemotherapy. He took a distinctly holistic approach, recognizing the importance of the individual's relationship with the universe and the harmony of the body, soul and spirit in order to achieve a state of continuing health. The father of homeopathy, Samuel Hahnemann took up his principle that *similia similibus curantur* ('like cures like') and his view of the importance of the invisible realm of energies and vibrations in healing.

40

Elias Artista

> Never look outside for what you need, until you have made
> use of the whole of yourself.
>
> Gerard Dorn

Although Paracelsus died in obscurity and poverty, his works soon inspired a cultural revolution not only in Switzerland and Germany but throughout Europe.[1] Calling themselves 'spagyrists', his followers scoured and ransacked nature for remedies from chemical, metallic and mineral sources. The movement went beyond mere science to become a philosophical, religious and even social one. Paracelsus predicted that a new Elijah would come fifty-eight years after his death, an 'Elijah the Alchemist' or an 'Elias Artista' who would transform the world, inaugurate a 'chemical' millennium, and bring about a golden age.[2] The roll-call of Paracelsians included the major alchemists of the sixteenth and seventeenth centuries. Many of them helped form the 'Fraternity of the Rosy Cross', later known as the Rosicrucians.

Petrus Severinus, one-time physician to the Danish king, set the tone. He advocated like Paracelsus in his *Idea Medicinae Philosophicae* (1571, 'Idea of Philosophical Medicine') giving up books and plunging into the Book of Nature:

> sell your lands, your houses, your clothes and jewellery; burn up your books. Instead buy yourselves stout shoes, travel to the mountains; search the valleys, the deserts, the sea-shores and the deepest recesses of the earth; mark the distinctions between several kind of animals, plants and minerals . . . Be not ashamed to study the heavenly and earthly lore of peasants. Lastly, buy coal, build furnaces, work with fire. Thus and thus only will you attain to knowledge of things and their properties.[3]

Among the leading Paracelsians was Joseph Duchesne, a graduate of
Basle, who became the physician of the French King Henri IV. His
advocacy of chemically prepared medicines was condemned by the
medical professors at the Sorbonne but he replied with the spirited
defence *On the Material of the Old Medicine of the Ancient Philosophers* (1603). Following Paracelsus, he not only believed that three
'principles' of salt, sulphur and mercury are present in all substances
but also that a certain *sal generalis* is capable of producing 'philosophical gold'. Thomas Thymme, an Elizabethan writer and clergyman who
spread Paracelsian ideas in England, translated from Latin Duchesne's
work as *The Practice of Chymicall and Hermeticall Physike by Quer-
cetanus* (1605).

The son of a Basle goldsmith, Leonhardt Thurneysser zum Thurn
also became interested in Paracelsus after coming across his works
while gathering herbs for a physician. After trying to sell a gilded lead
brick to some Jews at the age of seventeen, he set off on his travels
throughout Europe, developing his skills in mining and metallurgy. At
the same time, he combined his Paracelsian ideas with the study of the
Cabala and alchemy, and produced a great array of treatises, including
astrological herbal works as well as ones on mineral and metallic
waters. He combined his alchemical and medical ideas in the finely
illustrated *Quinta Essentia* published in Munster in 1570. He eventually became physician to the Elector of Brandenburg.

I found Gerard Dorn to be the most original and interesting of
Paracelsus' followers. Born in Belgium, he lived in Basle and Frankfurt
in the 1560s and 1570s and translated many of the master's works
into Latin. He developed Paracelsian alchemy in a spiritual direction
and had no doubt about the power of mind: 'As faith works miracles
in man, so this power, the *veritas efficaciae*, brings them about in
matter. This truth is the highest power and impregnable fortress
wherein the stone of the philosophers lies hid.'[4]

Dorn's alchemical writings include a work on the physical and
metaphysical skill in chemistry, to which he added a section on the
preparation of metals in both the major and minor works of the
Philosopher's Stone.[5] This was followed up by an account of Trithemius' ideas of the 'spagyric art', an illustrated collection of extracts from
the masters, and a number of his own tracts in Lazarus Zetzner's
Theatrum Chemicum (1602). They all show that he believed that the
Philosopher's Stone is to be found within rather than without. The

first condition of the Work is the integration of the self. This means at first concentrating and focusing on oneself: 'Never look outside for what you need, until you have made use of the whole of yourself.'[6] Indeed, Dorn boldly stated that the Stone is man, exclaiming in one of the most memorable sayings of alchemical literature: 'Transform yourselves from dead stones into living philosophical stones!'[7]

Dorn calls the celestial substance hidden in man *caeleum*. In the eyes of the world it is worthless, the cheapest thing, but 'to the wise more worthy of love than precious stones and gold, a good that passeth not away, and is taken hence after death'. He would seem to be describing, as Jung observed, nothing less than the Kingdom of Heaven on earth.[8] Dorn undoubtedly made a major contribution to the European tradition of spiritual alchemy.

The Flemish Paracelsian Joan Baptista van Helmont, on the other hand, became a major figure in the history of science for his discovery of gas. Born in Brussels in 1579, he went to Louvain University where he studied medicine but, impatient with the Aristotelian bias, turned to 'spagyric' alchemy. After touring Europe, visiting London and working during the plague epidemic in Amsterdam in 1605, he had sufficient private means to retire from the world and set up his own laboratory. He undertook his alchemical studies with a religious enthusiasm, devoted to what he called 'pyrotechnia', the art of the furnace.

He attracted the attention of the Jesuits for his unorthodox religious views expressed in a treatise on the Paracelsian theory of the cure of wounds which worked by sympathetic magic by anointing the weapon with a salve rather than the injury it caused. He was put under house arrest and the Inquisition nearly prosecuted him for heresy. Inspired by Paracelsus, he argued that an 'Archeus' or 'Master Workman' gave life and form to the human body in the form of a vital air. The idea undoubtedly helped him develop his notion of 'gas', a name he borrowed from the word for 'chaos' in Flemish. The discovery made him a founder of modern chemistry.[9]

Van Helmont's writings on medicine – *Ortus Medicinae* ('The Dawn of Medicine') – were only edited after his death by his son but they revolutionized the subject. They show that he never abandoned his belief in the possibility of alchemical transmutation. He left an intriguing account of a stranger who left him some saffron-coloured powder which he used in an alchemical experiment. He described his

method with scientific accuracy: he projected the powder on to mercury in a crucible in a furnace and when he lifted the lid found a
nugget of gold exactly the same weight as the original mercury.

*

While Dorn and van Helmot were historical figures the legendary
alchemist Basil Valentine (Basilius Valentinus), whose works were
published at the height of the Paracelsian influence, is a much more
elusive and mercurial character. My research threw up several anoma-
lies about him. His works were published early in the seventeenth
century yet it is claimed that he was a fifteenth-century Benedictine
who travelled to Egypt and went on pilgrimage like Nicolas Flamel to
St Jacques of Compostella in Spain. Some sources say he even spent
part of his youth in Belgium and England. The title page of his *Last
Will and Testament* claims that it was left under a marble table on the
high altar of the Cathedral of Erfurt.

His work had a great influence and still does, but did Basil
Valentine really exist? I could find no fifteenth-century texts to his
name and the ones printed in the following century contain anachro-
nistic allusions to America and tobacco. His name may have derived
from the Greek *Basileus*, the King, and the Latin *Valens*, the Powerful.
In reality, Basil Valentine may well have been the pseudonym of his
'editor' Johann Thölde, a salt boiler from Frankenhausen.

Valentine's most famous work was *Triumph-Wagen Antimonij*
('The Triumphant Chariot of Antimony'), printed in German in Leipzig
in 1604. It proposes antimony rather than mercury as the *prima
materia*. In the preface, Antimony claims that it contains the Paracelsian triad of principles which make up the universe: 'It is I, Antimony,
that speak to you . . . In me you find mercury, sulphur and salt, the
three great principles of health.' What fascinated many alchemists who
used antimony as the starting substance, including Isaac Newton, is
that after a process of purification through many heatings it changes
its crystal structure and its colour from silver to purple. The crystals
are long and slender and arrange themselves to look like fronds of
ferns on a stem. In special conditions they cluster around a centre and
produce a beautiful shape known as the Star Regulus.

The other well-known work published in Valentine's name was
called *Twelve Keys*.[10] The book is divided into twelve sections with an
emblem illustrating each of the twelve keys which are intended to open

'the doors of the knowledge of the ancient stone and unseal the most secret fountain of health'. Although it is called the *Practica* on the title page, it is very theoretical and full of obscure meanings. The work asserts that the 'Stone is derived from two things [male and female], and one thing [seed], in which is concealed a third thing [the Stone]'. It also makes clear that 'living man is an harmonious mixture of the four elements; and Adam was generated out of earth, water, air, and fire, out of soul, spirit and body, out of mercury, sulphur and salt'. In true Paracelsian spirit, the author declares that 'After the conflagration [at the end of the world], there shall be a new heaven and a new earth, and the new man will be more noble in his glorified state than he was before.'

How is the Stone to be prepared? The text of the twelfth key is far from clear: 'It is a stone, and no stone' we are told. 'It proceeds from one, and is one matter. Bind together the fixed and the volatile; they are two, and three, and yet one only. If you do not understand you will attain nothing.' Presumably this means that the Stone is to be made from sulphur (the fixed) and mercury (the volatile) which produce the Stone (the third) which is one. But the appendix then goes on to say: 'Know that the Stone is composed out of one, two, three, four and five. Out of five – that is, the quintessence of its own substance. Out of four, by which we understand the four elements. Out of three, and these are the three principles of all things. Out of two, for the mercurial substance is twofold. Out of one, and this is the first essence of everything which emanated from the primal fiat of creation.'[11]

Having deciphered the text that far I was still left with the problem of obtaining the three Paracelsian principles of all things: salt, sulphur and mercury.

I found the emblems of the *Twelve Keys* fascinating. They tell their own story. The king and queen represent the male and female principles of the work – Sol and Luna – from which the Stone is to be produced. The enigmatic emblem to the ninth key is in the form of the sign for *prima materia*, a cross over an orb. Within the circle three snakes emerging from hearts represent salt, sulphur and mercury, and the body, soul and spirit. Around a naked man and woman (Sol and Luna) birds symbolize the different stages and colours of the alchemical process: the raven under the man's feet (*nigredo*), the peacock's tail under the woman's (*cauda pavonis*), the white swan on her head (*albedo*) and the red eagle on his (*rubedo*). The twelfth key further shows the alchemist in his laboratory at his anathor, with a lion (sulphur) eating a snake (mercury).

The elusive twentieth-century alchemist Fulcanelli claimed that Valentine's work offers a short and easy 'dry way' as opposed to the long and arduous 'moist way' in alchemy. In another work called *Azoth* attributed to Basil Valentine, it is written: 'in order to arrive at this Art, neither great labour nor trouble is required and the expenses are small, the instruments of little worth. For this Art may be learnt in less than twelve hours and brought to perfection within the space of *eight days*, if it has its own principle within itself'.[12] I was warned by practising alchemists, however, that this quick 'dry' way can be very dangerous and should only be attempted by the advanced adept.

*

Valentine was not the only elusive Paracelsian alchemist. There are several stories of a mysterious stranger, a wandering 'Elias', claiming to have the Philosopher's Stone in the seventeenth century. The Swiss scientist Johann Friedric Helvetius left the most vivid account of one such encounter. His testimony carries considerable weight since he was the personal physician to the Prince of Orange, a respected scientist and a sceptic about alchemy.

Helvetius records that on the afternoon of 27 December 1666 an 'Elias' from North Holland called at his house in The Hague. The stranger said that he was a brass founder as well as a 'great lover of the Pyrotechnian Art'. He came 'in a plebeian habit, honest gravity, and serious authority; of a mean stature, a little long face, with a few small pock holes, and most black hair, not at all curled, a beardless chin, about three or four and forty years of age'.

After discussing the possibility of a universal medicine which could cure all diseases and prolong life, 'Elias' asked Helvetius whether he would know the Philosopher's Stone when he saw it. Helvetius writes:

> I answered not at all, though I had read much of it in Paracelsus, Helmont, Basilius, and others; yet I dare not say I could know the philosopher's matter. In the interim he took out of his bosom pouch or pocket, a cunningly-worked ivory box, and out of it took three ponderous pieces or small lumps of the stone, each about the bigness of a small walnut, transparent, of a pale

brimstone colour, whereunto did stick the internal scales of the crucible, wherein it appeared this most noble substance was melted; they might be judged able to produce about twenty tons of gold . . .

After handling it for almost a quarter of an hour, Helvetius returned this 'treasure of treasures' to its owner. To escape the gaze of passers-by, they then moved into a back room. Therein the stranger opened his doublet and showed Helvetius five large pieces of gold hanging on green silk ribbons. One said, 'Jehovah's wonderful and miraculous Wisdom in the Catholic Book of Nature. I was made the 26 August 1666.' Another announced under the alchemical symbols for gold, mercury and silver: 'God, Nature and the Spagyric Art make nothing in vain.'

The stranger then went on to tell him that an 'outlandish friend' had shown him how to make precious jewels out of ordinary stones, how to prepare a metallic liquor which cured all dropsies in four days, and how to turn a piece of leaden pipe with a little 'sulphureous powder' in a crucible over a hot fire into pure gold.

Helvetius begged to be shown the effect of transmutation. The stranger said he would be back in three weeks. On his return, he gave Helvetius a crumb of his Stone as big as a rape or turnip seed, saying 'receive this small parcel of the greatest treasure in the world'. When Helvetius asked for more, he took the piece, cut it in half with his nail, flung it into the fire, and gave him the rest neatly wrapped in blue paper, saying, 'It is yet sufficient for thee.'

'Elias' told him that only two metals and minerals are used in the preparation of the Stone and the menstruum was a 'heavenly salt, or of heavenly virtue'. The whole work lasts not more than four days and costs no more than three florins. But the stranger refused to tell Helvetius 'how the philosophers do make, and break open the glassy seal of Hermes, in which the Sun sends forth a great splendour with his marvellous coloured metallic rayes . . . by whose help the volatile metals may be fixed into the most permanent metals, either gold or silver'.

The wandering Elias told Helvetius that he would return the next morning to show him the manner of projection but he disappeared for ever. Nevertheless, Helvetius' wife entreated him to perform an experiment with the 'little spark of his bounty' which they had acquired. She wrapped the matter in wax while he cut half an ounce of old lead and melted it in a crucible. She then put in the medicine made up into a small pill which was soon hissing and bubbling and within a quarter of an hour all the mass of lead was totally transmuted into the best and finest gold. The couple were amazed. 'And indeed (had I lived in Ovid's age)', Helvetius wrote:

> there could not have been a rarer metamorphosis than this, by the art of alchemy. Yea, could I have enjoyed Argus's eyes, with a hundred more, I could not sufficiently gaze upon this so admirable and almost miraculous a work of nature; for this melted lead (after projection) shewed us on the fire the rarest and most beautiful colours imaginable; yea, and the greenest colour, which as soon as poured forth into an ingot, it got the lively fresh colour of blood; and being cold shined as the purest and most refined resplendent gold.[13]

They immediately had it tested by a goldsmith who declared it the most excellent gold in the world and offered him fifty florins for every ounce of it. The next day the rumour went about The Hague and they had many illustrious visitors, including the General Assay-Master and Examiner of the Coins of the Province of Holland. He had it properly assayed several times, first by mixing it with silver and then by combining it with antimony over fire, only to find that they lost nothing at all of the gold; indeed, it had grown heavier.

This extraordinary tale has all the earmarks of truth and shows how the influence of the Hermetic tradition, alchemy and Paracelsian ideas continued well into the seventeenth century. Even that other illustrious Dutchman, the rationalist philosopher Spinoza, wrote to a friend saying that he had to accept the evidence of Helvetius.

Unfortunately I had not yet encountered in my travels an unknown 'Elias' with a small 'piece of his bounty' to place in my hands. But I was sufficiently inspired by Helvetius' story to continue my search for the Philosopher's Stone amongst the shadowy Hermetic societies which emerged in the seventeenth century.

41

The Rosicrucian Illuminati

A Christian marking of ancient doctrines and signs.

Robert Fludd

The Moravian alchemist Michael Sendivogius in his *Novum Lumen Chymicum* ('New Chemical Light'), published simultaneously in Prague and Frankfurt in 1604, predicted the imminent coming of a New Age:

> The times are at hand when many secrets of Nature will be revealed to men. The Fourth or Northern Monarchy is about to be established; the Mother of Knowledge will soon come ... Mercy and truth will meet together; peace and justice will kiss each other; truth will spring up from the ground, and righteousness will look down from heaven ... and knowledge will be the common property of all.[1]

Because of the threat of prosecution, many alchemists preferred to publish anonymously and work in small secret societies. The Brotherhood of the Rosy Cross – the Rosicrucians – emerged from this milieu as a Hermetic and alchemical group intent on bringing about a novel and spiritual revolution throughout Europe. They marked a shift from practical to spiritual alchemy. Their organization and number remain shadowy, and even their manifestos, which first appeared in Germany, are couched in the veiled and mysterious language of the alchemists.

The famous Rosicrucian symbol is that of the Rose blossoming at the centre of the Cross. While the Rosicrucians warned against fraudulent alchemists, they undoubtedly believed in a genuine alchemy. The philosopher Robert Fludd, one of their number, asserted in no uncertain terms: 'The Philosophy of the brothers of the Rose and Cross relies completely on alchemical principles and alchemical theory, which means that it fully respects Hermetic philosophy and shares the Mosaic and Cabalistic complex of thoughts. It is a Christian marking of ancient doctrines and signs, but it does not change their character.'[2]

The first Rosicrucian manifesto called *Fama Fraternitatis* appeared in Cassel in 1614. It claims that the Brotherhood of the Rose and Cross was founded by a German monk, Father Christian Rosenkreutz, 'an illuminate man' who was allegedly born in 1378 and lived to 106. He was educated in a monastery from the age of five and then travelled widely from the age of sixteen in the Middle East where he met Turks who told him about the sages of Damascus. They knew his name and taught him many secrets. He learned about the Magia and the Cabala which enabled him to enter into 'the harmony of the whole world, wonderfully impressed on all periods of time'. They lent him a book known as 'M' which he translated into Latin.

After three years, he set out on a journey from the Persian Gulf to Egypt, and from there through the Mediterranean Sea to Fez in Morocco, still a centre of Islamic alchemy, where the masters taught him their wisdom. He stayed there for two years, then crossed to Spain and travelled back to northern Europe. Although he could make as much alchemical gold as he wished, he lived simply and devoted himself to drawing up his philosophy.

When Father Christian Rosenkreutz died he was buried in a spacious underground crypt on the doors of which was the inscription: POST CXX ANNOS PATEBO ('I will be opened after 120 years'). And true to its prophecy, a friar discovered the crypt illuminated by an inner sun one hundred years and twenty later and spread the Rosicrucian programme for the reformation of the world.

The brotherhood, it is said, was founded by R. C. and three other men. They created 'a magical language and writing' with the help of a 'large dictionary' and possessed the book 'M' as well as one called the 'rota'. One of their main tasks was to attend to the sick for no fee. The Brothers were advised to continue to live according to the manners of the countries in which they lived, only making themselves known by their seal and sign 'R.C.' Once a year they would meet in their 'House of the Holy Spirit'. The ninth grade of their ritual was that of the Alchemist-Magus.

Although it was related to medicine and healing, I soon realized that the new Rosicrucian philosophy was primarily alchemical. It was the gold of spiritual understanding that Father R.C. had found and was offering: 'he doth not rejoice that he can make gold,' the *Fama Fraternitatis* makes clear, 'but is glad that he seeth the Heavens open, and the angels of God ascending and descending, and his name written in the Book of Life'.[3] The goal was gnosis, the knowledge of mystical illumination. It was not to remain within the brotherhood but to be spread to all humankind. It is known that every man on entering the Order was given a white stone, possibly a symbol of the Philosopher's Stone itself.[4]

The *Fama Fraternitatis* declares that the unearthing of the vault heralds 'a general reformation, both of divine and human things, according to our desire and the expectation of others; for it is fitting, that before the rising of the Sun there should appear and break forth Aurora, or some clearness, or divine light in the sky'.[5]

I discovered another short Rosicrucian work known as the *Confessio Fraternitatis*, addressed to 'All the Learned of Europe', which was also published in Cassel in 1615. It declares that the brethren had 'by no means made common property of their Arcana' and that they will not admit into their Order 'any who are not actuated by the highest motives, and who are not proficient in *The Art*'. Reflecting the Renaissance interest in the Cabala and magic, it asserts that God has incorporated characters and letters in the Holy Scriptures and 'imprinted them most manifestly in the wonderful work of Creation on the heavens and on the Earth'. From these letters, the treatise claims, 'we have borrowed our magick writing, and thence have made for ourselves a *new language*, in which the nature of things is expressed'.[6]

Two years after the *Confessio* the *Chymische Hochzeit Christiani Rosenkreutz, Anno 1459*, was published in 1617. Calling itself a 'Hermetic Romance', it takes the form of an alchemical allegory in which dissolution and death are followed by the marriage of Sol and Luna, well-known symbols of sulphur and mercury. The book is written in seven chapters and festivities are divided into seven days, mirroring the stages of the alchemical process and the number of the planets.

Rosenkreutz is invited to the royal wedding but on the first day swoons away and dreams that he is fettered in a pit of darkness and despair. A ray of light comes and draws him up and he is able to dress for the wedding. On the second day, he travels through a forest and sees a tablet fastened to a tall cedar, signed with the planet Mercury, symbol of the *Magnum Opus*. The tablet warns him of four roads to the palace, one of which is the Royal Road. He chooses the right one and passes through several portals (using a gold piece and salt) to find himself in an assembly of philosophers. On the third day, he is weighed in a Great Balance, passes the test, and is invested into the Order of the Golden Fleece. He is then shown the wonders of the castle, the Great Phoenix, the Holy Sepulchre, the Globes of the Earth and the Planets. On the fourth day, he is presented to the king and queen, drinks a draught of silence from a crystal glass, and witnesses a drama in which a black man kills the royal couple and places them in coffins.

On the fifth day Rosenkreutz sets off for the seven-storeyed Tower of the Gods and on the sixth day begins to ascend it with other 'Artists' with the help of a ladder. On the third floor they come across a globe containing a snow-white egg from which hatches the phoenix, emblem of transformation. On the sixth floor, its breast is opened and its blood collected in a chalice. While some artists remain to transmute base metals into gold, Rosenkreutz and a few others are taken to the seventh chamber where they use the pure blood of the phoenix to bring the king and the queen back to life, thereby completing the *Magnum Opus*. Victorious, the artists return over the sea to celebrate the real wedding of the king and queen and are invested as Knights of the Golden and Rosy Cross.

I found the account of the chemical wedding to be a haunting and magical tale. Yet I learned that it was almost certainly written by Johann Valentin Andreae, a Lutheran pastor from Würtemberg who had studied at Tübingen. Indeed, he may have written all three Rosicrucian documents.

*

In Germany, the Rosicrucian manifestos and the *Chemical Wedding* had an immediate impact. Henry Khunrath, author of *Ampitheatrum Sapientiae Aeternae* ('The Ampitheatre of Eternal Wisdom') published in Hanover in 1609, was immediately won over to the cause. His famous engraving in modern perspective of an alchemist in his study-laboratory brings together the arts and the sciences, music and mathematics, in an intense religious atmosphere. The praying figure, with the help of the Magia, Cabal and Alchymia, clearly seeks the illuminating knowledge of gnosis in order to understand the secrets of nature.

Michael Maier, the alchemist and personal physician to Rudolf II, was a member of the Cassel chapter of the Rosicrucians. He wrote and published a tract defending the brotherhood in Germany and dedicated a work which explained the rules of the Rosicrucian Order 'To all lovers of true chemistry throughout Germany'.[7]

In England, Robert Fludd openly declared that he was a disciple of the Rosicrucians. Steeped in alchemy, he quoted extensively Ficino's translation of the *Hermetica* and declared 'Trismegistus, the most divine of all philosophers'.[8] His vast *Utriusque Cosmi, Maioris Scilicet et Minoris* (1617–19, 'History of the Macrocosm and Microcosm') was published by Theodor De Bry the Younger in Frankfurt. The marvellous plates of Matthew Merian have ensured that they are endlessly reproduced. They offer the quickest route into the Hermetic world view. To sit in the silence of the rare books section of the new British Library and turn slowly the pages of the *Utriusque* and see the circular engravings was for me an unforgettable experience.

One of the most famous illustrations depicts the Creator as 'Tetragrammaton' (the Hebrew name for God consisting of the four consonants VHVH) emanating energy through the spheres of angels. A naked woman represents nature, chained to God above and holding an earthly monkey on a chain below, who sits on a sphere at the centre of the animal, vegetable and mineral realms. It makes a graphic illustration of the Great Chain of Being which extends from God to the lowliest creature. Fludd declared, 'In the Great Rosarius is unfolded the sacred symbols the mystery of the Resurrection.' Fludd was a devout Christian, yet because of his use of the esoteric teachings of the *Hermetica* and the Cabala, the work was placed on the papal index of forbidden books.

After studying at Oxford, Fludd travelled and studied in France and Italy. Fludd was one of the greatest Hermetic philosophers England ever produced. Despite his unorthodox views, he was eventually accepted into the Royal College of Physicians. He accepted Paracelsus' view of matter as consisting of the *tria principia* of salt, sulphur and mercury and in a work called *Truth's Golden Harrow* compared the operations of alchemy to the germination of wheat.[9] In a remarkable passage which echoes Gerard Dorn, he made clear that he saw the Rosicrucian and Hermetic goal to be the transformed soul of spiritual alchemy:

In the centre of our Cross is a Rose the colour of Blood, to show that we have to plant and labour till the impure be made pure, and *perfect* growth transfixed in the *Centre*. This labour is the Divine and Sacred Alchemy, and the full Rose on the Cross is its completion . . . By progress in virtue, by sublimation, by tears, by the inhaling of the Divine Breath of God, thus will the Soul be sublimated, rendered subtle, able clearly to contemplate God, be conformed to a likeness with the Angels. Thus apparently dead and lifeless stones will become living philosophic stones.[10]

Fludd was not the only Englishman to come under the influence of the Rosicrucians. The works of Francis Bacon are suffused with their message. Bacon's *Advancement of Learning* (1605) is a serious survey of the state of knowledge and a call for more research and experimentation, especially in natural philosophy. But the work ends with a resounding demand for a 'fraternity in learning and illumination'. Indeed, Bacon was as much a Renaissance magus, steeped in the *Hermetic* and Cabala, as he was a forerunner of the experimental method in science.

In his *New Atlantis*, discovered amongst his papers after his death in 1626, Bacon described a Utopia on an island called Bensalem ('Blessed Peace') in which every kind of applied science and technology is used for the good of the whole. It is run by an Order called 'Solomon's House' who are devoted to the study of the works of the Creation. The High Priest rides in a chariot on which there is 'a sun of gold, radiant upon the top, in the midst'. Their organization recalls that of the temples of ancient Egypt. I felt sure that the vision of the *New Atlantis* came from the same Hermetic stream as Campanella's *City of the Sun*.

The work also echoes the 'Invisible College' of the Rosicrucians with its philosopher-priests emerging every twelve years from Soloman's House to gather knowledge of the world and to harmonize its movements. The brethren are called 'merchants of light'. Like the Rosicrucians, they heal the sick gratis and wear no special dress, merging with the citizens of the country they travel through. One of the visitors to the island observes: 'we were apt enough to think that there was something supernatural in this island, but yet rather angelical than magical'.[11]

Although the Rosicrucians formed a clandestine movement, they gave rise to what has been called the 'Rosicrucian Enlightenment' in the early seventeenth century.[12] In 1623 groups calling themselves the 'Invisibles Ones' put up placards saying that they knew many deep secrets of wisdom:

> We, being deputies of the principle College of the Brothers of the Rose Cross, are making a visible and invisible stay in this city through the Grace of the Most High, towards whom turn the hearts of the Just. We show and teach without books or marks how to speak all languages of the countries where we wish to be, and to draw men from error and death.[13]

The announcement, with reports of Rosicrucians on the move in Germany and Spain as well as in France, created a real stir in Church and State. A mysterious sect from Spain calling themselves the 'Illuminati' appeared in Paris. The rumour spread that there were thirty-six Invisible Ones dispersed through the world in groups of six. Their purses were full of money, they had the power to transport themselves wherever they wished and they could dwell unnoticed in any country.

The belief in the imminent spiritual enlightenment and moral reformation of the world was widespread throughout Europe. The last bishop of the Czech Brothers before it was suppressed was the great scholar Jan Amos Komenský (Comenius) who in his *Via Lucis* ('The Way of Light'), written in England in 1641, called for 'an Art of Arts, a Science of Sciences, a Wisdom of Wisdom, a Light of Light'.[14] Comenius corresponded with the Rosicrucian Johann Valentin Andreae who initiated him into the Brotherhood of the Societas Christiana which was founded in 1620 and worked under the motto of 'Truth, Freedom and Love'. Comenius' *Pansophine Prodromas* and his efforts to create a world peace academy and a universal language were part of the same movement for reform.

In England, Robert Boyle and Isaac Newton who were to transform chemistry and physics made a deep study of alchemy and were strongly drawn to the Rosicrucian ideal. Newton had a copy of the *The Fame and Confession of the Fraternity of R. C., commonly of the Rosie Cross* (1652) which was translated by Thomas Vaughan and dedicated to 'The most illustrious Truly Regenerated Brethren of the R. C.' Vaughan was the brother of the Metaphysical poet Henry Vaughan and tried to spread the 'Divine Alchemy' of the Rosicrucians.[15]

The young Boyle wrote in October 1646 to his former tutor that he was applying himself to natural philosophy according to the principles of 'our new philosophical college' and he asked him to send books 'which will make you extremely welcome to our Invisible College'. Writing to a friend in February 1647, he further confessed:

> The best on't is, that the cornerstones of the *Invisible* or (as they term themselves) the Philosophical College, do now and then honour me with their company ... men of so capacious and searching spirits, that school-philosophy is but the lowest region of their knowledge ... they take the whole body of mankind to their care.[16]

This college was the father of the Royal Society in England.

Splendour of the Sun

I am the Way and the Level Road.
Whosoever travels me without stumbling and stopping
Finds good lodging by day and night.

Splendor Solis

In my research into the plethora of alchemical treatises printed in the sixteenth and seventeenth centuries, three extraordinary illustrated texts stood out. They are called the *Splendor Solis* ('Splendour of the Sun'), *Rosarium Philosophorum* ('Rosary of the Philosophers'), and *De Lapide Philosophico* ('On the Philosopher's Stone') by Lambsprinck. The illustrations have been endlessly reproduced and provide striking insight into alchemy at its peak before it was forced underground by the triumph of the Scientific Revolution and the Age of Reason which followed.

I discovered that *Splendor Solis* was thought to be the work of one Salomon Trismosin and was called *La Toyson d'or* ('Golden Fleece') in French. Among his many alchemical papers in the Bodleian Library in Oxford, Elias Ashmole, the founder of the Ashmolean Museum in Oxford, left a copy of the work called 'The Golden Fleece, or The Flower of Treasures, in which is succinctly and methodically handled, the Stone of ye Philosophers, his excellent effects and admirable virtues . . .'[1] Ashmole made the copy himself from a translation of *La Toyson d'or* made by his alchemical teacher William Blackhouse of Swallowfield.

Who was Salomon Trismosin? Nothing is known of the adept behind the pseudonym except that he claimed to be the 'Master of Paracelsus'.

The most beautiful manuscript of *Splendor Solis*, with twenty-two painted illustrations, dates from 1582 and is held in the Harley collection in the British Library.[2] Looking at its stunning illustrations, I could see why the trustees acknowledge it to be one of their greatest treasures. The symbolism refers to the different stages of the alchemical process, both the outer physical work in the laboratory and the inner spiritual work in the soul. The text moves between the two levels, using physical analogies for spiritual changes. Both words and images inform each other.

The work is primarily concerned with the most ancient of alchemical themes, a theme which first clearly emerged in the Osiris myth in Egypt: the incarnation of spirit into matter through the cycle of death and rebirth. It unites the microcosm and the macrocosm, by bringing heaven down to earth, and by raising matter to spirit.

But could it help me in my quest for the Philosopher's Stone which I was in danger of forgetting by my immersion in the marvellous alchemical art and literature of the period? In the last part of the seventh treatise of *Splendor Solis*, the author describes the virtues and powers of the 'Noble Tincture' of the Philosopher's Stone. He claims that the ancient sages discovered four chief virtues in the laudable Art:

> First, it preserves man from all manner of diseases.
> Second, it makes perfect the metallic bodies.
> Third, it transforms all stones.
> Fourth, it makes malleable any glass.

The first virtue of the Stone, the author claims, surpasses all the medicines. Taken in a warm drink of wine and water, it will heal 'paralysis, dropsy, leprosy, jaundice, heart palpitations, ileus, fever, epilepsy, colic' as well removing all melancholy and depression. In short, as Senior (Ibn Umail) says: 'It makes a man glad and young, and keeps his body fresh and healthy.' What more could a person want!

Its second virtue enables it to transform all imperfect metals into gold. Of the third virtue, it can produce precious stones such as jasper, jacinth, red and white corals, emerald, chrysolite, sapphire, crystals, carbuncles, ruby and topaz which are 'far better and more efficacious' than the natural ones – and dissolve them as well. Fourthly, and most interestingly from the point of view of the stained glass of the great Gothic cathedrals, when the medicine of the 'noble tincture' is applied to molten or crushed glass, it can be cut and changed into all colours.[3]

As with most medieval alchemists, the recommended *prima materia* is mercury but it is not common mercury. It is acknowledged that the whole art of the 'Stone of the Wise' is based on it, but the author adds: 'There is no need to tell of it here: the natural teachers describe it very clearly and adequately in their books.'[4] But do they? In all my travels and researches, I have not yet been able to find out precisely the whereabouts of this 'philosophical mercury'. This of course does not mean that it does not exist.

The author of the *Splendor Solis* is keen to stress that his alchemical way is a natural way. In the first treatise, he declares that the Stone of the Wise is achieved through the 'Way of Greening Nature'; by this, he means that it arises by growing things. At the same time, the adept assists nature with his art: 'Nature serves Art, and then Art serves Nature.'[5] He is also eager to give natural analogies to alchemical procedures. The first stage of putrefaction, for instance, which is achieved by the power of fire is likened to a brood hen hatching an egg with steady and gentle warmth.

The first treatise is illustrated by an old man pointing to a flask with the banner proclaiming: 'Let us go and seek the nature of the four elements.' The second treatise then shows a knight standing with his feet in two fountains – one with golden liquid and the other silvery, representing sulphur and mercury, the sun and the moon. They flow into each other and then into the sea. On his shield is emblazoned in Latin: 'Make one water out of two waters. You who seek to create the Sun and the Moon, give them to drink of the inimical wine and you will obtain vision at their death. Then make earth out of water, and you will have multiplied the Stone.'[6]

In the next illustration, the purest mercury and sulphur are represented by a queen (Luna) with a full moon over her head and a crescent moon under her feet and a king (Sol) with the sun above and a lion's head underfoot. As it is said in the text: 'Dissolve it until it is sublimated, then distil and coagulate it; make it rise and fall; dry it inside out.' The aim is thus to invert the elements and thereby reunite them to create the Stone.

The third treatise takes the form of parables, the favourite way of alchemists to express their meaning. It opens with a quotation from Hermes: 'The one end of this world is when Heaven and Earth come together.'[7] The first parable shows men digging for ore in a mountain where the 'Philosopher's Quicksilver' is formed – 'decocted' by nature and by the influence of the sun and other planets. When it is brought to a 'fiery, earthy, subtle hardness', the 'Philosopher's Sulphur' is also formed. So this is where I should find my *prima materia*. But where is the mountain to be found? Where is the map of the territory?

The third parable depicts an old king drowning in the sea: the death of the old king (Osiris) begins the cycle of death and rebirth. In the fourth parable, the philosopher Menaldus provides the key to the whole process: 'I enjoin all my followers to make the bodies spiritual through dissolution, and again to make spiritual things corporeal by gentle decoction.'[8]

This principle is illustrated by a man who is 'black as a Moor stuck in clay or filthy, black, foul-smelling slime'. A beautiful young woman with wings made from the white feathers of a glorious peacock comes to his aid, clothes him with a purple garment and leads him with her to heaven: dark matter becomes spirit, the dead rises to immortal life.

The fifth parable has the intriguing illustration of a hermaphrodite with two heads and wings – the combination of sun and moon, earth and water, man and woman. It combines the male and female principles of the universe. They bring forth four elements and make a fifth element – the white 'Magnesia'. When they all come together in a single thing the Stone can be produced.

The next stages of the alchemical process are then illustrated by figures in flasks: a boy blowing bellows in the mouth of a dragon (the untamed forces of the soul), three red, white and black birds fighting (salt, sulphur and mercury as well as *nigredo*, *albedo* and *rubedo*); a three-headed eagle (the fusion of the previous three birds). All these are in flasks heated over fire.

The last figures are in closed flasks which mark the process of integration: a three-headed dragon (still resolving the three forces), a peacock with an iridescent tail (coagulation is taking place), a queen (the white tincture) and a king (the red tincture). These stages and colours of the process of dissolution and coagulation were well known since Egyptian times.

Unless one is steeped in the alchemical and Hermetic tradition, much of the text and its illustrations would seem incomprehensible. But after the labour of the early stages, it becomes clear that the final part is like 'child's play' and 'woman's work'. This is said to be one of the profound secrets of the Work: after the discipline and care of the early stages, the adept can be spontaneous and playful in his or her work.

In the conclusion of *Splendor Solis*, the most precious art of alchemy is acknowledged to be a gift from God. Meditation is therefore considered essential. Since for the most part alchemy is described in enigmatic sayings and figures and concealed in parables, one must be 'grounded and firm in contemplation' in order to understand the secret definitions and procedures. And since meditation is a 'subtle sense', it is not for all.[9] But a person who meditates on the Art of alchemy, whose mind and heart are illuminated through meditation, will soon grasp its meaning.

While *Splendor Solis* was illustrated with exquisite miniature paintings, the anonymous *Rosarium Philosophorum* has graphic woodcuts, some of which are distinctly erotic.[10] It describes the preparation of the Philosopher's Stone in a series of symbolic pictures with accompanying text. The themes are supported by quotations from the alchemical authorities Hermes, Geber, Rhazes, Senior (Ibn Umail), Arnald of Villanova, the author of the *Turba Philosophorum* and others.

The work opens with a mercurial fountain and in the woodcuts which follow a king (Sol) and queen (Luna) cross flowers and stand on the sun and moon. They represent the counter-crossing of male and female principles as well as of sulphur and mercury. Their immersion in a bath is the first stage of dissolution (*solutio*). They then come together in love (*coniunctio*), the union of opposites which produces the hermaphrodite. With one body and male and female heads, it lies in water in a sarcophagus: the alchemical vessel has become a tomb. Energy ceases: this is the stage of putrefaction (*putrefactio*).

The soul then leaves the lifeless corpse in the form of a cherub. But falling dew from heaven washes and purifies the lifeless black body in the grave. The soul returns, and the white stage of *albedo* is attained. The winged hermaphrodite rises with outstretched wings holding coiled serpents, symbolizing the red stage of *rubedo*. And then the final moment is reached with the risen Christ stepping out of the tomb, symbol of the Philosopher's Stone which brings eternal life.

I could see why the work caught Jung's attention for it is a brilliant summary of the alchemical process and the journey of the soul in death and rebirth. The woodcuts also offer a visual meditation on bringing together the individual's male (*animus*) and female (*anima*) sides and the ultimate integration of the self.[11]

Another well-known alchemical work of emblems circulating in manuscript form in the Rhineland and in the Netherlands in the 1580s was *De Lapide Philosophico* by Lambsprinck, later known as *The Book of Lambspring*. It was published in Frankfurt in 1625 with the subtitle 'A Noble Ancient Philosopher, concerning the Philosophical Stone'.[12] The stages in the alchemical process and in the journey of the soul are depicted by familiar alchemical symbols. Two fish swimming in the sea represent the soul and spirit in the body. A knight fighting a dragon stands for putrefaction. The Ouroboros snake eating its tail has the explanation: 'The Mercury is precipitated or sublimed, dissolved in its own proper water, and then once more coagulated.' A salamander in the fire represents 'augmentation' of the Philosopher's Stone. The blood of the salamander, we are told, is the 'most precious Medicine upon earth':

> For this blood drives away all disease
> In the bodies of metals,
> Of men and of beasts.
> From it the Sages derive their science,
> And through it they attain the Heavenly Gift,
> Which is called the Philosopher's Stone.

More disturbing images follow. The father (a king on his throne) devours his son, watched by a spiritual guide in the form of the winged Hermes. The father-king next sweats profusely in bed 'while oil and the true tincture of the sages flow forth from him'. And then he gives birth to a new son with whom he is joined for ever. A beautiful emblem shows the winged Mercurius with the son on the top of a 'mountain of India'. At the end they sit relaxed with the king: the three principles are united to form the Philosopher's Stone.

These beautifully illustrated works depict the classic stages of the alchemical process but they offer little practical advice on how to produce the Philosopher's Stone in the laboratory. They are undoubtedly works of spiritual alchemy, showing the passage of the soul through death and rebirth and the steps taken by the fragmented self towards wholeness and harmony.

The Golden City

In past times, long before the reign of princess Lbuse, who is said to have founded Prague around the year 700, seven monks came from the centre of Asia, the heart of the world. They did what they have done for a secret reason in various other places of the Earth – they planted a twig on a rock, on the left river-side of Vltava, on the place where Hradcany, Prague Castle stands today.

Gustav Meyrink

'Would you like to meet a practising alchemist?' said the voice on the telephone with a slight central European accent.

'Yes, certainly!' I replied immediately.

'Only joking!'

'Who am I speaking to?'

'This is Robert Vrum. I'm ringing from Prague Castle. It would give me much pleasure to talk to you about alchemy. When you arrive in Prague give me a ring.'

After a visit to the great city, a friend of mine had placed into my hands a book called *Rudolf II and His Prague* with the subtitle *Mysteries and Curiosities of Rudolfine Prague 1550–1650*. Its author was Robert Vrum.

Prague in the autumn: city of swirling mists, flying buttresses, dreaming spires, tumbling leaves and the coat-tails of alchemists disappearing round corners in the cobbled lanes of the Old Town. In the middle of a great basin, possibly created by a meteorite, in the centre of Europe, Prague has attracted over the centuries more alchemists than any other European capital. Their work reached its height during the reign of Rudolf II during the late sixteenth and early seventeenth centuries, when Hermetic philosophers, astronomers and alchemists came from all over Europe – including Giordano Bruno, Tycho Brahe, Johannes Kepler, John Dee and Edward Kelley – to study and practise in the congenial atmosphere.

Despite the triumph of the Scientific Revolution with its mechanical and rationalist philosophy, the Hermetic tradition continued in Prague, sometimes emerging from the underground only to disappear again like a figure on a bridge in winter fog. Even in the twentieth century during the Nazi and communist eras, the alchemists continued to work in cellars and flats, alone or in small circles, only to come forth in the Hermetic carnival at the beginning of the 1990s.

I arrived in Prague on a warm autumn night in late September. As I waited outside the airport wondering how to get to the city, an elderly gentleman suddenly appeared at my elbow and took me through the arcane and labyrinthine ways of the trams and underground of the golden city. Was this just a coincidence or was he a guardian angel in disguise? He left me at my Art Nouveau hotel on Wenceslas Square. Three naked golden graces danced at its summit. Its faded elegance seemed in keeping with the ancient city.

The next day, I crossed Charles Bridge, with its medieval sculptures of devils, angels and crucifixes, and climbed the hill to the castle which had figured so powerfully in Kafka's haunting novels. It was dominated by the Gothic spires of Vitus Cathedral. Vrum had given me some careful instructions:

'Just before you cross the bridge over the moat to the castle, you will see on your left a small green door in the wall. It will take you into a garden. The guard will not speak English but show him my telephone number. He will point you in the right direction.'

I knocked firmly on the green door in the ancient wall. A fresh-faced young soldier opened the door, waved me in with a smile and pointed through a courtyard to a building set amongst trees in a beautiful formal garden. It was a large modern villa, well furnished in light oak. There was no sign of life or of an entrance. Then suddenly an elderly woman, elegantly dressed and leading a small dog, appeared from behind a bush. She explained in perfect English that we were in the Royal Gardens and the villa had been built by the first president of independent Czechoslovakia as his home after the Second World War. The communist rulers had later preferred to live in grander settings. After the collapse of the old regime, the playwright and new president

Václav Havel had moved in for a while, but had decided to live out of town.

The unknown lady appeared exactly at the right time. She opened a door and took me to the office of Forum 2000. Vrum was its director. Again, I seemed to have been brought here by some unknown force, without being challenged and without any effort on my part.

Robert Vrum was a tall, slim man with fine features in his forties. He spoke excellent English with a slight Czech accent, having lived in Canada for several years. We went into a large room with old masters on the walls and beautiful views of the gardens through the large windows. We sat around a large circular table. An ancient clock ticked away.

Vrum came straight to the point:

'What is your interest in alchemy?'

'I'm mainly interested in the practice and theory of alchemy, not only as a form of early science but as a means of spiritual transformation.'

'I think the key is in spiritual transformation. It's a release of something present in matter. Actually, it was Paracelsus who said that a baker is an alchemist as he bakes bread or the wine maker as he makes wine!'

'Why do you think the alchemists spoke in riddles?' I asked.

'For me, it's quite simple. There are powers of nature that are significant, and there are methods which can be applied to direct them which are very practical. These might range from mind control to transforming matter. It does work, it has been proven over the centuries. There are also special techniques to expand your mind. But if they fall into the hands of people who do not know how to deal with them or who use them for the wrong means and purposes, there's a problem. With any knowledge comes responsibility.'

'Can you give me an example?'

'To give you a very simple one, have you heard of heliotropic breathing, a more socially acceptable alternative to LSD? It's intensive breathing in which oxygen gets into your brain, and you start to have visions or experience things which you can have under certain drugs. It's an old method which has been used for centuries, in Tibet and other places, but always confined to a circle of initiates. This is not because they don't want to share it but simply because you have to be prepared for it. If you open up the hidden powers of whatever is inside of you, it can be very damaging to you when you don't know how to deal with it. You can open up a Pandora's box if you're not ready for it. So it takes a certain discipline and understanding in order to deal with these things.'

'Yes, alchemy does deal with hidden forces . . .'

'To give you another example, I believe that the combustion engine was one of the possibilities for discovery which was never meant to materialize. Yet it did. Atomic power is another example.'

Turning to a central preoccupation of the alchemists, I asked whether he thought it possible to prolong life.

'No question about that in my mind. Prolonging life is not such a great mystery. Modern science will tell you how to prolong your life by ten years; why not by a hundred years? It's quite possible. There are some who would like to prolong their life simply because they want to enjoy life longer. But that's not the true goal of the alchemists. If life isn't enriched, it doesn't have a meaning. Prolonging your life can be pretty tricky then.'

'In China, the Taoist alchemists told me that they only want to prolong life in order to have more time to seek enlightenment and to become immortal.'

'Yes, that's how it should be. But prolonging life indefinitely is not the goal of alchemy. It's sometimes a necessity, which can be quite painful.'

'What for you then is the ultimate goal of alchemy?'

'First, to release something from matter. Second, to help something to be released from matter.'

'What's that?'

'The precious substance, the true gold of the philosophers.'

'Do you mean the soul?'

'Yes, soul would probably be the most logical word in the case of one individual soul. But there is more to life than just one individual soul . . .'

'I agree. That's what the Hermetic philosophers mean by the *anima mundi*, the world soul. But, tell me, why did you become involved in alchemy?'

'At first, it seemed exciting, a funny game, ancient alchemists making gold, living for ever, becoming invisible and all that. Only later did I realize what it really means. But there's, how shall I say . . .'

Vrum paused, searching for the right phrase. The clock ticked away in the silent room. Leaves drifted down in the still air through the wide windows. A conker fell and rolled on the grass.

'Yes, that's it, there's the poetry of occultism – not in the sense of actual poetry but in the tricky sense of a trap. Esoteric studies, the occult, alchemy, or whatever we call it, can be very attractive, very exotic, but you can fall into the trap of enjoying yourself, reading all the important books, attending all the important lectures. Some people travel to faraway, exotic places to find something, but in reality most of the time they are just enjoying themselves . . .'

I knew exactly what he meant. I could see the tendency in myself. Had I not travelled the world in the last eighteen months looking for the Philosopher's Stone? Was it just to write another book? A pleasant way of earning a living? Or was I really serious about my quest? Did I really want to find something that would enable me to transform matter and bring about my salvation?

Vrum continued: 'There has to be an inducement for a human being to lean towards alchemy in the first place. There's almost an erotic quality which draws you into it without realizing why. It draws you in, but then you realize that it's not what you thought it was in the first place.'

He was touching on something which was becoming increasingly clear to me: 'To me the idea of making gold in alchemy is a lure, a way of getting people interested and a means of keeping the tradition alive in difficult times. It's perhaps like the melody in a song which is passed down from generation to generation. The melody ensures that the song lives on although only a few singers may understand its deep meaning.'

'I would go even further,' Vrum added. 'There could be in the song, in the sound, or in a painting, something hidden which people do not understand on a conscious level, yet it can touch them in some other way, perhaps in an even more important way. For us reason is very important, logic is very important, so that we can summarize things, but there are other more important things. Plato said that *eros* is the driving force of the soul, yet it does not guarantee the direction. That's why you have to have Logos. You need a combination of the two.'

'But once you've got involved with alchemy, excited by its promise, it's difficult not to carry on . . .'

'It's a very personal thing,' Vrum replied. 'Indeed, in writing a book, finding out about these things, you are finding out about yourself . . .'

We stopped there. Robert Vrum, director of Forum 2000, had another meeting. We agreed to meet later. I found our conversation fascinating since it brought together many of the ideas and themes I had been thinking about since my journey had begun eighteen months before in China.

When I met Vrum again in the afternoon, he had just seen the chief of protocol from the Ministry of Foreign Affairs with whom he was arranging an 'informal gathering' of ambassadors from the European Union in a crypt 40 metres below St Vitus Cathedral in Prague Castle.

'Hardly anybody knows about it,' Vrum chuckled. 'The communists dug a tunnel there to create a nuclear bomb shelter. The hill on which Prague Castle was built has a very special energy. When you are inside the chamber in the rock below the cathedral, you can feel a very strong vibration. I see the meeting I'm organizing there as an example of practical alchemy. Putting certain elements together and mixing them, you get certain results! These things play an important role in the diplomatic world.'

I returned to the theme of our earlier conversation.

'There seems to be a great deal of interest in alchemy at the moment, worldwide. Perhaps it's because it's the beginning of the new millennium.'

'It's not just the date, it's the situation. If you look around, things are happening everywhere. I like to joke about it. If you believe in past lives, you may have hit someone in the Gothic era, and in the Baroque era somebody would hit you back, but now it's a matter of weeks! Everything's becoming more urgent; there's instant karma. Nature has a way of showing urgency. Things become more open. The information is being disseminated around the world: you can peep into almost any initiation rite these days. All the ancient secrets are being revealed.'

'I agree. You and I are part of this movement. I believe there's a new enlightenment taking place, not like the Enlightenment of the eighteenth century which was based on analytical reason, but an enlightenment based on the illumination of spiritual knowledge, on *gnosis* rather than Logos. That's why things are being said which were never revealed before. People recognize the urgency.'

'There's a new enlightenment and a new darkness. It's usually in the greatest darkness that you can see the light.'

'I also sense that the Invisible College which the Rosicrucians and Hermetic philosophers talked about in the seventeenth century is becoming more visible. In many parts of the world Illuminati are appearing . . .'

'The people of this kind, the philosophers, the mystics, they simply recognize each other, they don't need secret handshakes; it's just natural. And they do have their agenda which I hope is quite unselfish. Yes, I believe it.'

'Perhaps now is the time for a moral and spiritual reformation of the world.'

'I hope so. Rational science pushed alchemy underground in a very clever way by ridiculing it rather than suppressing it. Rational science is quite often successful in solving the big problems we have but we would not have them if we did not have this rational science in the first place! It's caught in its own salvation, so to speak, which is not very good for anybody.'

'I quite agree. For the last 300 years since the Scientific Revolution, we have had this mechanical and rational science separating the scientist from his work, but it's only a very temporary aberration. We are now recovering and developing a new alchemy.'

'Rational science simply made this world into a mechanical model, like a chessboard, either black or white, yes or no. If you're a chemist, you shouldn't meddle in philosophy, and if you're a philosopher you shouldn't do quantum mechanics. So science strictly divided knowledge into different compartments and the meaning of life was delegated to philosophy. In all the scientific disciplines, the key question of the end of knowledge disappeared, for it was not considered important. The only importance was the experimental results, but not the very basis of them, why they were performed in the first place. But now the questions of the quality of life, the meaning of life, and my position in life are becoming again important.'

'You can't escape these questions. Material comfort is not enough. You can't live by bread alone.'

'Humanity has been in this situation many times before. The technical and scientific advances are great today but the spiritual level is far below them. When there's a discrepancy between the two it brings about the end of civilizations. The Egyptians probably suffered from this. And we are now.'

'Yes, and before the Egyptians there was probably another civilization, which is remembered in Plato's myth of Atlantis.'

'You can call it Atlantis or by any other name', Vrum continued, 'but I'm sure there were previous civilizations or sources of knowledge. If one looks at the pyramids, it's clear that their knowledge came from somewhere else. After 6,000 years, we are not as advanced as some civilizations were before us. It's very obvious for anyone who has the mind to think.'

'In China and India too they talk about giants coming from across the sea bringing the knowledge of alchemy. Within these myths, there's invariably an element of historical truth.'

'Certainly.'

'What do you think about initiation rites in alchemy? Are they important?'

'A crucial point which involves all initiation rites is death. Comenius has a very interesting allegory about it in his *Labyrinth of this World and the Paradise of the Heart*. For Comenius the paradise of the heart is symbolized by the figure of Christ. He describes how in a symbolic city, he sees people being attacked by Death, who is shooting people with arrows. One person is hit and made sick, another is hit and dies. But there's a very strange thing. Death has the bow but she does not have the arrows herself. She takes the arrows from the people. They bring the arrows so that she has something to shoot them with.'

'I suppose he's saying that we are responsible for the time of our own death. The Chinese alchemists say the same thing.'

'Comenius writes about the death of true Christians, as he calls them, who are ready for death. The angels come to them and they're happy because they're waiting for death as a release. It's a very interesting allegory.'

'The preparation for death has always been a central aim of the Hermetic philosophers and alchemists.'

'Yes, I believe there're two things crucial to any real initiation. One is the experience of death. And the second is how to deal with human energy, how to get it, how to keep it, and how to direct it.'

'Does the initiation help you to prepare your soul for the voyage after death?'

'It actually shows you what death is. I believe you get a preview. You experience what you will experience in a real situation so you'll know what to expect.'

'Is it necessary to have a teacher to initiate us?'

'No one is between us and enlightenment. For anyone who has eyes to see, we have a teacher within us. Gurus are often interested in egotistical power. Anyone who says he's a great spiritual leader, you can be sure he's not. Mystics don't give lectures!'

'How can we find the truth then?'

'Truth is beyond laws. Everyday routine is the real killer. If you understand the laws of nature you can go beyond them. The key is to learn the rules and then to break them without talking about it. Then a miracle can happen!'

Since Vrum had written a book about the court of Rudolf II, I asked him about the alchemical tradition in his country.

'It's much older than Rudolf, beyond even Charles IV, the emperor who lived here two or three hundred years before. Rudolf was a very prominent personality who supported alchemy a great deal, although he's quite misunderstood. He was very knowledgeable. He first learned about it in the court of his uncle, Philip II of Spain.'

'And Spain had been occupied by the Moors . . .'

'Of course. There was a strong tradition of alchemy there, because of the Middle Eastern influence and the Mediterranean sea. What's also important is that Rudolf II and Philip II were the two greatest collectors of Hieronymus Bosch who for me is the ultimate alchemist.'

Vrum was chairman of the Bosch Foundation which was sponsoring the restoration of the 'Garden of Delights'.

'The depth of Bosch's knowledge of alchemy was exceptional and the way he could put it into his pictures. For some people images are much easier than words, and in Bosch's paintings, especially in the St Anthony triptych, there are volumes of alchemical books. The symbols, the secret language of alchemy, are all there. It's a book in which you don't have to use your Logos very much!'

'As you said earlier, the baker, the wine maker and the painter are all alchemists in their own way.'

'Yes, you can bake very ordinary bread and you can live by that, but you can also create bread which is a pleasure, which has all the nutritional qualities but at the same time has something more. The same goes for wine and for painting.'

'And it involves a transformation of nature . . .'

'Absolutely.'

'Which can only be achieved through an understanding of nature.'

'Of course – the alchemist offers a helping hand.'

'That's crucial, I think. The role of the alchemist is to assist not to conquer nature . . .'

'Yes, I would say that the true alchemist is more like a mystic than a magician. Spiritual alchemy is mysticism. Magic is wanting to transform something by your own will: you want to subdue something, you want to give it orders. To give you a parable, I would say the mystic is someone who knocks on the door to the Great Unknown and patiently waits until the door is opened. The magician will rush the door, try to force it open, in order to get in. Both can work, there's no question about that, both ways are very practical, but one of them is not for me!'

'Nor me either!' I added.

It was time to go, but before I took my leave I asked Vrum why he thought Prague had become such a centre of alchemy.

'It seems that about two billion years ago a meteorite created the Bohemian crater. It has a very special energy. Prague has a strange identity, with four main elements: the Celts, the Germanic tribes, the Slavs and, from the tenth century, the Jews. It is a melting pot – alchemy on a large scale! Its energies either attract or repel people; it has its own spirit of place. There's a prophecy that at the end of the world Prague will survive like an island in the sea!'

Rudolfine Prague

His Majesty is interested only in wizards, alchymists, kabbal-
ists and the like, sparing no expense to find all kinds of
treasures, learn secrets and use scandalous ways of harming
his enemies . . .

Proposition to the Archdukes in Vienna (1606)

As we sat in the former presidential villa in the royal gardens, Robert
Vrum pointed out to me a round tower growing out of the walls of
Prague Castle on the other side of a deep moat. 'It's called the Powder
Tower. It used to be an alchemical laboratory during the reign of
Rudolf II. The English alchemist Edward Kelley once worked there.'

Kelley was one of many European alchemists who flocked to the
court of Rudolf II (1552–1612). He was officially the Emperor of
the Holy Roman Empire, the *Dominus Mundi* ('World Ruler'), King
of Bohemia and Hungary, King of the Romans. The seat of his power
was Prague Castle at the centre of Bohemia which was at the centre of
Europe.

Born in Vienna, Rudolf was the eldest son of Emperor Maximilian
II. As Vrum pointed out, being a member of the House of Habsburg,
Rudolf went to Spain for his education from the age of eight to sixteen
in the court of his uncle, Philip II of Spain. First in Escorial and then
in Madrid, he came into contact with the rich and profound Hermetic
tradition bequeathed by the Muslims. After the imperial court moved
from Vienna to Prague, he become emperor in 1576.

Rudolf rapidly turned Prague into a centre of alchemy and occult
learning. One Venetian visitor at the court observed: 'He delights in
hearing secrets about things both natural and artificial, and whoever is

able to deal in such matters will always find the ear of the Emperor ready.'[1]

One such was Rabbi Löw, a mystical Jewish scholar who allegedly stopped the emperor's carriage on Charles Bridge at a distance by kinetic energy. His greatest claim to fame was the creation of a golem (Hebrew for 'unformed matter') from the mud of the River Vitava to work for him. When the artificial human went berserk, he was forced to withdraw its diet of *shemhamforash* – a magical formula for life written on a parchment – and it returned to clay. I visited Löw's grave in the cemetery of the Old Jewish Quarter and noticed that people still left candles and notes on his ornate tombstone in the hope of realizing their dreams.

Rudolf was interested in the arts as well as the sciences. He gathered together a unique collection of Renaissance artists, including Titian, Leonardo, Tintoretto, Caravaggio, Holbein, Dürer, Brueghel and Bosch. They provided him with a mirror of the world, a kind of cosmic theatre. He also kept a menagerie of lions, leopards, bears and wolves and an Indian raven. But it was alchemy which most intrigued him. He shared the alchemical dream of the Renaissance to go beyond the world of appearances and to penetrate the higher reality beyond.[2] He locked himself away behind the walls of his vast castle and welcomed anyone who might help him in his search for the Philosopher's Stone. Alchemical laboratories bubbled inside and outside the castle walls. As the title of a work by Daniel Stolcius puts it, he wished to create

> A Chemical Pleasure-Garden, decorated with handsome figures cut in copper, illustrated with poetic paintings and explanations, so that it may not only serve to refresh the eyes and the spirit but arouse at the same time a very deep contemplation of natural things . . .[3]

Following Vrum's advice, I visited the Powder Tower overlooking the Deer Moat where the Great Work was once performed. It still contained an alchemical laboratory with its furnaces, alembics tubes and vases. Nearby was Golden Lane where goldsmiths and alchemists reputedly had their workshops and where Kafka once lived. The Hermetic writer Gustav Meyrink placed in the lane a house called The Last Lantern which was the threshold between the visible and the invisible.

Kelley was imprisoned in the New White Tower at one end of Golden Lane. In the nearby Black Tower the renowned Czech alchemist and noble Bavor Rodovsky of Hustiran also spent three years imprisoned for debts during which time he translated works of Hermetic philosophy. In the old White Tower, of which only a part remains, there is a fresco of Hermes and Pallas Athene in the Coat of Arms Hall. Hermes, of course, was the Greek equivalent of Thoth, and Pallas Athene the Greek goddess of wisdom. The union of Hermes and Athena – Hermathena – represented the ideal of eloquent wisdom.

It seems that Rudolf patronized hundreds of alchemists and Hermetic thinkers in Prague during his reign.[4] Outstanding amongst the philosophers was the Italian Giordano Bruno. He published two papers in 1588 whilst residing in the city: *One Hundred and Sixty Articles against Mathematicians and Philosophers* and *On the Calculations and Combinations according to R. Lull.* From Bohemia Bruno travelled to Germany before returning to Venice where he was imprisoned and eventually burned at the stake for his Hermetic beliefs by the Inquisition.

The great mystic Jacob Boehme from Gorlitz, Silesia, came to Prague in 1619. He had served as an apprentice cobbler but came under the influence of Paracelsus. In 1598, he had a mystical experience for several days in which he felt surrounded by *lumen naturae*, the divine light at the centre of 'The Book of Nature'. He had another in 1600 whilst examining the lustre of a pewter dish in the sun and described the vision in *Morgenrote* (1634, 'Red Sky at Morning'). In this and other works, he expressed his view of the unity of the soul and God. He placed great stress on free will: 'For every person is free and acts as his own God, so he can transform himself into wrath or love.'[5]

Like Paracelsus, he wrote *On the Signature of Things* (1635) and developed the *tria principia* of salt, sulphur and mercury in *On the Three Principles of the Divine Being* (1660). His philosophy dealt with 'Alchemy in the cosmos: its first Matter and its Three Principles, Alchemical work in Man: the threefold life in him; The Eternal Essence and the Tincture in Man and Nature'. While he had not alchemy 'in the praxis', he wrote 'in the knowledge of the spirit' about the Philosopher's Stone. For him, the Word is the true Philosopher's Stone, by which I assumed he meant the Word of God as revealed to humanity.

The famous astronomer-astrologer Tycho Brahe was no less welcome at Rudolf's court. After seeing an eclipse of the sun in 1560 in Denmark, the fourteen-year-old boy decided to study astronomy and mathematics. At eighteen, when observing the conjunction of Saturn and Jupiter, he concluded that the *Alfonsine Tables* were a month out and he started to make new instruments and tables. In the same year he designed a great solar mirror to help make alloys of precious stones. After predicting the appearance of a comet in 1577, he went on to offer a modified form of the Copernicus heliocentric theory of the universe: all the planets revolve around the sun, but the sun revolves around the earth. On his death in 1601, Johannes Kepler inherited his position as Imperial Astronomer at Rudolf's court as well as his equipment, and used his careful observations to support the view that the sun is at the centre of our solar system.

During my stay in Prague I visited Tycho Brahe's tomb in the Church of Our Lady Before Týn in the centre of the old town. The false metal tip to his nose which replaced the one lost in a duel is clearly visible on his statue. He once read in the stars that Rudolf and his favourite lion had the same constellation and that they would share the same fate. When the lion died, Rudolf died three days later.

In the same district, I came across the House of the Three Plumes, also known as The Wolf's Throat. It was here the great Moravian alchemist Michael Sendivogius (c.1556–1646) lived. He was reputed to have transmuted alchemical gold for Rudolf although the temperamental Emperor threw him twice into gaol.

Sendivogius had studied in Krakow and was allegedly a pupil of the Scottish alchemist Alexander Seton. Seton claimed in 1602 to have visited the pilot Jacob Huassen in the Netherlands whom he had saved the year before off the Scottish coast. He showed the seafarer how to transform lead into gold. He then travelled around Europe, visiting Italy, Switzerland and Germany. In Fribourg he convinced the sceptical Professor Dienheim of the possibility of manufacturing gold with the help of a magic powder. Several documents claim that he performed the transmutation in Germany; in Cologne, he even used lapis lazuli as his first substance. When Christian II, the Elector of Saxony, heard of Seton's knowledge, he had him arrested and tortured but the Scot refused to reveal any secrets.

Sendivogius allegedly helped Seton to escape from prison but his mentor survived only another couple of years. After his death, he not only inherited his widow but also some of his alchemical powder.[6] Sendivogius' main work, *Novum Lumen Chymicum*, was published simultaneously in Prague and Frankfurt in 1604. In the preface, he enticingly offers to show 'Diana unveiled' and to open the 'gates of Nature' and 'enter her innermost sanctuary'. It was addressed to 'all genuine seekers of the great Chemical Art, or sons of Hermes'.[7]

The subtitle of Sendivogius' work declares that it is drawn from the fountain of nature and practical experiments. He warns that there are only a few true alchemists around and to understand their hidden meaning one must go beyond the 'outer husk' of their words. Modern learning, he argues, is greatly superior to the ancients, except in one respect: 'they knew the secret of preparing the Philosopher's Stone'.

This looked very promising; no wonder Isaac Newton spent so many years studying the work.[8] Nature, Sendivogius asserts, is divided into four 'places' and four 'qualities'. They are not, however, in accord as one is always striving to conquer the rest. It is therefore of the utmost importance to know the places of nature which are most in harmony. How to find this out is not clear. While comparing the growth of metals in the earth with a man inseminating a woman, and discussing the influence of the sun and the moon, Sendivogius falls back on Paracelsus' three principles of mercury, sulphur and salt in the composition of metals. He defines the Stone or Tincture as nothing other than 'gold digested to the highest degree'.[9]

Although in the history of science Joseph Priestley is usually credited with discovering oxygen, it would seem that Sendivogius discovered the gas 153 years earlier.[10] He found that heated saltpetre (potassium nitrate) produced the 'elixir of life' (oxygen). A Dutch inventor called Cornelius Drebbel took up the idea in 1624 and in the first-known working submarine made from wood and greased leather travelled along the River Thames from Westminster to Greenwich powered by twelve oarsmen at a depth of 4.5 metres.

It was probably Michael Maier who introduced Sendivogius to Rudolf II and he chose him as one of his twelve 'sophic apostles' in his *Symbola Aureae Mensae* (1617). Maier was born in Holstein, practised medicine at Rostock and then moved to Prague.[11] The Emperor was so pleased with him that he made him his personal physician, his private secretary and Count Palantine. Maier's first book, *Arcana Arcanissima* (1614, 'The Secret of Secrets'), interpreted Greek and Egyptian myth in an alchemical way. In an elaborate allegory, the protagonist undertakes a pilgrimage in search of the phoenix, which takes him to Egypt. In the Nile delta, he meets Mercury (Hermes), the 'god of culture and science', who shows him the dwelling of the fabulous bird.[12]

Maier next attempted the impossible in his *De Circulo Physico Quadrato* (1616): to square the circle. Two years later he composed *Viatorium* on 'The Seven Mountains of the Planets' which deals with the search for the prime matter of the alchemists.[13] But his most famous work was *Atalanta Fugiens* (1618, 'Escaping Atalanta') which wonderfully entwines words, music and the surrealist engravings of Matthew Merian to present a summary of Renaissance alchemy as a progressive realization of harmony. I studied the original work in the British Library only to find during my visit to Prague that it was on sale as a CD-ROM.

Maier was a key figure in the Rosicrucian movement and may well have acted as an ambassador and as a spy. On the death of Rudolf, he visited Holland and then travelled to England where he met Sir William Paddy, the personal physician of King James I, the future father-in-law of the King of Bohemia.

The alchemist Oswald Croll (c.1560–1609) also turned up in Prague in 1597 after studying in Marburg, Heidelberg, Strasbourg and Geneva and tutoring in France. But rather than working for Rudolf, he became the personal physician of Prince Christian I of Anhalt-Bernburg in the Upper Palatinate and dedicated his main work *Basilica Chymica* (1608) to him. He also visited the chateaux of other nobles interested in alchemy and made use of the huge library of Peter Vok von Rozmerk at Trebon to whom he dedicated his *Treatise on Signatures*.

Like Paracelsus, Croll developed a form of medicine inspired by alchemy. He went beyond his master in his astral mysticism to argue that each being has its own *astrum* or star, constellation and even heaven. At the same time, he rejected the claims of astrology that the stars directly influence events on earth: 'through dew, rain and seasonal changes, the upper stars and the zodiac awaken and promote life and growth, but do not influence'.[14]

Croll used the biblical account in Genesis to explain the existence of disease in the world. It was the Fall of Man which brought about corruption in the world: God sowed the 'tinctures' of disease as a curse for his disobedience. And yet Croll also took the view that the invisible inner spiritual nature of humans is pure if separated from its corrupt body: 'Man is a hidden world, because visible things in him are invisible, and when they are made visible then they are diseases, not health, as truly as he is the little world and not the great one.' It is therefore on the invisible, essential aspect of man, not on his body, that the alchemist-physician must work. By working on his spirit, he can cure his body: 'It is not the locall Anatomy of a man and dead corpses, but the Essentiated and Elemental Anatomy of the World and man that discovereth the disease and cure.'[15]

The title page of Croll's *Basilica Chymica* shows the tradition in which he stood. It has portraits of the alchemists Hermes Trismegistus, Morienus, Geber, Lull, Roger Bacon and Paracelsus. It also has an inverted triangle linking the triads of *animalia, vegetabilia, mineralia* with *anima, spiritus corpus* and *ignis, aer, aqua*. This is within a circle giving the main sources of his inspiration: *cabala, theologica, magia, astronomica, halchymia, medica.*

Croll believed that God and nature have put their signatures on all their works in the Creation, from the highest stars to the smallest pebbles. It is the task of the adept to read the divine book of signatures and to understand the correspondences, the sympathies and antipathies in all beings and things. The grammar to read this arcane language is to be found in the Hermetic hieroglyphs, in the sacred letters of Thoth, and in the universal language of the Logos, which correspond to the laws of geometry, form, movement and equilibrium. The adept must therefore seek to restore the lost wisdom of the ancients.

While being a great reformer of medicine and science, Croll was steeped in political intrigue and apparently acted as a spy for the Protestant cause. He returned to Prague in 1602 and died there in mysterious circumstances seven years later. Rudolf may have been offended by his working for other Bohemian nobles, both as a spy and alchemist, but was pleased to obtain certain precious manuscripts and other 'secret matters' from him. After Croll's death, his reputation grew. Robert Burton in his *The Anatomy of Melancholy* (1621) refers to him as a physician and alchemist who knew about 'magnetically cured' weapon salve and salt of corals 'to purify the blood for all melancholy affections'. He also knew about alchemical gold which 'shall imitate thunder and lightning, and crack louder than any gunpowder'.[16]

Although the court of Rudolf II inevitably attracted charlatans and puffers, the Martin Rulands, father and son, of Bavarian origin stand out as genuine alchemists. The father was not only a Paracelsian and author of medical and theological works in his own right, but compiled several dictionaries. His son was a physician during the 1590s at Regensburg and moved to Prague where he was ennobled as one of Rudolf's personal *chymiatrus* (chemical physician). He not only wrote a *Defence of Alchemy* (1607) but claimed to know *The True Method for Completing the Philosopher's Stone* (1606).

Just before Rulands senior died, he compiled a remarkable *Lexicon Alchemiae Sive Dictionarium Alchemisticum* which was dated Prague, 10 April 1611. I consulted the English translation of the work which appeared in Frankfurt in the following year. It contains a mine of information about everything from the elixir of life to the treatment of metallic ores. The various stages in the alchemical process (such as calcination, putrefaction, solution, coagulation, sublimation and projection) and the various methods (such as extraction, distillation and sublimation) are all defined.

There is only one line on the definition of alchemy as 'the separation of the impure from the purer substance' but five pages are devoted to the Philosopher's Stone. The *Lapis Philosophicus* is called 'the most potent virtue concentrated by art in the centre. Outwardly, it is a Tincture. Or it's the Universal Medicine by which age is renewed in youth, metals are transmuted, all diseases cured . . . It is the Stone of the Wise whereby the imperfect metals are improved'.[17]

*

The most famous English alchemist to come to Prague was John Dee, who spent six years in and around Bohemia in the 1580s and met Rudolf II at his court. Dee claimed that only one in a thousand philosophers would understand his work; he was probably seriously underestimating the number. Born in England in 1527, he studied at St John's College in Cambridge and then at the University of Louvain where he wrote an alchemical work in twenty-four books called *Mercurius Coelestie* ('Celestial Mercury') which was never published and is now lost. He became one of the most learned men in Europe, not only as a brilliant mathematician and astronomer, but as a Renaissance magus, steeped in alchemy, the Hermetic philosophy and the Cabala. At his home in Mortlake, he gathered together the largest library of natural sciences in England. Containing more than 3,000 volumes, it was more complete than those at Oxford or Cambridge at the time.[18]

Like Giordano Bruno, Dee felt that the mysteries of the cosmos could be understood through certain symbols, keys and combinations. He was therefore delighted by the discovery in Antwerp of Abbot Trithemius' *Steganographia* – 'a boke, nedefull and commonious, as in humanye knowledg none can be meeter or behovefull'.[19] He spent ten days in Antwerp making his own copy. At the same time, he admired Roger Bacon and composed an *Apologia* for him.

In the British Museum I tracked down in Room 44 in the Department of Medieval and Later Antiquities a showcase carefully controlled for humidity and temperature. It contains John Dee's famous 'shew stone' (a quartz crystal sphere) which he used for scrying – contacting his angel spirits – as one might use a computer to surf the Net. His *Private Diary*, edited in the nineteenth century from an Oxford manuscript, shows that he took the spirit world to be completely real. In addition, his *True and Faithful Relation* of his communications with spirits is a remarkable record of his visionary experiences. Like the Rosicrucians, he felt the time was ripe for a spiritual and moral restoration of the world and took his spirits, especially the 'Archangels' Uriel and Gabriel, as prophetic guides.[20]

Although imprisoned briefly during the reign of Mary I for allegedly casting spells against her life, Dee became the personal astrologer, adviser and probably secret agent of Elizabeth I. She frequently asked him to attend her court. He even calculated the astrologically favourable time for her coronation. But it was not to her but to Emperor Maximilian, the father of Rudolf II, that Dee dedicated his masterpiece *Monas Hieroglyphica* which was published in Antwerp in 1564.

The work contains a complex system of alchemy, Hermetic philosophy and Cabalistic numerology. The hieroglyph itself is a unified construction of alchemical symbols embodying the underlying unity, or *monas*, of the universe. The concept of unity is of course central to the Hermetic tradition as expressed in the *Emerald Tablet* and in the recently discovered *Corpus Hermeticum*, both works which Dee treasured. He called his hieroglyph the 'London seal of Hermes'.[21] Hermes in Dee's view had derived his wisdom from a divine source in ancient Egypt and the Hermetic texts were direct revelations of God. Moses too was instructed in the wisdom of the Egyptians and had magical power in his words and works. Since the ancient sages Moses and Hermes could practise magic, Dee saw no reason why he could not emulate them as a Renaissance magus.

Dee said that it took him twelve days to write the *Monas Hierogly-phica* after carrying it in his mind for seven years.[22] On the title page is the inscription: *Qui non intelligit, avt taceat, avt discat* ('He who does not understand should be silent or learn'). Dee was following a long tradition in alchemy of writing his treatise in such a way that only the initiated could understand it.[23] In his prefatory letter to the *Monas Hieroglyphica*, Dee asserts:

> Our hieroglyphic monad possesses hidden in its innermost centre, a terrestrial body. It teaches without words, by what divine force that [body] should be actuated. When it has been actuated, it is united in (perpetual marriage) to a generative influence which is lunar and solar, even if previously they were widely separated.[24]

On one level Dee's hieroglyph (see below) is the symbol of mercury on the sign of Aries. It contains the symbol of gold, the circle, joined to a symbol of silver, the crescent. Both rest on a rectilinear cross that represents the 'ternary' and the 'quaternary'. The 'magical ternary' of our earliest 'forefathers and wise men consisted of the body, spirit and soul' while the quartenary represent the four elementary compounds of heat, cold, moisture and dryness (fire, earth, water and air). Dee hints darkly that the cross in a 'most secret manner' signifies the 'octonary' which earlier magi did not understand but which the initiated reader 'will especially note'.[25] I mention this for the adepts among you.

Aries   gold   silver   heiroglyph

The complex symbol of the monad clearly has extraordinarily rich alchemical associations. The hieroglyph embodies the whole alchemical process, with the sign of Aries representing fire, the sign of mercury, the alembic, the point within the circle, gold. Interlaced with the crescent moon, they represent the chemical wedding of Sol and Luna which gives birth to the Philosopher's Stone. As such, the hieroglyph is a symbol which encompasses the whole cosmos and if it becomes engraved in the mind it will lead to an experience of divine gnosis. Indeed, if properly understood and used, it will bring 'great wisdom, power over other creatures, and large dominion'.[26]

Dee taught alchemy to the poet Sir Philip Sidney, which his friend

Thomas Moffet (the father of the little miss who sat on a tuffet) called 'that stary science, rival to nature'.[27] For Dee, alchemy was not just the art of transmuting base metal into gold; its primary objective was the transformation of the human spirit so that it could make contact with the divine mind. Dee's friend Thomas Thymme wrote in his preface to his proposed translation of the *Monas*: 'This noble science is the way to celestiall & supernatural things, by wich the ancient Wisemen were led from the works of Art & Nature to understand, even by reason the wonderfull powre of God in the creacion of all things.'[28] The *Monas Hieroglyphica* thus offers a ladder to reach the One and Only. It is also a fine example of spiritual alchemy in which the soul is transformed and the body made invisible:

> He who fed [the monad] will first himself go away into a metamorphosis and will afterwards very rarely be held by mortal eye. This . . . is the true invisibility of the *magi* which has so often (and without sin) been spoken of, and which (as all future *magi* will own) has been granted to the theories of our monad.[29]

Dee left England for Poland in 1583 after an introduction from Prince Laski. He then went from Krakow to Prague, where after seances he felt enjoined by his archangel Uriel to tell Rudolf II in 1584 that he possessed the secret of transmutation and had discovered the Philosopher's Stone. Unfortunately the red powder he had brought with him had lost its strengh. The Lutheran leader Budovec recollected that at the meeting Dee predicted a miraculous reformation would soon take place in the Christian world which would prove the ruin of Constantinople and of Rome. Fearful of his influence, the nuncio of the Vatican managed to persuade Rudolf to expel the English magus. Dee found refuge in Vilém of Rosenburg's castle in Trebon before finally returning to England in 1599. He published no more and died largely forgotten nine years later.

Edward Kelley (c.1555–94) collaborated with Dee both in England and in Bohemia. While Rudolf II's court astronomer Tycho Brahe had lost part of his nose, Kelley had no ears. They had been cut off after forging a document as a municipal scribe in his native town of Worcester. Although born an Englishman named Talbot he changed his name to Kelley and later passed himself off in Rudolf's court as 'of the knightly kin and house called Imaymi in the country of Conaghaku in the kingdom of Ireland'.[30] He soon earned a dubious reputation, having been accused of necromancy and of exhuming a corpse from Walton-le-Dale Park for magical purposes.

At the age of twenty-five, Kelley contacted Dee at Mortlake and soon ingratiated himself with the older man. In their 'angelic communications', Kelley claimed that the angels spoke to him in a special language called Enochian, named after Enoch, the Old Testament figure associated with Hermes. A female spirit called Madimi suggested to Kelley in a seance with Dee that they shared their wives which they apparently did for a while.

Kelley picked up enough alchemy on the way to appear impressive. In *The Theatre of Terrestrial Astronomy*, he described the *conjunctio* stage in the alchemical process – the chemical wedding – in the following terms:

> Mercury and Sulphur, Sun and Moon, agent and patient, matter and form are opposites. When the virgin or feminine, earth is thoroughly purified and purged from all superfluity, you must give it a husband to meet for it; for when the male and the female are joined together by means of the sperm, a generation must take place in the *menstruum*. The substance of Mercury is known to the Sages as the Earth and matter in which the Sulphur of nature is sown, that it may thereby putrefy, the earth being its womb.[31]

Elias Ashmole published in his *Theatrum Chemicum Britannicum* a work in verse entitled 'Sir Ed: Kelley concerning the Philosopher's Stone written to his special good friend, G. S. Gent'. The author reveals nothing new but adds the rider:

> If this my Doctrine bend not with they brayne,
> Then say I, nothing though I said too much:
> Of truth tis good will moved, not gaine . . .[32]

Two tracts on the Philosopher's Stone attributed to Kelley – *Tractatus Duo de Lapide Philosophorum* – were published in Amsterdam and Hamburg in 1676.

Kelley and Dee travelled to Poland and then to Bohemia where they worked together in the laboratories of Vilém of Rosenberg. In his diary on 10 May 1587, Dee noted: 'E. K. did open the great secret to me. God be thanked.' On 14 December he wrote: 'Mrs Edward Kelly gave me the divine water, earth and all!' Then in January 1588, Dee noted that he returned an elixir, possessing the properties of the

Philosopher's Stone, to Kelley who claimed to have found it himself in Glastonbury Abbey.

When Dee returned to England, Kelley stayed on. The Emperor invited him to his court to supervise a great alchemical work which was in progress in the Powder Tower in Prague Castle. Rudolf made him a 'Golden Knight' of Imana. After marrying a rich widow, he bought the house in Charles Square in Prague where the necromancer Dr Faust had once lived.[33] I visited it and found that around the bay window in the tower of the house murals have recently been discovered with alchemical symbols, including the phoenix.

Kelley's fame reached the court in England and Lord Burleigh even sent agents to ask him to return so that he could practise his 'Royal Profession'. In a letter to Sir Edward Dyer (a friend of Dee's) dated May 1591, Burleigh asked for some of Kelley's 'mystic powder' to be delivered in a 'secret box' so that he could demonstrate the possibility of transmutation to Elizabeth I.

Kelley was not to be enticed from Bohemia. But his wheel of fortune turned. He was imprisoned in Prague Castle after killing a servant of the imperial court in a duel. During an escape attempt, he broke his leg. Although eventually pardoned, he was jailed again. Dee recorded in 1595 'the newes of Sir Edward Kelley was slayne'.[34] It seems, however, that he was still alive two years later and some say he lived on until after 1600. He was not forgotten. Elias Ashmole reported the memory of Dee's son Arthur playing as a boy with some of Kelley's 'Plates of Gold made by Projection'.[35] The work of Dee was known by Isaac Newton and his Hermetic circle two generations later.

*

Despite the magical powers of all those around him, Rudolf II was unable to fend off the machinations of his younger brother Matthias, who eventually deposed him in 1612 for neglecting the affairs of the State. The alchemists and Hermetic philosophers were sent packing. But they took heart when in 1619 the wedding was announced of the new King of Bohemia Frederick V, known as the Palgrave, to the English poetess Elizabeth, daughter of James I. Francis Bacon and Sir Philip Sidney attended the wedding. It was widely hoped that the new Protestant regime would be based on the Rosicrucian ideals but such hopes were short-lived. The newly-weds were defeated one year later at the Battle of White Mountain by the Catholic Emperor

Ferdinand II. The ensuing conflict between Catholics and Lutherans led to the Thirty Years War (1618–48) which devastated central Europe. Bohemia alone lost almost a third of its population. The Rosicrucian movement was forced underground.

Ironically, outside the castle walls, on a mountain overlooking Prague, the French philosopher René Descartes was serving as an artillery surveyor in the Imperial Army at the time of the wedding. He spent the winter during the campaign which led to the Battle of White Mountain 'meditating in a stove', trying to place the edifice of his thought on clear and precise ideas. After concluding *cogito ergo sum* ('I think, therefore I am'), he went on to become the father of modern philosophy. Although admired by some Rosicrucians, the highly influential rationalist philosopher ensured that the Enlightenment of the eighteenth century was to be based on analytical reason rather than the spiritual illumination of the Hermetic philosophers and alchemists. A strict dualist, Descartes divided completely the mind and body, beginning the split between reason and feeling which has bedevilled Western philosophy ever since.

45

The Ultimate Magus

Nature, and Nature's Laws lay hid in Night,
God said, let Newton be, and all was light!

Alexander Pope

This was the prevailing view of Newton in the 'Age of Reason'. With
the publication in 1687 of his masterpiece *Philosophiae Naturalis
Principia Mathematica* ('The Mathematical Principles of Natural
Philosophy'), Newton transformed the Western world view and
depicted the universe as a machine governed by universal and fixed
laws. When I came to write a book on William Blake, I discovered
another side to the great scientist. Blake held Newton responsible for
the kind of mechanical and rationalist philosophy which enabled the
dark satanic mills of the Industrial Revolution to blight England's
green and pleasant lands. 'May God us keep', he wrote, 'from Single
vision and Newton's sleep.'[1]

Neither Pope nor Blake know what we know today: the greater
part of Newton's life was spent in the Great Work of alchemy. It is
perhaps the greatest irony in the history of science that its most
respected and famous figure, the exemplar of the rational and objective
scientist, should have spent more of his life involved with alchemy
than in any other intellectual pursuit.[2] For twenty-seven years in
Cambridge Newton ranged over a vast area of occult and Hermetic
knowledge and his central concern was the pursuit of the Philosopher's
Stone.

When the economist John Maynard Keynes acquired Newton's
papers, he was astonished to find that they contained a vast collection
of alchemical writings. In a famous speech in 1942 to the club of the

Royal Society (which emerged from the Invisible College of the Rosi-crucians), he declared:

> In the eighteenth century and since, Newton came to be thought of as the first and greatest of the modern age of scientists, a rationalist, one who taught us to think on the lines of cold and untinctured reason. I do not see him in this light. I do not think anyone who has pored over the contents of that box which he packed up when he left Cambridge in 1696 and which, though partly dispersed, have come down to us, can see him like that.
>
> Newton was not the first of the age of reason. He was the last of the magicians, the last of the Babylonians and Sumerians, the last great mind which looked out on the visible and intellectual world with the same eyes as those who began to build our intellectual inheritance rather less than 10,000 years ago . . . [He] was the last wonder-child to whom the Magi could do sincere and appropriate homage.[3]

Keynes was entirely right in this, except that Newton's pedigree goes back to ancient Egypt and Israel rather than to Babylon or Sumeria. Newton considered Egypt to be the source of all philosophy and religion and Israel the oldest and most advanced civilization. He was certain that the ancients had once held the key to all knowledge and that it had come down in a disguised form in the Hermetic tradition and alchemy. He believed that the original design of their temples mirrored the design or 'frame of the world'. In a notebook, he wrote:

> So then it was one design of the first institution of the true religion to propose to mankind by the frame of the ancient temples, the study of the frame of the world as the true temple of the great God they worshipped . . . So then the first religion was the most rational of all others till the nations corrupted it. For there is no way (without revelation) to come to the knowledge of the deity but by the frame of nature.[4]

Newton considered Solomon to be 'the greatest philosopher in the world' and spent a great deal of time trying to reconstruct the Temple of Solomon as a 'frame' for the whole system of the heavens and as a pattern for the future of the human race.[5] He also shared the view of the alchemists and the Rosicrucians that the secret wisdom of the ancients could only be recovered by the worthy. And just as he tried to understand the riddle of nature, so he sought to unravel the past and predict the future. In his *Chronology of Ancient Kingdoms Amended* which he called an 'alchemical history', he prophesied that the end of the world would occur in the middle of the twenty-first century.

The two aspects of Newton – the alchemist and the mathematician – led the American scholar Betty Jo Dobbs to entitle a work on the role of alchemy in his thought as *The Janus Faces of Genius* (1991).[6] A closer scrutiny, however, suggests that the mathematician and the alchemist were not looking in different directions; Newton always remained a Hermetic philosopher of nature. It seems unlikely that he would have been able to elaborate his doctrine of gravitation without the alchemists' understanding of the 'occult' forces in nature and their correspondences, sympathies and antipathies. The founding father of modern empirical and rational science was indeed the last great medieval alchemist, the ultimate magus.

*

What led Newton to undertake the quest which I was now on? He was born after the death of his father on Christmas day in 1642 and at the age of three was abandoned by his mother when she moved out of their home to marry a wealthy farmer. Newton grew up a lonely child in the country but this did not curb his early inventiveness which found an outlet in a passion for making models. His interest in alchemy was awakened when he went to Grantham School and lodged with the local apothecary who introduced him to the instruments and ingredients of his trade. Something of a hypochondriac, Newton for the rest of his life concocted for himself his own medicines, including laudanum (opium) whose curative powers he celebrated. He also read Aristotle who taught him the theory of elements and syllogistic logic; Plato who confirmed his developing notion of God as the divine mind and architect; and Francis Bacon who celebrated the experimental method and upheld the ideal of a scientific brotherhood.

By the time Newton reached Cambridge he believed in the Hermetic doctrine that truth is 'the offspring of silence and unbroken meditation'.[7] As a student, he was soon exposed to the spiritual alchemy of his tutor Henry More who in his greatest work on *The Immortality of the Soul* had described a personal, all-pervading Spirit at work in nature. Newton found no contradiction between his religion and science, between worshipping God and pursuing truth wherever it

might lead him. In 1663 he began his philosophical notebook with
Quaestiones Quaedem Philosophicae ('Some Problems of Philosophy')
which included 'Of Water & Salt', 'Attraction Magnetical', 'Of the
Sun Stars & Planets & Comets' and 'Of Gravity & Levity'.[8] His future
alchemical and astronomical interests were already taking shape.

As a fellow and then Lucanian professor at Trinity College, Cambridge, Newton by 1669 had become the most advanced mathematician of his age. In the process of establishing general principles to
investigate the motions of planets, he created the calculus (differentia-
tion and integration) in order to find the exact gradient of a curve. By
doing so, he clarified the fundamental principle behind the inverse
square nature of gravity.

He further developed in his work on optics a comprehensive theory
of the nature of colours. Both were influenced by his research in
alchemy which depicted hidden 'forces' at work in nature and stressed
the possibility of transformation. In his *Optics*, Newton wrote: 'The
changing bodies into light, and light into bodies, is very comfortable
to the course of Nature, which seems delighted with transformations.'[9]
From the earliest days of alchemy, changing colours of substances were
taken as signs of their transformation. His great discovery in optics
was that white light is composed of the colours of the spectrum.

Newton had an obsession with the colour crimson and decorated
his rooms at Cambridge in it. This has been dismissed as little more
than an odd quirk of personality.[10] In reality, the colour red symbolized
the last stage in the alchemical process. Moreover, the Red Elixir was
another name for the Philosopher's Stone which could be projected
onto base metal in order to turn it into gold. By decorating his rooms
in red, Newton was surrounding himself with the colour of the
ultimate goal of alchemy.

Why was Newton so drawn to the subject? In the first place,
alchemy was still mainstream in the study of chemical operations in
nature. Secondly, he was attracted by its belief in natural transformations. Thirdly, and probably most important of all, alchemy offered
Newton, an earnest and devout seeker after truth, a comprehensive
philosophy of nature and a unified theory of the universe. It did not
separate science from religion and held that a proper investigation of
nature would reveal the fingerprints of God.

Newton began his systematic studies in alchemy around 1667. In
his quest for the Philosopher's Stone, he first familiarized himself with

21. The tenth-century Muslim alchemist Muhammad ibn Umail (also known as Senior Zadith), entering the 'Treasure House of Wisdom' which contains the Philosopher's Stone.

22. Moorish Archway above the Puerta del Sol, Toledo, Spain. In the twelfth century countless manuscripts translated from Arabic passed through the arch to spread alchemy throughout Europe.

23. Hermes Trismegistus holding a tablet with alchemical symbols from the fourteenth-century work *Aurora Consurgens* ('The Rising Dawn').

24. 'Mercury of the Philosophers' from a sixteenth-century version of the *Turba Philosophorum* ('The Assembly of the Sages').

25. Anonymous fourteenth-century
drawing of new life emerging from
the dead body of the *prima materia,*
the first substance of alchemy.

26. Sol and Luna, symbolizing
sulphur and mercury, the two
fundamental principles of alchemy.

27. The chemical wedding of Sol
and Luna represented as a king and
queen in the waters of dissolution.

28. Albertus Magnus points to
the Hermaphrodite, the offspring
of Sol and Luna, which produces
the Philosopher's Stone.

29. The Great Work to produce the Philosopher's Stone presented in all its aspects. The alchemist stands in a copse of metals, with the lion at his feet symbolizing the union of Sol and Luna. The stag-headed figure on the right represents the seeker after truth.

30. A Renaissance alchemist in his study-laboratory prays before a tabernacle.

31. An adept seeks to square the circle. The accompanying emblem says: 'Make of man and woman a circle, from that a square, then a triangle, then another circle, and you will have the Philosopher's Stone.'

32. French alchemist Jean Dubuis, founder of The Philosophers of Nature, in his laboratory in Malesherbes, France.

33. Vladislav Zadrobílek, Hermetic philosopher, alchemist and publisher, at his home in Prague, Czech Republic.

the existing literature of alchemy, making careful notes in the books themselves and in his own notebooks. He gathered together what has been called the best collection of alchemical texts up to his time.[11] After his Cambridge years, Newton sold or gave away many of his alchemical volumes, but at his death his library still contained 169 volumes on the subject. They included eight works by Ramon Lull, four by Basil Valentine, nine by Michael Maier, works by Michael Sendivogius, the Rosicrucian Manifesto and *The Fame and Confession of the Fraternity R.C.*, whose high ideals he espoused. His first and most frequently consulted alchemical work was *Theatrum Chemicum Britannicum* compiled by his near contemporary Elias Ashmole.

Newton's manuscripts show that he made exact transcripts of alchemical works, translations of others writings, summaries, indexes and comparisons. He compiled a glossary of some 7,000 words which included alchemical names, different pieces of apparatus, and a list of terms. Perhaps out of respect for the long Hermetic tradition of secrecy, Newton left key words like 'Anima' and 'Elixar' (sic) undefined – or perhaps to be defined later after his own experiments. In keeping with his belief in the rule of silence and anonymity, he adopted in his alchemical work the pseudonym of Jeova Sanctus Unus ('One Holy God') inspired by an anagram of the Latinized version of his name, Isaacus Neuutonus.

Like all alchemists, Newton felt that it was essential to be pure in thought and action and worthy of the Great Work. In a note entitled 'Observations of the Matter in the Glass', he reminded himself of the religious nature of the Work and its importance in helping to alleviate the suffering of humanity. His alchemical work was not for personal wealth or prestige:

> so be it far from me to make myself a name or otherwise to use it excessively farther than for competent necessities for myself, but specially for thy honour & glory & maintenance of thy truth, & to the good of the poor fatherless, the poor widows & other thy distressed members here on Earth.[12]

As an old man, Newton confessed to John Conduit with rare candour: 'They who search after the Philosopher's Stone [are] by their own rules obliged to a strict and religious life. That study [is] fruitful of experiments.'[13]

In a surviving manuscript from a 'Mr F' (probably Ezekiel Foxcroft, a fellow of King's College), Newton recorded his view and approach to the Work:

> For alchemy does not trade with metals as ignorant vulgars think, which error has made them distress the noble science; but she has also material veins of whose nature God created handmaidens to conceive & bring forth its creatures ... This philosophy is not of that kind which tends to vanity & deceit but rather to profit & to edification inducing first the knowledge of God & secondly the way to find true medicines in the creatures ... the scope is to glorify God in his wonderful works, to teach a man how to live well ... This philosophy both speculative & active is not only to be found in the volume of nature but also in the sacred signatures, as in Genesis, Job, Psalms, Isaiah & others. In the knowledge of this philosophy God made Solomon the greatest philosopher in the world.[14]

In Newton's day, the main alchemists in England were in the circle of the Polish alchemist Samuel Hartlib who lived in London. They included Sir Kenelm Digby (who claimed to have discovered a weapon salve which operated by sympathy), George Starkey (Eirenaeus Philateles), Thomas Vaughan (Eugenius Philalethes) as well as the Neoplatonist philosopher Henry More.[15] Strongly influenced by Paracelsus, they were interested in alchemy as a spiritual discipline as well as an experimental science. Newton was in touch with the group and may have contributed papers to their meetings. Moreover, from 1669 he was introduced to an underground network of alchemists and specialist book-dealers who found him esoteric texts from all over Europe.

Robert Boyle was another key figure in Hartlib's circle. He carefully distinguished between 'alchemy' and 'chemistry' and kept most of his alchemical findings to himself and his friends. They inevitably overlapped; indeed the latter grew out of the former. Yet by introducing modern experimental methods and theories into alchemy he emptied it of its spiritual aspirations and thereby transformed it into chemistry. In *The Sceptical Chymist* (1661) and *Certain Physiological Essays* (1661), Boyle undermined the traditional Aristotelian view of the four elements at the heart of alchemy by arguing that matter is corpuscular and mechanical in character. He also elaborated Boyle's Law, which states that the pressure of a gas varies inversely with its volume at constant temperature.

Newton made notes on Boyle's work as a student and continued to follow his researches. They may have met before 1675 at a meeting of alchemists at Ragley estate in Warwickshire, the home of Anne Finch, the Viscountess Conway where Henry More had rooms. Their public correspondence began in the following year when Newton enquired about Boyle's paper 'Of the Incalescence of Quyicksilver with Gold', which dealt with alchemical matters and was published in the *Philosophical Transactions* of the Royal Society. The two subsequently became friends and colleagues in the Royal Society.

Although fifteen years his junior, Newton warned Boyle against revealing too much about alchemy to an ignorant and unworthy public. In a private letter sent to Henry Oldenburg, the Secretary of the Royal Society, Newton argued that Boyle should obey the traditional Hermetic rule of silence about his alchemical work:

> It may possibly be an inlet to something more noble, not to be communicated without immense damage to the world if thre [sic] should be any verity in the hermetic writers, therefore I question not but the great wisdom of the noble author will sway him to high silence till he shall be resolved of what consequences the thing may be either by his own experience, or the judgement of some other ... that is of a true hermetic philosopher ... thre being other things beside the transmutation of metals (if those great pretenders brag not which none but they understand).[16]

After his extensive reading in alchemical literature, Newton followed Boyle in using mercury as his *prima materia*. Newton first dissolved common mercury in nitric acid and then added lead filings. Since it only produced a white precipitate with a silver metal at the bottom which proved to be mercury, he tried adding different metals. When he realized that he was merely obtaining a purified form of mercury and dissolved compounds, he turned to his furnace. He spent several months at it night and day. His assistant and room-mate John Wickins records at this stage 'his forgetfulness of food, when intent upon his studies; and his rising in a pleasant manner with the satisfaction of having found out some proposition without any concern for or seeming want of his night's sleep which he was sensible he was lost thereby'.[17]

After spending several months performing this group of experiments, Newton was disappointed to find that all he could produce was still a precipitate along with the purified mercury. He therefore turned away from Boyle and experimented with antimony which had been recommended as the *prima materia* by Basil Valentine in *The Triumphant Chariot of Antimony*. Newton diligently copied extracts from the treatise in his notebooks. Antimony has the peculiar property of forming crystalline compounds with radiating shards when blended with various reducing agents. When mixed with iron, the substance forms a beautiful star-like crystal shape which the alchemists called the Star Regulus of Antimony or the Regulus of Mars. While some considered it to be the true substance of the Philosopher's Stone, Valentine insists that 'This Star is not so precious as to contain the Great Stone; but yet there is hidden in it a wonderful medicine.'[18]

In one of his early essays on alchemy, Newton gave a detailed account of preparing the Regulus and apparently produced it before the end of 1670. He knew that it was not the Philosopher's Stone, but he was doubtless impressed by the way the shards radiated outwards or – perhaps more importantly – inwards towards the centre. Newton's discovery of the Star Regulus four years after finding a mathematical relationship describing the receding force involved in planetary motion may well have been an important step towards his full-blown theory of universal gravitation.[19]

After 1673, Newton moved with his assistant John Wickins to new rooms in Trinity and set up a larger alchemical laboratory in an adjoining wooden shed. He continued his alchemical research with the same single-mindedness, drawing up his findings around 1675 in the 1,200-word document known as the *Clavis* or 'Key'. According to John Wickins, he thought that all hours not spent in his alchemical studies were wasted:

> So intent, so serious upon his studies that he ate very sparingly, he often forgot to eat at all . . . He very rarely went to bed, till 2 or 3 of the clock, sometimes not till 5 or 6, lying about 4 or 5 hours, especially at spring & fall of the leaf, at which times he used to imply [sic] about 6 weeks in his laboratory, the fire scarcely going out either night or day, he sitting up one night, as I did another until he had finished his chemical experiments, in the performance of which he was the most accurate, strict, exact. What his aim might be, I was not able to penetrate into . . .[20]

By the time Newton was forty-one, his shoulder-length hair was almost completely grey. He joked to Wickins that he had experimented so much with quicksilver that 'he took so soon the colour'.[21]

During the winter of 1677–8 whilst Newton paid a rare visit to the college chapel a fire burned a collection of his alchemical papers and nearly destroyed the laboratory. It was rumoured that he had lost in the fire a *Principia Chemicum* which according to William Stukely explained 'the principles of that mysterious art upon experimental and mathematical proofs and he valued it much'.[22] If true, it was a tragic loss. But Newton's years of alchemical study and experiment were not entirely wasted for they had revealed to him invisible forces at work in the universe which could not be explained away by a theory of mechanics. They undoubtedly contributed to his understanding of the nature of gravity.

By the mid 1670s Newton had shown mathematically that an inverse square law applies to the force experienced by a planet orbiting around the sun. Inspired by his alchemical studies, he then began to realize that there was an attractive force which holds the planets in their orbits. His observation of the movements in 1680 and 1682 of Halley's comet which made an elliptical path around the earth, confirmed his view of universal gravitation and of the existence of a hidden force in celestial mechanics. With their view of 'active principles' at work in the universe and of a 'spirit' infused in matter, the alchemists helped Newton to conceive of gravity as an active principle which operates by attraction at a distance. Indeed, it seems unlikely that Newton could have visualized attraction in this way without his previous alchemical work.[23]

As early as 1675 Newton had used in a paper 'An Hypothesis Explaining the Properties of Light' the phrase 'secret principle of unsociableness', echoing the Hermetic doctrine of correspondences, sympathies and antipathies. It is clear that he was deeply impressed by the transmutations in nature and the apparent purification of matter which he observed in his alchemical experiments:

> For nature is a perpetual circulatory worker, generating fluids out of solids, and solids out of fluids, fixed things out of volatile, & volatile out of fixed, subtle out of gross, & gross out of subtle, some things to ascend & make the upper terrestrial juices, rivers and the atmosphere; & by consequence others to descend for a requital to the former.[24]

Again, in a letter to Boyle written in early 1679, Newton put down the dissolution of materials to a 'secret principle in nature by which liquors are sociable to some things & unsociable to others'.[25]

Like the ancient alchemists, Newton believed that the divine principle infuses the entire creation like dye in water. In 1664, he had written in a notebook:

> He [God] being a spirit and penetrating all matter, can be no obstacle to the motion of matter; no more than if nothing were in its way.[26]

He always believed that God is responsible for planetary motion. In a paper 'Of Nature Obvious Laws & Proceses in Vegetation', probably written in 1672 at the height of his alchemical work, Newton further described how metals and other substances are influenced in their interactions by a subtle spirit which he called 'vegetable action'. It was this that allowed changes to take place in substances in the crucible:

> There is therefore besides the sensible changes wrought in the textures of the grosser matter a more subtle secret & noble way of working in all vegetation which makes its products distinct from all others & the immediate seat of these operations is not the whole bulk of matter, but rather an exceeding subtle & unimaginably small portion of matter diffused through the mass which, if it were separated, there would remain but a dead & inactive earth.[27]

By observing the power of attraction and repulsion in his crucible in his small alchemical laboratory at Cambridge, Newton was able to see the gravitational force which makes matter attract matter throughout the crucible of the universe. He followed the ancient Hermetic principles in reverse; as below, so above. By doing so, he felt he had unravelled the riddle of the universe. He had also totally overturned existing knowledge and transformed the world view of his contemporaries.

After the *Principia*, Newton continued to work at alchemy in search of the Philosopher's Stone. But it was a period of increasing stress and emotional turmoil. In the spring of 1693, he wrote a document called *Praxis*. It has been called the work of 'a man on the edge of madness' but in fact it contains many of the normal preoccupations and themes of alchemists.[28]

Tantalizingly, Newton records that he had at last achieved 'multiplication', the ultimate goal of alchemy:

> Thus you may multiply each stone 4 times & no more for they will then become oils shining in the dark and fit for magical uses.

You may ferment it with gold by keeping them in fusion for a day, & then project upon metals. This is the multiplication in quality. You may multiply it in quantity by the mercuries of which you made it at first, amalgaming the stone with mercury of 3 or more eagles and adding their weight of the water, & if you design it for metals you may melt every time 3 parts of gold with one of the stone. Every multiplication will increase its virtue ten times &, if you use mercury of the 2d and 3r rotation without the spirit, perhaps a thousand times. Thus you multiply to infinity.[29]

The term 'eagles' here of course is crucial and is left undefined.

Was this a delusion, mere wishful thinking, or did Newton really find out how to transmute matter and discover the Philosopher's Stone? If he had, would it not shatter the carefully built edifice of his mechanical philosophy recently outlined in the *Principia Mathematica*? If he accepted that multiplication was possible, would he not have to revise fundamentally his *Magnum Opus*? At all events the tension was too much. The work *Praxis* was left incomplete after five short chapters.

In the early autumn Newton suffered a breakdown, probably due to a combination of overwork, self-neglect, emotional strain and poisoning from an exotic cocktail of substances imbibed during a quarter of a century of alchemical experimentation. He decided to give up theoretical and experimental science. After leaving Cambridge in 1695, the man who had sought alchemical gold ironically became Master of the Mint in the Treasury. As late as August 1724, he was sending counterfeiters to the scaffold without any show of mercy.

Another final irony: the ultimate magus, whose understanding of gravity had only been made possible by his alchemical studies, created the mechanical and reductionist science which forced alchemy into a backwater and eventually underground. In the age of positivist science which followed, alchemy became primarily the interest of philosophers, artists and writers rather than experimental scientists. The blinding light of analytical reason chased it into the shadows, although it continued to glow like a stained-glass window in the penumbra of esoteric thought. Only in the twentieth century did it begin to re-emerge from the gloom and darkness.

Part Seven

The Dormant Volcano

Puffers and Prophets

Alchemy is only obscure because it is hidden.

Fulcanelli

Although the Scientific Revolution made possible by Newton forced alchemy underground, it was largely kept alive by isolated writers like Goethe, Victor Hugo and Nerval, who saw in it a metaphor for spiritual transformation. Many esoteric orders and semi-secret societies used its symbols and ideas in their rituals and ceremonies. Mary Anne Atwood attempted to bring its insights together for the Victorians while A. E. Waite in Britain and Marcelin Berthelot in France at the turn of the twentieth century outlined its history and reprinted many of its key texts. It was given new life by the psychoanalyst Carl Jung who believed that the alchemical process mirrored the development of the self towards wholeness.

But what of alchemy as a scientific discipline? Late in the seventeenth century the alchemist Johann Rudolf Glauber discovered sodium sulphate, Hennig Brandt discovered phosphorus and Johann Friedrich Böttger was the first to make porcelain in Europe. Throughout the eighteenth and nineteenth centuries isolated alchemists continued to work in their laboratories. Mainstream science still considered it nonsense, even though the Curies, the discoverers of uranium and the forerunners of nuclear physics, were rumoured to have been involved in alchemy.

The beginning of the twentieth century offered new hope of realizing the ancient dream of the alchemists to transmute base metal into gold. The physicist Ernest Rutherford from New Zealand undermined the orthodox view that elements cannot be altered by transmuting nitrogen into oxygen and hydrogen in a laboratory in England. The experiment used high-energy radioactivity and bombarded the nitrogen with helium. He also claimed that it was possible to produce minute quantities of gold, but 'only by the transmutation of even more costly element, platinum'.[1]

It is now generally accepted that transmutation is possible. Radio-activity can be defined as the property possessed by certain elements to transform themselves by disintegration into another element, as a result of modification of the atom. In nature it occurs all the time: lead is usually the result of the decay – what alchemists would call 'putrefaction' – in a radioactive series of nuclides. In addition, a dozen new elements which do not exist in nature have been made in laboratories in experiments with nuclear energy. This can only be done at the moment with vast amounts of energy and subatomic particles which travel at great velocity. Nevertheless, the experiments suggest that the alchemists may well have known things which modern science is only beginning to find out.

Within this more sympathetic atmosphere, practising alchemists re-emerged in the twentieth century. In France in the 1930s a group calling themselves '*hyperchimistes*', partly inspired by the historical work of Berthelot, set about combining traditional knowledge and modern methods. The most well-known was F. Jollivet Castelot who founded the Alchemical Society of France. He insisted that the alchem-ist should be a 'hylozoist, that is, consider that matter is living, and therefore respect it, manipulate it with awareness of its intellectual potential, and see it as Being multiplied, fragmented, divided, suffering, but tending by ceaseless evolution to reconstitute itself in the unity of substance'.[2] In one of his experiments, he mixed silver, '*trisulfure d'arsenic*' and '*oxysulfure d'antimonie*' and heated it to a temperature of 1200° centigrade. The result, he claimed, was a metal composed of many traces of gold. The French Academy of Sciences was not impressed and did not recognize the work.

At the same time, another *hyperchimiste*, the Parisian biologist C. Louis Kervran, argued that the growth of bacteria and plants shows how numerous spontaneous transmutations take place in nature. Oats, for instance, germinated in a medium containing no calcium, more than doubled the calcium content in their grains. If true, it suggests that it is not only by radioactivity that elements in nature are trans-muted.

Alchemists have claimed that they knew nuclear energy and its dangers long before it was discovered by orthodox scientists. Jacques Bergier recalls in *Le Matin des magiciens* how a 'mysterious personage' who was a practising alchemist warned him in June 1937 of the dangers of the explosive release of atomic energy and poisoning through radiation. Bergier was working at the time with André Helbronner, the noted French atomic physicist who was later killed by the Nazis. The stranger asked Bergier to tell Helbronner that 'certain geometrical arrangements of highly purified materials are enough to release atomic forces without having recourse to either electricity or vacuum techniques'. He claimed that alchemists had known about the secrets of nuclear power for centuries but for moral and religious reasons had not divulged them. He went on:

> You are on the brink of success, as indeed are several other scientists . . .
>
> May I be allowed to warn you to be careful? . . . The liberation of atomic energy is easier than you think, and the radioactivity artificially produced can poison the atmosphere of our planet in the space of a few years. Moreover, atomic explosives can be produced from a few grains of metal powerful enough to destroy whole cities. I am telling you this for a fact: the alchemists have known it for a long time . . .

Having looked forward to meeting a practising alchemist, Bergier asked the stranger to reveal to him the nature of the work. 'You ask me', he said,

> to summarize for you in four minutes four thousand years of philosophy and the efforts of a life-time. Furthermore, you ask me to translate into ordinary concepts for which such a language is not intended. All the same, I can tell you this much: you are aware that in the official science of today the role of the observer becomes more and more important. Relativity, the principle of indeterminacy, shows the extent to which the observer today intervenes in all these phenomena. The secret of alchemy is this: there is a way of manipulating matter and energy so as to produce what modern scientists call 'a field of force'. This field acts on the observer and puts him in a privileged position *vis-à-vis* the Universe. From this position he has access to the realities which are ordinarily hidden

from us by time and space, matter and energy. This is what we call 'The Great Work'.[3]

Does this mean that the alchemists knew how to alter the structure of atoms in the 'field of force' without the use of huge, costly and dangerous nuclear reactors?

Who was the mysterious stranger? Bergier was convinced that he was none other than Fulcanelli, the most elusive alchemist of the twentieth century. Two major works appeared under Fulcanelli's name – *Le Mystère des cathédrales* in 1926 and two years later *Les Demeures philosophales*. I came across two recent editions in a bookshop dedicated to esoteric subjects on the left bank of the Seine in Paris opposite the Cathedral of Nôtre Dame. The first not only seeks to reveal the Hermetic message of the Gothic cathedrals but attempts to restore the 'phonetic Cabala' by giving a highly idiosyncratic interpretation of the origins of words. The word 'Cabala', for instance, is said to derive from the Latin *caballus*, meaning 'a horse', whereas the word 'Kabbala' from the Hebrew Kabbalah means 'tradition'. The Cabala is said to be the lost key to the 'Gay Science' and the 'Language of the Birds'.[4]

The title *Les Demeures philosophales* ('Dwellings of the Philosophers') makes clear that it is about *le symbolisme hermétique dans ses rapports avec l'art sacré et l'ésotérisme du grand oeuvre*. It consists chiefly of a guide to sites in France where alchemy has left its mark since the Middle Ages. Interwoven in the narrative are different legends and discussions of the main principles of alchemy, illustrated by reference to alchemical texts. The author asserts that 'Alchemy is only obscure because it is hidden.' Alchemists of the past avoided in their works a common form to ensure that the profane would not misuse it. But while it has been relegated to the world of

> reveries, illusions and chimeras . . . one sees through its allegorical language and abundance of equivocal nomenclature, this ray of truth, this profound conviction born of certain facts, duly observed and which owes nothing to the fantastic speculations of pure imagination.[5]

But who was Fulcanelli? His name would appear to be a pseudonym, meaning 'the fire of the sun'. He may have been an individual having fun, leaving false clues in a typically alchemical manner. It is equally possible that a secret group of initiates wrote under his name. In the preface dated 1925 to the first edition of *Le Mystère des cathédrales* (published by Schemit in Paris in 1926) his self-styled 'disciple' Eugène Canseliet claims that the author was a member of an organization called the Brothers of Heliopolis but adds 'Fulcanelli is no more.'[6]

If, according to Canseliet, Fulcanelli was 'no more' in 1926, how could he have informed Bergier of the dangers of nuclear science in 1937? The French writer on alchemy Louis Pauwels further claimed that he met an alchemist in the Café Procope in Paris in March 1953 who said he was thirty-five but who had full features, white curly hair and many deep wrinkles in a pink skin, with eyes that laughed in a detached sort of way. 'Everything about him suggests another age . . . I asked him about Fulcanelli, and he gave me to understand that Fulcanelli is not dead.' Pauwels became convinced that the alchemist was Fulcanelli himself. To add a further twist to the legend, Walter Lang reported in the 1957 introduction to the English translation of *Le Mystère des cathédrales* that Canseliet had received a message from the alchemist and met him at a pre-arranged rendezvous. 'The reunion was brief, for Fulcanelli once again severed contact and once again disappeared without leaving a trace of his whereabouts.' Lang adds, however, that Fulcanelli had grown younger: he had been an old man of eighty when Canseliet had first met him, but thirty years later he appeared to be a man of fifty.

After the Second World War, Bergier asserted that members of the CIA who were investigating German research on atomic energy wanted to trace Fulcanelli because he was thought to hold the secrets of the atom bomb.[7]

Does Fulcanelli still exist? Having discovered the Philosopher's Stone is he capable of manifesting himself in different parts of the world from time to time? Some claim that he has been seen in New York. He has become such a legend that he even appears in science fiction magazines.

One intriguing theory is that the published works of Fulcanelli were taken from the research of René Schwaller. Born in 1887, Schwaller studied chemistry and Hermeticism and then went on to become a brilliant Egyptologist. As a young man before the First World War, Schwaller came to Paris and joined the Brothers of Heliopolis, a group organized by the painter Jean-Julien Champagne,

the writer Pierre Dujois, the alchemist Eugène Canseliet, Gaston Sauvage – and, so it is claimed – Fulcanelli.[8] Fulcanelli is said to have
obtained an oath of secrecy from Schwaller and given him in return
the name of Aor (Light). The poet Oscar V. de Lubicz soon after
'ennobled' René Schwaller by giving him his surname; henceforth, he
became known as R. A. Schwaller de Lubicz.

Aor is said to have identified an alchemical manuscript which was
removed from Chacornac's famous esoteric bookshop where Fulcanelli
worked. Jacques Sadoul prepared a 'red powder' made according to the
instructions given in the manuscript. In a little laboratory at the factory
of the gasworks at Sarcelles, he then allegedly projected it in 1914 onto
lead and made gold in the company of Champagne and Sauvage.[9]

After the First World War, Schwaller was involved in Paris with
an elitist group called Les Veilleurs ('The Watchmen'). A photograph
of some of its members includes the future Nazi Rudolf Hess. This is
not surprising since in Germany between the wars there was considerable interest in alchemy and the Nazis saw it as a possible means of
fund-raising. In the early 20s, Franz Tausen, a chemical assistant in
Munich, published a pamphlet called '180 Elements, the Atomic
Weight, and Their Incorporation in the System of Harmonic Periods'.
Every atom of an element, according to Tausen, has a characteristic
frequency of vibrations which is related to the atomic weight of the
nucleus and various orbital rings of electrons around it. This subsequently was verified. But Tausen further claimed that matter could be
'orchestrated' and that by adding a substance to one element to change
its vibration frequency, it could be transmuted into another.

The rumour circulated in Munich that Tausen had made gold and
it was not long before Hitler's fund-raiser General Erich von Ludendorff arranged a demonstration with four other Nazi associates,
including a chemical engineer. The substances, mainly iron oxide and
quartz, were melted in a crucible which Tausen kept in his hotel room
overnight. The next morning the crucible was heated again in an
electric furnace. Tausen added a small quantity of white powder and
the molten mass was left to cool. On being broken open, the crucible
revealed a nugget of shining gold weighing 7 grams.

Greatly excited, General von Ludendorff formed 'Company 164'
and a large laboratory and factory were set up. Investors rushed in.
After diverting much of the investment to Nazi party funds, the general
resigned. But Tausen persevered and on 16 June 1928 claimed that he

had produced 723 grams of gold in one operation. A year later, he was arrested for fraud and after a sensational trial in 1931 was found guilty.

At the same time, a Polish engineer called Dunikovski declared that he had found a new kind of radiation, capable of transmitting sand or quartz into gold, which he termed 'Z' rays. To prepare the mineral, it was first ground down, spread on copper plates and melted by a current of 110,000 volts so that the 'Z' rays could then do their work. Again investments poured in. When no gold was forthcoming Dunikovski was arrested, tried and found guilty of fraud. After his release from prison, he settled down in San Remo in Italy, but rumours of his experiments attracted the French chemist Albert Bonn. In October 1936, he gave a demonstration in front of an invited audience of scientists. Claiming that minerals in the earth contain 'embryonic atoms' which grow over thousand of years, he declared that his process could accelerate the growth of the atoms and thereby turn quartz into gold. The demonstration stirred up considerable public interest, and Mussolini sent an Italian professor to look into it. An Anglo-French syndicate was formed and plans were drawn up for a large factory in England to process sand brought from Africa. The project was abandoned when the Second World War broke out.

*

The War did not stop Archibald Cockren in Britain from publishing in 1940 *Alchemy Rediscovered and Restored* in which he claimed to have discovered the Philosopher's Stone. Qualified as an osteopath, he had been in charge of hospital departments of electrical massage and physiotherapy during the First World War. Afterwards in his private practice, he experimented with injections of microscopic doses of gold as a therapy. In his view, 'in the medicine of metals, there is a perfect curative system; that is in the seven metals, gold, silver, iron, copper, tin, mercury and lead, can be found elements to cure all discords in the human body, and that when this system is properly understood and practised, the multitude of remedies may be discarded. Be it understood that this is not my system, but one which is as old as man himself'.[10]

Cockren set out to produce 'philosophical mercury' from an unnamed metal which he discovered after much experimentation. 'This metal,' he announced, 'after being reduced to its salts and undergoing special preparations and distillation, delivered up the Mercury of the Philosophers, the *Aqua Benedicta*, the *Aqua Celestis*, the Water of

Paradise.' The first intimation he had of this 'triumph' was 'a violent hissing, jets of vapour pouring from the retort and into the receiver like sharp bursts from a machine-gun, and then a violent explosion, whilst a very potent and subtle odour filled the laboratory and its surroundings'. A friend who was present described the odour 'as resembling the dewy earth on a June morning, with the hint of growing flowers in the air, the breath of wind over heather and hill, and the sweet smell of the rain on the parched earth'.

Cockren eventually managed to distil this sweet-smelling gas into a 'clear golden-coloured water'. By adding salts of gold to it and distilling the mixture, he was able to produce 'oil of gold'. From this, he allegedly obtained 'a white water, and a deep red tincture which deepens in colour the longer it is kept; these two are the mercury and the sulphur described by the alchemists'. In order to prepare the Philosopher's Stone, he then heated the black dregs left after the extraction of the golden-coloured water until they became a white salt. Next he took some of this 'salt' and heated it moderately in a sealed flask with the 'mercury' and the 'sulphur'. The 'leaden mud' slowly rose like dough to produce a crystalline formation. The writer Edward Garstin visited Cockren at the time and saw:

> a glass vessel of oval shape containing layer upon layer of basic matter in the traditional colours of black, white, grey and yellow. At the top these had blossomed into a flower-like form, a pattern arranged like petals around a centre, all of a glowing orange-scarlet.[11]

By gradually increasing the heat and adding more 'mercury', Cockren claimed that the mixture continually changed colour until it became 'white and shining; the White Elixir'. When the heat was gradually increased, the colour changed from white to citrine and finally to red – the Elixir Vitae, the Philosopher's Stone, the medicine of men and metals. The colour changes are exactly those described by the Alexandrian alchemists nearly 2,000 years earlier. Unfortunately, Cockren's experiment could not be verified for he was killed soon afterwards in the Blitz. Although his secret of the Philosopher's Stone died with him, old people in London were still said to be sipping his elixir as late as 1965.

*

After the Second World War, Armand Barbault in France used ancient methods of alchemy for medicinal purposes, although he preferred to work with plants rather than metals. In *L'Or du millième matin*, he outlined his approach. His starting point is a mixture of earth and plants, moistened with dew, baked in an alembic, and remoistened. The whole process is repeated until a black substance is obtained. It eventually will produce a 'liquor of gold' which can be used as an elixir, capable, Barbault claims, of curing a variety of diseases, and of stimulating the effects of ordinary medicine. He openly admits: 'My medicine does not, therefore, seek to operate on the same wave-length as official medicine.'

Inspired by the seventeenth-century wordless book *Mutus Liber*, Barbault uses dew as his medium, which he collects by dragging a sheet across plants and wringing it out. His *prima materia* is a 'germ' which he calls 'Philosopher's Peat', which is said to grow 10 centimetres below the surface in black earth in a woodland clearing. In order to have maximum potency, both dew and germ have to be collected in the right location, at the right time of day and in the right season when the stars are favourable. He was helped by a female companion who acted as a kind of psychic guide. On one occasion, he records 'in the evening, a dream revealed to her a whole spectrum of colours whose source was the sun, concentrated exactly where the germ of our Matter was. She reports that she saw for the space of a minute the most beautiful colours in the world. I believe that at this moment the stone was fertilized'.[12]

After collecting the materials, the tips of young plants are fermented in the dew for forty days. The liquid is then added to the Philosopher's Peat contained in a closed flask by means of a faucet. The flask is kept at a steady temperature of 40° centigrade for forty days. The temperature is then raised until a dry ash is obtained. Some dew and 2.5 grams of powdered gold are added and the mixture is placed into long test tubes which are inserted partway into an oven so that the contents in the lower part of the tubes boil and then condense in the upper part of the tubes. The tubes are boiled at a temperature between 150° and 200° for four hours and then left to stand for four hours, the whole process repeated seven times. Barbault calls the resulting gold liquor 'vegetable gold' although he accepts that spectrum analysis does not reveal the presence of gold. He claims that the elixir, which is similar to a homeopathic remedy, has brought about some remarkable cures, especially for multiple sclerosis, uraemia and syphilis. Who can tell?

*

During my travels and research, I was conscious of Eugène Canseliet's dictum that 'No author does more harm than he who discusses alchemical operations of which he has not carried out not even the simplest one.'[13] I was therefore determined to undertake some experiments myself in order to understand the terms and processes as well as to see how the fundamental principles are put into action. At first I followed the instructions of the Swiss alchemist Frater Albertus who founded the Paracelsus Society in the USA in the 1970s.

I quickly realized that it is something anyone can do with the minimum of equipment. It is the subjective factors and the interpretation which are crucial. As with great chefs and wine makers, there is always a certain *je ne sais quoi* which makes all the difference. The work revolves around the furnace. The rest consists of a few flasks, a distillation train, an extractor and a condenser. Skill and more than a little patience help.

My alchemical experiments began with preparing herbal elixirs. There are three main ways of obtaining an essence from herbs. The first is by *maceration*, in which the fresh or dried herb is soaked in water, or preferably alcohol or ether (known as the menstruum) and left to stand at room temperature. The second is by *circulation*, in which the fresh or dried herb is circulated or percolated. In this case a condenser is placed over the flask which allows the moisture or vapour to condense and drip back into the flask; the process, which occurs repeatedly, is also known as reflux. And finally, through *extraction*, in which the herb is placed in an extractor.

I started with the herb known as balm, lemon balm or Melissa (*Melissa officinalis*) which was growing in profusion in my garden in North Wales. After picking and drying the flowering herbs, I ground them as small as possible and placed them in a glass flask. Over this I poured the menstruum, in this case a medium of grape brandy although any strong alcohol can be used. I then closed the flask firmly with a rubber bung leaving one half empty to allow for expansion. Next I placed it close enough to a heater in order to obtain the steady temperature required for hatching chicken's eggs. In former times, alchemists would have used fermenting horse dung.

I allowed the process of 'maceration' to take place for three days after which time the menstruum had turned green. I poured off the liquid – the 'essence' – into a clean glass container. I then placed the remaining herbal substance into a dish and burned it to black ashes. The alchemists call this 'faeces', for the obvious reason that the ashes seem like waste. But they play a crucial role in the preparation of the herbal elixir. I burned them in a small porcelain dish and ground them several times until they turned light grey. This produces what the alchemists call 'Salt'; it is considered to be a dead, negative and passive recipient, but it is essential. This process of burning is called 'calcination'. I then placed the Salt in a preheated flask (so as not to break it) and poured in the essence. After sealing the flask tightly with a rubber bung so that no fumes could escape, I left it for two weeks for the process of 'digestion' to take place. And hey presto, after that time the elixir or tincture was ready for use. When taken with a few drops of the Salt and the Essence in a glass of distilled water, it produces, according to Frater Albertus 'exhilarating results'.[14] It certainly did me no harm and may well have done me some good.

On the face of it, this experiment seems simple in the extreme. 'It's child's play!' you may well exclaim. But there are deep and obscure principles at work, the fundamental principles of alchemy.

In the case of my herbal elixir made from lemon balm, this involves bringing together the positive forces of sulphur and mercury in the Essence (made from the macerated liquid) and the negative or passive recipient of the Salt (made from the calcinated ashes). The Essence is the active force in the vegetable kingdom and is the same in all plant life, while the Salt or ashes to which a plant can be reduced distinguish it from other plant forms. Dividing substances into vegetable, animal and mineral, Frater Albertus asserts that each kingdom has its own mercury which is the life-giving energy manifest in all matter. Clearly it is in this obscure area that science becomes 'alchemystical', based on untestable axioms and intuitions.

Alchemical medicine differs radically from allopathy (which treats diseases like most Western medicine by inducing a condition different from the cause of the disease), homeopathy (which uses a small amount of a drug that in healthy persons produces symptoms similar to those of the disease being treated), and biochemistry (the basis of the pharmaceutical industry). Alchemy cures by using a healing positive force – usually called the 'quintessence' – against negative forces. It is a kind of vital life force which is similar to the Chinese concept of chi or the Hindu notion of prana. The result is medicine allegedly more potent than any other.

Gateway to the Soul

> Alchemy provides the psychology of the unconscious with a
> meaningful historical basis.
>
> C. G. Jung

During my search for the Philosopher's Stone, I was repeatedly struck
by the profound psychological insights of the alchemists which they
expressed in words, images and symbols. I was therefore fascinated to
discover that Jung, the greatest pupil of Freud and the founder of
depth psychology, was equally impressed. Indeed, his life and work
were totally transformed by contact with the alchemical tradition.
'Only after I had familiarised myself with alchemy', he wrote at the
end of his life,

> did I realise that the unconscious is a *process*, and that the psyche
> is transformed or developed by the relationship of the ego to the
> contents of the unconscious. In individual cases that transforma-
> tion can be read from dreams and fantasies. In collective life it has
> left its deposit principally in the various religious systems and their
> changing symbols. Through the study of these collective transfor-
> mation processes and through an understanding of alchemical
> symbolism I arrived at the central concept of my psychology: *the
> process of individuation*.[1]

Jung became an alchemist of the psyche who assisted men and women
through the dangers and trials of the inner process of transformation
towards wholeness.

Jung was particularly struck by the close resemblance between the
imaginary world of the alchemists and the dream world of his patients.
He observed that certain symbols in alchemy, such as the rose, the

eagle, the king and queen, and the fighting dragons, appeared in the dreams of individuals who had no knowledge of alchemical literature. He concluded that the alchemical symbols are archetypes, describing the development of the human psyche as unavoidably accompanied by conflict, crisis and transformation. By understanding the archetypes and recognizing the variety of forms they take, he was able to interpret his patients' dreams and fantasies as parallels of different alchemical stages. Far from being merely the precursor to modern chemistry, Jung believed that the world of alchemical symbols stands 'in a very real and living relationship to our most recent discoveries concerning the psychology of the unconscious'.

I found one of the most enduring images of Jung's *Memories, Dreams, Reflections* was of him finding himself by a lake making a circle with stones on the shore. It was during a period of emotional crisis in his life and he later interpreted his action as an unconscious projection of a desire for wholeness. It was part of his own quest for 'individuation'. Jung believed that the alchemists in their search for the Philosopher's Stone – and I see this in my own quest – were unconsciously following a similar path. Their wish to square the circle was thus an attempt to realize the apparent paradox of becoming fully individual and yet part of the whole.

How did Jung come to alchemy? He says that after his break with Freud he first came across the tradition in Herbert Silberer's *Problems of Mysticism and Symbolism* (1917). Silberer recognized the unconscious foundations of the *opus alchymicum*, particularly in its use of symbols. In the Hermetic writings, he detected the eruption of repressed unconscious forces, notably the Oedipus complex and the dynamics of introversion, regression, parricide, incest, castration, anxiety and rebirth – the Freudian works, no less. The *opus alchymicum* is a journey of the soul leading the alchemist to final death and rebirth inside an Oedipus complex of religious proportions. Indeed, the goal to discover the Philosopher's Stone is an attempt to attain psychic wholeness similar to that of Indian mystics.

After reading Silberer, Jung still dismissed alchemy as 'something off the beaten track and rather silly'.[2] But in 1926, he had a prophetic dream which preceded his deep involvement in the subject. He found himself entering a courtyard through a gateway; the doors then slammed shut behind him and a voice said: 'Now we are caught in the seventeenth century.' Two years later he read and analysed *The Secret*

of the Golden Flower, the late Taoist work on alchemy translated by
Richard Wilhelm. After reading a work called *Artis Auriferae Volu-
mina Duo* (1593), given to him by a bookseller, he concluded that the
alchemists were talking mainly in a symbolic language. Jung polished
up his Latin and Greek and began to study alchemical texts in earnest.

As a result, his understanding of Christianity underwent a transformation. One night in 1939 he awoke and saw bathed in bright light
the figure of Christ on the Cross at the foot of his bed. The body was
made of green gold which Jung interpreted as the 'the living quality
which the alchemists saw not only in man but in organic nature'.[3] It
was an expression of the life-spirit or the *anima mundi* which animates
the whole cosmos.

A study of the work of Paracelsus further led him to discuss the
nature of alchemy and its relation with religion in *Psychology and
Alchemy* (1944). His alchemical explorations, however, reached their
apotheosis in his *Mysterium Coniunctionis* (1955). The original intention of his *magnum opus* was to represent 'the whole range of alchemy
as a kind of psychology of alchemy, or as an alchemical basis for depth
psychology'. The result was that 'my psychology was at last given its
place in reality and established upon its historical foundations. Thus
my task was finished, my work done, and now it can stand'.[4]

Alchemy was thus as central to Jung's life and work as it had been
to Newton's. It provided him with material which he could use 'to
describe the individuation process at least in its essential aspects'.[5] It
also offered a treasure house of symbols which were extremely helpful
not only for an understanding of neurotic and psychotic processes but
for their treatment and healing.

*

I was greatly heartened by Jung's appreciation of the psychological
and spiritual insights of alchemy. He saw that from its earliest days
alchemy had a double face: 'on the one hand the practical chemical
work in the laboratory, on the other a psychological process, in part
consciously psychic, in part unconsciously projected and seen in the
various transformations of matter'.[6] He knew that while the physical
goal of alchemy was gold, the panacea and the elixir of life, the
spiritual one was healing self-knowledge, the illumination of spiritual
light, and the rebirth of the soul from the corruption of the flesh.

At the same time, Jung valued alchemy not only for its revelation of the depths of the psyche but also for its spiritual wisdom. He recognized that 'alchemy did not merely change into chemistry by gradually discovering how to break away from its mythological premises, but that it also became, or had always been, a kind of mystic philosophy'.[7] Whereas the interest in alchemy in his own day had been mainly in its contribution to the history of chemistry, Jung brought out its importance in the history of religion and philosophy. There could be no doubt that the *opus alchemycum* is also an *opus divinum*.

But this was not all. Jung's own view of the psyche shared similar assumptions with alchemy. From the beginning, alchemy held that there is one substance out of which all things are made; that change occurs through the union of opposing forces; that there is a definite structure in the ultimate components of matter; and that there is a mutual interpenetration of soul and body which makes matter alive. In the same way, Jung believed that the self is a unitary process, change takes place in the mind through a conflict of opposites, the archetypes provide an underlying structure to the psyche, and individual psyches affect each other.[8]

In addition, the symbolism of alchemy provided Jung with the basic idea of the individuation process in three fundamental ways. Jung called the contra-sexual components of the psyche the *anima* and *animus*: as a man, I have a female *anima* side and my lover as a woman has a male *animus* side. These correspond to the most obvious archetypes in alchemy, the male and female principles of Sol and Luna. Secondly, the initial dark stage of the alchemical process, *nigredo*, corresponds to Jung's notion of the 'shadow', which in its personal form represents the repressed inferior side of the ego and in its transpersonal form the collective evil of humanity. Finally, the *lapis alchemycum*, the Philosopher's Stone, which is produced at the apotheosis of the alchemical process, symbolizes the fully individualized self which transforms old structures and unites body and soul, the lower and the higher, the male and female into an organic whole.

*

While providing great insight into the alchemist's use of symbols and brilliantly using them himself to illuminate the psyche and its processes, I found that Jung often misinterpreted the nature and meaning of alchemy. Rather than trying to see alchemy in terms of its own traditions, he tends to ransack alchemical texts for symbols to confirm his own version of analytical psychology. He always liked to appear the scientist, not only making the doubtful claim that psychology is an objective and progressive science but implying that the moderns know much more than the ancients. He asserts with some arrogance that 'the misfortune of the alchemists was that they did not know what they were talking about', as if they were projecting the archetypal images welling up in their unconscious in an undirected and incoherent way.[9] The alchemist, he argued, 'experienced his projection as a property of matter; but what he was in reality experiencing was his own unconscious'.[10] Projection for Jung was a process of transferring one's own feelings onto an object or person; the qualities of the goddess Venus, he would say, are an unconscious projection of our own sexuality.

Jung's understanding of alchemy was also undoubtedly coloured by his own Christian cultural bias. He often seems to forget that it developed its own traditions in China based on Taoism, in India on Hinduism, and in Egypt on the sacred science of the temples. As we have seen, even in the Western tradition, alchemy did not enter Europe until the eleventh century and then only thanks to the Muslim Arabs who in turn drew on the pagan works of Hellenistic Greeks, Egyptians and Persians.

Nevertheless, I agreed with Jung that within Europe at least alchemy became an important undercurrent in mainstream Christianity. Just as a dream often compensates for the conflicts of the conscious mind, so alchemy endeavoured to fill in the gaps left by the Christian tension of opposites between male and female. The fundamental idea of alchemy pointed back to the 'primordial matriarchal world' which was overthrown by 'the masculine world of the father' in medieval Christianity.[11]

It also sought to recover the original unity of the universe. The famous alchemical wedding between sulphur and mercury, which represent the male (Sol) and female (Luna) principles, produces the figure of the hermaphrodite (uniting Hermes and Aphrodite). When the union takes place between the opposites, male and female, body and soul, conscious and unconscious, bright and dark, something new is born, a 'third thing'. The rebis (double) figure of the hermaphrodite is a symbol of this 'third thing' beyond gender which points to the underlying structures which link all humanity together. It is not the antithesis of Christ but rather his counterpart from the unconscious, a fabulous being conforming to the nature of the primordial mother.

And just as in Christianity the redemption of man the microcosm is the task of Christ, so the hermaphrodite has the function of saving the macrocosm of the world.

The hermaphrodite is neither one thing nor the other. Whereas Western logic rejects the middle term between affirmation and negation, between 'yes' and 'no', nature consists largely of such 'excluded middles' or 'thirds'. Nature, moreover, has many effects which resolve an opposition, just as a waterfall 'mediates' between 'above' and 'below'. The alchemists sought for that effect which could heal not only the disharmonies of the physical world but the inner psychic conflicts and afflictions of the soul as well. As Jung observed: 'What the alchemist tried to express with his Rebis and his squaring of the circle, and what the modern man also tries to express when he draws patterns of circles and quaternities, is wholeness – a wholeness that resolves all oppositions and puts an end to conflict, or at least draws its sting.'[12]

The combination of opposites symbolized by the hermaphrodite is not, however, the personification of the goal of alchemy but an intermediate state before the birth of the Philosopher's Stone. Since it is a transcendental entity and not found in nature it can only be described by paradoxes; it is, for instance, called a stone which is not a stone, a rare thing which can be found on a dung heap. It requires discipline and wisdom to produce and yet it can also be child's play.

In this way, Jung thought that alchemy compensated for the one-sidedness of Christian spirituality and the patriarchal suppression of the feminine. It completes it by bringing the opposites, male and female, Sol and Luna, closer together and by giving greater importance to sexual life than Christianity does.[13] In the process, the body is spiritualized as much as the spirit is made flesh.

*

I found in Jung's analysis of alchemy a confirmation of my growing awareness that the quest for the Philosopher's Stone mirrors the search of the self for wholeness. It seemed to me that the stages of the alchemical process reflect the various stages of the growth of the self as it moves from confusion, darkness and despair towards harmony, light and tranquillity. Indeed, I was beginning to suspect that after years of searching for the 'prime matter' and the Philosopher's Stone they might well be found in myself.

The initial black stage of *nigredo* in alchemy, when the *prima materia* dissolves and the spirit is separated from its dross, marks the beginning of the dark night of the soul's journey when it must face terror, despair, abandonment and dissociation. This is the stage of 'dissolution' in alchemy.

The alchemists often talked of seeking out 'our *nigredo*' in a similar way to Jung's call to acknowledge the 'shadow' in ourselves; it is a process of embracing or befriending the darkness. In this way, creative change is seen as a source of stability rather than its enemy. The old sages identified *nigredo* with melancholia and saw it as a necessary stage to pass through before attaining enlightenment and calm. When Morienus, for instance, was asked why he chose to live in mountains and deserts, he said: 'I do not doubt that in hermitages and brotherhoods I would find greater repose, and fatiguing is work in the deserts and mountains: but no one reaps who does not sow . . . Exceeding narrow is the gateway to peace, and none may enter save through the affliction of the soul.'[14]

The alchemists saw their art as a means of ending such affliction, as a practical and spiritual technique of healing themselves and of finding everlasting joy. Michael Maier wrote:

> There is in our chemistry a certain noble substance, in the beginning whereof is wretchedness with vinegar, but in its ending joy with gladness. Therefore I have supposed that the same will happen to me, namely that I shall suffer difficulty, grief and weariness at first, but in the end shall come to glimpse pleasanter and easier things.[15]

After the dissolution of the *nigredo* stage follows coagulation. It is the moment when the opposites of Sol and Luna, male and female, mercury and sulphur, body and soul, come together in the *coniunctio* of the 'chemical wedding'. If the relation is compulsive, the fusion will not be successful and it may produce gruesome forms, often represented by poisonous snakes, toads or dogs. The union must then be further purified. This is seen as the white stage of *albedo* in which the rebis of the hermaphrodite figure is born.

The final purification of desire and the perfection of matter occur at the *rubedo* or red stage. In early alchemical works it is symbolized by the resurrected Osiris, while in the medieval *Rosarium Philosophorum*, it appears as the risen Christ. Desire is no longer experienced as a threat but can be integrated as a creative fire which animates the whole self. Then follows the culmination of the art of alchemy and therapy: the birth of the Philosopher's Stone and the full individuation of the self.

As Jung wrote:

> [In the] state of 'whiteness' one does not live in the true sense of the word. It is a sort of abstract, ideal state. In order to make it come alive it must have 'blood', it must have what the alchemists called the *rubedo*, the 'redness' of life. Only the total experience of being can transform this ideal into a fully human mode of existence. Blood alone can reanimate a glorious state of consciousness in which the last trace of blackness is dissolved, in which the devil no longer has an autonomous existence but rejoins the profound unity of the psyche. Then the *opus magnum* is finished; the human soul is completely integrated.[16]

The alchemists believed that the inner and outer work can only be achieved through meditation; it is essential to the task. But it is not just calm contemplation or emptying of the mind. Ruland in his seventeenth-century lexicon of alchemy says: 'The word *meditatio* is used when a man has inner dialogue with someone unseen. It may be with God, when He is invoked, or with himself, or with his good angel.' Imagination, too, is essential, defined by Ruland as 'the star in man, the celestial or super celestial body'.[17] Jung himself saw the alchemical operations as the equivalent of the psychological processes of the 'active imagination' in the development of the self.[18]

Jung was right to see alchemy as a way of freeing the suffering and terror locked up in our psyches and a means of healing the dissolution of the mind. The alchemists called it the Philosopher's Stone, the Elixir of Life, or the universal panacea. From my own experience, I can confirm that *nigredo* can lead to *rubedo*, dissolution to coagulation, dismemberment to reunion: the cold-blooded snake and dragon of melancholy and depression can be transformed into the lion and eagle of energy and illumination.

48

The Salamander

In man's inner alchemy higher substances are distilled.

G. I. Gurdjieff

Throughout my researches, I realized that alchemy played an important role in the world view and rituals of many clandestine societies and semi-secret movements which continue to exercise an important influence in the affairs of the world. However unattractive the environment, the Hermetic tradition has survived like a salamander which lives in a fire. Among the most persistent groups are the Rosicrucians and, to a lesser extent, the Freemasons.

In a description of Perth in Scotland, Henry Adamson wrote in 1638:

> For we are Brethren of the Rosie Cross;
> We have the Mason word and second sight.[1]

This is the first known mention of the Masons. It shows that by the seventeenth century they were not only associated with the Rosicrucians but claimed to possess occult powers and used secret words in their rites.

The origins of Freemasonry are shrouded in mystery. The order seems to have emerged from the guilds of masons who worked on the Gothic cathedrals. They would have been in contact with the returning Crusaders, especially the Knights Templar, who brought back secrets of building and alchemy from the Middle East.[2] After 1200 the first secular building fraternities arose, endowed with many privileges, such as the right of sanctuary and the right to have their own judicial courts. Their members were 'free' – free from serfdom – and could travel unhindered throughout the world.

The masons organized themselves into lodges, with apprentices, journeymen and masters, and carefully protected their knowledge. The journeymen were expected to travel to at least three lodges to increase their understanding and skill and to become proficient in drawing, design and geometry. They would recognize each other with special handshakes or by particular ways of walking, posing or knocking on doors. The lodges were exclusive bodies and few were initiated into them, hence their reputation for secrecy.

Speculative freemasonry claims to be descended from these guilds of masons but while its members took over their symbols (such as the angle-iron, pair of compasses, level, measuring stick, hammer and trowel), they lost their practical skills and sacred knowledge.[3] The first known Freemason on British soil was the Hermetic writer Elias Ashmole, founder of the Ashmolean Museum in Oxford and editor of the alchemical compendium *Theatrum Chemicum Britannicum*. His diary says that he was made a mason in a lodge at Warrington in 1646, eight years after Adamson wrote his lines on Perth. His adoptive father was the alchemist William Blackstone, who called him from his sickbed to tell him 'in Silables' the secret of the 'true Matter of the Philosopher's Stone'.[4]

It would seem that Freemasonry originated in Britain from an alchemical crucible full of Hermetic philosophy, the Cabala, alchemy, astrology, and Paracelsian and Rosicrucian ideas. A mock advertisement in the satirical *Poor Robin's Intelligence* in 1676 shows how closely these ingredients were associated at the time:

> These are to give notice, that the Modern Green-ribbon'd Caball, together with the Ancient Brotherhood of the Rosy-Cross; the Hermetick Adepti and the Company of Accepted Masons, intend all to dine together on the 31st November next, at the Flying-Bull in Windmill-Crown-Street . . .[5]

There is a tradition within Freemasonry that Hermes played a major part in preserving the knowledge of the mason craft and transmitted it to mankind after the Flood. Indeed, in the early days Freemasons took up much Egyptian symbolism and considered Hermes as their patron.[6] In Mozart's opera *The Magic Flute*, the name of the head priest Zarastro reflects the association of Zoroaster with Hermes in alchemical genealogies of ancient wisdom.

The Freemasons have always had an ambivalent relationship with those in power. In the eighteenth century, they were considered to be a serious threat to the status quo. They played an important role in the American War of Independence, with George Washington being made a Master of a Parisian lodge. Their influence was immortalized in the dollar bill with its Hermetic emblem of an utchat eye at the top of a pyramid. It was also claimed that during the French Revolution the Masonic lodges were hotbeds of republican sedition. In the twentieth century, they were persecuted under the Nazis and disapproved of by the communist authorities in Eastern Europe. Yet now they are often seen as part of the Establishment, as an organization which draws members from business, the police, the armed forces, the judiciary and the civil service. My grandfather was a mason, as were most of the successful businessmen in the seaside town where I grew up in southern England.

In what way can the members of the modern Masonic lodges be called followers of the Hermetic arts? In theory, just as the alchemist seeks to create the perfection of gold, so the good mason chisels at the rough stone of himself to form a perfect cube. He wishes to transform himself from dull physical lead to resplendent spiritual gold. Since it is a gradual process and happens by degrees, there are different stages of initiation. The symbols, mottos, secret gestures and words are intended to protect those seekers on the path. This was the principal aim of traditional Freemasonry but in practice it would seem that Mammon has replaced Hermes in many lodges and more than a few join the brotherhood mainly for mutual support and the promotion of their material interests.

*

While sharing common roots and similar aims with the Freemasons, the Rosicrucians in the inhospitable period following the Scientific Revolution evolved into different groups. The self-styled 'Real Rosicrucians' renamed their organization the Order of the Golden Rose and Cross. They were eventually integrated with the Freemasons. Around 1760 the Order of the German Golden and Rose Cross was established which had branches as far as Russia. Some say that the brothers of the R + C separated again and disappeared into India or Tibet.

Today there are many organizations associated with the name Rose and Cross which share the original aims of the brotherhood. The most influential are the Dutch-based association Lectorium Rosicrucianum and AMORC, the Ancient and Mystical Order Rosae Crucis of the Great White Brotherhood, which has its headquarters in the USA.

The Lectorium Rosicrucianum defines itself as 'a gnostic spiritual school' and aims to guide its pupils through 'an inner process of renewal and transformation' leading to 'the rebirth of Spirit, Soul and Body'. They look forward to a new age after 26,000 years of development which will bring forth a new Man. Their emblem is a triangle within a square within a circle, a well-known alchemical symbol for the Philosopher's Stone. They place the rose at the centre of a cross within a pentagram (the title of their journal) to represent the reborn human being. One of their favourite symbols is a pelican which feeds its young with the blood from its heart, another old alchemical symbol.

Two of the leading twentieth-century thinkers of Lectorium Rosicrucianum were Jan van Ricjkenborgh and Catharose de Petri. They wished to shift the 'I-central consciousness' from being 'king' in the inner being to its proper role as 'servant' to the 'growing Spirit-Soul, the true self, the inner Christ'. They clearly stand in the Hermetic tradition. Fundamental to their teaching is that there are two orders of existence: the one of time and space in which we live; the other the divine order which is eternal. Every individual is connected with the latter via a divine spark in the heart. Lying dormant in most of us, it can be awakened and reconnected with the pure energy of the divine world.

The Supreme Grand Lodge of AMORC is based in San Jose, California, and its Commonwealth Administration used to be in Bognor Regis on the south coast of England where I was born. The 'First Imperator' Dr H. Spencer Lewis compiled in 1918 a *Rosicrucian Manual* for the organization. It has an old photograph of 'A Modern Alchemist in his Laboratory', depicting F. Jollivet Castelot, Past President of the French Alchemical Society and High Officer of La Roise-Croix of France who allegedly produced gold by transmutation.

The *Rosicrucian Manual* asserts that 'the ancient Rosicrucians claimed that it was possible to transmute the baser metals into the more refined and they demonstrated this in their day, as we do in our day, in a material or chemical world, by the transmutation of gross metals into gold or platinum'. But what most interests Rosicrucians now 'is to transmute the baser elements of our physical natures into the highest ideal expressions and to transmute our desires and thoughts into living spiritual ideals. Thus all of us are striving to become true alchemists and demonstrate the real art of transmutation'.[7]

The stated aims of AMORC are to train the 'Master in the Holy Temple' (the body) and 'Workers in the Divine Laboratory' so that members can become unselfish servants of God to mankind. It prepares 'Mystics, Adepts and Magi' so that they can become creators of their own destiny.

While finding some of its ideals inspiring and its courses interesting, I was not drawn to the organization of AMORC. As it declares in its 'Great American Manifesto', it adopts 'strictly autocratic principles of government' with a hierarchy of lodges and chapters. It has *fratres*, *sorores* and *colombes* (brothers, sisters and doves) as members and students who can attempt to pass through twelve degrees of knowledge and initiation. A key part of initiation rites is an oath of secrecy.[8]

The rectangular plan of their temple in San Jose is very similar to the ancient temples I had visited in Egypt. The first initiation takes place in the so-called 'Chamber of the Cross', also known as the 'Abiding Place of Life and Death', the 'Tomb of Silence' and the 'Tomb of Terror'. As with the Freemasons, God is conceived as the Master Architect.

The main symbol of the Order is a cross within an upturned triangle. The cross, it is claimed, came from the first person in Egypt or possibly Atlantis who raised and outstretched his arms in adoration of the sun rising in the East, turned to the West to salute the place where life ended and then noticed the shadow of the cross made by his body on the ground. The upturned triangle is said to have been used by the ancient mystics of Egypt to represent the divine creations in the world. The most interesting emblem for me, however, is the 'Seal of the Founder', which reflects the continuity of the Hermetic tradition. Within an oval cartouche (symbolizing eternity) a crown separates a beetle (the Egyptian god Khepri, emblem of rebirth) and a circle with a point at its centre (symbol of gold and perfection).

I was intrigued to learn that AMORC believes that Great Masters are incarnated from the Cosmic Plane into this world as members of the Great White Lodge which has no visible meeting place. 'True members of the path' prepare for admission through 'cosmic initiation' once they have developed 'cosmic consciousness'.

According to the *Rosicrucian Manual*:

> The Master K-H-M is *Deputy Grand Master* of the Great White Lodge of the Great White Brotherhood. He was at one time known on earth as Thutmose III of Egypt, and at one time resided at Lake Moeris (Morias) ... The Master K-H-M (often called 'K-H') passed through a number of reincarnations and was an important character on this earth many times, and has lived for over a hundred and forty years in many incarnations. During his most recent incarnation on the earth plane, he lived at the secret monastery and temple near Kichingargha [in Tibet].[9]

If this is the case, I had visited K-H-M's tomb – that of Tuthmosis III – on the West Bank of the Nile at Luxor.

An influential offshoot of the Rosicrucians was the Martinists founded in the late eighteenth century by Louis Claude de Saint Martin, author of the *The Unknown Philosopher*. The Martinists believe that we are 'incarnate souls' and that we pass through a span of 144 years before we are reincarnated. If I die at ninety, I must therefore wait fifty-four years before I am reincarnated. The Martinists are fatalistic, insisting that we can do little about our past karma.

Present-day Martinists operate under the umbrella of AMORC. They introduce the initiate to the Hermetic interpretation of God, nature and Man. Its symbols are the cloak and the sword-cross, the former to remind the initiate of the need for discretion and self-possession, and the latter to stand as 'an emblem of the union of contrary forces and eternal generation and regeneration'. Saint Martin was strongly influenced by the mystery schools of ancient Egypt, the Cabala and early Christian mysticism. Standing in the Hermetic tradition, the Martinists claim:

> Everything within the universe itself is in motion. This motion is rhythmic, and the nature of the objects is maintained or changed by the vibratory rate established in them by differing rhythms. Vibration and rhythm are the means by which the harmony of the universe is maintained.

Before 'entering the temple' and being accepted as a member of the Order, the initiate must be successful in tests of fire, water, earth and air and be 'victorious in his combat against the dragon'. One of their initiation rituals is to be placed in a coffin and left overnight in a dark chamber. By passing the third superior degree (in twenty-four lessons) the master will find the password for the 'Circle of Unknown Philosophers'. Their invocation for meditation is: 'At the gateway to the Path of Return, we stand humbly seeking permission to enter. May we ever dwell in the eternal light of Cosmic Wisdom!'[10]

*

The Rosicrucians played an important part in the founding of the Hermetic Order of the Golden Dawn. Established in London in 1888 by S. L. MacGregor Mathers, it counted among its members the writers W. B. Yeats and George Bernard Shaw, the magician Aleister Crowley, and the historian A. E. Waite. The interest was more on spiritual than practical alchemy. As MacGregor Mathers wrote, the real work takes place inside the laboratory of the soul:

> The subject is man ... The work of the alchemists was one of contemplation and not a work of the hands. Their alembic, furnace, cucurbit, retort, philosophical Egg ... in which the work of fermentation, distillation, extraction of essences and spirits, and the preparation of the salts is said to have taken place was Man ...[11]

Claiming to teach 'the principles of occult Science and the Magic of Hermes', the Order concocted a heady brew of alchemy, astrology, the Tarot, numerology, Masonic symbolism, magic and visionary experience. It admitted men and women on equal terms, but the penalty for breaking the oath of membership was to be subjected to a magical 'current of will' which allegedly could paralyse or kill like lightning. Its members were organized into an elaborate hierarchy of orders, with titles such as *Philosophus*, *Adeptus Exemptus*, *Magus* and *Ipsissimus*.

The most striking ritual of the Order of the Golden Dawn was conducted in a replica of Christian Rosenkreutz's funeral vault. It re-enacted the Crucifixion: the initiate was bound to the Cross and was obliged to swear an oath which had obvious alchemical overtones: 'I will, from this day forward, apply myself to the Great Work – which is, to purify and exalt my Spiritual Nature so that with the Divine Aid I may at length attain to be more than human, and thus gradually raise and unite myself to my higher and Divine Genius, and that in this event I will not abuse the great power entrusted to me.'[12]

Aleister Crowley broke with the London Temple of the Order of the Golden Dawn and went on to found his own society called the Order of the Silver Star. He identified himself with the 'Beast of the Apocalypse', whose number is 666. During a visit to the Cairo Museum in Egypt in 1904, his wife, who acted as his seeress, received a message from the gods telling them to invoke Horus. They felt impelled to stop before an image of the Egyptian god in the form of RA-Hoor-Khuit, painted on a wooden stele of the twenty-sixth dynasty. The number of the exhibit was 666. A few days later another message came through his wife from an angel called Aiwass and Crowley wrote it down and later published it as *Liber Legis* ('Book of the Law'). It called for a new order for humanity founded with the aid of a 'stele of revealing' in the Cairo Museum.[13] Calling himself the Messiah of the New Age of Horus, he experimented with drugs and later wrote a commentary on the Tarot called *The Book of Thoth*.

One dictum which Aiwass seems to have borrowed from Rabelais was: 'Love is the law, love under will.' Crowley expected his followers to say in reply: 'Do what thou wilt shall be the whole of the law.'

When in 1920 Crowley set up a villa in Sicily for the practice of erotic magic, he called it the Abbey of Thelema, also mentioned by Rabelais. In the following year, he claimed to have reached the highest grade of *Ipsissimus* ('The Absolute'). Crowley's interest in erotic magic led him to investigate yoga and tantrism as an ecstatic technique to prolong life and to transcend normal human limits.

Crowley was head of the British section – or rather was the representative for Ireland, Iona and all the Britains – of the Ordo Templi Orientis (OTO), the Order of the Templars of the Orient. He adopted the name of Baphomet – the hermaphrodite deity which the Knights Templar had been accused of worshipping.

Founded in Germany in 1902 by the Freemason Karl Kellner (d.1905), OTO was part of the German occult revival although it was later suppressed by the Nazis. It claimed to have rediscovered the 'great secret' of the Knights Templar – the magic of sex. In the light of this discovery, alchemy was reinterpreted as a technique of erotic magic. Alchemy not only provided the key to the ancient Egyptian and

Hermetic tradition but explained 'all the secrets of Nature, all the symbolism of Freemasonry and all systems of religion'.

Kellner went to India, as I had done, to study tantric sexual alchemy and was one of the first to bring back its teaching to Europe. In the nine degrees of ritual, the highest was the sexual union of the tantric alchemist. In the light of tantra, Western alchemy was given a sexual interpretation: the athanor is the phallus; the cucurbit, the vagina; the serpent, or blood of the Red Lion, is semen. The mysterious first matter is composed of vaginal secretions mixed with semen. The base metals were seen as the animal appetites which are capable of being transformed and purified into spirituality – the gold of the alchemists.[14]

*

Towards the end of the nineteenth century, several other spiritual teachers and societies turned to alchemy and the Hermetic tradition for inspiration. The Theosophical Society, founded in New York in 1875 by Madame Helena P. Blavatsky, took up the seventeenth-century Rosicrucian programme of building a bridge between science and religion and of developing the latent spiritual powers of humanity. The Masters of Theosophy were said to guide humanity's destiny from their headquarters in Tibet, the centre of Buddhist alchemy. The teachings of Ku-Hu-Mi, mentioned by the Rosicrucians, were made known to advanced Theosophists by Madame Blavatsky who claimed to have been one of his personal students in Tibet.

The educational reformer Rudolf Steiner was Secretary General of the German branch of the Theosophical Society and a member of the Order of the Golden Dawn before leaving to found the Anthroposophical Society which he hoped would fulfil the Rosicrucian ideal. He wrote extensively on alchemy, including a commentary on the *Chymic Wedding of Christian Rosenkreutz*. His distinctive version of Hermetic philosophy is still taught in Waldorf schools throughout Europe and the United States.

The Armenian G. I. Gurdjieff was also interested in alchemy. He declared in his work *All and Everything*, which contained his famous *Beelzebub's Tales to His Grandson* (first published in English in 1950), that because of their false beliefs the majority of humanity are half-asleep, unable to tap their higher consciousness. He presented the basic ideas of spiritual alchemy in his 'science of consciousness' in which a person can 'wake up' to his possibilities. 'In man's inner alchemy', Gurdjieff declared, 'higher substances are distilled out of other, coarser material which would otherwise remain in a coarse state.' To achieve this end, he devised activities from his base in Fontainebleu which involved dancing, meditation and close contact with nature. In his *Tertium Organum*, first published in Russian in 1913, his Russian associate P. D. Ouspenky described the fourth dimension of the world and offered an original version of reincarnation in which when a person dies he passes backwards and becomes another person. He saw his work as an advance on Aristotle's *Organon* and Bacon's *Novum Organum*.

The Bulgarian Omraam Mikhaël Aïvanhov who settled in France in 1937 took up the Rosicrucian belief in the Great White Brotherhood and founded the Universal White Brotherhood. Aïvanhov insisted on the need for a spiritual master as a mirror reflecting the truth and was more than willing to do the reflecting. He was particularly interested in spiritual alchemy as a means of self-purification and transformation. Gold for him is 'condensed sunlight', and since man is made in the image of the sun, he called for a new 'solar civilization'.

In *True Alchemy or the Quest for Perfection*, Aïvanhov advocated the sublimation of sexual energy and the transformation of the matter of everyday life through spirit. Once you know the 'rules of spiritual alchemy', he declared, 'you will learn how to transform and use even the poisons in you'. He recognized that producing the Philosopher's Stone is less a physical than a psychic and spiritual process:

> The true alchemist knows that, in addition to the chemical elements he has to prepare according to the formula, he must also be capable of emanating a force, which, alone, can trigger the process of transmutation.[15]

*

The Hermetic tradition continues to exert its influence in journals and societies. Otakar Grise founded *Isis*, a major journal of Hermetic studies, and until recently Adam McLean edited the *Hermetic Journal* from Edinburgh. The Association for Research and Information on Esotericism regularly publishes the journal *Aries* in France. The German alchemist Frater Albertus founded the Paracelsus Research Society in the United States and the French alchemist Jean Dubuis was a founding member of the Philosophers of Nature in France which now have their headquarters in Wisconsin in the USA. David Fideler at Phanes Press in Grand Rapids edits the journal *Alexandria* and reprints many alchemical texts. On the Internet, there is an Alchemy Virtual Library and Alchemy Forum archive with a very active web site for alchemists throughout the world.[16]

These groups and societies raise the question of whether there is a self-styled elite of 'Spiritual Masters' or 'Illuminati' at work in the world. As humanity faces the possibility of cataclysmic annihilation in this millennium, are they transmitters of ancient wisdom and harbingers of a new dawn of spirituality? Do they share anything in common with the Rosicrucian 'Invisibles', the 'Superior Unknowns' of the Freemasons, or the masters of the 'Great White Lodge' of the Theosophists? Will they be invisible pilots in the coming storm?

At their best, the Hermetic societies and movements which have drunk deeply at the well of alchemy share a similar goal: spiritual transformation and perfection. They seek the Philosopher's Stone of universal knowledge and the gold of understanding. Above all, they believe that however asleep and ignorant they may appear, all people are capable of salvation and enlightenment. The Great Work of this new century is to see whether this can be achieved.

49

Philosophers of Nature

No one can transmute any matter if he is not transmuted himself.

Paracelsus

I met Jean Dubuis and his companion Josette in a restaurant in St Germain des Prés in the Latin Quarter of Paris in late October. He was a tall thin man with delicate hands and straight white hair. He wore a tweed jacket and pressed trousers, with an American bootlace tie with a silver toggle decorated with turquoise stones. Born in 1919, he looked ten years younger than his age.

Dubuis had come up to Paris to meet me and to see his lawyer about a pending legal case involving the association of alchemists called Les Philosophes de la Nature which he had founded in 1979. He had been the President for twelve years but had recently dissolved the French organization after accusing other members of trying to make money out of his knowledge and instruments. It had been moved to the USA where it was called the Philosophers of Nature. His former French colleagues had retaliated with a court case.

I was strongly attracted by Dubuis' stress on the freedom of enquiry and expression and his refusal to hide behind a cloak of secrecy. During our conversations, Dubuis said with a twinkle in his eye: 'The person who puts a finger on his mouth to make the sign of silence in effect hides the great cavern behind!'

'Is there ever any danger in revealing knowledge?' I asked him.

'No. If a person isn't ready to receive the knowledge, it won't work. If his heart is not right, he will not understand the secrets. It only works if you have a certain maturity, if you're internally developed.'

'What about symbols? Alchemy is difficult for most people because of them . . .'

'Symbols are useful. They are a kind of language. They are useful to begin with.'

At our first meeting in Paris, Dubuis handed me two pieces of metal about a square centimetre in size. They had been cooled in a crucible and then cracked open: one was silvery and with small crystals and the other tinged violet and with larger crystals. 'They're made from antimony; the violet one has undergone about twenty-five operations. It already has some gold in it. You can handle it, but I would wash your hands after touching the other piece . . .' It was already on the way to becoming the Star Regulus which had so fascinated Newton.

Dubuis also placed in my hands the copy of the manuscript of the French alchemist Nicolas Flamel, dated 1470, which had been taken from his illustrated *Book of Abraham*. 'There are only five copies in existence, two with Russ House, the President of the Philosophers of Nature in the United States. It took a friend of mine two years to transcribe it from the original in the Bibliothèque Nationale in Paris.'

Each page of the copy of the virtually illegible manuscript was peppered with symbols.

'Basil Valentine is important, but Nicolas Flamel is the best. I have been repeating some of his experiments.'

I asked him how he had come to alchemy.

'My first experience of eternity was when I was ill for eighteen months as a boy; my life was never the same after that.'

He also had a profound spiritual experience on his own at the age of twelve in the Mont St Michel. It taught him that the visible world is supported by an invisible realm and that there is Oneness hidden behind the apparent multiplicity of things.

He had studied electrical engineering and during the Second World War worked on nuclear research. In 1944 he was at the laboratory of Synthèse Atomique of Ivry with Jean Frédéric Joliot-Curie, the son-in-law of Pierre and Marie Curie who had discovered uranium.

'I'm sure that the old Curies knew about the esoteric,' he told me. 'Joliot was the first to discover how to split the atom. If I hadn't worked with him, I would have been taken off to a slave labour camp in Germany. We had some uranium but kept it well hidden from the Germans. Alchemists have long known about the power of nuclear energy. I'm sure that if some adepts hadn't informed the Americans of certain secrets, they would not have been able to develop the atomic bomb so early.'

'Why should they want to do that?' I asked, surprised at the revelation.

'The people were members of an esoteric organization who knew what they were doing. It was part of a larger plan which has not yet been completed . . .'

After the war, Dubuis had worked in the computer industry. In the meantime, for twenty years he was a member of the AMORC group of Rosicrucians in San Jose, and then a dozen years with the circle of 'unknown philosophers' amongst the Martinists. Throughout this period, he deepened his studies of the Cabala and alchemy. He eventually became acquainted with the German alchemist Albert Riedel, known as Frater Albertus, the founder of the Paracelsus Research Society in the US, some of whose experiments I had performed. However, he broke with him because he felt he was too concerned with secrecy and with making money. He preferred the more open approach of the Italian Swiss alchemist Augusto Pancaldi and with him founded Les Philosophes de la Nature in France as a research and teaching centre for esoterism, the Cabala and alchemy.

Dubuis argued that the reason why modern science has not found the 'Hermetic secret' is simply because it has not looked for it properly. The experiments are not repeatable since so much depends on the role of the alchemists and their state of being. Alchemy, moreover, is concerned with the metaphysical as well as the physical; it leads to 'a unitary knowledge which includes a conception of the world'.

Alchemy assumes that the whole of the Creation is a field of energy. Everything is evolving and has consciousness although there are degrees of consciousness in the mineral, vegetable and animal realms. Where modern science seeks to find out how matter created life, alchemy declares that life created matter for its further evolution. This is attained through the universal process of life, death and rebirth. Alchemy seeks to change the level of energy in life – a change which cannot be attained without the inner transformation of the alchemist himself. As Paracelsus observed: 'No one can transmute any matter if he is not transmuted himself.'

Out of the original chaos of primal matter emerges negative and positive energy, represented by nitrate (*nitre*) and salt (*sel*). The former divides into active fire and passive air, while the latter separates into active water and passive earth. Air and water produce 'philosophical mercury' or the 'spirit of things' – the key of alchemy since it possesses the energies of life and of matter. For a body to be usable in alchemy it must be alive, that is to say, it must have three principles – Paracelsus' triad of sulphur, mercury and salt, which represent in turn soul, spirit and body.

For Dubuis, bodies completely deprived of their sulphur and mercury are dead. With their energy being lost in chaos, they become radioactive. Indeed, the difference between alchemy and modern science may be illustrated by nuclear transmutations. Since they involve water and earth, nuclear changes are physically dangerous but have little direct effect on the psyche. The alchemist on the other hand influences matter through the elements of life, fire and air. There is little physical risk but in case of error there can be serious psychic repercussions.

Dubuis insists that alchemical processes imitate the processes of nature and the Great Work only seeks to accelerate them. The most fundamental is the process of life, death and rebirth. This is mirrored in the method of distillation which charts the level of the life of a liquid. Just as sea water is evaporated by the sun, transformed into vapour, only to be reborn through condensation in the form of rain, so a liquid is distilled in the alchemist's distillation apparatus by becoming a vapour with heat and then being cooled to form a liquid. What takes place in the alchemist's flask mirrors the operations of the cosmos.

The alchemist can distil liquids in different ways: by the classical manner of separating impurities; by 'cohobation', in which the residual impurities are burned and what is distilled is mixed with the residues of the calcination; by circulating and redistilling, in which case there is a process of 'distillation-purification-evolution'. Dubuis claims that at least seven 'cohobitations-distillations' are necessary to get a sensible result in an experiment. Another method of distillation is through 'circulation': a flask of a particular form is placed in an environment which assures a slow but continuous distillation in a closed circuit. At least a month and sometimes a year or more is necessary: 'patience' is a word, Dubuis suggests, to be written on the door of the alchemist's laboratory.

The second great method – and more mysterious – is the first truly alchemical realization. It involves the separation of the three principles of sulphur, mercury and salt. But these are 'philosophical principles' within living matter, and not actual chemicals. A long circulation of the three principles will, according to Dubuis, give a living elixir with therapeutic powers.

The third method is that of 'fecundation', involving a chemical wedding. Sulphur is considered as male, mercury as female, and salt the matrix. The three are placed within a 'Philosophical Egg' – a flask – and put in an incubator with a temperature around 40° centigrade. Circulation will then begin within the egg.

Using the three above methods, Dubuis claims you can obtain a 'Vegetable Stone' from which one can immediately extract an elixir by soaking it in water.

Because of the reactions between the alchemist and his operations, his work in his laboratory is inevitably solitary. If he wishes to do experiments in the realm of metals, physical and psychic preparation is necessary. He must therefore clean the sulphur, mercury and salt – his soul, spirit and body – within him before he proceeds.

Having once produced vegetable elixirs from plants, Dubuis suggests that taking a few drops every day of the week will help cleanse the psychic centres. After eighteen months the operator should be ready to begin to work on metals. Virgin metals must be used directly from mines in the earth. The separation of the three metallic principles – sulphur, mercury and salt – requires the possession of 'Philosophical Mercury' or an 'alkahest'.

Dubuis defines an alkahest as the philosophical mercury extracted from a non-metallic mineral. This can be obtained from the dry distillation of tartre, natural sulphur crystallized in the earth, or the very ancient volcanic sulphur from the Massif Central in France. The great problem is the manipulation of the 'Philosophical Mercury' which is very volatile and boils at room temperature and can only be conserved in a glass ampoule closed by flame. Working on it can, however, liberate the spiritual energies of the operator. And, according to Dubuis, the seven metals – gelene, cassiterite (tin oxide), marcasite (iron pyrrhites), gold, green vitriol (a copper mineral), cinnabar (mercuric sulphide) and silver – can all produce a Stone and each marks a step towards the ultimate goal of the Philosopher's Stone.

'Where do you get your minerals from?' I asked him.

'For a real operation, you must get your substances in their natural state. For instance, saltpetre which grows on walls with bacteria in a cellar is better than industrial saltpetre. In the same way, the sal ammoniac made by the Egyptians by distilling the urine of camels is preferable to that made by electrical synthesis. They bear the signature of nature . . .'

*

After our dinner, Jean Dubuis and Josette invited me and my companion Elizabeth to their home on the outskirts of Malesherbes in the Seine-et-Oise, about 60 kilometres to the south of Paris. Their house was a modest villa with a garden on the edge of town. There was no visible sign of great wealth. We slept upstairs next to the laboratory. The whole floor was decorated in browns and yellows. On the wall of the landing, there was a reproduction of the golden mask Tutankhamon (the original of which I had seen in Cairo), a portrait of Rudolf II visiting an alchemist (which reminded me of Prague), and a modern symbolic table and periodical classification of the elements.

The next morning Dubuis showed me around his laboratory and then left me to explore it for myself. Over his desk, he had a good library of alchemical classics in French and English as well as works on magic and the Cabala. The authors included Joseph Needham, Aleister Crowley and Eliphas Levi. He admitted to having three libraries in the house, one of which was private.

On his long workbench he had two modern distillation stills as well as an assortment of phials and alembics. 'This is a special extractor I made with the Italian alchemist Augusto Pancaldi and a glazier for alchemical work. I use it for distilling essential oils from herbs and for preparing the Vegetable Stone.'

It looked like a customized version of the modern Soxlet extractor for the preparation of the herbal elixir. The extractor has three parts – a flask to contain alcohol, an extractor with a thimble to contain herbs, and a condenser – which together permit the process of refinement and filtering.

He showed me a glass receptacle which still had the residue of the 'Stone'.

On his laboratory bench, there was also a modern *bain-marie*. Although better manufactured and more accurate than Maria the Prophetess's, the basic instruments for heating and distillation had not changed.

He then showed me his incubator made from an old refrigerator with two compartments which warmed rather than cooled its contents. It could keep his chemical mixtures warm at a steady temperature with an accuracy only dreamt of by medieval alchemists who had to rely on fermenting manure for gentle heat. Some of his colourful liquids had been incubating for years, slowly cooking, slowly transforming. One compartment was set at 37°, the other at 40°.

'You should leave a stone of antimony in it for one or two years. When the essential oils have become red they are ready to use,' he observed.

His athanor consisted of two small stoves: one could heat to 900° and the other, made by himself from quartz, to 1300°. 'At that temperature, terracotta crucibles are no good,' he observed, 'so I use graphite ones.'

To cool the heated minerals, he poured them into a stainless steel crucible.

'I agree with Basil Valentine,' Dubuis went on, 'that you should work with antimony on the days only when the sun is out.'

'And the position of the moon?'

'Not important. Saturday morning is always a good day.'

He showed me some of the minerals he had been working on. These included cinnabar from Spain in an enclosed jar as its fumes were toxic, sal ammoniac, untreated antimony, and antimony powder. There was a silvery block of antimony which had been heated in his athanor.

'This is dead,' he said, discarding it with contempt. 'There's no life in it.'

Like Basil Valentine and Isaac Newton, he used antimony as his primary matter rather than the more traditional mercury. The piece of silvery metal with a violet tinge he had given me and which was in my pocket had been heated about twenty-five times to more than 1200° centigrade.

'Antimony is the only body whose energy can be transferred to another without it being lost. The problem for Nicolas Flamel was how to transfer this energy. It's not possible to transfer it directly into mercury. There are different ways: first you have to make the Star Regulus of antimony. For this, you need the intermediary of the alchemist's art.'

'Alchemy is like agriculture,' he went on. 'If you sow metal seeds, you get a metal crop. If you sow gold, you get gold; if you sow uranium, you get uranium – although the last is very dangerous.'

Dubuis showed me a piece of graphite with small yellow pieces in it which came from the Massif Central in France. With a Geiger counter he demonstrated how radioactive it was. 'It's oxide of uranium. It's not dangerous. There's some radioactive Thorium 135 which is in gas mantles which the ecologists recommend. A little radioactivity can be good for you; light doses are beneficial since it stimulates the cells. It's only dangerous when there's too much. If there's too much it leads to chaos and cancer.'

He had made his own Geiger counter. 'Normal counters only detect one type of radioactive particles, but this one detects three,' he explained. 'I made it after realizing that whenever antimony is transformed, there's a loss of energy.'

'Where do you think it goes?'

'I have my ideas but they're not official ideas. In effect, I believe in alchemy there's an exchange between the visible and the invisible world, between this world and the one above, otherwise you cannot explain the loss of energy.'

'Is it really necessary to do experimental work?' I asked him.

'Both study and laboratory work are important. You need head, hands and heart to be a good alchemist. The head to think with, the hands to do the experimental work and the heart to contact the inner life.'

'Do you need a teacher?'

'No, I say neither master nor guru! The only true master is the one you have in the heart. Once you've got it, then you can follow Sendivogius's advice: "Burn all your books, including mine!"'

'But what about the earlier stages? Do you need someone to help you?'

'You can learn in courses and books. The equipment is simple and cheap.'

'Is there a quick, dry way of attaining the Philosopher's Stone?'

'You have to do both, a wet and then a dry path. They are different phases. According to Nicolas Flamel, when one wants to transfer energy, one goes through liquid states, and when one wants to develop the energy, one incubates the dry parts. But there's a rare way, the way of direct knowledge without books . . .'

He wouldn't be drawn so I asked: 'How can I know whether I am making any progress or not ?'

'I've developed a method to measure it. By distilling and testing a few drops of your own blood, you can see how far you have developed on the path.'

Ultimately, for Dubuis and other modern adepts, alchemy is the science of a spiritual civilization. For this reason, no one can transmute matter without first being transformed himself. Alchemy finds no place within a materialist scientific community which rigidly separates the experimenter from his or her experiment.

Nevertheless, Dubuis was heartened by recent scientific developments in the United States: 'Scientists there have already questioned the claim that one cannot act by chemical means on the nucleus of an atom, the place of transmutations. It would now appear that a transfer of energy between the exterior layers and the nucleus is possible. The nucleus changes to re-establish equilibrium. The theoretical impossibility of transmutation by action on the external layers is not therefore a certainty.'

He also predicted a revolution in hard science in Europe:

'I believe that a great revelation will be made from CERN in Switzerland in the next ten years or so. It will turn upside down existing knowledge and overthrow all existing theories. CERN is the scientific centre in the world for breaking the atom into its smallest components. In its research into high-energy particle physics, it uses accelerators to bombard atoms to reveal their secrets. It is working to show that elementary particles can go faster than light. These experiments will be in agreement with quantum mechanics but delicate to reconcile with the theory of relativity.'

'In what way will the revelation upset existing knowledge?' I asked.

'It will give access to what's at present invisible, access to higher levels of consciousness.'

'What effects will it have?'

'By bringing about the unity of knowledge, there'll be a rapprochement between modern science and the spiritual world. It will lead to the collapse and disappearance of the world religions and cults. Islam and the Catholic faith will be the first. We are in an era when the invisible is being made visible.'

'But doesn't the world look dark at the moment at the beginning of the third millennium?'

'You have to descend into darkness in order to ascend into the light. There will be a sudden ascent soon . . .'

50

The Wings of Love

I have come to tell you what you do not know: the Work is
with you and within you. Once you find it in yourselves,
where it continuously resides, you will possess it forever
right where you stand.

Anon., *Seven Chapters of Hermes*

Before I left Prague, the historian Robert Vrum suggested that I should
visit Vladislav Zadrobílek. 'He's an author and publisher who has a
bookshop called the Trigon in district 7 of Prague. He's chairman of
Universalia which organized a very interesting exhibition called "Opus
Magnum" last year which showed a variety of Hermetic initiation
rites, secret societies and alchemical texts. It attracted more than
70,000 visitors.'

Following his advice, I caught a tram from my hotel in Wenceslas
Square, crossed the river and climbed the hill to district 7, east of the
castle. It was a warm and still Saturday morning in late September and
the dry leaves were beginning to fall. On my way, I noticed advertisements
on billboards for lectures on Rosicrucianism. After some difficulty, I
managed to find the corner bookshop, its triangular shape reflecting its
name. From above its windows, I read the words: '*Nakladatelství, Knihy,
Trigon, Grafika, Antikvariat*' but the metal shutters were firmly down.

In my mind I called Vladislav Zadrobílek 'Z'. Perhaps like the
letter in the alphabet, he would be at the end of my quest. Determined
to meet him, I returned early on Monday morning, the day of my
departure from the ancient city. As we climbed the same hill to the
bookshop, my companion Elizabeth noticed a tall man with silver hair
and beard striding along in a long, dark overcoat. She said: 'I think he
could be the man we've come to meet!'

The antiquarian bookshop was open and there was a young assistant looking after it. I immediately noticed works on sale of the classic alchemists Ramon Lull, Paracelsus and Salomon Trismosin. The assistant with startling blue-green eyes was called Pavel Suchanek. Having spent some time in Australia, he spoke good English. He said Zadrobílek had just gone out but should be back by lunchtime. Since I had to catch a plane out of Prague that evening, I hoped he was right. He told me that Z had been in his time a musician, a Surrealist, and a Hermetic philosopher as well as a publisher. He used the pseudonyms D. Ž. Bor and Vladimír Kuncitr for some of his writings. Although he had been a practising alchemist, he had, as the young man put it, 'lost the rope' and had turned to theoretical reflections.

Pavel explained that the organization 'Universalia' had been founded in the 20s by two legendary Czech illuminati. Their work was interrupted during the Second World War when some of its members were sent by the Nazis to concentration camps. They were also part of the underground opposition during the communist era. When the old regime collapsed, there had been a boom in Hermetic literature which culminated in the exhibition 'Opus Magnum' in 1997. There were now three Rosicrucian societies active in the country, with German, American and Polish links. The euphoria of independence had been followed by a degree of disillusion: 'There's a jungle of corruption in political circles, and the biggest cakes have already been eaten. People are full of ideas about the future but everyday reality is a kick!'

When I asked Pavel whether he was involved in the Hermetic movement, he replied: 'I'm just dancing on the surface.'

We went away for lunch and when we returned Z was there. He looked like a rabbi with his flowing grey beard.

'I have seen you before,' he said, smiling warmly at Elizabeth – he was indeed the man in the long, dark coat whom she had seen striding down the hill. He spoke Latin and German, but no French, English or Spanish, so we had to rely on Pavel to interpret our conversation. We went up in an old Russian lift to Z's flat on the sixth and top floor of the building. It was spacious and full of rare and curious books, icons and paintings.

Z offered to show me his 'printing house'. I thought it was in another part of the building but he took me to his study which was full of ancient books. During the communist regime he said he had published thirty samizdat titles on Hermetic subjects, printing about

200 copies of each book, some of which had been coloured and illustrated by his two daughters. They even produced some in the basement of a building which had been used by officials of the communist government. He gave me a magnificently produced copy of *Opus Magnum* which he had edited and partly written for the great exhibition on alchemy. He also showed me some wonderful first editions in his curious library of the works of Johann Valentin Andreae, Jacob Boehme and Robert Fludd. I had seen a copy of the latter in the British Library a few weeks before.

We went next door and sat around a square table in the corner of a room which had a large wooden medieval crucifix and Japanese paintings on the wall.

I came straight to the point.

'Are you an alchemist?'

As Pavel translated the words carefully, Z looked steadily at me with his clear blue eyes, smiling enigmatically. He said nothing. I did not find the silence awkward because he had a calm and gentle presence.

'Have you discovered the Philosopher's Stone?'

Same enigmatic smile, same amused glance, same silence.

'Do you know any practising alchemists?' I persevered, thinking that our conversation was going nowhere and perhaps I should leave.

After a pause, he said in a quiet voice: 'I had a friend who was an alchemist who disappeared after the political change. He worked in his laboratory for ten years, beginning again and again. He made many mistakes but there was some success; he went far. My friend had access to the Stone by the mystic path doing spiritual work. Jesus was a teacher for him. He was mad and had visions.'

I had an uncanny feeling that Z was talking about himself.

'Do you believe that the Philosopher's Stone exists?'

'It exists!' he said with conviction, an intense glint in his eye.

'Is there a quick path – what some call the dry path – to discover it?'

'No. You have to follow the classical line.'

Z then volunteered something for the first time:

'I had another friend who was a doctor of natural sciences. He followed the scientific method. One day he got a stone which was radioactive; he measured it with a Geiger counter and the level of radioactivity was very high. He feared it and put it into a box and threw it into a lake. He died soon after.'

'What substance did he start with?'

'He started with cobalt – not the radioactive isotope but ordinary cobalt. He melted his radical stuff; it turned black, then white and then had a yellow surface on it like a cake. His method was correct but he used the wrong material.'

Again, I had a strong intuition that Z was talking about his own work. I recalled that he had been a practising alchemist and that he had a penchant for pseudonyms. He said he now had no time for practical alchemy; he wanted to reach as wide an audience as possible amongst those interested in the Hermetic tradition.

'I now believe all spiritual paths lead to the same arena,' he declared.

'What for you then is the key?' I asked. 'What is the important point of alchemy?'

'The alchemist wants to meet God. The goal of alchemy is not just gold but a golden heart, the transformation of the inner self.'

Remembering my own preliminary experiments, I went on: 'Is it essential to work in the laboratory?'

'You can work at practical experiments and inner alchemy at the same time. I work now in a spiritual way. For me, alchemy is a parable about inner transformation. The changing colours in alchemy, going from the dark to white and then to red, are signs that you are on the right path. The alchemist pursues gold but after finding gold he goes on and then he's a winner. What comes after gold is the secret. The alchemist who discovers this definitely gets a new name too.'

'What is the Philosopher's Stone then?'

'For me, it's a stage of matter which turns other metals into silver or gold. But there's a difference between the Stone of the Philosophers and the Philosopher's Stone. You start with the former and end with the latter. Fulcanelli makes this distinction.'

'Do you think Fulcanelli is still alive? I've heard that someone saw him at a bullfight in Spain. Others claim to have seen him in New York.'

'He doesn't send me postcards! Is he alive? Are we all alive?'

Z added on a more serious note that he had been deeply involved with Fulcanelli and had taken ten years to understand the meaning of his works and to translate them into Czech.

'The *Dwellings of the Philosophers* is his master book. I was talking about it to Stanislas Klossowski de Rola recently. For him Fulcanelli is the peak.'

De Rola was the son of the French painter Balthus and a writer on alchemical symbolism. Just as I was about to raise the subject, Z said: 'Ah, yes, the elixir of life. The other goal of the alchemists. There's nothing unusual about living to 200 years. Contemporary science has a similar goal. But relative immortality will be a big problem for the world. If they prolong life through genetic engineering it will be a tragedy. For the alchemist the maximum life span is a thousand years. God gave that limit. It's the maximum time that the human organism can make itself young again.'

'The elixir vitae is different from contemporary medicine then?'

'Yes. There're three types of stones: the stone of transformation, the stone which leads to the elixir, and the stone which is a material substance which you can boil and then make such things as immortal lamps.'

'Immortal lamps?'

'Lamps that don't go out!'

As I looked around the room, he laughed and said: 'You can't go from stage three back to stage two!'

Aware that I would have to leave soon to catch my plane out of Prague, I returned to our theme.

'Where can I find the Stone of the Philosophers to make the Philosopher's Stone? I've read that it can be found on a dung heap and the whole process is child's play . . .'

'Nothing happens by chance. Chance is just for the silly man. The Stone is everywhere – the thing is to take it in the hand. He who has it has taken a long step on the way . . .'

'Do you think there's any point me coming to Prague in my quest for the Philosopher's Stone?'

'Let me tell you a story. There are two people. One stays at home and observes an anthill for years. Another travels around the world and returns with tired legs. It might seem that they have similar experience and the same wisdom. But the man by the anthill may have more experience since he sees the moment when the ants turn into adults. Nature gives them wings and they fly away.'

'So there's no need to travel?' I thought of Lao Tzu who said that you can see the way to heaven from your window without going outside.

'The ants' wings are love,' Z went on. 'Human creatures, too, have wings but people forget why nature gives them wings. Maybe our task is like the ants to use our wings and to fly to another world and to give life and civilization there. But it will be a different civilization from the one on earth. We are exiles here but we can learn to love and then get back to where we came from . . .'

51

A Crucial Message for Our Time

Transform yourself from dead stones to living philosophical stones!

Gerard Dorn

I ended my quest for the Philosopher's Stone and the secrets of alchemy where I began, in the magic square of my house by the sea in North Wales, looking west over a valley between a hill covered in ancient oaks and a bare and rugged mountain. I wrote this book in one of its nine squares, inspired by its sacred geometry and the spectacular view. By a happy coincidence, the name of the house is Bromebyd, which means in Welsh 'the place of my growing'. After several years of intensive travelling and research, I had certainly been transformed by the experience.

My quest had opened my mind to new and strange ideas, beliefs, symbols and images. It had taken me on a marvellous journey to the four corners of the earth and through the three realms of existence – the physical, the mental and the spiritual. I had been greatly inspired by my conversations with Chinese Taoists, Indian Hindus, Tibetan Buddhists and European alchemists. I would never forget my moments of meditation in the White Cloud Temple in Beijing, under Buddha's bodhi tree and in the subterranean chamber of the Great Pyramid. The suffused pink light of the mosque of Córdoba, the deep glow of the stained glass of Chartres, the musty stillness of the necropolis under St Peter's, and the bustle of the golden lane of Prague Castle would always be with me.

I was still left with the mystery of the origins of alchemy. I had found out that it had emerged independently in China, India and Egypt thousands of years before Christ and that all these civilizations sought to discover an elixir or stone which would transmute base metal into gold, prolong life, and even bring about immortality.

How could this be explained? Firstly, by the common nature of our human condition. Since we are born to die and live in a world of scarcity, it is not surprising that human beings should dream of immortality and abundance. Secondly, it can be explained by the universal character of the human mind. The common symbols and images of alchemy can be seen as archetypes in the collective unconscious which take on different cultural forms in different civilizations. I had found, for instance, that the male and female principles at the heart of alchemy are represented by the dragon and the tiger in China, Shiva and Shakti in India, Isis and Osiris in Egypt and Sol and Luna in Europe.

For me, however, the most compelling explanation is that alchemy originated in a lost civilization which sent off envoys to China, India and Egypt before it collapsed under some catastrophe. There is an element of historical as well as psychological truth in myths and legends and all three countries have stories that the knowledge of alchemy was brought across the sea by a group of sages, known as the 'Sons of Reflected Light' in China, the Siddhas in southern India and the 'Companions of Horus' in Egypt. The most likely place where this lost civilization – possibly the lost civilization of Plato's Atlantis – might be is somewhere between all three countries in the Indian Ocean. If this is the case, alchemy and the Hermetic tradition contain in a disguised form profound wisdom from the earliest times.

During my travels and research, my respect for the true alchemists undoubtedly deepened. They were passionately dedicated to their art in their search to understand the secrets of nature. They chose to work anonymously in their laboratories, studies and retreats, often losing touch with their families and friends. They were never interested in pursuing worldly power, fame and riches and had to suffer the persecution of the Church and the State. While wishing to prolong life for others, they often shortened their own. Their vocation was a lonely quest for knowledge which took them beyond the boundaries of normal existence to mysterious and uncharted regions of the mind. They were potholers of the unconscious, mountaineers of the spirit, surf riders of the infinite.

With their consistent attempt to unite theory and practice, the alchemists were the first scientists in the full sense of the word. They did not merely contemplate phenomena and observe their regularities but boldly attempted to understand the nature of their operations. Not resting in theory, they tested their ideas in the laboratory. They accepted nature for what it is, careful to observe its ways rather than to impose their own preconceptions. They did not interfere deeply in the processes of nature but simply wished to manipulate time by speeding up the growth of metals and slowing down the rhythm of ageing. With their art, they tried to assist nature to unfurl its potential, to change *what is* into *what might be*. They worked *with* rather than *against* nature.

Unlike those scientists who hide behind a cloak of 'objectivity', the alchemists felt a profound responsibility for their work and recognized the dangers of pushing nature to the extreme. They knew they were playing with fire, hence their warning about the dangers of nuclear energy. Since they considered nature to be sacred, they always respected and revered it. Theirs was never a 'value-free' science for they saw values involved in every phase of the Work. They did not distinguish sharply between ritual and experiment, vision quest and research. They worked for the benefit of the whole: of society, of the planet and of the universe.

I can understand the frustration and irritation of the critics of alchemy. The theories of the alchemists are not based on premisses which can easily be confirmed or refuted. It is difficult to repeat their experiments under controlled conditions, especially as they do not reveal openly their essential ingredients. The alchemists have many more variables than the modern scientist to take into consideration, not only the quality of the substances and apparatus used, but the favourable time, the correct position of the stars, and their worthiness as experimenters. If they have not undergone the alchemy of the inner self, they will not be able to obtain good results in the laboratory. And however much they try to assist nature, they cannot succeed without the assistance of God.

Yet alchemists are not naive. In the past, their reasoning and observations of nature from the development of science offered reasonable grounds for their hopes. If grains of opaque sand could be transformed into clear glass, then it seemed reasonable to expect that mercury could be transmuted into gold. If the skill of humans could transfer earth into iron by means of fire, why should not other substances be transformed? And if a small piece of yeast can turn flour and water into bread, what might the ferment of the Philosopher's Stone produce?

Although alchemy was forced underground by the Scientific Revolution in the late seventeenth century, the world view of the new science is remarkably close to that of the ancient alchemists. Werner Heisenberg's uncertainty principle has confirmed the insight of alchemy that the observer affects the observed; indeed, the scientist might be said to 'participate in' rather than just observe the experiment.[1] The very fact of observing subatomic particles will influence the life of the particles.

Quantum physics reaffirms the fundamental unity of the universe. The more one penetrates nature, the more one realizes that it is not made up of discrete building blocks or isolated atoms. It is a field of forces in which the part is inseparable from the whole. Nature now appears as a web of relations, confirming the old alchemists' principle: 'All is One, and One is All.' Indeed, to talk of Gaia as a living organism is to speak a very ancient alchemical language.[2]

Relativity theory has placed interdependency at the heart of matter. Space and time are interdependent and our experience of events is modified by our relative position and velocity in space. In his general theory of relativity, Einstein described the gravitational field as a space-time continuum 'curved' or 'warped in the presence of matter'. Chaos theory has further revealed indeterminacy as a fundamental aspect of the universe although it does necessarily deny an underlying pattern.

The notion of a completely objective science in which the scientist merely observes the external word therefore no longer holds. Modern physicists now accept that we cannot speak about nature without, at the same time, speaking about ourselves. Indeed, the world view of modern science as a constant flow of transforming energy is so close to that of the ancient Chinese alchemists that it makes sense to talk of the 'Tao of Physics'.[3]

It seems likely that mechanical science and not alchemy will prove to be the aberration in the history of thought. The roots of alchemy are very old, but it is a sacred science which is beginning to unfurl again after a period of relative neglect. The questions raised by the alchemists of the place of humanity within nature and of the relationship between the visible and invisible are being asked with renewed urgency. In the twenty-first century, the alchemists will no doubt be seen not as the confused and naive eccentrics of the past but as visionaries of the future.

There could be a major revelation to come from the cutting edge of science within the next decade or so which will turn upside down existing knowledge and pick up where the traditional alchemists left off. It may well give access to levels of consciousness which are at present invisible. Science and spirituality will no longer be seen as enemies, ritual will return to experiment, and vision will be part of research. And by bringing about the unity of knowledge and making science sacred once again, it could lead to the collapse of the prevailing orthodoxies of the world's organized religions.

*

In the process of researching and writing this book, I have become convinced that there is a great mystery from ancient times, a mystery whose meaning was largely lost but which is now gradually being recovered and revealed in many different fields. Alchemy provides a fresh perspective and new light on this ancient wisdom – that we reap what we sow, that life is a preparation for death, and that death itself is only another stage on our journey. Alchemy has kept alive the possibility of the transformation and realization of the self, of the passage of the soul from darkness to light, from ignorance to knowledge, from chaos to harmony, from perishable matter to immortal spirit.

Ancient alchemists in China, India and Egypt knew that there is a unity behind the myriad diverse forms in the world. They understood that true knowledge requires illumination and intuition, not just reasoning and proof. They recognized that there is an intelligence of the heart as well as of the mind. They knew that we human beings are not just complicated machines or instinctive animals but have a divine spark and potential for immortality. They could see that we are not just accidental combinations of atoms but are purposeful and self-directing creatures. They were aware that a human being is the cosmos in miniature, and that there are stars in our bodies as well as in the heavens. More than any other field of knowledge, alchemy has kept these beliefs alive during the last 300 years of false enlightenment.

The growing interest in alchemy is a sign of a general reformation of the world in this dawn of the third millennium. We are now living through a period when the old mechanical and reductionist model of the universe is crumbling and a new one is emerging which is organic, holistic, dynamic and living.

After his lament of the end of Egyptian civilization, Asclepius prophesied in the second century a time when 'The gods who rule the earth will [withdraw], and they will be stationed in a city founded at Egypt's farthest border towards the setting sun, where the whole race of mortals will hasten by land and by sea.'[4]

I sense this time is now about to come, 2,000 years after the collapse of Egyptian civilization. It is time for a New Atlantis to emerge in the East and the West, where the sun rises and sets. The twilight of the gods is no more. The Invisible Ones are making themselves known. The Illuminati are abroad. The ancient wisdom of the alchemists is beginning to awaken the earth from a long and deep slumber and in the new dawn this could lead to a miraculous transformation of the world. As the *Emerald Tablet* prophesied, it will be a time of 'marvellous adaptations' when one will possess 'the glory of the brightness of the whole world' and all obscurity will fly away. And leaving behind the chrysalis of materialism, we will then be able to ride the wind on wings of love.

*

But what of my own vision quest? Has it brought me untold material and spiritual riches? Has it prolonged my life? Has it enabled me to decipher the riddle of the universe? Yes and no. My travels and research have lightened my pockets and threatened my health. Yet I feel infinitely richer, richer not in material possessions but in the true wealth of wisdom.

I believe I have a greater understanding of myself and my place within the scheme of things. I now know that the universe is not a random collection of dead atoms, but a vibrating field of energy, an *anima mundi* with subtle correspondences and sympathies across the entire span of nature's web. I acknowledge and embrace the shadow within my unconscious. I celebrate life and do not fear death, knowing that although I am born to die I may live again. I look forward to death with hope and feel better equipped for the voyage in the hereafter. I am confident that as the dross of my body dissolves, so my soul will coagulate into a more refined and ethereal form.

But what of the Philosopher's Stone? During my long journey, I often felt close to discovering it. I would sometimes catch a glimpse of it out of the corner of my eye, but when I turned around it was gone. I often thought of it as a stone on a mountainside which glows in the swirling mist but which becomes invisible in the bright light of the noonday sun.

For all my research, I must confess that I have not yet discovered the Stone as a physical object or as a substance which can transmute metal into gold. I started out on the gradual moist path but have not yet found the quick dry one. This does not mean that it does not exist nor that I will not one day discover it.

But does it mean that I have failed in my quest? I think not. I recall the old alchemical story of a man on his deathbed who told his sons that he had buried gold in his vineyards. They dug them up and discovered no gold. But this improved the soil for the vines and for the rest of their lives they had wonderful harvests which produced the headiest of wine. I, too, have engaged in celestial agriculture and enjoyed some exquisite elixirs which have opened the gateways of my mind.

When the Hermetic philosopher Z in Prague asked me what I was looking for, I said without thinking: 'Self-harmony and harmony with the universe.'

'Then you don't need the Stone. You are the Stone!' he replied. 'The Stone might need some cleaning and purifying but wherever you go, you have it!'

What a revelation that was! I am what I am looking for. I am what I am. I had travelled around the world, visited many ancient sites, ransacked libraries and met countless people only to realize that I was carrying with me what I was searching for! You can indeed know the whole world without leaving your house and see the way to heaven through the window. The ant watcher can know more than the globetrotter. But I also see that I had to go around the world and do so much research in order to realize that I already had what I was looking for.

Z was right. I have a great deal of polishing and refining to do, but at least I now know that the Philosopher's Stone is deep within me. Its colour has changed from black to white as night passes into day. It has all the colours of the rainbow and of the peacock's tail. I can already see tinges of silver and gold appearing . . .

And its effect on me? I feel I am moving from confusion to clarity, chaos to harmony, desert to home.

The Philosopher's Stone is a divine spark within us all which can become a candle to illuminate our whole self. It is the embryo of our subtle body which lives on after the decay of our flesh. It is a crystal in the cave of our consciousness. It is a seed which can put forth golden shoots and blossom into a golden flower. It is a symbol of the wholeness and fulfilment to be attained when our body, soul and spirit sing together in unison, when the stars within dance with those without, when the sun and the moon lie in tender embrace, and when the original harmony between heaven and earth is finally restored.

As the ancient alchemists said, the Philosopher's Stone is a stone and not a stone. It is the most precious thing in the world and the most common, the most difficult and child's play, to be found nowhere and everywhere. If allowed to grow, it will indeed bring everlasting life and untold riches, both here on earth and in the world around the corner.

Whatever may happen to us in our lives, we can all be transformed from dead stones into living philosophical stones. Of that I am certain.

Notes

Chapter 1

1. See Joseph Needham, *Science and Civilisation in China*, vol. 5, part 2 (Cambridge University Press, 1974), pp. 303–4.

Chapter 3

1. John Maynard Keynes, 'Newton the man', *Royal Society: Newton Tercentenary Celebrations* (Cambridge University Press, 1947), pp. 27–34.

Chapter 4

1. See Needham, *Science and Civilisation in China*, vol. 5, part 3 (1976), p. 2.
2. See ibid, part 2 (1974), p. 157.
3. See Mircea Eliade, *The Forge and the Crucible: The Origins and Structure of Alchemy*, 2nd edn. (University of Chicago Press, 1982), pp. 109, 212–14; and his *Shamanism: Archaic Techniques of Ecstasy* (Princeton University Press, 1972), p. 447.
4. See Arthur Waley, *The Nine Songs: A Study of Shamanism in Ancient China* (London, Allen & Unwin, 1955), p. 9.
5. See Chee Soo, *The Taoist Ways of Healing: The Chinese Art of Pa Chin Hsien* (London, Aquarian Press, 1986), pp. 12–13.
6. Lao Tzu, *Tao Te Ching*, trs. Gia-Fu Feng & Jane English (New York, Vintage, 1972), ch. 15.
7. See Jessica Rawson (ed.), *Mysteries of Ancient China: New Discoveries from the Early Dynasties* (London, British Museum Press, 1996), p. 17.
8. See Yü Ying-shih, 'Life and immortality in the mind of Han China', *Harvard Journal of Asiatic Studies*, 25 (1964–5), 104–5.
9. See also Needham, *Science and Civilisation in China*, vol. 2 (1956), p. 240. Nathan Sivin, *Chinese Alchemy: Preliminary Studies* (Harvard University Press, 1968), p. 2.
10. Needham, *Science and Civilisation in China*, vol. 2 (1956), pp. 240–1.
11. Ibid., vol. 5, part 3, pp. 29–31.

12. Ko Hung, *Phao Phu Tzu*, ch. 16, in Needham, *Science and Civilisation in China*, vol. 5, part 3, p. 38.

Chapter 5

1. See my *Nature's Web: Rethinking Our Place on Earth*, 2nd edn. (London, Cassell, 1995), ch. 1. My *Riding the Wind: A New Philosophy for a New Era* (London & New York, Cassell, 1998, Continuum 2000) is also greatly inspired by Taoism.
2. Herbert A. Giles (tr.), *Chuang Tzu* (London, Unwin Paperbacks, 1980), p. 256.
3. Cf. Needham, *Science and Civilisation in China*, vol. 2, pp. 56–73.
4. Lao Tzu, *Tao Te Ching*, ch. 6.
5. See Liu-I-ming, commentary on Chang Po-tuan's *Understanding Reality: A Taoist Alchemical Classic*, tr. Thomas Cleary (Honolulu, University of Hawaii Press, 1987), p. 98.
6. Lao Tzu, *Tao Te Ching*, ch. 4.
7. Needham, *Science and Civilisation in China*, vol. 2, p. 227.
8. Ibid., vol. 4, p. 226.
9. Ibid., vol. 2, p. 279 f.; vol. 4, p. 306.
10. *Huai Nan Tzu* (c.125 BC), ch. 9.
11. Needham, *Science and Civilisation in China*, vol. 2, p. 287.
12. Lao Tzu, *Tao Te Ching*, ch. 55.
13. A. C. Graham (tr.), *The Book of Lieh-Tzu: A Classic of Tao* (London, Mandala, 1991), p. 97.
14. Edward H. Schafer, *Pacing the Void: T'ang Approaches to the Stars* (Berkeley, University of California Press, 1977), p. 39.
15. Ibid., pp. 135–6.
16. Lu Yen, *Chu T'ang shu*; ibid., p. 134.
17. Ibid., passim.
18. D. Hawkes, *The Songs of the South* (Harmondsworth, Penguin, 1985), p. 196.

Chapter 6

1. Wei Boyang, *The Secret of Everlasting Life* [*Can Tong Qi*], tr. Richard Bertschinger (Shaftesbury, Element, 1994), p. 146. The old spellings for his name and work are Wei Po-yang, *Ts'an T'ung Ch'i*. It was translated by Needham as 'The Convergence of the Three'. See Needham, *Science and Civilisation in China*, vol. 5, part 3, p. 51.
2. *The Convergence of the Three* is one of approximately 100 Chinese alchemical books still in existence. They are almost all found in a collection of Taoist canonical writings, known as the *Taoist Patrology* (*Dao Zan*, or in old spelling *Tao Tsang*). It was first collected about 730, completed in 1019, and printed in 1444 or 1447. There are only two

substantially complete copies, one in the library of the White Cloud Temple in Beijing, and the other in the Imperial Household Library in Tokyo. The White Cloud copy, comprising 1,421 works in 1,057 volumes, was reprinted in 1924–6 by Commercial Press.

3. Wei, *The Secret of Everlasting Life*, pp. 91–2.
4. Ibid., pp. 120–1.
5. Ibid., p. 241. Needham attributes the experiment to Wei Boyang (Needham, *Science and Civilisation in China*, vol. 5, part 3, p. 68 f.); Bertschinger to his disciple Xu Congshi, *The Secret of Everlasting Life*. p. 155.
6. Arthur Waley's translation in Needham, *Science and Civilisation in China*, vol. 5, part 3, p. 72.
7. John Blofeld, *The Secret and the Sublime: Taoist Mysteries and Magic* (London, Allen & Unwin, 1973), pp. 49, 132.
8. In Needham, *Science and Civilisation in China*, vol. 5, part 2, p. 295.

Chapter 7

1. Ko Hung, *Alchemy, Medicine and Religion in the China of AD 320. The Nei P'ien of Ko Hung*, tr. James R.Ware (New York, Dover, 1981), p. 3. The author is also known as Phao Phu Tzu.
2. Ibid., p. 270.
3. See Needham, *Science and Civilisation in China*, vol. 5, part 3, p. 77.
4. Ko, *Alchemy, Medicine and Religion in the China of AD 320*.
5. Ibid, p. 36.
6. Needham, *Science and Civilisation in China*, vol. 2, pp. 439–40.
7. Ko, *Alchemy, Medicine and Religion in the China of AD 320*, p. 50.
8. Ibid., pp. 296, 300.
9. Ibid., p. 310.
10. Ibid., p. 269.
11. Ibid., p. 75.
12. Ibid., p. 63.
13. Ibid., p. 99.
14. Ibid., p. 54.
15. Ibid., p. 269.
16. Ibid., p. 138.
17. Ibid., p. 77.
18. Needham, *Science and Civilisation in China*, vol. 3, pp. 83–4.
19. Cf. ibid., vol. 3, p. 103.
20. Ko, *Alchemy, Medicine and Religion in the China of AD 320*, p. 45.
21. Ibid., p. 310.

Chapter 8

1. Sun Ssu-mo, in Sivin, *Chinese Alchemy*, p. 250.
2. Ibid., pp. 147–8.

3. Ibid., p. 150.
4. Ibid., p. 181.
5. Ibid., p. 130.
6. See Chang Po-tuan, *Understanding Reality: A Taoist Classic*, tr. Thomas Cleary (Honolulu, University of Hawaii Press, 1987).
7. Lao Tzu, *Tao Te Ching*, ch. 16.
8. Chang, *Understanding Reality*, p. 141.
9. Ibid., p. 66.
10. Ibid., p. 165.
11. Ibid., p. 51.
12. Ibid., p. 38.
13. Thomas Cleary (tr.), *The Secret of the Golden Flower: The Classic Chinese Book of Life* (New York, HarperSanFrancisco, 1991), p. 10.
14. Ibid., p. 14. Richard Wilhelm's translation of *The Secret of the Golden Flower: A Chinese Book of Life* first appeared in 1929 with a commentary by C. G. Jung and was later translated from the German by Cary F. Baynes. It misleadingly translates 'energy', 'illumination' and 'celestial mind' as Eros, Logos and intuition in keeping with Jungian psychology. Cf. Needham, *Science and Civilisation in China*, vol. 5, part 5 (1983), pp. 246–7 and Cleary, *The Secret of the Golden Flower*, pp. 80–2.
15. Cleary, *The Secret of the Golden Flower*, pp. 15, 16.
16. Ibid., p. 33.
17. Ibid., p. 48.
18. Ibid., p. 49.
19. Ibid., p. 61.
20. Ibid., p. 64.
21. Ibid., p. 11.

Chapter 9

1. See illustration, Needham, *Science and Civilisation in China*, vol. 5, part 5, p. 157.
2. Ibid., p. 161.
3. Wei, *The Secret of Everlasting Life*, introduction, p. 7.
4. Needham, *Science and Civilisation in China*, vol. 5, part 5, pp. 143–4.
5. These remedies can be found in Sun Ssu-mo, *Chhien Chin Yao Fang* ['A Thousand Golden Remedies'] (c.652).
6. Ko, *Phao Phu Tzu*, ch. 13.
7. Needham, *Science and Civilisation in China*, vol. 5, part 2, p. 286.
8. Ko, *Phao Phu Tzu*, ch. 16.
9. Needham, *Science and Civilisation in China*, vol. 2, p. 146.
10. Ibid., vol. 5, part 5, p. 104, fig. 1580.
11. Ibid., vol. 5, part 4, p. 246n.
12. Ibid., vol. 5, part 5, p. 189.

Notes 471

13. Thomas Cleary (tr.), *Sex, Health, and Long Life: Manuals of Taoist Practice* (Boston & London, Shambhala, 1994), p. 15.
14. Needham, *Science and Civilisation in China*, vol. 5, part 5, p. 192.
15. *Su Nü Ching*, 'The Immaculate Girl' (c.third century BC); ibid., pp 192–3.
16. Needham, *Science and Civilisation in China*, vol. 5, part 5, p. 198.
17. See Cleary, *Sex, Health, and Long Life*, pp. 134–8.
18. Needham, *Science and Civilisation in China*, vol. 5, part 5, p. 200.

Chapter 10

1. In Needham, *Science and Civilisation in China*, vol. 5, part 3, p. 227.
2. E. V. Cowdry, 'Taoist ideas of human anatomy', *Annals of Medical History*, III (1925), 307.
3. Needham, *Science and Civilisation in China*, vol. 5, part 3, p. 250n.
4. Ibid., vol. 5, part 2, p. 130.
5. Lao Tzu, *Tao Te Ching*, ch. 1.
6. Ibid., ch. 8.
7. See Needham, *Science and Civilisation in China*, vol. 5, part 5, pp. 115–6.
8. Ibid., vol. 2, p. 293
9. See ibid., vol. 5, part 5, p. 301 and Robert Temple, *The Genius of China: 3,000 Years of Science, Discovery and Invention* (London, Prion, 1991), pp. 127–9.

Chapter 12

1. François Bernier, *Voyage dans les États du Grand Mogol* (Paris, Fayard, 1981), p. 245.
2. See K. M. Sen, *Hinduism* (Harmondsworth, Penguin, 1975), p. 44.
3. See my *Nature's Web*, p. 26.
4. Prafulla Chandra Ray, *A History of Hindu Chemistry*, 2nd edn. (2 vols., Calcutta, 1925), vol. 1, pp. iii, 79; vol. 2, p. iv.
5. Ibid., vol. 1, pp. ix–x. See also David Gordon White, *The Alchemical Body: Siddha Traditions in Medieval India* (University of Chicago Press, 1996), p. 13.
6. Ray, *A History of Hindu Chemistry*, vol. 1, p. i.
7. White, *The Alchemical Body*, p. 53.
8. Needham, *Science and Civilisation in China*, vol. 1, pp. 207, 209; White, *The Alchemical Body*, pp. 53, 63.
9. Ibid., pp. 66–7.
10. Eliade, *The Forge and the Crucible*, pp. 130–1.
11. See Ray, *A History of Hindu Chemistry*, vol. 1, p. 2; Eliade, *The Forge and the Crucible*, p. 215; White, *The Alchemical Body*, p. 104.
12. Ray, *A History of Hindu Chemistry*, vol. 2, pp. 7–8.
13. Ajit Mookerjee & Madhu Khanna, *The Tantric Way: Art, Science, Ritual* (London, Thames & Hudson, 1993), p. 110.

14. See Mira Roy & B. V. Subbarayappa (eds.), *Rasarnavakalpa* (New Delhi, Indian National Science Academy, 1993), p. 3.
15. Ibid., p. 82.
16. Ibid., p. 63.
17. Ibid., p. 81.
18. White, *The Alchemical Body*, p. 171.
19. Ibid., pp. 57, 174.
20. See Eliade, pp. 127–8. See also his *Yoga, Immortality and Freedom*, tr. Willard R. Trask (Princeton University Press, 1958); *The Forge and the Crucible*.
21. Eliade, *The Forge and the Crucible*, p. 134.
22. See Ray, *A History of Hindu Chemistry*, vol. 1, pp. 55–9; Eliade, *The Forge and the Crucible*, pp. 135–6.
23. See Mookerjee & Khanna, *The Tantric Way*, p. 19.
24. Eliade, *The Forge and the Crucible*, p. 140.

Chapter 13

1. Katha Upanishad, in Nik Douglas, *Tantra Yoga* (New Delhi, Munshiram, Manoharlal, 1971), p. 33. See also Sen, *Hinduism*, pp. 80–1.
2. Chandogya Upanishad; Taittiriya Upanishad; in Douglas, *Tantra Yoga*, pp. 33, 34.
3. Ibid., pp. 95–6.
4. See R. H. Singh, *The Holistic Principles of Ayurvedic Medicine* (Delhi, Chaukhamba Sanskrit Pratishthan, 1998), pp. v, 12.
5. See *Acharya Charaka*, sutra 11:54; C. Dwarakanatha, *Introduction to Kayachikitsa* (Varanasi, Chaukhambha Orientalia, 1986), p. 9.
6. Cf. Singh, *The Holistic Principles of Ayurvedic Medicine*, p. 17; Dwarakanatha, *Kayachikitsa*, pp. 20, 24–5.
7. See Singh, *The Holistic Principles of Ayurvedic Medicine*, pp. 318; 159–60.
8. Cf. Dwarakanatha, *Kayachikitsa*, p. 35.
9. See Singh, *The Holistic Principles of Ayurvedic Medicine*, p. 162.
10. Ibid., pp. 162–3.
11. See Thiru N. Kardaswamy, *History of Siddha Medicine* (Madras, Manorama Press, 1979), p. 254.
12. See Joseph Caezza, 'Alchemy and Tamil Siddhars', Alchemy web site http://www.levity.com/alchemy/home.html; Needham, *Science and Civilisation in China*, vol. 5, part 5, p. 285; Cf. White, *The Alchemical Body*, p. 61.
13. In Layne Little, 'An Introduction to the Tamil Siddhas' in alchemy web site above.

Chapter 14

1. White, *The Alchemical Body*, pp. 336–7.
2. Ibid., p. 337.
3. In Douglas, *Tantra Yoga*, introduction.
4. White, *The Alchemical Body*, p. 1.
5. Ibid., p. 5.
6. Ibid., pp. 301–2.
7. M. P. Pandit, *Kundalini Yoga* (Twin Lakes, Wisconsin, Lotus Light Publications, 1993), p. 47.
8. Douglas, *Tantra Yoga*, p. 63.

Chapter 15

1. Mookerjee & Khanna, *The Tantric Way*, p. 15; Cf. Sir John Woodroffe (Arthur Avalon), *The Serpent Power*, 9th edn. (Madras, Ganesh, 1973), introduction.
2. Heinrich Zimmer, *Myths and Symbols in Indian Art and Civilization*, ed. Joseph Campbell, (New York, Pantheon, 1953), p. 105.
3. Douglas, *Tantra Yoga*, after p. 65.
4. Kamil V. Zvelebil, *The Poets of the Powers* (London, Rider, 1993), pp. 101–2.
5. Pandit, *Kundalini Yoga*, p. 55n.
6. In Joseph Caezza, 'Alchemy and Tamil Siddhars'.
7. White, *The Alchemical Body*, p. 235.
8. Mookerjee & Khanna, *The Tantric Way*, p. 184.
9. White, *The Alchemical Way*, p. 28.
10. Douglas, *Tantra Yoga*, p. 89.
11. Anon., *Khajuraho* (New Delhi, Rupa, 1997), p. 4.
12. See Pramila Poddar & Pramod Kapoor, *Temples of Love: Khajuraho* (New Delhi, Lustre Press, 1992), p. 15.
13. Ibid., p. 75.

Chapter 16

1. Ho-Shan's memorial, *Buddhist Scriptures*, tr. Edward Conze (Harmondsworth, Penguin, 1975), p. 217.
2. See Francesca Fremantle & Chögyam Trungpa (trs. & eds.) *The Tibetan Book of the Dead: The Great Liberation through Hearing in the Bardo* (Boston, Shambhala, 1987), p. 23.
3. See ibid., pp. 4, 58n.
4. In Douglas, *Tantra Yoga*, p. 40.
5. Freemantle and Trungpa, *The Tibetan Book of the Dead*, p. 91.
6. Ibid., p. 68.

7. Edward Conze (tr.), *Buddhist Wisdom Books, containing the Diamond Sutra and the Heart Sutra* (London, Allen & Unwin, 1980), p. 36.
8. Ibid., pp. 47–8.
9. Ibid., p. 68.
10. Ibid., p. 70.

Chapter 17

1. Plato, *Timaeus*, tr. H. D. P. Lee (Harmondsworth, Penguin, 1965), p. 35.
2. See E. A. Wallis Budge, *From Fetish to God in Ancient Egypt* (Oxford University Press, 1934), p. 155. See also W. B. Emery, *Archaic Egypt* (Harmondsworth, Penguin, 1987), p. 192.
3. Plato, *Timaeus*, p. 38.
4. See Robert Bauval & Adrian Gilbert, *The Orion Mystery* (London, Heinemann, 1994).
5. See Peter Tompkins, *The Secrets of the Great Pyramid* (New York, Harper & Row, 1971); John Anthony West, *The Traveller's Key to Ancient Egypt: A Guide to the Sacred Places of Ancient Egypt* (London, Harrap Columbus, 1987), pp. 85–103.
6. See E. A. Wallis Budge (ed. & tr.), *The Book of the Dead* (London & New York, Arkana, 1985), pp. lxiv–lxxi.
7. See W. Marshall Adams, *The House of the Hidden Places* (Kildonan, Banton Press, 1991).
8. *Egyptian Gazette*, 1 March 1998.
9. See West, *The Traveller's Key to Ancient Egypt*, pp. 139–40. See also Robert Bauval & Graham Hancock, *Keeper of Genesis: A Quest for the Hidden Legacy of Mankind* (London, Heinemann, 1996).

Chapter 18

1. See R. T. Rundle Clark, *Myth and Symbol in Ancient Egypt* (London, Thames & Hudson, 1993), p. 91.
2. Summary in West, *The Traveller's Key to Ancient Egypt*, p. 382.
3. Wallis Budge, *The Book of the Dead*, ch. xliii, p. 184.
4. Ibid., p. 622.
5. West, *The Traveller's Key to Ancient Egypt*, pp. 283–4.
6. Ibid., p. 293.
7. Cf. Rundle Clark, *Myth and Symbol in Ancient Egypt*, p. 160.
8. West, *The Traveller's Key to Ancient Egypt*, pp. 389–92.

Chapter 19

1. West, *The Traveller's Key to Ancient Egypt*, p. 393.
2. Ibid., p. 402.

3. See Richard H. Wilkinson, *Symbol and Magic in Egyptian Art* (London, Thames & Hudson, 1994), p. 83.
4. See Geoffrey Cornelius, *The Secret Language of the Stars* (London, Pavilion, 1996).
5. See R. A. Schwaller de Lubicz, *Sacred Science: The King of Pharaonic Theocracy* (Rochester, Inner Traditions, 1988), appendix V.
6. E. A. E. Reymond, *The Mythical Origin of the Egyptian Temple* (Manchester University Press, 1969), p. 4.
7. Ibid., p. 77.

Chapter 20

1. See Iamblichos, *Theurgia, or The Egyptian Mysteries*, tr. Alexander Wilder (London, Rider, 1911), p. 246.
2. Christian Jacq, *Egyptian Magic*, tr. Janet M. Davis (Warminster, Aris & Phillips, 1985), p. 5.
3. See Geraldine Pinch, *Magic in Ancient Egypt* (London, British Museum Press, 1994), pp. 9–10.
4. *Coffin Texts*, spell 261.
5. E. A. Wallis Budge, *Egyptian Magic* (New York, Dover, 1971), p. 126.
6. Wallis Budge, *The Book of the Dead*, p. 152.
7. Wallis Budge, *Egyptian Magic*, pp. 187–8.
8. See Jacq, *Egyptian Magic*, p. 57.
9. Wallis Budge, *Egyptian Magic*, p. 20.
10. See J. F. Bourghouts, *Ancient Egyptian Magical Texts* (Leiden, Nisaba, 1978), vol. 9, p. 2.
11. See Wallis Budge, *Egyptian Magic*, p. 91.
12. Ibid., pp. 147–52.
13. Ebers Papyrus in Jacq, *Egyptian Magic*, p. 111.
14. Ibid., p. 126.
15. Ibid., Edwin Smith Medical Papyrus, p. 110.
16. In Jack Lindsay, *The Origins of Alchemy in Graeco-Roman Egypt* (London, Frederick Muller, 1970), pp. 347–8.
17. Jacq, *Egyptian Magic*, p. 135.
18. See *Coffin Texts*, spell 269; ibid., p. 68.
19. 'The chapter of Coming Forth by Day in the Underworld', Wallis Budge, *The Book of the Dead*, pp. 214–5. Two forms of this chapter which is the summary of the whole were in use. The shorter form dated as far back as the time of Hesepti, a king of the first dynasty, about 4300 BC. The second longer form was attributed to the reign of Men-kau-Ra (Mycerinus), a king of the fourteenth dynasty, about 3600 BC.

Chapter 21

1. Plato, *Timaeus*, tr. H. D. P. Lee (Harmondsworth, Penguin, 1965), p. 67.
2. Ibid., p. 92.
3. Aristotle, *Metaphysics* in A. J. Hopkins, *Alchemy: Child of Greek Philosophy* (New York, Columbia University Press, 1934), p. 21.
4. Aristotle, *De Caelo* in Hopkins, *Alchemy*, p. 22.
5. See Aristotle, *De Anima* in Hopkins, *Alchemy*, p. 26.
6. 'The Isis myth' in Hopkins, *Alchemy*, p. 245; Marcelin Berthelot, *Collection des anciens alchimistes grecs* (Paris, Georges Steinheil, 1888), pp. 31–6.
7. In Lindsay, *The Origins of Alchemy*, pp. 194–5.

Chapter 22

1. See Brian P. Copenhaver, *Hermetica* (Cambridge University Press, 1992), pp. xiv–v. This work contains a translation of the Greek *Corpus Hermeticum* and the Latin *Asclepius*.
2. Quoted in Robert A. Armour, *Gods and Myths of Ancient Egypt* (American University in Cairo Press, 1986), pp. 154–5.
3. See Garth Fowden, *The Egyptian Hermes: A Historical Approach to the Late Pagan Mind* (Cambridge University Press, 1986), p. 196.
4. See Armour, *Gods and Myths of Ancient Egypt*, p. 158.
5. Cf. *Hermetica*, pp. lxi–vii. The dating of the *Hermetica* to the first century AD was confirmed by the discovery in 1945 of the Nag Hammadi library of Coptic Gnostic texts which included several Hermetic treatises and one which was not previously known. It also contained two texts from the Hermetic 'Perfect discourse', only surviving in Latin and known as the *Asclepius*, the Latin name for the Egyptian physician-alchemist Imhotep. Of the existing collection of Hermetic texts, the *Corpus Hermeticum*, the Stobaean fragments, the Vienna and Nag Hammadi papyri, and the 'Perfect discourse' probably date from the fourth century. See Fowden, *The Egyptian Hermes*, pp. xiv–xv, 4–5, 10.
6. Nag Hammadi codices in *Hermetica*, p. 192n.
7. *Corpus Hermeticum*, *Hermetica*, Discourse, XIII, pp. 52–3.
8. Ibid., IX, p. 29.
9. Ibid., IV, p. 17.
10. Ibid., see pp. 33, 38, 39, 40, 48, 51, 52, 67, 78.
11. *Corpus Hermeticum*, *Asclepius*, I, p. 2.
12. Ibid., I, p. 4.
13. Ibid., XVI, p. 59.
14. *Asclepius*, p. 68.
15. *Corpus Hermeticum*, XII, p. 47. Cf. XI, p. 40.
16. Ibid., XII, p. 46.
17. Ibid., X, p. 35.

18. Ibid., X, p. 36.
19. *Asclepius*, p. 69.
20. *Corpus Hermeticum*, pp. i, 3.
21. Ibid., XIII, p. 30. Cf. VII, p. 24.
22. Ibid., X, p. 35.
23. *Asclepius*, p. 70.
24. Ibid., p. 77.
25. Ibid., p. 92.
26. *Corpus Hermeticum*, XI, p. 41.
27. *Asclepius*, p. 84.
28. Ibid., p. 79.
29. *Corpus Hermeticum*, I, p. 6.
30. Ibid., XI, p. 42.

Chapter 23

1. See Hopkins, *Alchemy*, p. 2.
2. See Berthelot, Les Papyrus de Leide, *Collection des anciens alchimistes grecs*, pp. 3–73. The Leiden papyrus, along with the Stockholm Papyrus, is reprinted in Robert Halleux (ed. & tr.), *Les Alchimistes grecs* (vol. 1, Paris, Les Belles Lettres, 1981).
3. See Hopkins, *Alchemy*, p. 63n. See Berthelot, *Collection des anciens alchimistes grecs*, pp. 46–7.
4. See Joseph Needham, *The Refiner's Fire: The Enigma of Alchemy in East and West* (London, n.d.) pp. 10–11, 30.
5. Lindsay, *The Origins of Alchemy*, p. 91 f.
6. Hopkins, *Alchemy*, p. 6n.
7. Plinius, in Lindsay, *The Origins of Alchemy*, p. 132.
8. Synesius to Dioscoros, ibid., p. 141.
9. Hopkins, *Alchemy*, p. 67
10. In Lindsay, *The Origins of Alchemy*, p. 103. For an interpretation of this dream, see Jung, *Psychology and Alchemy*, *Collected Works* (20 vols., London, Routledge & Kegan Paul, 1979), vol. 12, p. 360. I have changed the translation of Ostanes' formula.
11. In Hopkins, *Alchemy*, p. 65.
12. See Fowden, *The Egyptian Hermes*, p. 90.
13. Hopkins, *Alchemy*, pp. 64, 66.
14. Zosimus, *Thirty-five Chapters from Zosimos to Eusebios*; Berthelot, *Collection des alchimistes grecs*, p. 167.
15. In Hopkins, *Alchemy*, p. 68.
16. Synesius to Dioscoros, in Fowden, *The Egyptian Hermes*, p. 167, n. 41.
17. In Lindsay, *The Origins of Alchemy*, p. 121.

Chapter 24

1. In Lindsay, *The Origins of Alchemy*, pp. 254–5.
2. Ibid., p. 258.
3. Cleopatra, Chrysopia, MS 2325, Bibliothèque Nationale, Paris; reprinted in Berthelot, *Collection des alchimistes grecs*, p. 132.
4. 'Olympiodorus the philosopher to Petasios King of Armenia on the divine and sacred art' in Lindsay, *The Origins of Alchemy*, p. 301.
5. R. H. Charles (ed.), *The Book of Enoch* (Oxford, Clarendon Press, 1912), vol. 7, p. 2; vol. 8, pp. 1, 2.
6. See Lindsay, *The Origins of Alchemy*, pp. 243–4.
7. In Hopkins, *Alchemy*, p. 73.
8. Raphael Patai, *The Jewish Alchemists* (Princeton University Press, 1994), p. 64.
9. Ibid., p. 63.

Chapter 25

1. In Lindsay, *The Origins of Alchemy*, p. 365.
2. Ibid., p. 324.
3. Ibid., p. 331.
4. Ibid., p. 335.
5. Zosimus of Panopolis, Berthelot, *Collection des anciens alchimistes grecs*, p. 233.
6. Zosimus, in Lindsay, *The Origins of Alchemy*, pp. 344–5. For Jung's interpretation, see his *Alchemical Studies* (1968), *Collected Works* (London, Routledge & Kegan Paul), vol. XIII, pp. 57–60.
7. See 'A Discourse of Hermes to Tat: the mixing bowl or the monad', *Corpus Hermeticum*, *Hermetica*, Discourse IV.
8. In Fowden, *The Egyptian Hermes*, p. 121.
9. 'On Apparatus and Furnaces', ibid, p. 123.
10. In Lindsay, *The Origins of Alchemy*, p. 328.
11. Zosimus, 'The Final Quittance', in Fowden, *The Egyptian Hermes*, p. 126.
12. Ibid.
13. Ibid., pp. 122–3.
14. Ibid., p. 125.
15. In Lindsay, *The Origins of Alchemy*, p. 324.
16. In Hopkins, *Alchemy*, pp. 74, 75.
17. Ibid., p. 76.
18. Ibid., p. 71.
19. John of Antioch, in Hopkins, *Alchemy*, appendix II, p. 246.
20. Ibid., p. 78
21. In Lindsay, *The Origins of Alchemy*, pp. 372, 373.
22. Hopkins, *Alchemy*, p. 79.
23. *Asclepius*, *Hermetica*, pp. 74, 82–3.

24. For the view that alchemy came from China in the eighth century, see Tenney L. Davis, 'The Chinese beginnings of alchemy', *Endeavour*, II (1943), 159. For an opposing view, see Homer H. Dubs, 'The beginnings of Alchemy', *Isis*, XXXVIII (1947), 62–86; 'The origin of alchemy', *Ambix: Being the Journal of the Society for the Study of Alchemy and Early Chemistry*, IX (1961), 23–36.

Chapter 26

1. J. W. Fück (ed.), 'The Arabic literature on alchemy according to An-Nadim (987)', *Ambix*, IV, 3, 4 (1951), 90.
2. See Georges C. Anawati, 'L'alchimie arabe' in Roshdi Rased (ed.), *Histoire des sciences arabes* (Paris, Editions du Seuil, 1997), vol. 3, pp. 112–21.
3. See H. E. Stapleton, R. F. Azon, & M. Hidayat Husain, 'Chemistry in Iraq and Persia in the tenth century', *Memoirs of the Royal Asiatic Society of Bengal*, VIII, 6 (1927).
4. See H. S. Nasr, *Science and Civilization in Islam*, 2 edn. (Cambridge, Islamic Texts Society, 1987), p. 26.
5. In Idries Shah, *The Sufis* (London, Octagon Press, 1977), pp. 195–6; see also H. S. Nasr, 'Hermes', *Islamic Studies* (Beirut, Librairie du Liban, 1967), ch. 6.
6. In Nasr, *Science and Civilization in Islam*, p. 35.
7. Ibid., p. 191.
8. For the Morienus story, see *Book of the Composition of Alchemy*, the first alchemical work to be translated from Arabic into Latin by Robert of Chester in 1144.
9. Fück, 'The Arabic literature on alchemy according to An-Nadim (987)'.
10. See E. J. Holmyard, Preface, *The Arabic Works of Jabir ibn Hayyan* (Paris, P. Geuthner, n.d.).
11. Jabir, 'Livre des balances' in M. Berthelot, *La Chimie au moyen-âge*, vol. 3, p. 140.
12. See Nasr, *Science and Civilization in Islam*. p. 258.
13. Quoted by Shaikh Ahmad Ahsa'i, 'Alchemy and the resurrection body' in Henry Corbin, *Spiritual Body and Celestial Earth: From Mazdean Iran to Shiite Iran*, tr. Nancy Pearson, Bollingen Series XCl:2 (London, I. B. Tauris, 1990), pp. 205–6.
14. E. J. Holmyard, *Alchemy* (London, Pelican, 1957 but reprinted by Dover, New York in 1990), p. 72.
15. See F. Sherwood Taylor, *The Alchemists* (London, Heinemann, 1951 but reprinted by Paladin in 1976), p. 69; Holmyard, *Alchemy*, p. 73.
16. Nasr, *Science and Civilization in Islam*, p. 260.
17. Holmyard, *Alchemy*, p. 80.
18. Holmyard, *The Arabic Works of Jabir ibn Hayyan*, vol. 1, pt 1, p. 54.
19. See Miguel Cruz Hernández, *Historia del Pensamiento en el Mundo*

Islámico 1: Desde Los Origenes Hasta el Siglo XII en Oriente (Madrid, Alianza, 1996), vol. 1, p. 134.

20. Jabir, 'Livre de royauté' in Berthelot, *La Chimie au moyen-âge*, vol. 3, pp. 111, 126.

21. See in Laleh Bakhtiar, *Sufism: Expressions of the Mystic Quest* (London, Thames & Hudson, 1976), p. 104.

22. See the table of numerical and geometrical correspondences in Bakhtiar, *Sufism*, p. 105.

23. Geber's *Summa Perfectionis Magisterii* (Rome, 1485) turned up in the *Pretiosa Margareta Novella* collection in 1557 in Germany. Much of the material was gathered in Jean-Jacques Manget's anthology *Bibliotheca Chemica Curiosa* published in two large folios in Geneva in 1702. For a list of the works of Geber in the British Library, see B. L. Sloane MS 1068.

24. Richard Russell (tr.), *The Works of Geber, the Most Famous Arabian Prince and Philosopher, of the Investigation and Perfection of the Philosopher's Stone*, translated from Latin (London, William Copper, 1686), p. 23.

25. Holmyard, *Alchemy*, p. 135.

26. Russell, *The Works of Geber*, pp. 5–6.

27. Holmyard, *Alchemy*, pp. 140–1.

Chapter 27

1. Fück, 'The Arabic literature on alchemy according to An-Nadim (987)', p. 8.

2. See A. J. Arberry (tr.), *The Spiritual Physik of Rhazes* (London, John Murray, 1950).

3. For the full story, see Nasr, *Science and Civilization in Islam*, pp. 197–200.

4. Ibid., pp. 270–1.

5. See Anawati, 'L'alchimie arabe' in Rased, *Histoire des sciences arabes*, vol. 3, pp. 126–7.

6. Rhazes, *The Secret of Secrets*, in Nasr, *Science and Civilization in Islam*, p. 273.

7. *Encyclopaedia Britannica*, 9th edn, p. 464.

8. See R. Steele, 'Practical chemistry in the twelfth century; Rasis' *De Aluminibus et Salibus*, *Isis*, XII (1929), 10–46.

9. G. S. A. Ranking, 'Life and works of Rhazes', *XVIIth International Congress of Medicine*, XXIII (1913), 237.

10. Avicenna, *De Mineralibus*, in Holmyard, *Alchemy*, p. 95. See also L. Makour, 'Avicenne et l'alchimie', *La Revue du Caire*, XXVII (1951), pp. 120–9.

11. Daniel Stolcius, *Viridrium Chymicum Figuris* (Frankfurt, 1624), British Library MS.717. d. 63, figura XX, sig. F 4.

12. See Holmyard, *Alchemy*, pp. 96–7.
13. Ibid., pp. 78–9.

Chapter 28

1. Washington Irving, 'The legend of the Arabian astrologer' in Miguel Sánchez (ed.), *Tales of the Alhambra* (London, Granada, 1994), p. 118.
2. Ibid., pp. 119–20.
3. In Ian Robertson, *Blue Guide to Spain* (London, A & C Black, 1993), p. 532.
4. See *La Belleza de Córdova* (Barcelona, Editorial Escuela de Oro, n.d.).
5. See William C. Atkinson, *A History of Spain and Portugal* (Harmondsworth, Penguin, 1967), p. 59.
6. Ibid., p. 60.
7. In Julio Samsó, *Las Ciencias de los Antiguos en Al-andalus* (Madrid, Editorial Mapfre, 1992), pp. 259–60.
8. The attribution of *Picatrix* to Al-Majriti has been questioned; it was probably enlarged and heavily edited after his death in 1007. See Anawati, 'L'alchimie arabe' in Rased, *Histoire des sciences arabes*, vol. 3, p. 131.
9. See Jung, *Psychology and Alchemy* (1944), *Collected Works*, vol. XII.
10. On the Cabala and alchemy, see Patai, *The Jewish Alchemists*, pp. 152–69.
11. Zohar, vol. 1, 156b, in Vladimír Sadek, 'The world of the Kabbala', *Magnum Opus*, ed. Vladislav Zadrobílek (Prague, Trigon, 1997), p. 304.

Chapter 29

1. In Claud Addas, *Quest for the Red Sulphur: The Life of Ibn 'Arabi*, tr. Peter Kingsley (Cambridge, Islamic Texts Society, 1993), p. 105.
2. Ibn al-'Arabi, *The Tarjuman Al-Ashwaq*, tr. R. A. Nicholson (London, 1911).
3. In Rom Landau, *The Philosophy of Ibn 'Arabi* (London, Allen & Unwin, 1959), p. 27.
4. Ibn 'Arabi, *The Meccan Revelations*, in Landau; ibid., p. 81.
5. See R. A. Nicholson, *Studies in Islamic Mysticism* (Cambridge University Press, 1921), p. 154.
6. Ibn 'Arabi, *Bezels of Wisdom* in Shah, *The Sufis*, p. 140.
7. Ibn 'Arabi, *Bezels of Wisdom* in Toshihiko Izutsu, *Sufism and Taoims: A Comparative Study of Key Philosophical Concepts* (University of California Press, 1984), pp. 9, 39.
8. In Addas, *Quest for the Red Sulphur*, p. 156.
9. In Landau, *The Philosophy of Ibn 'Arabi*, p. 84.
10. Cf. Toshihiko Izutsu, *Sufism and Taoism*, pp. 469–93.
11. *The Turba Philosophorum, or Assembly of the Sages, called the Book of Truth in the Art and the Third Pythagorical Synod*, tr. A. E. Waite

(London, G. Redway, 1896), p. 69. The work was first published in Latin at Basle in 1572. Von Julius Ruska published a scholarly German edition in 1931.

12. See Holmyard, *Alchemy*, p. 86; Martin Plessner, *Natural Sciences and Medicine in the Legacy of Islam* (Oxford, Clarendon Press, 1998).

13. *Turba Philosophorum*, pp. 66–8.

14. Ibid., p. 206.

15. Ibid., p. 193.

16. Robert Steele & Dorothea Waley Singer (trs.), 'The Emerald Tablet' (1927) in Holmyard, *Alchemy*, pp. 97–8.

17. See ibid., p. 99.

18. See Halleux, 'La réception de l'alchimie arabe en Occident', *Histoire des sciences arabes*, vol. 3, p. 147.

Chapter 30

1. See Halleux, 'La réception de l'alchimie arabe en Occident', *Histoire des sciences arabes*, vol. 3, p. 145.

2. My translation from a French translation of the Latin. For the Latin, see Halleux, ibid., p. 147. The work was partially translated into German by Goethe in *Die Schriften zu den Naturwissenchaften*.

3. See José S. Gil, *La Escuela de Traductores a Toledo y los colaboradores judios* (Toledo, Diputación Provincial de Toledo, 1985).

4. For the translations of the school, see Julio Samsó et al, 'Las traducciones toledanas en los siglos XII y XIII', *La Escuela de Traductores de Toledo* (Toledo, Diputación Provincial de Toledo, 1996).

5. In Shah, *The Sufis*, pp. 155, 163.

6. See Samsó, 'Las traducciones toledanas en los siglos XII y XIII', p. 20.

7. See J. F. Alemparte, 'La escuela de nigromancia de Toledo', *Anuario de Estudios Medievales* (Madrid), XIII (1983), 208.

8. The Castilian translation of the Picatrix has been lost. A German translation by H. Ritter & M. Plessner of the Arabic text was published in *Studies of the Warburg Institute*, xxvii (1962).

9. See Frances Yates, *Giordano Bruno and the Hermetic Tradition* (London, Routledge & Kegan Paul, 1964), pp. 6–72. See also Lynn Thorndike, *A History of Magic and Experimental Science* (New York, Macmillan, 1923), vol. 2, ch. LXVII.

10. See Charles S. Haskins, *Studies in the History of Medieval Science* (Cambridge University Press, 1924), p. 19.

11. *Picatrix*, Lib. IV, cap. 3 (Sloane Latin MS 1305) in Yates, *Giordano Bruno and the Hermetic Tradition*, p. 54. In the Arabic version of the text the city is called 'al-Asmunain'.

12. See Alemparte, 'La escuela de nigromancia de Toledo', pp. 205–68.

13. Wolfram de Eschenbach, *Parzival*, trs. Helen M. Mustard & Charles E. Passage (New York, 1961), pp. 243 ff.

14. Ibid., pp. 251–2.
15. See Emma Jung & Marie-Louise von Franz, *The Grail Legend* (1960), tr. Andea Dykes (London, Hodder & Stoughton, 1971), pp. 148–50 and Michael Baigent, Richard Leigh & Henry Lincoln, *The Holy Blood and the Holy Grail* (London, Arrow, 1996), pp. 310–11.

Chapter 31

1. See R. Barber, *The Knight and Chivalry*, 2nd edn. (Ipswich, 1974), p. 126. Cf. Baigent, Leigh & Lincoln, *The Holy Blood and the Holy Grail*, pp. 302–3. *Perlesvaus* was translated by Sebastian Evans as *The High History of the Holy Grail* (1893; new edn., Cambridge, 1969).
2. See Louis Charpentier, *The Mysteries of Chartres Cathedral* (1966), tr. Sir Ronald Fraser (London, Research into Lost Knowledge Organisation Trust, 1972), p. 37.
3. Cf. ibid., chs. vii, vii.
4. Abbot Suger, *De Consecratione Ecclesiae Sancti Dionysii* in Otto von Simson, *The Gothic Cathedral: The Origins of Gothic Architecture & the Medieval Concept of Order* (London, Routledge & Kegan Paul, 1956), pp. 95–6.
5. See Adelard of Bath, *Theologica Christiana*, in von Simson, *The Gothic Cathedral*, p. 38.
6. See A. Bothwell-Gosse, *The Knights Templars* (London, Co-Mason, n.d), p. 10.
7. Ibid., p. 43.
8. Ibid., p. 63.
9. See Y. Delaporte, 'Un Clou et le soleil', *Nôtre-Dame de Chartres: l'énigme du labyrinthe* (Chartres, n.d), p. 20.
10. See Jean Villette, 'L'énigme du labyrinthe de la cathédrale', ibid., p. 12.
11. Jean Favier, *The World of Chartres* (London, Thames & Hudson, 1990), p. 40.
12. See ibid., p. 172 & drawing. See also von Simson, *The Gothic Cathedral*, pp. 41, 155, 211.
13. See Von Simson, *The Gothic Cathedral*, pp. 199, 123.
14. See Malcolm Miller, *Chartres Cathedral: Medieval Masterpieces in Stained Glass and Sculpture* (Andover, Pitkin, n.d.), p. 7.
15. See Charpentier, *The Mysteries of Chartres Cathedral*, p. 70.
16. Von Simson, *The Gothic Cathedral*, p. 219.

Chapter 32

1. Roger Bacon, *Opus Maius* (1268) in Shah, *The Sufis*, p. xii.
2. Roger Bacon, *De Mirabili Potestate Artis et Naturae* (1542).
3. In Holmyard, *Alchemy*, p. 120.

4. Note on Rhazes, *Secretum Secretorum* in Bacon, *Opera Quaedam Hactenus Inedita*, ed. J. S. Brewer (London, Rolls series, 1859).

5. Holmyard, *Alchemy*, p. 116.

6. See Thorndike, *A History of Magic and Experimental Science*, vol. 2, p. 568.

7. See Albertus Magnus, *Libellus de Alchimia*, tr. Virginia Heines (Berkeley & Los Angeles, University of California Press, 1958). See also Michael Best & Frank Brightman (eds.), *The Book of Secrets of Albertus Magnus* (Oxford, Clarendon Press, 1973); Pearl Kibre, 'Albertus Magnus on alchemy' in James A. Weishepl (ed.), *Albertus Magnus and the Sciences: Commemorative Essays* (Toronto, Pontifical Institute of Medieval Studies, 1980), pp. 187–202. Gareth Roberts mentions thirty-two titles attributed to Albertus, in *The Mirror of Alchemy: Alchemical Ideas and Images in Manuscripts and Books* (London, British Library, 1994), p. 32.

8. See J. R. Partington, 'Albertus Magnus on alchemy', *Ambix*, I (1937), 3–20.

9. See Marie-Louise von Franz (ed.), *Aurora Consurgens: A Document Attributed to Thomas Aquinas*, Bollinger series (New York, Pantheon Books, 1966). The illustrated MS was originally in the monastery at Rheinau and is now held in Zentralbibliothek, Zurich. Illustrations from the MS are reproduced in Jacques van Lennep, *Alchimie: contributions à l'histoire de l'art alchimique*, 2nd edn. (Brussels, Crédit Communal, 1985), pp. 56–70.

10. Marie-Louise von Franz, *Alchemy: An Introduction to the Symbolism and the Psychology* (Toronto, Inner City Books, 1980), p. 181.

11. Ibid., p. 196.

12. Ibid., pp. 187–9, 195.

13. Ibid., pp. 204, 244–5.

14. Ibid., p. 244.

15. Ibid., pp. 266–7.

16. Ibid., p. 270.

Chapter 33

1. See Vatican codice, fols. 230 ss. Arnald was also known as Arnaldo de Vilanova, Arnalodus Villenueve and Arnaldus of Villa Nova.

2. See Menéndez y Pelayo, D. Marcelino, *Historia de los Heterodoxos Españoles* (Madrid, Biblioteca de Autores Cristianos, 1986), p. 484.

3. See Roberts, *Mirror of Alchemy*, p. 36. For a list of his manuscripts in the British Library, see ibid., appendix, pp. 122–3. See also Thorndike, *A History of Magic and Experimental Science*, vol. 3, pp. 654–78, for a noble attempt to separate the wheat from the chaff.

4. See René Verrier, *Études sur Arnaud de Villeneuve 1240–1311* (Leiden, E. J. Brill, n.d.).

5. See Michael Maier, *Symbola Aureae Mensae* (Frankfurt, Lucas Jennis, 1617).

6. Eugenius Philalethes, *LONG LIVERS: A CURIOUS HISTORY OF Such Persons of both Sexes who have liv'd several AGES and grown Young again* (London, n.d), pp. 165–70. The work is kept in the British Library.

7. Menéndez y Pelayo, *Historia de los Heterodoxos Españoles*, p. 486.

8. See Frances Yates, 'Ramon Lull and John Scotus Erigena', *Journal of the Warburg and Courtauld Institutes*, XXIII (1960), 1–44.

9. See Shah, *The Sufis*, pp. 203, 204, 388–9.

10. See Frances Yates, 'Lull & Lullism', *Renaissance & Reform: The Italian Contribution, Collected Essays* (vol. 2, London, Routledge & Kegan Paul, 1983), p. 84.

11. See Frances Yates, 'The art of Ramon Lull: an approach to it through Lull's theory of the elements', *Journal of the Warburg and Courtauld Institutes*, XVII (1954), 115–73. See also Anthony Bonner (ed. & tr.), *Selected Works of Ramon lull (1232–1316)* (Princeton University Press, c.1985) and *Doctor Illuminatus: A Ramon lull Reader* (Princeton University Press, c.1993).

12. See Michael Pereira, *The Achemical Corpus Attributed to Raymon Lull, Warburg Institute Surveys and Texts XVlll* (London, Warburg Institute, 1989), pp. 61–107.

13. Maier, *Symbola Aureae Mensae*.

14. See Raimondo Lullo, *Opera Chimica* (Firenze, Biblioteca Nationale Centrale) HP 1652, MS B 52. Some of the illustrations are reproduced in van Lennep, *Alchimie: contributions a l'histoire de l'art alchimique.*

15. The *Testament* attributed to Lull first appeared with a commentary by Giordano Bruno in vol. 4 of Lazarus Zetzner's *Theatrum Chemicum* (6 vols., Strasburg, 1659–61).

16. Bodleian Library, Oxford, MS Ashmole 1508. The Latin text was edited in 1572 by Michael Toxites and the English translation made by William Atherton in 1558.

17. In F. Sherwood Taylor, *The Alchemists: Founders of Modern Chemistry* (London, Heinemann, 1951), pp. 113–14.

18. Ibid., p. 115.

19. See Elias Ashmole, *Theatrum Chemicum Britannicum* (London, 1652), pp. 189, 443.

Chapter 34

1. See Gareth W. Dunleavy, 'The Chaucer ascription in Trinity College, Dublin, Manuscript D.2.8', *Ambix*, XIII (1965), 2–21. At one time the manuscript came into the hands of the Elizabethan magus John Dee.

2. See Ashmole, *Theatrum Chemicum Britannicum*, pp. 165, 467.

3. F. N. Robinson (ed.), 'Introduction', *The Works of Geoffrey Chaucer*, (London, Oxford University Press, 1957), p. 15.

4. Chaucer, 'The Canon's Yeoman's Prologue & Tale', ibid., pp. 213–23.

5. Sir George Ripley, *The Compound of Alchymy; or, The ancient hidden Art of Alchemic; conteinning the right ... means to make the Philosopher's Stone, Aurum potabile, with other excellent Experiments*, tr. Ralph Rabbards (London, T. Orwin, 1591) in Ashmole, *Theatrum Chemicum Britannicum*, p. 374.

6. George Ripley, *Cantilena*, verse 17.

7. Eirenaeus Philalethes, *Ripley Reviv'd: or, an Exposition upon Sir George Ripley's Hermetic-Poetical Works* (London, 1678).

8. *The Ripley Scrowle*, British Library Additional MS 5025. The scroll consists of four rolls of various lengths with watercolour drawings. On the second roll, it is written: 'This long roll was Drawne for me in Cullers at Liubeck in Germany 1588.'

9. Thomas Norton, *Ordinall of Alchemy*, ed. John Reidy, Early English Text Society (London, New York, Toronto, Oxford University Press, 1975), p. xii. See also Reidy, 'Thomas Norton and the *Ordinall of Alchimy*', *Ambix*, VI (1957), 59–85.

10. Norton, 'Ordinall' in Ashmole, *Theatrum Chemicum Britannicum*, p. 6. Ashmole gives Norton pride of place at the beginning of his collection. In order to find the best version, Ashmole compared fourteen manuscripts. One is beautifully written and illustrated on vellum and bears the arms of George Nevill, Archbishop of York. (See British Library Additional MS 10, 302, fol. 2.) The work was translated into Latin by Michael Maier and printed in Frankfurt in 1618 in his *Tripus Aureus* ('Golden Tripod'). It was reprinted in *The Museum Hermeticum* in 1625 and 1678. Thomas Norton's grandson Samuel continued the family tradition and wrote *A Key to Alchimie* (1577).

11. See F. Sherwood Taylor, 'Thomas Charnock', *Ambix*, II, 3, 4 (1938), 148–76.

12. Holmyard, *Alchemy*, p. 200.

13. See the holograph copy in Charnock's hand, dated November 1565 from his house in Stockland, Bristol, with Lord Burleigh's autograph. (British Library, Lansdowne MS 703, ffol. 1–53 a.)

14. Ashmole, *Theatrum Chemicum Britannicum*, p. 425.

15. Holmyard, *Alchemy*, p. 201.

16. British Library, Sloane MS 2640.

Chapter 35

1. Victor Hugo, *Notre Dame de Paris*, bk V, ch. ii, bk IV, ch. v, in Xavier Coadic, *L'alchimie autrefois* (Lyon, Horvath), p. 137.

2. See Fulcanelli, *Le Mystère des cathédrales*, ed. Eugène Canseliet (Paris, J. J. Pauvert, 1964) p. 53.

3. Ibid., p. 140.

4. Ibid., p. 53.

5. Abbé Villain, *Histoire critique de Nicolas Flamel* (Paris, Desprez, 1761).
6. See Holmyard, *Alchemy*, p. 244.
7. See *Nicholas Flamel, his exposition of the hieroglyphicall figures which he caused to bee painted upon an arch in St Innocent's Church-yard, in Paris* (1624), a translation of *Les Livres de figures hieroglyphiques de Nicolas Flamel* (1612). His tombstone is now in the Musée de Cluny.
8. An illustrated sixteenth-century work ascribed to Abraham called *Livre des figures hieroglyphiques* is now in the Bibliothèque Nationale, Paris.
9. Holmyard, *Alchemy*, p. 245.
10. See Coadic, *L'alchimie autrefois*, p. 116.
11. Nicolas Flamel, 'Short Tract or Philosophical Summary', *The Hermetic Museum*, tr. A. E. Waite, (London, 1893), vol. 1, p. 146.

Chapter 36

1. Holmyard, *Alchemy*, p. 217.
2. Haskins, *Studies in the History of Medieval Science*, p. 19.
3. Holmyard, *Alchemy*, p. 149.
4. Ibid., p. 150.
5. *The Worke of John Dastin* in Ashmole, *Theatrum Chemicum Britannicum*, pp. 263–4.
6. Petrus Bonus, *Pretiosa Margarita Novella* (c.1330), ed. Janus Lacinius Therapus (Venice, 1546), fol. 48 v.
7. Holmyard, *Alchemy*, pp. 145–6.
8. Ibid., p. 147.

Chapter 37

1. See Simon Schama, *Landscape and Memory* (London, HarperCollins, 1995), p. 285.
2. Giordano Bruno, *Spaccio de la Bestia Triofante* (1584), dialogue 3. See also Yates, *Giordano Bruno and the Hermetic Tradition*, pp. 213, 268.
3. Bruno, *La Cena de la Ceneri* (1584) in Yates, *Giordano Bruno and the Hermetic Tradition*, p. 206.
4. Giordano Bruno, *De la Causa, Principio, et Uno* l; Yates, *Giordano Bruno and the Hermetic Tradition*, p. 256.
5. See Yates, *Giordano Bruno and the Hermetic Tradition*, pp. 191–2.
6. Cf. Yates, 'Giordano Bruno', *Renaissance & Reform: The Italian Contribution, Collected Essays*, p. 104.
7. See Tommaso Campanella, *La Città del Sole*, ed. E. Solmi (Modena, 1904), pp. 3–5.
8. *Obeliscus Aegyptiacus*, in Joscelyn Godwin, *Athanasius Kircher: A Renaissance Man and the Quest for Lost Knowledge* (London, Thames & Hudson, 1979), p. 6.

9. Athanasius Kircher, *Oedipus Aegyptiacus*, vol. 3 (Rome, 1652), in Yates, *Giordano Bruno and the Hermetic Tradition*, pp. 417–18.
10. See Michele Basso, *Guide to the Vatican Necropolis* (Vatican City, 1986), p. 85.
11. See Michele Basso, *Eschatology and Symbolism in the Vatican Necropolis* (Vatican City, 1980).
12. Cf. Yates, *Giordano Bruno and the Hermetic Tradition*, pp. 115–16.

Chapter 38

1. See Biblioteca Laurenziana, Florence, MS ASH 1166. c.21.
2. Biblioteca Nazionale Centrale, Florence, MS BR52 HP 1652.
3. Torre Philosophici, Magl 1.2.149. tor II.
4. See Copenhaver, introduction, *Hermetica*, pp. xlviii–l.
5. Marsilio Ficino, *Opera Marsilii Ficini florentini insignis philosophi plantonici medici atque theolgi clarissimi opera omnia et quae hacentus extirere* (Basel, 1576), in Copenhaver, introduction, *Hermetica*, p. xlviii.
6. In Yates, *Giordano Bruno and the Hermetic Tradition*, pp. 70–1.
7. Giovanni Pico della Mirandola, 'Oration on the Dignity of Man' (1486), *The Portable Renaissance Reader*, eds. James Ross & Mary Martin McLaughlin (Harmondsworth, Penguin, 1977), p. 479.
8. See Yates, *Giordano Bruno and the Hermetic Tradition*, p. 143.
9. See G. G. Scholem, *Major Trends in Jewish Mysticism* (New York, Schocken Books, 1946).
10. Giovanni Pico della Mirandola, 'Oration on the Dignity of Man' in Yates, *Giordano Bruno and the Hermetic Tradition*, p. 91.
11. Brunot Santi, *The Marble Pavement of the Cathedral of Siena* (Firenze, Scala, 1993), pp. 13–14.

Chapter 39

1. Diana Fernando, *Alchemy: An Illustrated A to Z* (London, Blandford, 1998), p. 123. Cf. Mark Haeffner, *Dictionary of Alchemy* (London, Aquarian, 1994), p. 174.
2. See John Stillman, *The Story of Early Alchemy and Chemistry* (1924; New York, Dover, 1960).
3. Johannes Trithemius, *Steganographia* (Frankfurt, 1606).
4. Cornelius Agrippa, *De Occulta Philosophia* (1533), in Yates, *Giordano Bruno and the Hermetic Tradition*, p. 132.
5. Holmyard, *Alchemy*, p. 168.
6. See Walter Pagel, 'The prime matter of Paracelsus', *Ambix*, IX (1961), 119 f. and his *Paracelsus: An Introduction to Philosophical Medicine in the Era of the Renaissance* (Basle and New York, S. Karger, 1958).
7. In Fernando, *Alchemy*, pp. 124–5.
8. Paracelsus, *Volumen Paramirum* in Holmyard, *Alchemy*, pp. 174–5.

9. Paracelsus, *Paragranum* (c.1530–4), in Holmyard, *Alchemy*, p. 172.
10. Ibid., p. 173.

Chapter 40

1. See Hugh Trevor-Roper, 'The Paracelsian movement', *Renaissance Essays* (London, Fontana, 1986), pp. 149–99; R. P. Multhauf, 'Medical chemistry and the "Paracelsians"', *Bulletin of the History of Medicine*, XXIV (1954). Johannes Huser edited Paracelsus' work in ten volumes (Basle, 1589–91).
2. See Trevor-Roper, 'The Paracelsian movement', p. 157.
3. Petrus Severinus, *Idea Medicinae Philosophicae* (Basle, 1571), ch. vii, p. 73.
4. Gerard Dorn, *Speculativa Philosophia*, in Lazarus Zetzner (ed.), *Theatrum Chemicum*, (vol. 1, Ursel, 1602), p. 266.
5. See Gerard Dorn, *Artificii Chymistici Physici, Metaphysici, secunda pars and tertia . . . accessit etiam tertiaede parti, de praeparationibus metallicis in utroque lapidis philosophorum opere maiore minoreque* (1569).
6. Dorn, *Physica Trithemii* in Zetzner, *Theatrum Chemicum*, vol. 1, p. 472.
7. Dorn, *Speculativa Philosophia* in Zetzner, *Theatrum Chemicum*, vol. 1, p. 267.
8. Nathan Schwarz-Salant (ed.), *Jung on Alchemy* (Princeton University Press, 1995), p. 112. For more on Dorn, see Marie-Louise von Franz, *Alchemical Active Imagination* (Irving, Texas, Spring, 1979).
9. See Walter Pagel, *Joan Baptista van Helmont: Reformer of Science and Medicine* (Cambridge University Press, 1982).
10. Basil Valentine 's *Twelve Keys* first appeared in German in 1599. Michael Maier reprinted it in Latin in 1618 with striking emblems in his *Tripus Aureus*. It was incorporated seven years later in the *Musaeum Hermeticum* (Frankfurt, 1625) by Lucas Jennis. Enlarged edition, 1678.
11. Valentine, *Twelve Keys*, in *The Hermetic Museum*, vol. 2, pp. 351, 353.
12. Valentine, *Azoth, ou le moyen de faire l'or caché des philosophes* (Paris, Pierre Moet, 1659), p. 140.
13. In Holmyard, *Alchemy*, pp. 259–62. Helvetius, *Vitulus Aureus, quem mundus adorat et orat* (Amsterdam, 1667) was reprinted in Jean and Jacques Manget's *Bibliotheca Chemica Curiosa* (Geneva, Chonet, 1702) in the *Musaeum Hermeticum* of 1678. In Waite's 1893 edition it was called *The Golden Calf*.

Chapter 41

1. Michael Sendivogius, *Novum Lumen Chymicum* (Frankfurt & Prague, 1604) in *The Hermetic Museum*, p. 145.
2. Robert Fludd, in Vladimir Kuncir, 'Fraternitatis Rosae Crucis', *Opus Magnum*, p. 307.

3. *Fama Fraternitatis* (Cassel, 1614) in Frances Yates, *The Rosicrucian Enlightenment* (London, Routledge & Kegan Paul, 1964), appendix, p. 230.

4. See H. C. & K. M. B. Brothers, *The Rosicrucians* (Paddington, The Office of the Co-Mason, n.d.), p. 23.

5. Yates, *The Rosicrucian Enlightenment*, p. 249.

6. *Confessio Fraternitatis* (Cassel, 1615), ch. ix.

7. See Michael Maier, *Silentium post clamores, hoc est, Tractatus apologeticus quo causae non solum clamorum seu Revelationem Fraternitatis Germanicae de R. C. sed et silentii* (Frankfurt, 1617) and *Themis Aurea; hoc est de legibus Fraternitatis R. C. tractatus* (Frankfurt, 1618).

8. Fludd, dedication, *Utriusque Cosmi, majoris scilicet et minoris, metaphysica atque technica historia* (2 vols., Frankfurt, 1617–18), vol. 1, pp. 11–12.

9. See Fludd, 'Truth's golden harrow', ed. C. H. Josten, *Ambix*, III, 3, 4 (1949).

10. In Brothers, *The Rosicrucians*, p. 64.

11. Francis Bacon, *New Atlantis* (London, 1627).

12. See Yates, *The Rosicrucian Enlightenment*.

13. Ibid., p. 103.

14. Ibid., p. 179.

15. See Eugenius Philalethes (pseudonym for Thomas Vaughan), *Anthroposophia Theomagia, or A Discourse of the Nature of Man and his State after Death; grounded in his Creator's Protochimistry* (London, 1650).

16. In Yates, *The Rosicrucian Enlightenment*, p. 183.

Chapter 42

1. Bodleian Library, Oxford, MS Ashmole 1395.

2. Harley collection, British Library, MS Harley 3469. The work was first published in German by Rorschach in 1598 as part three of a collection called the *Aureum Vellus*. A Berlin MS version dates from 1532–5.

3. Salomon Trismosin, *Splendor Solis*, tr. Joscelyn Godwin, introduced by Adam McLean (Grand Rapids, MI, Phanes Press, 1991), p. 76. This edition reprints the engravings from the Hamburg edition of 1708.

4. Ibid., p. 19.

5. Ibid., p. 21.

6. Ibid., pp. 95–6.

7. Ibid., p. 29.

8. Ibid., p. 36.

9. Ibid., p. 78.

10. *Rosarium Philosophorum* (Frankfurt, 1550; Lubeck, 1588). The best illustrated version is held in the Stadtbibliothec Vadiana in St. Gallen. An early *Rosarium Philosophorum* was attributed to Ramon Lull.

11. See Jung, 'The Psychology of the Transference' (1946) in *Jung on Alchemy*, pp. 189–214.
12. *De Lapide Philosophico* ('On the Philosopher's Stone') by Lambsprinck. It was translated by Nicholas Barnard Delphinas into German and published in Lucas Jennis' *Museaum Hermeticum* in Frankfurt in 1625 and appeared in English in Waite's *The Hermetic Museum*.

Chapter 44

1. R. J. W. Evans, *Rudolf II and his World: A Study in Intellectual History 1576–1612* (Oxford, Clarendon Press, 1973), p. 196.
2. See A. G. Debus, *The Chemical Dream of the Renaissance* (Cambridge, W. Heiffer, 1968).
3. See Daniel Stolcius, *Chymisches Lustgärtlein* (Frankfurt, Lucas Jennis, 1624), with some plates from Michael Maier.
4. See H. C. Bolton, *The Follies of Science at the Court of Rudolf II* (Milwaukee, 1904), p. 129.
5. In Fernando, *Alchemy*, p. 28.
6. See A. E. Waite, *Lives of the Alchemystical Philosophers* (London, G. Redway, 1888).
7. Sendivogius, *Novum Lumen Chymicum*, reprinted in *The Hermetic Museum*, translated by Waite.
8. See Isaac Newton's annotated copy of *Novum Lumen Chymicum* in the British Library, c.112 aa. 3 (i).
9. Sendivogius, *Novum Lumen Chymicum* in Waite, *The Hermetic Museum*.
10. See Richard Brzezinski & Zbigniew Szydlo, 'A new light in alchemy', *History Today*, XIIIL, 1 (January 1997), 17–23.
11. See J. B. Craven, *Count Michael Maier* (Kirkwall, William Peace, 1910).
12. Michael Maier, *Arcana Arcanissima* (London, 1614).
13. See John Read, *Prelude to Chemistry* (London, G. Bell, 1936), pp. 212–54.
14. In Pagel, *Joan Baptista van Helmont*, p. 49.
15. Oswald Croll, 'Admonitory Preface' to *Basilica Chymica continens philosophicam propria laborum, experientia confirmatam descriptionem et usum remediorum chymicorum ...* (Frankfurt, 1608). H. Pinnell, a former chaplain in the New Model Army, translated Croll's preface in his *Philosophy Reformed & Improved in Four Profound Tractates. The I. discovering the Great and Deep Mysteries of Nature: by OSW. Crollins* (London, 1657).
16. In Fernando, *Alchemy*, p. 52.
17. See Martin Ruland, *A Lexicon of Alchemy or Alchemical Dictionary*, tr. A. E. Waite (London, 1892).
18. See Peter French, *John Dee: The World of an Elizabethan Magus* (1972; London, Ark, 1987), p. 28. See also J. Roberts & A. D. Watson (eds.), *John Dee's Library Catalogue* (London, Bibliographical Society, 1990).

Notes

19. In Evans, *Rudolf II and his World*, p. 219n. See also Nicholas Clulee, *John Dee's Natural Philosophy* (London, Routledge & Kegan Paul, 1988).

20. See J. O. Halliwell (ed.), *The Private Diary of Dr John Dee and the Catalogue of his Library of Manuscripts* (London, Camden Society Publications, 1842); and Meric Casaubon (ed.), *A True and Faithful Relation of what passed for many yeers between Dr John Dee ... and some spirits tending (had it succeeded) to a General Alteration of most States and kingdoms of the World* (London, 1659).

21. French, *John Dee*, p. 78.

22. See John Dee, 'A Translation of John Dee's "*Monas hieroglyphica*"', tr. and ed. C. H. Josten, *Ambix*, XII, 2, 3 (1964), 88–221. See also John Dee, *Essential Readings*, ed. Gerald Suster (Wellingborough, 1986).

23. See D. Ž. Bor, 'An attempt to explain the introductory engraving to John Dee's *Hieroglyphic Monad*', *Opus Magnum*, p. 289.

24. Dee, Prefatory Letter, *Monas Hieroglyphica*.

25. Dee, *Monas Hieroglyphica*, pp. 157–9.

26. Ibid., p. 217.

27. French, *John Dee*, p. 127.

28. Bodleian, Ashmole MS 1459, fol. 478.

29. Dee, *Monas Hieroglyphica*, pp. 135–7.

30. Evans, *Rudolf II and his World*, p. 226n.

31. Edward Kelley, 'The theatre of terrestrial astronomy' in R. Grossinger (ed.), *Alchemy* (California, 1979).

32. Ashmole, *Theatrum Chemicum Britannicum*, pp. 332–73.

33. Josef Tellc, 'The testimony of Dr Faust's house', *Opus Magnum*, p. 299.

34. Evans, *Rudolf II and his World*, p. 227.

35. Ibid., p. 228.

Chapter 45

1. Peter Marshall, *William Blake: Visionary Anarchist* (London, Freedom Press, 1988), p. 29.

2. See Michael White, *Isaac Newton: The Last Sorcerer* (London, Fourth Estate, 1997), pp. 2, 105.

3. John Maynard Keynes, 'Newton the man', pp. 27–34.

4. Jewish National and University Library, Jerusalem, Yahuda MS 41m fols. 6–7.

5. King's College Library (KCL), Cambridge, Keynes MS 33, fol. 5 v.

6. See Betty Jo Dobbs, *The Janus Faces of Genius* (Cambridge University Press, 1991). See also her earlier work *The Foundations of Newton's Alchemy, or 'The Huntinig of the Greene Lyon'* (Cambridge University Press, 1975).

7. KCL, Cambridge, Keynes MS 130, fol. 7.

8. In White, *Isaac Newton*, p. 53.

9. Newton, *Opticks or A Treatise of the Reflections, Refractions, Inflections & Colours of Light* (London, 1706), bk III, pt 1, query 30.
10. See White, *Isaac Newton*, p. 97.
11. See John Harrison, *The Library of Isaac Newton* (Cambridge University Press, 1978), p. 59.
12. Trinity College Library, Cambridge, Trinity Notebook, fol. 126.
13. KCL, Keynes MS 130.
14. Ibid., MS 33, fol. 5 v.
15. See Allen G. Debus, *The English Paracelsians* (New York, Oldbourne, 1965).
16. H. Turnbull (ed.), *The Correspondence of Isaac Newton* (Cambridge University Press, 1960), vol. 2, p. 2.
17. Bodleian, Oxford MS Don. b.15.
18. Basil Valentine in *The Triumphal Chariot of Antimony* (London, Vincent Stuart, 1962), p. 175.
19. See White, *Isaac Newton*, pp. 145–6.
20. KCL, Keynes MS 135.
21. Ibid., MS 137.
22. William Stukely, *Memoirs of Isaac Newton's Life*, ed. A. Hasting White (London, Taylor & Francis, 1936), p. 59.
23. See Richard Westfall, 'Newton and alchemy' in Brian Vickers (ed.), *Occult and Scientific Mentalities in the Renaissance* (Cambridge University Press, 1984), p. 330. See also his *Never at Rest: A Biography of Isaac Newton* (Cambridge University Press, 1980).
24. Newton, *Correspondence*, pp. 365, 368–70.
25. Ibid., vol. 2, pp. 288, 291.
26. Trinity Notebook, fol. 126.
27. Sotheby lot No. 113; Smithsonian Institute Library, Washington DC, Dibner Library of the History of Science & Technology, MSS 1031 B.
28. White, *Isaac Newton*, p. 250.
29. 'Praxis', Babson College Library, Massachusetts, Babson MS 420, p. 18a.

Chapter 46

1. See Ernest Rutherford, *The Newer Alchemy* (Cambridge University Press, 1939) p. 3. See also Dorothy M. Fish, *Modern Alchemy* (London, Faber & Faber, 1936), p. 178.
2. F. Jollivet Castelot, *La Loi de l'histoire* (1933) in Pierre Andremont, *Les Enigmes de l'alchimie* (Paris, Magellan, n.d).
3. Louis Pauwels & Jacques Bergier, *The Morning of the Magicians* (London, Avon Books, 1968), p. 24.
4. Eugène Canseliet, introduction, *Fulcanelli: Master Alchemist; Le Mystère des cathédrales*, tr. Mary Sworder (London, Neville Spearman, 1971), p. 17.

5. Fulcanelli, *Les Demeures philosophales* (Paris, J. J. Pauvert, 1965), vol. 1, p. 101.

6. Fulcanelli, *Le Mystère des cathédrales*, pp. 6–7.

7. In Neil Powell, *Alchemy: The Ancient Science* (London, Aldus Books, 1976), p. 53.

8. See Eugène Canseliet, *L'Alchimie expliqueé sur ses textes classiques* (Paris, J. J. Pauvert, 1974).

9. See Jacques Sadoul, *Le Trésor des alchimistes* (Paris, J'ai lu, n.d.).

10. Archibald Cockren, *Alchemy Rediscovered and Restored* (London, Rider, 1940).

11. Powell, *Alchemy*, p. 138.

12. Armand Barbault, *Gold of a Thousand Mornings* (London, Neville Spearman, 1975).

13. Canseliet, *L'Alchimie expliqueé sur ses textes classiques*.

14. See Frater Albertus, *The Alchemist's Handbook: Manual for Practical Laboratory Alchemy* (York Beach, Maine, Samuel Weiser, 1974), p. 38.

Chapter 47

1. C. G. Jung, *Memories, Dreams, Reflections* (London, Collins Fountain Books, 1977), p. 235.

2. Ibid., p. 230.

3. Ibid., p. 237.

4. Ibid., p. 248.

5. Epilogue, *Mysterium Coniunctionis* (1955–6) in *Jung on Alchemy*, ed. Nathan Schwartz-Salant, p. 113. For Jung's writings on alchemy, see also volumes 9, *Aion*; 12, *Psychology and Alchemy*; and 13, *Alchemical Studies*, of his *Collected Works*.

6. Jung, 'Religious ideas in alchemy' (1937), *Jung on Alchemy*, p. 65.

7. Jung, 'The psychology of transference' (1946), ibid., p. 165.

8. See Schwartz-Salant, introduction, ibid., p. 13.

9. Jung, 'The personification of opposites' (1955–6), ibid., p. 71.

10. Jung, 'Individual dream symbolism in relation to alchemy' (1936), ibid., p. 81. See also 'Epilogue', *The Practice of Psychotherapy*, ibid., p. 214.

11. Jung, 'Symbols of transformation' in Shwartz-Salant, introduction, ibid, p. 25.

12. Jung, 'The psychology of transference', ibid., p. 213.

13. Cf. von Franz, *Alchemy*, p. 260.

14. Morienus, *De Transmutatione Metallorum* in *Artis Aurisferae* (vol. 2, Basel, 1593), p. 17f; in Jung, 'Religious ideas in alchemy', *Jung on Alchemy*, p. 66.

15. Maier, *Symbola Aureae Mensae*, p. 568; in Jung, 'Religious ideas in alchemy', *Jung on Alchemy*, pp. 66–7.

16. William McGuire & R. F. C. Hull, *C. J. Jung Speaking* (Princeton University Press, 1977), p. 229.

17. Ruland, *A Lexicon of Alchemy*; in Jung, 'Religious ideas in alchemy', *Jung on Alchemy*, pp. 92–3, 95.
18. See Jung, 'Rex and regina' (1955–6), *Jung on Alchemy*, p. 62.

Chapter 48

1. Bothwell-Gosse, *The Knights Templars*, p. 108.
2. See Michael Baigent & Richard Leigh, *The Temple and the Lodge* (London, Corgi, 1997), pp. 127 f., 263–70.
3. See B. E. Jones, *Freemason's Guide and Compendium* (London, 1950); ibid, pp. 174, 207.
4. See C. J. Hosten, 'William Blackhouse of Swallowfield', *Ambix*, IV, 1, 2 (1949), 1–33.
5. Baigent & Leigh, *The Temple and the Lodge*, p. 221.
6. Cf. David Stevenson, *The Origins of Freemasonry* (Cambridge University Press, 1990), p. 85.
7. H. Spencer Lewis (ed.), *Rosicrucian Manual* (1918; San Jose, California, AMORC, 1971), p. 193.
8. Ibid., p. 17.
9. Ibid., p. 142.
10. See the correspondence courses of the Martinists from AMORC, San Jose, California.
11. Powell, *Alchemy*, p. 126.
12. See Israel Regardie, *The Golden Dawn* (4 vols., Chicago, 1937–40).
13. See John Symonds, *The Great Beast: The Life of Aleister Crowley* (London, Hamilton, 1963).
14. See Powell, *Alchemy*, p. 127.
15. Omraam Mikhaël Aïvanhov, *True Alchemy or the Quest for Perfection* (Fréjust, Prosveta, 1988), pp. 16, 31–2.
16. Alchemy website and virtual library *http://www.levity.com/alchemy/home.html*

Chapter 51

1. See my 'The cosmic joy of the new science', *Nature's Web*, ch. 27.
2. See 'The resurrection of Gaia', ibid., ch. 28.
3. See Fritjof Capra, *The Tao of Physics* (London, Wildwood House, 1975).
4. *Asclepius*, p. 83.

Glossary and Symbols

This list contains key words and symbols but is not exhaustive. For a fuller glossary see Gareth Roberts, *The Mirror of Alchemy* (British Library, 1994). For more detailed explanations, consult Mark Haeffner, *Dictionary of Alchemy* (Aquarian, 1994) and Diana Fernando, *Alchemy: An Illustrated A to Z* (Blandford, 1998).

ablutio – washing which precedes the white stage in the alchemical process.

albedo – the white stage that produces the white elixir which can turn base metal into silver.

alcohol – (Arabic *al-kohl*), originally a metallic powder used by Egyptians as eye make-up, hence essence and then spirit of wine.

alembic – (Arabic *al-anbiq*, from the Greek *ambix* for cup), the upper part of a still, often used to refer to the whole still. ⋈

alkali – (Arabic *al-qali* for plant ashes), originally a substance from burned seaweed.

alkahest – (German *allgeist* for all spirit), a universal solvent.

aludel – (Arabic *al-uthal*), a pear-shaped condensing receiver used to receive sublimates. ᘓ

amalgamation – softening of metals by mixing with mercury, thereby creating alloys. ͞aaa͞

ambix – (Greek for cup), iron saucer, often used to heat cinnabar to obtain mercury.

antimony – brittle metallic substance extracted from stibnite which forms crystal shapes when heated repeatedly. Sometimes used as first material in the alchemical process. ♁

aqua fortis – nitric acid. ⋎

arsenic – yellow orpiment; red realgar. o—o

athanor – (Arabic *al-tannur*), furnace, usually in the form of a tower and fed by charcoal, which provides a constant heat.

azoth – (Arabic *al-zauq*), mercury, particularly 'philosophical mercury' considered to be the first principle of all metals. ☿

bain-marie – water-bath for gradual heating. ♏

caduceus – magical wand of Hermes, usually entwined with two serpents.
calcination – reduction of a substance to powder or ash by roasting. ♈
calx – product of calcination. ♇
cement – a paste or powder of a penetrating mineral substance. ♌
ceration – conversion of a substance to a wax-like state; softening. ♐
cibation – feeding the ingredients of an alchemical process.
cinnabar – brilliant red ore of mercury; mercuric oxide. 33
circulation – reflux distillation; continual distillation of a liquid.
coagulation – conversion of a liquid into a solid; fixation of a volatile
    substance; crystallization. Sulphur famously coagulates or fixes liquid
    mercury, forming a chemical wedding (*conjunctio*). ♄
cohobation – return of a liquid distillate to its residue followed by repeated
    distillations.
congelation – (*congelatio*) conversion of liquid into a solid state; crystalliza-
    tion. ♉ (Taurus)
conjunction – (*conjunctio*), union or mixture of elements or opposites,
    usually depicted as the chemical wedding of Sol and Luna, producing a
    hermaphrodite.
copper – ♀ (Venus)
crucible – vessel which can be heated to high temperatures, used for melt-
    ing. ♉
crystal – ♃
cucurbit – (Latin for gourd), flask forming bottom part of a still. ○
cupel – shallow cup made of bone ash or porous material for testing or
    refining gold and silver.
cupellation – method of blasting out refined gold in a cupel.

dissolution – separation into constituent parts; decomposition. ♋ (Cancer)
distillation – key process in alchemy of boiling a liquid and reconverting the
    vapour into a liquid by cooling; a means of separating the volatile from
    the fixed, the pure from the impure. ♍ (Virgo)

egg – oval alchemical vessel which gives birth to the Philosopher's Stone;
    sometimes called the Philosophical or Cosmic Egg.
elixir – (Arabic *al-iksir* from Greek *xerion*, a powder for healing wounds),
    medicine of life; medicine of metals; the agent of transmutation; a ferment;
    sometimes a synonym for the Philosopher's Stone.
elements – fundamental principles of matter ○-E. In China, five elements:
    water, fire, wood, metal and earth; in India, five: earth, fire, air, water
    and ether; in the Middle East and Europe, four: earth ▽̶, fire △, air △̶
    and water ▽.

essence – extract or tincture obtained by distillation.
exaltation – the elevation of a substance to a higher quality.

ferment – substance which works like yeast in the process of transmutation; seed of metal; often considered to be a property of the Philosopher's Stone.
fermentation – the process of transmutation. ♑ (Capricorn)
fixation – making a substance non-volatile; turning spirit into a body. ♊
furnace – ⊕

gold – ductile and enduring metal; symbol of purity and wholeness. ☉ (sun)

hermaphrodite – (Greek: Hermes+Aphrodite), result of the chemical wedding of the opposites sulphur and mercury, Sol and Luna, male and female; also known as rebis (Latin for 'double thing') or androgyne (Greek for man and woman).

incineration – ♐ (Saggitarius)
iron – ♂ (Mars)
kerotakis – (possibly Greek for artist's palette), reflux apparatus for treating metals with vapours which is said to change their colours from black, white, yellow to red.

lead – ♄ (Saturn)
Luna – moon, representing mercury; silver; the female principle; often depicted as a queen. ☽
lute – cement used in sealing joints in alchemical apparatus.

magisterium – (Latin for 'mastery'), transmuting agent; sometimes used for the Philosopher's Stone.
magnesia – used to describe several mineral substances, such as manganese dioxide, magnetite and modern magnesia; like sulphur and mercury, a 'philosophical' principle. ♂♌
marcasite – pyrites. ♍
menstruum – a solvent, the action of which on a metal is compared to the supposed action of an ovum in menstruation.
mercury – one of the two principles of all metals, sulphur being the other; often personified as Luna, representing the female principle; yin; associated with the spirit. The most common *prima materia* of the alchemists. ☿
mortification – (*mortificatio*) the 'killing' of mercury, sometimes associated with slaying the dragon; the stage after the chemical wedding of mercury and sulphur; also called putrefaction.
multiplication – transmutation; alchemically induced growth of gold or silver; concentration of the multiplying power of the Philosopher's Stone. ≋

nigredo – the initial black stage of the alchemical process; by association, a state of melancholy or depression.

orpiment – bright yellow substance; yellow sulphide of arsenic, thought to contain gold. ⬭

peacock's tail – (*cauda pavonis*), the multi-coloured stage in the alchemical process, between *albedo* and *rubedo*.

pelican – form of circulatory still with two side-arms, shaped like a pelican pecking at its chest, which works by reflux distillation.

Philosopher's Stone – the great arcanum; the ultimate goal of the Work; a transmuting agent which can turn base metal into gold, heal diseases, prolong life and bring about immortality.

phoenix – fabulous bird which rises from its own ashes; symbol of death and resurrection mirrored in the alchemical process.

potable gold – gold in a solution. ☿

prima materia – the first matter or substance used by alchemists which has many different names; most commonly 'philosophical' mercury, and then antimony; represents chaos at the initial *nigredo* stage of the process. ⊕

projection – the final stage in the alchemical process when a tiny amount of the Stone, powder, or elixir is thrown onto a molten metal to be transmuted and 'multiplied' into silver or gold. ♓

puffers – alchemists who make excessive use of the bellows; by extension, false alchemists who puff themselves up.

putrefaction – decomposition of a substance or its conversion into an outwardly inert mass or powder. ♐

quicksilver – mercury.

quintessence – most refined essence of a substance; the fifth element; spirit.

realgar – red sulphide of arsenic. ♉

retort – glass vessel with a long neck; round vessel with a small neck bent over into a pipe which resembles a stork with outstretched beak. ↄ

rubedo – final red stage of alchemical process which produces the red elixir or gold.

sal ammoniac – ammonium chloride, used in washing and purifying processes. ✳

salt – a 'philosophical' principle, with mercury and sulphur, thought by some alchemists to be in all metals; associated with the body. ⊖

separation – (*separatio*) dividing the pure from the impure. ♏ (Scorpio)

silver – ☽ (moon)

Sol – sun, representing sulphur; gold; the male principle; often depicted as a king. ☉

solution – dissolving a solid into a liquid. ⬭

Soxlet extractor – modern alchemical apparatus for extracting a herbal elixir which has three parts: a flask, an extractor and thimble, and a condenser.

spirit – volatile substance which sublimes on heating, such as mercury, sulphur, sal ammoniac, orpiment and magnesia; what links the body and soul together.

stone – a 'philosophical' substance which can be animal, vegetable or mineral, although usually the latter.

sublimation – the key process in alchemy: the conversion of a solid into vapour, followed by condensation of the vapour into a solid form on a cool surface. The process is often compared to the circulation of rain or of the soul rising towards heaven. ☖

sulphur – one of the two principles of metal, mercury being the other; personified as Sol, representing the male principle; yang; associated with the soul. ♄ ♆ ♅

tin – ♃ (Jupiter)

tincture – a colouring liquid; substance used for tingeing metals; a penetrating spirit; another name for the elixir or the Philosopher's Stone. The white tincture gives rise to silver; the red, to gold.

transmutation – the transformation of a base metal into gold; of body into spirit.

tria prima – the three 'philosophical' principles in all metals – salt, sulphur and mercury – which correspond respectively to body, soul and spirit. All three are said to be in perfect balance in gold.

vitriol – ⊕

white water – 'philosophical' mercury.

Work completed – ☿

Bibliography

Bibliographies

Doberer, Kurt Karl, *A Bibliography of Books on Alchemy in the British Museum* (London, 1946).

Ferguson, J., *Bibliotheca Chemica*, 2 vols. (Glasgow, Maclehose, 1906).

Heym, Gerard, 'An introduction to the bibliography of alchemy', *Ambix*, I, 1 (1937).

Kren, Claudia, *Alchemy in Europe: A Guide to Research* (New York, Garland, 1990).

Pritchard, Alan, *Alchemy: A Bibliography of English-Language Writings* (London, Routledge & Kegan Paul, 1980).

Collections

Artis Auriferae, 2 vols. (Basel, 1593; reprinted 1610, 1752).

Ashmole, Elias, *Theatrum Chemicum Britannicum* (London, Nath. Brooke, 1652).

Aureum Vellus (Rorschach, 1598).

Berthelot, Marcelin P. E., *Collection des anciens alchimistes grecs*, 3 vols. (Paris, Georges Steinheil, 1888).

Collectanea Chymica Leidensia (Leiden, 1693).

De Alchemia (Nuremberg, 1541).

De Alchimia, 2 vols. (Frankfurt, 1550).

Esclava Galan, Juan (ed.), *Cinco Tratados Españoles de Alquimia* (Madrid, Tecnos, c.1987).

Halleux, Robert (ed. & tr.), *Les Alchimistes grecs* (Paris, Société d'édition, Les Belles Lettres, 1981–).

Klossowski de Rola, Stanislas, *Alchemy: The Secret Art of Alchemy* (London, Thames & Hudson, 1973).

——— *The Golden Game: Alchemical Engravings of the Seventeenth Century* (London, Thames & Hudson, 1997).

Manget, Jean-Jacques, *Bibliotheca Chemica Curiosa*, 2 vols. (Geneva, Coloniae Allobrogum, 1702).

Musaeum Hermeticum Reformatum et Amplificatum (Frankfurt, Hermann van de Sande, 1677), tr. A. E. Waite as *The Hermetic Museum Restored and Enlarged* (London, J. Elliott, 1893).

Regardie, Israel, *The Philosopher's Stone* (London, Rider, n.d.).

Waite, A. E. (ed.) *Collectanea Chemica* (London, J. Elliott, 1893; Edmonds, WA, The Alchemical Press, 1991).

Westcott, William Wynn, *Collectanea Hermetica* (London, Theosophical Publishing Society, 1893).

Zetzner, Lazarus, *Theatrum Chemicum*, vols. 1–3 (Ursel, 1610), vol. 4 (Strasbourg, 1613), vol. 5 (1622–4), reprinted 6 vols. (1659–61).

CHINA

Texts

Chang Po-tuan, in Davis, Tenney, L. & Chao Yun-tsung, 'Chang Po-tuan of Tien-t'ai, *Wu Chen P'ien*, essay on the understanding of the truth, a contribution to the study of Chinese alchemy', *Proceedings of the American Academy of Arts and Sciences*, 73 (1939), 97–117.

———— 'Three alchemical poems by Chang Po-tuan', *Proceedings of the American Academy of Arts and Sciences*, 73 (1940), 377–8.

———— *Understanding Reality: A Taoist Alchemical Classic*, tr. Thomas Cleary (Honolulu, University of Hawaii Press, 1987).

Chan Wing-Tsit (ed. & tr.), *A Sourcebook in Chinese Philosophy* (Princeton University Press, 1963).

Chou I ts'an t'ung ch'i (The Convergence of the Three; an apocryphal tradition of interpretation of the *Book of Changes*, c.AD 142).

Chuang Tzu, *The Way of Chuang Tzu*, tr. Thomas Merton (Boston, Shambhala, 1992).

———— *Chuang Tzu: A Taoist Classic*, tr. Fung Yu-Lan (1931; Beijing, Foreign Languages Press, 1995).

Chuang Tzu: Taoist Philosopher and Chinese Mystic, tr. Herbert A. Giles (1889; London, Mandala, 1980).

Cleary, Thomas (ed. & tr.), *Zen Essence* (Boston, Shambala, 1989).

———— (ed. & tr.), *The Spirit of Tao* (Boston, Shambala, 1993).

———— (ed. & tr.), *Sex, Health, and Long Life: Manuals of Taoist Practice* (Boston & London, Shambala, 1994).

Ko Hung, *Alchemy, Medicine and Religion in the China of AD 320. The Nei P'ien of Ko Hung*, tr. James R. Ware (New York, Dover, 1981).

Lao Tzu, *Tao Te Ching*, trs. Gia-Fu Feng & Jane English (New York, Vintage, 1972).

Lieh Tzu, *The Book of Lieh Tzu: A Classic of Tao*, tr. A. C. Graham (1961; London, Mandala, 1991).

Over, Raymond van (ed.), *I Ching*, tr. James Legge (New York, Mentor, 1971).

The Secret of the Golden Flower: A Chinese Book of Life, tr. Richard Wilhelm, with commentary by C. G. Jung. Translated from the German by Cary F. Baynes (San Diego, Harcourt Brace Jovanoch, 1961).

The Secret of the Golden Flower: The Classic Chinese Book of Life, tr. Thomas Cleary (New York, HarperSanFranscisco, 1991).

Wei Boyang, *The Secret of Everlasting Life* [*Can Tong Qi*], tr. Richard Bertschinger (Shaftesbury, Element, 1994).

Books and articles

Akira Ishihara, *The Tao of Sex*, tr. Howard S. Levy (New York, Harper & Row, 1968).

Album for Taoist Deities and Divine Immortals (Beijing, Hua Xia Publishing House, 1994).

Blofeld, John, *The Secret and the Sublime: Taoist Mysteries and Magic* (London, Allen & Unwin, 1973).

Chang, K. C., *Art, Myth and Ritual: The Path to Political Authority in Ancient China* (Harvard University Press, 1983).

———— *The Archaeology of Ancient China*, 4th edn. (Yale University Press, 1986).

Chao Pi Chen, *Taoist Yoga: Alchemy and Immortality*, tr. Lu K'uam Yu (New York, Samuel Weiser, 1973).

Chee Soo, *The Taoist Ways of Healing: The Chinese Art of Pa Chin Hsien* (London, Aquarian Press, 1986).

Chkashige, Masumi, *Oriental Alchemy* (New York, Samuel Weiser, 1974).

Cooper, J. C., *Chinese Alchemy: The Taoist Quest for Immortality* (Wellingborough, Aquarian Press, 1984).

Cowdry, E. V., 'Taoist ideas of human anatomy', *Annals of Medical History*, III (1925), 307.

Da Liu, *T'ai Chi Ch'uan and I Ching* (London, Routledge & Kegan Paul, 1974).

———— *The Tao of Health and Longevity* (London, Routledge & Kegan Paul, 1979).

Davis, Tenney L., 'The Chinese beginnings of alchemy', *Endeavour*, II (1943), 159.

Davis, Tenney L. & Chao Yun-tsung, 'The secret papers in the jade box of Chi'ing-ua', *Proceedings of the American Academy of Arts and Sciences*, 73 (1940), 385-9.

Dubs, Homer H., 'The beginnings of alchemy', *Isis*, XXXVIII (1947), 62-86.

———— 'The origin of alchemy', *Ambix*, IX (1961), 23-36.

Ebrey, Patricia Buckley, *China: Cambridge Illustrated History* (Cambridge University Press, 1996).

Famous Centres of Taoism (Beijing, Chinese Taoist Association, 1987).

Fêng Yu-lan, *A History of Chinese Philosophy* (London, Allen & Unwin, 1937; Princeton University Press, 1967).

Giles, Herbert A., *Religions of Ancient China* (1905; Singapore, Graham Brash, 1989).

Gulik, R. H. van, *Sexual Life in Ancient China: A Preliminary Survey of Chinese Sex and Society from ca. 1500 BC till 1644 AD* (Leiden, E. J. Brill, 1961).

Hawkes, D., *The Songs of the South* (Harmondsworth, Penguin, 1985).

Ho Ping-yü & Needham, Joseph, 'Elixir poisoning in medieval China', *Janus*, XLVIII (1959), 221–51.

———— 'Theories of categories in early medieval Chinese alchemy', *Journal of the Warburg and Courtauld Institutes*, 22 (1959), 173–210.

Johnson, Obed Simon, *A Study of Chinese Alchemy* (Shanghai, Commercial Press, 1928).

Kohn, Livia, *Early Chinese Mysticism: Philosophy and Soteriology in the Taoist Religion* (Princeton University Press, 1992).

Liu, Xinru, *Ancient China and Ancient China: Trade and Religious Exchanges, AD 1–600* (Delhi, Oxford University Press, 1994).

Loewe, Michael, *Ways to Paradise: The Chinese Quest for Immortality* (London, 1979).

Lu K'uan Yü (Charles Luk), *Taoist Yoga* (London, Rider, n.d.).

Maspero, Henri, *Le Taoisme et les religions chinoises* (Paris, Gallimard, 1971).

Mishio Kushi, *Nine Star Ki: Introduction to Oriental Astrology* (Becket, Mass., One Peaceful World Press, 1991).

Needham, Joseph, *Science and Civilisation in China* (Cambridge University Press, 1954–).

Palmer, Martin, *Yin & Yang* (London, Piatkus, 1997).

Rawson, Jessica (ed.), *Mysteries of Ancient China: New Discoveries from the Early Dynasties* (London, British Museum Press, 1996).

Schafer, Edward H., *Pacing the Void: T'ang Approaches to the Stars* (Berkeley, University of California Press, 1977).

Sivin, Nathan, *Chinese Alchemy: Preliminary Studies* (Harvard University Press, 1968).

Temple, Robert, *The Genius of China: 3,000 Years of Science, Discovery and Invention* (London, Prion, 1991).

———— 'The tao of immortality: the body as laboratory', *Helix*, I (1993), 36–41.

———— 'The autumn mineral: the Chinese origins of endocrinology', *Organon's Mag* (Netherlands).

Waley, Arthur, 'Notes on Chinese alchemy', *Bulletin of SOAS*, University of London, 6 (1930), 1–24.

———— *The Nine Songs: A Study of Shamanism in Ancient China* (London, Allen & Unwin, 1955).

Yü Ying-shih, 'Life and immortality in the mind of Han China', *Harvard Journal of Asiatic Studies*, 25 (1964–5), 104–5.

Zeng Qingnan, *Believe It or Not – Ancient and Mysterious Chinese Qigong*, ed. Jianguang Wang (Beijing, Foreign Languages Press, 1991).

INDIA

Texts

Aurobindo, Sri, *On Tantra*, ed. M. P. Pandit (Pondicherry, 1967).

Buddhist Scriptures, tr. Edward Conze (Harmondsworth, Penguin, 1975).

Buddhist Wisdom Books, containing the Diamond Sutra and the Heart Sutra, tr. Edward Conze (London, Allen & Unwin, 1980).

Fremantle, Francesca & Trungpa, Chögyam (eds. & trs.), *The Tibetan Book of the Dead: The Great Liberation through Hearing in the Bardo* (Boston, Shambala, 1987).

Mookerjee, Bhudeb, *Rasa-Jala-Nidhi Ocean of Indian Chemistry, Medicine and Alchemy*, 5 vols., 3rd edn. (Varanasi, Chaukhamba, 1926).

Radhakrishnan, Sarvepalli & Moore, Charles A. (eds.), *A Sourcebook in Indian Philosophy* (Princeton University Press, 1971).

Rasaratnakara, attributed to Nagarjuna (Louvain, 1944).

Roy, Mira & Subbarayappa, B. V. (eds.), *Rasanarvakalpa* (New Delhi, Indian National Science Academy, 1993).

Books and articles

Banerji, Sures Chandra, *New Light on Tantra: Accounts of Some Tantras, Both Hindu and Buddhist, Alchemy in Tantra, Tantric Therapy etc.* (Calcutta, Punthi Pustak, 1992).

Bernier, François, *Voyage dans les États du Grand Mogol* (Paris, Fayard, 1981).

Bharati, Aghehananda, *The Tantric Tradition* (London, Rider, 1965).

Bose, D. M. (ed.), *A Concise History of Science in India* (New Delhi, Indian National Science Academy, 1971).

Calasso, Roberto, *Ka: Stories of the Wind and the Gods of India* (London, Jonathan Cape, 1998).

Dash, Vaidya Bhagwan, *Alchemy and Metallic Medicine in Ayurveda* (New Delhi, Concept Publishing, 1986).

Dash, Bhagwan & Kashyap, Lalittesh, *Iatro Chemistry of Ayurveda (Ras Sastra)* (New Delhi, Concept Publishing, 1994).

Douglas, Nik, *Tantra Yoga* (New Delhi, Munshira Manoharlal, 1971).

Dwarakanatha, C., *Introduction to Kayachikitsa* (Varanasi, Chaukhambha Orientalia, 1986).

Eliade, Mircea, *Yoga, Immortality and Freedom*, tr. Willard R. Trask (Princeton University Press, 1958).

Humphreys, Christmas, *Buddhism* (Harmondsworth, Penguin, 1971).

Ions, Veronica, *Indian Mythology* (London, Hamlyn, 1983).

Kardaswamy, Thiru N., *History of Siddha Medicine* (Madras, Manorama Press, 1979).

Madhishassan, S., *Indian Alchemy, or Rasayana in the Light of Ascetism and Geriatrics* (New Delhi, Motital Banarsidass, 1991).

Mookerjee, Ajit & Khanna, Madhu, *The Tantric Way: Art, Science, Ritual* (London, Thames & Hudson, 1993).

Pandit, M. P., *Kundalini Yoga* (Twin Lakes, WI, Lotus Light Publications, 1993).

———— *The Yoga of Transformation* (Pondicherry, Dipti, 1994).

Poddar, Pramila & Kapoor, Pramod, *Temples of Love: Khajuraho* (New Delhi, Lustre Press, 1992).

Rajneesh, Bhagwan Shree, *The Ultimate Alchemy* (Poona, Rajneesh Foundation, 1976).

———— *The New Alchemy, to Turn You On*, ed. Ma Satya Bharti (Poona, Rajneesh Foundation, 1978).

Rawson, Philip, *The Art of Tantra* (London, Thames & Hudson, 1978).

Ray, Prafulla Chandra, *A History of Hindu Chemistry*, 2 vols. (London, Williams & Norgate, 1902; Calcutta, 1925).

———— (ed.) *History of Chemistry in Ancient and Medieval India* (Calcutta, Indian Chemical Society, 1956).

Sen, K. M., *Hinduism* (Harmondsworth, Penguin, 1975).

Sharma, P. V., *History of Medicine in India* (New Delhi, Indian National Science Academy, 1992).

Singh, R. H., *The Holistic Principles of Ayurvedic Medicine* (Delhi, Chaukhamba Sanskrit Pratishthan, 1998).

Venkataraman, R. A., *History of the Tamil Siddha Cult* (Madurai, Ennes, 1990).

White, David Gordon, *The Alchemical Body: Siddha Traditions in Medieval India* (University of Chicago Press, 1996).

Woodroffe, Sir John (Arthur Avalon), *Principles of Tantra*, 2 vols. (Madras, Ganesh, 1953).

———— *The Serpent Power* (Madras, Ganesh, 1953).

Yeshe, Lama, *Introduction to Tantra* (London, Wisdom Publications, 1987).

Zimmer, Heinrich, *Myths and Symbols in Indian Art and Civilisation*, ed. Joseph Campbell (New York, Pantheon, 1953).

Zvelebil, Kamil V., *The Poets of Powers* (London, Rider, 1973).

———— *The Smile of Murugan: On Tamil Literature of South India* (Leiden, E. J. Brill, 1973).

EGYPT

Texts

Ancient Egyptian Magical Texts, tr. J. F. Bourghouts (Leiden, Nisaba, 1978).

Ancient Egyptian Pyramid Texts, tr. R. O. Faulkner (Oxford University Press, 1969).

Berthelot, Marcelin P. E. (ed.), *Collection des anciens alchimistes grecs*, 3 vols. (Paris, Georges Steinheil, 1888).

Charles, R. H. (ed.), *The Book of Enoch* (Oxford, Clarendon Press, 1912).

Clement of Alexandria, *Stromata*, eds. O. Stählin & L. Früchtel (Berlin, 1970–85).

Halleux, Robert (ed. & tr.), *Les Alchimistes grecs* (Paris, Société d'édition, Les Belles Lettres, 1981–).

Hermetica, tr. Brian P. Copenhaver (Cambridge University Press, 1992).

Hermetica, tr. Walter Scott (Oxford, 1924–36).

Herodotus, *The Histories* (c.440 BC), tr. Aubrey de Selincourt (Harmondsworth, Penguin, 1972).

Iamblichos, *Theurgia, or The Egyptian Mysteries*, tr. Alexander Wilder (London, Rider, 1911).

Nock, A. D. & Festugière, A.-J. (eds.), *Corpus Hermeticum* (Paris, 1946–54).

Piankoff, Alexandre & Drioton, E. (eds. & trs.), *Le Livre du jour et le livre de la nuit* (Cairo, Institut français d'Archéologie Orientale, 1942).

Plato, *Timaeus*, tr. H. D. P. Lee (Harmondsworth, Penguin, 1965).

Plotinus, *The Enneads*, tr. Stephen MacKenna (London, Faber & Faber, 1962).

Rambora, Natacha (ed.), *Egyptian Religious Texts and Representations*, tr. A. Piankoff, 5 vols. (New York, Panther Books, 1954–74).

Stephanus, 'The alchemical works of Stephanos of Alexandria', ed. & tr. F. Sherwood Taylor, *Ambix*, I, 2; II, 1 (1937).

The Book of What is in the Duat, tr. R. O. Faulkner (Warminster, Aris & Phillips, n.d.).

Wallis Budge, E. A. (ed. & tr.), *The Book of the Dead* (London & New York, Arkana, 1985).

Zosimus of Panopolis, *Fragmenta Graeca* in P. E. Marcelin Berthelot, *Collection des anciens alchimistes grecs* (Paris, Georges Steinheil, 1888).

——— *Fragmenta Syriaca* in P. E. Marcelin Berthelot, *La Chimie au moyen âge* (Paris, Imprimerie Nationale, 1893).

——— *Zosimos of Panopolis. On the Letter Omega*, ed. & tr. H. M. Jackson (Missoula, Montana, 1978).

Books and articles

Adams, W. Marshall, *The House of the Hidden Places* (Kildonan, Banton Press, 1991).

Armour, Robert A., *Gods and Myths of Ancient Egypt* (American University in Cairo Press, 1986).

Bauval, Robert & Gilbert, Adrian, *The Orion Mystery* (London, Heinemann, 1994).

Bauval, Robert & Hancock, Graham, *Keeper of Genesis: A Quest for the Hidden Legacy of Mankind* (London, Heinemann, 1996).

Bernal, Martin, *Black Athena: The Afroasiatic Roots of Classical Civilization* (London, Vintage, 1991).

Berthelot, Marcelin P. E., *Les Origines de l'alchimie* (Paris, Georges Steinheil, 1885).

Chassinat, E., *Le Temple d'Edfu* (Cairo, 1928).

Daumas, F., 'L'Alchimie a-t-elle une origine egyptienne?', in *Das romisch-byzantinische Agypten, Akten des internationales Symposions*, 26–30, September 1978 in Trier (Mainz am Rhein 1983), 109–18.

Deiber, A., *Clement d'Alexandre et l'Egypte* (Cairo, IFAO, 1904).

Emery, Walter B., *Archaic Egypt* (Harmondsworth, Penguin, 1987).

Festugèire, A.-J., *La Révélation d'Hermès Trismegiste*, 4 vols. (Paris, Études Bibliques, 1950).

——— *Hermetisme et mystique païenne* (Paris, 1967).

Flinders Petrie, W. M., *The Pyramids and Temples of Gizeh* (London, Histories & Mysteries of Man, 1990).

Forster, E. M., *Alexandria: A History and a Guide* (London, Michael Haag, 1982).

Fowden, Garth, *The Egyptian Hermes: A Historical Approach to the Late Pagan Mind* (Cambridge University Press, 1986).

Fraser, P. M., *Ptolemaic Alexandria* (Oxford, Clarendon Press, 1972).

Frobes, R. J., *Studies in Ancient Technology I* (Leiden, Brill, 1964).

Gardner, Alan Henderson, *Egyptian Grammar* (Oxford University Press, 1950).

Gillain, O., *La Science égyptienne* (Brussels, 1927).

Glanville, S. R. K. (ed.), *The Legacy of Egypt* (Oxford, Clarendon Press, 1942).

Habachi, Labib, *The Obelisks of Egypt* (Cairo, American University Press, 1988).

Hancock, Graham, *Fingerprints of the Gods* (London, Heinemann, 1995).

Hart, George, *Egyptian Myths* (London, British Museum Press, 1990).

Hopkins, Arthur John, *Alchemy: Child of Greek Philosophy* (New York, Columbia University Press, 1934).

Jacq, Christian, *Egyptian Magic*, tr. Janet M. Davis (Warminster, Aris & Phillips, 1985).

Jung, C. G., *The Collected Works* (London, Routledge & Kegan Paul), vol. 12, *Psychology and Alchemy* (1953); vol. 13, *Alchemical Studies* (1968).

Lamy, Lucie, *Egyptian Mysteries* (London, Thames & Hudson, 1986).

Lefebvre, G., *Essai sur la médicine éyptienne de l'époque pharaonique* (Paris, Presses Universitares de France, 1956).

Lichtheim, Miriam, *Ancient Egyptian Literature* (University of California Press, 1975).

Lindsay, Jack, *The Origins of Alchemy in Graeco-Roman Egypt* (London, Frederick Muller, 1970).

Lloyd, G. E. R., *Magic, Reason and Experience. Studies in the Origin and Development of Greek Science* (Cambridge University Press, 1979).

Lucas, A., *Ancient Egyptian Materials and Industries* (London, Edward Arnold, 1952).

Mead, G. R. S., *Thrice Greatest Hermes*, 3 vols. (London, John M. Watkins, 1949).

Momigliano, A., *Alien Wisdom: The Limits of Hellenization* (Cambridge University Press, 1975).

Nock, A. D., *Essays on Religion and the Ancient World*, ed. Zeph Stewart (Oxford, Clarendon Press, 1972).

Patai, Raphael, *The Jewish Alchemists: A History and Source Book* (Princeton University Press, 1994).

Pinch, Geraldine, *Magic in Ancient Egypt* (London, British Museum Press, 1994).

Quirke, Stephen, *Ancient Egyptian Religion* (London, British Museum Press, c.1992).

Reymond, E. A. E., *The Mythical Origins of the Egyptian Temple* (New York, Manchester University Press, 1969).

Rundle Clark, R. T., *Myth and Symbol in Ancient Egypt* (London, Thames & Hudson, 1993).

Saleh, Mohamed, *Cairo: The Egyptian Museum on Pharaonic Sites* (Cairo, Egyptian International Publishing Co-Longman, 1996).

Scheel, Bernd, *Egyptian Metalworking and Tools* (Bucks, Shire Egyptology, 1992).

Schwaller de Lubicz, R. A., *Le Temple de l'homme*, 3 vols. (Paris, Caractères, 1957).

———— *The Temple in Man*, trs. A. & G. VanderBroeck (New York, Inner Traditions, 1977).

———— *The Egyptian Miracle: An Introduction to the Wisdom of the Temple*, trs. A. & G. VanderBroeck (Rochester, Inner Traditions, 1985).

———— *Esoterism & Symbol*, trs. A. & G. VanderBroeck (Rochester, Inner Traditions, 1985).

———— *Sacred Science: The King of Pharaonic Theocracy*, trs. A. & G. VanderBroeck (Rochester, Inner Traditions, 1988).

Shorter, Alan W., *The Egyptian Gods* (London, Kegan Paul, Trench, Trubner & Co, 1937).

Taylor, F. Sherwood, 'The origins of Greek alchemy', *Ambix*, I (1937), 30–47.

Tompkins, Peter, *The Secrets of the Great Pyramid* (New York, Harper & Row, 1971).

Wallis Budge, E. A., *From Fetish to God in Ancient Egypt* (Oxford University Press, 1934).

———— *Egyptian Magic* (New York, Dover, 1971).

———— *Egyptian Ideas of the Afterlife* (New York, Dover, 1995).

West, John Anthony, *The Traveller's Key to Ancient Egypt: A Guide to the Sacred Places of Ancient Egypt* (London, Harrap Colombus, 1987).

———— *Serpent in the Sky: The High Wisdom of Ancient Egypt* (Wheaton, IL, Quest, 1993).

Wilkinson, Richard H., *Symbol and Magic in Egyptian Art* (London, Thames & Hudson, 1994).

ISLAM

Texts

Al-Ghazzali, Muhammad ibn Muhammad, *The Alchemy of Happiness*, tr. H. A. Holmes (New York, Albany, 1873).

Geber, *Summa Perfectionis Magisterii* (Rome, 1485).

———— *The Works of Geber, the Most Famous Arabian Prince and Philosopher, of the Investigation and Perfection of the Philosopher's Stone*, tr. Richard Russell (London, William Copper, 1686; York Beach, Maine, Samuel Weiser, 1994).

———— *Works*, ed. & tr. E. J. Holmyard (London, Dent, 1928).

———— *The Summa Perfectionis of Pseudo-Geber*, ed. R. Newman (Leiden, E. J. Brill, 1991).

Ibn 'Arabi, *La Sagesse des prophètes*, tr. Titus Burckhardt (Paris, A. Michel, 1955).

Jabir ibn Hayyan, *The Arabic Works of Jabir ibn Hayyan*, ed. E. J. Holmyard, 2 vols. (Paris, P. Geuthner, n.d.).

Picatrix, German translation by. H. Ritter & M. Plessner in *Studies of the Warburg Institute*, XXVII (1962).

Rhazes, *The Spiritual Physik of Rhazes*, tr. A. J. Arberry (London, John Murray, 1950).

Rumi, Jalal al-Din, *Discourses of Rumi*, ed. A. J. Arberry (London, John Murray, 1961).

———— *The Mathnawi*, tr. R. A. Nicholson (London, 1969).

The Turba Philosophorum, or Assembly of the Sages, called the Book of Truth in the Art and the Third Pythagorical Synod, tr. A. E. Waite (London, George Redway, 1896).

Books and articles

Addas, Claud, *Quest for the Red Sulphur: The Life of Ibn 'Arabi*, tr. Peter Kingsley (Cambridge, Islamic Texts Society, 1993).

'Al-Kimiya', *Encyclopédie de l'Islam*, ed. C. E. Bosworth et al., 3rd edn., V (Leiden, E. J. Brill, 1991).

Anawati, Georges C., 'L'alchimie arabe', *Histoire des sciences arabes*, ed. Roshdi Rashed, vol. 3 (Paris, Éditions du Seuil, 1997), 111–33.

Arnold, Thomas, *The Legacy of Islam* (Oxford University Press, 1960).

Bakhtiar, Laleh, *Sufism: Expressions of the Mystic Quest* (London, Thames & Hudson, 1976).

Burckhardt, Titus, *Moorish Culture in Spain*, tr. A. Jaffa (London, Allen & Unwin, 1972).

Collins, Rogers, *Spain. Oxford Archaelogical Guides* (Oxford University Press, 1998).

Corbin, Henry, *Avicenna and the Visionary Recital*, tr. W. Trask (New York, Patheon Books, 1960).

———— *Creative Imagination in the Sufism of Ibn 'Arabi*, tr. Ralph Manheim (Princeton University Press, 1969).

———— *Spiritual Body and Celestial Earth: From Mazdean Iran to Shi'ite Iran*, tr. Nancy Pearson, Bollingen Series XCI:2 (London, I. B. Tauris, 1990).

Cruz Hernández, Miguel, *Historia del Pensamiento en el Mundo Islámico 1: Desde los Origenes Hasta el Siglo XII en Oriente*, vol. 1 (Madrid, Alianza, 1996).

Fück, J. W. (ed.), 'The Arabic literature on alchemy according to An-Nadim AD 987', *Ambix*, IV, 3, 4 (1951), 81–144.

Fuentes Guerra, R., *La Evolución de las Ciencias Exactas y Aplicadas en el Intercambio Cultural de Oriente y Occidente* (Madrid, Tipografia Artística, 1962).

Halleux, Robert, 'La Réception de l'alchimie arabe en Occident', *Histoire des sciences arabes*, 3, ed. Roshdi Rashed (Paris, Éditions de Seuil, 1997), 144–52.

Haskins, Charles S., *Studies in the History of Medieval Science* (Cambridge University Press, 1924).

Landau, Rom, *The Philosophy of Ibn 'Arabi* (London, Allen & Unwin, 1959).

Makour, L., 'Avicenne et l'alchimie', *La Revue du Caire*, XXVII (1951), 120–9.

Nasr, Seyyed Hossein, 'Hermes', *Islamic Studies* (Beirut, Librairie du Liban, 1967).

———— *Jalal al-Din Rumi, Supreme Persian Poet and Sage, Sufi Essays* (London, Allen & Unwin, 1972).

———— *An Introduction to Islamic Cosmological Doctrines* (London, Thames & Hudson, 1978).

———— *Science and Civilization in Islam*, 2nd edn. (Cambridge, Islamic Texts Society, 1987).

Nicholson, Reynold A., *Studies in Islamic Mysticism* (Cambridge University Press, 1921).

Partington, J. R., 'The chemistry of Razi', *Ambix*, I (1937), 192–6.

Plessner, Martin, 'The place of the *Turba Philosophorum* in the development of alchemy', *Isis*, XLV (1954), 331–8.

———— 'Hermes Trismegistus and Arab science', *Studia Islamica*, II (1954), 45–59.

———— *Natural Sciences and Medicine in the Legacy of Islam* (Oxford, Clarendon Press, 1998).

Ranking, G. S. A., 'Life and works of Rhazes', *XVIIth International Congress of Medicine*, XXIII (1913).

Samsó, Julio, *Las Ciencias de los Antiguos en Al-andalus* (Madrid, Editorial Mapfre, 1992).

Samsó, Julio et al., '*Las traducciones toledanas en los siglos XII y XIII*', *La Escuela de Traductores de Toledo* (Toledo, Diputación Provincial de Toledo, 1996).

Sezgin, Füaad, *Geschichte de arabischen Schrifttums*, vols. 3–5 (Leiden, E. J. Brill, 1970–4).

Shah, Idries, *The Sufis* (London, Octagon Press, 1977).

Stapleton, H. E. & Husain, Hidayat M., 'Three Arabic treatises on alchemy by Muhammad ibn Umail al-Tamimi', *Memoirs of the Royal Asiatic Society of Bengal*, XII, 1 (1933).

Stapleton, H. E., Lewis, G. L. & Taylor, F. Sherwood, 'The sayings of Hermes quoted in the *Ma' Al-Waraqi* of Ibn Umail', *Ambix*, III (1949), 69–90.

Stapleton, H. E., Azon, R. F. & Husain, Hidayat M., 'Chemistry in Iraq and Persia in the tenth century', *Memoirs of the Royal Asiatic Society of Bengal*, VIII, 6 (1927).

Steele, Robert, 'Practical chemistry in the twelfth century: Rasis, *De Aluminibus et Salibus*', *Isis*, XII (1929), 10–46.

Toshihiko Izutsu, *Sufism and Taoism: A Comparative Study of Key Philosophical Concepts* (Berkeley, University of California Press, 1984).

Ullman, Mandfred, *Die nature und Geheimwissenschaften im Islam* (Leiden, E. J. Brill, 1972).

Vernet, J., *La Alquimia: Historia de la Ciencia Arabe* (Madrid, 1981).

Washington, Irving, *Tales of the Alhambra*, ed. Miguel Sánchez (London, Granada, 1994).

EUROPE

Texts

Agrippa, H. Cornelius, *Three Books of Occult Philosophy*, tr. J. F. (London, 1651; Chthonios, 1986).

Aïvanhov, Omraam Mikhaël, *True Alchemy or the Quest for Perfection* (Fréjust, Prosveta, 1988).

Albertus, Frater, *The Alchemist's Handbook: Manual for Practical Laboratory Alchemy* (York Beach, Maine, Samuel Weiser, 1974).

Altus (pseud.), *Mutus Liber* (La Rochelle, 1677).

Andreae, J. V., *The Chemical Wedding of Christian Rosenkreutz*, tr. Joscelyn Godwin (Grand Rapids, MI, Phanes Press, 1991).

Aquinas, Thomas, *Aurora Consurgens: A Document attributed to Thomas Aquinas*, ed. Marie-Louise von Franz, Bollinger Series (New York, Pantheon, 1966).

Artephius, His Secret Booke, concerning the Philosopher's Stone, tr. Eirenaeus Orandus (London, 1624).

Atwood, Mary Anne (née South), *A Suggestive Enquiry into the Hermetic Mystery* (London, Trelawney Saunders, 1850).

Bacon, Francis, *New Atlantis* (London, 1627).

Bacon, Frier (Roger), *De Mirabili. His Discovery of the Miracles of Art, Nature & Magick. Faithfully translated out of Dr Dee's own copy, by T. M.* (London, Simon Miller, 1659).

——— *Secretum Secretorum* in *Opera Quaedum Hactenus Inedita*, ed. J. S. Brewer (London, Rolls series, 1859).

——— *Opus Maius* (1268), ed. J. H. Bridges, 3 vols. (Oxford, Clarendon Press, 1897).

——— 'The mirror of alchemy (*Speculum Alchimiae*)', tr. T. L. Davis, *Journal of Chemical Education*, VIII (1945–53).

Barbault, Armand, *Gold of a Thousand Mornings* (London, Neville Spearman, 1975).

——— *L'Or du millième matin* (Paris, Denvy-Livres, 1987).

——— *Entretien avec Eugène Canseliet*, ed. R. Amadou (Paris, Pauvert, n.d).

Bernardus, Trevisanus, *A Treatise of Bernard, Earl of Trevisan, of the Philosopher's Stone* (London, 1683).

Boehme Jacob, *De Signatura Rerum* (Amsterdam, 1635).

——— *Signatura Rerum, or the Signature of Things*, tr. J. Ellistone (London, Gyles Calvert, 1951).

Boyle, Robert, *Certain Physiological Essays* (London, 1661).

——— *The Sceptical Chymist* (London, 1661).

Bruno, Giordano, *De la Causa, Principio, et Uno* (Venetia, 1584; in fact London, John Charlewood, 1584).

—————— *De l'Infinito Universo et Mondi* (Venetia, 1584; in fact London, John Charlewood, 1584).

—————— *La Cena de la Ceneri* (London, John Charlewood, 1584).

—————— *Spacio de la Bestia Triofante* (Parigi, 1584; in fact London, John Charlewood, 1584).

Campanella, Tommaso, *La Città del Sole*, ed. E. Solmi (Modena, 1904).

Chaucer, Geoffrey, *The Works of Geoffrey Chaucer*, ed. F. N. Robinson (London, Oxford University Press, 1957).

Cockren, Archibald, *Alchemy Rediscovered and Restored* (London, Rider, 1940).

Confessio Fraternitatis (Cassel, 1615).

Croll, Oswald, *Basilica Chymica* (Frankfurt, 1608; Frankfurt, Gottfried Tampach, 1614).

—————— In *Philosophy Reformed & Improved in Four Profound Tractates. The 1. discovering the Great and Deep Mysteries of Nature by Osw. Crollius*, ed. H. Pinnell (London, 1657).

Dee, John, *A True and Faithful Relation of what passed for many years between Dr John Dee . . . and some spirits tending (had it succeeded) to a General Alteration of most States and kingdoms of the World*, ed. Meric Casaubon (London, 1659).

—————— *The Private Diary of Dr John Dee and the Catalogue of His Library of Manuscripts*, ed. J. O. Halliwell (London Camden Society Publications, 1842).

—————— 'A translation of John Dee's *"Monas Hieroglyphica"*', ed. C. H. Josten, *Ambix*, XII, 2, 3 (1964), 88–221.

—————— *Essential Readings*, ed. Gerald Suster (Wellingborough, 1986).

—————— *John Dee's Library Catalogue*, eds. J. Roberts & A. D. Watson, (London, Bibliographical Society, 1990).

—————— *The Diary of John Dee*, ed. Edward Fenton (Oxfordshire, Day Books, 1998).

Dorn, Gerard, *Artificii chymistici physici, metaphysici, secunda pars and tertia . . . accessit etiam tertiaede parti, de praeparationibus metallicis in utroque lapidis philosophorum opere maiore minoreque* (1569).

Eschenbach, Wolfram von, *Parzival*, trs. Helen M. Mustard & Charles E. Passage (New York, 1961).

Fama Fraternitatis (Cassel, 1614).

'*Fama Fraternitatis*' and '*Confession Fraternitatis*': *The Fame and Confession of Fraternity of R. C.: Commonly of the Rosie Cross*, tr. Eugenius Philathes (London, 1652).

Flamel, Nicholas, *Le Livre des figures hiéroglyphiques de Nicolas Flamel* (Paris, 1612).

—————— *Explanation of the Hieroglyphical Figures* (London, 1624).

—————— *Nicholas Flamel, his exposition of the Hieroglyphicall figures which he caused to bee painted upon an arch in St Innocents church-yard, in Paris* (1624), ed. L. Dixon (New York, 1994).

Fludd, Robert, *Utriusque Cosmi, majoris scilicet et minoris, metaphysica atque technica historia*, 2 vols. (Frankfurt, 1617–18).

———— 'Truth's golden harrow', ed. C. H. Josten, *Ambix*, III, 3, 4 (1949).

———— *Essential Readings*, ed. W. H. Huffman (London, 1992).

Fulcanelli, *Le Mystère des cathédrales* (1926), ed. Eugène Canseliet (Paris, J. J. Pauvert, 1964).

———— *Fulcanelli: Master Alchemist, Le Mystère des cathédrales* (1922), tr. Mary Sworder, introd. Eugène Canseliet (London, Neville Spearman, 1971).

———— *Les Demeures Philosophales et le symbolisme hermétique dans ses rapports avec l'art sacré et l'esoterisme du Grand Oeuvre* (Paris, 1928).

Helvetius, J. F., *Johannis Friderici Helveti Vitulus Aureus, quem mundus adorat et orat* (Amsterdam, 1667).

Kelley, Edward, *The Alchemical Writings of Edward Kelley* (1676), tr. A. E. Waite (London, J. Elliott, 1893).

———— 'The theatre of terrestrial astronomy' in R. Grossinger (ed.), *Alchemy* (California, 1979).

Khunrath, Heinrich, *Amphitheatrum Sapientiae Aeternae* (Hanau, Erasmus Wolfart S., 1609).

———— *The Ampitheatre Engravings of Heinrich Khunrath*, ed. Adam McLean, tr. Patricia Tahil (Grand Rapids, MI, Phanes Press, n.d.).

Lacinius, Janus Therapus, *The New Pearl of Great Price*, tr. A. E. Waite (London, J. Elliott, 1894).

Lambsprinck, *De Lapide Philosophico* (Frankfurt, Lucas Jennis, 1625).

Lull, Ramon, *Selected Works of Ramon Llull* (1232–1316), ed. & tr. Anthony Bonner (Princeton University Press, c.1985).

———— *Doctor Illuminatus: A Ramon Llull Reader*, ed. & tr. Anthony Bonner (Princeton University Press, c.1993).

Lullo, Raimondo, *Opera Chimica* (Firenze, Biblioteca Nationale Centrale) HP 1652, MS B 52.

McLean, Adam (ed.), *Rosarium Philosophorum* (Frankfurt, 1550; Lubeck, 1588), tr. Patricia Talil (Edinburgh, MOHS, 1981).

———— (ed.), *The Rosicrucian Emblems of Daniel Cramer* (Grand Rapids, MI, Phanes Press, 1991).

Magnus, Albertus, *Libellus de Alchimia*, tr. Virginia Heines (Berkeley & Los Angeles, University of California Press, 1958).

———— *The Book of Secrets of Albertus Magnus*, eds. Michael Best & Frank Brightman (Oxford, Clarendon Press, 1973).

———— *The Book of Secrets* (York Beach, Maine, Samuel Weiser, 1999).

Maier, Michael, *Arcana Arcanissima* (London, 1614).

———— *Silentium post clamores, hoc est Tractatus Apologeticus, quo causae non solum clamorum seu revelationem Fraternitatis Germanicae de R. C. sed et Silentii, seu non redditae ad sinulorum vota responsionis . . .* (Frankfurt, 1617).

———— *Symbola Aureae Mensae* (Frankfurt, Lucas Jennis, 1617).

——— *Atalanta Fugiens* (Oppenheim, Theodor de Bry, 1618), ed. &. tr. Joscelyn Godwin (Grand Rapids, MI, Phanes Press, 1989).

——— *Themis aurea de legibus fraternitatus* (Frankfurt, 1618).

——— *Tripus Aureus* (Frankfurt, Lucas Jennis, 1618).

Mylius, Johann Daniel, *Philosophia Reformata* (Frankfurt, Lucas Jennis, 1622).

Newton, Isaac, *Opticks or A Treatise of the Reflections, Refractions, Inflections & Colours of Light* (London, 1706).

——— *The Correspondence of Isaac Newton* (Cambridge University Press, 1960).

Norton, Samuel, *Key to Alchimie* (London, 1577).

Norton, Thomas, *Ordinal of Alchemy*, ed. John Reidy (London, New York, Toronto, Oxford University Press, 1975).

Paracelsus, *Parcelsus on the Secrets of Alchemy*, tr. R. Turner (London, 1656).

——— *The Hermetic and Alchemical Writings of Aureolus Philippus Theophastrus Bombast* (Paracelsus), tr. A. E. Waite, 2 vols. (London, J. Elliott, 1894).

——— *Paracelsus: Selected Writings*, ed. Jolande Jacobi, tr. Norbert Guterman (London, Routledge & Kegan Paul, 1951).

Pauwels, Louis & Bergier, Jacques, *Le Matin des magiciens. Introduction au realisme fantastique* (Paris, 1961), translated as *The Morning of the Magicians* (London, Avon Books, 1968).

Perlesvaus, translated by Sebastian Evans as *The High History of the Holy Grail* (1893; Cambridge, 1969).

Petrus Bonus, *Pretiosa Margarita Novella*, ed. Janus Lacinius Therapus (c.1330; Venice, 1546).

——— *Pretiosa Margarita Novella de Thesaro, ac Pretiosissimo Philosophorum Lapide* (Venice, 1656).

——— *The New Pearl of Great Price*, tr. A. E. Waite (London, J. Elliott, 1894).

Philalethes, Eirenaeus, *Ripley Reviv'd: or an Exposition upon Sir George Ripley's Hermetic-Poetical Works* (London, 1678).

Philalethes, Eirenaeus Philoponos, *The Marrow of Alchemy* (London, E. Brewster, 1652).

Philalethes, Eugenius, *Long Livers: A Curious History of Such Persons of both Sexes who have liv'ed several Ages and grown Young again* (London, n.d.).

Pico della Mirandola, 'Oration on the dignity of man' (1486), *The Portable Renaissance Reader*, eds. James Ross & Mary Martin McLaughlin (Harmondsworth, Penguin, 1977).

Reidy, John, 'Thomas Norton and the ordinall of alchimy', *Ambix*, VI (1957), 59–85.

Ripley, Sir George, *The Compound of Alchymy; or The ancient hidden Art of Alchemic; conteining the ... meanes to make the Philosopher's Stone, Aurum potabile, with other excellent Experiments*, tr. Ralph

Rabbards (London, T. Orwin, 1591; Norwood, N. J., Walter J. Johnson, 1977).

———— *The Marrow of Alchymie* in *Medicina Practica*, ed. W. Salmon (London, 1692).

Robert of Chester, *Book of the Composition of Alchemy* (London, 1144).

Ruland, Martin, the Elder, *A Lexicon of Alchemy or Alchemical Dictionary*, tr. A. E. Waite (London, J. Elliott, 1892; John M. Watkins, 1964).

Rutherford, Ernest, *The Newer Alchemy* (Cambridge University Press, 1937).

Sadoul, Jacques, *Le Trésor des alchimistes* (Paris, J'ai lu, n.d.).

Sendivogius, Michael, *Novum Lumen Chemycum* (Frankfurt & Prague, 1604).

Severinus, Petrus, *Idea Medicinae Philosophicae* (Basel, 1571).

Stolcius, Daniel, *Viridrium Chymicum Figuris* (Frankfurt, 1624).

———— *Chymisches Lustgatlein* (Frankfurt, Lucas Jennis, 1624).

———— *The Hermetic Garden of Daniel Stolcius*, ed. Adam McLean, tr. Patricia Tahil (Edinburgh, MOHS, n.d.).

Tausend, Franz, *180 Elements, the Atomic Weight, and their Incorporation in the System of Harmonic Periods* (Munich, c.1922).

Trismoson, Salomon (pseud.), *Aureum Vellus* (Basel, Rorschach, 1598–1608).

———— *La Toyson d'or, ou la fleur de thresors* (Paris, Sevestre, 1612).

———— *Splendor Solis*, ed. Adam McLean, tr. Joscelyn Godwin (Grand Rapids, MI, Phanes Press, 1991).

Trithemius (of Sponheim), Johannes, *Steganographia* (Frankfurt, 1606; Grand Rapids, MI, Phanes Press, n.d.).

Valentine, Basil, *Triumph-Wagen Antimonij* (Leipzig, J. Apels, 1604).

———— *Les Douze Clefs de philosophie de Frère Basile Valentin* (Paris, Perier, 1624).

———— *Azoth, ou moyen de faire l'or caché des philosophes* (Paris, Perier, 1624; Pierre Moet, 1659).

———— *The Triumphant Chariot of Antimony*, tr. I. H. Oxon (London, Thomas Bruster, 1660; J. Elliott, 1893; Vincent Stuart, 1962).

———— *The Last Will and Testament of Basil Valentine* (London, Edward Brewster, 1670).

Vaughan, Thomas, *Lumen de Lumine; or, A New Magical Light*, ed. A. E. Waite (London, G. Redway, 1888).

———— *The Works of Thomas Vaughan, Eugenius Philalethes*, ed. A. E. Waite (London, Theosophical Publishing House, 1919).

———— (Eugenius Philalethes), *Anthroposophia Theomagia* (London, 1650).

Books and articles

Abraham, Lyndy, *A Dictionary of Alchemical Imagery* (Cambridge University Press, c.1999).

Alemparte, Jaime Ferreiro, 'La Escuela de nigromancia de Toledo', *Anuario de Estudios Medievales*, XIII (1983), 205–68.

Alleau, René, *Aspects de l'alchimie traditionnelle* (Paris, Éditions de Minuit, 1977).

Andremont, Pierre, *Les Énigmes de l'alchimie* (Paris, Magellan, n.d).

Arnold, P., *Histoire des Rose-Croix e les origines de la Franc-Maconerie* (Paris, 1955).

Arnold, Thomas, *The Legacy of Islam* (Oxford University Press, 1960).

Atkinson, William C., *A History of Spain and Portugal* (Harmondsworth, Penguin, 1967).

Baigent, Michael & Leigh, Richard, *The Temple and the Lodge* (London, Corgi, 1997).

———— *The Elixir and the Stone: The Tradition of Magic and Alchemy* (London, Viking, 1997).

Baigent, Michael, Leigh, Richard & Lincoln, Henry, *The Holy Blood and the Holy Grail* (London, Arrow, 1996).

Barber, R., *The Knight and Chivalry*, 2nd edn. (Ipswich, 1974).

Basso, Michele, *Eschatology and Symbolism in the Vatican Necropolis* (Vatican City, 1980).

———— *Guide to the Vatican Necropolis* (Vatican City, 1986).

Berman, Madeleine, *Hieronymus Bosch and Alchemy; A Study of the St Anthony Triptych* (Stockholm, Almquist & Wiksell, 1979).

Berthelot, Marcelin P. E., *Les Origines de l'alchimie* (Paris, Georges Steinheil, 1885).

———— *La Chimie au moyen âge*, 3 vols. (Paris, Imprimerie Nationale, 1893).

Bolton, H. C., *The Follies of Science at the Court of Rudolf II* (Milwaukee, 1904).

Bothwell-Gosse, A., *The Knights Templars* (London, Office of the Co-Mason, n.d.).

Brothers H. C. & K. M. B., *The Rosicrucians* (London, Office of the Co-Mason, n.d.).

Burckhardt, Titus, *Alchemy: Science of the Cosmos, Science of the Soul*, tr. William Studdart (London, Stuart & Watkins, 1967; Wellingborough, Element, 1986).

Burland, C. A., *The Arts of the Alchemists* (London, Weidenfeld & Nicolson, 1967).

Bzezinski, Richard & Zbingniew Szydlo, 'A new light on alchemy', *History Today*, VIIII, 1 (Jan. 1997), 17–23.

Canseliet, Eugène, *Alchimie, études diverse de symbolisme hermétique et pratique philosophale* (Paris, 1964).

———— *L'Alchimie expliqueé sur ses textes classiques* (Paris, J. J. Pauvert, 1974).

Capra, Fritjof, *The Tao of Physics* (London, Wildwood House, 1975).

Caron, M. & Hutin, S., *The Alchemists* (London, Evergreen, 1961).

Charpentier, Louis, *The Mysteries of Chartres Cathedral* (1966), tr. Sir Ronald Fraser (London, Research into Lost Knowledge Organisation Trust, 1972).

Clarke, Lindsay, *The Chymical Wedding. A Romance* (London, Jonathan Cape, 1989).

Clulee, N. H., *John Dee's Natural Philosophy* (London, Routledge & Kegan Paul, 1988).

Clymer, Reuben Swinburne, *Alchemy and the Alchemists*, 4 vols. (Alentown, Philosophical Publishing Co, 1907).

———— *The Science of Spiritual Alchemy* (Quakertown, Philosophical Publishing Co, 1959).

Coadie, Xavier, *L'Alchimie d'autrefois* (Paris, Horvath, 1996).

Coelho, Paulo, *The Alchemist: A Fable about Following Your Dreams* (New York, HarperSanFrancisco, 1993).

Collins, Rogers, *Spain. Oxford Archaelogical Guides* (Oxford University Press, 1998).

Coudert, Allison, *Alchemy; The Philosopher's Stone* (London, Wildwood House, 1980).

Craven, J. B., *Count Michael Maier* (Kirkwall, William Peace, 1910).

Crow, W. B., *A History of Magic, Witchcraft & Occultism* (London, Abacus, 1972).

Cruz Hernández, Miguel, *Historia del Pensamiento en el Mundo Islámico, I: Desde los Origenes Hasta el Siglo XII en Oriente* (Madrid, Alianza Editorial, 1996).

Davis, Erik, *TechGnosis: Myth, Magic and Mysticism in the Age of Information* (London, Serpent's Tail, 1999).

Debus, Allen G., *The English Paracelsians* (New York, Oldbourne, 1965).

———— *Alchemy and Chemistry in the Seventeenth Century* (Los Angeles, University of California, 1966).

———— *The Chemical Dream of the Renaissance* (Cambridge, W. Heiffer, 1968).

De Jong, H. M. E., *Michael Maier's Atalanta Fugiens: Sources of an Alchemical Book of Emblems* (Leiden, E. J. Brill, 1969).

Dobbs, Betty Jo Teeter, *The Foundations of Newton's Alchemy; or, 'The Hunting of the Greene Lyon'* (Cambridge University Press, 1975).

———— *The Janus Faces of Genius: The Role of Alchemy in Newton's Thought* (Cambridge University Press, 1991).

Doberer, Kurt Karl, *The Goldmakers, 10,000 Years of Alchemy*, tr. E. W. Dickes (London, Brussels, Nicholson & Watson, 1948).

Drury, Nevill, *Shamanism* (Shaftesbury, Element, 1996).

Dunleavy, Gareth W., 'The Chaucer ascription in Trinity College, Dublin, Manuscript D.2.8', *Ambix*, XIII (1965), 2–21.

Eliade, Mircea, *Yoga, Immortality and Freedom*, tr. W. R. Trask (Princeton University Press, 1958).

———— *The Forge and the Crucible: The Origins and Structure of Alchemy*, tr. Stephen Corrin, 2nd edn. (University of Chicago Press, 1982).

———— *Shamanism: Archaic Techniques of Ecstasy*, tr. W. R. Trask (Princeton University Press, 1972; Harmondsworth, Penguin, 1989).

Eslava Galan, Juan, *Cinco Tratados Españoles de Alquimia* (Madrid, Tecnos, c.1987).

Evans, R. J. W., *Rudolf II and His World: A Study in Intellectual History 1576–1612* (Oxford, Clarendon Press, 1973).

Evola, Julius, *Eros and the Mysteries of Love: The Metaphysics of Sex* (Rochester, Vermont, Inner Traditions, 1991).

———— *The Hermetic Tradition: Symbols & Teachings of the Royal Art*, tr. E. E. Rehmus (Rochester, Vermont, Inner Traditions, 1994).

Fabricius, Johannes, *Alchemy: The Medieval Alchemists and Their Royal Art* (Copenhagen, Rosenkilde & Bagger, 1976; Wellingborough, The Aquarian Press, 1989).

Favier, Jean, *The World of Chartres* (London, Thames & Hudson, 1990).

Feild, Reshad, *Steps to Freedom: Discourse on the Alchemy of the Heart* (Putney, Vermont, Threshhold Books, 1983).

———— *Alchemy of the Heart* (Longmead, Element Books, 1998).

Fernando, Diana, *Alchemy: An Illustrated A to Z* (London, Blandford, 1998).

Fish, Dorothy M., *Modern Alchemy* (London, Faber & Faber, 1936).

Franz, Marie-Louise von, *Alchemical Active Imagination* (Irving, Texas, Spring, 1979).

———— *Alchemy: An Introduction to the Symbolism and the Pyschology* (1959; Toronto, Inner City Books, 1980).

French, P. J., *John Dee: The World of an Elizabethan Magus* (London, Routledge & Kegan Paul, 1972; Ark, 1987).

Fuentes Guerra, R., *La Evolución de las Ciencias Exactas y Aplicadas en el Intercambio Cultural de Oriente y Occidente* (Madrid, Tipografía Artística, 1962).

Gil, José S., *La Escuela de Traductores a Toledo y los Colaboradores Judios* (Toledo, Diputación Provincial de Toledo, 1985).

Gilbert, R. A., *The Golden Dawn: Twilight of the Magicians* (Wellingborough, Aquarian Press, 1983).

Gilchrist, Cherry, *Alchemy: The Great Work* (Wellingborough, Aquarian Press, 1984).

———— *The Elements of Alchemy* (Shaftesbury, Element, 1991).

Gillispie, Charles (ed.), *Dictionary of Scientific Biography* (New York, Charles Schribner's Sons, 1970).

Godwin, Joscelyn, *Athanasius Kircher: A Renaissance Man and the Quest for Lost Knowledge* (London, Thames & Hudson, 1979).

———— *Robert Fludd: Hermetic Philosopher and Surveyor of Two Worlds* (Grand Rapids, MI, Phanes Press, 1997).

Gray, Ronald D., *Goethe, the Alchemist. A Study of Alchemical Symbolism in Goethe's Literary and Scientific Works* (Cambridge University Press, 1952).

Grof, Stanislav, *Books of the Dead* (London, Thames & Hudson, 1994).

Grove, H. Stanley Red, *Alchemy Ancient & Modern* (London, 1911; E. P. Publishing, 1973).

Haeffner, Mark, *Dictionary of Alchemy* (London, Aquarian, 1991).

Harpur, Patrick, *Mercurius, or The Marriage of Heaven and Earth* (London, Macmillan, 1990).

Harrison, John, *The Library of Isaac Newton* (Cambridge University Press, 1978).

Haskins, Charles S., *Studies in the History of Medieval Science* (Cambridge University Press, 1924).

Holmyard, E. J., *Alchemy* (London, Pelican, 1957; New York, Dover, 1990).

Hopkins, Arthur John, *Alchemy: Child of Greek Philosophy* (New York, Columbia University Press, 1934).

Hosten, C. J., 'William Blackhouse of Swallowfield', *Ambix*, IV, 1, 2 (1949), 1–33.

Hutin, Serges, *L'Alchimie*, 3rd edn. (Paris, Presses Universitaires de France, 1966).

Johnson, Ken, *The Fulcanelli Phenomenon* (London, 1980).

Jones, B. E., *Freemason's Guide and Compendium* (London, 1950).

Jung, C. G., *Mysterium Coniunctionis* (London, Routledge & Kegan Paul, 1963).

————— *Memories, Dreams, Reflections*, trs. R. & C. Winston (London, Collins Fountain Books, 1977).

————— *C. G. Jung Speaking*, eds. William McGuire & R. F. C. Hull (Princeton University Press, 1977).

————— *Collected Works*, 20 vols. (London, Routledge & Kegan Paul, 1979): *Aion* (vol. 9); *Psychology and Alchemy* (vol. 12); *Alchemical Studies* (vol. 13).

————— *Jung on Alchemy*, ed. Nathan Schwartz-Salant (Princeton University Press, 1995).

Jung, Emma & Franz, Marie-Louise von, *The Grail Legend* (1960), tr. Andea Dykes (London, Hodder & Stoughton, 1971).

Keynes, John Maynard, 'Newton the man', *Royal Society: Newton Tercentenary Celebrations* (Cambridge University Press, 1947), 27–34.

Kingsley, Peter, *Ancient Philosophy, Mystery and Magic* (Oxford, Clarendon Press, 1995).

Lennep, Jacques van, *Alchimie: contributions à l'histoire de l'art alchimique* (Brussells, Crédit Communal, 1984).

Lewis, H. Spencer (ed.), *Rosicrucian Manual* (1918; San Jose, California, AMORC, 1971).

Lindsay, Jack, *The Origins of Alchemy in Graeco-Roman Egypt* (London, Frederick Muller, 1970).

Lippmann, E. O. von, *Entstehung und Ausbreitung der Alchemie* (Berlin, 1919–31).

McIntosh, Christopher, *Rosy Cross Unveiled, the History, Mythology, and Rituals of an Occult Order* (Wellingborough, Aquarian Press, 1980).

McLean, Adam, *A Commentary on the Mutus Liber* (Grand Rapids, MI, Phanes Press, n.d.).

———— *The Spiritual Science of Alchemy* (Edinburgh, Megalithic Research Publications, 1978).

Mahdihassan, S., 'Alchemy and its connection with astrology, pharmacy, magic and metallurgy', *Janus*, XLVI (1957), 81–103.

Marshall, Peter, *William Blake: Visionary Anarchist* (London, Freedom Press, 1988).

———— *Nature's Web: Rethinking Our Place on Earth* (London, Simon & Schuster, 1992; Cassell, 1995).

———— *Riding the Wind: A New Philosophy for a New Era* (London, Cassell, 1998; London & New York, Continuum, 2000).

Meinel, Christop (ed.), *Die Alchemie in der eruopäischen Kultur und Wissenschaftgeschichte* (Wiesbaden, Harrassowitz, 1986).

Menéndez y Pelayo, D. Marcelino, *Historia de los Heterodoxos Españoles* (Madrid, Biblioteca de Autores Cristianos, 1986).

Merkur, D., 'The study of spiritual alchemy: mysticism, gold-making, and esoteric hermeneutics', *Ambix*, XXXVII (1990), 35–45.

Metzner, Ralph, *Maps of Consciousness: I Ching, Tantra, Tarot, Alchemy, Astrology, Actualism* (New York, 1971).

Miller, Malcolm, *Chartres Cathedral: Medieval Masterpieces in Stained Glass and Sculpture* (Andover, Pitkin, n.d.).

Miller, Richard & Iona, *The Modern Alchemist: A Guide to Personal Transformation* (Grand Rapids, MI, Phanes Press, 1994).

Multhauf, Robert P., 'Medical chemistry and the "Paracelsians"', *Bulletin of the History of Medicine*, XXIV (1954).

———— *The Origins of Chemistry* (New York, Oldbourne, 1966).

Needham, Joseph, *Science and Civilisation in China* (Cambridge University Press, 1954–).

———— *The Refiner's Fire: The Enigma of Alchemy of East and West* (University of London, 1971).

Newman, W., 'Prophecy and alchemy: the origin of Eireneaus Philalethes', *Ambix*, XXXVII (1990), 97–115.

Nicholl, Charles, *The Chemical Theatre* (London, Routledge & Kegan Paul, 1980).

Nôtre-Dame de Chartres: l'énigme du labyrinthe (Chartres, n.d).

Pagel, Walter, *Paracelsus: An Introduction to Philosophical Medicine in the Era of the Renaissance* (New York, 1958; London, S. Karger, 1982).

———— 'The prime matter of Paracelsus', *Ambix*, IX (1961).

———— *Joan Baptista van Helmont: Reformer of Science and Medicine* (Cambridge University Press, 1982).

Partington, J. R., 'Albertus Magnus on alchemy', *Ambix*, I (1937), 3–20.

———— *A History of Chemistry*, 4 vols. (London, Macmillan, 1961–70).

Patai, R., *The Jewish Alchemists* (Princeton University Press, 1994).

Peat, F. David, *The Philosopher's Stone* (London, Bantam Books, 1991).

Pereira, Michael, *The Alchemical Corpus Attributed to Raymon Lull, War-*

burg Institute Surveys and Texts XVIII (London, Warburg Institute, 1989), pp. 61–107.

Powell, Neil, *Alchemy, the Ancient Science* (London, Aldus Books, 1976).

Principe, L. M., 'Robert Boyle's alchemical secrecy: codes, ciphers and concealments', *Ambix*, XXXIX (1992), 63–74.

Pritchard, Alan, 'Thomas Charnock's book dedicated to Queen Elizabeth', *Ambix*, XXVI (1979), 56–73.

——— *Alchemy* (London, Routledge & Kegan Paul, 1980).

Ramón Luanco, D. Jose (ed.), *La Alquimia en España. Escritos Inéditos, Noticias y Apantamientos que Pueden Servir para la Historia de los Adeptos Españoles* (Madrid, Collección Alatar, 1980).

Ramsay, Jay, *Alchemy: The Art of Transformation* (London, Thorsons, 1997).

Raphael, A., *The Philosopher's Stone* (London, Routledge, 1965).

Read, John, *Prelude to Chemistry* (London, G. Bell, 1936).

——— *The Alchemist in Life, Literature and Art* (London, T. Nelson, 1947).

——— *Through Alchemy to Chemistry* (London, G. Bell, 1957); *From Alchemy to Chemistry* (New York, Dover, 1995).

Redgrove, Peter & Shuttle, Penelope, *Alchemy for Women* (London, Rider, 1995).

Regardie, Israel, *The Golden Dawn*, 4 vols. (Chicago, 1937–40).

Roberts, Gareth, *The Mirror of Alchemy: Alchemical Ideas and Images in Manuscripts and Books from Antiquity to the 16th century* (London, British Library, 1994).

Robertson, Ian, *Blue Guide to Spain* (London, A & C Black, 1993).

Roob, Alexander, *The Hermetic Museum: Alchemy & Mysticism* (Köln, Taschen, 1997).

Rutherford, Ernest, *The New Alchemy* (Cambridge University Press, 1937).

Sadoul, Jacques, *Le Trésor des alchimistes* (Paris, J'ai lu, n.d.).

——— *Alchemists and Gold* (London, Neville Spearman, 1972).

Samsó, Julio, *Las Ciencias de los Antiguos en Al-andalus* (Madrid, Editorial Mapfre, 1992).

Samsó, Julio et al., *La Escuela de Traductores de Toledo* (Toledo, Diputación Provincial de Toledo, 1996).

Sapere, Aude, *The Science of Alchemy* (London, Neptune Press, 1979).

Sarton, George A. L., *Introduction to the History of Science* (Baltimore, 1950).

Schama, Simon, *Landscape and Memory* (London, HarperCollins, 1995).

Scholem, G. G., *Major Trends in Jewish Mysticism* (New York, Schocken Books, 1946).

Secrets of the Alchemists (New York, Time-Life Books, 1990).

Sheppard, H. J., 'Gnosticism and alchemy', *Ambix*, VI (1957), 86–101.

——— 'Alchemy: origin or origins?', *Ambix*, XVII (1970), 69–84.

Silberer, Herbert, *Hidden Symbolism of Alchemy and the Occult Arts*, tr. S. E. Jellife (1917; New York, Dover, 1971).

Simson, Otto von, *The Gothic Cathedral: The Origins of Gothic Architecture*

& the Medieval Concept of Order (London, Routledge & Kegan Paul, 1956).

Singer, June, *Androgyny* (New York, Anchor/Doubleday, 1976).

Skinner, Stephen, *In Pursuit of Gold: Alchemy in Theory and Practice* (New York, Samuel Weiser, 1976).

Smith, Pamela H., *The Basics of Alchemy: Science and Culture in the Holy Roman Empire* (Princeton University Press, 1997).

Spencer Lewis, H. (ed.), *Rosicrucian Manual* (1918; San Jose, California, AMORC, 1971).

Stapleton, Henry Ernest, 'The antiquity of alchemy', *Ambix*,V, 1/2 (1953).

Stevenson, David, *The Origins of Freemasonry, Scotland's Century 1590–1710* (Cambridge University Press, 1990).

Stillman, John, *The Story of Early Alchemy and Chemistry* (New York & London, Apleton, 1924; New York, Dover, 1960).

Stukely, William, *Memoirs of Isaac Newton's Life*, ed. A. Hasting White (London, Taylor & Francis, 1936).

Sutherland, C. H. V., *Gold* (London, Thames & Hudson, 1959).

Symonds, John, *The Great Beast: The Life of Aleister Crowley* (London, Hamilton, 1963).

Szulakowska, Urszula, *John Dee and European Alchemy* (University of Durham, c.1996).

Taylor, F. Sherwood, 'The origins of Greek alchemy', *Ambix*, I (1937), 30–47.

———— 'The alchemical works of Stephanos of Alexandria', *Ambix*, I (1937), 116–39.

———— 'Thomas Charnock', *Ambix*, I, 3, 4 (1938), 148–76.

———— 'George Ripley's song', *Ambix*, II (1946), 177–81.

———— *The Alchemists: Founders of Modern Chemistry* (London, Heinemann, 1951; Paladin, 1976).

Theissen, W. R., 'John Dastin's letter on the philosopher's stone', *Ambix*, XXXVIII (1986), 81–7.

Thompson, C. J. S., *The Lure and Romance of Alchemy* (London, Harrap, 1932).

Thorndike, Lynn, *A History of Magic and Experimental Science*, 8 vols. (New York, Macmillan & Columbia University Press, 1929–58).

———— *Magic, Witchcraft, Astrology and Alchemy* (Cambridge University Press, 1936).

———— *Michael Scot* (London, Nelson, 1965).

Trevor-Roper, Hugh, 'The Paracelsian movement', *Renaissance Essays* (London, Fontana, 1986).

Verrier, René, *Études sur Arnaud de Villeneuve, 1240–1311* (Leiden, E. J. Brill, n.d.).

Villain, Abbé, *Histoire critique de Nicolas Flamel* (Paris, Desprez, 1761).

Vrum, Robert, *Rudolf II and His Prague: Mysteries and Curiosities of Rudolfine Prague 1550–1650* (Prague, 1997).

Waite, A. E, *The Real History of the Rosicrucians* (London, G. Redway, 1887).
———— *Lives of the Alchemystical Philosophers* (London, G. Redway, 1888).
———— *The Doctrine and Literature of the Kabalah* (London, Theosophical Publishing House, 1902).
———— *Raymond Lully, Illuminated Doctor, Alchemist and Christian Mystic* (London, Rider, 1922).
———— *The Brotherhood of the Rosy Cross* (London, Rider, 1924).
———— *The Secret Tradition in Alchemy* (London, Kegan Paul, 1926).
———— *The Key to the Tarot* (London, Rider, 1999).
Weishepl, James A. (ed.), *Albertus Magnus and the Sciences: Commemorative Essays* (Toronto, Pontifical Institute of Medieval Studies, 1980).
Westfall, Richard S., *Never at Rest: A Biography of Isaac Newton* (Cambridge University Press, 1980).
———— 'Newton and alchemy' in Brian Vickers (ed.), *Occult and Scientific Mentalities in the Renaissance* (Cambridge University Press, 1980).
White, Michael, *Isaac Newton: The Last Sorcerer* (London, Fourth Estate, 1997).
White, Ralph (ed.), *The Rosicrucian Enlightenment Revisited* (Lindisfarne Press, n.d.).
Whitman, Edward C., *The Alchemy of Healing* (Berkeley, North Atlantic Books, 1994).
Wilson, Colin, *The Philosopher's Stone* (London, Antler Books, 1969).
Wilson, Frank Avray, *Alchemy as a Way of Life* (London, C. W. Daniel, 1976).
Yates, Frances, 'The art of Ramon Lull: an approach to it through Lull's theory of elements', *Journal of the Warburg and Courtauld Institutes*, XVII (1954), 115–73.
———— 'Ramon Lull and John Scotus Erigena', *Journal of the Warburg and Courtauld Institutes*, XXIII (1960), 1–44.
———— *Giordano Bruno and the Hermetic Tradition* (London, Routledge & Kegan Paul, 1964).
———— *The Art of Memory* (London, Routledge & Kegan Paul, 1966).
———— *The Rosicrucian Enlightenment* (London, Routledge & Kegan Paul, 1972).
———— *Lull & Bruno* (London, Routledge & Kegan Paul, 1982).
———— *Renaissance & Reform: The Italian Contribution, Collected Essays*, 2 vols. (London, Routledge & Kegan Paul, 1983).
Zadrobílek, Vadislav (ed.), *Magnum Opus* (Prague, Trigon, 1997).

Index

St John the Baptist 276
Saint Martin, Louis Claude de 438
St Peter's Church (Rome) 326, 331–2
St Peter's Square, obelisk in 327
St Thomas Aquinas 14, 282–3
sal ammoniac 229, 449
'Salon of Elements' (Palazzo Vecchio) 337–8
salt 350–1, 354, 365, 389, 447
samadhi 89, 90–1, 114
Samana 115
Samarkhand 6
Samber, Robert 291
Samkhya school 101
sandhyabasa 114
sansara 132
Saqqara 142, 150, 169
Sarnath 125–6
sattva 102, 103
Saturn 29, 115, 310, 351
Sauler, James 307
Sceptical Chymist, The (Boyle) 404
Schwaller de Lubicz, R. A. 157, 417–18
science 8, 9, 15–16 377, 378, 398–409, 446–7, 452, 460–3
in China 8, 9, 27
in India 111
and religion 335
see also chemistry, nature
Science and Civilisation in China (Needham) 6
Scotti, Andrea 343–4
Scotus, Michael 320
Secret of Everlasting Life, The 36
Secret of the Golden Flower, The 50, 56, 57, 59, 426–7
Secretum Secretorum (Rhazes) 228, 280
Sefer Yetzirah 242
self 103, 111–12, 114, 145, 186–7, 247, 432, 463, 465–6 *see also* psychology
Semita Recta (Albertus Magnus) 282
Semita Semitae (Arnald) 288, 321
Sendivogius, Michael 361, 388–9, 403

Senior Zadith *see* Ibn Umail, Muhammad
Sephiroth 242, 341–2
Serapis 176, 196
Set 152, 164
Seti I 156
Seton, Alexander 388
Seven Chapters of Hermes (Anon) 453
Severinus, Petrus 353
sex 8, 46, 64–9, 88, 89, 113, 119–20, 121–2, 187, 430, 440–1
depicted in temple sculptures 122–4
see also 'chemical wedding'
Shabistari, Mahmud 244
Shah, Idris 292
Shakti 89, 93, 94, 117–18, 119, 121, 460
shamans 20–1, 26
shaman's step 33
shape changing 45
Shastri, Krishna Pal 109–10
Shastri, Lobsang Norbu 126–9
Shaw, George Bernard 439
shen 61, 74–5
Shiah 217, 219, 239
Shih Ching 28
Shiva 89, 93, 94, 98, 106, 115, 117–18, 460
Shu 151
Shu Ching 28
Shuchirch, William 299
Shui 38, 39
Shukla, J. S. 101–5
Sicily 270, 286, 319
Siddha medicine 105–6
Siddhas 22, 91, 113, 165, 460
siddhis 113
Sidney, Philip 394, 397
Siena Cathedral 342
Silberer, Herbert 426
silver, making into gold 222
silver-making 109, 193, 289, 314
artificial silver 190–1, 194
Sirius 145
Sixtus V, Pope 326